REIMAGINE PHARMA MARKETING

Make it Future-Proof!

REIMAGINE PHARMA MARKETING

Make it Future-Proof!

Subba Rao Chaganti

Pharma Med PRESS
An Imprint of
BSP Books Pvt. Ltd.

PharmaMed Press
An imprint of BSP Books Pvt. Ltd.
4-4-309/316, Giriraj Lane,
Sultan Bazar, Hyderabad - 500 095.

Reimagine Pharma Marketing: Make it Future-Proof!
by *Subba Rao Chaganti*

Published by

PharmaMed Press
An imprint of BSP Books Pvt. Ltd.
4-4-309/316, Giriraj Lane, Sultan Bazar, Hyderabad - 500 095.
Phone: 040-23445688, 23445600; Fax: 91+40-23445611
E-mail: info@pharmamedpress.com
www.pharmamedpress.com/pharmamedpress.net

Cover Design

J. Siva Prasad, Amita Designs

ISBN: 978-93-95039-46-8 (Hardbound)

REIMAGINE
PHARMA MARKETING

Make it Future-Proof!

Subba Rao Chaganti

PharmaMed Press

An imprint of BSP Books Pvt. Ltd.

4-4-309/316, Giriraj Lane,

Sultan Bazar, Hyderabad - 500 095.

Reimagine Pharma Marketing: Make it Future-Proof!
by *Subba Rao Chaganti*

Published by

PharmaMed Press
An imprint of BSP Books Pvt. Ltd.
4-4-309/316, Giriraj Lane, Sultan Bazar, Hyderabad - 500 095.
Phone: 040-23445688, 23445600; Fax: 91+40-23445611
E-mail: info@pharmamedpress.com
www.pharmamedpress.com/pharmamedpress.net

Cover Design

J. Siva Prasad, Amita Designs

ISBN: 978-93-95039-46-8 (Hardbound)

Dedicated to:

I dedicate this book to all those Re-Imagineers for reimagining products, devices, treatments, and overall healthcare, making them accessible, affordable, and improving patient care and disease outcomes.

PREFACE

Over the years, a lot has changed and not changed in the pharmaceutical marketing environment.

Firstly, what has changed? Consider these, for example. The blockbuster drugs targeting large populations of patients are on the wane. The developmental product pipelines are drying up. A continuous pressure to reduce costs and demonstrate greater value and a shift from treatment to prevention and personalized treatments disturb the status quo. Pharmaceutical sales teams' access to physicians has come down to half of what it was only a few years ago. The patient, who was at the periphery all these years, has moved to the center of healthcare decision making. The rules of customer engagement are changing. Pharmaceutical marketing teams continue to push messages to convince prescribers about the relative superiority of their therapies over competitors, albeit through multiple channels.

Now, let us consider what has not changed. Pharma's search for new blockbusters has not changed despite the shrinking of drug targets. Pharma's 'inside-to-outside' way of working has not changed.

Besides, an exciting range of disruptive technologies is catalyzing the pharmaceutical industry to reimagine its future. Yet, the pharmaceutical industry, except for a few leading companies such as Novartis, Pfizer, Roche, and UCB, remains a laggard in digital transformation.

The recent COVID-19 pandemic added rocket fuel to the digital transformation of the pharmaceutical industry. COVID-19 has changed every aspect of life for every person in the world, not just pharmaceutical companies. It has changed everything. It is transforming the entire model of care, including pharmaceutical sales and marketing. Telemedicine, for example, has quickly become ingrained in the healthcare ecosystem. Digital transformation has become inevitable and imminent. COVID-19 is serving as a wake-up call for pharmaceutical companies to evaluate their digital maturity and ability to serve customers with personalized experiences.

A new era is shaping as the business world strives to move beyond the coronavirus. To do well in this new post-COVID world, pharmaceutical companies need to reimagine their marketing and communication strategies.

In a world where change accelerates and the marketing environment becomes more complex, it is no longer sure that the current business model is appropriate for its future. Buzzwords of Pharma managers like cash cows, stars, sales force effectiveness (SFE) are not enough. You need to include a series of frameworks such as Design Thinking, Sprints, SCRUM, Omni-channel, Closed Loop Marketing, Blue Ocean, Lean Canvas, Kanban, Personae, Net Promotion Score, and Personalized Healthcare.

The time to reimagine is now. As Rahm Emanuel, the former White House Chief of Staff under President Barrack Obama said: *Never allow a good crisis to go waste. It's an opportunity to do the things you once thought were impossible.*

A well-thought-out reimagining process is repeatable and can make it future-proof. While you are reimagining, the key questions to ask and answer are:

A. Does market acceleration make structured planning and management irrelevant to tomorrow's market situation?
B. Is structured planning more relevant to cross-functional implementation to be customer-focused in a rapidly changing marketing environment?
C. Is Scenario Planning an appropriate tool?
D. Is the company's leadership ready to walk the talk of breaking silos and move power down to the teams?

Empowered teams need to think strategically while ensuring agile tactical implementation. Paul Hudson, Sanofi's CEO, commented in a recent Fortune Magazine: *Pharma needs to stop chasing shiny objects and start embracing practical technology. It may sound counterintuitive, but if we want to leapfrog into the next innovation era, Pharma companies must first pause and develop a strategic vision for adopting the new tech*.

Reimagine Pharma Marketing: Make it Future Proof presents the reader with a current view of the changing Pharma marketing environment. It shows how the new tools of the technology and approaches, and organizational structures are needed to thrive in a rapidly changing market place.

Subba Rao Chaganti

ACKNOWLEDGEMENTS

First and foremost, my sincere thanks and heartiest congratulations to all those digitally savvy brand teams who created all those great digital campaigns discussed in this book. The one hundred and two cases in this book show us how to use digital and other technologies and social media in the highly restrictive pharmaceutical marketing. They had done some brilliant and outstanding work. They taught many valuable insights and practical lessons to pharmaceutical marketers and all aspiring pharmaceutical brand managers. Without them, there is no Reimagining Pharma Marketing book. They are the *raison d'être* for this book.

I must express my gratitude to all those who have helped me in this long journey of fifty-five years in pharmaceutical marketing. But, unfortunately, there are far too many to mention here.

However, I must mention two individuals who were great re-imagineers in their own right and might and who have been an inspiration to me for reimagining this *book, Reimagine Pharma Marketing: Make it Future-Proof!*

They are the Late Prof. Tarun Gupta, director of marketing at Glaxo (GSK, now), who reimagined pharmaceutical marketing in India in the early seventies and created a strategic model that the entire pharmaceutical industry followed India for over fifty years, and many still do. The other is the late Prof. Chitta Mitra, founder-chairman of C Marc. He pioneered prescription research and taught the entire industry how to use it as a powerful and indispensable strategic marketing tool in India.

There are two more individuals— Mr. S Chandrasekhar and Mr. V. Thiagarajan to whom I am grateful for encouraging me to experiment and learn at work during my formative years in the industry.

One cannot claim a book of this magnitude as the work of one individual. Many people have helped me in producing this book. It is impossible to acknowledge all those who helped me create this book individually. I sincerely thank all my teachers and peers who have helped me widen my horizon and broaden my perspective of marketing in general and pharmaceutical marketing in particular.

Here are a few individuals whose help and support have been truly significant. Without their physical, intellectual, and moral support, this book would still be in a conceptual stage. I sincerely thank Mr. J. Siva Prasad, Managing Director of Amita Designs, for designing a fantastic cover for the book.

My thanks to Mr. Anil Shah for his faith in this project. Apart from being a publisher with vision, he has been pushing me to bring about this book. I must also thank Mr. Nikunjesh Shah for making digital versions of this book available. Finally, my thanks are also to Mr. Naresh Daver for designing this book beautifully.

Last but not least, I owe my thanks to Mahalakshmi, my better half, both literally and figuratively. I must also thank my three children and their spouses (Srinivasa Phanindra, Geetha, Lavanya, Aditya, Soumya, and Chaitanya) for supporting and pushing me to write the Reimagine Pharma Marketing book. More importantly, I thank my grandchildren - Aditi, Eesha, Surya, and Shriya. They watched me with awe while I was writing this book, which inspired me greatly and gave me tremendous satisfaction.

Subba Rao Chaganti

CONTENTS

LIST OF ABBREVIATIONS

ADA	American Diabetes Association
ADHD	Attention Deficit Hyperactivity Disorder
AF	Atrial Fibrillation
AI	Artificial Intelligence
AMD	Age Related Macular Degeneration
ANA	Association of National Advertisers
AR	Augmented Reality
AWS	Amazon Web Services
BLA	Biological License Application
BMI	Body Mass Index
BMS	Bristol-Myers Squibb
CDC	Centers for Disease Control
CDC	Centers for Disease Control and Prevention
CDRH	Center for Devices and Radiological Health
CDS	Clinical Decision Support
CIO	Chief Information Officer
CKD	Chronic Kidney Disease
CLM	Closed-Loop Marketing
CME	Continuing Medical Education
CMO	Chief Marketing Officer
CMS	Centers for Medicare and Medicaid Services
CNS	Central Nervous System
COPD	Chronic Obstructive Pulmonary Disorder
CPC	Cost-per-Click
CPT	Cost per Thousand
CPT	Current Procedural Technology
CRM	Customer Relationship Management
CTA	Call-To-Action
CTC	Click to Conversion
CTO	Chief Technology Officer
CTR	Click-Through-Rate
CVS	Consumer Value Stores

CX	Customer Experience
DOL	Digital Opinion Leader
DSCSA	Drug Supply Chain Security Act
DTC	Direct-to-Consumer
DTx	Digital Therapeutics
EBITDA	Earnings Before Interest Tax Depreciation and Amortization
ECG	Electro Cardiogram
EFCCA	European Federation of Crohn's and Colitis Association
EHR	Electronic Health Record
ELN	Electronic Lab Notebook
EMR	Electronic Medical Record
e-MSL	Electronic Medical Science Liaison
F2F	Face-to-Face
FHIR	Fast Healthcare Interoperability Resources
GRPs	Gross Rating Points
GSK	GlaxoSmithKline
HCP	Healthcare Professional
HIPAA	Health Insurance Portability and Accountability Act
HMD	Head-mounted Display
HNCA	Head and Neck Cancer Alliance
IBD	Inflammatory Bowel Disease
IIOT	Industrial Internet of Things
IoT	Internet of Things
ISP	Indication-Specific Pricing
IVR	Interactive Voice Response
KOL	Key Opinion Leader
KPI	Key Performance Indicator
LIMS	Laboratory Information Management Systems
MCCPDC	Mark Cuban's Cost Plus Drug Company
MCM	Multichannel Marketing
MDD	Major Depressive Disorder
ML	Machine Learning
MLR	Medical Legal Regulatory
MOA	Mechanism of Action

MOA	Mechanism of Action
MOD	Method of Delivery
MR	Mixed Reality
MSD	Merck Sharp and Dohme
MSL	Medical Science Liaison
NCDs	Noncommunicable Diseases
NHS	National Health Service
NLP	Natural Language Processing
NPS	Net Promoter Score
NUHS	National University Health System (Singapore)
OAB	Over Active Bladder
PAG	Patient Advocacy Group
PBM	Pharmacy Benefit Manager
PDT	Prescription Digital Therapeutics
PDUFA	Prescription Drug Use Fee Act
POV	Point of View
PPC	Pay-Per-Click
PQRS	Physician Quality Reporting System
PRO	Patient Reported Outcome
PSP	Patient Support Program
PSSD	Psoriasis Symptoms & Signs Diary
PTSD	Post-Traumatic Stress Disorder
RCT	Randomized Clinical Trial
RCT	Randomized Clinical Trials
ROE	Return on Engagement
ROI	Return on Investment
RPA	Robotic Process Automation
RWD	Real-World Data
RWE	Real-World Evidence
SaaS	Software as a Service
SaMD	Software as a Medical Device
SDGs	Sustainable Development Goals
SDoH	Social Determinants of Health
SEA	Search Engine Advertising

SEM	Search Engine Marketing
SEO	Search Engine Optimization
SERPs	Search Engine Result Pages
SMS	Short Messaging Service
sNDA	Supplementary New Drug Application
TAM	Total Addressable Market
TRPs	Television Rating Points
UCPMP	Universal Code of Pharmaceutical Marketing Practices
UHC	Universal Health Coin
URL	Universal Resource Locator
USB	Universal Serial Bus
USPTO	United States Patent and Trademark Office
UX	User Experience
VR	Virtual Reality
XR	Extended Reality

CHAPTER

1

Reimagine Everything

Reimagine every element of the Pharmaceutical Marketing Mix

Plug into the anti-obvious power of the rebel,
or get those opposing minds to
Plug into your purpose, to solve your problem,
to reimagine your process.

— *Max McKeown*

Why Reimagine?

Just when the caterpillar thought, the world was over, it became a butterfly!

—*Proverb*

What is Reimagining?

Reimagining, in simple terms, means to imagine or conceive something in a new way. However, there is more than mere semantics to the word *Reimagine*. Reimagining is an organizational vision that challenges its members to push the limits of innovation and look beyond traditional industry norms.

Why Reimagine?

Before answering the question, Why reimagine, let us understand what we exactly mean by 'reimagining.' Reimagining means to think again or anew, especially to change or improve. Why Reimagine? The emergence of an era of consumerism and digital and data disruption are placing new demands on business, and operational models make reimagining the new strategic imperative. Additionally, two major reasons necessitate reimagining. One is digital disruption. The other is the COVID-19 Pandemic.

Digital Disruption

Digital disruption affects every industry, and the pharmaceutical industry is no exception. Consequently, it is creating a host of problems for companies. Here are some of the major problems. Digital disruption is:

- breaking down long-standing business models
- changing customer expectations rapidly
- blunting the competitive edge of leading firms

What is the best way to solve these problems? The only way to solve these problems is by embarking on a digital transformation. Companies should transform and reinvent themselves as digitally powered, next-generation enterprises to remain competitive. However, digital transformation is not just about technology, nor should it be led by it. Instead, the transformation process should begin with the customer. Because digital disruption often manifests itself as a disruption of the customer experience. Digital disruptions offer superior customer value propositions across the dimensions of cost, control, convenience, customization, and community. Consider, for example, how Uber has transformed the experience of hailing a taxi or how Tesla has changed the experience of owning and driving a car.

That is why the most affected functions in organizations by digital disruptions are customer-facing functions such as sales and marketing. Digital disruption reaches a company through its marketing function because it impacts the customer experience more directly and immediately than manufacturing, finance, or human resources. Marketing, therefore, is ideally positioned to combat digital disruption and become the firm's competitive edge by leading its digital transformation program.

Marketing, therefore, must reimagine and transform itself to harness the power of new and emerging technologies. The outcome of such a transformation is a new concept of marketing that looks very different in terms of strategy, processes, people, and systems. Data drives the reimagined marketing while automation powers it and analytics optimize it.

Many people mistakenly think that reimagining marketing means becoming more digital or adopting digital marketing. However, digital is just a channel providing new mechanisms for engaging customers. Rather, reimagining marketing is about transforming operations and skillsets across the entire marketing organization.

Reimagining marketing involves reimagining every element of the marketing mix. It involves all aspects such as how work gets done, how technology is used, how to engage with customers, and how to organize people and processes.

Disruption in a business environment is inevitable. When disruption is inevitable, there is only one option. To be the disruptor because i you don't disrupt your business, someone else will disrupt. The message is loud and clear! Disrupt, or be disrupted!

The COVID-19 Pandemic

That the novel coronavirus (COVID-19) pandemic has changed the world would be an understatement. In less than a year since the virus emerged, it's upended day-to-day lives across the globe. It has changed how we work, learn and interact and interact. Its social distancing guidelines have led to a more virtual existence, both personally and professionally. How and when did it originate?

While the exact origin of the COVID-19 is not clear yet (at the time of writing), WHO (World Health Organization) was informed on December 31, 2019, that a few cases of pneumonia of unknown origin in Wuhan City, China. A week later, on January 7, 2020, the Chinese authorities identified a novel coronavirus as the cause and temporarily named it '2019-nCOV.' Very soon, the virus spread worldwide in an unprecedented manner, causing the worst-ever damage globally, resulting in huge loss in terms of human lives and economy. The number of human lives lost globally due to the pandemic was over 167.4 million between January 7, 2021, and May 23, 2021. The world economy too suffered heavily, resulting in a 4.5 percent drop in 2020, which in monetary terms is a huge loss of 3.94 trillion US dollars in one year.

Impact on Pharma Industry

The rapid onset of the COVID-19 pandemic at its peak brought in-person engagement to a grinding halt. The 'in-person' engagement has been the standard that health and life sciences companies use to interact with their physician customers and other healthcare provider customers. Even after its slowing down, in-person engagement levels have come down significantly. COVID-19 forced pharma companies to explore alternative ways to engage their customers. Pharma companies, who have already started engaging their customers remotely through digital channels, have stepped it up. Those who have not started digital or remote engagement began adopting digital engagement. The standard practices are changing because of COVID-19 and will likely continue to change as this is a behavioral trigger point for the industry.

The New Normal

COVID-19 has transformed nearly every aspect of life as we know it. No other event has so pervasively affected our lives, from work to family to home. Virtually every aspect of our day-to-day activities has been profoundly altered. Everything has changed. Consider these, for example:

- Social distancing has become common.
- Telemedicine is being encouraged even though medical centers and physicians' offices are reopened.
- Most health authorities and governments recommend no gathering of >100 people, avoiding certain rotating geographic hotspots.
- Conferences, major sporting events, and concerts are not expected to return until fall 2021, and to their former levels ever any time soon.
- Some level of contact tracing is in place in most countries.
- Contactless transactions, including healthcare, will become the norm for payments and data transfers.

Can we ever go back to how we managed our business pre-COVID-19? Unlikely. The changes have set in for too long and significantly impacted us adapting quickly, and trying many new things to keep our businesses afloat during this global pandemic.

Managing in the Post-COVID-19 Times

Managing the post-COVID-19 times offers us unique challenges as well as opportunities. Consider the challenges first. The key questions to answer are:

- What changes to healthcare will affect our industry?
- How will consumer behavior evolve?
- What will the Pharma brand launches look like in the future?

- What shifts are likely in the sales-rep access to physicians in the future?
- How can pharmaceutical companies remain viable, profitable partners in the healthcare exchange?

Opportunities for Pharma

The COVID-19 pandemic has accelerated many pre-existing trends such as:

- an increase in the use of health tech and telemedicine
- a decrease in sales-rep access
- a focus on customer experience
- the momentum of digital transformation across pharma organizations, which have been lagging

The pandemic has sharpened the focus on these trends and brought urgency. Also, it revealed new opportunities to upend a stagnant status quo to make dramatic improvements in areas that, until now, had not received focus. In May 2020, The Intouch Group and DHC Group released a white-paper titled—*The Aftermath: COVID-19 Insights & Recommendations - How the Pandemic Will Forever Change Pharma Sales & Marketing* that highlights the following opportunities:

- Opportunities to support telemedicine and a broader ecosystem of connected health
- A shift toward a data-driven, customized concierge approach for medical reps
- Virtual medical events offering further reach
- Enhanced PSPs (Patient Support Programs) with the patient at the center
- More meaningful methods of decreasing the cost burden on patients
- A movement toward remote clinical trials and the digitization of product launches
- Enhanced access to, and interoperability of health data interoperability of health

The pandemic has created two significant opportunities for pharmaceutical companies—one is at the convergence of health and technology, the other being to improve its declining reputation. Above all, the pandemic offers an unprecedented opportunity to positively affect the pharmaceutical industry's image, moving from the present perception of a greedy, profit-focused industry to a more authentic, life-saving, game-changing value the industry brings.

Rahm Emanuel, former Chicago mayor and former White House Chief of Staff under President Barrack Obama, said some time ago: *Never allow a crisis to go waste. It is an opportunity to do the things you once thought were impossible*.

Organizations waiting for change can never be disrupters as they wait to be disrupted.

Reimagine the Pharmaceutical Market

The Pharmaceutical Market

Traditionally, pharmaceutical companies worked to develop mass-produced, mostly chemically developed drugs to treat various disease conditions, large afflicting patient populations, and promote these to physicians who then prescribe to patients. Although this blockbuster model is rapidly becoming outdated, many global pharmaceutical companies still cling to this model, which is bound to change soon. Consider these reasons for the impending change, for example:

1. *Rising costs*: Costs have been rising continuously for over two decades across the Pharma value chain—from R&D to manufacturing to marketing, making the discovery and development of new products very expensive. In addition, increasing generics competition, patent expirations, dwindling new product pipelines, the growing importance of biosimilars, and the ever-increasing cost-containment pressures from payers and the various governments have led to more price pressure on the pharmaceutical market.
2. *Changing consumer preferences*: Modern consumers (patients), having used seamless, integrated experiences across devices offered by other industries such as travel, entertainment, and retail, expect the same from pharmaceutical companies.
3. *A basic shift* from curative to preventative approach in treating disease

Changing Landscape

The healthcare landscape is changing rapidly. With the advancement of technologies and changing needs of patients, clinicians, and payers for care outside the hospital, breadth of treatment is increasingly available at ASCs (Ambulatory Surgery Centers) and patients' homes. Thus, examinations, therapies, and treatments are migrating outside the hospital and into new points of care. Factors driving this trend are:

- The rising cost of care pushes patients to find more accessible care options that meet their needs better.
- As hospitals acquire independent practices, the growing cost of care makes patients seek alternative care options.
- Sites of care are shifting.
- Providers' organizations are consolidating.
- Health data is exploding.
- Reimbursement rules are changing.
- Telehealth has reached high levels of adoption.

COVID-19 pandemic pushed some of these care delivery changes, and others are the result of the increasing influence and mandate of key stakeholders like empowered patients and their increasing influence on the ecosystem.

Shifting of Points of Care: Implications for Pharma Marketers

The digital revolution has impacted the environment in physicians' offices too. The average waiting time for patients in a physician's office is twenty minutes past their appointment time to see the doctor, according to *The Vitals Eighth Annual Wait Times Report 2017* in the US. As a result, physicians' offices have redecorated their waiting areas to engage the waiting patients. While the medical practices still have posters and wallboards, most POC (Point-of-Care) marketing now takes place digitally.

What are the implications for Pharma marketers of this shifting and expansion of points-of-care? First, the increased digital channels such as interactive exam room tablets, touchscreen wallboards, check-in tablets, and sponsored Wi-fi connections offer brands more ways to engage with patients, extending the reach and impact of the brand's digital assets. Thanks to the advanced technologies, patients can now access brand websites, method of administration videos, safety information, patient testimonials, and other materials online from the waiting areas in the physician's office, including the exam room. In addition, some companies offer digital content on mobile devices to help educate and inform patients.

As Nancy Phelan, Outcome Health's senior vice president of commercial growth, has rightly observed, *Leveraging technology during the moment of Care to inform and empower patients in the minutes before, during, and after their consultation has a measurable impact on the patient/doctor discussion as well as treatment adoption*.

Impact of POC (Point-of-Care) Messaging

Pharma brand managers believe POC (Point-of-Care) messaging has significant advantages over the digital display as it targets specific patient groups. In addition, It provides a greater opportunity to impact patients when choosing a treatment or a prescription drug. As a result, there seems to be a change in the focus of POC channels from brand awareness to patient education and adherence or support program registration.

The Point of Care Communication Council noted a high patient-reported impact from POC messaging. According to a study on the effect of POC messages on patients, 68 percent of patients asked for a brand they had been exposed to in POC marketing, and 65 percent indicated that they were more likely to switch brands after seeing POC messages. Furthermore, the study showed an impact beyond the office too. Thirty-one percent of patients were more likely to fill the prescriptions after seeing healthcare advertising at the point of Care.

While Point-of-Care marketing is allowed in the US, most countries do not permit it. For example, In Spain, Italy, and the UK, only healthcare professionals (HCPs) or patient organizations can communicate about PSPs (Patient Support Programs) to patients. Therefore, pharmaceutical companies in these countries must not promote any PSP openly and to the general public. Moreover, the communication materials in the context of PSP must be factual, educational, and neutral and not contain any promotional overtures.

Change in Approach

So far, Pharma has been following its traditional one-to-one customer approach. However, its success in the changing healthcare ecosystem calls for a shift in customer approach for a more dynamic business-to-ecosystem (B2E) mindset, observes Pratap Khedkar in his article, *It's time for biopharma to elevate its role from 'supplier' to 'partner'* published on July 6, 2021, on ZS Associates blog, zs.com.

An ideal healthcare ecosystem is full of life and activity with many partnerships and collaborations to provide a better patient experience, improve health outcomes, and control costs. However, some key players, such as pharmaceutical companies, HCPs (Healthcare professionals), provider organizations, and health plans, largely carry out their functions in silos.

Pharmaceutical companies should dive deep into the huge data available and understand and acknowledge each stakeholder's goals and objectives to uncover new opportunities to align priorities and collaborate. Pharma should think beyond their current level of thinking and center their business operations on HCPs (Healthcare Professionals), and other stakeholders as the decision-making power of other stakeholders, such as patients and provider organizations, is increasing.

Future of Healthcare

The healthcare market is in for a transformation. While several factors drive it, two factors play a major role in mandating it. Firstly, customers, being almost pampered by other industries providing seamless experiences with their products and services, also expect similar experiences from pharmaceutical companies.

Secondly, the outside players, including big tech players and startups entering the field, make it more competitive. For the past few years, tech companies have invested in machine learning and artificial intelligence solutions in data & analytics, genomics, and administration to launch products and services addressing the unmet needs of patients with regular therapies and chronic diseases.

While pharmaceutical companies focusing on the curative part of the disease have often not paid adequate attention to this overlooked area, this is an area of great importance in the holistic picture of medical treatment. In contrast, innovators and disruptors like tech companies and startups enter the market by discovering and capturing the uncovered opportunities across the patient journey.

Therefore, healthcare companies, including pharmaceutical companies, must accelerate their digitalization of internal processes and upping their offering.

In addition, the changing regulatory environment is also driving the change toward the digitalization of the healthcare industry.

Evolving Healthcare Ecosystems

The Healthcare industries are moving toward new digital ecosystems and data-driven services to unlock new revenue streams by providing holistic solutions throughout the patient journey. These ecosystems help deliver superior patient care by connecting different players in mutually beneficial collaborations.

Why A New Ecosystem?

Although an old English phrase, *A Jack of all trades is a master of none but often better than a master of one,* is often used in a derogatory sense, it may be more apt to describe the current situation of our healthcare in general. While the highly specialized contribution of specialists and super specialists is quite significant in our healthcare, a gap exists in our traditionally siloed, treatment-specific approach to providing optimal patient care. It seems to result in fragmented, even uncoordinated Care perpetuating the exponential increase in the utilization and cost of Care. As a result, health equity remains a dream and, if not remedied, may remain so even in the future. So, the dilemma continues, and the key question remains: *How do we help patients address their health and wellness challenges before they face significant personal and financial problems*?

The answer to this question may lie in a new ecosystem that is collaborative and multi-disciplinary to meet the healthcare challenges of today and tomorrow because these challenges are becoming increasingly medically complex, socially diverse, and technologically sophisticated populations.

So far, pharmaceutical companies and other healthcare stakeholders' approaches have focused on healthy patient outcomes. However, they have not paid the required attention to behavioral health initiatives. Yet, these initiatives are increasingly gaining importance in addressing a patient's health and well-being. Pharmaceutical companies cannot afford to ignore these factors as they are related to health equity and social determinants of health (SDoH).

The following five cases illustrate how some big tech firms and healthcare players powered by technology are transforming the healthcare landscape as we know it. For example, whoever has thought of Amazon, the world's largest online store, would be a leading primary care provider in the US? And Walmart, the global retail giant's foray into healthcare? Also, could anyone visualize that an unstaffed *Ping AI Doctor One-Minute clinic* powered by artificial intelligence will help bridge the physician shortage and improve healthcare access?

CASE

1

Amazon's Foray into Health Care: Too Big to Fail!

Amazon, the e-commerce behemoth, has been serious about entering healthcare for some time now.

Why Healthcare? Why Pharmacy? The size of the opportunity is the primary reason. According to the *US Primary Care Physicians Market Size Report, 2030*, the healthcare industry was worth $808 billion in the US as of 2021. About a third of revenue comes from patient care. The primary care physician market was around $260.1 billion in 2021 and is expected to reach $266 billion in 2022.

Let us now consider the pharmacy market. For example, the US pharmacy market alone was worth a whopping $312.6 billion in 2021, with a growth rate of approximately 3 percent since 2018. The UK pharmacy sector was around $15.52 billion in 2021. In addition, the global online pharmacy business has become a giant of an industry in its own right is expected to grow from $68.4 billion in 2021 at a CAGR (Compound Average Growth Rate) of 16.1 percent to reach $261.7 billion by 2030 according to a report by Prescient & Strategic Intelligence.

The Beginning

Amazon has been eyeing this huge market opportunity and making strategic movies to enter it, for over two decades. It all started in February 1999, when Amazon bought a 40 percent stake in drugstore.com Inc to get a foot in the door on the retail side of the prescription drug business. However, it eventually ran into the existing web of middlemen, and regulators, bringing its ambitions to a halt.

The Strategy

Amazon has, then identified an unmet need— a pain point for patients in the current healthcare system. It has realized that patients are tired of a healthcare system that doesn't put them first and addressed that with its patient-centric service to change that one visit at a time. They have brought on-demand urgent and primary care services to patients nationwide.

The four foundational principles of Amazon's core strategy are:

1. Firstly, introduce a customer-friendly product with user experience and create a customer experience superior to the competition. It helps the company to build economies of scale, network effects, and the power to negotiate with other suppliers.
2. Invest in upfront fixed costs to function better and provide customers with an outsourced version of the services. For example, FBA (Fulfilled By Amazon) and AWS (Amazon Web Services) allow companies to use warehousing, data storage, and analytics, which are traditionally expensive on a rent-to-own basis.
3. Once your platform reaches a critical mass of users, standardize users' (suppliers') offerings.
4. Ensure standardization that removes messy, fragmented back-office functions and creates transparent and competitive markets for buyers and suppliers.

Sticking to these four principles, Amazon has followed a strategic acquisition path for its healthcare strategy to achieve the domain expertise and talent needed to create its mark in the new business. The following table presents a snapshot of Amazon's acquisitions in the healthcare space.

Amazon took another shot in 2018 at entering healthcare by forming a joint venture, Haven, with two of America's most powerful companies—Berkshire Hathway and JP Morgan Chase to lower costs and improve outcomes in healthcare. However, three years

Table 1.1 Amazon's Acquisitions and Initiatives in Healthcare Space

Year	Acquired	Purpose
1999	40 percent stake in drugstore.com, an online pharmacy.	To enter into online pharmacy business
2018	PillPack for $ 753 million. PillPack delivers most of the medications consumers can get from their local drugstores pac kaged in convenient white packets so people will remember to take them, along with automatic refills and 24/7 customer support.	To gain access to the highly lucrative pharmacy business in all the fifty states in the US and attract customers with PIllPack's customer-centric approach and Amazon's obsession in creating great customer experiences.
2019	Launches Healthcare service (Amazon Care) for Amazon employees in Seattle.	Piloting the Amazon's Healthcare Program, Amazon Care.
2019	Acquires Health Navigator, which provides technology and services to digital healthcare.	To augment Amazon Care in creating superior customer experiences.
2020	Launches Amazon Pharmacy, rebrands PIllPack.	To increase and expand its pharmacy business.
2021	Expands Amazon Care, by opening it to other companies.	Amazon Care extended to other companies and plans to extend it to 20 cities, including Seattle, and Los Angeles by the end of 2022. Plans to cover all 50 States in the US.
2022	Acquires One Medical, the primary care company for $3.9 billion.	To enter the primary care business, expand the reach and scope of Amazon Care, and to reinvent 'healthcare'.

(Source: Multiple blog articles and the company websites, amazon.care, amazon.com)

later, it had to be shut down as each of the three founding companies (Amazon, Berkshire Hathway, and JP Morgan Chase) seemed to be executing their projects separately with their employees, obviating the need for the joint venture, to begin with, according to some unidentifiable sources. However, Amazon's determination to enter healthcare continues and is evident from its subsequent strategic moves.

Acquires PillPack

Amazon's acquisition of PillPack, an online pharmacy that lets users buy medications in pre-made doses, underscores how it wants a more direct and commercial role in the healthcare business. The acquisition has made significant headway for Amazon in the pharmaceutical distribution space.

PillPack is a good fit for Amazon. Customers love PillPack as it serves them efficiently and effectively with its prescription management platform, *pharmacyOS*, similar to Amazon's order management and fulfillment services, Fulfillment by Amazon (FBA). PillPack has an NPS (Net Promoter Score) of 80 compared to the pharmacy average of 20, which shows how customers love It. In addition, with its PillPack acquisition, Amazon gained a $100 million revenue run-rate business, a built-out pharmacy supply, and pharmacy licenses in all 50 states. In addition, Amazon rebranded PillPack as Amazon Pharmacy, making its strategic intent to disrupt the online pharmacy business.

Launches Amazon Pharmacy

In 2020, Amazon announced the launch of Amazon Pharmacy. Amazon Pharmacy provides discounts on prescription drugs through its subscription program, Amazon Prime, which allows customers to track their orders through Prime. Also, it allows cash-paying customers to price-shop their prescriptions through a partnership with InsideRx, which allows Amazon to reference prices from Express Scripts.

Advantage, Amazon Pharmacy!

With its razor focus on hassle-free experiences, personalization, and ease of use, Amazon has a distinct advantage over its competitors in the pharmacy business. The company reinforces its differentiators to disrupt the pharmacy business. Marina Turea identifies *Six Ways Amazon Plans to Disrupt the Pharmacy Business* in a blog article of the same title in Healthcare Weekly published on August 6, 2021. Here is the gist:

1. *Amazon boasts a large, loyal customer base* of over 300 million active customers, 100 million Prime members, and about five

million sellers on the site, which could prove useful for its health solutions business.

2. *Home delivery of pills*: PillPack (Amazon Pharmacy now) will handle the medication dispensing, monitoring, and support to individual patients, payers, manufacturers, and new companies in the form of a pharmacy delivery API (Application Programming Interface) to plug into. In addition, the acquisition of Whole Foods allows Amazon to set up in-store pharmacies to complement PillPack's online business.
3. *Ability to offer discounted drug prices*: Amazon can afford to pursue low-profit initiatives owing to the cash that its ecosystem helps to generate. For example, Amazon now offers Medicaid beneficiaries a discounted prime membership. It could even allow them to use SNAP (Supplemental Nutrition Benefits) on the site directly.
3. *Superior customer experiences*: For example, Amazon Web Services (AWS) can help handle the enormous data loads and analysis necessary to create great customer experiences in healthcare.
4. *Amazon's holistic approach to healthcare*: Amazon now offers Medicaid beneficiaries a discounted prime membership. The company is working to create a wholesome or one-stop shop for every healthcare need the patient might have, say from diagnostics and treatment to wellness and recovery. In addition, Amazon's ability to cover food and groceries allows it to offer disease-specific meal kits to people in locations where access to fresh produce might be difficult. Also, Amazon could differentiate its meal kit offering to meet the health needs of Medicaid and Medicare populations as a differentiating tactic.
5. *Alexa*, the AI (Artificial Intelligence)-powered digital voice assistant of Amazon, can help patients and shoppers to fill their prescriptions and pick up other wellness products or consumables. Furthermore, Amazon has partnered with several developers and healthcare firms to empower Alexa to help with chronic disease management. Alexa can help automate the process with PillPack, scheduling prescriptions and delivering medications as required. In addition, Amazon's

Echo, its voice-controlled speaker with video capabilities, is ideal for monitoring purposes, especially at home, once it becomes HIPAA (Health Insurance Portability and Accountability)-compliant. The Echo could be used to monitor adherence and give notifications about medications. It could also be a hub for services like telemedicine, digital therapeutics companies, coaches, and more to help manage Medicaid and Medicare members in their homes. Amazon, for example, has patents for monitoring blood flow and heart rate through the camera and could expand to *fall detection* and *gait monitoring*. Additionally, Alexa could integrate into EMRs (Electronic Medical Records) as a passive note taker during visits and address the pain points of doctors who find the EMR process inefficient and time-consuming, requiring them to take down information from patients during the visits manually. Over time, Alexa could help shift Amazon from the middleware that populates an EMR system into an EMR.

Amazon Care

In 2019, Amazon launched its initial Amazon Care pilot to its employees in the Seattle area. However, the company has been aggressively planning to expand it to the general population ever since.

Amazon Care's model is based on a virtual and physical approach, offering in-person visits from healthcare professionals and other digital services coordinated through an app.

Amazon acquired One Medical, a concierge primary care company, for $3.9 billion to expand Amazon Care's reach into primary Care. The acquisition allows Amazon Care to address many pain points patients undergo in accessing primary care, such as—booking an appointment, waiting weeks or even months to be seen, taking time off work, driving to a clinic, finding a parking spot, waiting in the waiting room then the exam room for what is too often a rushed few minutes with a doctor, then making another trip to a pharmacy. As a result, Amazon Care sees a huge opportunity to improve the quality of the experience significantly.

Amazon Care plans to extend its services to over twenty cities by the end of 2022 and eventually to all the fifty states in the US.

Amir Dan Rubin, president and CEO of One Medical said in the press release that Amazon's acquisition of One Medical reflects the company's strategic intent. He said:

The opportunity to transform healthcare and improve outcomes by combining One Medical's human-centered and technology-powered model and exceptional team with Amazon's customer obsession, history of invention, and willingness to invest in the long-term is so exciting. There is an immense opportunity to make the healthcare experience more accessible, affordable, and enjoyable for patients, providers, and payers. We look forward to innovating and expanding access to quality healthcare services together.

With a patient satisfaction score of 4.7 out of 5, Amazon is becoming the partner of choice for organizations looking to offer workplace benefits. The three reasons customers cite for embracing Amazon Care are its main differentiators. These are:

1. Amazon Care's comprehensive solution
2. On-demand access to high-quality clinicians through Care Medical, Amazon Care's clinical services provider, and
3. A seamless patient experience

More Healthcare Initiatives

Besides Amazon Pharmacy and Amazon Care, Amazon is taking more initiatives in the healthcare space signaling its intent to make a big difference in the healthcare market. Consider these, for example:

- AWS (Amazon Web Services) has been helping genomics organizations accelerate the translation of raw sequencing data into actionable insights through scalable, secure, and cost-effective solutions. Many industry leaders such as Ancestry, AstraZeneca, Illumina Genomics, DNANexus, Genomics England, and GRAIL use AWS to reduce costs, enhance security and do more with their data.
- In December 2020, Amazon announced its Amazon HealthLake, a HIPAA (Health Insurance Portability and

Accountability Act)-eligible service for healthcare organizations that aggregates an organization's complete data across various silos and disparate formats into a centralized AWS (Amazon Web Service) data lake, and automatically normalizes this information, using machine learning. Amazon HealthLake identifies each piece of clinical information, tags and indexes events in a timeline view with standardized labels to make it highly searchable, and structures all data into the Fast Healthcare Interoperability Resources (FHIR) industry-standard format for a complete view of the health of individual patients and entire populations. Thus, Amazon HealthLake can help healthcare professionals, providers, health insurers, and pharmaceutical companies provide patients and populations with data-driven, personalized, and predictive care.

- Amazon has also announced the AWS Diagnostic Development Initiative, committing $20 million to support projects using AWS to support research-oriented workloads across four program areas: early disease detection, diagnostics, prognosis, and public health genomics.
- Amazon is almost DSCSA (Drug Supply Chain Security Act) Ready. The Drug Supply Chain Security Act in the US in 2023 requires that all pill bottles be traceable from end to end. In addition, all parties involved in the pharmacy supply chain should be a part of a universal interoperable tracking system. With its robust logistics framework and the requisite licenses, Amazon could run a fulfillment system for healthcare companies like the Fulfillment By Amazon (FBA) service. It can meet all interoperability and tracking requirements called for by the DSCSA.

What Could Amazon Do?

Finally, what Amazon could do in the healthcare space could be summed up by what Robin Gaster, an Amazon expert and author of the book *Behemoth, Amazon Rising: Power and Seduction in the Age of Amazon*, told Home Health Care News:

Amazon has made a business out of dis-intermediating existing businesses and markets, and that's what they're going to do here.

Further, it seems that the healthcare space is pretty well set up for what they want to do, and businesses are desperate to try and find cheaper ways to address health issues.

Amazon Care's Shutting Down in a Strategic Move

Amazon plans to cease its operations of Amazon Care from December 31, 2022, and the company has sent an email to Amazon Health Services employees accordingly. The company's decision to pull the shutters down on Amazon Care just three years after it began piloting a primary care service for its employees, blending telehealth and in-person medical services is a strategic move and not a withdrawal.

While some healthcare experts opine that Amazon Care's shutdown represents a failure of the company to understand the complexity of Healthcare, Forrester Research believes that Amazon's closing Amazon care is not the end of the retail titan's healthcare ventures. Instead, the shutdown of Amazon Care is a strategic plan to move the focus of healthcare offerings from the employee to the consumer. Natalie Schibell, VP, Research Director, and Kara Wilson, Researcher, explain the reasons why the shutdown of Amazon Care is a strategic move, not a failure, in their Forrester blog article, *Amazon Pulls the Plug on Amazon Care, Signaling A New Dawn of Healthcare Disruption*, published on August 28, 2022. Here are the reasons in brief:

- *Shifting the focus from employees to customers*: Amazon is moving away from employee healthcare (with Amazon Care) and setting its sights on direct-to-consumer (DTC) opportunities, offering patients convenient care that is timely, personalized, and more affordable. It can remove barriers to healthcare access.
- *Moving the needle on value-based care*: Amazon's customer-centric model can potentially reinvent the patient experience by putting the patient at the center of the patient journey to drive value-based, quality care at every touch point and provide proactive rather than reactive care.

- *Targeting the entire care continuum*: By closing the doors of Amazon Care, moving to acquire One Medical, and bidding for Signify Health signal the retail giant's strategic intent of targeting the full care continuum. These moves can make Amazon a patient's one-stop shop for all health products and primary care services, health food, and prescriptions.

(Source: Adapted from CB insights Report, Amazon in Healthcare: *The E-Commerce Giant's Strategy for A $3 Trillion Market* published on September 5, 2018, in their blog, cbinsights.com; and blog articles—Heather Landi, *Amazon Care is Shutting Down at the End of 2022. Here's Why*, Fierce Healthcare, August 24, 2022; and Natalie Schibell, VP, Research Director, and Kara Wilson, Researcher, forrester.com/blog, August 28, 2022)

CASE

2

Walmart Health's Disruptive Moves!

Walmart's journey into healthcare began in 2014 when it launched a program called, *Healthcare Begins Here* as a passport to the healthier living event at local Walmart Stores throughout the country. The program provided consumers with healthcare information to guide them on their journey to live healthier lives. In addition, consumers also had access to several preventative services such as free blood pressure, blood glucose, and vision screenings and access to immunizations and a one-stop-shop health insurance enrollment platform. The program's success reinforced the company's faith that it could make a difference in healthcare. In addition, it has led to other successful initiatives, including new supplier collaboration opportunities beyond the pharmacy to create great customer experiences.

In 2019, Walmart launched its first Walmart Health 'Superstore' in Dallas, Georgia, to provide medical access to patients with no or poor insurance coverage in underserved areas. Since then, Walmart has expanded its network of Walmart Health Centers.

Walmart launched its health superstores initiative in Georgia at low cash prices, such as a flat $40 for an adult primary care visit. Compared to this, Walmart, which contracts with roughly 90 percent of the payers in Florida for its new centers, has been charging $90 for an annual adult checkup.

Walmart is vying with competitors like CVS and Walgreens to expand primary care networks as COVID-19 continues to drive demand for low-cost care outside the physician's office or hospital. With a huge customer base of about 5,000 physical stores and a strong customer-focused approach, Walmart has a distinct competitive advantage in penetrating the healthcare business.

Walmart is keen on expanding its network of health centers to all 50 states. However, it prioritizes rural areas in states with aging demographics, growing populations, and access challenges for near-term growth.

Walmart Health Centers deliver primary and urgent care, labs, X-rays, diagnostics, dental, optical, hearing, and behavioral health and counseling under one roof, with transparent pricing for patients at the point of service.

The highly customer-centric Walmart provides an omnichannel experience for its patients. Walmart has added Telehealth by acquiring MeMD, a telehealth provider, to its healthcare strategies to provide in-person and digital care across its multiple assets and solutions.

Walmart Health aims to provide access to virtual care across the US, including urgent, behavioral, and primary care complementing their in-person Walmart Health Centers.

Walmart has partnered with EPIC, the EHR (Electronic Health Record) Services, a leading technology provider for managing its health-center operations. In addition, patients can access telemedicine seven days a week through MeMD, which it plans to rebrand soon.

Walmart, the retail giant, has been interested in healthcare for a long time and has been building assets in medication management, telemedicine, and health insurance plans.

(Source: Rebecca Pfifer, *Walmart Opening 5 Health 'Superstores' in Delayed Florida Launch*, HealthcareDive, April 5, 2022, and *A Case Study on Walmart's Healthcare Begins Here Program*, PriceWaterHouseCoopers, pwc.com, 2017))

CASE 3

CVS Health: Not Just Rebranding, but Reimagining!

After acquiring Aetna, the health insurance giant in the US, CVS Pharmacy has not only rebranded itself but reimagined its purpose as CVS (Consumer Value Stores) Health.

CVS Health is a healthcare corporation and parent company of CVS Pharmacy, which operates about 9,900 retail locations in 49 states, the District of Columbia in the US, and Puerto Rico.

In 2019, the company acquired Aetna, a health insurance giant, for $69 billion as part of its overall goal to make healthcare more affordable and accessible to consumers.

CVS Health did a great job combating the coronavirus during the pandemic by administering over 15 million COVID tests and 20 million vaccinations.

CVS Health: Key Strategic Pivots

CVS Health aims to build on its existing relationships to deliver personalized care in a seamless, full-circle way and to end systemic inequities in the healthcare system. Here are the key elements on which its strategy revolves:

- *Improving Primary Care Delivery Capabilities:* CVS healthcare teams will address the *whole* patient's physical and emotional needs. CVS will bring care to where people want it— in nearby CVS® HealthHub® and MinuteClinic® locations, at home, or virtually.

- *Optimizing Retail Locations to Serve As Community Health Destinations*: Moving beyond a traditional drug store model, CVS will continue to provide a broader range of health services from COVID-19 testing to depression screenings and more at CVS Pharmacy locations throughout the country.
- *Expanding New Health Services:* The company will harness the power of digital to help people schedule care, connect with physicians and get quality and affordable care.
- *Digital-First Approach Across Businesses*: CVS Health will digitally connect its pharmacy capabilities to give people more options using artificial intelligence to deliver superior customer experience and position cvs.com as a premier health and wellness destination.
- *Enhancing Omnichannel Health Experiences*: The company vows to achieve a wow performance by delivering greater choice and range of services where people want them—in their stores, in people's homes, and virtually through integrated cross-channel solutions. While CVS Health offers several healthcare services to ensure the health and wellbeing of patients across the country, it has two main service delivery arms. These are— CVS Pharmacy and MinuteClinic.

CVS Pharmacy

CVS Pharmacy delivers innovative, community-based solutions to make healthcare simpler, more affordable, and more accessible, offering customers convenience and value across various health, wellness, personal care, and beauty products. Also, consumers can access expanded health services and pharmacy support. In addition, CVS Pharmacy's pharmacists help drive medication adherence, close gaps in care, and recommend more cost-effective drug therapies through face-to-face counseling with patients. Here is a brief account of services offered by CVS Pharmacy to help patients manage their conditions:

- **ScriptPath™** automatically reviews the patient's current CVS Pharmacy prescription information and prescriber instructions. It then uses clinical data to generate a schedule of the most convenient times of day to take each medication. Patients receive an overview of their regimen, a prescription schedule, and corresponding prescription labels that take the guesswork out of what to take and when.

- **ScriptSync™** helps patients refill their prescriptions easily and conveniently. The pharmacy staff can reschedule eligible maintenance prescriptions so patients can pick up all their refills in a monthly CVS Pharmacy visit or delivery through ScriptSync.
- **SimpleDose™** improves patient adherence by simplifying the management of their daily medications with presorted prescription packs at no added cost. A box containing a 30-day supply is delivered to the home or local CVS Pharmacy.
- **Pharmacy Advisor®** helps CVS Caremark plan members achieve better health outcomes. Through the program, a pharmacist engages plan members diagnosed with chronic conditions either at the pharmacy counter or by phone when the member chooses a mail service pharmacy.
- **Transform Diabetes Care** service uses CVS Health data insights and analytics to create personalized plans for individuals across five clinical areas. This service is available to patients with Caremark and Aetna benefit plans, which also identifies gaps in care, and responds to patient needs before they arise.

CVS pharmacists are trained to provide vaccination services, offering patients a safe and convenient way to adhere to vaccination schedules recommended by the Centers for Disease Control and Prevention (CDC). In addition, patients can conveniently schedule appointments via the cvs.com website or the CVS app.

Lastly, pharmacists at CVS Pharmacy use the CVS Pharmacy Savings Finder to identify or verify lower-cost options for patients to drive medication compliance and adherence.

CVS MinuteClinic

CVS has 1,100 Minute Clinic locations across the US, offering convenient, high-quality care for common family illnesses. In addition, MinuteClinic offers expanded services where clinicians can screen, diagnose and treat customers and provide follow-up care for chronic conditions and provide services for minor injuries or illnesses, immunizations, and annual exams, in-store or virtually. Further, MinuteClinic locations inside HealthHub stores offer sleep apnea assessments and phlebotomy services.

The MinuteClinic services are also available for patients without health insurance at an affordable cash payment option, with visits costing $59. In addition, most Aetna insurance plans also cover video visits. Video visits are available 24 hours a day, seven days a week, and can be accessed via a mobile device or computer.

CVS Pharmacy: Many Firsts

CVS Pharmacy's commitment to better health is evident from the number of initiatives it undertook over the years. As a result, CVS has many 'firsts' to its credit, putting the company ahead of the curve. Consider these, for example:

- CVS Pharmacy became the first and only major drugstore to stop selling tobacco in 2014.
- The first national retailer to require third-party testing and verification of all vitamins and supplements through its *Tested to Be Trusted* program. CVS Pharmacy tests national and *store* brands to confirm that ingredients listed on the label are accurate and free from certain additives and contaminants through an independent lab.
- CVS pharmacy became the first and only national retailer to ensure Sun Protection standards in 2016 by removing sunscreens with an SPF (Sun Protection Factor) below 15 from their shelves. In addition, the CVS Pharmacy expanded its commitment to healthy sun protection by removing oxybenzone and octinoxate from all CVS Health brand sunscreens with an SPF below 50.
- Truth in Imagery: In 2018, CVS Pharmacy committed not to materially alter beauty imagery created for in-store or online advertising and social media. At the same time, the company introduced the *CVS Beauty Mark,* a watermark designed to highlight imagery that has not been altered.

- In 2019, CVS Pharmacy ran a *Beauty in Real Life campaign* highlighting beauty's authentic and more realistic image to empower women to feel comfortable and confident in their skin through traditional advertising and influencer campaigns.
- CVS Pharmacy's commitment to ensuring safety in manufacturing its store brands can be seen in the fact that it removed parabens, phthalates, and formaldehyde donors from nearly 600 CVS Store brand beauty and personal care products.
- Also, CVS Pharmacy was the first major retailer to announce the removal of trans-fats from all CVS Store Brands Food products, 18 months ahead of the FDA requirement.

Focusing on Primary Care

CVS Health wants to broaden its care delivery strategy into a primary care model, including a physician-led primary care center integrated with virtual and home assets. The company plans to add a few hundred primary care centers to its MinuteClinics, drugstores, and health-focused HealthHub locations launched a few years ago. In addition, CVS plans to move from an episodic to a more longitudinal approach to care and eventually add more specialty services to compete effectively in the rapidly growing healthcare market.

The company's primary care strategy is to directly own some primary care clinics and forge relationships with others through management services organization agreements, wherein an organization manages multiple affiliated physician practices and clinics.

CVS Health is looking to acquire a primary care provider in the country before the end of 2022. Furthermore, In the first week of September 2022, CVS Health announced that it agreed to acquire Signify Health, a healthcare platform that uses analytics and technology to pair clinicians with patients for home-based visits.

(Source: Several blog articles and websites—fortune.com, retailpharmacy.cvshealth.com)

CASE

4

Walgreens Healthcare Reimagines Retail Healthcare!

The retail industry has been in a constant state of change for many years. Consumers expect personalized interactions, connected online and in-store experiences, and high-quality customer service when they shop. Consumers of healthcare services, too, expect similar seamless experiences, be it online or offline.

Walgreens, a leading retail pharmacy giant, is taking some big steps to meet the increasing expectations of healthcare consumers. Walgreens is one of the largest drugstore chains in the US, with more than 9,000 drugstores in all 50 states, the District of Columbia, Puerto Rico, and the US Virgin Islands.

Walgreens plans to leverage Microsoft's Dynamic 365 Power Platform along with Adobe Experience Cloud to provide a unified, 360-degree view of the customer and Adobe's customer experience management solutions to deliver great customer experiences through the industry's only end-to-end solution for analytics, content management, personalization, and campaign orchestration. In addition, the new platform will help the company to achieve mass personalization, delivering the right offers and content to the right customer whether they shop in the store, online, or through the mobile app.

In addition, Walgreens collaborates with technology company Philips to offer sleep solutions and digital tools through its digital marketplace to sharpen its focus on chronic disease management.

Strategic Initiatives

As a part of its digital transformation to remain competitive in the highly competitive retail healthcare, Walgreens is taking key strategic initiatives. Consider these, for example:

- Walgreens takes a majority stake of 63 percent in VillageMD, the primary care company, for $5.2 billion to expand into value-based primary care, a $1 trillion, a fast-growing segment of the healthcare system. VillageMD's physician-led care teams include pharmacists, nurses, lab technicians, behavioral health specialists, and other providers with a national network of clinical best practices to help provide coordinated, personalized care for each patient. Walgreens Boots Alliance (a global pharmacy-led healthcare company operating in nine countries) and VillageMD have 52 co-located primary care practice locations. In addition, they plan to open at least 600 co-located Village Medical at Walgreens primary care practices in more than 30 US markets by 2025 and 1,000 by 2027.
- Walgreens Boots Alliance launched a new business segment, Walgreens Health, focused on consumer-centric, tech-enabled healthcare to leverage the company's capabilities in primary care, post-acute care, and home care.
- As a part of its new strategy, Walgreens acquires an initial 55 percent stake in CareCentrix, a post-acute and home care company. CareCentrix will operate under Walgreens Health. The post-acute care market, one of the fastest-growing healthcare segments in the US, is estimated to be around $75 billion annually.

Walgreens Health

With the launch of Walgreens Health, the healthcare giant is reimagining retail through expanded health and wellness offerings and mass personalization, accelerating its digital offerings and aiming to become a leading provider of local clinical services.

Walgreens Health aims to provide equitable, personalized, whole-person healthcare to local communities across America to meet wherever consumers are— in the store, at home, in the doctor's office, and via mobile app.

(Source: Wikipedia and blog articles—1. Heather Landi, Walgreens Doubles Down on Primary Care, Home Health With Major Investments in VillageMD, CareCentrix, Fierce Healthcare, October 14, 2021; 2. Heather Landi, How Walgreens Leveraged its Microsoft Partnership to Respond to COVID-19, Fierce Healthcare, June 26, 2020; 3. Bruce Japsen, Walgreens CEO: We're Opening A New VillageMD Clinic 'Every Three Days', Forbes.com, August 22, 2022)

CASE

5

Ping An Good Doctor Launches the World's First AI-Powered, Un-staffed Clinic in China!

Can you imagine a future visit to the doctor could mean visiting a local mall and dipping into an AI-powered booth? You don't have to. You can do that in China now.

In November 2019, *Ping An Good Doctor*, a one-stop healthcare ecosystem platform, showcased a tiny unstaffed clinic that employs artificial intelligence. Patients can sit in the three-square meter *One-minute clinics* and chat about their symptoms with a cloud doctor called AI Doctor.

The AI Doctor will gather medical history and develop a diagnosis plan, which will then be passed on to a specialist consultant via Telehealth. And the One-Minute Clinic can connect patients with a clinician on Ping An Good Doctor's in-house medical team.

The system also includes a smart medicine cabinet where patients can get their medication after diagnosis. It will include upwards of 100 common medications.

The One-Minute Clinics have already been piloted in the Wuzhen Scenic Area outside of Shanghai. The virtual clinics could be anywhere from pharmacies to schools and shopping malls to highway service stations so patients can access them easily.

The One-Minute Clinics address a long-felt need of shortage of doctors in China. Ping An Good Doctor One-Minute Clinics show a way to significantly meet the challenges of physician shortages and improve healthcare access to patients.

The growing influence of Ping An across Asia is evident from the memorandum of understanding signed with Bangkok Dusit Medical Service, the largest healthcare network in Thailand.

The company raised $1.1 billion in its IPO (Initial Public Offering) in Hong Kong in April 2019.

(Source: Adapted from a blog article of Laura Lovett, Ping An Good Doctor Showcases AI-powered, unstaffed clinics, MobileHealth News, November 29, 2019).

Changing Role

In the new healthcare ecosystem, pharma companies can improve the efficacy of treatments not only with the drugs they produce but also with digital supportive services. For example, pharma companies can co-create services to improve the coordination of different healthcare providers, with innovators using the data to improve the treatment path, develop services to support caregivers and families, and help patients improve their quality of life by adopting healthy nutrition habits. In addition, digital services can also help patients prepare for the physician's visit, keep track of symptoms, and remind prescriptions to improve adherence. Since digital solutions are connected to creating an ecosystem, they help you throughout the journey from finding what ails you through the treatment.

At the same time, medical technology players entering the healthcare ecosystem focus on connecting medical devices to the integrated digital platform, improving efficiency, reducing human errors, and reducing costs. According to research by Simon-Kucher, global pricing, and strategy consulting firm, although most Medtech companies (70 percent) face price pressures coupled with increasing costs in the market, many of them are investing in the digitalization of services and products to reduce costs.

The new healthcare ecosystem allows you to analyze the huge data generated mostly by users, providing new insights into patients' health to all the stakeholders working to improve patients' health outcomes. Thus the data-driven approach in the new ecosystem replaces the previous fragmented journey and helps provide better care and outcomes.

Pharma and Medtech companies can leverage the business value offered by data, develop better solutions, and improve their ability to react and respond to emerging needs of patients or problems such as the COVID-19 breakout, stay relevant, and become future-proof.

Reimagine the Pharmaceutical Product

Reimagine the Product

Several factors are redefining and transforming the future landscape of healthcare. Consider these, for example:

- Ground-breaking digital technologies coupled with changing needs in wellness such as nutrition, weight management, physical activity, and managing and sharing personal health data.
- Escalating priorities in treating chronic diseases such as respiratory, diabetes, cardiovascular
- Empowered consumers with ever-increasing exposure to technologies such as digital, mobile, personalization, and social media demand enhanced customer support, education, and reminders to improve medication adherence

All these trends are driving pharma marketers to rethink their products to be more relevant to the current needs of patients and other key healthcare stakeholders. Reimagining the product, therefore, is not a nice-to-have but mandatory.

Reimagine Product Launch

Pharma marketers often focus on clinical efficacy, ease of use, adverse events profiles, and superiority over the competition when they launch new products. However, they miss out on a very important aspect of the new product, the customer experience (CX). Customer experience is omnipresent in many industries such as boutique hospitality, retail, retail banking, transportation and others. These industries are strongly committed to building the customer journey with the strategic intent of creating a superior customer experience. In addition, they continue to measure it to improve the experience over time. So, as a pharma marketer, can you reimagine your product launches by building customer experience into your strategy? Because today customer experience is the strategy!

Product to Platform

Several companies across all industries are transitioning from *Product-based* to *Platform-based* business models. The pharmaceutical industry, too, has started moving from a traditional *Pill* to *a Platform* (Pill + Service + Data +Software) model to deliver value beyond treating illness and start facilitating wellness.

Why Reimagine the Product Strategy?

It looks like the blockbuster era for new pharmaceutical products is over, as pharmaceutical companies cannot develop products that make the big difference they used to in the past. In addition, the drug development costs and the time it takes from concept to commercialization have become prohibitively high.

Further, patient satisfaction has become the most crucial prerequisite for success in the pharmaceutical industry. Patient satisfaction, of course, has always been paramount, but now it has a much broader significance that is beyond therapeutic effectiveness. For example, patient satisfaction represents nearly a third of all Medicare incentive payments in the US.

Therefore, it is time for Pharma to re-look at its product strategy and reimagine. So what is Pharma doing to rethink its product strategy? Here are some of the strategic approaches that pharmaceutical companies are adopting:

- Mining and analyzing real-world data to unearth the unmet needs of patients so they can develop products that can be highly relevant to patients
- Unable to create meaningful differentiation in products, some leading pharmaceutical companies are trying to create differentiation by providing services that address the patients' latent needs and beyond their products right from the clinical developmental stage.

Service-Around-the-Pill

How can Pharma help hospitals and large provider groups improve patient experience and satisfaction? By improving the patient experience with therapy. The patient's experience with a drug includes the therapeutic effectiveness of the molecule. But now, it also includes a new set of expectations. To successfully compete for formulary status and physician preference now requires non-drug support. Support and service around the Pill (the molecule). Everything from patient communication to lifestyle support. Therefore, it is time to focus on building around the Pill instead of trying to move beyond it. David Ormesher, CEO of *closerlook*, a leading digital marketing agency, cogently argues in a LinkedIn blog article: *Pharma: Build around the Pill, not beyond the Pill* — published on October 7, 2015. Here are the main points:

- Around-the-pill thinking will challenge the new product teams to consider the entire experience of the therapy. The product touches everyone, from provider to patient to caregiver to patient community to financial counselors. Think of it as the local neighborhood of a drug. A community experience that impacts the patient experience.
- Around-the-pill is less about new businesses or new sources of revenue. It is more about surrounding an existing product portfolio with support services.
- Around-the-pill even includes finding new ways to identify which patients will benefit the most.

Roadside Assistance

David Ormesher presented a very appropriate analogy to the around-the-pill approach in Pharma. He quotes an example of a similar service from the automobile industry. Here is the example he gave:

When Mercedes Benz was the first auto manufacturer to offer roadside assistance for the vehicle's life, they didn't do it because it offered a new revenue stream. Instead, they did it to back their quality product. The new service offering didn't change Mercedes' business model or product — It created more value for their current products by assuring quality.

Pharma's around-the-pill service is similar to what Mercedes did. Pharma needs to develop adjacent services to support its current products by creating a well-rounded solution. Building around the Pill is not only more attainable but will also be more valuable for Pharma's primary customers. And it will be a source of a distinctive competitive advantage.

Four Examples

Smart Pharma Consulting gave four examples of how pharmaceutical companies have provided services around the Pill in their position paper of November 2016 titled: *Patient-centric strategy — what patient services pharma companies should provide*. Here are the examples:

1. *Disease monitoring and progression monitoring*: in 2014, Biogen partnered with PatientsLikeMe to distribute Fitbit to 248 multiple sclerosis patients to collect data to improve treatment protocols and prove the value of their medication to payers, physicians, and other patients.
2. *AstraZeneca's community website, Living with Lung Cancer for lung cancer patients*: After completing a patient research survey, AstraZeneca co-developed a website with more than 100 patients dedicated to building a community for lung cancer patients, where they can share their emotional journeys and everyday experiences and thus feel better.
3. *Merck's connected device to improve adherence*: In 2014, Merck launched a new device to inject Rebif (interferon beta-1a) for patients with multiple sclerosis, which collects and stores data that can be sent to a secure server. The system can prompt patients to better adherence to treatment.
4. *Cornerstones4Care, a patient support program*: Cornerstones4Care is an online service from Novo Nordisk providing diabetes patients with personalized tools, resources, and information to help them reach their diabetic goals and improve their quality of life.

Service-beyond-the-Pill

For many years, the pharmaceutical industry has put the Pill at the center of its commercial strategy development. It is understandable given the enormous financial and time investments made for each product during the blockbuster era. However, now that the blockbuster model is almost vanishing, the pharmaceutical industry needs to identify the unmet needs among patients, physicians, and payers and sharpen its competitive edge.

The healthcare industry stakeholders are looking for the pharmaceutical industry to join them as a partner to track and measure the products they provide and their impact on health outcomes. In addition, they are looking at the pharmaceutical industry to provide services beyond the Pill. The potential benefits of developing services around and beyond the Pill are significant. Consider, for example, adherence to long-term treatment as one of the greatest unmet needs in delivering treatment. The estimated size of the adherence market in the US is $46 billion for heart failure and $71 billion for diabetes. And that is just treatment adherence. Several other unmet needs, such as increasing diagnostic accuracy or developing tools and measurement solutions that could help improve outcomes. Services can give a company its distinct competitive advantage.

Pharmaceutical companies can learn a lesson from Tony Hsieh, Chief Executive of successful online shoe company Zappos. Consider these, for example:

1. Tony Hsieh explains Zappos' philosophy when he calls his company a service company that happens to sell shoes. Can pharmaceutical companies redefine themselves as service companies that happen to make and sell medicines (pills)? In other words, can they build service around their pills? Pharmaceutical companies must acknowledge that products on their own are not enough, and services around are essential to give the products the best opportunity to succeed. Pfizer acknowledged this fact when Adele Gulfo, President of US

Primary Care at the company, said: *The days of just selling the Pill are over*.

2. Seventy-five percent of Zappos sales come from repeat customers. That speaks volumes about the level of customer satisfaction and customer loyalty. Pharma could achieve similar levels of customer satisfaction by providing services beyond the Pill. To accomplish that, Pharma should put all its key stakeholders' needs at the center, with a package of services (including the Pill) developed to match them.

Beyond-the-Pill: Critical Success Factors

Mark Pesse and Lea Bucher of Executive Insight, a leading healthcare consulting firm, suggest five critical success factors in their insightful article, *Going beyond the Pill — Part Four: Preparing for implementation* in the Executive Insight Report published in PharmaFocus. The critical success factors are:

- Begin development of service-beyond-the-pill well before the launch of a product
- Always keep stakeholders' needs (including the patient) at the center.
- Consider that some non-traditional stakeholder groups (caregivers and pharmacists) may be central to a particular disease area.
- Co-Develop solutions directly with consumers to ensure complete relevance and adoption from an early stage
- Consider involving experienced external partners as and when required to assist with the execution of the strategy.

The following case shows how a global pharma major implemented an integrated service-beyond-the-pill service and gained.

CASE

6

Bayer's *Gateway* to Success!

Bayer has set up MS Gateway (www.ms-gateway.com), an online patient resource for people with multiple sclerosis. The MSGateway is not just a website. It is a well-thought-out service strategy, providing solutions for each stage of the patient pathway. Also, Bayer offers an *Ask a Neurologist* service to newly diagnosed patients, enabling patients to consult with these specialists in a completely anonymous environment. Patients at an early stage find this service more comfortable.

Apart from being a great benefit to the patient, the service raises Bayer's profile as a provider of genuinely useful, value-adding patient resources helping to build trust with patients and healthcare professionals, and payers.

Beyond the Pill, or injection?

Additionally, Bayer has another service offering — BETAPlus via the MS Gateway for patients down the pathway who are prescribed Betaseron, Bayer's interferon-based therapy for multiple sclerosis. The service includes access for each patient to a BETANurse — where MS-trained nurses are available for individual consultation through regular visits and phone calls to aid patients with injection training, side effect concerns, and other general queries. The BETANurse service is a tremendous resource for patients and saves significant time for general practitioners and other healthcare professionals involved in these patients' care.

One more service that complements MS Gateway, BETAPlus, and BETANurse is called My BETAApp. My BETA App is a smartphone app that allows patients to schedule, track, and record Betaseron injections. Again, these may greatly help improve compliance —an outcome that would benefit all stakeholders.

The MS Gateway also offers a Wellness Corner. The service provides exercise advice and several online games to positively influence patients' feelings of well-being, helping to keep motivation and compliance high. All these patient-centric services, beyond the Pill, help further down the patient pathway. They help patients optimize their care and therapy to improve outcomes.

Bayer thus offers a full pathway of value-adding services, such as MS Gateway, BETAPlus, BETANurse, BETAApp, and Wellness Corner, fulfilling three functions.

1. First and foremost, it provides something of genuine value to the end-user and improves the overall patient experience.
2. Secondly, it helps optimize outcomes benefiting the patients, HCPs, payers, and society
3. Finally, it demonstrates the company's commitment and the added value provided by the brand.

(Source: Adapted from the article: Marc Pesse, Lea Bucher, *Going beyond the Pill — Part Two: Why services are the next blockbuster*, A Report by Executive Insight, PharmaFocus, A Wiley Publication)

Reimagine the Pharmaceutical Price

The ever-escalating costs of prescription drugs and the overall healthcare costs are increasingly pressurizing all governments, providers, and payers to contain the healthcare costs. A recent BMJ (British Medical Journal) article observed that pharmaceutical prices are often unfair, many prices exceed affordability, and value for money thresholds are not justified by research and development costs. As a result, according to the Gallup Poll, pharma's reputation has sunk to the lowest levels among the US industries in 2019. Moreover, high prices act as a barrier to access. Realizing this, some pharmaceutical companies have started reimagining their pricing strategies and pursuing value-based pricing strategies to improve access. As a result, there is a surge of 'Paying for Value' as the new reimbursement paradigm for innovative costly therapies in all markets with high levels of health insurance.

However, there is nothing new in the 'Pay for Value' approach because all new products had to demonstrate their value in therapy in the pharmaceutical industry. It is a prerequisite for new product launches.

So, what's new? Traditionally, pharmaceutical companies have been judged primarily by whether or not a new treatment has exhibited significant and meaningful improvements in key study endpoints in randomized clinical trials (RCT). However, in recent years what has markedly changed is the demand for certainty on how that clinical data translates into the real-world setting and what impact a new product promises. In other words, payers are less inclined to accept theoretical arguments to bridge perceived gaps between observed clinical trial efficacy and promised real-life value. Consequently, real-world effectiveness considerations beyond RCT (Randomized Clinical Trials) efficacy claims increasingly influence formulary decision-making.

Emerging Approaches

Outcomes-based performance agreements. Christopher Bradbury, senior vice president of integrated clinical and specialty drug solutions for Cigna Pharmacy Management, says *competitive drug prices are important. Still, equally important is in ensuring that customers' medications are working as or better than expected.*

Outcomes-based performance agreements can have different criteria and goals. Consider these, for example:

- *Population-level outcomes guarantee*: An ideal population health outcome metric should reflect a population's dynamic state of physical, mental, and social well-being.
- *Patient-level outcomes guarantee* is a relatively new strategy aiming to achieve the best outcomes for the lowest cost and thus maximize patient value. In value-based care, the only true quality measures are the outcomes that matter to the patient.
- *Conditional treatment continuation (CTC)* is a performance-based scheme where the payer continues to cover the cost of the drug or medical device based on short-term treatment goals to ensure that only patients that benefit from the treatment will remain on treatment coverage.
- Coverage with evidence development (CED) represents a specific approach to coverage for promising technologies for which the evidence remains uncertain. CED (Coverage with Evidence Development) demands that additional evidence is generated to address the sources of uncertainty and secure ongoing coverage.

Future Models

Here are some novel and alternative payment schemes under the value-based pricing approach:

- *Indication-specific pricing*: The concept of indication-specific pricing (ISP) means that the cost of a drug will vary depending on its use. Even though ISP is a novel value-based pricing approach, it is fraught with many administrative, ethical and regulatory challenges.
- *Blockchain-enabled platforms (example: Healthcoin)*: Universal Health Coin (UHC), a public benefit corporation, plans to launch

an anonymous, token-based healthcare system that employs blockchain technology to arbitrage, decentralize, fund, and provide the fair payment of health services worldwide. It eliminates third-party intermediaries who bog down the healthcare delivery process by creating a trusted personal relationship between doctor and patient using blockchain technology, machine learning and artificial intelligence.

- *Fund-based payment*, including re-insurance risk pools: Pooling is a system in which many people purchase insurance as a group to lessen the cost of coverage as the members of the pool are deemed low risk and compensate for the increased cost of insuring those who are high-risk.
- *Annuity Models (example: Health impact bonds)*: Social impact bonds (SIBs) represent a new way to finance social service and health promotion programs whereby different investors provide an upfront capital investment. The government will pay back investors with interest if a program meets predetermined criteria for successful outcomes.

Money-back Guarantee

It is common to have money-back guarantees for most consumer goods but not prescription drugs. However, a relatively new phenomenon is emerging in the pharmaceutical sector. Some prescription drugs now promise to perform, or the manufacturer or pharmacy benefit company will provide a discount or refund. Still, the refund or discount will not go to the patient. Instead, it goes back to the health plan or the employer.

Cigna, a leading health insurance company in the US, says it entered into 'Value-based contracts' for medications designed to treat conditions such as heart failure and multiple sclerosis, which are based on agreed-upon health metrics to measure whether a drug meets expectations. Under these contracts, the manufacturer will reduce the cost to Cigna's benefit plans if a drug doesn't perform as expected.

Here are some more examples of value-based contracts between pharmaceutical companies and health insurance companies:

- Express-Scripts offers its own guarantees and has lowered the cost of treatment to payers by nearly 50 percent since 2015, and has granted 50,000 patients access to care on its Hepatitis-C program.
- Novartis, a global Pharma major, offers rebates and guarantees on some drugs by collaborating with payers on outcome-based contracting solutions to drive a shift toward value pricing in the healthcare system.

It is important to note that value-based pricing is not suitable for all types of treatments. Value-based pricing should meet two criteria. One is that the results or outcomes are measurable and directly attributable to the product. Second, there should be no cheaper generic alternatives available as this would negate the cost side of the use of care.

No Cure, No Pay

Some leading pharmaceutical companies have used a *no cure, no pay* strategy as a competitive strategy, instilling confidence in their products about twenty-eight years ago. Here's a table presenting eight examples of money-back guarantees offered by pharmaceutical companies between the years 1994 and 2005:

Table 1.2 Money-back Initiatives by Some Pharma Companies

Year and Company	Money-back Offer
1994: Merck-Frost	Offered refunds to patients who had been prescribed finasteride if they required surgery for benign prostatic hyperplasia after one year of treatment.
1995: Sandoz	Introduced a money-back guarantee for clozapine for treatment resistant schizophrenia. The reimbursement covered the costs of the drug, dispensing fees, and pharmacy markups.
1998: Merck	Promised to refund patients and insurers up to six months of their prescription costs if simvastatin plus diet did not help them lower LDL cholesterol to target concentrations identified by their doctors.

Table 1.2 Contd...

Year and Company	Money-back Offer
2004: Novartis	Launched a *no cure, no pay* initiative for valsartan hydrochlorothiazide as part of a 'take action for healthy blood pressure program' in the US. In addition to a money back guarantee for the patient only, the program also provides the option of a 30-day trial product package, the opportunity to buy a blood pressure measuring device cheaply, and various on-line compliance systems.
2004: Novartis	Launched a *no cure, no pay* initiative for valsartan in Denmark, independent of the initiative in the US.
2004: Lilly ICOS	Launched a *no cure, no pay* on tadalafil for erectile dysfunction in the US. Patients who were not satisfied with the treatment were issued with voucher for the oral treatment of their choice.
2005: Novartis	Launched a money back initiative in Denmark for nicotine chewing gum. If the patient does not like the taste (four tastes to choose from), a refund offered.
2005: Bayer	Launched a *no cure, no pay* initiative on vardenafil for erectile dysfunction in Denmark. Patients who are not satisfied with the treatment can get the cost refunded.

(Source: Adapted from a blog article, No Cure, No Pay

Later in 2015, a few more companies such as Merck, Eli Lilly, Novartis, Sanofi, Amgen, and Regeneron entered into pay-for-performance deals similar to *no cure, no pay* ones. Consider these pay-for-performance agreements, for example:

- In 2016, Merck&Co and Aetna, the second largest health insurer in the US, entered into a value-based agreement for Merck's Januvia and Janumet used to treat type 2 diabetes. The contract requires Merck to pay rebates to Aetna if certain portions of patients in the population who are prescribed Januvia and Janumet do not achieve the treatment goals and require further therapy, as determined by their physicians.
- In 2016, Cigna, a leading health insurance company in the US, entered into a pay-for-performance agreement with Novartis for the drug Entresto, approved by the US FDA to treat heart failure with reduced ejection fraction. The agreement ties the financial terms to how well the drug improves the relative health

of Cigna's customers and reduces the proportion of customers with heart failure hospitalizations.

- Harvard Pilgrim, a leading health insurance company in the US, entered into two value-based contracts— one with Amgen Inc. to cover the rheumatoid arthritis medicine, Enbrel, and the other with Eli Lilly for its osteoporosis medicine, Forteo. These pay-for-performance deals aim to curb spending on drugs while giving patients access to costly treatments. Enbrel costs nearly $45,000 per patient annually, while Forteo costs about $29,000 annually in the US.
- In 2017, Amgen entered into an outcome-based pricing deal with Harvard Pilgrim, a leading health services company in the US, for its low-density lipoprotein (LDL) cholesterol-reducing drug, Repatha (evolocumab). Repatha costs about $14,000 per patient annually but reduces LDL cholesterol by 60 percent. Amgen announced a first-of-its-kind offer: the company would pay a refund for all eligible patients who had a heart attack or stroke while taking the cholesterol-fighting injection.
- In 2018, Regeneron, Sanofi, and Express Scripts agreed to improve affordability and access to Praluent (Alirocumab) to help reduce LDL cholesterol. As per the agreement, Express Scripts will pay a net price consistent with the value-based price benchmark ICEE (Institute for Clinical and Economic Review) established this year, and will give the drug an exclusive placement on Express Scripts' national formulary, presenting fewer administrative hurdles when prescribing the treatment to physicians will face fewer administrative hurdles, and will share the financial savings directly with patients.

Dr. Mark Frendrick, MD, Director of the University of Michigan Center for Value-Based Insurance Design, believes as the guarantees become more common, patients will get a share of the refund.

With so many new pricing models being tried and tested, the pricing scenario will see more innovative approaches to pharmaceutical pricing, which are value-based and not necessarily based on reducing prices.

All the money-back initiatives and innovative pricing models are based on what some pharmaceutical companies are trying out in chronic therapy areas and very expensive therapies in biopharmaceuticals to treat diseases for which currently there are no effective treatments and some rare diseases in research-based Pharma markets such as the US, Western Europe, and Japan. They may not work in treating acute medical conditions.

Many pricing models and money-back guarantees may not be possible in branded-generics markets, including emerging markets today. Still, there is a need to reimagine the pharmaceutical pricing strategies demonstrating value based on pharmacoeconomic rationale because these markets are also under continuous pressure to contain increasing prescription drug costs and total healthcare costs.

Moreover, the classic epidemiological transition theory states that as countries become more developed, the disease burden shifts from most infectious diseases to most chronic diseases. In addition, demographic changes related to aging populations result in a nutrition transition where people increase their consumption of fats, sugars, and processed foods and a physical activity transition, wherein people are becoming more sedentary. And with increasing urbanization and patients becoming more literate and aware of their diseases, and taking greater control of their health will likely demand seamless experiences from healthcare just like their counterparts in highly developed countries of today. Therefore, if pharmaceutical companies in emerging and branded-generics markets do not understand what is happening in healthcare globally and do not reimagine now, they will likely find it too late when the change hits them in their markets. Remember, like in war, in business too, Forewarned is Fore-armed!

A Grand Bargain!

The 2018 agreement between Regeneron, Sanofi, and Express Scripts is hailed as a Grand Bargain because it is, for the first time, a manufacturer demonstrating its willingness to responsibly price an innovative medicine in line with its clinical benefits based on an independent assessment of what is fair, the value-based price would be for their drug, Praluent, and Express Scripts the health insurer making it financially and administratively easier for eligible patients to access this life-saving therapy. It is a win-win for the manufacturers, payers, and patients and could be a model for the rest of the industry to contemplate.

Steve Miller, chief medical officer of Express Scripts, commented on the agreement: *We think this is a new model. You've got a company that looks at what fair drug price is, puts itself through an external evaluation, and then negotiates on that price with us. We believe that this can change the marketplace.*

Commenting on the agreement, Leonard Schleifer, Co-founder and CEO of Regeneron Pharmaceuticals said:

I hope the world will take notice, and other payers will follow, and other drugs will follow. Because there is no point in us discovering all these things if we can't figure out a way to get them to patients, get them paid for, and have an adequate incentive for the people funding this research.

New Disruptor on the Block

Besides the outcome-based or pay-for-performance deals for chronic therapy and costly treatments, a new kind of disruptor entered the arena of reducing the prices of generic prescription drugs in the US. Here's a case that highlights the disruptive moves of the new entrant.

CASE

7

Mark Cuban's Disruptive Move To Make Generic Drugs Affordable!

Mark Cuban, serial investor, TV personality, Dallas Mavericks owner, and Shark Tank judge, is set to disrupt the drug pricing model in the US with the launch of a generic drug company, *Mark Cuban Cost Plus Drug Company (MCCPDC)*, to cut out costly PBMs (Pharmacy Benefit Managers) and help patients with huge cost savings.

Mark Cuban's Cost Plus pharmacy (MCCDPC) is registered at launch as a 503 (B) compounding pharmacy that is an outsourcing facility. Although a 503 (B) company is less regulated than a typical generic drug company, it will still need to register with the FDA, be inspected by the FDA, and adhere to specific manufacturing requirements. The distinction between operating as a generic company and as a compounding pharmacy is that a compounding pharmacy won't be submitting its generic drug applications to the FDA for new generic products. Instead, it piggybacks on other generic drug submissions. However, the company would like to register itself as a full-fledged outsourcing facility and plan to get a biological license application (BLA).

Strategic Entry

Mark Cuban's Cost Plus pharmacy entered the business with Albendazole, a drug for treating hookworm infestation, and there is a strong strategic reason behind it.

It's common for disadvantaged populations in the US to suffer from rampant outbreaks of hookworm. Unfortunately, Albendazole, commonly used to treat hookworm, could cost as much as $500 per course, making the drug out of reach for many in need. So, Mark Cuban started by donating more than 10,000 tablets of Albendazole to cure parasitic infections in the most affected areas of the southern US.

So, Mark Cuban started the company with the main goal of dramatically reducing the costs of drugs like Albendazole and introducing transparency to the pricing of drugs so that patients know they are getting a fair price.

Simple, Transparent Pricing Model

Cost Plus pharmacy's pricing model is simple. It is cost (manufacturing or procurement) + 15%, plus the pharmacy fee, if any. For example, the acquisition cost of Albendazole for the company is $26.08 per course. When you add the 15% overhead and administration expenses incurred by the company to continue to provide this disrupting service, it makes the base price of the drug $30. Then, the company adds the cost of $3.00 that its pharmacy partners charge to prepare and provide the prescription to the patients. That makes the sales price on the company website $33, far lower than it costs in the marketplace. Every product that the Cost Plus Drug Company sells is priced similarly.

Here is a table showing some examples of costs that patients can save on different drugs.

Table 1.3 Cost Savings with Mark Cuban's Cost Plus Drug Company: Some Examples

Generic (Reference Brand)	Maximum Retail Price (MRP) in $	Cost Plus Drug Company's Price ($)	Savings ($)
Albendazole (Albenza) Tablet	437.68	33.00	404.68

Table 1.3 Contd...

Generic (Reference Brand)	Maximum Retail Price (MRP) in $	Cost Plus Drug Company's Price ($)	Savings ($)
Acetazolamide (Diamox) Tablet	69.60	9.30	60.30
Amlodipine (Norvasc) Tablet	50.00	3.60	46.40
Amoxycillin + Clauvulanate (Augmentin) Tablet	65.40	9.30	56.10
Azithromycin (Zithromax) Tablet	150.35	11.10	139.25
Calcitriol (Rocaltrol) Capsule	40.50	5.10	35.40
Carbidopa-Levodopa (Sinemet CR) tablet	35.10	6.60	28.50
Cefdinir (Omnicef) Capsule	89.70	14.10	75.60
Chlorpromazine HCL (Thorazine) Tablet	231.30	6.60	225.00
Desvenlafaxine Extended Release Tablet (Pristiq)	289.53	18.30	271.23

(Source: Mark Cuban Cost Plus Drug Company Website, costplusdrugs.com)

Vertical Integration is the Way

Alex Oshmyansky, CEO of Mark Cuban Cost Plus Drug Company, believes the only way to ensure affordable prices get through is to integrate vertically. Accordingly, the company has been taking initiatives to integrate vertically and has already moved in that direction. Consider these, for example:

- Partnered with Truepill, a digital health platform that delivers diagnostics, Telehealth, and pharmacy infrastructure to power consumers with health experiences.
- In November 2021, the MCCPDC launched its pharmacy benefit manager (PBM) and pledged to be transparent about the costs it pays for drugs to those who work with it.
- The company plans to integrate its pharmacy and wholesaler with its PBM so that the PBM's clients have access to wholesale pricing through the pharmacy.
- Also, the company plans to build a state-of-the-art pharmaceutical facility in Dallas, Texas, to produce high-quality medicines at the lowest possible prices.

(Source: Adapted from many blog articles and the company website, costplusdrugs.com)

Reimagine Everything

Reimagine the Business Strategy

Pharmaceutical companies must reimagine their business strategy as healthcare start-ups and technology giants invade the traditional pharmaceutical business. Also, as digital technologies continue to disrupt the pharmaceutical industry, the pharma companies must address whether they can tie digital to their assets. It is exciting to note that digital technologies can supplement or support pharmacological therapies to improve patient outcomes. The time to reimagine the business strategy for pharmaceutical companies is now. Therefore, pharma companies must decide if they can move from a *products-and-pills* company to a *solutions* company. It could make a big difference between success and failure.

Reimagine the Marketing Strategy

Pharma has been focusing on its products for far too long. It is time to shift that and sharpen the focus on the customer. The Digital revolution has disrupted customer experience in several industries. Consider, for example, how Uber has transformed the experience of hailing a taxi, how Tesla has changed the experience of owning and driving a car, or how Amazon has created a seamless online purchasing experience. Healthcare consumers used to these delightful customer experiences expect and even demand similar experiences in healthcare delivery. Therefore, product differentiation, the major source of competitive advantage for the pharmaceutical industry, is no longer enough. Pharma needs to reimagine its marketing strategy and provide a differentiated delightful customer experience to thrive. Customer Experience is the new strategy!

Reimagine Marketing Communications

Marketers tend to focus on the message they want to communicate. Instead, they must focus on the information the customer seeks to be relevant and valuable to them. Use journey mapping to identify what message will resonate at each relationship stage and customers' media choices. It is crucial to deliver the right content to the right person in the right place at the right time. Remember, your customers will always be in one of the relationship stages across the customer journey. Therefore, you need to develop an always-on, balanced content program to be effective.

Reimagine Customer Engagement

Although the virtual sales reps' and physicians' engagement has been well underway before the pandemic, the COVID-19 outbreak put the digital transformation process on steroids. About 52 percent of specialists in Europe showed interest in virtual engagement even before the pandemic, according to research by Across Health, a pharma marketing consultancy firm. In a poll conducted by Global Data during the COVID-19 pandemic, seventy-five percent of the physician participants saw virtual interaction remaining (either as a stand-alone option or phygital (a mix of in-person and virtual interactions). It is vitally important that pharma companies reimagine their customer engagement strategies and embrace digital transformation because their customers embrace it. The rules of customer engagement in the pharma industry are changing. The cardinal principle of customer engagement is engaging with your customers when they want, where they want and how they want!

Reimagine Market Research

Traditional market research is too time-consuming and expensive. The Internet explosion has revolutionized market research. It has evolved from pen-and-paper surveys, one-on-one interviews, and focus group discussions into something more mobile, instant, and convenient process. Philip Graves, the author of *ConsumerOlogy*, says that *traditional market research violates basic neuroscience or human consciousness and lacks the empathy necessary to uncover the authentic truth within customers. Traditional market research strategy and insights rely too heavily on the head (rational being). But customer beliefs and decisions are also unconsciously emotional (the heart) and intuitive (the gut)*. Can you reimagine your marketing research practices using qualitative, observational techniques and online and social media research tools?

Reimagine R&D

Declining R&D productivity is one of the major challenges biopharmaceutical companies face today. A recent study by Deloitte showed that the return on pharmaceutical R&D investment for a cohort of 12 large pharmaceutical companies showed a continuous decline from 10.1 percent in 2010 to 1.9 percent in 2020. The only way out of this gloomy outlook is that promising new and emerging digital technologies can help pharma companies optimize the clinical development process across the R&D value chain, including patient recruitment, improving adherence, capturing and analyzing the data, and making decisions using intelligent algorithms and big data.

Digitization can simplify patient enrollment, which is crucial for clinical trials by optimizing a complex patient eligibility workflow after aggregating live data from disparate sources. In addition, digitization can make the process of patient selection much faster. For example, IAG (Image Analysis Group), a company that helps to accelerate novel drug development by using the right analytical tools and modern trial infrastructure, could shrink the process of patient workflow optimization, which would usually take seven days to just four hours, using digital technologies.

Furthermore, digital technologies help researchers combine historical information from electronic health records (EHRs) with imaging, genetic and molecular test data to drive the development of highly targeted treatments such as CAR-T (Chimeric Antigen Receptor and T-Cell) and other cell therapies in oncology giving hope to patients resistant to more conventional approaches.

Realizing what technology can do to reduce the costs of drug discovery, regulatory authorities are encouraging the use of new technologies and capabilities and approving more drugs and devices faster than before, particularly in smaller patient populations and under-served therapeutic areas based on real-world data.

As Tom O'Leary, Chief Information Officer at ICON, a leading contract research organization (CRO), says, *the whole area of digital often requires the patient to engage via devices. Therefore, it will be essential to show that the drug or device a company has developed is the best option for the patient*. Pharma can achieve this by taking the patients' voices into account at all stages of development.

McKinsey's Vision for the Future of R&D

Sastry Chilukuri, Edd Fleming, and Ann Westra of Mckinsey & Company have visualized the future R&D in their insightful article,

Digital R&D: The $100 billion Opportunity, published on McKinsey & Company blog on December 1, 2017. Here is their vision in a capsule form:

- In the future, drug discovery will be driven by machine learning and advanced analytics mining large datasets, enabling researchers to understand and visualize interaction with targets and to predict *in silico* a molecule's likelihood of success and reach approval in the market.
- Regulators will approve new products based on real-world evidence (RWE) generated in clinical trials conducted where patients are enrolled as part of their routine care, and rich data is collected through non-interventional means to improve the speed and quality of operations to demonstrate the efficacy, safety, and outcomes of products. Thus, the patients generate the data continuously through the widespread use of sensors to collect information, and artificial intelligence and deep learning help diagnose and treat patients.

In the future, McKinsey believes pharma will be completely digital, not simply digitized. Going digital implies applying digital technologies to our current way of working, like moving from manual processes to paperless systems. In addition, it requires a complete rethink of deploying digital technologies to reimagine value chains and drive innovation.

Finally, Nicolo Paraggio, Managing Director, Life Sciences and R&D Strategy Lead at Accenture, suggests that pharma companies can achieve savings of $1.2—1.7 billion per successful molecule (including the cost of capital and cost of failure) and will create additional future revenue opportunities for $150— 450 million in her article, *Billions to Millions: Improving R&D Productivity* published in accenture.com on October 25, 2021. Also, she suggests the Accenture strategic model with three strategic plays— digital and data-led research, faster, smarter development, and a new science portfolio.

Reimagine Supply Chain

While supply chain disruptions are not uncommon, the recent COVID pandemic exposed the vulnerability of the pharma supply chain, identifying many of its weak points or gaps. Therefore, pharma should reimagine the supply chain to make it future-fit and be obsessed with a customer-centric approach to ensure seamless delivery of its products and services to improve patient care.

Pharmaceutical companies can transform their operations with digitization, enabling them to operate with greater agility, cost-efficiency, and control to provide better patient care.

Digital technology helps pharma companies increase visibility into their supply chain operations and make better and faster decisions. Furthermore, it allows companies to fully integrate their supply chains, making them more adaptive and responsive. As a result, pharma can improve its planning accuracy, manufacturing efficiency, productivity, inventory, and service levels. The following table lists several areas where digital technology can help the pharma operational value chain realize its potential.

Table 1.4 Digital Technology Applications in Pharma Operations

Planning	Sourcing	Manufacturing	Delivering
• Real-time supply chain monitoring • Near-real-time-scheduling • Demand management • Inventory management • Compliance management • Supply chain optimization	• Automated order processes • Online / mobile approval • Enterprise-level spend analysis and dashboards • Supplier relationships and quality management • Contract management	• Real-time shop floor and production flow monitoring • Automated, real-time process analytics • Equipment downtime monitoring • Predictive maintenance • Additive manufacturing / 3D Printing	• End-to-end product visibility • Automated product stocking • Automated inventory and delivery via drones • Improved internal logistics via automated guided vechicles

Source: Dr. Marcus Ehrhardt and Peter Behner, Digitization in pharma: Gaining an edge in operations, Strategy&, PWC

Reimagining the supply chain in pharma requires building a digital supply chain ecosystem that includes:

- Virtual supply chain control tools such as analytics, mobile interfaces, industrial apps, and social listening

- Cloud-based information architecture
- The digitally enabled physical supply chain includes collaborative networks, sensors, IoT (Internet of Things), smart warehousing, 3D Printing, RFID (Radio Frequency Identification), and Drones.

Integrating all these elements will improve all stages of the operations value chain, including planning, sourcing, manufacturing, and delivering your products and services, and help you overcome any possible disruption.

According to Strategy&, digitization in the pharmaceutical industry will help achieve real-time visibility and faster decision-making. In addition, it improves operational processes and maintenance, and productivity by reducing downtime significantly in manufacturing plants by 30 to 40 percent.

Reimagine Technology

Several new and emerging digital technologies such as Artificial Intelligence (AI), Machine Learning (ML), Virtual Reality (VR), Augmented Reality, Telemedicine, Telehealth, Mobile Health, Robotics, Cloud Computing are revolutionizing and transforming health care, and creating new healthcare ecosystems. Pharmaceutical companies must embrace these technologies and harness them to improve patient outcomes and business performance.

Reimagine the Pharma Sales Rep Model

Traditionally, pharmaceutical companies relied on face-to-face salesforce and physician interactions. Pharma sales reps were pivotal in promoting their products as they were the most important communication channel of pharma's products and services. Later, the digital revolution and the wide availability of online media and digital channels became important sources of information to physicians, reducing the pharma sales rep's exclusive role in providing information. Later, in 2019, the global pandemic COVID-19 accelerated the digital transformation trend, changing how they operate. During the pandemic, pharma companies were forced to replace face-to-face contacts with physicians with virtual ones. Digital transformation is no longer nice to have but a need to have. Therefore, reimagining the role of pharma sales representative has become mandatory!

■

Reimagining the Patient

Patient-Centricity

The role of the patient in healthcare is changing from a passive recipient of healthcare to an active participant in managing his health. For far too long, the patient has been at the periphery of his healthcare, with the physician is in command. Patients have no choice other than to trust the doctor entirely. However, the tide is shifting. The patient is becoming increasingly empowered. What is driving this patient empowerment? Marrie Ennis-O'Connor writes about the seven essential components of patient empowerment in a blog article titled *What does it mean to be an empowered patient* on Patient Empowerment Network in May 2018. These components are–Information, Health Literacy, Digital Literacy, Self-Efficacy, Mutual Respect, Shared Decision-Making, and A Facilitating Environment. At the same time, consumers (patients) demand that the healthcare system catches up with other industries that have embraced the perks of the digital age, such as instant communication, patient education support, information availability, information storage, 24/7 access, and social connectivity. Pharma companies will do better to reimagine the patient in the light of this changing healthcare ecosystem.

The Cardinal rule to customer-centricity is this: Serve your customers' problems. Make sure that every change, every action, and every improvement your company makes has the end goal of solving a customer problem. Since the end consumer is the patient in Pharma, customer-centricity means patient-centricity. However, physicians remain critically important (intermediate) customers as they decide what medicines patients need.

Moreover, today, patients are more empowered than ever before. What is patient empowerment? WHO (World Health Organization) defines patient empowerment as *a process through which people gain greater control over decisions and actions affecting their health*. The shift of patients from passive consumers of healthcare to active decision makers on matters regarding their healthcare calls for a change in operations and culture of healthcare organizations, including Pharma, ushering in the patient-centered movement in healthcare. The patient-centered healthcare describes efforts by patient advocates and the healthcare industry to put the patient, not the system, in the center of healthcare priorities and operations. Can pharma lag behind when the entire healthcare system puts the patient at the center? Certainly not. It's time for Pharma to reimagine the patient. Realizing this, pharma has been making patient-centric initiatives for some time now. Consider these, for example:

- Many leading global pharmaceutical companies are increasingly listening to the patients to understand their pain points, experiences, and unmet needs, addressing them in their clinical, drug development, and discovery programs.
- They are also partnering with patient advocacy groups (PAGs) and communities to know and understand what patients need and want.
- Pharma has also started studying patient journeys more actively to understand their pain points across various touchpoints during their journey to make timely, relevant, and meaningful interventions.
- Some leading pharma companies, such as Merck, Pfizer, Sanofi, and Astellas among others have started having Chief Patient Officers (CPO) at the senior level to focus on patients' needs.

Pharma's Patient-Centric Moves

Pharma's relationships with patient associations in the past have been mainly transactional. But that is changing now. Some pharmaceutical companies like Sanofi are trying to reframe and reimagine their patient focus by exchanging more information – exchange of expertise, ideas, support in policy, and engagement from the present transactional relationship. They are trying to put patient needs at the center of their activities, striving for the highest standards of transparency and integrity, and communicating with patients and patient organizations.

The bond between pharma and patient associations has grown stronger and stronger in recent years. As a result, pharma companies are increasingly employing former patients as ambassadors. Here are some examples of the patient-centric moves by select pharmaceutical companies:

1. *Sanofi Genzyme*: Genzyme focuses on the rare disease side of the business. It can be very different because sometimes more people are working on a drug than taking it. Henry Featherstone, Director of Public Affairs at Sanofi Genzyme, described a case of the first patient treated on Genzyme therapy, who might have otherwise died as a child, who is now a father and an ambassador for the organization. There are many individual patient stories like that, which are important. The company believes that an individual and the personal approach can become the norm across the organization, not just for rare diseases.
2. *Merck & Co*: A key pillar of Merck's current patient engagement activities is its embracing carer's initiative to catalyze external stakeholder insight exchange and collaboration to power innovation and transformation in patient care. In 2017, Merck launched *Embracing Carers,* an initiative guided by eight leading carer organizations worldwide to raise awareness and drive a call to action for the support of carers worldwide. This multi-year initiative aims to drive substantial change for carers and focuses on four main audiences—media, policy, stakeholders, and healthcare systems. The Embracing Carers project received the prestigious award from the World Congress and Wego Health for its collaboration and building a mutually beneficial relationship with advocacy groups, elevating the patient voice and positively impacting their lives.
3. *AbbVie*: AbbVie has a PCR (Patient-Centered Research) team to bring patient-centricity— the voice of the patient to its product development and discovery programs. Apart from gathering data from patient-reported outcomes (PROs) or the data that comes directly from the patients, the PCR team listens to patients to understand their unmet needs in medical

care and applies that knowledge to its clinical programs and specific clinical trials. AbbVie sharpens its patient focus by generating high-impact and compelling evidence to optimize patients' access to their medications access through their HEOR (Health Economics and Outcomes Research). In addition, AbbVie links its programs to what's happening in the real world and works towards its vision to be a pioneer in strategic evidence generation.

4. *Astellas*: Although Astellas has been taking patient inputs into account, it did not have any formal process or program until recently. However, towards the end of 2019, Astellas created a new position, Senior Vice President of patient-centricity, to show its commitment to patient-centricity internally and externally. The role involves establishing the structure and process needed to facilitate and act on patient engagement throughout the entire development life cycle from discovery to market launch. Astellas understands that patient focus and engagement are crucial for the company's future growth. The company believes that Pharma should engage patients and partner with patients, caregivers, and physicians to understand their perspectives on the disease. More importantly, it's crucial to utilize that information.
5. *UCB*: As patients play an increasingly active role in the medicine development lifecycle, pharmaceutical companies like UCB engage with patients to gather their perspectives and even co-create at key decision points in their drug development programs. UCB is actively participating in this area by collaborating on the PARADIGM project. PARADIGM is an industry and public partnership program with players designed to advance patient engagement focusing on three key decision-making points: research priority setting, design of clinical trials, and early dialogue with regulators and health technology bodies.

It is not only the pharmaceutical industry that is becoming patient-centric; the regulators like FDA (Federal Drug Agency) in the US, and the EMA (European Medical Agency) in Europe are also becoming patient-oriented.

In the US, the FDA is developing guidance documents on how to collect, analyze and report data on patient experience appropriately. These guidelines illustrate that regulators recognize the value of patient-reported outcomes and offer practical information on how this information can impact product labeling, including the uses and effective treatments.

The European Medicines Agency (EMA) and regulators in most countries take patient-centered outcomes evidence into evaluating treatment efficacy and approval. Furthermore, the FDA and EMA are collaborating on strategies to include the patient voice in their regulatory decision-making.

All these trends highlight patients' increasingly important role in their healthcare. Pharma companies will do better to reimagine the patient and heed their voices.

Reimagine the Pharmaceutical Sales Representative

The Changing Landscape of Pharmaceutical Selling

What's up with the pharmaceutical selling arena? What is changing and what is not? Pharmaceutical sales representatives access to physicians has been getting increasingly difficult. Representatives have been the main channel for transmitting marketing information through 'detailing' to physicians for over sixty years. The personal selling effort has accounted for 60 percent of all sales and marketing expenditures in the US. Even in a branded-generics market like India, the total cost of personal selling effort accounts for the most significant chunk of total sales and marketing expenditures.

Declining Physician Access

Physicians' access to pharmaceutical representatives has been steadily declining over the past 10— 12 years in the research-based Pharma markets like the US. Today almost one-half of the physicians in the US have moderate-to-severe restrictions on representatives' visits. A dramatic increase in the number of representatives over the years, turbulent market conditions with dwindling R&D pipelines, drastic cost-containment methods, increasing generic competition, and a frenzy of M&A (Merger and Acquisition) activities are some of the primary reasons for the steadily declining physician access. It is observed that 19 out of 25 mergers corresponded with additional decreases in Pharma sales rep access within one year following the merger. What is more, an increasing number of medical schools and university-affiliated health systems (especially top-tier programs) restrict access to physicians by pharmaceutical companies— a behavior these graduates often take with them when they enter the workforce at hospitals or start their practice with minimal exposure to Pharma reps during their medical training and fellowship program; leading the new generation of physicians to limit in-person visits with pharmaceutical representatives. Another important reason is that today physicians do not see much value-added in the information provided by pharmaceutical sales representatives as much of the data is already available to them at the click of a button thanks to the internet explosion.

While it is discouraging that doctors may not meet as often as before with pharmaceutical representatives, most physicians still view these representatives as valuable sources of information.

Compared to the physician-access restrictions in the US, the access restrictions in many emerging markets are not that severe, but they are declining albeit slowly. The restrictions are more qualitative than quantitative. There are a few 'no-see' doctors in India too. The restrictions are more regarding the frequency of visits by a representative and the time allotted to him. The duration of a call is anywhere between 30 seconds to 2 minutes today compared to an average of four to five minutes a few years before. Very few representatives with thorough product knowledge and excellent communication skills can get more time with doctors.

The main reason for the lack of interest and apathy towards personal visits of representatives and their detailing is the significant drop in the sales force's quality of information and presentation skills. In a study conducted by the Mumbai-based brand communications consultancy firm, Brandcare a few years ago, over 85 percent of doctors said that the communication skills of medical representatives are inferior, and their knowledge about the drugs too, is shallow. Many doctors felt that most of the representatives are working as a postman, delivering samples and gifts. A representative with inadequate product knowledge and inferior communication skills cannot get the physician's attention, let alone engage.

Despite all these reasons discussed, most physicians worldwide think that pharmaceutical representatives would be an essential source of information provided they add value. What is needed is a paradigm shift from the current transactional selling to transformational selling.

Accessing the In-accessible

How do you meet the challenge of this declining access of physicians? How do you gain access to the less accessible and inaccessible physicians who matter? Pharma companies internationally are trying to make up for the reduced access to their representatives through other channels. These include telesales (call center), direct mail, email marketing, e-detailing, speaker programs, self-serve digital content (content that is available on the physicians' professional social media sites, clinical product presentations, Pharma branded sites, e-detailing, and other digital channels) and mobile alerts among others. An Affinity Monitor Study conducted a few years ago by ZS Associates, a leading consultancy firm specializing in pharmaceutical sales and marketing, showed that some Pharma companies had sent nearly 50 percent more digital messages, including emails and mobile alerts—than the number of personal face-to-face calls attempted. The physicians' response to this avalanche of digital messages can be understood from this comment of a specialist physician, who said: *More than anything, they (the Pharma companies) are taking a big dartboard and picking up the darts and just flinging them and hoping one of them will stick*.

It's like Pharma companies saying that here's all our ammunition and that's the target— let's throw. Blanketing customers with marketing messages is not likely to yield the desired results because even if some messages hit the target, the customers may not pay attention to them. What is the solution? How do you get the attention of the physicians? Empathy is the solution. Yes, Pharma companies need to apply some compassion and consider the situation from the physician's perspective. No single channel always works today. Therefore, it is essential to understand what kind of content doctors want to receive, which channels they prefer, and how frequently they wish to be contacted to tailor their marketing communication. That way, they can make sure that messages resonate. Focus on the quality of the customer interaction and not on their reach at all costs.

New Rules of Engagement

It is the steady onslaught of marketing messages that are causing an information overload, which is making the physicians deliberately tune out. Like you label unwanted and unsolicited information as spam, physicians label most marketing messages as spam. To avoid this and to more effectively engage with physicians, Pharma companies need to do three things. These new rules of engagement are:

Empathize: Determine the type of content that interests the physician and will engage him. Understand their preferences. Some prefer clinical information communicated by a peer. Others may want patient education material. Some others may wish to access the information themselves from a library of self-serve content. Pharma companies should also understand the channels by which physicians prefer to be contacted.

Be Relevant: Pharma companies that understand physicians' preferences can design and deliver the most relevant communication to their target doctors through the channels of their interest.

Resonate: Pharma companies should also understand the impact of frequency. Different channels show different saturation points. It is essential to know how often is too often? Research shows that doctors tend to open the first few emails for a given brand, but they stop after receiving about ten emails. In messages through mobile apps, the saturation point is lower— doctors stop responding after four or five messages. Direct mail, on the other hand, has a higher saturation point but a lower engagement rate.

Pharma companies can use the alternative channels to access the *hard-to-see* and *no-see* doctors and reinforce their access to currently accessible physicians. It may be difficult to determine the preferences of individual physicians. Still, it is increasingly feasible to systematically track and measure the types of content that the companies put out and the relative response to different content types. It is also possible to analyze the new highly granular data like 'rep-doctor iPad' interactions. Also, Pharma companies can use analytics to understand how marketing channels reinforce each other. They can, based on this understanding, develop the desired set of actions—at the right time and in the correct sequence, supporting the sales reps to increase their engagement with individual physicians.

Pharma companies can optimize their engagement with physicians in general, and *hard-to-see* and *no-see* doctors in particular, by using the data to understand the affinities of the doctors they are trying to reach and tailoring the content, channel, and frequency of their marketing messages accordingly.

What is needed is a higher engagement rate and better customer experience than a higher message transmission rate. In marketing, as in medicine— a little empathy goes a long way!

The COVID-19 Pandemic's Impact on Pharma Selling

In 2019, the outbreak of the coronavirus pandemic commonly known as COVID-19 added fuel to the already declining physician access to pharma field forces. From the very start of the pandemic, traditional in-person sales reps' visits to physicians declined sharply due to social distancing and lockdown measures worldwide. Pharmaceutical companies had to adapt to the rapidly changing marketing environment and train their sales forces to use virtual tools to stay connected to physicians. With restrictions around in-person interactions and hospitals continuing, the relationship between physicians and pharma sales reps will be altered significantly, creating a substantial demand for virtual and online meeting software and tools. The pharma companies need to respond to this shift in physician's behavior, reimagine engagement, and recreate the in-person experience using virtual technologies and tools to deal with HCP (Healthcare Professionals) challenges during the pandemic and when the pandemic recedes. According to a 2019 Global Data poll, seventy-five percent of the physician participants in the US said virtual interactions will remain (either as a stand-alone or a mix of in-person and virtual interactions) after the COVID-19 recedes. Only twenty-five percent of the physicians believed that in-person interactions would go back to the pre-pandemic levels. These findings clearly reflect the change in physician's preferences, and pharma companies will need to reimagine the customer engagement process and the role of the pharma sales rep in the new normal.

The Changing Role of the Pharma Sales Rep

COVID-19 acted as a catalyst in redefining the sales reps' role in the pharmaceutical industry. Sales forces provide the vital link between the pharmaceutical industry and healthcare providers (HCPs) by introducing their prospects, innovative therapies, and clinical insights. However, the digital revolution is changing the exclusive role of the sales reps by offering alternative communication channels. As a result, the role of the traditional pharma sales rep may also significantly change. The reimagined salesforce will have a greater need for tech-savvy sales reps knowing how to build brands, respond to customers' needs and deliver messages using hybrid or phygital (physical + digital) methods and virtual tools. COVID-19 dramatically changed all that pharmaceutical companies had relied on— traditional face-to-face sales force and physicians' interactions, reinforcing the need for virtual communication approaches.

The longer social distancing restrictions continue, the more changes they are expected to bring to future interactions. For pharmaceutical companies, it means that sales forces will need to move away from a one-size-fits-all communication approach and adapt to varying customer needs.

Changing Preferences

Physicians' interaction preferences with Pharma are changing. As a result of the wide availability of online media and digital channels, the face-to-face rep is no longer the sole source of information. Two fundamental changes are driving this change.

1. One is demographics. The *digital native* physicians (51 percent) have, for the first time, exceeded the number of digital immigrant ones (49 percent) in 2014. Digital natives are the new generation of young people born into the digital age, while digital immigrants learned to use computers at some stage in their adult life. Being exposed to technologies from their early life, digital natives see everyone on an equal level and not hierarchically. They think and process what they see and listen differently to digital immigrants.

2. The other is changing channel preferences. Many specialist physicians now spend significantly more time online for professional purposes than with sales reps. Digital channels, therefore, provide a significant opportunity for pharmaceutical companies to engage physicians outside normal business hours. Consider, for example, that specialists in Northern Europe, according to an Across Health research report, spent 37 hours online for professional purposes compared to only 0.9 hours with pharma sales reps in 2017.

Physicians tend to receive over twenty professional emails daily, and with their increasing administrative burdens, their time for face-to-face (F2F) meetings with reps has become quite limited. The pandemic has reduced it even further with its social distancing and lockdown measures. And, to top it all, the pharma sales rep is no longer the only influential channel in the mix today. Many impactful pharma-owned channels exist that rep can orchestrate to increase engagement levels with customers. Therefore, the way out for Pharma is best summed up by Pratap Khedkar of ZS Associates, a leading management consulting and professional services firm, when he says: *While it is discouraging that doctors may not meet as often with Pharma reps, most physicians still view these reps as valuable sources of information. Pharma Companies just need to find new ways to reach these customers*.

Orchestrator Reps

What the pharma sales forces need today are the *Orchestrator reps*. Jaideep Bajaj, Chairman of ZS Associates, a leading sales and marketing consulting firm globally, helped develop the *Orchestrator rep* concept. The orchestrator rep is an evolution of the traditional rep. According to Saby Mitra and Jaideep Bajaj of ZS Associates, this new sales rep model integrates sales, marketing, and other customer-facing functions and leverages technology to facilitate an integrated multichannel customer engagement. While this application is new, he says it is really a logical extension of the sales rep role, which capitalizes on a new idea, tools, and training. The new technology and tools enable reps to orchestrate multiple channels seamlessly to engage their HCPs (Healthcare Providers). As the orchestrator rep is in the center of all actions and events, he can use them to tailor sales call to the physician's unique situation and preferences, making them highly relevant to his needs. The whole idea behind the orchestrator rep is that the sales call is a continuum of all other interactions, so that call can be most effective. And it is not just about just one call. The objective is to keep incorporating all interactions to continuously improve all future interactions and align the relationship solidly around the needs of the physician over time. And they need to be tech-savvy to be able to:

- increase access through additional channel touchpoints
- prolong the conversations through digital channels
- create higher impact through improved insights gained through remote engagement
- generate and prioritize leads through historical Chanel affinity insights

The field force is increasingly considered the conductor of all channels for engaging their customers, leveraging F2F (face-to-face), email, remote engagement, web visits, and providing and leveraging the key customer insights in the process. Why should Pharma embrace the multichannel rep strategy? Here are some important reasons:

1. Enhanced customer engagement to achieve superior customer experience based on physicians' channel preferences.
2. To deliver the right content through the right channel and at the right time.
3. To optimize resource allocation.

Changing Role

The changing role of the pharma sales rep from a predominantly face-to-face one to a multichannel rep is challenging. The challenge is to *be there, where and how the physician wants*! What is more, he has to manage and orchestrate many personal and non-personal channels.

The *Personal Channels* are Tele-detailing, F2F (face-to-face) interactions, Local meetings, Call center, e-MSL (e-Medical Science Liaison), and Congresses.

The *Non-personal Channels* are Website (Pharma & 3rd party), Direct mail, SMS, Apps, Webinars, Virtual Detail, Banners and Advertising, and Social media.

Orchestrator Rep: Key Tactics

There are four key digital tactics that Orchestrator reps use today:

1. *Tablet Detailing*: This *push* strategy increases the impact of face-to-face visits.
2. *Rep Email*: This is also a *push* strategy to increase frequency on top of F2F (face-to-face) visits.
3. *Remote engagement*: Remote engagement or virtual detailing is another push strategy to increase customer reach on top of face-to-face or in-person visits.
4. *HCP Self-service website*: HCP-Self-Service Website can be used as a very influential *pull* channel. It is far more interesting as physicians are willingly drawn into it.

In a ZS Associates white paper titled Pharma Sales: *Why you need orchestrator reps now*— Jaideep Bajaj explains the evolutionary process of the orchestrator rep. Orchestration is a continuum, and it has three steps, and the choice of the step depends on the company's culture and its need to manage the rate of change. Here is the essence of what he said in the white paper:

1. Step one is the *Inform Stage*. In this phase, the rep knows the doctor's preference for how he or she receives information and what content or offers he or she prefers to receive, along with all the past and future interactions with the pharma company. That's a lot of information to harmonize the content of a sales call and make it more effective.
2. Step two is the *Influence Stage*. At this point, the rep can put information back into the system so that marketing can shape both the pace and the content of messages based on the doctor's preferences. So reps are actually influencing future interactions.

3. Step three is the *Orchestration Stage*. At this point, the reps can pause, stop, or trigger specific interactions based on what they know about the physician. For example, the rep might hold a marketing email until after her visit to lay the groundwork for these messages, and the email will then have more impact. Or she might want to cancel mailing a kit to a doctor because she wants to take it herself or decide not to use the kit at all as she doesn't think the message will resonate with the physician. The rep can also trigger follow-up actions based on available personal and non-personal tactics to meet the needs of a particular physician.

Implementing Orchestrator Rep Sales Model

While transforming the traditional pharma sales reps into orchestrator reps can boost the company's reach, engagement, and performance, it is not an easy task. Pharma companies must integrate their sales, marketing, and other customer-facing departments and ensure firm commitment from their top management. Before implementing the orchestrator rep model, they should first design integrated customer engagement strategies for reps. Here five important points to consider before implementing the transformation program:

1. Customer behavior and preferences are moving toward digital engagement. Companies, therefore, must leverage technology, grow digital capabilities and equip their sales reps with the ability to maximize the use of alternate digital channels. They must empower their reps to build digital relationships with their customers.
2. The sales force needs a 360-degree view of the customers and the physician engagement with sales and marketing to access, sort through and make the best use of available customer data and insights for building enduring relationships. To do this, pharma companies must create a robust data, analytics, and technology infrastructure.
3. Make it easy for reps. Create a simple mobile solution. Integrate it into the sales force automation (SFA) platform. Train reps on orchestration capabilities and not just tools.

4. Don't let other Salesforce Excellence (SFE) levers stand in the way. Review sales rep competencies, hiring profiles, incentive plans to include orchestration dimensions.
5. Perhaps the most important and difficult aspect of implementation is change management. The organization should secure buy-in for the orchestrator rep model from the top management and key stakeholders across hierarchies. It involves training the reps in a new, enhanced role that requires a huge shift in the mindset.

Essential Pre-requisites

How do you make your change process from traditional sales rep to orchestrator successful? The following infrastructure and capabilities are essential for improving reach, engagement, and performance in the evolving omnichannel environment in healthcare.

A. **Infrastructure:** You need to have the right data collection protocol to capture the information that really matters. All the data that is sufficiently precise and at the pace you need. Once you gather the data, you need to build a customer data repository to develop a 360-degree view of the customer based on all interactions and data. You also need to set up a user interface in Customer Relationship Management (CRM) and link with marketing operations so that reps can easily access and use the data.

B. **Capabilities:** To deliver and organizing customer journey across multiple touchpoints:

- Train to transform your field force into orchestrator reps
- Change the focus of field force from product-centricity to customer-centricity
- Up-skill the entire organization to achieve multichannel management capabilities.
- Gain a thorough understanding and insights into the omnichannel ecosystem
- Shift your Focus from HCP-centricity to patient-centricity

Not a Nice-to-Have, but a Need-to Have

Once a leading competitive advantage, product differentiation is no longer enough to win in the rapidly changing pharma marketplace. A seamless, holistic customer experience is what the customers want. Customer experience is the new strategy. A differentiated customer experience, therefore, is your competitive edge. Physicians will have an experience whether you design one or not, and sales reps will continue to face declining access despite your efforts to stem the tide. Transforming your customer engagement model to orchestrator rep is your big opportunity to win in the evolving healthcare ecosystem.

Here is a case (The Orchestrator Rep: Imagine the Possibilities) showing how an orchestrator rep can improve customer experience to cement a customer relationship. It requires an orchestrator rep who is aware of all interactions between the company and a particular physician, can shape the sales and marketing outreach to make it more effective.

CASE

8

The Orchestrator Rep: Imagine the Possibilities!

Consider a sales rep heading into a physician visit who gets an update on his tablet that the physician recently logged on to the company's website to look into side effects. Immediately, the sales rep changes his talking points and tailors the discussion to the doctor's concerns. The meeting goes well, and as the rep is leaving, the doctor asks about the efficacy and mentions that she hates unsolicited emails. Immediately, the rep updates the doctor's profile to pause future marketing emails and asks the company's Medical Science Liaison (MSL) to call the physician directly with concise answers to her questions.

(Source: ZS Interview with Jaideep Bajaj, Pharma Sales: Why You Need Orchestrator Reps Now, ZS Sales+Marketing)

Customer Experience

The pharmaceutical industry has contributed significantly towards improving people's health worldwide and continues to do so. For example, it has recently developed a handful of vaccines to help the world get past the most deadly pandemic ever, COVID-19. And yet, its public perception is very poor. According to the Harris Poll, only 53 percent of consumers (patients) hold a positive view of Pharma. In addition, a recent Gallup poll on consumer perceptions found Pharma rated below electric utilities and oil and gas!

Why is it that the Pharma brands, despite their disease-treating, health-restoring, and even life-saving nature, cannot connect with consumers (patients) like some leading consumer companies such as Apple and Spotify do? What differentiates them? The answer is Customer Experience!

Great consumer brands create a strong emotional connection with their consumers, whereas Pharma does not create that with consumers, who are patients. The best consumer brands have gone beyond engaging their customers and moved further to focus on creating a great customer experience, and the whole company is solidly aligned with that. They map every aspect of customer experience with extreme care from first engagement to first purchase and continued usage. They cover all possible touchpoints and leave nothing to chance.

However, the Pharmaceutical industry focuses on building relationships with their intermediate customers, such as healthcare practitioners (HCPs), and not with patients, their ultimate customers, or consumers of their products and services. Some major pharma companies have realized the need to focus on patients and initiated patient-centric moves in their overall strategy for some years. A look at their mission statements confirms this.

Table 1.5 Mission Statements of Select Pharma Companies

Company Name	Mission Statement
Pfizer	At, Pfizer, we innovate everyday to make the world a healthier place. It was the vision of Charles Pfizer at the very beginning, and it holds true today in everything we do. From Scientific discovery to breakthrough products to our essential partnerships around the world, we 're committed to quality healthcare for everyone. Because every *individual matters.*
Roche	Doing what *patients* need next.
Novartis	Our mission is to discover new ways to improve and extend *peoples lives.*
Johnson & Johnson	Our credo stems from a belief that *consumers, employees,* and the community are all equally important.
Merck &Co	We share one vision and one mission: to save and improve *lives.*
Sanofi	Everyday, Sanofi's 100,000 employees are committed to improve the *lives of people* around the world with sustainable and responsible solutions and initiatives.
AbbVie	Create an innovation-driven, *patient-focused* specialty biopharmaceutical company capable of achieving sustainable top-tier performance through outstanding execution and a consistent stream of innovative new medicines.
GlaxoSmithKline	A science-led global healthcare company with a special purpose to help *people* do more, feel better, live longer.
Amgen	To serve *patients.*
Gilead Sciences	To discover, develop, and commercialize innovative therapeutics in the area of unmet medical needs that improve *patient* care.
Bristol-Myers Squibb	Bristol-Myers Squibb is a global biopharmaceutical company whose mission is to discover, develop, and deliver innovative medicines that help *patients* prevail over serious diseases.
AstraZeneca	We push the boundaries of science to deliver *life-changing* medicines.

Source: Sean McDade, PhD, Founder-CEO, PeopleMetrics, *Pharma Customer Experience: 20 Secrets to 10X Your CX and Boost Patient Outcomes*, Lioncrest Publishing, 2021)

All their patient-centric strategies aim at increasing and improving Pharma's engagement with patients. However, while engaging patients is very important, it is not enough. Thanks to the internet explosion and ever-increasing healthcare information and knowledge, the patients today, are more health-literate, aware, and empowered. In addition, they are getting used to great customer experiences from companies in other industries and expect the same from the pharma industry. Therefore, Pharma has to move from engagement to delivering a great customer experience because customer experience has become the crucial differentiator. Moreover, customer experience overtakes everything, including price and product quality. Therefore, customer experience is the new imperative for Pharma's success.

What is Customer Experience?

Exactly, what is customer experience? A clear understanding of customer experience is a necessary first step to creating it.

Annette Franz, founder-CEO of CX Journey Inc, defines *Customer Experience as the sum of all the interactions a customer has over the life of the relationship with the brand, including the feelings, emotions, and perceptions of those interactions*. This definition makes customer experience everyone's job, and every employee plays a role in delivering a customer experience that matters.

Organizations, including pharma companies, must deliver an amazing customer experience to succeed in today's hyper-competitive marketplace. But then, how do you deliver an amazing customer experience? The first step is understanding how the best customer-focused companies deliver a winning customer experience. Here are three foundational principles to deliver a superior customer experience based on what they do:

1. *Clearly define* your customer experience vision and constantly communicate it across the organization to remind and reinforce.
2. *Listen to your customers*— what they are saying and not saying to understand how they perceive their interactions and experiences with your brand and organization. Because, in the

final analysis, customer experience is about how customers perceive their interactions and experiences with you, which is their reality. They can walk away from your interactions and experiences instantly with just one click if they feel that your offerings (products and services) do not meet their needs and wants, and are not likely to return.

3. *Consistency* is the key to success in creating a remarkably memorable customer experience. Delivering a customer experience that lights up a customer's eyes every time she interacts with your brand and company is crucial to building customer loyalty. Consistency needs to be ever-present. Leveraging communication technologies to help you reach your customers whenever they have questions or concerns is a powerful way to achieve consistency.

As every customer is different, so is their definition of a great customer experience. Integrating these three foundational elements mentioned above as a core customer experience philosophy will help deliver personalized experiences that delight customers.

Why Customer Experience (CX) is a Must for Pharma?

Loyalty— customer loyalty is incredibly profitable for any business, including Pharma. Loyal customers increase opportunities to cross and up-sell as they are more likely to try other products and recommend you. However, in the face of increasing healthcare consumerism and customer choice, the pharmaceutical industry finds it difficult to build loyalty among its customers. But, how do you create loyalty when it is increasingly difficult and traditional promotional methods and customer engagement fall short? Many pharma companies find that adopting a customer experience (CX) approach is the answer. The only way to improve brand perception and customer satisfaction is to consistently meet and exceed your customers' expectations across their journey. As a result, customer experience has overtaken price and product as the key brand differentiator. That is why Gartner, a leading consulting firm with research and advisory expertise, calls *customer experience the new battlefield, with 80 percent of companies competing mostly or completely based on customer experience*.

Moreover, patients who have positive experiences with Pharma are more likely to join clinical trials, successfully onboard to new medications, adhere over time, and enjoy positive medical outcomes.

Remember, patients are also consumers, who have a smartphone, smartwatch, shop on Amazon, listen to Spotify, watch Netflix, and hail a Uber or Lyft taxi. All these services provide consumers with very satisfying experiences. And these experiences influence patients to expect whether they are boarding onto a new medication or continuing their medication in chronic conditions.

Also, look around the best-in-class companies worldwide and understand their strategic approaches. Increasingly, they organize their businesses around what customers want as they realize that the new and recent technological advances enable and empower customers to choose their products. Today, customers can learn more about the products before buying and using them daily. Therefore, the value delivery of the product depends not just on the product or service itself but on the customer's entire experience across his journey.

CX: Two Essential Ingredients

The two aspects to consider when bringing CX (Customer Experience) into an organization are— Strategy and Design.

A Customer Experience Strategy outlines the vision and objectives for driving CX across the organization. It encompasses all activities across all functions to optimize customer value and experience. Also, it involves a strong alignment across the business to identify who your customer is, what you want to achieve by creating better customer experiences, and how you plan to implement the strategy. When developing a Customer Experience Strategy, consider the following questions:

- Who are our customers?
- What do great customer experiences look like for them?
- What experiences will our customers compare us to?
- How will we better empathize with our customers?

Customer Experience Design is the coordinated approach a company takes to empathize with customers and create solutions to optimize the customer experience. It involves a range of research activities; developing customer personas, mapping customer journeys, identifying moments of truth, design-thinking activities to ideate, prototype, and test solutions, executing omnichannel campaigns, and measuring impact through the voice of the customer (VOC).

Ten Guiding Principles

Finally, as Blake Morgan, a well-known customer experience expert and author of the book**,** *The Customer of the Future: 10 Guiding Principles for Winning Tomorrow's Business,* says, today's customers are already demanding friction-less, personalized, and on-demand experiences from their products and services. In addition, tomorrow's customers will insist on experiences that make their lives significantly better and easier. Therefore, to win, customers will have to do better than merely proclaiming that customer experience is a priority, but build customer focus into every aspect of their business. The following table summarizes the ten guiding principles described by Blake Morgan in her book.

Table 1.6 CX (Customer Experience: Ten Guiding Principles)

	Customer Experience: Ten Guiding Principles
1.	Customer Experience Mindset
2.	Building a customer-centric Culture
3.	Developing customer-focused leadership. It's all about investing in your leaders who will invest in their employees and provide a superior customer experience.
4.	Designing a smooth, no-friction customer experience. We can create a zero-friction customer experience by walking through the customer journey and learning from customer service champions like Amazon.
5.	Customer-focused marketing
6.	Customer Experience Technology, which is critical in creating, improving and growing customer experience
7.	Digital Transformation
8.	Personalization and the customer experience of the future
9.	Using Customer Experience Analytics
10.	Ethics and Data Privacy in Customer Experience

The pharmaceutical industry can do better by imbibing these ten guiding principles into its strategic framework and intentionally creating an experience that delights all its customers, namely the patients, physicians, and other stakeholders. Therefore, Pharma has to move from managing customer engagement to creating customer experiences.

CE (Customer Engagement) to CX (Customer Experience)

For a long time, the pharmaceutical industry has mastered the art and science of customer engagement, mainly with their physician customers. However, today's customers need more than engagement. They want meaningful engagement that enriches their experience. That is why great consumer brands emotionally connect with their customers consistently. Pharma has to up its act from engagement to experience if they want to continue to thrive.

Creating a Great Customer Experience

First, we must understand what a great experience is. Is it all about our interactions with customers? There is more to customer experience than interaction. Yes, interactions are important, but then there is more. We must meaningfully engage customers at every single touchpoint that matters across their journey. A clear understanding of touchpoints, interactions, and engagement is necessary to create a great customer experience.

Touchpoints are those points where a customer comes into contact with your brand or organization. For example, it could be through a visit to your website, contact with an employee, brand message, product, and across different channels. Here's a brief list of some possible *touchpoints*:

- Exploring the website
- Social media posts, ads
- Recognizing the company's brand image on digital platforms
- Receiving Emails
- Reading a company's blog, annual reports, news, updates

Interactions are the communication processes between customers and employees. Consider, for example, the following possible interactions:

- Communicating with the company's medical representatives
- Messaging and contacting the support team
- Sending an email, filling out a company form
- Sharing the company's resources on social media
- Interacting with a company's product, such as going through the product information leaf-let

Engagement is the quality of interaction. Here are some examples of some possible engagement activities:

- Signing-Up for a free trial, freemium, or a newsletter
- SigningUp for a free webinar
- Agreeing to a call with the medical representative or MSL (Medical Science Liaison)
- Buying a product or service

CX, UX, and Customer Service

Before learning to create a great customer experience, it is important to understand the differences between User Experience, Customer Service, and Customer Experience— the three terms whose meanings are often blurred.

UX (User Experience) refers to the feeling users experience when using a product, service, application, or system. It is a broad term covering how well a user can navigate the web site, how easy it is to use, how well the content is displayed, etc.

Customer Service is the support you offer your customers— both before and after they buy and use your product or services— that helps them have an easy and enjoyable experience with you.

UX (User Experience) and *Customer Service* make up part of the *CX (Customer Experience).*

How to Create a Customer Experience?

First, you must create a customer experience strategy to get and stay ahead of the competition. A Customer Experience strategy is a holistic plan to increase customer satisfaction and engagement across all touchpoints and interactions with your brand (Product and Corporate), from discovery to post-purchase. It can be the foundation to ensure your organization provides the best service across all touch points. Here is a table presenting an outline of the customer experience strategy process:

Table 1.7 Customer Experience Strategy Process

Customer Experience Strategy Process
Customer • Understand your audience and create buyer personas • Define what customers can expect from you, what makes you stand out from competition and what benefits and experiences you promise
Journey Create a clear roadmap of your customer journey, including touchpoints with customer engagement levels
Measurement Decide on the methodology and frequency of customer experience measurement and define the metrics set to be applied
Analysis Determine the way you will analyze the customers' feedback and steps to be taken to improve their pain points
Improvement Plan the efficiency enhancement aimed at customer experience boost via proper corrective actions

Nikoletta Bika, the senior content specialist at Acquire, a digital platform for creating a customer experience, explains fourteen ways to create a great customer experience in her blog article, *How to Create Customer Experience: 14 Ways*, published on December 3, 2021. Here is the gist**:**

1. Understand your customers and create buyer personas
2. Analyze your business objectives
3. Reverse-engineer the experience you want to deliver

4. Select team players and get them invested in the process
5. Use the right design in the Game
6. Pay attention to customer feedback
7. Research your competitors
8. Build systems for quick and effective resolutions
9. Incorporate a memorable brand personality
10. Apply Artificial Intelligence Technology
11. Redefine your marketing
12. Understand how to measure your customers' experiences
13. Use the right technology and tools
14. Optimize your customer experience strategy

1. **Understand Your Audience and Create Buyer Personas**: Who are your customers? What are their motivations? You need to understand your customers and know what makes them do what they want to do, to build customer personas you can use to shape your customer experience strategy.

   Research shows that over two-thirds (66 Percent) of consumers expect companies to understand their needs. So it is important to find out what they're looking for across their entire buyer journey and personalize their experience. Therefore, creating detailed buyer personas is crucial. How to do this? Create detailed customer profiles and segment your customers to understand where they are coming from, their buying behavior, and what they will need from your brand/ company throughout their journey and across all your channels. Then, use a CRM (Customer Relationship Management) tool to collect the relevant data and get useful insights.

2. **Analyze Your Business Objectives:** What type of customer experience do you need to create? To decide on this, you must first define your business goals. What are your business goals? New customers? Entering a new market? For example, if you are launching products and services into a current marketplace, you need to review brand studies and identify the barriers. How can you overcome these barriers? Next, you need to

create a customer experience strategy to help you achieve your long-term goals. Finally, ask and answer the following questions to shape your customer experience strategy better:

- Where do we stand today in terms of a customer-centric experience?
- What gaps can you identify between customer expectations and actual experiences? How can you bridge them?
- What technology, people, and processes do we need

3. **Reverse-engineer the Experience You Want to Deliver**: Steve Jobs, the founder of Apple Inc., showed the best way to create a meaningful customer experience when he said: *Begin with the customer experience and work backward to ward the technology*.

   How do we do this? First, you can start listing your brand's customer experience stages. Where are the opportunities to make a great impression? For Amazon, for example, it is delivery. What is it for you? Then, start from there and ask: What do we need to ensure customers go through this stage seamlessly?

4. **Select team players and get them invested in the process:** It is humans that create and deliver customer experiences. And an exceptional customer experience begins from within. So if employees are not having a meaningful experience and don't even know what a good customer experience looks like, you can't expect them to deliver that to customers. Therefore, you must hire and train people to cultivate and develop a customer-centric mindset.

5. **Use the Right Design Early in the Game:** A good User Experience (UX) can create a great customer experience. UX design is essential for the main contact points for your customers when they come into contact with your brand, namely your brand or company website. Here are three points to remember and act upon for improving UX design for a better customer experience:

- Create a consistent brand experience across your website, apps, email, and social media channels.

- Make it easy to navigate so your customers can find the right information or service.
- Factor in emotion where applicable. For example, Wufoo, the cloud-based form-filler that makes it easy to create registration forms, application forms, surveys, and contact forms, added emoji faces ranging from *super smiley* to *mega grumpy* to their app. And then, they asked customers to rate their feelings on this scale.

6. **Pay Attention to Customer Feedback:** Bain & Company's research showed that while **80 percent of** companies believe they are providing great customer service, only **8 percent** of customers agree. Therefore, it is very important to close this gap; customer feedback is the only way to do this. The three ways to ask for customer feedback are:

- Conduct post-interaction and real-time feedback surveys regularly.
- Usually, customers are more honest and vocal on social media and therefore practice social listening. Over 80 percent of customers use social media to engage with brands. Furthermore, according to Ameyo (a leading CX solutions company) research, fifty-seven percent of customers would rather contact companies via digital media such as email and social media rather than use voice-based customer support. Also, Sprout Social, a social media management solutions company, observed that thirty percent of customers would go to a competitor if the brand did not respond on social media.

7. **Research Your Competitors**

   Analyzing competitors and market trends give the company a clear picture of what competitors are doing to serve their customers. It helps you identify gaps, such as customer experience tactics that no one is using. It also helps you catch up with what your competitors are doing to avoid being left behind. Determine your competitors, their products, and services, and consider the following questions:

- What are their marketing strategy, pricing, sales tactics, and results?
- What is their content strategy?
- What is their level of engagement?
- What are their social media presence, strategy, and go-to platforms?
- What technology stack are they using?

  Do a SWOT analysis to learn their strengths, weaknesses, opportunities, and threats.

8. **Build Customer Support Systems for Quick and Effective Resolutions:** Build effective and efficient customer support systems which can be the pillars of your customer experience strategy. Consider, for example, using a *live chat* which is very convenient for customers browsing your website. It is non-distracting and provides easy access when needed. You can also integrate it with *video chat* and *chatbots* for greater support

9. **Incorporate a Memorable Brand Personality:** How people perceive your brand personality may be subjective but is extremely important. Consumers often have strong and personal gut reactions to brands— as they do to certain people. And these emotional connections have a direct impact on sales and business. According to Harvard Business School, 95 percent of purchasing decisions are based on feelings instead of logic.

   A unique, distinctly different brand personality can set your brand apart from the pack. A set of human characteristics give a brand its distinctive personality in the customer's eyes. A brand's personality shapes the public perception of a brand based on how it acts and what it says and looks like. Thus, a brand personality, in essence, implies the company's reputation or demeanor or the *felt sense*, as psychotherapists call it.

   Creating a brand personality is not enough. First, you must ensure your brand personality is represented in all your branding efforts, from your logo to your website to the tone of voice of your customer service reps. A successful brand personality should meet the following essential five criteria:

- *It must be authentic*. Your brand personality must reflect your business goals and company culture.
- *It must be memorable.* It would be best if it stood out to be remembered.
- *It must provide value*. What value does it provide for customers that they can't get elsewhere?
- *It must be trustworthy.* Like a real person, your brand must deliver what it promises to earn customers' trust.
- It must have the *authority* of an expert in its field. A brand personality that has expertise and confidence and is helpful will earn loyalty from its customers.

While your brand personality deals with the human characteristics of your brand, *your brand identity* is the manifestation of your brand personality, like your logo, color scheme, and tone of voice in all your brand communications.

Further, *brand voice* is vital as customers conclude your brand personality based on how you communicate on social media, websites, blogs, ads, press releases, and other product messages.

10. **Apply AI (Artificial Intelligence) Technology:** Today, most customers (for example, 6 out of 10 in the US) prefer digital self-service tools like websites, mobile apps, or online tutorials over a call or video chat for resolving issues. AI can enhance this experience. Here are some of the many benefits that AI can offer to enhance customer experiences:

- Enables auto-responses to routine customer queries, guiding your customers with carefully curated content.
- By automating common, regular customer service interactions, AI can free up your time to focus on more complex issues.
- Can segment your user base and increase personalization. AI can send personalized messages and even track their response automatically by sifting through the records of a subscriber's email browsing data, web pages visited, and past interactions.

- AI can send the customers the most relevant promotional messages based on past interactions.
- An AI Chatbot on your website can help you provide more personalized experiences and faster, automated service.

11. **Redefine Your Marketing:** Today's customers do not wait for your ads, emails, or sales representatives to make buying decisions. Instead, they actively research their options and are more well-informed than ever. Digitalization has drastically shifted customers' decision-making process.

    That is why you must redefine your marketing and enable proactive and educational marketing in addition to traditional campaigns, like content, reviews, word-of-mouth marketing, and more to create the best possible customer experience.

12. **Understand Your Customer Experience Metrics**: Measuring and monitoring customer experience is necessary to deliver a great customer experience. Remember the axiom? What can't be measured can't be improved.

    According to a 2019 Gartner CEM (Customer Experience Study), seventy-five percent of businesses showed customer satisfaction leads to positive business outcomes, such as revenue growth, increased customer retention, or increased lifetime value. Also, Adobe's 2020 Digital Trends Report found brands that effectively managed experiences were three times as likely to have exceeded their top company goals in 2019. Moreover, the 2018 PWC's (Price Waterhouse Coopers) *Experience is Everything Report* revealed that more positive brand experiences than great advertising persuaded 65 percent of US customers. That is why measuring customer experience is the new imperative for defining your product or service's success and improving customer loyalty.

    Customer experience tools help you understand how customers view and interact with your brand. While there are several experience metrics that you can use to monitor customer interactions, the following six are more important:

- Net Promoter Score
- Customer Satisfaction Score

- Customer Effort Score
- Customer Churn Rate
- Customer Retention Rate
- Customer Lifetime Value

13. **Use the Right Technology and Tools:** Customer experience strategy is increasingly driven by technology. Also, the customer journeys and purchasing behaviors have increasingly shifted to digital, almost forcing the companies to get strategic about delivering consistent digital customer experience across all touchpoints and consumer-facing channels. Therefore, it would help if you had a robust customer experience platform and the right technology and tools to deliver a superior customer experience. The recent *Digital Trends Report 2019* by Econsultancy and Adobe emphasizes the need for marketing and technology integration when it says: *The successful companies deliver first-class, personalized customer experiences built on a foundation of integrated marketing and technology*.

    Richard Buettner, the marketing head at STYLA, the fastest StoreFront Technology company, recommends a combination of the following ten customer experience tools:

- Customer Relationship Management (CRM) platforms
- Customer Journey Management Software
- Social Media Tools
- Customer Feedback Management Tools
- Customer Experience Management Platforms
- Customer Engagement Platforms
- Helpdesk Platforms
- Personalization Platforms
- Post Purchase Platforms
- Front-end Experience Platforms

These ten platforms and tools are essential for businesses in general. However, Pharma needs to adapt these to its specific requirements to make them more relevant wherever necessary.

14. **Optimize Your Customer Experience Strategy:** A customer experience strategy is not a one-time exercise but an ongoing process. *Customer experience optimization*, therefore, is a continual process of using data to gather feedback on customer's experiences throughout their lifecycle to improve it. So what is the mantra for a successful customer experience strategy? Measure, Optimize, Repeat.

CX and Pharma

Customer-centricity is at the core of the customer experience strategy. Patients are the ultimate consumers or end-users of their products and services, so every pharma company claims to be patient-centric. For example, if you read any pharma company's mission statement, you will undoubtedly see the prominently mentioned patient-centricity. Yet, few companies are patient-obsessed and always create, measure, and manage customer experiences because they understand there is more to patient-centricity than developing innovative, safe drugs that improve the quality and the length of a patient's life. Why so? Why is it that very few pharma companies adopt a customer experience strategy? There are many reasons. Firstly, there are different levels of customers and many stakeholders. Secondly, Pharma faces regulatory and compliance constraints that other industries do not, limiting the extent to which Pharma can create and manage customer experiences. Before we get into details, it is useful to understand who Pharma's customers are and its regulatory constraints.

Pharma's Customers

Who are Pharma's customers? Traditionally, they have been physicians who prescribe medications for patients. However, the definition of customers has expanded to include other HCPs (Healthcare Practitioners) such as physician assistants, nurse practitioners, caregivers, and patients. The two main reasons that have caused this shift in the customer make-up are:

A. Pharma has shifted from mass-market drugs to specialties. The specialty drugs now represent almost half the overall market and often require close patient interaction. Although the specialty drugs were the first to adopt this close interaction with patients, this is a need even mass-market drugs will have to satisfy in these days of hyper-competition.

B. The second reason is the growing consumerization of health care. Patients are more involved in their healthcare decisions and expect to have support throughout their treatment journey and demand access to that support where, when, and how they choose.

Pharma's Regulatory Constraints

While there are many regulatory constraints that the pharmaceutical industry faces, let us focus primarily on those that may impact its ability to deliver great customer experiences. Also, a detailed analysis of the pharmaceutical regulatory environment is beyond the scope of this book.

Here are some of the perceived and real constraints affecting the customer experience strategy implementation in the pharmaceutical industry:

- The federal anti-kickback law in the US prohibits any form of remuneration intended to reward or influence prescribing behavior, such as providing a gift to HCPs (Healthcare Practitioners) to encourage prescribing a specific medication, awarding research grants to high-prescribing physicians, or purchasing services from HCPs at exorbitant fees.
- The Physician Payments Sunshine Act (PPSA) is another US federal law aiming to improve transparency regarding payments to HCPs. Under this law, Pharma manufacturers must disclose to the Centers for Medicare and Medicaid Services (CMS) any payments or other transfers of value made to physicians.

The notion of a transfer of value under the PPSA (The Physician Payments Sunshine Act) has broad implications for Pharm CX. As per this law, Pharma can't communicate to HCPs that patient support programs will reduce their workload because that would be *something of value*, which is not allowed for compliance. However, these programs improve access to medicines for patients.

In addition, Pharmaceutical Research and Manufacturers of America (PhRMA) has created a voluntary Code governing the relationships between industry and HCPs that most Pharma companies abide by. The Code puts commonsense guardrails on Pharma-sponsored meals and entertainment, gifts, continuing medical education, and consulting arrangements.

In most countries, direct-to-patient pharmaceutical product advertising is not permitted, the United States being the major exception. Even in the countries where it is permitted, Pharma companies must conduct it in full compliance with country laws, regulations, and relevant codes of practice.

Even in India, the government has proposed a voluntary code—UCPMP (Uniform Code for Pharmaceutical Marketing Practices) to control the Pharma-Physician nexus and to curtail kickbacks and other payments to physicians by Pharma for prescribing specific medications. Other countries are also likely to follow this trend sooner or later.

While there is less clarity in Pharma's interactions with patients, PhRMA (Pharmaceutical Research and Manufacturers of America) offered *Principles on Interactions* with patient organizations essentially to prevent Pharma companies from exerting undue influence on the actions of patient organizations. However, PhRMA has nothing to date on Pharma interactions with individual patients. But, the International Federation of Pharmaceutical Manufacturers and Associations (IFPMA) provides some guidance on Pharma-patient interactions suggesting the ethical boundaries that Pharma need to observe when interacting with patients and caregivers, individually or as part of patient organizations. For example, they focus on ethical guidelines around hiring patients as consultants, advisors, or speakers at internal company meetings.

Considering these regulatory constraints, do pharmaceutical companies have the same opportunity with Pharma CX as in other industries? Certainly! Because exceptional and meaningful customer experiences are not about kickbacks but about fostering positive emotional interactions between customers and the company. Pharma must carefully consider regulatory and compliance guidelines, especially regarding HCPs. Of course, this is true for everything that Pharma does. Pharma faces those same regulatory hurdles when creating promotional campaigns, but have they prevented Pharma from conducting those campaigns? Further, Pharma has delivered positive feelings to its customers more effectively than any other industry. Above all, Pharma saves lives and provides better quality of life!

What is Pharma CX?

Pharma CX (Customer Experience) is the key to patient-centricity, says Sean McDade, the founder, CEO, and visionary of PeopleMetrics, a leading provider of experience management software and advisory services. He defines Pharma CX quite succinctly as *intentionally creating, continuously measuring in real-time, and proactively managing the customer experience* in his book, 'Pharma Customer Experience: 20 Secrets to 10X And Boost Patient Outcomes.' He further unpacks in his book the three steps involved in this definition to deliver an exceptional customer experience:

1. The first step is to be intentional about creating the customer experience. Customers engage with Pharma constantly, from simple experiences like onboarding onto new medications to larger ones like joining clinical trials and choosing which drug to prescribe. Every one of these interactions is an opportunity to connect emotionally. Yet many a Pharma company overlooks this vast opportunity to connect emotionally and sees customer experiences as unavoidable steps to get through.
2. The second step is to measure customer experience continuously and in real-time to understand its effectiveness. It is important to measure continuously and in real-time at touchpoints that matter the most because these are the *moments of truth*.

3. Finally, Pharma must proactively manage CX (Customer Experience). For example, when a customer has a poor experience, there should be a process to follow up with that customer to resolve their issue.

Thus, Pharma CX acts as a critical feedback loop that allows for continuous improvement. It is a mindset shift from developing products to intentionally creating, continuously measuring, and proactively managing experiences across every important touchpoint (moment of truth).

Two Key Questions

Two important questions separate a Patient-centric or Pharma CX organization from the rest of the pack.

- As an organization, what can we do today to put the patient first and deliver the best possible experience to our patients?
- Also, the leadership at a Pharma CX organization encourages and ensures that each employee asks this daily question: What can I do today to create a better patient experience?

CX is More than Market Research

Whatever we have discussed so far about customer experience in Pharma sounds like market research, and Pharma does a lot of market research. While Pharma CX is similar to market research, a few distinctions are important.

Before we discuss the differences between market research and Pharma CX, one similarity is vital to both— adverse-event reporting. In market research and Pharma CX, any patient comment that references an adverse event from their current medication must be reported by CX leaders and communicated to pharmacovigilance teams.

Now, the key differences between market research and Pharma CX are highlighted in the following table:

Table 1.8 Market Research and Pharma CX: Key Differences

	Market Research	Pharma CX (Customer Experience)
Communication with customer	One-way	Two-way (encouraging dialogue)
Analysis	Aggregate	Individual and aggregate
Audience	Sample	Census
Access to results	Market research team and product sponsor	Everyone
Length of survey	Long	Short/brief
Timeframe	weeks/months	Real-time
Incentives	Usually required	Limited/optional
Timing	Point in time	Continuous
Purpose	Strategic	Strategic and operational
Participant identity	Anonymous	Identified

Source: Sean McDade, Pharma CX: 20 Secrets to 10X and Boost Patient Outcomes, Lion Crest Publishing, 2021

Pharma CX: Three Areas of Focus

Pharma must focus on three vital areas to create and deliver great customer experiences:

1. Customer segmentation— identifying and understanding target customers
2. Mapping journeys of identified target customers
3. Identifying all the touchpoints, mainly the moments of truth (the touchpoints that matter most) to connect emotionally

1. **Customer Segmentation and Defining A *Segment of One***: A segment is a grouping of potential customers. It is about making choices as we cannot be all things to everyone. So we must choose which customers we will pursue in our effort to build a relationship and which ones we will not pursue. Finally, it is about making sacrifices for the greater good of the brand. Kim Mullarkey, former vice president of marketing for LifeScan, the maker of the OneTouch BSL (blood sugar level) monitor, says that *marketers need to practice the discipline of sacrifice*.

You must identify and then find a strategically appropriate match between different target segments and your ability to *create meaning* with them. The segment you choose will represent the most likely prospects with similar values, attitudes, and needs that our product or service can satisfy better than the competition. It is important that you go beyond defining the target segment by demographic profiles, past practices, or how the competition is doing it.

Once we have chosen our target segment, we need to clearly define the prospective customer within it to have a clear profile of her. In other words, we must create a *Persona* representing our most likely prospects.

Personas in Pharma Marketing

About twenty-two years ago, software designer Alan Cooper introduced the concept of *user personas* in his book T*he Inmates Are Running the Asylum: Why High Tech Products Drive Us Crazy and How to Restore Sanity*. Personas have initially become an important tool for software and web design, which marketers in other industries adopted later.

What is a User Persona? A User Persona is a qualitative tool that helps you create a fictional character to serve as an archetype to guide design development. A user persona brings the concept of a targeted audience to life as it is based on quantitative, qualitative, and ethnographic research. As Personas include demographic, psychographic, and technographic information and personal narrative elements, creating a complete picture of the user's behaviors, environment, and needs, they provide brief biographic profiles of your prospective customers that you can depend on. That is how and why, through personas, we get to know *why* our customers behave the way they do. More importantly, it allows us to segment in terms of value, attitudes, and behavior instead of just in terms of demographics. Such segmentation is even more important in healthcare, including Pharma, where user emotions can range from empowerment to frustration and even hopelessness. Once you understand how customers feel and what they value on key dimensions, you can create personalized experiences that echo emotionally and promote the desired feeling and experience, whether that is convenience, care, comfort, etc.

Further, personas help us avoid relying on our perceptions, such as *I know what my customers need-bias*, a common stereotypical depiction of the customer. Therefore, it is useful to create multiple personas for all traditional segments such as patients, physicians, and other stakeholders to get a well-rounded, representative view of the customer base across the segments to make thoughtful, educated, and unbiased decisions that satisfy customer needs.

So, how do we define our Persona or the Target Customer? We must move beyond mere abstraction and deal with something concrete. We must find that *one person*, a real living and breathing human being. Once you can see her clearly in your mind, you define her, using the following seven essential components to arrive at our bullseye— target *customer one*:

- Demographics
- Psychographics
- Patient condition / Lifestage/ Targeted Occasion
- Attitudes about her situation as related to the product category or therapeutic area
- Current Brand/Product usage and dissatisfactions
- Other relevant telling behaviors
- Needs, both rational and emotional

This Persona definition will result in a more relevant and actionable target segment with matching psychographic profiles and similar feelings and attitudes about the category, specific situation, and shared needs.

It is important to fix this relevant Persona clearly in our minds. For example, some great copywriters fixed a picture of a Persona on their desks and wrote a copy to that individual. It helped them relate to a real human being, not an abstraction.

Once we zero in on the bullseye Customer in our mind, it is time to answer a host of questions about him to draw a complete profile of our target customer. The questions are similar to those in an 'Attitude, Awareness, and Usage (AA&U)' marketing research study and cover three basic areas, personal, category, and brand-specific information. The answers are specific responses about what you know of this real, Persona (bullseye target customer).

Building Personas

Matt Hummel, Chief Experience Officer at Paragon Inc., suggests a three-step approach for building personas in healthcare in his insightful blog article, *Using Personas to Develop Relevant Marketing Messages*, published in their blog, Paragon Inc, on August 3, 2020. Here are the three steps:

1. **Talk to Real People**: The best way to build healthcare personas is by conducting a one-on-one interview with key customer groups such as patients, physicians, providers, and caregivers. While interviewing, it is more important to focus on what the prospective customers value and how they feel and behave. One more thing. You should conduct at least three to five interviews in each category before you can begin to spot patterns and commonalities that categorize your primary patient of *one*. Some of the key questions to ask in the process of categorizing: What are their pain points and feelings during these touchpoints? What outcomes do they expect? What day-to-day behaviors impact their goals, motivation, and interactions with pharmaceutical companies on their journey?
2. **Find the Commonalities**: After conducting the interviews, the next step is to analyze them to derive commonalities across customer segments (patients, physicians, providers, and caregivers) and categorize them into personas as broadly or as narrowly as you want. However, you must find the right balance and ensure that your personas adequately reflect your customer segments and can be the most useful reference when making marketing decisions.
3. **Write the Brief Persona Profile:** It would help if you wrote a profile, which is a fictional story for each Persona you create across the segments to understand and empathize with for the customer experience you want to create. The persona profile should consist of things like:

- A persona name (that describes the Persona)
- A fictional name
- Basic demographics such as education, ethnicity, and family status
- A quote that sums up feelings

- A photograph
- A summary of the person and their day-to-day life, and the key points as they relate to the dimensions studied in the research. The main aim of creating a persona's profile is to create a real-life snapshot to which employees and key stakeholders can relate.

How Can We Use A Persona?

You can use healthcare personas in many ways. Often marketers develop personas and file them away in a market research folder. Instead, your cross-functional teams should use them as a reference and ensure you put the *customer at the center* of your customer experience design strategy.

Here are some applications you can think of for using the personas you have developed:

- Designing products or services
- Creating personalized marketing messages
- Building patient journey maps for improving customer experience
- Prioritizing marketing decisions

Healthcare personas are a useful tool for synthesizing your qualitative and quantitative research to understand your customers as real people. This insight can help you focus on where it needs to be: on patients, which can significantly improve the customer experience.

Two Customer Personas (Patient and Physician)

Here are two tables that provide two examples of personas— one each for patients and physicians to give a feel of what a *persona* looks and feels like.

Table 1.9 Patient Persona: An Illustrative Example

Patient: Anita, Age: 52, Background: Rheumatoid arthritis (RA) patient suffering from depression, Location: Chicago, Needs support from the company's RA ambassadors regarding education on side effects, appointment management

Behaviors	Needs and Pain Points
• Maintains a healthy diet and feels good about taking care of her own health and wellness • Husband is her primary caregiver • Talks regularly to a neighbor with RA who took part in a clinical trial • Doctor recommended medication to protect joints from further damage but she declined • Takes supplements to help with symptoms • Does online research and has joined RA panels	• Was misdiagnosed 20 years ago • Wrist rotation no longer flexible enough to paint • Has difficulty carrying things and is not as strong as she was • Anxious about worsening symptoms • Scared by reading about the disease; tries not to think about it • Fearful of injections and possible side effects of medication • Unsure whether some symptoms are caused by the disease, aging, or other factors

Source: Jan Ascher, Daniel Höglund, Arafat Milka, Ivan Ostojic, and Maxence Vancauwenberghe, *From product to customer experience: The new way to launch in Pharma*, McKinsey & Company, August 15, 2018

Table 1.10 Physician Persona: An Example

Physician: Dr. Peter Harrison, Age: 47, Role: Key Opinion Leader in Oncology, Experience: 20 Years, Location: Academic Medical Center, Wants to participate and be respected in the scientific community, but frustrated by operational logistics

Role	Needs and Pain Points
• Be a recognized leader in his field by contributing to publications and participating in steering committees Contribute to the development of step changes in treatment • Build long-term research collaborations with pharma companies	• Paucity of opportunities to participate in steering committees as an emerging thought leader • Expertise is taken for granted (unclear expectations, lack of institutional memory) • Non-standardized and inefficient clinical trial processes with unprepared and inexperienced monitors are frustrating and time-consuming

Source: Jan Ascher, Daniel Höglund, Arafat Milka, Ivan Ostojic, and Maxence Vancauwenberghe, *From product to customer experience: The new way to launch in Pharma*, McKinsey & Company, August 15, 2018

Customer Journey Mapping

The digital revolution in its wake has disrupted traditional pharmaceutical promotion significantly. Add to this the rise of patient consumerism, which means that patients are increasingly empowered by ever-expanding information and choices. As a result, they feel increasingly confident and willing to take greater control of their health.

In such a changing marketing environment, as a pharma marketer, you need to know which triggers and touchpoints are most impactful for patients, physicians, and other stakeholders and how you should maximize your influence on them.

It is not just the patient's journey being disrupted. For many years, the gold standard of communication and engagement between pharma companies and physicians has been a combination of sales representatives, advisory boards, medical congresses, and brochures. But today, it has changed a lot with medical professionals making as much as 70 percent decision journey before even they talk to pharma company's sales representatives.

Therefore, it is time for pharma marketers to understand the physician's journey to engage them effectively. Mapping the customer journey thus becomes rather mandatory!

What is customer journey mapping like? Customer journey mapping is a visual representation of every customer interaction with your organization, which can significantly improve the customer journey. Today, it has become necessary as the path to conversion is no longer linear, with customers often using various devices and channels. Moreover, Econsultancy's report, *The Business Case for Customer Journey*, shows that companies who embed mapping in their culture are twice as likely to exceed their top business goals than their competitors.

Many Benefits

Understanding how a customer interacts throughout their entire journey helps marketers to elevate it. Here are some of the more important benefits of customer journey mapping. It helps to:

1. **Enhance Personalization**. Marketers can provide consumers with more contextually relevant and valuable interactions at every important touchpoint across the journey. For example, marketers can guide the customer toward the point of decision-making when a customer transitions from *awareness* to *research and consideration* by delivering the right message at the right time.
2. **Uncover Inconsistencies**. Customer journey mapping helps uncover the gaps between what customers want and their experience. These issues could be related to customer service or communication. Some examples are identifying customers who are left waiting for a response on social media or customers who are being sent irrelevant emails. Marketers could easily fix those issues once they know these gaps. Thus, customer journey mapping can help businesses to bridge the gaps between strategy and execution, correcting and eradicating the poor mistakes within the customer journey that can damage the overall perception of the brand and the company.
3. **Identify Pain Point**s. Customer journey mapping can also help marketers to reduce the amount of time, and effort customers have to put into getting what they want and make the path to purchase and conversion seamless.
4. **Achieve Strategic Goals**. Customer journey mapping can also help organizations to achieve their overall strategic goals by making them more customer-centric and enabling marketers to turn insight into action.

Three Phases

For a customer's healthcare journey map there are three basic phases. Here is a table that describes broadly the three phases of a healthcare journey map.

Table 1.11 Three Phases of A Healthcare Journey Map

Before Treatment	During Treatment	After Treatment
Deciding to Act New symptoms or a life event prompts action	**Pre-Service** Addressing insurance issues, completing intake forms, getting medical records, and related issues	**Follow-up** Receiving prescriptions, booking follow-up appointments, and related issues
Researching Care Options Doctors, locations, specialities	**Arrival** Getting and waiting at the physical location or virtual waiting room	**Maintenance** Managing health and maintaining wellness
Making Contact Reaching out to learn more or to schedule by phone, online, web chat or other means	**Appointment** Time spent with clinicians	**Maintenance** Managing health and maintaining wellness
	Diagnostics Additional labs, imaging, or other diagnostic tests	
	Treatment Plan Providing a program or advice to treat or manage a health issue	
	Discharge Patient departs, follow-up instructions provided	

Source: Linda Watts, Your guide to healthcare personas, Perficient Blog, February 8, 2022

Mapping the Patient's Journey

Pharma marketers should develop a deeper understanding of how patients move through the healthcare system and how they are influenced by various stakeholders along the way, which is called a patient's journey. The main objective of mapping the patient journey for any given condition or disease is to identify leverage points, which, if activated, drive patients to the desired outcome. The analogy of a flowing river represents the flow of patients better. For example, leverage points are like damns in the river, which will direct the flow of patients to a particular brand.

The patient's journey in the marketing context represents a qualitative map of the flow and various touchpoints. Opportunities to improve outcomes lie hidden in these touchpoints. The following table presents an overview of the different phases and leverage points in a typical patient's journey.

Table 1.12 Patient Journey Phases

Awareness & Recognition	Presentation & Diagnosis	Treatment Selection	Brand Selection & Access	Switching & Persistency
Symptoms, experiences, emotions, and actions taken prior to seeking care	Motivations to seeking care and to whom patients present (including referral patterns)	Characteristics and external forces that drive and influence physician treatment selection	Characteristics and external forces that drive and influence physician brand selection	Drivers: switching, compliance/ non-compliance and disease progression

Source: Paula Fullman and Derek Evans, A More Holistic Approach to the Patient Journey, PM360, September 18, 2013

When you are constructing your patient journey, considering the following questions will help you to understand and leverage the key touchpoints:

- How quickly do patients move to second-line or later? Can you shrink that time lag?
- What is the top first-line choice? Who is making the decision? Which specialty?
- Are there any diagnosis issues? Is there a need to drive awareness?
- Does a treatment lag behind diagnosis?

Example of A Patient's Journey Using A Pharma Company's Patient Support Program

Let's consider the journey of a patient who has been prescribed a new medication and is using a pharma company's patient support services provided by a pharma company to seek the onboarding process, and with managing the disease.

The following table presents a snapshot of the patient's onboarding steps:

Table 1.13 Patient Onboarding on Pharma's Patient Support Service

Step	Engagement Oppotunities	Rules of Engagement	Key Questions
Digital	Websites, Apps, and Portals :Usually the first point of contact or touchpoint is through digital engagement technologies	• Enable easy enrollment process • Easy navigation through the site to search for relevant information quickly • Provide information on available treatment centers and transport options • Enable physicians through a website or a physician portal with guidance on preauthorization help regarding health approval to prescribe the new drug	• Was it easy to enroll in the patient support program? • Was it easy to find the most important information? • Was it well organized? • Easy to log in? • Personalized?
Contact Center	Patients often turn to the Contact Centers, which are important hubs of information and support to get answers to their questions regarding the management of their disease. Contact centers are invaluable resources of information particularly for patients with rare diseases.	• Easy access • Prompt and friendly service in answering queries • Correct and complete information	• Are patient support service phone numbers easily accessible? • Is it easy to enroll in a patient support program? • Was it easy for the physician to share this information with patients?Are case managers and the company representatives knowledgeable? Empathetic? Available? Treating patients with respect?

Contd...

Step	Engagement Oppotunities	Rules of Engagement	Key Questions
In-Person, or Tele-health	• Nurse educators meet patients in their homes or via Telehealth with certain complex diseases and new medication to answer questions about disease and the new medication, and • To teach them how to take it properly • Nurse educators also visit HCPs either face-to-face or via Telehealth to educate on their company's medication	• Timely visits by nurse educators • Simple and complete information that is easy-to-understand • Ease of access and smooth Telehealth appointments	• Did the nurse educator arrive on time? • Are nurse educators clear in their comm-unication? • Was the patient comfortable ad-ministering their new medication after meeting with the nurse educator? Did the nurse educator leave behind literature that is easy to understand? • Was it easy for the patient to enroll into the patient support program directly in a Telehealth visit with their physician?
Post-Onboar-ding	• Follow-up with patients to ensure adherence to medication and care • Six-monthly and Annual relationship surveys with patients about their overall patient experience	• Timely surveys • Simple, and less time-consuming surveys	• Has the patient had any issues traveling with their medication? • How easy has the medication been to administer? • Has the patient been able to understand their case manager or the company representative clearly to answer questions?

Source: Adapted from *Sean McDade, Ph.D, Pharma Customer Experience: 20 Secrets To 10X And Boost Patient Outcomes*

Creating Great Patient Experiences

While there are many touchpoints in a typical patient's journey, identifying which ones are *moments of truth* is key to creating great experiences. So what is a moment of truth? How can you determine it? It is not as difficult as it sounds to identify a moment of truth. The key question is: *how much pain will your customer incur if a touchpoint does not go well*?

You must prioritize those touch points with the biggest potential impact and take great care to ensure you will meet and exceed each customer's expectations during all those moments.

Consider, for example, transportation to treatment centers is often a moment of truth for patients. It has become even more important during the COVID-19 pandemic since transportation options for patients and caregivers are limited.

Here are two cases showing how leading international health insurance giants addressed the pain point of transporting patients to health centers by collaborating with On-demand Transportation Services!

CASE

9

CVS Health, Uber Collaboration Identifies a Moment of Truth and Addresses Patients' Pain Point!

CVS Health, a healthcare giant from the US, through its health insurance arm Aetna's Medicare Advantage (MA) Program, collaborates with Uber Health, a division of the leading international hail-taxi firm, to address an important pain point in the patients' journey.

The collaboration will provide free transportation to low-income patients needing transportation to medical care, work, or educational programs. The partnership is part of CVS's *Health Zones* initiative, which aims to reduce health disparities in high-risk communities by addressing social determinants of health such as housing, transportation, access to food, and healthcare. As a result, transportation for medical and non-medical needs is becoming an increasingly important benefit in MA plans.

Eileen Howard Boone, CVS Health senior vice president of corporate and social responsibility and philanthropy and chief sustainability officer, said in this regard: *Our Health Zones initiative allows us to make a real impact on the health of communities across the country by working closely with organizations that share our commitment to addressing social determinants of health*.

Anne Tumlinson, CEO of ATI Advisory, a services firm based in Washington DC, helping businesses and government in transforming healthcare delivery and aging services for highest-need older adults, told McKnight's Home Care Daily Pulse in an email: *The new partnership around services in Health Zones is broader than the Aetna-MA membership. It will benefit any plan member in the community where it is offered. In general, though, MA is a much more flexible financing tool for paying for home-based medical and social services. I'm sure the CVS CEO has their MA Plan in mind as the larger organization pushes into the home community.*

According to CVS executives, part of the strategy is building a strong base of in-home care by delivering patients the products and services they need. In addition, dual eligible seniors who qualify for both Medicare and Medicaid offer tremendous potential to CVS because most live within a 10-mile radius of a CVS store.

Source: Diane Eastabrook, New CVS, Uber Collaboration Could Be A Boon To Aetna MA Members, McKnights Home Care, January 21, 2022, https://www.mcknightshomecare.com/new-cvs-uber-collaboration-could-be-a-boon-to-aetna-ma-members/

CASE

10

Uber Ties Up with Cerner EHR System for US Providers to Schedule Non-Emergency Transportation for Patients, Caregivers, and Staff!

Uber, the global hail-taxi platform giant, launched Uber Health in March 2018, to set up rides for patients, caregivers, and staff. An Uber Health API (Application Programming Interface) allows for integration into existing healthcare products and for transportation to be scheduled for follow-up appointments while still at the healthcare facility. The company also rolled out a HIPAA-compliant dashboard (Health Insurance Portability and Accountability Act) that providers can use to set up rides for patients, caregivers, and staff.

Further, Uber Health entered into a collaboration with Cerner, a global leader in the EHR (Electronic Health Records) System business, to deepen its ties to healthcare providers by embedding its platform into Cerner's EHR system.

The partnership will help reduce transportation barriers that can lead to delayed care, poor management of chronic conditions, and declining health outcomes for patients. In addition, the integration of Uber's platform with Cerner's EHR will streamline operations and support greater interoperability, according to the companies. For example, providers who use Cerner's EHR will be able to access the tools to book transportation, including name, phone number, and pick-up addresses will auto-populate from Cerner technology directly into a ride request with Uber.

The integration will be available to Cerner-client hospitals and health systems soon.

Dan Trigub, head of Uber Health, said on this occasion: *Joining forces with Cerner marks a new chapter for Uber Health and our mission to provide accessible, efficient transportation for patients and caregivers. Reliable transportation to and from appointments can help reduce operating costs and patient no-show rates and help improve patient outcomes. Our goal is to simplify the way healthcare providers can access transportation options—and our work together will accomplish just that.*

Source: Heather Landi, Uber Announces Integration With Cerner EHR System for US Providers, Fierce Healthcare, October 28, 2019,

What Pharma Can Do?

What can Pharma learn from these case studies of collaboration between on-demand transportation service companies and companies providing EHR System services? Sean McDade, the CEO and Founder of PeopleMetrics, suggests in his book, *Pharma CX: 20 Secrets to 10X and Boost Patient Outcomes*, that Pharma ask these important questions:

1. Have we listed treatment centers on a patient support services website (or available with case managers and executives at contact centers)?
2. Have we listed treatment centers plus public transportation options (including directions from the public transportation drop-off site to the treatment center) on patient support websites?
3. Do we use a company like Circulation to offer patients a coupon code for a free or a discounted round-trip ride on Uber or Lyft to the closest treatment center?

Pharma must think beyond access to create exceptional customer experiences. Pharma can find many opportunities to create customer experiences patients will remember and tell others about. The only thing is that Pharma should expand its thinking around how to help people— not just about medication access. It's about helping people live better lives. Consider these opportunities, for example:

- Childcare services
- Parking assistance
- Housework assistance, including cleaning or handy work
- Meals
- Mental Health Support
- Access to Meditation Apps or techniques
- Fitness and nutrition help
- Concierge transportation services

While some of these services may not be possible in Pharma due to regulatory hurdles, all these services would provide a frictionless experience for patients to obtain their medication and achieve better outcomes. You must find a balance between *the Do no harm* mentality of internal regulatory teams and creating customer experiences that customers love.

If you dig deep enough, you are sure to find many opportunities to create memorable experiences for your customers. Consider these, for example:

- Close to a third of diabetes patients also have depression. Can we think of helping them through meditation or access to mental health professionals to help these patients for better outcomes?
- Also, it is widely known and well established that exercise is a natural way to reduce depression and anxiety. Can Pharma partner with fitness organizations like Peloton or a local gym to offer complimentary indoor exercise classes and content for patients on certain medications? Would that help adherence and result in better outcomes?

Maybe, these are beyond the scope of Pharma's role in the patient experience. The point here is to think beyond what is possible concerning creating an emotional connection with your customers. When Pharma changes its current mindset of providing prescription drugs to cure ailments (that's vital, no doubt about that) to what it means to support patients, they can find incredible opportunities to deliver exceptional customer experiences.

Mapping the Physician's Journey

In the past, the sales representative meeting the doctor and managing their relationship was all that mattered. The sales representative used to be the primary and usually the only contact point for the doctor, which tended to be more promotional and transactional, but not any longer.

The Digital revolution has changed all that and ushered in an era of virtual engagement model for Pharma's stakeholders. Today, physicians can engage with multiple channels over multiple touchpoints. Moreover, Pharma's customers (physicians) and consumers (patients) started expecting, nay, even demanding seamless experiences from Pharma, which they are getting from other industries such as hospitality, travel, and retail, among others.

Therefore, pharmaceutical companies must create and deliver great customer experiences to earn customer loyalty. And mapping the customer journey is crucial to emotionally connecting with physicians, patients, and other stakeholders at every touchpoint to exceed the expectations of customers and consumers. Here's a brief checklist to map the customer experience:

1. Identify all the touchpoints the customer would go through. From the physician's perspective, how would they navigate through the touchpoints? Where and how can you help them?
2. Visualize the different needs and expectations that could arise at different points in the physician's journeys. Which needs and expectations can you fulfill and how?
3. Critically evaluate the end-to-end experience. Are there any gaps or barriers that could hinder the experience? Are there any opportunities where you can help physicians perform better?
4. Simplify the interaction design. Avoid processes that can be complex for the physician.
5. Track and measure. Regularly capture measurements that matter at critical points in the journey (moments of truth).

Content is the Key to Effective Physician Engagement

How do you effectively engage your physicians on all key touch points (moments of truth) across their journey? Content, relevant content holds the key to the successful engagement of physicians.

You must create content according to your customer journey maps for each physician's Persona across all touchpoints that matter, and remember every touchpoint matters!

Here is a table that shows the stages of a physician's journey and key questions to ask in each stage to develop relevant content (Table 1.14).

When you create and deliver relevant content that meets the needs of the physician at all the touchpoints across their journey, you will have created a seamless customer experience that delights and converts them into loyal prescribers and even advocates in time. The following table presents a picture of what a great, seamless customer experience looks like (Table 1.15).

Table 1.14 Physician's Journey Mapping for Matching the Content: An Example

	Awareness	Evaluate	Decision-making	Advocate	Retention
Description of what happens during these stages	• Physician at this stage is aware of his want or need for a product or service. • Example: • The Need • A Private physician's practice recognizes the airborne infectious nature of the COVID-19 virus. He realizes they need FFP2 masks to protect staff and patients.	• Starts researching their options. • Investigates FFP2 vendors looking for a product, affordable bulk orders and fast delivery	• Weighs down the options, selects a vendor • Finds the vendor that meets the criteria and places an order	• Uses the product or service and is happy with the experience • Refers other consumers to the product or service provider • In our example, the physician satisfied with the FFP2 product and customer experience and recommends the vendor to a fellow practitioner who also needs FFP2 masks	• The consumer continues to use the product without switching to a different vendor. • The Physician becomes a recurring customer placing a new bulk order every month
Key Questions to Ask	• How will the person seek a solution to the problem they have	• What points are important to the person? Price, convenience? Any other?	• What touchpoints will the person	• What will convenience the person to advocate the	• What will keep the person coming back? Reliable delivery? Special deals etc?

Table 1.15 *Contd...*

	Awareness	Evaluate	Decision-making	Advocate	Retention
	identified? Via Google, healthcare publications, industry thought-leader web sites etc?		come into contact with to arrive at a decision? Visiting the company web site? Calling a healthcare sales rep?	brand they end up choosing? What channels will they use to spread the word? Word of mouth? Social media?	
Content Analysis and Deciding on Appropriate Content	Info-packed content in the form of blog posts or infographics can drive awareness	Web site landing data analysis such as sales pages, or live demos can help evaluate	Free-trial sign-Up pages can help drive decision-making	Shareable social media posts and forward-friendly emails can encourage advocacy	Engagement boosters like user guides, webinars, podcasts can help improve retention

Source: Adapted from an article—Scott Adams, How to Map Your Content to the Customer Journey in Healthcare, ShareMovingMedia Inc, February 11, 2021

Table 1.15 Great Customer Experience for A Physician: An Example

Every morning the surgeon Dr. Peter Anderson starts the day by checking his emails.
Today, Dr. Peter reads an email from a pharmaceutical company that has launched a new molecule. The surgeon clicks on the link and reads about the details of the drug that has been provided. He reads this information for about three minutes.
The doctor's data regarding the email, clicking on the link, and engaging with the information has been captured.
The sales rep has access to this data; he knows the doctor has shown interest in this new drug.
Later in the day, the sales rep calls on the surgeon and e-details only the newly launched product, giving some additional information as an extension to the email article that the doctor had read in the morning. More value is added during the rep call.
Later that evening, the doctor gets to see some ads for the drug in the online medical journal that he subscribed to.
With a click on the ad, the doctor is directed to the drug's website (which is customized for this surgeon— the content on the drug is all relevant to the doctor's specialty). The surgeon also goes over the published studies on the site.
Data on the doctor's website visit is also captured.
In the following days, the doctor Tweets about the new drug, has social chats with other fellow doctors, and gathers their opinion.
Few days later, the doctor prescribes the drug to a patient and forwards patient assistance program details to the patient.

(Source: Adapted from pharmalive.com)

Big Pharma's Take On CX

How is Big Pharma responding to the changing business landscape? How are they adapting to the changing marketing and business environment? Understanding their strategic approaches to the changing customer landscape can significantly help us formulate our strategies. Here are four cases of how some leading global pharmaceutical companies approach the customer experience strategy.

CASE

11

Pfizer's Customer Experience Strategy!

Mike Bellis, Customer Experience Specialist, and former Customer Experience Lead for Pfizer, Europe, explains their approach to customer experience strategy:

Loyalty is incredibly profitable. Creating loyalty means you don't have to work so hard to sell, improving your operational efficiency and profit margins. Loyal customers are more likely to try other products and services, increasing opportunities to cross-and-up-sell. Most valuable of all, loyal customers are more likely to recommend you, an incredibly low-cost way to acquire new customers. Creating loyalty can be very profitable for running a business.

But how do you create loyalty? For a growing number of Pharma companies, the answer is to adopt a customer experience approach. Consistently meeting or exceeding your customers' expectations right across the journey leads to improved brand perception and customer satisfaction. Put simply, this means the next time they need something, they are much more likely to come back to you.

While Pharma is rarely the first guest to arrive at a party, many companies are embracing customer experience. For me, customer experience is the answer to some of the fundamental challenges that face Pharma; declining customer engagement, a greater emphasis on profit margin, and capabilities that haven't changed in

10, 15, or 20 years and are bordering on irrelevance. The world has changed, and we have to change with it.

Yet, making a move to a customer experience model is not an easy one. Part of the problem is that some companies think they are already customer focused, but they are driven by revenue and profit, not customers' priorities. As a result, adopting CX management requires a change of mindset that puts the customers' requirements first and the businesses' requirements second.

(Source: Hugh Gosling, Through the Thick and Thin, PharmaTimes Online, January 2017)

CASE

12

Teva's Customer Experience Strategy!

Tim White, head of the customer experience at Teva Pharmaceuticals speaks about how Teva is going about its customer experience strategy:

We need to provide an experience that offers value to customers, so they prefer us over a competitor or other service provider. So how did we go about this? Firstly, we looked at the many examples of great customer experience in other sectors.

The former US President Barack Obama was an early adopter of CX. Obama brought customer experience principles into the political arena— fourteen years ago. He provided great information and the resources his supporters needed to get out there and share his message— and It worked.

The key to delivering a good experience lies in understanding customer behavior in a very granular way. When we execute projects now, we focus on individual customer behavior. It is no longer good enough to know that you sold your top decile physicians ten times last week. That's not focusing on individual behavior. We are trying to get to the core insights. What are their needs? What does their daily job look like, and where do we fit into this picture of their lives? We need to ensure that we are present where our customers are. It's not about pushing messages. It's about being relevant. We want to get to a point where we're customizing all of our experiences through all channels so that every interaction is timely, relevant, and iterative.

Teva focuses on service, not just selling. When we bring our medicines to market, we do not lead with product messages; rather, we use a service mode. For example, we were asked to launch a new product into the Dutch market without a sales force. While I don't believe it is feasible to do this in today's world, we had no sales targets, so the project was designed to get learning. We went to the market last month—November 2016 successfully— with an oral contraceptive that has a unique value proposition. We created a customer engagement strategy and a lot of good content, media, editorial content, etc., and put that out through different channels to create a good customer experience, funneling through inbound marketing into more product-focused discussions with customers. We were able to gain a lot of brand awareness this way, and now we are combining push and pull using customer experience principles.

(Source: Hug Gosling, Through the Thick and Thin, PharmaTimes Online, January 2017)

CASE 13

UCB's Customer Experience Strategy!

Eddie Chan, vice-president and head of global marketing at UCB speaks about customer experience at UCB:

While the attention so far has been on 'experience,' the definition of the term 'customer' should not be taken for granted. At UCB, our customers are our patients— full stop. Of course, HCPs remain a key interface and will continue to be a critical factor for the foreseeable future. Still, we have restructured our organization along the lines of how we generate and deliver value to the patient. We examined touchpoints along the value chain, beginning with how we more actively involve patients and create positive experiences in clinical development and progressing through to how we support patients while in therapy.

While the CX transformation at UCB remains a work in progress, the response has been significant. Consistent feedback from patients and stakeholders is that our sentiment is authentic, and we are acknowledged to be genuinely acting upon it. The entire industry has been searching for 'beyond the pill' opportunities for some time, but Pharma tends to fall prey to the bright and shiny object syndrome, dazzled by technology as the answer rather than technology as merely the enabler. The mindset change in the industry must continue to evolve to understand behavioral science and how people utilize information and services in the real world. Patients are people, and people are consumers.

In particular, UCB is taking a service and value-driven approach in the US market. Throughout 2016, we have conducted several live pilots to see how we can modify our go-to-market approach in response to some of the changes in the healthcare landscape. For example, accountable care organizations or integrated delivery networks often have standardized protocols that impact— which is to say limiting— face time between sales professionals and prescribers. So how can one convey value in the absence of an interface?

UCB's approach has been to offer a much more consultative, service-based model. Again this is no longer about reach and frequency, especially as our brands are well-recognized for their effectiveness and tolerability. With a service approach, we can have value-driven discussions at the C-Suite level around population health and convey new expressions of our therapies' value. I am unaware of other organizations that proactively advise customers to discontinue therapy in the absence of meaningful improvement during an initial pre-defined period, which is the case for Cimzia. We see the right patients at the right time for the right response to deliver value. This approach resonates with patients and other stakeholders.

(Source: Hug Gosling, Through the Thick and Thin, PharmaTimes Online, January 2017)

CASE 14

Customer Experience Strategy at Takeda!

Hicham Naim, head of business model innovation and strategic projects at Takeda, tells about how they are approaching customer experience:

Takeda has recently taken its first steps on the CX journey. Designing a great customer experience is becoming increasingly important in our industry. However, the expectations of our different customers for the quality of experiences are set by all their interactions with brands and services outside of Pharma, where many other sectors are far ahead of our industry. At Takeda, we set our ambition and sought to understand the outside-in perspective to explore what our customers want. At the start, we set the stage to create this ambition, explaining to our leaders what CX is and how it differs from customer-centricity and multichannel.

However, there is a perception issue to overcome. Customer experience sounds fluffy, but the world is much more complex now, and customers need a different set of conversations with us that will help them provide the best health they can to patients. Consequently, companies need to raise the bar in experience-design capabilities to deliver better interactions at particular touchpoints and an integrated and coherent customer experience across all touchpoints. Superior engagement requires creating compelling stories and experiences enriched by strong content.

CX starts with a different approach to customer engagement. Personas and Customer journey maps are important strategic enablers that help provide an in-depth understanding of who our customers are, what they need, and how they interact with our company across all touchpoints. They allow targeted actions to better deliver against customer expectations.

With so many customers and variables, you need to deconstruct the overall customer experience into individual journeys. So we asked ourselves: What are the different customer journeys we need to identify to deliver the right customer experience?

Yet, converting colleagues to the concept of customer experience can take time. If you want to win with customer experience, you first need a shared vision and ambition. It would help if you also had time to introduce new capabilities gradually so that employees can absorb them and provide evidence through 'Proof-of-Concepts' to learn and change the mindset, culture, and practices. It's a transformative journey that can take three, four, or even seven years to complete. It is a journey that is incredibly complicated because it involves nearly every function. The key is to make it simple.

(Source: Hug Gosling, Through the Thick and Thin, PharmaTimes Online, January 2017)

CASE

15

AstraZeneca's Customer Experience Strategy!

Phil Matton, vice-president and head of international projects at AstraZeneca shares his experience on implementing customer experience:

In 2010, AstraZeneca undertook a program to transform how it interacted with its customers. We knew the world was changing, and so were our customer expectations. Our new approach put service at the center, with selling arranged around that centra core, driving customer and patient loyalty.

In common with many others, the company faced a range of challenges. In Pharma, we have real access issues with our customers. Even though we know prescribers still prefer face-to-face visits, the number of decent conversations with customers about products and services has diminished greatly. So we're all asking, how can we add value and improve the experience?

In response, we introduced a new channel— *The Service Rep*— and a call center capability, plus experimented with channel mix to optimize them. Our focus was to move from products to services to drive the experience and create customer loyalty, regardless of whether the brand was growing, mature, or launched. One mistake we made was to put too great a focus on cost, and we had to go back in time and time again to make the point that the service channel was about customer experience and not about saving money. The channel does save money, but, first and foremost, it's about the experience we create for our customers.

As a part of this approach, we went back to basics. To ensure that marketing teams and sales leaders focused on what customers need from our brands and services, we took everyone back to the fundamental basics of marketing. We rewrote the AZ Way of marketing to ensure we focused on customer experience. Through that process, we reinforced the message by getting senior management teams in the markets to challenge brand teams on what they were trying to achieve with every customer segment, building a channel experience in an integrated way. We also had a strategic group that developed a framework to embed the behaviors across all markets and make it 'business as usual,' as people move according to their behaviors.

We took away several important lessons in the process. A key learning was the critical role of the change management process; senior management buy-in was essential. A really hard part for marketers to get their heads around was how to develop more patient-centric, customer-centric materials. It was also vital to engage the sales force and management team as there was a real danger that they would kill the new channels if they saw them as a threat to their livelihoods. So we had to reinforce the huge importance of their role— to sell the product.

(Source: Hug Gosling, Through the Thick and Thin, PharmaTimes Online, January 2017)

CASE

16

Five Customer Experience Lessons from Pharma Giant Eli Lilly & Co!

Colonel Eli Lilly, a man committed to creating high-quality medicines that met real needs in an era of unreliable elixirs peddled by questionable characters, founded Lilly in 1896. His message to the generations of employees who have followed was this: *Take what you find here and make it better and better*.

More than 145 years later, the team at Lilly remains committed to its vision and is driven by the core values of integrity, excellence, and respect for people. And their commitment to serving people starts in-house— creating positive experiences for the employees who bring life to the brand.

Empowered employees serve customers better. So, employees play a vital role in the customer journey, whether those customers be patients, healthcare professionals, or the communities in which they live. Therefore, enhancing experiences for your employees and customers can help your company achieve 1.8 times faster revenue growth, according to recent research from Forbes Insights and SalesForce.

Christine Hill, global customer experience strategy and measurement leader at Eli Lilly & Co, says Lilly seeks to optimize the customer experience from drug development to the point where the customer acquires and uses the developed drug. It also endeavors to scale effectively and efficiently and ultimately reinvest in drug discovery, closing the loop.

Lilly's experience offers five lessons in understanding the relationship between customer and employee experience, which is crucial to delivering an exceptional customer experience. Nigel Holloway distills these five lessons in his insightful article, *Five Lessons On Customer Experience From Pharma Giant Eli Lilly And Co*, in **forbes.com**, published on June 7, 2022. These five lessons are:

1. **Stay focused on adding value:** It is important to understand the shared value proposition for the employee, the customer, and the company because it's possible to create many positive experiences that don't add value. Remember, often, a pain point for an employee will also be a pain point for the customer. The key is understanding the interdependencies of these pain points and then figuring out the root causes and the best way to solve them.
2. **You need to know all of your customers**: Improving customer experience requires measuring it, which in turn requires mapping it. But that's a complex task because customers rarely fall into a single category. In Pharma, the market consists of not only patients but also healthcare professionals, patient-support groups, insurance companies, and even entire communities. Mapping customer experience helps companies determine which customer interactions align with their goals. It also helps them to make changes, if necessary.
3. **Identify points of disconnect**: Assessing customer and employee experience is a challenge, and it is best done in a spirit of open inquiry. For example, when the team at Eli Lilly tracked how their customers engaged with the company, they realized that there were things they thought they knew but didn't. So customer experience mapping becomes this continual learning opportunity to research more about the interactions between employees and customers. The insights that tracking offers can be surprising. What seems like an insignificant interaction with a customer could be *incredibly painful* for them. This disconnect is because we don't understand the customer's expectations.

4. **Mapping the customer journey is the key**: Marketers often use the Net Promoter Score (NPS), which measures the likelihood that customers recommend a company. But as useful as the NPS is, it's insufficient. It doesn't tell you where you are disappointing the customer and where you have gaps in the experience you deliver. Therefore, NPS, when used as a score and not a complete system, is at best a directional diagnostic. Mapping is a strategic prioritization tool as it helps people understand what touchpoints are most important and painful.
5. **Aligning revenue growth and the experiences of customers and employees pays big dividends**: While the goal of engaging employees and improving customer experience is to add corporate value, improving results depends on integrating customer and employee experience management. The recent Forbes Insights and SalesForce research found that alignment is the key. Christine Hill *says that when people know how their work matters to a customer, it increases their alignment, engagement, innovation, and collaboration. Good employee morale means good employee output*.

(Source: Nigel Holloway, Five Lessons On Customer Experience From Pharma Giant Eli Lilly And Co, forbes.com, December 8, 2020)

Reimagine the Technology

How Pharma can Harness the Power of New and Emerging Technologies?

The Technology you use impresses no one.

The experience you create with it is everything.

Artificial Intelligence (AI) and Machine Learning (ML)

Although research into artificial intelligence (AI) started in the 1950s, the industry has only recently used AI terminology. However, according to Veeva, one of the most successful and innovative cloud software companies, AI technology will soon transform pharmaceutical sales.

What is Artificial Intelligence?

Artificial Intelligence (AI) is the development of intelligent computers that can perform several human-like tasks. The technology should develop reasoning, problem-solving, perception, planning, and learning from past experiences. Finally, artificial intelligence (AI) should think and behave rationally like humans. AI has progressed significantly and is now integrated into our daily lives, which we can experience with Apple's Siri and Amazon's Alexa. Even though these systems perform specific tasks well, they require direction and are considered weak systems. Artificial Intelligence (AI) aims to develop robust systems that would make their own decisions and intelligently handle various situations.

Machine Learning (ML)

Machine learning (ML), another buzzword in the area, is an artificial intelligence (AI) branch. There is one difference, however. In contrast to AI, which imitates human capabilities, machine learning (ML) trains computers using vast data to recognize patterns and make decisions without direction. Machine learning (ML) algorithms have been around for some time, but a recent development can now apply machine learning to big data. Netflix offers an excellent example of how to use machine learning. It uses the technology to tell you which film to watch or a series to binge on next.

Many Benefits of AI and ML

While artificial intelligence, with all its capabilities, remains a work in progress like any other evolving technology, many industries are already reaping its benefits. For example, banks use AI to cut costs, increase efficiency, and security. In addition, improved voice and chatbots offer an alternative to human customer service and potentially save the industry up to $450 billion by 2030. Besides, you can train the pattern recognition capabilities of machine learning to spot fraudulent activity in real-time, making it an asset in the fight against cybercrime. Also, AI and ML have made self-driving cars a possibility, with Tesla leading the way with its autopilot hardware. Similarly, Japanese shipping companies are developing self-navigating vessels using AI to calculate the safest and most fuel-efficient route to their destinations.

Artificial Intelligence (AI) and the Healthcare Industry

Artificial Intelligence (AI) has also been helping the healthcare industry in many ways. For example, in the oncology segment, in 2018, cancer caused 9.6 million deaths worldwide. AI technology now helps oncologists diagnose cancer early, making safer treatment possible, allowing fast and accurate biopsy analysis, reducing error and the need for repeat tests. Also, an algorithm is being developed to identify lower, tumor-shrinking doses of drugs that provide effectiveness with reduced toxicity.

Artificial Intelligence and Pharma Industry

Artificial Intelligence (AI) has already proved itself as a useful tool to support the research and development activity carried out by pharmaceutical companies. However, with increasing investments in AI, Pharma companies are exploring ways to exploit its potential in marketing. In January 2019, Paul Shawah, senior vice president of Veeva Commercial Cloud, opined that AI would significantly impact the life sciences industry 2019. He said: *We will move towards an AI-driven workforce as artificial Intelligence becomes a standard capability across commercial applications. AI will not only continue to improve sales force effectiveness with suggestions on their next best activities... It will also automate references-linking in content management for marketing operations.*

According to Accenture, one of the leading global strategy consulting firms, AI could help workers to use their time more efficiently, increasing labor productivity by up to 40 percent — just the sort of boost that sales reps need.

The impact of AI on pharmaceuticals can start before the sales rep meets a customer. Machine learning (ML) can separate customers into highly specific segments allowing sales teams to personalize their activity to a higher degree. You can, for example, segment doctors based on factors such as interest in new drugs, location, and availability in addition to therapy areas and specialization.

David Keane, Co-Founder, and CEO of Bigtincan, a leading sales enablement platform, outlines four best practices in implementing AI-based technology to improve physician engagement in his Pharmaceutical Executive article titled, *Can AI Improve Sales Productivity in Pharma?* Here's a gist of what he has suggested:

1. *Prioritizes Pre-Call Planning*: Artificial intelligence (AI) technology can provide the required training and certification materials to prepare sales reps adequately for meeting the physicians and other key stakeholders in advance. AI can also recommend the most relevant information and content that can impact the meeting. It can provide the most relevant and personalized content that is physician-specific marketing collateral to the sales force. AI thus offers two significant advantages. One is, it minimizes the time consumed by reps looking to gather these materials. Also, by implementing more effective pre-call preparation, Medical reps can maximize their effectiveness in every customer meeting. Consider this scenario: *Medical reps can ascertain in advance that a particular doctor is more interested in making time for reps with more treatments to offer. Recognizing this need ahead of time empowers the representative to come armed with details on all the drugs relevant for that particular physician. Besides, AI can recommend the most important reprints, detail aids, abstracts, and leave-behinds for each call with a prescriber determined by the marketing team's best practices and sales leadership. The company's sales force can spend more time with physicians, physician assistants (PAs), and nurse practitioners by optimizing the pre-call planning process with artificial Intelligence.*

2. *Reduces Administrative Tasks*: You can use AI technology to automate manual administrative tasks to free up representatives' time, engage with physicians, and cultivate relationships effectively. For instance, technology can help automatically log calls with physicians, nurses, pharmacists, and other key customers into the company's customer relationship management (CRM) systems such as SalesForce, Veeva, and the like. You can also take advantage of using smart forms, which enable digital data entry and connect to back-end systems, which allow representatives to complete them while in the field from their mobile devices. It eliminates time-consuming paper-based forms enabling your sales force to place orders on-site and in real-time, increasing overall productivity. You can feed this content, in turn, into an AI-powered tool to help inform the self-learning algorithms and automatic content recommendations to salespeople based on factors such as where they are in the sales cycle, their role, and what their peers are using — and a significant reduction in time spent seeking for the right content. Pharmaceutical salespeople will spend more time in the field and call on more customers since the administrative tasks that traditionally forced them to spend more time at their desks, like inputting their sales calls into their CRM systems and emailing a reprint to a physician, are now automated.
3. *Identifies and Shares Best Practices*: By measuring the actions of every user and learning from this process, an artificial intelligence-powered solution can determine what works and what doesn't for engaging prospects, generating prescriptions, and closing the deals. AI-based solutions can make real-time content recommendations for sales representatives tailored to where they are in the sales cycle and significantly improve their chances of a successful outcome. Consider this scenario: I*f the top 10 percent of salespeople use a particular presentation during their initial meetings, the system will push that content to other salespeople as they are headed toward their introductory session with their prospects because of AI's (and Machine Learning) capability*

to measure and learn from the successes and failures of other salespeople across the team. And by identifying the habits of their best reps, organizations can improve outcomes by elevating the performance of the entire sales team. In other words, artificial intelligence (AI) can always become a sales trainer and mentor for the sales representatives. Further, in the traditional setting, pharmaceutical sales representatives typically meet to share thoughts and advice with their peers only at quarterly plan-of-action or national sales meetings, usually held once or twice a year. Artificial Intelligence (AI) technology enables the representatives to share and implement these best practices in real-time and potentially translate to immediate improvements.

4. *Enables Real-World Step-by-Step Guided Selling*: By taking the input data, AI-powered sales enablement technology helps guide the salespeople throughout the entire sales cycle suggesting the best next steps, activities, and assets based on that information. This approach, often called Guided Selling, offers a real-world way to help salespeople be successful, especially when they have limited time with physicians. Further, artificial intelligence (AI) provides customized prescriber profiles and call history to better prepare sales representatives before engaging with physicians, physician assistants (PAs), and nurse practitioners to share the best practices of the top sales representatives in the organization to maximize the time in front of the physician.

Artificial intelligence (AI) technology thus acts as a virtual mentor to the entire sales force in an organization, recommends the most relevant, personalized content to each physician, and allows them to benefit from the marketing's expertise. In fact, according to Sirius Decisions, a global B2B (Business-to-Business) research and advisory firm, aligning sales and marketing is proven to deliver 19 percent more growth. It is because artificial intelligence (AI) technology aligns sales and marketing in the best possible way.

Artificial Intelligence can do a lot more. Dr. Andrea Bates, Founder of EULARIS and AI Academy, presents the big picture of what AI can do to Pharma in her insightful three-part article, *16 Examples of Successful Application of Artificial Intelligence in Pharma Marketing*, on their blog, EULARIS. Here is the summary:

1. *Identifying Rare Diseases*: According to Shire Pharmaceuticals, it takes an average of 7.6 years to diagnose a rare disease without technology and comes after countless tests and physician visits, leading to a huge cost to the healthcare system. However, Artificial Intelligence can help us identify these patients within the data sets such as EHR (Electronic Health Record) and clinician data within minutes after initial data wrangling, creating the algorithms.
2. *Enhances Content Engagement in Marketing and Sales*: Artificial Intelligence-powered clustering linked to customer data can help us create personalized product recommendations like Amazon and Netflix do. Using AI technology, pharma companies can identify the optimal next message to give a physician to enable greater engagement.
3. *Predicting and Modifying Patient Adherence*: Automated Artificial Intelligence can help us ensure that each patient gets the right message or solution relevant to that patient to improve adherence.
4. *Precision Physician Targeting*: Most pharmaceutical companies still rely on historical information to make physician targeting decisions. But the market is not about yesterday. It is about tomorrow. Artificial Intelligence can help marketers to make more precise decisions about physician targeting by analyzing numerous things. It can help us predict which doctor has the most potential to prescribe for a patient appropriate for our brand today. AI can also help the rep understand the priority, based on the most recent data, to gain more prescriptions for our brand.
5. *Puts Content Marketing on Steroids*: Content marketing has become fiercely competitive, with more companies joining the content marketing game. Artificial Intelligence can help you stay ahead of the game with algorithms to produce content, source, optimize, and distribute it to reach your customers when they want it, where they want it, and how they want it.

6. *Customer Segmentation and Personalized Marketing*: Pharma marketers' current segmentation practices depend on a limited number of variables siloed by the brand. Therefore, you are likely to find the same physician in multiple brand target lists within the company. However, AI helps unify the data silos and enables you to find far richer information by combining unlimited customer variables into algorithms for a 360-degree view of the customer and data in real-time. Thus, you can segment dynamically, focus on preferred channels, and send a relevant message to connect with individual physicians based on their specific needs and behaviors at any given time.
7. *Next Best Action Recommendations and Omnichannel Marketing*: Using Artificial Intelligence technology, we can predict the most likely outcomes from a set of interactions with a customer or customer segment. The technology allows us to identify the next best content, in the next best channel, in the right sequence, at the right time, in a customer-specific manner, enabling maximum customer engagement and a faster journey to the brand, disrupting the journey positively and fulfilling all the customers' expectations to maximize engagement.
8. *Customer Journey Mapping*: Artificial Intelligence takes customer journey mapping to the next level. It can help you uncover the changing nature of the customer's relationship with the brand, ensure that you disrupt the journey positively, and fulfill all the customer's expectations to maximize engagement.
9. *Social Listening Analysis*: Social media is a goldmine of data as it generates enormous data 24/7. Artificial Intelligence helps marketers to analyze conversations around the brand and provide helpful insights.
10. *Predicting Signs of Physician-Switching*: By applying Artificial Intelligence, it is possible to predict the brand-switching behaviors of physicians. Knowing this will significantly help pharma marketers to plan their customer acquisition and retention strategies effectively.

11. *Pricing and Market Access*: Artificial Intelligence can help pharma marketers leverage the changing pricing scenario to deliver value-based pricing strategies that address the varying needs of payers globally.
12. *Better Sales Forecasting*: Artificial Intelligence analyzes the previous sales data, competitors' sales data, and product comparison to predict future sales.
13. *AI Search Engines and Chatbots in Pharma Marketing Research*: Using Artificial Intelligence, you can create a huge knowledge database with all the market research data collected and analyzed over the searchable years. The analyses provide meaningful insights.
14. *Enhances Customer Call Centers*: Artificial Intelligence, with its natural language processing (NLP) and machine learning (ML) capabilities, can take the call center customer experience to a new level. Unlike IVR (Interactive Voice Response), AI could provide a different output for different people depending upon the system's learning about the persons and the probability of their needs. AI could also capture all the data from the call centers to predict topics and optimal answers for the call center teams to predict topics for call-center teams around specific drugs. With sentiment analysis added, more information and insights can be gained, enabling the staff to detect early signs of annoyance before a human advisor can spot it.
15. *Faster Reimbursement*: A combination of NLP (Natural Language Processing) and ML (Machine Learning) can create great value for Pharma by assisting in faster reimbursement. AI can do this by understanding the varying needs of different payers globally and delivering a payer-specific communication strategy.
16. *Key Opinion Leader (KOL) and Thought Leader (TL) Mapping*: AI can significantly augment your Key Opinion Leader (KOL) and Thought Leader (TL) mapping. The main difference with AI is that it is constantly updated and analyzed automatically and can identify things that traditional approaches miss.

AI in the Pharmaceutical Industry

Apart from Marketing, you can implement artificial intelligence in almost every aspect of the pharmaceutical industry across its entire value chain. Consider the following areas, for example:

1. *Research and Development*: Pharma companies globally use AI and advanced ML algorithms to streamline drug discovery processes.
2. *Drug Development*: According to MIT (Massachusetts Institute of Technology), only 13.8 percent of drugs successfully pass through clinical trials. Not only that, a pharma company has to spend up to $2.6 billion for the drug to go from concept to commercialization. AI and advanced ML technologies can improve the success rate of clinical trials and reduce development costs.
3. *Diagnosis*: Artificial Intelligence technologies enable physicians to rapidly analyze the vast amount of data in patients' electronic health records (EHRs) and help them arrive at a diagnosis.
4. *Treatments for Rare Diseases*: Generally, pharmaceutical companies do not spend their time and resources on finding rare disease treatments since the ROI (Return on Investment) is very low compared to the time and effort invested in them. According to Global Genes, a Non-profit advocacy organization for individuals and families fighting rare and genetic diseases, nearly 95 percent of rare diseases do not have FDA-approved treatments or cures. AI and ML have innovative capabilities that can change the scenario by reducing the time to diagnose and saving costs.
5. *Epidemic Prediction*: Many pharmaceutical companies and healthcare providers globally already use AI and ML technologies to monitor and forecast epidemic outcomes. The ML-based malaria outbreak prediction model that functions as a warning tool for predicting possible malaria outbreaks and aiding healthcare providers in taking the best course of action to combat it is a good example.

6. *Remote Monitoring*: Remote monitoring is a significant breakthrough in the pharma and healthcare sectors. Many pharma companies have already developed wearables powered by AI algorithms that can remotely monitor patients suffering from chronic and life-threatening diseases.
7. *Manufacturing*: Pharmaceutical companies can implement AI in manufacturing for higher productivity, improved efficiency, and faster production of life-saving drugs. Pharma can use AI to manage and improve manufacturing areas, including quality control, predictive maintenance, waste reduction, design optimization, and process automation.

Implementing AI

The pharmaceutical industry is finding many applications to use Artificial Intelligence across its value chain. However, the process of transformation is not without challenges. One is that its current IT (Information Technology) infrastructure is based on legacy systems that are not optimized for AI. The other is a shortage of expertise and people with AI skills to implement and integrate AI across the organization. Therefore, it is best for pharmaceutical companies to partner and collaborates with academic institutions specializing in AI to guide the adoption process. In addition, they also need to embark on a company-wide learning and development program to train their people to implement AI tools and techniques properly for optimal productivity.

What the Future Holds for AI?

The future of Artificial Intelligence in the pharmaceutical industry looks promising. Top pharmaceutical companies, including Roche, Pfizer, Novartis, Merck, AstraZeneca, GSK (GlaxoSmithKline), Sanofi, AbbVie, Bristol-Myers Squibb, and Johnson & Johnson have already collaborated or acquired AI Technologies. In addition, nearly half of the global healthcare companies will implement AI strategies by 2025.

Augmented Reality (AR) and Virtual Reality (VR)

What do Pokémon Go and Excedrin have in common? Both are using Augmented Reality (AR) and Virtual Reality (VR) to persuade consumers to be more active (Pokémon Go) or to be more compassionate (Excedrin). However, Pokémon Go is the revolutionary Augmented Reality-based mobile game that made the underlying technology extremely popular and accessible. In contrast, GlaxoSmithKline's branded Excedrin Migraine Experience is the world's first Virtual-Reality (VR)-based migraine simulation that provides a new level of understanding of migraine. The migraine experience is designed to give non-sufferers the chance to safely experience migraine symptoms, including disorientation, aura, sensitivity to light, and blurred vision.

What is Augmented Reality (AR)?

Thomas Caudell, a researcher at Boeing, coined 'Augmented Reality' (AR) in 1990 to describe how the head-mounted displays that electricians used when assembling complicated wiring harness worked. However, Augmented Reality made it into the news when Google Glass was tested in 2013.

Techopedia, the well-known IT education website, describes Augmented Reality (AR) as *an interactive experience of a real-world environment where objects in the real world are enhanced by computer-generated perceptual information, sometimes across multiple sensory modalities, including visual and auditory, haptic, somatosensory, and olfactory*. Augmented Reality thus combines real and computer-based scenes and images to deliver a unified but enhanced view of the world.

Augmented Reality employs computerized simulation and techniques such as image and speech recognition, animation, head-mounted, hand-held devices, and powered display environments to add a virtual display on top of real images and surroundings.

What is Virtual Reality (VR)?

Virtual Reality (VR) is a three-dimensional, computer-generated environment with which you can explore and interact. It completely replaces the user's world environment with a simulated one— virtual Reality. The person experiencing virtual Reality becomes a part of this virtual world or immersed within this environment and can manipulate or perform a series of actions while he is present there.

Virtual Reality (VR) uses computer technology to create a simulated environment. Unlike traditional user interfaces, VR places the user inside an experience. Instead of viewing a screen in front of them, users are immersed and interact with three-dimensional worlds. By simulating as many senses as possible, such as vision, hearing, touch, and even smell, the computer is transformed into a gatekeeper to this artificial (virtual) world.

Virtual Reality creates this immersive experience with the help of devices such as HTC Vive, or Oculus Rift. These devices help transport the users into several real-world and imagined environments, such as the middle of a squawking Penguin colony or the back of a dragon, or even into a bloodstream, respiratory tract, or any other physiological processes like medical and pharmaceutical environments.

Difference between AR and VR

Augmented Reality (AR) enhances the real-life environment with some computer-generated elements. So the virtual scenes are mixed with the real ones, overlaying the digital details on the real world. In addition, augmented Reality often adds digital elements to a live view by using the camera on a smartphone. Snapchat lenses and the Pokémon Go game are some notable examples of Augmented Reality.

Virtual Reality (VR), on the other hand, completely replaces the real world with a virtual environment. That means everything you see looks quite life-like, though, in fact, it is just a simulation.

To dive into the Virtual Reality world, you need to use a head-mounted controller or glasses. At the same time, Augmented Reality mostly uses commonplace devices like tablets, smartphones, or laptops. Of course, Augmented Reality can also be applied through Microsoft HoloLens, which is currently very expensive to be widespread.

Why AR or VR?

Why do marketers in general and pharma marketers, in particular need AR or VR? Are they really necessary? Here are at least five compelling reasons for making AR and VR an integral part of your marketing strategy.

1. VR sessions can increase the quality and attractiveness of visits by medical representatives.
2. Modern VR builds upon mechanisms of action (MOA) animations, which have become a mainstay in pharmaceutical marketing. For example, today, no blockbuster drug gets released without a 3-D animation. While MOA provides a piece of clear and concise information about a drug, they pale compared to the experience of being in the bloodstream or penetrating a cell wall to deliver a drug, which only Virtual Reality can create.
3. Both AR and VR significantly improve patient-HCP communications, which result in better outcomes. As Drew Griffin, senior technical architect at Razorfish Health, said: *Given that patient-HCP communication can be qualitatively dense, any technology such as AR/VR that can provide just-in-time, easy-to-digest, context-sensitive data will be an unprecedented and invaluable tool to educate patients during diagnosis and treatment of their conditions. This gives pharmaceutical companies an excellent opportunity to reach healthcare professionals and patients with their creative communication*.
4. With most healthcare professionals (HCPs) and patients using the web to access health, medical or prescription drug information, we find ourselves in the middle of an ocean full of

digital health information. How can you stand out in such a scenario? Creating visual and educational content without being ad-driven can be highly interesting and involving. Augmented Reality and Virtual Reality can help us achieve these communication objectives as they can create immersive experiences.

5. In the US, less than 50 percent of the pharmaceutical sales force has access to physicians. Still, each year, US drug companies spend up to $5 billion sending their representatives to meet doctors. In 2015 alone, it is reported that pharmaceutical companies in the US wasted 1 to 1.5 billion dollars on marketing by making infeasible calls to physicians. The Pharma industry needs an effective communication tool that can extend its reach to reluctant physicians. AR and VR are probably excellent means to achieve this.

Augmented or Virtual Reality?

There are several marketing situations ideally suited for implementing Augmented Reality or Virtual Reality. As these technologies become more affordable, it is crucial to know when and how to deploy them most effectively. The core philosophy for AR and VR revolves around empathy. Both technologies are experiential. However, when you have decided on using these technologies, the first critical decision is: whether to use AR or VR? Besides their technical differences, these approaches have different applications in marketing. Here are two broad distinctions between AR and VR:

1. Virtual Reality (VR) is typically an enclosed environment enabling an immersive, utterly experience. Therefore, one can use virtual reality to let healthcare providers and caregivers experience another person's symptoms, providing a more definite sense of how a disease affects their lives.
2. On the other hand, Augmented Reality (AR) often involves projecting onto an external surface and provides a shared experience. Augmented Reality is a good fit for educational campaigns. It can also demonstrate a novel therapeutic approach and a new drug's mode of action.

Like any other marketing technology, it is also essential to know when not to use Augmented Reality and Virtual Reality. These new technologies' 3-D functionality and immersive nature should be a supplement, and they do not replace traditional approaches. When a print ad accomplishes the campaign's goal, it does not make sense to use a VR or AR version just because they are more appealing and advanced. A good rule of thumb is that VR and AR are not the choices if there is no pressing need for empathy or hands-on education.

AR and VR in Healthcare

Early adopters in the healthcare and life sciences are starting to use Augmented Reality to explain complex concepts and treatments. Because it helps you engage healthcare professionals (HCPs) and patients with three-dimensional images by optimizing today's digital channels to provide an attention-grabbing new content type. One company, for example, created a 3D heart model to demonstrate how a medicine moves through the organs as a part of a new treatment producing a much more significant impact than a simple video. Another example of where Augmented Reality has been used is mapping an individual's body for surgery and showing the exact locations of veins in a patient's arm, helping HCPs treat patients better and improve outcomes. Arno Sosna, general manager, Veeva Systems, a leading cloud computing company focused on pharmaceutical and life sciences industries, suggests three areas — sales, marketing, and customer service, where Augmented Reality can be a game-changer in his article titled, *The New (Augmented) Reality*, published in the Pharmaceutical Executive on April 18, 2018.

1. *Enhance Personalized Customer Engagement:* Augmented Reality creates highly engaging experiences for healthcare professionals (HCPs) and patients to enhance customer involvement. Finding new ways to interact with them can serve as a real differentiator and help foster more personal relationships. Augmented Reality can create a better connection with customers by spurring emotions such as wonder or surprise. Pharmaceutical companies can

innovatively tell their stories and demonstrate the value that their products offer compellingly with the help of Augmented Reality. Healthcare practitioners (HCPs) can understand how a treatment works in the body, even in a particular type of patient's body. The contextual experience allows HCPs to more fully appreciate the treatment benefits, making the information more memorable.

2. *Improve Understanding of Complex Treatments*: Pharmaceutical marketers face challenges when communicating highly specialized and complex treatments with just words. Videos help but are still limited. Today, Augmented Reality technology offers a multi-dimensional way to communicate complex concepts for greater comprehension and retention. Researchers have concluded that Augmented Reality is more effective because it allows people to engage in the learning process with multiple senses to produce better results. As Benjamin Franklin, an American polymath and one of the Founding Fathers of the United States, said: *Tell me, and I forget. Teach me, and I remember. Involve me, and I learn*. Augmented Reality involves the viewer in multiple ways to learn faster. In healthcare, Augmented Reality can teach medical practitioners complex medical procedures — not just in theory but also in practice — allowing them to virtually touch and manipulate objects to see their effect or practice the procedure. Yan Fossat, vice president of Klick Health Labs at Klick Health, the world's largest independent health marketing and commercialization agency, said: *AR is a beautiful new addition to the visual toolbox and can be spectacular in telling a story with impact. AR is a particularly suitable medium for cases where a contextual understanding of a medical concept is required. For instance, giving someone the ability to see a disease or skin condition on their skin instantly or enabling them to see someone with macular degeneration sees with their reduced vision is much more impactful than other forms of visual or textual representation.*
3. *Create A Powerful Brand Differentiation*: Today's hyper-competitive business landscape demands and dictates that

you differentiate your product or service to achieve success. Augmented Reality can provide an important point of differentiation for pharmaceutical and life science companies. Marketers will be able to use Augmented Reality to stand out in the crowd with compelling content. They can create a powerful visual experience and demonstrate their products' novel mode of action, efficacy, and more. With the help of Augmented Reality, they can dramatically raise brand and disease awareness.

Virtual Reality technology plays a significant role. As Erin Fitzgerald, vice president of marketing at AccentHealth, says, *Virtual Reality is incredibly engaging. More importantly, the potential to interact with patients and influence behavior by delivering deeply relevant content in a new vivid format. Data shows that 96 percent of physicians agree that Virtual Reality engagement can be more valuable than websites and other clinical tools. In 2017, as healthcare marketers concentrate on delivering immersive, individualized patient experiences, we expect Virtual Reality to take hold at the point of care. Anatomical models are already being integrated into exam room tablets, and, before long, therapeutic and behavioral visualizations will be standard educational tools for patients throughout the medical journey.*

Here are three examples of how Virtual Reality is playing a crucial role in improving treatment outcomes:

1. *Virtual Reality for Post-traumatic Stress Disorder (PTSD)*: Post-traumatic Stress Disorder (PTSD) is a psychiatric disorder that can occur in people who have experienced or witnessed a traumatic event such as a natural disaster, a severe accident, a terrorist act, war, or combat, rape or other violent personal assault. Studies have shown that Virtual Reality can help improve outcomes in PTSD. How does Virtual Reality achieve this? The affected person wears a pair of VR glasses or Head Mounted Display (HMD). It contains two tiny monitors which display images of the source of the disorder— a battlefield, for example. The rationale is that exposing someone to the source of their condition combined with relaxation skills will

enable them to cope and adapt. As they are exposed to this over time, the threat level is removed, decreasing their anxiety levels and feelings of anxiety. The person can revisit the painful memories to develop new forms of behavior that will change these and any other existing beliefs. It will cause them to learn new ways of thinking, which will positively impact their lives. (Source: Virtual Reality treatment for PTSD, Virtual Reality Society, UK)

2. *Virtual Reality is twice as effective as morphine in treating pain*: Over 100 million Americans suffer from chronic pain. Since the 1990s, opioid prescriptions (for treating chronic pain) have tripled in the US. As a result, today, the US, a country with a mere 5 percent of the world's population, consumes around 80 percent of opioids. There is a definite need to find an alternative to treating chronic pain. Howard Rose, the Virtual Reality industry veteran who has been working on VR for more than twenty years at the Human Interface Technology Lab (HIT Lab) at the University of Washington, believes that Virtual Reality is the alternative.
3. *Virtual Reality eases phantom limb pain*: If a hand, an arm, or a leg is amputated due to an accident or disease, eight out of ten amputees experience discomfort in the limb that is no longer there. The phenomenon is called phantom limb pain. Dr. Bo Geng, Postdoc at the Faculty of Medicine at Aalborg University in Denmark, explained how phantom limb pain occurs. She said: T*he tactile representation of different body parts is arranged in the brain on a map. If the brain no longer receives feedback from an area, it tries to reprogram its signal reception map. Tests have shown that phantom limb pain can be relieved if the brain is tricked into thinking that the amputated limb is still attached to the body.* By placing a mirror at an angle in front of the chest, you can create the visual illusion that the body is symmetrical. If you then pretend to do the same movements simultaneously with both hands, the brain, in many cases, can be convinced that it is in contact with an amputated hand. Virtual reality makes it possible to create an experience

of being present in a three-dimensional world where you can move around freely, grab things, and interact with them. Mirror therapy has some limitations because you have to physically sit in front of a mirror, do the same movement in a confined space with both hands at the same time and keep your eyes on the mirror to break the illusion. With Virtual Reality, there is a much better chance of creating a convincing alternate way. In the new method, the patients have to put on VR goggles and a glove. At the same time, small electrodes are placed on the residual limb, known as the stump. The amputees play much different virtual Reality (VR) games that involve doing the same thing with both hands, such as grabbing a pole that has to be twisted into different shapes or pushing different virtual buttons. Virtual Reality makes you feel as if you were using both hands. Dr. Bo Geng Says: *Of course, we need to do more tests, but the results so far look promising. (source: Aalborg University, Virtual Reality Eases Phantom Limb Pain, ScienceDaily, May 31, 2017)*

Virtual Reality in Pharma Marketing Communications

One thing is for sure. Virtual Reality certainly increases user interaction. It, therefore, offers significant opportunities and benefits to pharmaceutical marketers. It gives them a chance to deliver to their audiences the closest experience possible with a product, service, or place without actually being there. In short, Virtual Reality helps Pharma to engage with its customers in an ideal way. Consider, for example, the following areas in pharmaceutical marketing suggested in a PitStop blog article titled, *Using Personas to Develop Relevant Marketing Messages*, where Virtual Reality can be of significant help in boosting engagement levels with its audiences:

1. *Branding*: Virtual Reality technology helps pharmaceutical companies create, promote, and uniquely raise brand awareness. It offers a memorable and even an unforgettable experience to consumers. Virtual Reality allows pharmaceutical equipment manufacturers to market their products more cost-effectively. The marketers can provide the viewers with an

immersive virtual reality experience instead of lugging around expensive heavy machinery or arranging a physical tour of their facilities. Also, consider, for example, how an immersive simulation supplied by a brand treatment can help healthcare professionals (HCPs) experience a migraine for themselves while creating a better understanding of its mode of action within the body. This enhanced understanding and added value can market a treatment while complying with the strict regulatory framework.

2. *Storytelling*: Virtual Reality enables pharmaceutical marketers to tell stories in a completely new way, thus creating an innovative approach to visual storytelling. It creates a buzz and excitement about a product. You can make even mundane products such as a syringe or tubing come alive with Virtual Reality. Above all, Virtual Reality helps pharmaceutical marketers make even the most complex product information easily understandable and simple leading consumers to the eureka moment of real understanding of the potential therapeutic benefits of a particular product as it is engaging and exciting. Virtual Reality helps pique and retain an interest in biochemical processes, clinical trials, manufacturing and R&D equipment, and others by creating an interactive, intuitive, and playful learning environment. As a result, it allows pharmaceutical marketers and healthcare professionals to become active rather than passive consumers of information.
3. *Immersive Experience*: Virtual Reality provides a tangible, powerful, and immersive experience not possible with any other media such as brochures, speech, websites, PowerPoint, or even videos. Your audience can test drive the content, be it a piece of equipment or a physiological process. Moreover, it builds empathy. Virtual Reality helps clinicians and caregivers experience what it is like to have a condition such as Parkinson's or chronic migraine. They feel their hands shake or see as a migraine aura distorts their vision. The experience engages them in a way that makes them receptive to your brand messages.
4. *Training*: Virtual Reality can facilitate training in a big way. For example, if you are marketing stents, you can use it to let

clinicians experience how it feels to use the device without the fear of failure. You can also use Virtual Reality to provide experiential training on production or physiological process. You can also use it as a powerful training tool to market your new drugs throughout their lifecycle. In the introductory stage, Virtual Reality helps in raising awareness among doctors. At the product growth and maturity stage, it reinforces the additional promotional tools to increase market penetration, leading to the more frequent use of the drug and more new patients.

AR and VR in Pharma Marketing

Increasingly, pharmaceutical companies are exploring the possibilities of Augmented and Virtual Realities to increase awareness of diseases, novel therapeutic approaches, and brand differentiation. Consider the following examples:

1. Pfizer has previously adopted Augmented Reality using holographic technology to demonstrate treatment for strokes at a World Heart Federation conference. Sharad Kumar, Co-Founder of holographic services at Virtual Presence, a technology company that provides virtual content and events, said that *holography allows key opinion leaders (KOLs) and medical specialists to be available in multiple locations simultaneously*.
2. In 2015, Bayer teamed up with DJM PAN. This leading multichannel agency developed Augmented Reality to communicate with healthcare professionals (HCPs) to help promote the treatment of age-related macular degeneration (AMD) and diabetic macular edema. Physicians at an industry event were given a smartphone headset with an app programmed to simulate some of the effects of poor vision and understand how this might affect their patients.
3. Boehringer Ingelheim used Virtual Reality in a campaign to provide an immersive experience to 400 cardiologists at an American College of Cardiology conference in April 2016. The conference attendees were immersed in the bloodstream via a Samsung Gear VR headset as part of the Pradaxa reversal

agent — Pradaxa Bind (Idarucizumab) campaign. All the cardiologists received the campaign enthusiastically.

Cases in AR and VR

Here are three cases showing how forward-thinking pharmaceutical companies have used Augmented Reality and Virtual Reality to raise awareness, drive home their product differentiation, and enhance brand recognition and recall value.

CASE 17

Digital Pharma: Genzyme's Augmented Reality Heart!

Genzyme, the third-largest biotechnology company globally, was acquired by Sanofi in 2011 and became a wholly owned subsidiary of Sanofi. Genzyme developed Renvela (Sevelamer), a phosphate-binding drug used to treat hyperphosphatemia in patients with chronic kidney disease (CKD). While the product looked very promising, the company faced some significant challenges in marketing. The company launched Renvela in Europe in June 2009.

Major Challenge

Low awareness of the consequences of prescribing calcium-based phosphate binders has been a major challenge. Calcium-based phosphate binders are the mainstay in treating hyperphosphatemia in patients with chronic kidney disease. However, evidence suggests that the consequent raising calcium levels may introduce coronary artery and cardiac calcification, thereby imposing a higher risk of death than with a non-calcium binder. Unfortunately, however, the awareness of such a risk seems to be very low. Maybe because doctors do not see calcification unless they look specifically for it, they probably continue to prescribe calcium-based phosphate binders they have been using all along. Changing this perception and, thereby, their prescribing behavior from calcium-based phosphate binders to non-calcium phosphate binders is quite challenging.

Innovative Approach

Suzanna Van Straaten, senior renal marketing manager at Genzyme Europe, and her team came up with a creative, even ingenious approach to raise awareness of the consequences of continuing treatment of chronic kidney disease with calcium-based phosphate binders and the importance of switching over to calcium-free phosphate binders. In addition, they developed an innovative digital tactic to support their strong product strategy.

The current low awareness is because doctors do not see calcification as they are not specifically looking for it. What if you can make them see the calcification for themselves and how it is happening. A sort of a calcification-preview like In 3-D animation? That was the eureka moment! The team sought the help of the Windsor-based advertising agency, Lang Land, which developed an augmented reality gateway that aims to shock doctors by showing the risk of using calcium-based phosphate binders rather than calcium-free phosphate binders.

The team at Genzyme Europe launched a new website as a home for their augmented reality-based campaign, calcifiedheart.com. The website allowed users to take a peek inside their hearts, or so the site's use of augmented reality makes it seem.

They demonstrated their Augmented Reality based calcified heart at their booth at a big European Congress to draw attention to a broader audience. They later developed it as a multipurpose e-tool for online and offline use. The demonstration at the nephrology conferences across Europe has been a phenomenal success. Technology grabbed the attention of doctors. It boosted conversation between doctors and booth staff about what they saw at the booth. Many doctors even said: *I'll not give my patient calcium because I can see the consequences*. Thus, the battle for awareness was won. But, when the battle for awareness is won, will the success lag behind?

Suzanna Van Straaten, the Augmented Reality-based digital initiative architect at Genzyme, said: *This digital magic has been a great success. It has created a new interest in treating chronic kidney disease, but it has helped them visualize the dangers of calcification*.

(Source: Adapted from articles: 1. Dominic Tyer, Digital Pharma: Genzyme's Augmented Reality heart, Pharmafile, October 12, 2010; 2. Suzanna Van Straaten, Senior Renal Marketing Manager, Genzyme, Pharmaceutical marketing: Augmented Reality — a new way to engage at Digipharma Europe Conference, YouTube, April 17, 2012)

CASE

18

GSK's Migraine Simulator for Excedrin Wins Creative and Consumer Praise!

Seeing is believing in GlaxoSmithKline's Excedrin campaign for migraine. GlaxoSmithKline (GSK) teamed with DDB Remedy, a leading marketing, and advertising agency, to create a migraine simulator using Augmented Reality (AR) and Virtual Reality (VR). Working with migraine sufferers, GSK and DDB recreated what migraines feel like. While pain is not included, the experience does simulate the different visual symptoms such as disorientation, aural, and sensitivity to light that often signal the beginning of a migraine.

Virtual Reality (VR) is an emerging technology for healthcare, and its popularity in Pharma is growing as a way for marketers to understand better and communicate patient conditions and experiences. While the campaign is based on virtual reality, it is not about celebrating the latest technology and creating a difference. Instead, the goal of the work is to induce empathy for sufferers. In making the viewers understand and feel what it is like living with migraines.

GSK focused throughout the campaign on the idea that 36 million people in the US suffer from migraines. The one thing they find common is how debilitating it is and how difficult it is to explain that to their partners and others around them. The debilitating nature and the difficulty of migraines can only be experienced but not explained. GSK wanted to make its target audience experience what it feels like to have a migraine. The most appropriate technology to achieve that is Virtual Reality. This feel of migraine is best captured in its TV ad, which features:

One mother who wears the Virtual Reality headset and experiences what her daughter Elisabeth goes through breaks down, saying: I'm sorry that you go through this. Three other migraine sufferers and their loved ones or co-workers have similar experiences posted in online videos at the Excedrin migraine experience website.

(excedrin.com/migraine-experience).

Social media comments about the campaign reveal similar experiences. For example, one commentator on Facebook wrote:

For those who suffer from migraines, this commercial says it all. If you don't have them, watch it for someone who does. The only thing that can come with one... my daughter has had them since she was 11. The first time she got one, I took her to the emergency room. The doctor took me aside and said she was faking. Really.

Amardeep Kahlon, marketing director of GSK Consumer Healthcare for respiratory care and pain relief, said: *One of the best things about this has been watching online conversations... Migraine sufferers finally feel that people understand them and what their experience is.*

The Migraine Experience

Here's a transcript of GlaxoSmithKline's video, The Migraine Experience, that explains it all:

She gets up in the morning, and boom, she has a migraine; there are 36 million migraine sufferers in the US. Most people think a migraine is just a bad headache. You're just saying that so you can call in sick today. They could think that you are overdramatic. I think she thought I was lying. Migraine sufferers felt misunderstood until, together with Excedrin, the head pain expert, we created the first Augmented Reality migraine simulator, which consisted of a Virtual Reality headset-twin mounted HD cameras and a wireless controller to manage the intensity of the symptoms with virtual Reality developed— we can mirror exactly what a sufferer goes through when a migraine strikes. Friends, family, and co-workers were then challenged to experience the symptoms of a migraine.

Next, we shared their experience online the second that the aura starts, everything else stops, any sort of bright light will make me feel like the room is spinning, or I start to see little; Oh, are you okay, we've made the migraine experience fully accessible by developing the app. Now anyone can experience the symptoms of migraine. Experience where you can experience the symptoms of a migraine.

Our campaign reached millions of people and touched the hearts of everybody who saw it — Sufferers and non-sufferer alike. I mean, you described it to me, but it's nothing like actually seeing it. Experience because the whole world can see that a migraine is more than just a headache.

The Excedrin Migraine Experience Campaign took about a year to create and bagged three creative awards at Cannes Lions Health 2016. It won two Silver Lions in Health & Wellness, Education and Awareness for the use of technology, and a Bronze Lion for Health & Wellness in OTC oral medications to use technology.

In addition to winning creative awards, the campaign has generated substantial online attention with almost 19 million views and more than 11 million on Facebook. The campaign generated more than 285,000 social engagements, including comments, retweets, likes, and shares. GlaxoSmithKline recently added to its marketing mix a new app that works with virtual reality viewers like Google Cardboard to create a three-dimensional version of symptoms.

The Augmented Reality Excedrin Migraine Experience Campaign unlocked a new level of understanding of migraines and their impact on the daily lives of the millions of people who suffer from this condition worldwide.

(Source: Adapted from articles: 1. Beth Snyder Bulik, Pain, and empathy: GSK migraine simulator for Excedrin wins creative and consumer praise, Fierce Pharma, June 23, 2016; 2. News provided by Weber Shandwick, and Weber Shandwick celebrates Grand Prix Award Five Cannes Health & Wellness Lions with clients, agency partners at Lions Health 2016, CISION PR Newswire, June 20, 2016)

CASE

19

Salix's New Virtual Reality Film Gives Doctors an *Insider* Tour of the Human Gut!

Irritable Bowel Syndrome (IBS) conveys a similarity of syndromic symptoms — abdominal pain associated with bowel habits, form, and frequency changes. However, there is a multitude of different causes.

Salix Pharmaceuticals, a division of Valeant, the specialty Pharma company in the US, launched a unique learning tool— a 3-D Virtual Reality (VR) tool on May 9, 2017, that offers a tour of the gastrointestinal tract. The virtual reality film is viewed through a VR headset as a 3-D tour through the human digestive system. Along the way, the possible causes of IBS — such as food intolerance, history of gastrointestinal infections, and altered microbiomes— are discussed. Salix launched this VR virtual tour of the human gastrointestinal tract to a target audience of gastroenterologists at Digestive Disease Week.

The Virtual Reality tool is expected to help primary care physicians diagnose IBS, exploring various causes of the sometimes difficult-to-diagnose condition. The tool offers doctors a new perspective and an educational experience simultaneously as the disease, IBS. Salix representatives later took the VR film on their office visits. While speaking about this unique tool, Dr. Brooks Cash, a Salix gastroenterology advisor, said in an interview: *This learning tool is designed to educate clinicians regarding varying pathophysiologies at the heart of IBS*.

How did Salix get the idea for the tool? The idea came out of a Salix advisor meeting, where someone showed an iPhone clip featuring a 3-D roller coaster ride during a break. The Salix team took the idea and ran with it to develop an experiential tour of the human gastrointestinal gut. Dr. Brooks Cash, along with other advisors, worked to make the tour accurate and educational.

Why is the focus on primary care physicians? Because primary care physicians are second only to gastroenterologists in diagnosing IBS. Salix-funded research published in the American Journal of Gastroenterology— found that 45 percent of IBS patients were diagnosed by gastroenterologists while 42 percent by primary care physicians. Also, when you consider that approximately 70 percent of IBS-D patients initially present their symptoms to a primary care physician, it makes eminent sense to focus on primary care physicians for their XIfaxan, Salix's IBS-D treatment.

(Source: Adapted from the article: Beth Snyder Bulik, New Salix Virtual Reality film gives doctors an 'insider' tour of the human GI tract, Fierce Pharma, May 9, 2017)

Beyond AR and VR

There are two more 'realities' beyond Augmented Reality and Virtual Reality. These are Mixed Reality (MR) and Extended Reality (XR).

Mixed Reality (MR) is a hybrid between AR (Augmented Reality) and VR (Virtual Reality). It superimposes an interactive experience over the real world, allowing for both simulated Reality and true Reality. For example, in augmented reality (AR), your ability to interact with simulation does not exist or is significantly limited. Likewise, in virtual reality (VR), you cannot interact with the real world. Whereas, in MR (Mixed Reality), digital and real-world objects co-exist and interact in real-time. Microsoft's HoloLens is an example of Mixed Reality (MR). It allows you to place digital objects into the room you are standing and lets you spin them around or interact with the digital object in any way possible.

Extended Reality (XR) is an emerging umbrella term for all the immersive technologies, AR (Augmented Reality), VR (Virtual Reality), and MR (Mixed Reality). All immersive technologies extend the Reality we experience by blending the virtual and real worlds or creating a fully immersive experience. While the XR (Extended Reality) can be applied across many areas in Pharma and healthcare, it offers three significant opportunities for Pharma marketers:

1. *Product Demonstration*: With XR (Extended Reality), you can effectively communicate complex concepts about your new product's mechanism of action through demonstration. You can help healthcare providers visualize how your product acts inside the body through an immersive experience. Pharma sales reps can use XR (Extended Reality) technology to create interactive and immersive product demonstrations and enhance the e-detailing of their new products.
2. *Experiential Marketing*: Using the power of AR (Augmented Reality) and VR (Virtual Reality), pharmaceutical companies can offer highly engaging visual experiences to HCPs. This experiential marketing opens many exciting avenues, such as showing a patient an accurate 3D simulation of what their *future*

self might look like. Consider, for example, what they look like if they continue a particular type of cancer treatment or have undergone a cosmetic procedure.

3. *Learning and Development*: XR (Extended Reality) takes learning and development activity to a new level. It provides an excellent way of visualizing complex information in a distraction-free environment and endless opportunities for repetition, opening up many opportunities to enhance learning and development. Many Pharma Majors have already started investing in developing XR (Extended Reality) projects for many different purposes. For instance, Johnson & Johnson Institute's Global VR training program for surgeons helps many surgeons worldwide to improve their skills. Also, Pfizer has developed, using AR (Augmented Reality), a guide that answers patients' questions about one of their product lines at the point of purchase.

The Future Outlook

The number of companies embracing the idea that making scientific content come alive through Virtual Reality is increasing slowly but steadily. Virtual Reality can grab attention and improve interest in new products during medical conventions, conferences, and other events where physicians gather. As a result, many pharmaceutical companies utilize Virtual Reality to engage physicians and create a memorable brand experience.

Pharmaceutical and life sciences companies are testing the waters in new and exciting ways. Industry experts and analysts opine that in the foreseeable future, the integration of Augmented Reality applications into a conventional workflow, such as Customer Relationship Management (CRM), Electronic Medical Records (EMR), and other analytical platforms, will lead to even more exciting possibilities.

Today, Virtual Reality (VR) is on the cusp of mass consumer adoption. From ubiquitous smartphones to headsets such as Oculus Quest 2, HP Reverb, and Sony Play Station VR are available.

Furthermore, the VR-based initiatives by huge companies such as Facebook and YouTube are making more desirable content and pushing VR technology into the daily lives of the mass population.

The number of Virtual Reality headsets is proliferating. In 2016, there were about 7 million Virtual Reality headsets; the number is estimated to grow to 37 million by 2020 and reach a whopping one billion in 2021. In addition, recent research revealed that more than sixty percent of respondents believed that extended Reality (XR) would be mainstream in the next five years.

So, is everything about Extended Reality hunky-dory? Alternatively, are there any obstacles? Perhaps, the biggest obstacle to XR is simply the resistance to change and inertia. However, forward-thinking companies will lead the way, provide the industry with key learnings, and create a broader acceptance of XR as a Killer App with endless possibilities.

Pharmaceutical companies will likely release all-in-one mobile apps that give customers an immersive XR (Extended Reality) experience, from realizing animations showing the effects of a prescribed medicine inside their body to facilitating virtual consultations with doctors in the foreseeable future.

Every which way you think, Extended Reality will be increasingly important in pharmaceutical and life sciences marketing strategy because of its ability to create extraordinary experiences for healthcare practitioners (HCPs) and patients.

The Internet of Things (IoT)

Wikipedia defines The Internet of Things (IoT) as the extension of Internet connectivity into physical devices and everyday objects. With internet connectivity, embedded in electronics, and other forms of hardware, these devices can communicate and interact with others over the Internet, which you can monitor. IoT devices for consumer use have several applications, including home automation, connected vehicles, and connected health devices with remote monitoring capabilities.

Internet of Things (IoT) has several applications for medical and health-related purposes such as data collection, analysis for research, and monitoring. These have evolved and continue to evolve so much that they have connected available medical resources and healthcare services to create a digitized healthcare system. Today, IoT devices have achieved a high degree of remote monitoring and emergency notification capabilities. These smart healthcare devices range from blood pressure and heart rate monitors to advanced devices capable of monitoring specialized implants such as pacemakers, Fitbit electronic wrist bands, Apple Watches, and more. In addition, several consumer wearable devices such as connected scales and wearable heart monitors have also been introduced to encourage healthy living. Research is on to apply IoT to the clinical laboratory industry, and your smartphone could be your diagnostic laboratory in the foreseeable future.

All these devices and wearables are collectively called the Internet of Medical Things (IoMT). Its contribution could be quite significant, as a 2015 Goldman Sachs report indicated that healthcare IoT devices "can save the United States more than $300 billion in annual healthcare expenditures by increasing revenue and decreasing costs".

IoT benefits all Stakeholders in Healthcare

Internet of Things (IoT) enabled devices have made remote monitoring possible in the healthcare sector for all stakeholder groups such as patients, families, physicians, hospitals, and insurance companies. Dr. Rajasekharan Karjagi, Head Analytics and Solutions, and Manish Jindal, Manager, Analytics and Solutions at Wipro, summarized the benefits IoT offers multiple stakeholders in healthcare to engage remotely in their article on the Wipro Blog. Here is the gist:

1. *IoT for Patients*: Wearable devices like fitness bands and other wirelessly connected devices like blood pressure and heart rate monitoring cuffs, glucometers, etc, give patients access to personalized attention. You can tune these devices to track and remind calorie count, check exercise, appointments, blood pressure variations, and much more.
2. *IoT for Physicians*: Physicians can keep track of patients' health more effectively using these devices and other home monitoring equipment embedded with IoT. They can also track patients' adherence to treatment plans or any need for immediate medical attention. As a result, IoT enables healthcare professionals to be more watchful and connect with patients proactively. In addition, data collected from IoT devices can help physicians identify the best treatment process for patients and improve outcomes.
3. *IoT for Hospitals*: IoT devices are useful in monitoring patients' health and many other areas in hospitals. IoT devices triggered with sensors are used for tracking the real-time location of medical equipment like defibrillators, nebulizers, oxygen pumps, wheelchairs, and other monitoring equipment. IoT devices are also helpful in asset management like pharmacy inventory control and environmental monitoring, such as checking refrigerator temperature, humidity, and temperature control.
4. *IoT for Health Insurance Companies*: Health insurers have many opportunities with IoT-connected intelligent devices. Insurance companies can leverage data captured through health monitoring devices for their underwriting and claims operations and bring transparency to the underwriting, pricing, and claims processing. The IoT-captured, data-driven decisions in all the

operation processes enhance the visibility of the customer into the underlying thought process behind every decision made, making the whole process more customer or patient-centric.

COVID-19 Accelerates IoT Adoption

The global COVID-19 pandemic significantly enhanced the risk of getting infected while diagnosing or treating patients, and many hospitals and diagnostic centers have started adopting IoT systems to offer contactless services. In addition, the pandemic has accelerated IoT adoption in the health care industry. In 2020, for instance, the World Health Organization (WHO) medical staff and patients at a field hospital in Wuhan, China, started adopting Cloud-Mind's Artificial Intelligence (AI)-synched smart medical devices such as bracelets and rings. These wearable devices monitor vital signs such as heart rate, the temperature in the infected patients, such as heart rate, temperature, blood oxygen levels, and more during the COVID-19 pandemic.

The rapid spread of the virus and a limited number of medical staff led the governments to take quick initiatives to adopt advanced technologies, including IoT, artificial intelligence, blockchain, and machine learning. These technologies help physicians to consult, diagnose and treat patients even in remote locations.

IoT in Pharma

Internet of Things (IoT) has incredible potential to help pharma and device companies. It can help improve quality, reduce cost, and even change how a medication is delivered to patients. IoT offers significant benefits to the pharmaceutical industry across its entire value chain, starting from R&D, drug discovery, manufacturing, supply chain management, sales, and marketing, and helps improve efficiency and productivity.

In today's highly competitive marketing environment, where the customer is hyper-connected, marketing should be data-driven, and IoT-enabled devices are the goldmine of data. These data and analytics enable marketers to create a seamless customer experience that is significantly superior to the competition. Marketo, an American Software company, specializing in marketing automation software, sums up best the role of IoT in marketing: *IoT is the interconnectivity of our devices that provides endless opportunities for brands to listen and respond to the needs of their customers with the right message, at the right time and on the right device*.

In sum, consider this illustrative list of benefits that the Internet of Things (IoT) brings to the pharmaceutical industry:

- IoT technology helps patients connect to physicians with remote monitoring and virtual visits.
- It helps hospitals track staff and patients.
- IoT healthcare devices facilitate the care of patients with chronic diseases.
- Automates patient care workflow.
- Artificial Intelligence (AI)-powered devices and analytics quickly cull, analyze, and disseminate data to keep everyone on the same page.
- Reduces inefficiency and errors.
- Optimizes the pharmaceutical manufacturing processes and productivity and helps reduce drug prices.

Some IoT applications in Pharma and Healthcare

Apart from the many IoT and other connected devices such as fitness bands, watches, glucometers, and blood pressure monitors, there are many applications of the Internet of Things in healthcare. Mike Thomas introduces some IoT applications by healthcare companies that are changing the landscape of remote monitoring of patient's health in a BulletinIn.com article, *6 IoT in Healthcare Applications Leading to an Improved Industry*.

1. *SystemOne* uses IoT in healthcare with Vodafone's global IoT network and managed IoT connectivity platform, barcode, label system, and specialist. SystemOne transmits medical diagnostics data in real-time to physicians and other healthcare

workers in the world's technology deserts to stay better connected to patients and more effectively manage public health situations, including infectious diseases.

2. *Chronic Disease Management*: Quio, a connected-health company, is a cloud platform that wirelessly connects various devices related to medicines. Healthcare providers and caregivers can see trends and more effectively respond to data with the tools for mobile and web. Users can also get personalized tips on dealing with conditions and have opportunities to participate in research studies anonymously.
3. *Pfizer and IBM*: The Pfizer and IBM partnership uses IoT technology to track the effectiveness of Parkinson's drugs and make any necessary doctor-patient communication. For example, Pfizer and IBM recently developed 'Parkinson's Room' decked out with sensors on everything from the fridge handles and cupboards to doors and beds that detect even the smallest variations in a patient's movements. The data collected in their wirelessly beamed devices to scientists who analyze their progress and medication responsiveness.
4. *Spry Health*: Spry Health's loop device delivers 'the monitoring power of a hospital bed in the form of a fitness tracker.' Among its capabilities are facilitating continuous vital sign data monitoring and patient status via the cloud and gleaning actionable insights that spur better care.
5. *Honeywell*: Honeywell's 'Genesis Touch' keeps patients connected with remotely located care providers that receive transmitted biometrics data via a patient dashboard. The 'Genesis Touch' can also host video visits, give multiple providers access to a patient's vital statistics, and be integrated with an oximeter, blood pressure monitor, and precision health scale.
6. *AdhereTech*: Patients receive a free AdhereTech smart pill bottle with their specialty medication that's used just like a normal bottle and issue reminders for missed doses via a text or phone. It also facilitates personalized support for medication refills and health issues. Avella Speciality Pharmacy, which

issues AdhereTech's smart bottles for five medications from four companies, stated in a report that AdhereTech had improved the duration of therapy by 26 percent, fill rates by 9 percent, and dose-level adherence by 15 percent. AdhereTech generates 1 to 2 percent additional fills of specialty medications per patient per year.

Here's a case of UCB, a leading international pharmaceutical company, that has launched a wellness program with Garmin for rheumatoid arthritis patients in the pharmaceutical industry.

CASE

20

UCB Launches a Wellness Program with *Garmin* for Rheumatoid Arthritis Patients!

UCB, one of the leading multinational pharmaceutical companies, worked with Garmin, a well-known wearable devices company, to launch Wellness4U, a health and wellness platform for people with immunological disorders. The platform has an activity tracker as a pilot program. Speaking about this initiative, Todd Edwards, Vice President and head of US immunology at UCB, told Mobile Health News in an email: *Our medicines treat thousands of people worldwide, and we are engaging with patients, their families, and healthcare professionals to address their unmet needs. We recognize that radical changes are taking place in the ecosystem of care and that we need to evolve accordingly to deliver on our vision. The key element of our evolution is to focus on delivering individual patient values. Wellness4U is an example of a program that supports patients beyond therapeutic intervention by addressing more psychosocial elements that impact people living with immunological disorders*.

The company launched its activity-tracker pilot in select cities across the United States by giving selected patients a *Garmin VivoFit* activity tracker to measure steps and sleep. In addition, patients can access the data and educational materials, and social support through a wellness platform, an online community. The company enrolled fifty rheumatoid arthritis patients for its pilot program.

(Source; Adapted from the article: Jonah Comstock, UCB works with Garmin on Wellness program for rheumatoid arthritis patients, Mobile Health News, March 20, 2017)

IoT: Future Outlook

The proliferation of healthcare-specific IoT products opens up immense opportunities. In addition, the vast data generated by these connected devices hold the promise to transform healthcare. Small wonder that the connected health and IoT devices industry is poised for major growth in the coming years. The global Internet of Things (IoT) in the healthcare market is projected to grow from the present US $89.07 billion in 2021 to a whopping US $446.52 billion in 2028 at a CAGR of 25.9 percent during this period.

■

Chatbots

What is a Chatbot? A chatbot is a computer program designed to simulate conversation with human users, especially over the internet. Chatbots are automated conversational interfaces powered by artificial intelligence that fulfill specific needs or deliver appropriate content requested by users. Chatbots can be divided into two broad categories— informational and transactional. They are available on various messaging and communication platforms globally, such as Facebook Messenger, Skype, WhatsApp, WeChat, and more. They are also coming to IoT (Internet of Things) devices such as Alexa.

Why Chatbots? Because people are spending more time on messaging apps these days than on social media. That is a huge turning point, as Peter Rojas, Entrepreneur in Residence at Betaworks, the New York-based startup that makes essential products that thoughtfully combine art and science, says. He adds that messaging apps are the future platforms, and bots will be how their users access all sorts of services.

Chatbots in Pharma Industry

While Chatbots are relatively new to the healthcare space, patients have been chatting about their health-related matters on message boards and Facebook groups for some time now. As a result, the pharmaceutical industry can find many ways to use Chatbots to help and engage patients. Consider these, for example:

- Chatbots can boost awareness initiatives by pharmaceutical companies on different disease conditions.
- Newly diagnosed patients can use Chatbots to find doctors and specialists in the area.
- Instead of using a call center, a newly prescribed patient can receive treatment onboarding and adherence support through a Chatbot at a fraction of the cost.
- With Chatbots, you can connect with patients in the always-on, always-accessible way they want.
- Chatbots allow you to help patients efficiently with information related to side effects and adherence. A Chatbot can efficiently

deliver that to patients to understand and, more importantly, through a channel they are comfortable with.

Also, Chatbots have an advantage over channels like email and direct mail. Pharmaceutical brands invest a lot into these channels. Still, research reported by AdWeek shows that people are 3.5 times more likely to open a message notification than an email and four times more likely to click through a link found in a message.

Many Touchpoints

There are many possible touchpoints where Chatbots can be of great use in pharmaceutical and healthcare businesses. Santosh Maharshi summarizes the various touchpoints where Chatbots can be used effectively in a Gray Matrix 360 blog article titled, *Chatbots for Pharma Industry*.

1. *Customer Support*: A Chatbot can power your website or be present on a platform of your choice to answer frequently asked questions by existing customers, generate a support ticket, track the status of the service request or be a simple user guide to customers.
2. *Branding and Marketing*: A Chatbot can help you connect with current and prospective customers via regular brand information and news and market your products or services. It can also help you get instant customer feedback and provide simple and short services to your marketing campaigns.
3. *Sales*: A Chatbot can take orders and process individual orders from stores to track the sales team and the daily feedback status of your sales team.
4. *Education and News*: It can let you and your stakeholders know what is happening with you and your industry. A Chatbot can also pass on regular information and educate them on a particular topic.
5. *Human Resources (HR)*: A Chatbot can simplify some HR functions and save time. It can, for example, process leave requests and applications to being a mini intranet on a smartphone.

6. *Business Tools*: Chatbots can convert any multiple steps oriented process into a simple flow, such as conducting surveys, polls, questionnaires, and more.

How Chatbots can Help?

The use of Chatbots in the pharmaceutical and healthcare industry has been increasing slowly and steadily. Here are some notable examples of how Chatbots can help:

1. *Virtual Nurse*: Virtual Nurse is a Chatbot in the hands of your patients, providing all the technology-based assistance, care, and support to patients. It asks the patients daily about medicines they have to take, reminds them of activities suggested by the doctor, keeps track of all the data fed into the system by doctors and patients, and provides a full summary of the patients' progress. It can even fix tests with the lab and appointments with the doctor.
2. *Personal Health Assistant*: This app powered by Gray Matrix's Chatbot is geared to positive affirmations and assistance to lead a healthy life through activity and diet and keeping records of health markers.
3. *Health QnA*: This Chatbot answers your health-related questions 24/7. You can create a specialized bot for a particular disease and provide frequently asked questions (FAQ) and answers. You can also create a brand-specific Bot, which will cover multiple conditions.
4. *Chatbot for Doctors*: As it is becoming increasingly difficult to keep track of the latest research regarding your products and other developments in the industry, creating a Chatbot will help your stakeholders in general and doctors in particular self-serve all this information with the touch of a button. It can also help the doctors to schedule a conference call or a meeting with your sales representative or medical science liaison (MSL).

Top Chatbots in Healthcare

In the past few years, smart algorithm-powered Chatbots have multiplied, easing the burden on doctors in primary care and helping patients learn to take care of their health. The Medical Futurist has summarized the top Chatbots and shows how they are changing the healthcare scenario in their blog post, *The Top 12 Chatbots*, on May 29, 2018.

1. *SafeDrug Bot*: SafeDrugBot is a chat messaging service that offers assistant-like support to healthcare professionals and doctors who need appropriate data about using the drug during breastfeeding. Besides, it provides information about the active ingredients in the medications and alternative medicines.
2. *Izzy*: Izzy, the yellow fluffy little bird, could become the loyal friend of every woman using Facebook Messenger. The cutie takes care of the user's period and keeps menstruation dates and fertile windows in mind. She asks about emotional rollercoasters or period pains and learns to give information about menstrual health and sexual issues. It's a handy companion for the most difficult days in a woman's life.
3. *Babylon Health*: Babylon Health is a British online medical consultation and health service available on subscription founded in 2013. It is powered by artificial intelligence (AI). It offers consultation based on personal medical history and common medical knowledge and live video consultation with a real doctor whenever a patient needs it. In the first case, users report the symptoms of their illness to the app, which checks them against a database of diseases using speech recognition and then offers an appropriate course of action. In the second case (live video consultation with a real doctor), which already goes beyond the usual service of a Chatbot, doctors listen and look carefully to diagnose the patient and then write prescriptions or refer to a specialist if required. Even the UK's National Health Service (NHS) started to use the Chatbot for dispensing medical advice for a trial period in 2017.
4. *Florence*: Florence Chatbot is a personal nurse in the color blue and works on Facebook Messenger, Skype, or Kik Messenger. Florence can remind patients to take their pills, which might be a handy feature for older patients. You write the name of the medicine in the chat, the number of times you must take it a day, and at what time. Then, Florence sends you a message in chat every time you must take the pill. In

addition, Florence can track the users' health parameters such as body weight and mood, thus helping them reach their goals. The Chatbot also has the skills to find the nearest pharmacy or doctor's office if one needs it.

5. *YourMD*: YourMD is a free platform that offers actionable health information based on highly accurate sources, and lets users make the best choices for their health. It is a symptom-checker powered by artificial intelligence (AI) and is available on iOS, Android, Facebook Messenger, Slack, Kik, and Telegram. It is also an excellent source of online medical service providers such as pharmacies, diagnostic test centers, and doctors' offices. YourMD was awarded the prestigious UNESCO/ Netexplo Award for Innovations that can improve society in 2017.
6. *Ada Health*: Ada Health was the fastest-growing medical app in Europe in 2017, with over 1.5 million users. According to Daniel Nathrath, CEO of Ada Health, Ada will become a standard diagnostic tool for doctors. It can assess the user's health based on the indicated symptoms using its AI-based database. That is already the case; users can share their health assessment with their doctor, or, in the UK, they can choose to consult with a qualified GP (General Practitioner) via its Doctor Chat feature. Ada will also become much more of an ongoing health companion, helping patients and doctors intelligently monitor health data over the long term to enable predictive and proactive care.
7. *Sensely*: Sensely is an avatar-based, empathy-driven clinical platform that helps clinicians and patients better monitor and manage their health. Their virtual assistant, *Molly*, focuses on bringing the human touch into automated healthcare. Molly can assess patients' symptoms using speech, text, images, and video. As the user wishes, she can use text or speech to communicate. Based on the gathered data and the information fed into its algorithm, Sensely interprets the users' symptoms and recommends a diagnosis. *Molly* uses the colors of the triage system well-known in emergency care to decide the case's urgency. In Sensely's symptom triage, it means assessing whether self-care is enough or the patient should

turn to a doctor. Also, it offers a local service discovery and rich resources for self-care.

8. *Buoy Health*: Buoy Health was developed by a team of doctors and computer scientists through the Harvard Innovation Laboratory. It was based on massive clinical data from 18,000 clinical papers to mirror the literature referenced by physicians. The data included over 5 million patients and approximately 1,700 disease conditions. With Buoy Health, you can check your symptoms online or browse its vast database to figure out what might be wrong with your health. The Chatbot thoroughly asks you about the details of your medical state and offers various solutions and actionable steps to take.
9. *Symptomate*: Infermedica leverages artificial intelligence (AI) and machine learning (ML) technology to power its symptom-checker Chatbot, Symptomate. It runs online and on mobile phones as a Chatbot or voice-based application. It assesses the user's health status, and based on the symptoms, it sets up a possible diagnosis and gives actionable recommendations.
10. *Gyant*: Gyant combines messaging, AI, and medical experts to radically improve the diagnosis and treatment of non-urgent conditions. It is a health Chatbot that asks patients to understand their symptoms and then sends them to doctors who provide diagnoses and prescribe medications in real-time. The service is available on Facebook Messenger or Alexa currently. The team at Gyant, However, plans to release it on every messaging platform soon. Gyant provides its services to English-speaking patients and users who speak Spanish, Portuguese, and German. The company says it has already screened over 200,000 people in Latin America for diabetes, out of which 5,000 people were diagnosed with the condition.
11. *Bots4Heal*th: Bots4Health is a Chatbot created by the Spain-based digital transformation agency, The Neon Project, specializing in conversational user experience (UX) solutions. In 2016, they released a woman's health Chatbot, Eva, a tool that first concentrated on young women and accessed their sexual and reproductive health information. However, it has widened the target audience after an update, expanding the range of health issues.

12. *Cancer Chatbot*: It is a helpful resource for cancer patients, caregivers, friends, and family on Facebook Messenger. The Chatbot offers many resources for patients, from chemo tips and tricks to free services. It provides resources for caregivers to ease the burden of caring. It also gives friends and families advice on what to say and how to help cancer patients best. It has well-thought-out solutions.

Some health Chatbots can connect patients with clinicians for diagnosis or treatment. It is almost certain that those talking or texting Chatbots through their smart algorithms might become the first contact point in primary care in the future. Patients will not get in touch with physicians, nurses, or any medical professional with every one of their questions but will turn to Chatbots first. If the Chatbot could not comfortably respond to the raised issues, it would transfer the case to a real-life doctor.

Pharmaceutical companies seem to be warming up to the idea of using Chatbots in their marketing programs. Here are three cases showing how Pharma companies can put Chatbots to use in many ways, such as providing personalized training for its sales force, delivering patient education, and improving adherence.

CASE

21

The Generics Major, Teva Launches *Braltusbot* to Improve HCP Engagement!

In 2018, Teva, the generics major, created Braltusbot, a chatbot for HCPs on their UK Braltus website. Braltusbot combined cutting-edge Natural Language Processing and Artificial Intelligence with a robust research process, feedback, and content creation to launch the UK's first pharmaceutical brand chatbot.

Teva also took Braltusbot to HCPs by embedding it in online advertising. It allows HCPs to converse with the Chatbot without leaving the website they are in. These innovative adverts have delivered industry-leading metrics for Teva. Kim Innes, General Manager, Teva UK and Ireland, said: *The experience for a worried HCP must be seamless. Braltusbot uses technology to make care better where and when it matters*.

(Source: Chris Finch, AI is transforming Pharma R&D—Now It Can Transform Pharma Marketing, PharmaLiVE, August 12, 2019)

CASE

22

Norgine Launches *Ava* Chatbot to Provide Patient Support!

A successful colonoscopy may prevent cancer from being missed. Norgine, a leading European specialty pharmaceutical company, developed Ava, a chatbot to maximize colonoscopy success rates by providing patients with answers to questions about problems with the procedure and their bowel preparation. Ava might help save lives.

Kim Jacks Bryant, Global Digital Marketing Lead at Norgine, said: *Norgine is looking beyond standard channels to choose the right technology for each problem we want to solve. For example, we felt a chatbot was the most effective way to provide 24/7 patient support*.

(Source: Chris Finch, AI is transforming Pharma R&D—Now It Can Transform Pharma Marketing, PharmaLiVE, August 12, 2019)

CASE

23

Lupin Launches India's First Chatbot for Patients!

Lupin, an Indian Pharma major, started to digitize the patient journey in the overall healthcare space with Anya, India's first Chatbot for patients to address queries related to diabetes. Anya in Sanskrit means inexhaustible or limitless, and this is the prime quality of the bot. As it evolves, Anya will address all queries of patients and ensure their health conversations continue. Anya is primarily a disease management partner who aims to facilitate users in partnering with doctors in their journey to manage their ailments. Lupin created Anya as a platform where patients can get easy and ready access to medically verified information for their queries at any given time. Anya will not replace a doctor's diagnosis but act as a trusted information partner.

Lupin launched Anya at the 46th annual meeting of the Research Society for the Study of Diabetes. Anya is an intelligent and patient-friendly chatbot trained to help patients with health-related concerns as part of their disease management. As a start to digitize the patient journey in the overall healthcare space, Lupin has started with Anya to address queries related to diabetes.

According to recent research, India is estimated to have had 72 million cases of diabetes in 2017, and the figure is expected to double to 134 million by 2025. Patients today are technologically advanced and like to be well informed on managing their health conditions.

However, there is a lack of trusted, comprehensive, doctor-verified sources of disease management information for patients. Lupin has launched Anya with the idea of bridging this gap by providing medically verified information and acting as a preferred partner for doctors in resolving patient queries anytime.

Speaking about the launch of Anya, Rajeev Sibal, President, Lupin India business, said: *At Lupin, we continue to explore ways to integrate technology to support effective patient care. Chatbot as a technology has enormous potential to aid in medical assistance and help build awareness and break myths associated with various therapies. We are taking this first step to offer this Artificial intelligence-based Chatbot for patients and health givers, and we believe this will be a game-changer in disease management in the future. It will also be a significant step in providing better access in rural markets as we adopt and launch digital healthcare platforms for better outreach*.

(Source: Adapted from the article: Lupin launches India's first Chatbot for patients, BioSpectrum, November 26, 2018)

Advantage Chatbots!

Chatbots have many advantages to offer pharma marketers. The significant ones are:

1. Chatbots can engage 24/7, handling basic questions, allowing the medical affairs teams more time to address more complex questions.
2. Chatbots are eminently trainable. By analyzing the questions received, Chatbots can be trained to answer increasingly complex questions. Their data also provides insights into the needs of HCPs and patients, which can be used to improve services and the quality of the Chatbot's answers.
3. Chatbots play a key role in helping patients self-manage their conditions, providing opportunities for pharma marketers to add more value to their support services.
4. Chatbots present a low-risk, low-cost opportunity for pharma marketers, creating an image of solution providers for themselves.

Digital Voice Assistants

Today, most of us are familiar with digital assistants such as Siri on iPhones, Google Assistant on Android phones, and Bixby on Samsung phones on other smartphones, tablets, laptops, and other devices. We also find them on smart speakers like the Amazon Echo, Google Home, and Cortana on personal computers with Microsoft Windows 10 operating systems. But, what is exactly a digital assistant?

A digital assistant is a computer program to assist users by answering questions and performing specific tasks. Because these digital assistants respond to voice commands, they are called voice assistants. Jack Krupansky, a freelance consultant and software developer, offers a more comprehensive definition of a digital assistant in his article on Medium: *An intelligent digital assistant is a software service coupled with a specialized hardware device such as a smart speaker or simply a feature offered on a general-purpose computing device such as a personal computer (PC), tablet, smartphone, or wearable computer (such as a digital wristwatch), which offers some interesting set of abilities of a traditional, human assistant, most notably answering questions and performing tasks using voice and natural language processing (NLP) backed by artificial intelligence (AI), rather than providing purely canned responses*. Jack Krupansky also listed several tasks that these digital assistants can perform:

1. Voice-enabled, voice control, voice interaction, and voice queries
2. Natural language interaction, commands, and results
3. Find information about weather, traffic, news, and more.
4. Answer questions almost like a digital encyclopedia
5. Make recommendations
6. Perform simple actions around the home, controlling devices, home automation
7. Media control selecting content, controlling volume, music, audio, video, movies, and TV shows

8. Make and take phone calls.
9. Send and receive messages.
10. Chat, converse with the machine
11. Foreign language translation
12. Dictionary look-up
13. Managing to-do lists
14. Setting alarms, timers, reminders, and alerts.
15. Shopping
16. Ordering takeout for delivery
17. E-commerce
18. Concierge functions, reservations, tickets, services
19. Access specialized internet services and open-ended modules developed by third parties.
20. Proactively perform tasks to provide information without being explicitly asked (to a limited extent today)
21. Support for multiple users on a single device
22. Personalization, adaptation, responses, and action; take users' data (personal data, preferences, usage history)

Although designed initially to perform some basic tasks, these digital assistants are gaining intelligence and slowly working their way into the fabric of daily consumer's life, leisure, and now their health. Their capabilities are gradually expanding, unfolding many new possibilities.

Digital Assistants and Pharma

Hands-free digital or voice assistants like Apple's Siri, Google's Google Assistant, and Amazon's Alexa are fast becoming common names. There are many ways pharmaceutical companies can use these to reach customers and promote their products and services. The opportunities for pharmaceutical companies currently include:

- Enhanced patient engagement
- Better reach to HCPs (Healthcare Practitioners)
- Tracking sales representatives

Beth Snyder Bulik presents a plausible scenario of how pharmaceutical companies could use digital voice assistants in the future in her insightful article published in Fierce Pharma titled, *Ask and get health answers: Will 2018 be a tipping point for Pharma voice assistants?* Picture the following scenario that presents some of the longer-term potential for these devices:

Imagine, for instance, Amazon Echo or Google Home devices in physician offices. A Pharma company could create a skill, which Amazon calls its voice apps, that could be downloaded onto the Echo to allow a physician to order samples by simply saying a few words. It's an exciting avenue for pharmaceutical companies to explore these devices as virtual 24/7 sales representatives who sit electronically in the doctor's office and work with live human services, and physicians with the latest information and resources.

Digital Assistants and Physicians

According to DRG Digital, the Digital Voice Assistant trend is already increasing among HCPs, as the life science industry's partner for data-driven physician and patient engagement. Almost one-third of doctors already use Amazon Echo voice services or Electronic Health Records (EHR) with voice capabilities. They are using these voice assistants to search Google to hunt for a website. DRG Digital research suggests the most common ways doctors use voice assistants to:

- ask drug or dosing questions (24 percent)
- diagnostics, disease, or clinical information (22 percent)
- communicate with colleagues (7 percent)

The present rate of usage of these digital voice assistants among physicians, according to research, is:

- 78 percent of users utilize voice on the phone
- 48 percent dictate on phone or tablet
- 31 percent use digital voice assistants, 29 percent use voice in EHR (Electronic Health Records)

Doctors seem to use most of the voice tools to search for content on the web. They are using to search Google to hunt for a website. Will they be put to more robust use in the future? As Jeff Greene, Vice President, Digital Strategy and Insights at DRG Digital, says: *You can bet on it if Apple, Google, and Amazon are behind it*.

Specialized devices could be used to help doctors find information just by talking, keeping their hands free for examining patients. For example, doctors could ask the device about symptoms, treatments, and dosages. The system would then be able to respond with appropriate answers. The more advanced devices might even offer advice on when to send patients for further tests with a specialist and when to send them home with a prescription — and suggest what to write on that prescription.

Digital Assistants and Patients

As these digital assistants improve their skills and increase, patients will be talking to Amazon's Alexa, Google Assistant, and Apple's Siri about which drugs to take and their side effects, reminders to stick to, and dosing schedules. They will also talk to these devices to determine the symptoms, diseases, and treatment options and even determine which doctor or hospital to consult. In addition, they will likely migrate from a manual search to a voice search for the information they need and want.

Coleman Bigelow, the senior brand partner at Google, explains that many consumers turn to digital assistants to connect to relevant information on behavioral requests. They expect convenience out of digital as Google observed a significant uptick in health-related near-me searches such as pharmacies near-me, hospitals near-me, and doctors near-me, among others. Digital assistants provide this convenience to patients. All that they need to do is ask!

Digital Assistants and Disease Diagnosis

Digital assistants are gaining intelligence and slowly working their way into healthcare. The way the voice-activated technology is evolving, there is always a likelihood that these AI-powered small yet powerful devices will work alongside doctors to collect and analyze patient audio for more significant medical insights. For example, the short voice clips from these digital assistants may have the potential to help diagnose a range of diseases and conditions, revealing the research conducted at New York University's Langone Medical Center.

Researchers hope to find patterns of speech that might serve as signals of illness through complex algorithms, machine learning (ML), and cataloging many voice clips over time. In addition, researchers aim to determine whether conditions like PTSD (Post-traumatic Stress Disorder) and even heart disease could be detected much earlier than previously thought possible over a five-year study. Here are a few examples indicating the research efforts to determine how digital assistants can help physicians diagnose some diseases and conditions.

- In a recent study, voice analysis software detected which Veterans had PTSD and who did not, with 89 percent accuracy. Dr. Charles Marmar, Chair of psychiatry at New York University School of Medicine in New York City, stated: *Our findings suggest that speech-based characteristics can be used to* diagnose *this disease. With further refinement and validation, it may be employed in the clinic in the foreseeable future*.
- In a study conducted with Beyond Verbal, an Israel-based voice analytics company, Mayo Clinic identified 13 voice features associated with coronary artery disease (CAD). One of these is associated with a 19-fold increased likelihood of CAD. Researchers wrote in their poster presentation to the American Heart Association Scientific Session that voice features analysis can assist physicians in estimating the pre-test probability of CAD among patients presenting chest pain, especially in the telemedicine setting.
- Voca AI, specializing in voice assistant development, is working to develop voice technology in partnership with Carnegie Mellon University that could identify people infected with Coronavirus simply by the sound of the voice. The start-up is

collecting data from voice recordings to identify patterns in the speech of those infected.

It is also possible in the future that digital voice assistants, which can identify speech patterns signifying a particular disease or condition, will be able to indicate the development of other diseases such as Alzheimer's disease or dementia. It is because, in these cases, speech patterns are known to deviate from the norm. Thus, specialized voice assistants sensitive enough to pick up these signals could be a significant breakthrough for the pharmaceutical industry.

The healthcare industry is discovering the benefits of voice assistants in increasing efficiency and improving patient experience. As a result, many healthcare brands are utilizing voice technology effectively. Archana Oberoi presents *7 interesting use cases of Voice Assistants in Healthcare* on April 22, 2019, on daffodil.com. Here are the details:

1. *Voice assistants help patients manage diabetes*: Sugarpod is a type 2 diabetes management solution with custom tasks for patients based on their preference.
2. *Assuring medicine adherence for patients*: Non-adherence to medication is a major issue in chronic disease management. Boston-based voice platform start-up *Orbita* has developed an Alexa Skill to resolve this problem. It reminds elders to take the medication on time and helps the family involved in caregiving activities.
3. *Insurance Purchase and Claims Management*: Many people find buying the right healthcare insurance difficult and complex. Liberty Mutual, an American insurance company, developed an Alexa Skill to simplify this. It allows the insurers to navigate their plans and helps manage the policy using Amazon Echo. If the voice assistant fails to find a policy match according to the prospect's profile and budget, it directs the call to an independent agent.
4. *Voice-Activated Instructions for First-Aid*: Mayo Clinic, a non-profit academic medical center, introduced an Alexa Skill that allows its users to get first-aid information. Users can ask relevant questions like, "Alexa, ask Mayo first-aid how do I

treat burn blister?" to get first-aid information.

5. *Health Tips for a Better LifeStyle*: Voice assistants can help users with day-to-day tips for a healthy lifestyle. For example, they can offer tips to treat insomnia, create a diet chart to improve protein intake in the diet, etc. Cleveland Clinic is developing an Alexa Skill for this, allowing its users to take advantage of the vast knowledge base that the academic medical center delivers.
6. *Live Information About the Healthcare Provider*: According to a Deloitte study, average wait times at the doctor's office cost around $43 per person a year. New Hanover Regional Medical Center in northern California has an Alexa Skill for patients to have live updates about the hospital. The users can have real-time information about parking, lost and found information, bill payment details, directions to the hospital, information about the medical center team, availability, etc.
7. *Diagnostic Suggestions Using AI (Artificial Intelligence)*: A visit to a virtual doctor to have an empathic conversation about one's symptoms and disease conditions is no longer science fiction. With AI (Artificial Intelligence)-powered virtual doctor, it is a possibility. Dr. AI Alexa uses artificial intelligence, deep learning, and emotional intelligence to offer diagnostic suggestions to users. The skill leverages the medical know-how and experience of over 107,000 physicians across more than 143 specialties.

The COVID-19 and Digital Assistants

COVID-19 has put tremendous strain on the healthcare systems globally, with virtually no established treatment, an exponential rise in cases, and inadequate resources. Moreover, medical staff is vulnerable to catching the virus. For the industry struggling to cope with the unprecedented crisis of COVID-19, Artificial Intelligence (AI) came as a boon, and the industry rapidly embraced AI and digital assistants with open arms. Consider the rapid strides the industry is making in its adoption of technology:

- For instance, in Singapore, the National University of Health System (NUHS) and BotMD have partnered to launch the NUHS-BotMD Artificial intelligence clinical assistant app for frontline medical staff to access hospital-specific information on COVID-19 guidelines and operational directives quickly. It immediately answers questions from hospital staff about protocols, instructions, drug dosage information, drug formulary, and on-call rosters.
- In 2019, Unified Physician Management rolled out a voice-enabled digital assistant, Suki, that uses Artificial Intelligence(AI) to help doctors with medical charting during patient visits.
- In July 2019, Amazon and the UK government announced Alexa devices would use the NHS (National Health Service) website to provide information to users seeking health advice. Using NHS data will give users the credibility of the source of information and increase their confidence.
- In March 2020, Digital Health Company Babylon launched a new care assistant to help patients during the COVID-19 pandemic. The service provides information and cares for patients according to their needs, allocating doctors' time to patients who need it most. Patients can check their symptoms and consult doctors; the tool also helps people cope with self-isolation.

Here is a case study that shows Merck, a global Pharma major, is planning to use digital assistants in the foreseeable future creatively.

CASE

24

Sugarpod Wins Alexa Diabetes Challenge!

Merck, the global Pharma major, sponsored the Alexa Diabetes Challenge, which called on innovators to create Alexa voice-enabled solutions to improve patients' lives with type 2 diabetes. Alexa is Amazon's voice-activated digital assistant, providing real-time information through devices, including Amazon Echo and Echo Dot. Alexa is one of the several new digital assistants, such as Apple's Siri, Microsoft's Cortana, and Google Assistant.

Speaking about the Alexa Challenge, Tony Alvarez, president of the primary care business line and customer strategy at Merck, said: *Technology advances create digital health opportunities to improve support for people managing their lives with a chronic disease. The principal purpose of the Alexa Diabetes Challenge was to identify new ways to use technology already present in a patient's daily routine*.

The challenge pitted five teams against each other to showcase the potential of voice technology in diabetes care. Each of the five contestants of the Alexa Diabetes Challenge presented a unique way for patients to use the Alexa platform for diabetes management.

1. Sugarpod used an interactive diabetes care plan that included a smart foot scanner.
2. Personal Intelligent Agent (PIA) is an intelligent agent that was NASA-licensed artificial-intelligence technology integrated with the internet of things (IoT) device data.

3. Taming of Type2Diabetes Together (T2D2) is a virtual nutritional assistant.
4. GluCoach is a holistic management solution.
5. DiaBetty is a virtual diabetes educator sensitive to a patient's mood based on acoustics.

Sugarpod Wins the *Alexa Diabetes Challenge*!

Sugarpod, developed by Wellpepper, is a clinically validated platform in digital patient treatment plans that can deliver actionable and highly engaging task-based treatment plans based on personalized protocols for each patient. It won the grand prize of $125,000 in the Alexa Diabetes Challenge.

Sugarpod is an interactive diabetes care plan solution that provides tailored tasks based on patient preferences. The solution is a comprehensive end-to-end plan. According to Annie Weiler, Co-founder and Co-inventor of Sugarpod, the solution's voice, and mobile interactive treatment plans help people newly diagnosed with type 2 diabetes integrate new information and routines into the fabric of their daily lives, self-manage, connect to care and avoid complications. Wellpepper already delivers patient experiences via SMS, email, web, and mobile application. Integrating voice was the natural next step to make the platform more convenient to use at home — where diabetes management mainly occurs.

Sugarpod Weight and Foot Scanner

What is unique about Sugarpod is that it first includes a voice-powered scale and foot scanner that monitors diabetic foot ulcers and takes pictures of the feet. These pictures are classified for the provider, care team, and patient. Why a foot scanner? Because foot complications associated with diabetic peripheral neuropathy can lead to foot ulcers, amputation, increased hospital visits, and deaths and account for up to $9 billion in healthcare costs. By continuously monitoring for foot ulcers, sugarpod can save time and money and improve the quality of life.

Sugarpod's distinct advantage is that it ensures early scanning for patients with neuropathy at the time of diagnosis, and at the same time, patients weigh themselves. Clinicians do not interpret the image; Sugarpod flags foot ulcers and looks for hotspots.

Another significant advantage of Sugarpod is that while paper-based information is overwhelming for the patients, Sugarpod is comprehensive but not overwhelming. As Annie Weiler says, *it breaks down the activities associated with managing type 2 diabetes into manageable, interactive tasks — all personalized for the user and delivered via voice, mobile, or device*.

The prototype of Sugarpod developed for the competition was trained on 370 images of feet and wounds, and 100 people tried it. Sugarpod uses Echo with the user care plan. Besides, a mobile application has several capabilities, such as tracking meals and recording mental health surveys.

Sugarpod was originally conceived as a home device to be used by patients. Still, during the prototype setting, it was determined that the solution could also be used in the clinic for early diagnosis. As a result, the team is developing the device and integrating the voice as a part of the patient care plan.

While commercializing Sugarpod might take some more time as it has to go through the regulatory approval process, one thing is sure. Sugarpod is poised to take personalized diabetes management to the next level.

(Source: Adapted from the article: Alexander M. Castellino, Ph.D., Sugarpod wins Alexa diabetes challenge, Medscape, October 16, 2017)

Possible Threats

Although users increasingly rely on digital assistants as a part of their daily routines, the increased usage is not without threats and risks. One is the monitoring of people's ultimate environment can seem intrusive. Many articles in the media have raised concerns about the devices supposedly listening to private conversations and sharing recordings. In addition, the digital voice assistants may record snippets of audio from homes, potentially making whole new types of data for analysis for companies. Data security threats such as these may hinder the growth of digital assistants. However, companies and developers are working towards overcoming these risks.

Digital Assistants: Future Outlook!

What does the future hold for digital assistants? One thing is for sure. New uses of these devices are likely to emerge as digital voice assistants proliferate. They are indeed increasing at an unprecedented rate. They are expected to cross the human population number of 7.5 billion by 2021. In addition, there will be greater integration of digital assistants' voice user interfaces (VUI) with health applications, significantly improving patient engagement and experience and leading to better outcomes.

As Vinod Khosla, a well-known technologist and investor, posited, almost 80 percent of what human physicians currently do would soon be done instead by technology allowing physicians to focus their time on the essential elements of patient-physician interaction. The AI-powered digital assistants can free doctors a significant amount of time by automating the data generation and consumption tasks in their interactions with repetitive and time-consuming patients.

Norman Winarsky, Author, advisor to start-ups, and investor, presents an overview of what these digital voice assistants could do to assist physicians and patients in health care in a VentureBeat article titled, *What AI-enhanced healthcare could look like in 5 years*.

Digital voice assistants powered by artificial intelligence (AI) technology have the potential to bring a revolutionary change in healthcare. Here are a few examples of what they can do.

- Physicians will practice with artificial intelligence-powered digital assistants using, for example, software tools similar to Apple's Siri but specialized to specific healthcare applications. They will provide real-time and ongoing support and recommendations to the physician for diagnosis and treatment and administrative tasks.
- The digital assistants will enable physicians to treat 5 to times more patients with chronic illnesses as they do today, with better outcomes than in the past.
- The digital voice assistants will have the conversational ability and will support the physician in messaging with patients, answering routine questions, suggesting treatment options, and more.
- AI-powered digital assistants will support patients and healthy individuals in health maintenance with ongoing and real-time intelligent advice.

Winarsky ends his article by painting a metaphoric picture of these digital voice assistants: *Many of today's familiar AI engines personified in Siri, Alexa, Google Assistant, and Cortana are learning as humans learn, and they are in their infancy, just starting to crawl. However, Healthcare digital assistants will soon be able to walk and run. Within the next five years, they will be conversational, learn from the user, maintain context, and provide proactive assistance, to name a few of their emerging capabilities.*

Electronic Health Record (EHR)

An Electronic Health Record is a digital version of a patient's paper chart. EHRs are real-time, patient-centered records that make information available instantly and securely to authorized users. The providers and their staff use EHRs to manage a broad range of patient care, such as administrative, lab test ordering and reporting, prescribing, and patient communication. A complete EHR system includes both patient health records and an e-prescribing interface. Currently, over 90 percent of physicians in the United States are using EHR technologies, according to CMI/Compas Media Vitals Research. The EHR adoption rate in other countries, too, is considerably high. For example, In China, it is at 96 percent, Brazil at 92 percent, Russia at 93 percent, and France at 85 percent. This very high and nearing universal adoption rate means a massive opportunity for pharmaceutical companies to communicate with their target physicians at the point of care. Additionally, with declining access to physicians via sales representatives, EHRs are likely to play a more significant role in the Pharma's engagement with healthcare providers within the patient care setting to stay top-of-mind while prescribing decisions are made.

EHR: An Opportunity for Pharma

EHR offers pharmaceutical companies an excellent opportunity. It can be an additional channel for reaching healthcare professionals (HCPs), providing more tools and resources to physicians when prescribing. Healthcare professionals, including nurses, office staff, and administrators, use an EHR system throughout the day for everything related to their practice management. Physicians also use the EHR in the exam room with the patient present.

Perhaps one of the most important reasons for Pharma to seriously consider EHR in their multichannel strategy is the amount of time physicians spend on EHR systems every day. Manhattan Research indicates that the average time a physician spends using EHR had gone up from 3.3 hours per day in 2015 to 4.3 hours per day in 2017.

The most significant opportunity for pharmaceutical companies is to integrate their messaging to physicians during two key moments:

1. To influence the prescribing decision within the health records, and
2. To reinforce the prescribing decision within the e-prescribing interface

Integration can thus help a brand stay top-of-mind and offer a competitive advantage by addressing specific barriers to treatment such as dosing or cost or increasing awareness of support services. In addition, Pharma marketers can influence physicians' prescribing decisions in two ways; through advertising and technology solutions.

Pharma companies can use banner advertising within either administrative tasks or consultative workflows, which will help in enhancing brand awareness or increasing reminders messages to improve brand recall or assist in identifying appropriate patients. Pharma marketers can target their messages by physician specialty, target list, geography, past prescribing behavior, patient demographics, current therapy, or patient diagnosis.

Pharmaceutical companies can also implement technology solutions at the institutional level assisting the providers in availability checks and decision support services. Angelo Compano, senior vice president, the customer experience at Ogilvy CommonHealth Worldwide, and Kristen Kohler, media director at CMI Media, suggest the opportunities available for Pharma to influence and reinforce the prescribing decision and promote adherence in their April 2018 white paper titled, *An EHR Overview for Pharma Marketers*:

Banner ads within the e-prescribing interface triggered by selected therapy and potentially layering geographic, access, or diagnosis targeting:

- Integration of e-coupons, enrollment forms, or printed patient education materials
- Prior-authorization assistance technologies
- Closed-Loop pharmacy programs
- Discharge paper sponsorships

Advertising within EHR

While EHRs offer a big opportunity for pharmaceutical companies to reach their target audience with their marketing messages when prescribing, many EHR platforms do not allow brand promotion. Those that do have been historically limited to banners and text ads. Pharma companies, therefore, need to approach EHR advertising creatively and follow the best practices. Pharmaceutical companies actively using the EHR platforms for advertising are repurposing their digital banner ads. However, physicians prefer messages that make their workflow more efficient and provide more value in patient interactions.

Analyze your audience to identify their needs. Also, it would help if you explored tactics your competitors do not currently use. The best approach is to go back to marketing basics, taking your audience into account first and foremost. Always focus on physician and patient needs. Start with a few fundamental questions:

1. How is your audience engagement across the healthcare IT landscape?
2. How can your brand bring value to the HCPs and Patients at the point of care?
3. What information does your target audience want? Need?
4. Discuss with all key stakeholders such as partners, brand teams, and service teams, and determine what integration (not promotion) opportunities exist.

EHR advertising needs a different approach. Do not bombard and turn physicians off with your brand promotional messages. Instead, provide value to physicians and patients with clinical information and resources. Focusing on the needs of the physicians and patients instead of just promotional messages will create and enhance the perceived value of your brand in their minds. Make your brand communication highly relevant to the needs of your target audiences in terms of tone, brevity, and visual appeal. Always use an active voice. Avoid vagueness. Support your brand claims with supporting data. Do not use acronyms. Persuade, do not demand. Liz Sporrer and Samantha Bogus of CMI Media Inc. suggest some important points in their September 2015 blog article on cmimedia.com titled, *Electronic Health Records and Pharmaceutical Advertising*, which offer simple yet powerful tips to follow while advertising within EHRs:

- Keep messages short and to the point, with a clear call-to-action (CTA)
- Use active verbs combined with time statements (example: Send today)
- Use brand names upfront, be as clear as possible, and ensure regulatory compliance.
- Design visually distinct banners to grab attention
- Refresh creative often to avoid wearing out
- Provide solutions to the problems that patients may face at the point of prescribing (example: highlight common side-effects and provide treatment suggestions, suggest supportive therapy, and offer financial assistance such as coupons, discounts, and others).

These messaging factors have proven their effectiveness. According to CMI, when you take all of these messaging factors into account for a brand campaign across two partners, the brand's EHR prescribing increased by 388 percent throughout the six-month campaign. At the same time, the prescribing of its competitor decreased by 36 percent.

What is the success principle for brand messaging within the EHR system? Can it be distilled into one axiom? Yes, and it is this: Rather than focusing on glossy promotional messaging, focus on better equipping HCPs with necessary information as they navigate their EHR system. It means providing patient instructions, informing how brands are coded in specific systems, formulary coverage information, pictures of devices such as inhalers and injectables for use, trial-based evidence, and drug initiation and titration recommendations. In a capsule, your messaging should deliver value to the physicians and patients.

Two Examples

Pharma marketers need to understand that they have to approach EHR platforms as distinct marketing channels rather than marketing tactics. Therefore, they need to formulate a strategy for EHR platforms. Beth Snyder Bulik describes how two pharmaceutical companies have successfully used Electronic Health Records (EHR) platform to promote their brands in her Fierce Pharma article titled, *Ogilvy CommonHealth takes deep dive on EHR as a marketing strategy for Pharma clients* published on May 9, 2016.

1. A large pharmaceutical company decided to promote one of its hospital antibiotics using the EHR platform. The company wanted to remind providers about the drug at the point of care, and EHR was its strategy. Beginning with 320 hospital targets, the Pharma company and its distribution partners found 192 active EHR systems users and targeted messages to them. The results were more than encouraging. The EHR program achieved a 28 percent engagement rate with physicians in the first month, followed by 36 percent and 26 percent in the following two months – the first three of an ongoing six-month campaign. The key takeaway for the company is that in the closed system of EHRs, whether cloud-based or enterprise software means, the marketing and communications from Pharma to physicians are not scattershot web ads but much more targeted inside communications that can inform doctors at a critical moment.
2. Practice Fusion, a cloud-based EHR provider, offers the second example. Practice Fusion launched an obesity clinical decision support program. The EHR notified physicians with messages at the point of care about recording patients' Body Mass Index (BMI) stats and, if high, noting a treatment plan. The program reached over 50,000 physicians and 3.7 million patients resulting in 25,000 Plus more patient plans, a five-fold increase. The key insights from this are best summed up by Dorothy Gemmell, senior vice president of life science practice, and strategic partnerships at Practice Fusion, when she said: *As*

healthcare moves from volume-based to value-based, novel solutions are needed to drive better outcomes. The (big) data will eventually help identify how certain treatment plans may improve weight management.

Two Cases

AstraZeneca, a global Pharma major, has been making pioneering efforts in exploring the Electronic Health Record platform to provide value-added information to improve patient adherence in chronic disease conditions such as asthma and COPD (chronic obstructive pulmonary disease). Here are two cases highlighting AstraZeneca's initiatives in the EHR space.

CASE

25

Geisinger and AstraZeneca Create New Asthma App Suite!

Geisinger, one of America's most innovative health services research organizations, and AstraZeneca, a global Pharma major, partnered to improve asthma care by creating a suite of products integrated into electronic health records (EHR). The new app aims to engage patients and providers in co-managing the disease, especially during intervals between office visits. The partnership uses scientific expertise from both companies in disease management, patient engagement, adherence, healthcare innovation, research, and technology to fundamentally redesign how asthma patients are diagnosed and treated.

The mobile app connects the data to a real-time, web-based application called Provider Asthma Management Assistant. The assistant combines EHR, and patient-reported data feeds to enable asthma educators and respiratory therapists to triage patients on the fly and bring specialists as needed.

Asthma symptoms can be unpredictable, and breathing issues don't always occur in the doctor's office. Therefore, a tool to help patients and physicians stay connected and share information is immensely useful. That's what connected health is all about. The partnership between AstraZeneca and Geisinger focuses on how they can help patients and physicians with digital tools for speeding up diagnosis and treatment decisions.

The new asthma app suite includes a mobile app that allows patients to view asthma-related weather forecasts, log symptoms and asthma triggers, establish medication reminders, track health status over time, and, more importantly, communicate with their healthcare team.

While describing the unique benefits of the app suite, Paul Simonelli, MD, Ph.D., Chair of Pulmonary and Critical Care Medicine at Geisinger, explained: *Patients sometimes do a lot worse with their asthma than we know based on three to six or nine-month periodic visits. Therefore, it is easy for this new suite of products to adapt to any long-term chronic respiratory illness that needs monitoring, including COPD (Chronic Obstructive Pulmonary Disease).*

Some asthma patients may have multiple attacks per week, and it is not feasible or necessary to see a doctor every time. With the new app suite, attacks and symptoms can be tracked and easily monitored in real-time by the full spectrum of the healthcare team.

(Source: Geisinger Caring, News Release, July 17, 2018)

CASE

26

Time for an Asthma Check, Doc?!

In 2015, AstraZeneca, a global Pharma major, acquired a couple of respiratory products — Tudorza Pressair and Daliresp from Actavis. Although Forest Labs developed both these products, Actavis acquired them in 2014. Tudorza Pressair (aclidinium bromide inhalation powder) is an anti-cholinergic used in the long-term maintenance treatment of bronchospasm associated with chronic obstructive pulmonary disease (COPD), including chronic bronchitis and emphysema. Daliresp (roflumilast) is a prescription medicine used in adults with severe COPD to decrease the number of flare-ups or worsening of COPD symptoms.

To strengthen its respiratory product portfolio, AstraZeneca acquired the respiratory business of Almirall, a Spanish pharmaceutical company, for US $2.2 billion, including a combo med Duaklir (aclidinium bromide and formoterol fumarate dihydrate inhalation powder). Duaklir is used to relieve symptoms of chronic COPD in adult patients. The competition in the respiratory therapeutic area was very intense. Long-term respiratory rival GlaxoSmithKline (GSK) was launching several brand new products.

To reinforce its position in the respiratory segment, AstraZeneca thought of a beyond-the-pill strategy. So it teamed up with Practice Fusion, a San Francisco-based company that developed a free electronic health record (EHR) system for physicians as software as a service (SaaS). The software, also called Practice Fusion, includes modules for patient management, e-prescribing, scheduling, and billing.

Physicians who use Practice Fusion for their health records know the software alerts them when certain patients need checkups or shots. In addition, AstraZeneca has funded a new program designed especially for asthma and COPD management. The new AstraZeneca program identifies current asthma or COPD patients who have not met specific clinical guidelines. The software then creates an advisory on each patient's EHR (Electronic Health Record). When clicked open, that advisory lists the funding source in the third line: AstraZeneca.

With AstraZeneca alerts program, doctors can check aggregate data on their asthma and COPD patient populations, including the percentage diagnosed with each condition. They can see how their patients stack up against other Practice Fusion groups. The program shows the percentage of patients meeting clinical guidelines compared with the Practice Fusion average.

Patient management features of Practice Fusion include:

- A library of shared charts for physicians within a practice or network.
- A live feed of patients' medical and diagnostic history.
- Lab tests.
- Immunization records.
- Centers for Disease Control (CDC) growth charts.

In addition, the e-prescribing feature maintains a patient prescription history and includes a medication library from which physicians can add custom medication. Also, there is an email feature for drug information and dosage instruction.

The asthma advisory sponsored by AstraZeneca is one of the fourteen Clinical Decision Support (CDS) systems that Practice Fusion can note in its EHR system. The electronic notes appear at the top of a patient's digital record. Various factors trigger the notes in the patient's medical records, such as history, chronic conditions, previous diagnoses, and demographics.

The majority of the advisories are typical Physician Quality Reporting System (PQRS) items that remind doctors and nurses to ask certain questions or follow up upon screenings. For example, they nudge HCPs about eye and foot exams for diabetics, documentation on allergies, medication, and screening or follow-ups on a patient's body mass index (BMI).

Practice Fusion comes in two versions. A free version for the physicians gets its revenue by showing relevant pharmaceutical advertisements to its users. In addition, Google provides targeted ads based on patients' conditions. Physicians who do not want to participate in the ad-supported version can use the subscription-based version by paying a monthly fee.

Programs like these empower HCPs (Health Care Practitioners) with data giving them a qualified view of their patient's health, which ultimately has the potential to help them identify at-risk patients and promote treatment compliance.

(Source: Adapted from the article: Tracy Staton, Time for an asthma check, doc? AstraZeneca-sponsored EHR reminder will tell you, Fierce Pharma, April 29, 2015)

Insights are Important

The widespread implementation of digital record keeping has revealed new opportunities for life sciences companies. Extensive segmentation is now possible and starts with access to up-to-date details on healthcare providers. Pharmaceutical companies need current email addresses and institutional affiliations to facilitate appropriate direct messaging. When marketing and salespeople are served with demographic and specific hospitals or doctors, they can tailor their emails appropriately.

EHRs (Electronic Health Records) can offer even more and greater insights. The more pharma companies know about the conditions doctors treat and the products they use, the more effectively they can customize and send relevant messages tying treatment information from the insurance claims to details drawn from EHRs, giving marketing a huge advantage.

Pharma marketers should be alert to spot emerging opportunities from the shifts in everyday record-keeping, diagnostics, and prescriptions brought by EHRs and practice management systems (PMS). With the knowledge that marketers gain from the relevant business intelligence, marketers and salespeople can communicate more reliably with healthcare professionals and offer product information most relevantly.

EHR: The Way Forward

Previously considered a tactic within our point-of-care digital plans, Electronic Health Record (EHR) space, with increasing adoption, soon emerged as a separate channel with unique advantages. EHR allows Pharma marketers to showcase the product value throughout the patient journey while supporting HCPs within their daily workflows. Therefore, EHR is a medium worth considering for Pharma brands in all stages of their lifecycle.

The growth of Electronic Health Records (EHRs), including efforts such as the drive to e-prescriptions led by substance abuse prevention efforts, resulted in a whopping 2 billion prescriptions in

2016. Besides improving the physicians' workflow effectiveness, EHR is also growing in importance as a marketing strategy. Therefore, pharmaceutical companies need to start exploring and experimenting with this emerging marketing channel.

EHRs have evolved today from being a tactic among the digital plans of pharmaceutical companies into a separate channel by themselves. It has emerged as a unique point of care channel. You cannot rely on standard advertising opportunities such as banners and text links to reach HCPs in this channel. Instead, it would be best to showcase your value proposition throughout the patient journey while supporting HCPs within their daily workflow. Such an approach to building strategic partnerships helps pharma companies to serve physicians best.

EHRs continue to show an upward usage trend, and the high ROI of campaigns and proven success metrics validate that it's a medium to watch and worth considering for brands in all stages of their lifecycle.

If you have not yet adopted EHR as a marketing channel in your strategy, consider what William J. Febbo, CEO of EHR service provider, Optimize Rx, said: *If you're not too late today, you will be by this time— next year.*

Telehealth

What is Telehealth?

The American Academy of Family Physicians defines Telehealth as a broad collection of electronic and telecommunication technologies and services that support at-a-distance healthcare delivery and services.

The Covid-19 pandemic has largely driven Telehealth and is increasing rapidly. As a result, the point of care is rapidly shifting from in-person appointments to digital channels like telemedicine visits, remote monitoring, and virtual consultations. In addition, regulatory support, technological advancements, and the need to reduce patient exposure to the new coronavirus are accelerating this shift.

When you think of it, Telehealth is more than a channel for delivering care. Instead, it reflects a fundamental shift in how brands reach patients and physicians. Until now, the focus of brand marketing has been on in-person delivery of care specific to geographical locations like sales territories, DMA (Direct Market Access), and managed care tactics. In contrast, geography is less significant in Telehealth, making digital marketing more critical.

The Telehealth Way

How does Telehealth work? There are two ways in which physicians provide Telehealth services to patients. One is that there are vertically integrated virtual practices like *PlushCare* or *98point6*. And then, there are brick-and-mortar offices, where physicians provide Telehealth services by signing up with companies providing Telehealth services like Teladoc Health or Amwell to deliver Telehealth during their off hours or by offering Telehealth services to existing patients in place of in-person visits using zoom, FaceTime, and other teleconference platforms. In addition, the Practices using teleconference platforms like Zoom and others are rapidly integrating their workflows and EMR (Electronic Medical Record) systems into these platforms.

The rise of Telehealth with all its virtual consultations, reminders, and mobile health, among other services, has important implications for pharmaceutical companies. Consider these, for example:

- As digital pharmacies and the market for direct-to-consumer prescription services continue to grow, many patients will obtain their prescriptions through an online provider. So companies must re-evaluate their supply chain strategy and technologies.
- Telehealth can contribute to combating patient non-adherence with services like smartphone apps, emails, or e-health platforms providing usage directions and alerts to remind patients to take their medications regularly. In addition, pharma companies can think of partnering with Telehealth companies to improve patient adherence.
- Telehealth platforms could provide a site of exchange for Pharma marketers and HCPs (Healthcare Professionals) where they can provide relevant and timely information. It can be a good opportunity for engaging prescribers and patients. Pharma, of course, has to tread this space cautiously owing to regulatory concerns and ensure compliance.

Although it is COVID-19 that pushed healthcare to a new frontier, Telehealth, it has now been so ingrained in the delivery of care, so there is no going back. Therefore, Pharma should rethink and adapt its sales and marketing approach to the fast-growing Telehealth platform. Victoria Summers and Vijesh Unnikrishnan suggest six ways to tap into the opportunities that Telehealth offer in their insightful zs.com blog article, *While Telehealth Continues to Evolve, Pharma Needs to Keep an Eye on the Future*. Here's the gist:

1. **Factor Telehealth into Your Annual Plans**: Include Telehealth in your annual marketing plans, including territory mapping and sales force alignment. You can understand which physicians are engaging in Telehealth and how much of their practice is via Telehealth and in-person through claims analysis. This information can help your representatives to plan a mix of in-person and virtual details accordingly. Also, you may plan a

key account management strategy for large Telehealth platforms and virtual practices. In addition, you can engage physicians and patients with relevant messages and materials by including the *next-best action* artificial intelligence (AI) algorithms in Telehealth as a trigger to provide digital educational and patient materials.

2. **Adapt a Patient-centric marketing Strategy for the Telehealth Platform**: Explore the media opportunities in Telehealth, such as virtual waiting room messages, ads, and digital materials. It is important to restructure the content and align the tactical calendar with Telehealth partners to engage with physicians and patients effectively.
3. **Understand the Role of Telehealth in the Customer Journe**y: Telehealth can help activate patients early in their treatment journey in some therapeutic areas. And Telehealth can play an important role in follow-up and adherence in some chronic diseases like diabetes, for example, by replacing some of the frequent in-person visits. It is critical to understand whether and when Telehealth can play an important role in a patient's journey so you can map the patient experience with Telehealth to augment and improve the patient experience.
4. **Customize Content**: Integrating customer-centric messages with Telehealth triggers to drive highly relevant messages to patients after a Telehealth visit can be very useful in accelerating patient consideration. Also, you can customize the content differently for patients using Telehealth and those who don't. Further customization by patient type (new patient vs. those who have been on therapy for a while), geography, or type of insurance coverage can make your communication specific to patients' needs.
5. **Use Digital Engagement to Improve Customer Outcomes**: You can use Telehealth to help patients to start and stay on treatment. For some therapies, Telehealth support is more effective in activating patients by answering patients or providing a link to physicians. For others, it can be very helpful in adhering to a treatment plan. You can prioritize your

Telehealth efforts and programs by understanding where telehealth can provide maximum impact. For instance, you can increase enrollment, fulfillment, and adherence by integrating copay cards, remote monitoring, and patient support programs with Telehealth.

6. **Measure What Matters**: Whenever you add a new channel to the marketing and support landscape, you generate new data, which increases measurement opportunities. It is important to monitor various types of data from claims processing, platform usage, patient and physician satisfaction, and prescribing behavior to get the big picture. The important areas to monitor are:

- Measuring the Telehealth platform messages in *Virtual Waiting Rooms* to learn what resonates with patients.
- Account for the patients enrolling on Telehealth platforms who do not have primary care providers, as these disengaged patients provide a new opportunity.
- Appointment compliance rates and treatment rates with Telehealth to design virtual-friendly treatments to drive patient engagement.

Challenges

While Telehealth is highly promising, it is not without challenges. However, its acceleration does have some speed bumps. Shiv Rao, MD, the co-founder, and CEO of Abridge, a company focusing on bringing context and understanding to every medical conversation, observed three challenges in implementing Telehealth in his article, *Industry Voices— 3 Challenges Exposed in the New World of Telehealth (and how to overcome them)* published on fiercehealthcare.com. on August 10, 2020. Here are the three challenges:

1. **Access**: Internet access is an issue for many people. In the US, for example, more than a quarter of people 65 years of age and older say that they don't use the internet, and for about 21 percent of rural Americans, access to high-speed internet is an issue. If this is the case in a first-world country, the situation will not likely improve in emerging and developing

countries. Therefore, video conferencing is not an option for everyone. In addition, mobile data could be very expensive for some populations. So, how can we overcome this? Providers should include traditional phone calls and text messaging to deliver Telehealth services and healthcare education. A text-based conversation is preferable as opposed to waiting for a doctor to appear on screen, which could be 20-plus minutes from the time a patient logs on.

2. **Recall**: At-home distraction can be an issue with Telehealth. The distracting factors could be many. Consider, for example; the TV may be too loud; children may need attention; a patient's dog could be barking uncontrollably, and many more negatively impact how well patients comprehend and follow the information and advice that the physicians give. As it is, it is already difficult for patients to remember everything their providers cover during a visit, and Telehealth can make it even worse. Telehealth could introduce a system where physicians can quickly summarize key takeaways for patients to overcome this problem of comprehension and recall.
3. **Coordination**: Patients, particularly seniors, usually bring a family member to clinical consults to help them better understand the conversation. As social distancing measures introduced during COVID-19 are still in effect, this isn't easy to do for Telehealth and in-person appointments. At the same time, as Harvard Public Health Review puts it, the quality of care health workers provide doesn't matter if patients don't understand what they're being told. Therefore, coordinating care and keeping people on the same page is a significant factor in positive outcomes. How to do this? By tracking the dialogue between patients and doctors. Providers can make care coordination more seamless and efficient if they can create a record of what was discussed and the next steps in the patient's care pathway.

Reimagine Strategy

Finally, Pharma has a significant opportunity to be at the forefront of delivering great patient value as the point-of-care shifts to a digital on-demand model. Pharmaceutical companies must quickly reimagine and adapt their sales and marketing strategy to maximize this opportunity. To do this, Pharma must shift its mindset from traditional thinking and upend the go-to-market strategy. And the time to transform is, Now!

Digital Therapeutics (DTx)

Digital Health Landscape

The Digital revolution has been sweeping across the industries, including healthcare, for some time, forcing businesses to reimagine their processes to be online and automated. Therefore, it is important to understand the digital landscape before we discuss digital therapeutics.

What is the digital universe, and how do we define digital health? Digital health is healthcare companies utilizing information technology (IT) or software as a primary means of differentiation. The companies cover the entire spectrum of the healthcare sector, addressing all three key stakeholders— payers, providers, and patients.

The companies working in digital health are spread across a wide range, from start-ups to established unicorn companies (that reach a valuation of $1 billion without being listed on the stock market) to large conglomerates such as Google and Apple. The following table presents a snapshot of the digital health landscape.

Table 2.16 Digital Therapeutics Landscape

Pharma	Providers	Insurance & Benefits	Consumer Health & Wellness
Digital Thera-peutics • Supply chain • R&D (Real-world Evidence and clinical trial support	• Telemedicine & virtual visits (primary and specialty care) • Electronic Medical Record (EMR) systems • Clinical Decision Support (CDS)	**Consumer-focused health and coverage** • Stride Health • Bright Health • League • Devoted Health • Oscar • Modern Health	**Wearables & Wireless devices** **Wellness, Fitness trackers and Nutrition Apps** • Dreem • Citizen • Headspace • Lumosity • Calm

Table 2.16 *Contd...*

Pharma	Providers	Insurance & Benefits	Consumer Health & Wellness
DTx Companies • Pear Thera-peutics • Omada Health • Akili Inter-active • Livongo Health • Proteus	**Providers** • American Well • Lyra Health • One Medical • Healthverity • Babylon • Quartet • TallSpace	**Genomics** **DNA genetic testing** **Early cancer detection** • Nebula Genomics • Freenome • Nomad • 23andMe • Grail	**Diagnostics** **Imaging** **Pathology** • PathAI • Butterfly Network • Aldoc HeartFlow • Proscia

Source: Digital Therapeutics and the Future of Pharma, A Report by Torreya, February 2020

What are Digital Therapeutics (DTx)?

Digital Therapeutic Alliance, a global non-profit trade association of industry leaders and stakeholders engaged in advancing evidence-driven digital therapeutics, defines Digital Therapeutics (DTX) as *products that deliver evidence-based therapeutic interventions driven by high-quality software programs to prevent, manage, or treat medical disorders or disease*. They are used independently or in concert with medications, devices, or other therapies to optimize patient care and health outcomes.

Digital therapeutic products empower patients, clinicians, and payers with intelligent and accessible tools for addressing various conditions through high-quality, safe, and effective, data-driven interventions.

How do digital therapeutics help patients? Patients engage with digital Therapeutics through mobile apps that:

- Offer basic guidance, such as techniques to overcome insomnia or administer first aid.
- Work in conjunction with a drug regimen in complex conditions like asthma or cancer treatment

- Use cognitive or motivational stimulation (gamification) to promote behavioral change to improve adherence and help healthcare institutions to delay or prevent the onset of chronic disease by providing preventative measures.
- Connect with wearables and consumer electronics to track and capture data and communicate with patients
- Interface with medical equipment, such as tracking blood sugar levels, by picking up wireless signals from sensors embedded in the patient's skin

Furthermore, digital Therapeutics can collect, synthesize, and analyze patients to help physicians personalize treatment and work with patients to avoid complications.

Digital Therapeutics (DTX): Product Types

Digital therapeutics utilizes software or applications to treat diseases and may include ancillary components such as connected hardware device(s), adjunctive pharmacotherapy, or live clinical support. However, the software component could still drive meaningful outcomes as an independent contributor to treatment.

Unlike traditional pharmacological therapeutics, digital therapeutics typically have shorter development and commercialization timelines and smaller investments. They may or may not require FDA approval depending upon the type of product.

There are two types of digital therapeutics— Monotherapy or Standalone and Combination products.

Monotherapy or Standalone products are software or application-only products.

Combination products can be subdivided into:

- *Companion products* do not usually require FDA approval and can be used to treat a condition alongside pharmacological products and HCP (Healthcare Professional) treatment.
- *Combination products* are applications or sensors designed to be used in conjunction with a specific pharmacological product, such as (a type of insulin).

- *Adjunct products* are apps or sensors that are designed to be used with pharmacological intervention (such as all types of insulins) or HCP treatment.

Here is a table that presents some examples of these two broad categories of digital therapeutics.

Table 2.17 Digital Therapeutics (DTX): Broad Categories and Examples

Monotherapy Products		Combination Products	
1. Akili	Adaptive sensory stimulus software delivered via a video game for ADHD, autism, major depressive disorder (MDD), multiple sclerosis (MS) and inflammatory diseases	1. Chrono Therapeutics	Transdermal drug delivery wearable that integrates biologically timed drug delivery with personalized data support
2. Big Health	Automated and personalized cognitive behavioral programs for mental health, including insomnia and anxiety	2. Glooko	Diabetes software products providing insights to improve outcomes for people with diabetes and their care teams
3. Med-Rhythms	Uses neurologic music therapy via a combination of sensors, music, and AI (Artificial Intelligence) to measure and improve walking	3. Propeller	Digital companion connected to inhaled medication devices for asthma and COPD (Chronic Pulmonary Obstructive Disease) that transmits data to patients, physicians and healthcare organzations

Table 2.17 *Contd...*

Monotherapy Products		Combination Products	
4. Click Thera-peutics	Proprietary cognitive and neurobehavioral platform that optimizes user engagement for a variety of indications, including MDD (Major Depressive Disorder) migraine, insomnia and acute coronary syndrome (ACS)	4. Proteus	Formulates digital drugs with ingestible sensors to communicate when ingested via a wearable patch that captures physiologic response, apps to support patient and physician decision making in cardiovascular and infectious disease
5. Welldoc	Welldoc's BlueStar® helps guide individuals with chronic diseases like type 2 diabetes by helping them self-manage their conditions , while connecting them to their healthcare team	5. Voluntis	Mobile and web apps to deliver personalized recommendations to the patient and the care team so that they can, for example, adjust treatment dosage, manage side effects or monitory symptoms in diabetes and oncology

Source: Digital Therapeutics and the Future of Pharma, A Report by Torreya, February 2020

DTx and Therapeutic Areas

Digital therapeutics demonstrated their potential to favorably impact CNS (Central Nervous System) and other chronic disorders. For example, the impact can be seen in two main areas within CNS—behavioral mediated disorders like depression, anxiety, insomnia, panic attacks, ADHD (Attention-Deficit Hyperactivity Disorder), Parkinson's, and stroke recovery. Also, digital therapeutics could be used to manage chronic disorders such as diabetes, asthma, COPD (Chronic Obstructive Pulmonary Disease), and other cardio-metabolic conditions, which need significant behavioral, lifestyle, and drug compliance.

Value Beyond the Pill

Digital Therapeutics can help Pharma improve patient outcomes and performance in several ways. Consider these, for example. Digital Therapeutics can:

- Help Pharma address unmet patient needs that traditional treatments and therapies have been unable to provide.
- Enable pharmaceutical and biotech companies to differentiate products with a relatively low capital investment compared with R&D costs usually associated with the development of a new drug or medical device
- Help extend product lifecycles and differentiate products in development.

Considering these potential benefits and the value beyond the pill that digital Therapeutics offers pharmaceutical companies in improving their competitive edge, they must seriously consider including digital Therapeutics in their product strategies.

Digital Therapeutics (DTx): Ten Foundational Principles

Digital Therapeutics can be used independently or with medication, devices, and other therapies to treat physical and behavioral health conditions, including pain, diabetes, anxiety, post-traumatic stress disorder (PTSD), and asthma.

Five years ago, people had questions about their efficacy when digital Therapeutics were still being tested and validated. Therefore, the Digital Therapeutic Alliance, the trade association of digital therapeutic companies, laid down ten foundational principles to which a digital therapeutic must adhere. These are:

Table 2.18 DTx: Ten Foundation Principles

1. Prevent, manage or treat a medical disorder or disease
2. Produce a medical intervention that is driven by software
3. Incorporate design, manufacture, and quality best practices
4. Engage end users in product development and usability processes
5. Incorporate patient privacy and security protections
6. Apply product deployment, management, and maintenance best practices
7. Publish trial results inclusive of clinically meaningful outcomes in peer-reviewed journals
8. Be reviewed or cleared, or certified by regulatory bodies as required to support product claims of risk, efficacy, and intended use
9. Make claims appropriate to clinical evaluation and regulatory status
10. Collect, analyze, and apply real-world evidence and product performance data

Source: Digital Therapeutic Alliance Website, digitaltherapeuticalliance.org

Three Main Categories

According to Digital Therapeutic Alliance, there are three main product categories for digital Therapeutics: products to treat a disease, manage a condition, and improve a health function. DTx products that meet Industry Core Principles are generally classified into one of the three categories based on the product's primary purpose. Furthermore, all products, irrespective of their categories, must deliver a therapeutic intervention and use clinical endpoints to support product claims.

The following table presents details of these three product categories of digital Therapeutics:

Table 2.19 Digital Therapeutics (DTX)Categories

	Disease-Treating DTx Products	Disease-Managing DTx Products	Health Function-Improving DTx Products
Clinical Endpoints	Must deliver a therapeutic intervention and use clinical end points to support product claims	Must deliver a therapeutic intervention and use clinical endpoints to support product claims	Must deliver a therapeutic intervention and use clinical end points to support product claims

Table 2.19 *Contd...*

	Disease-Treating DTx Products	Disease-Managing DTx Products	Health Function-Improving DTx Products
Clinical Evidence	Clinical trials and ongoing evidence generation required	Clinical trials and ongoing evidence generation required	Clinical trials and ongoing evidence generation required
Level of Medical Claims	Medium to high risk claims	Medium to high risk claims	Low to medium risk claims
Regul-atory Over-sight	Third-party validation of efficacy and safety claims by regulatory or equivalent national body	Third-party validation of efficacy and safety claims by regulatory or equivalent national body	Degree of oversight depends on local regulatory frameworks
Patient Access	Prescription	Non-prescription or prescription	Non-prescription or prescription

Source: Digital Therapeutic Alliance Website, digitaltherapeuticalliance.org

Benefits All Stakeholders

Why is it that Pharma is very keen on embracing digital therapeutics? That is because digital therapeutics significantly benefit all stakeholders. Here is a table presenting digital therapeutics' benefits to all stakeholders— patients, Pharma, Payers, Providers, and health systems.

Table 2.20 Digital Therapeutics (DTx) Benefits All Stakeholders

Patient Benefits	Pharma Benefits	Payer Benefits	Provider and Health System Benefits
• On-demand or easy access to treatment and care	• More favorable risk/reward product development with higher PTRS (Probability of Technical and	• Improved clinical and health economic outcomes and reduction in overall medical costs, including decreased HCP	• Digital therapeutics can be used as a monotherapy or in concert with other therapies to optimize patient care and health outcomes

Table 2.20 *Contd...*

Patient Benefits	Pharma Benefits	Payer Benefits	Provider and Health System Benefits
• Personalized treatment programs, using machine learning and AI (Artificial Intelligence) to continuously update and tailor software to meet patient needs based on real-tine data and analytics • Increased access to evidence-based interventions	• Regulatory Success) and shorter timeframe for product development • Potential for increased patient compliance to pharmacological interventions • Increased direct and earlier patient engagement	and reduction in pharmacological intervention • Improvement in overall health and wellness and disease prevention • Compelling safety profile could be a step-edit before pharmacological intervention	• Increased access to novel treatment options

Source: Digital Therapeutics and the Future of Pharma, A Report by Torreya, February 2020

DTx and Pharma

Realizing the many benefits that digital therapeutics offer to all healthcare stakeholders, leading pharmaceutical companies have collaborated with several DTx companies. The following table presents an overview of important Digital-Biopharma deals in the last few years.

Table 2.21 Significant Digital Therapeutics (DTx)-Biopharma Deals

Pharma Company	DTx Company	Purpose
1. Astellas	Welldoc	• Jointly develop and commercialize BlueStar® in Japan and certain other Asian markets for patients with diabetes, collaborate to broaden the adoption of BlueStar in the US, and jointly develop and commercialize digital therapeutics in other therapeutic areas globally • Astellas will make an upfront payment of $15 million to Welldoc, as well as development and commercialization milestones and royalties on future sales
2. Ironwood	Pear Therapeutics	• Evaluate prescription digital therapeutics for selected indications within the gastrointestinal space
3. Abbott	Omada Health	• Integrate Abbott's FreeStyle Libre system, a continuous glucose monitoring technology, with Omada Health's pioneering digital care program
4. Novo Nordisk	Noom	• Collaboration on digital health solutions focusing on weight management • Follows a successful 8-month pilot that combined Noom's behavior change programs with Novo Nordisk's experience with chronic diseases
5. Bayer	OneDrop	• Bayer led $40 million Series B financing • Commercial licensing deal for Bayer to use OneDrop's platform in Bayer's global bio-digital efforts in oncology, cardiovascular disease and women's health
6. Sanofi	Happify	• Focusing on developing app-based solutions for management and improvement of physical outcomes in people with multiple sclerosis (MS)

Table 2.21 ***Contd...***

Pharma Company	DTx Company	Purpose
7. Orexo	Gaia	• Orexo has partnered with Gaia to create a new digital therapy for people with opioid use disorder (OUD) which is expected to launch in the US in 2022 • Orexo to carry out clinical development, regulatory approval and commercialization, while Gaia is eligible for royalties, milestone payments and compensation during development
8. SHIONOGI	Akili	• Shionogi oversees clinical development, sales and marketing for ADHD and Autism Spectrum Disorder digital therapeutics in Japan and Taiwan • Upfront, development and potential milestones for commercialization valued up to $125 million
9. Otsuka	Click Therapeutics	• To develop and commercialize a prescription digital therapeutic (PDT) for MDD (Major Depressive Disorder) • Upfront, development and potential milestones for commercialization up to $302 million • Click Therapeutics will receive double-digit royalties on global sales

Digital Therapeutics (DTx) in Use: Some Examples

Over the last few years many digital therapeutic products have been developed under the three categories discussed above. Here are some notable examples of DTx products approved by US FDA and are in use.

Table 2.22 Digital Therapeutics Approved by US FDA: Some Examples

1. **Kaia Health** offers MSK Solution, a musculoskeletal digital therapeutic focusing on pain relief. The DTX solution guides patients through physical therapy using an algorithm to evaluate performance and adapt exercises to patient needs. It also connects users to coaches and medical providers when necessary.

Table 2.22 *Contd...*

2. **Applied VR** became the first company to receive US FDA approval in 2021 for its *EaseVRx*, a virtual reality (VR)-based digital therapeutic for pain relief. *EaseVRX* is a virtual reality headset preloaded with software content that guides chronic low back pain patients through an eight-week program. According to one study, *EaseVRX* users reported an average 42 percent reduction in pain.
3. **Omada Health's** digital therapeutic solution, *Prevent® Program*, combines data from continuous glucose monitoring devices with virtual physician visits, peer support, and health coaches to improve diabetics' health metrics. In addition, it shows that digitally enabled self-management education and support can improve hemoglobin A1C levels and medication adherence.
4. **Better Therapeutics**, a prescription digital therapeutics (PDT) company, provides a form of cognitive behavioral therapy focused on nutrition (nCBT) to improve outcomes among people with type 2 diabetes.
5. **Akili Interactive** uses gamification to provide a prescription video game treatment, *EndeavorRX*, to improve attention function in children with attention-deficit/hyperactivity disorder (ADHD). The treatment deploys sensory stimuli and motor challenges to target and activate specific networks in the brain. According to a study, A novel digital intervention for actively reducing the severity of a pediatric ADHD (STARS_ADHD): a randomized control trial, published in Lancet Digital Health on February 24, 2020, *EndeavorRx* improved objective attention in children with ADHD between 8 and 12 years.
6. **Freespira** provides the only FDA-cleared, evidence-based, medication-free digital therapeutic that incorporates a sensor, a physiological feedback display, and coaching to help patients alleviate anxiety attacks and post-traumatic stress disorder symptoms. Research shows that 93 percent of users experienced a clinically significant reduction in panic symptoms one-year post-treatment.
7. **Pear Therapeutics** focuses on substance use disorders and provides two digital therapeutics— Reset and Reset-O to treat substance and opiate disorders, respectively. They are 12-week programs that provide a specific type of cognitive behavioral therapy called the community reinforcement approach, says Corey McCann, president, and CEO of Pear Therapeutics.

(Source: Anuja Vaidya, Senior Editor, What Are Digital Therapeutics and Their Use Cases? mHealth Intelligence, May 20, 2022)

Digital Therapeutics (DTx): Major Players

Let us now look at some companies transforming the digital therapeutics space.

1. **Meru Health** is revolutionizing mental healthcare with its clinically proven treatment program for depression, anxiety, and burnout with long-lasting outcomes. It is a 12-week app-based program that divides into weekly themes focusing on

tackling mental health challenges with multiple approaches and building habits to prevent relapses. The clinically proven treatment program combines the latest evidence-based therapy modalities with HRV (Heart Rate Variability)-biofeedback, sleep science, nutritional psychiatry, emotional intelligence coaching, and anonymous peer support group help participants achieve transformational results.

2. **Livongo Health** simplifies diabetes management with quick checks, unlimited strips, a smart meter that automatically uploads your blood sugar readings to your secure account on the Livongo app, personalized tips, and expert coaching. Also, it helps improve your habits to lower your risk of developing type 2 diabetes. In addition, the Livongo app helps you track your health trends, such as high blood pressure and weight management.
3. **Propeller Health** makes it easy for patients with Asthma and COPD (Chronic Pulmonary Obstructive Disease) to stick to their treatment plan and helps them to learn what may be causing their flare-ups so that they can have more symptom-free days. How does Propeller work? Propeller sensors attach to the inhalers that patients already have and track where, when, and how often the patients use their medication and send that information to an app on their phones. Thus, over time, the app learns about the patient's flare-ups and medication use and can help them become an expert at managing their symptoms and identifying their triggers. In addition, Propeller creates reports that help the patients and caregivers to understand their asthma or COPD and to work with their physicians to adjust treatment plans as needed. Propeller is doctor-recommended, clinically proven, and cleared by the FDA and has more than 100,000 users in the US.
4. **Omada Health** is a virtual-first chronic care provider helping members make lasting changes to improve health and reduce healthcare costs for organizations. Omada's approach tackles various chronic conditions, including diabetes, hypertension, and musculoskeletal (MSK) pain. Each virtual care program of

Omada combines behavior science and clinical protocols to improve the patients lasting health. Omada has enrolled 1,500 organizations so far, saved $1,000 per member in the first year, and achieved 95 percent customer satisfaction.

5. **Virta Health** delivers continuous remote medical care in diabetes reversal via its app powered by technology and data science, with physicians and nurses providing expert medical care via Virta's custom-designed app medical records system. Patients on the Virta Treatment get daily support and answers to questions from a dedicated health coach, continuous medical supervision by physician-led care team facilities, safe de-prescription of medications, meters, strips, connected scale, educational resources, and a private, opt-in forum for discussion and support among peers. In sum, Virta provides 100 percent online, just on-demand care with no waiting rooms.
6. **Vivante Health** offers *GI-Thrive®*, an all-in-one digestive health program that delivers category-defining digital health solutions with personalized, comprehensive care for people with digestive conditions. GI-Thrive® combines clinically backed interactive technology, targeted nutrition, and 24/7 personal support to improve digestive disease outcomes and reduce the cost of care.
7. **Pear Therapeutics**, a pioneer in prescription drug therapeutics (PDTs), discovers, develops and delivers clinically validated software to provide better patient outcomes, smarter engagement and tracking tools for clinicians, and cost-effective solutions for payers. Pear's leading product, reSet® for treating substance use disorder, was the first PDT (Prescription Drug Therapeutic) to receive authorization from the FDA to improve disease outcomes. Pear's second product, reSet-O® for treating opioid use disorder, was the first PDT to receive Breakthrough Designation and was authorized in December 2018. Pear's third product, Somryst® for treating chronic insomnia, was the first product submitted through FDA's traditional 510 (k) pathway while simultaneously reviewed through FDA's Software Pre-certification Pilot Program and was authorized in March 2020. (*Source: peartherapeutics.com,*

8. **Akili Interactive** is creating a new class of digital medicines for people with cognitive impairment, delivered through captivating video game experiences. In June 2020, Akili received FDA clearance for its EndeavorRx®, the first-and-only prescription treatment delivered through a video game. EndeavorRX® improves attention function in children 8 - 12 years with ADHD (Attention-Deficit Hyperactivity Disorder). It is a safe add-on alongside other treatments. Endeavor RX® targets key areas of the brain that play a role in attention function, and gameplay adapts to each child, and parents can follow progress via the EndeavorRx insight app. EndeavorRx is clinically proven, with 73 percent of children reporting an improvement in their attention and parents reporting improvement in ADHD-related symptoms after two months of treatment. In addition, no serious adverse events were seen in any clinical trials of EndeavorRx.(*Source: akiliinteractive.com*)
9. **Click Therapeutics** develops, validates, and commercializes software as prescription medical treatments for people with unmet needs. The company's digital therapeutics are designed to be used independently or in conjunction with biomedical treatments and enable individuals through cognitive and neurobehavioral mechanisms. Click Therapeutics has entered into partnerships with two of the big Pharma companies— a $ 300 million collaboration with Otsuka to develop and commercialize digital therapeutics for patients with a major depressive disorder (MDD) and a $500 million collaboration with Boehringer Ingelheim to develop and commercialize CT-155, a novel Prescription Digital Therapeutic (PDT) to aid in the treatment of Schizophrenia. In addition, Click Therapeutics is working with Magellan Health to launch a fully digital integrated, and comprehensive smoking cessation program. (*Source: clicktherapeutics.com*).
10. **Welldoc** is leading the way with AI-driven digital coaching across multiple chronic conditions such as type 1 and type 2 diabetes, hypertension, heart failure, and pre-diabetes. (Source: welldoc.com).

11. **Voluntis,** an Aptar Pharma company and a leader in digital therapeutics, provides drug-specific digital solutions and drug-digital combinations with a robust regulated technology platform and unique expertise. Voluntis develops DTx (Digital Therapeutics) solutions on their dedicated platform, *Theraxium* leveraging off-the-shelf modules addressing common needs of digital therapeutics out-of-the-box. All their solutions go through robust validation processes based on international standards for Software-as-a-Medical Device (SaMD). Voluntis, so far, has 14 regulatory approvals for DTx. In 2002, Voluntis announced two partnerships with pharmaceutical companies— one with Tilak Healthcare to help patients with cancer better manage ocular toxicities by giving access to Tilak Healthcare's OdySight® Care and the possibility to measure their visual health anytime, anywhere. The second partnership is with a leading innovator in FDA-cleared personal electrocardiogram (ECG) technology to improve the management of atrial fibrillation (AFlb) for patients with cancer. Under the collaboration, AliveCor's KardiaMobile device will be integrated with Theraxium, Voluntis' regulated platform for digital therapeutics (DTX), to help address the challenges associated with cardio-toxicity management for patients undergoing cancer treatment and facilitate remote self-monitoring for atrial fibrillation (AFlb). (Source: voluntis.com)
12. **Kaia Health** offers digital programs to help people with chronic musculoskeletal pain, including back, hip, and knee pain — and COPD (Chronic Obstructive Pulmonary Disease). In February 2021, Kaia Health unveiled its complete musculoskeletal care solution with Kaia Gateway and Premium Partners. Kaia Gateway includes a case review service and clinical triage algorithms, while Kaia Premium Partners provide native interoperability with select providers— all within Kaia's existing solution. Kaia has already evaluated this in the industry's largest randomized control trial (RCT) involving 1,245 patients. With this offering, Kaia extends its support to chronic, acute, and pre-surgery care for back, neck, hip, knee, shoulder, hand/wrist, and foot/ankle pain. Kaia Health has over 500,000 users today in the US. (Source: kaiahealth.com)

DTx and Regulatory Environment

In recent years, there has been an increase in regulatory acceptance globally for digital therapeutics as the evidence of their ability to reduce healthcare costs mounts. Consider these facts, for example:

- The 21st Century Cures Act of December 2016 sets the pace for accelerating drug and medical device development and improving mental health delivery by including several provisions pushing for greater interoperability, adopting electronic health records (EHRs), and supporting human service programs.
- US legislation is encouraging the adoption of new digital technologies. The Centers for Medicare and Medical Services (CMS) is looking at HCPS (Healthcare Common Procedure Coding System) codes in the US. There is a move to get Medicare to design a new benefit category for DTx with appropriate coding.
- CDRH (Center for Devices and Radiological Health) of FDA in the US, launched the pilot program known as the Digital Health Software Pre-certification (Pre-Cert) program to establish a new regulatory framework for digital health. The Pre-Cert program is for products that develop a *software-as-a-medical device* (SaMD).
- According to the National Drug Control Strategy Report, the US could consider coverage for providing motivational incentives within health plans.
- Senators Shelley Moore Capito and Jeanne Shaheen are pushing to introduce the Access to Prescription Digital Therapeutics Act of 2022, establishing separate benefit categories for DTx and creating a coverage and reimbursement framework with product-specific codes.
- Germany has adopted a national level of access for DTx by involving clinicians much earlier in the decision-making process.
- France, Belgium, Italy, and Spain will soon roll out their framework.

Recently (2020), the FDA in the US created the Digital Health Center for Excellence (DHCoE) to provide advice and support for the regulatory review of digital health technology.

While the overall regulatory environment is supportive and encouraging, DTx manufacturers should work closely with all stakeholders, such as government, public and private payers, and providers, to help streamline prescription and reimbursement processes to realize the full benefit of digital therapeutics.

Finally, it is common knowledge that patients can benefit hugely from the digital bumper harvest, but only when we separate the wheat from the chaff, as the experts say. The regulatory environment is moving in that direction.

DTX Commercialization: Which Path to Take?

Big Pharma is keen on embracing digital therapeutics to create the much-needed differentiation in their products and therapies. However, the optimal path to commercialize DTx is not yet clearly determined. The multiple methodologies for arriving at a business model to scale and commercialize a digital therapeutic under evaluation are:

1. **Direct-to-Consumer** model offers advantages like early revenue opportunities by demonstrating product capabilities. However, the downside is— the high commercialization costs, and consumers expect insurance to cover healthcare costs.
2. **The fee-for-service** model allows a digital therapeutics firm to contract directly with a payer to set a rate for app usage. Further, CVS (Consumer Value Stores) Health and Express Scripts, an online pharmacy and a leading PBM (Pharmacy Benefit Manager) in the US, have launched digital formularies, enabling the fee-for-service model. The challenges here are that it may require a pilot or testing period and a long contracting process.
3. **Value-based Reimbursement** can offer cost savings for health systems and payers, but it isn't easy to allocate cost savings to a particular product.

4. **Device-like Reimbursement** requires dedicated CPT (Current Procedural Terminology) and HCPCS (Healthcare Common Procedure Coding System) codes for billing. It requires FDA approval, and the path from FDA approval to reimbursement is still undefined.

There is no well-established framework to determine pricing and reimbursement for new products in the digital therapeutics space, as the commercialization of DTx products is fairly recent. In addition, a broad range of digital therapeutic products makes it difficult to have a singular or formulaic approach for securing reimbursement like traditional pharmaceutical products.

Notwithstanding these limitations, payers are highly receptive to digital therapies because they offer many benefits such as a favorable safety profile, the potential to drive healthcare costs down such as decreased HCP visits, increased patient access to care, and enabling patients to self-manage chronic conditions that carry significant cost burdens.

In the future, developers of digital therapeutics must integrate health-economic evidence generation and payer value communication activities into their commercialization plans. They can draw parallels from their pharmaceutical counterparts' access and reimbursement evidence requirements and follow those. The following table outlines the steps to improve access and reimbursement of digital therapeutics.

Table 2.23 DTX: Steps to Improve Access and Reimbursement

Policy Makers	Payers	Developers
• Establish centralized reimbursement pathways • Include eHealth and telemedicine in a list of reimbursable services (Codes)	• Dedicate budgets/ funds to digital health technologies • Provide guidance or data requirements fo decision making	Develop appropriate evidence - Disease specific endpoints - Robust trial Design - Clinical & economic comparators - Patient adoption & adherence data - HEOR (Health Economic and Outcomes Research) data - Ensure patient adherence through optimal product design

Table 2.23 ***Contd...***

Policy Makers	Payers	Developers
Expected Benefits Improved patient care and Faster & broader access	**Expected Benefits** Price control fo new technologies and Cost-effective use of resources	**Expected Benefits** Predictable product forecasting and Drive in innovation & investment

Source: Francesca Boggio, Stephen Focsa, and Michele Casanova, Access & Reimbursement to Reward Innovations, Digital 'BTP' Solutions, Executive Insight.ch, April 11, 2018

Developing structured access and reimbursement pathways for digital therapeutics is crucial for their success as they can positively impact multiple stakeholders in the healthcare industry. Generating the right data holds the key to success in this regard.

Francesca Boggio, Stefan Focsa, and Michele Casanova suggest four key aspects regarding what makes the right data in their insightful article, *Access & Reimbursement to Reward Innovations* in Digital "BTP' Solutions, published on executiveinsight.ch on April 11, 2018.

1. Endpoints that are disease-specific and comparable to other treatments should be chosen (e.g., pharmaceutical products)
2. Measures that can be associated with cost savings or cost offsets should be included (e.g., reduction in hospitalization)
3. Data generated should demonstrate patient adoption and adherence (payers can be skeptical of the use of new technologies)
4. Data must be robust enough to convince payers (e.g., the number of patients in the trial should represent the disease area)

Here is a case of a DTx (Digital Therapeutics) company that has achieved successful reimbursement for its Digital Therapeutics:

CASE

27

Livongo Health Achieves Successful Reimbursement with Many Insurers!

Although there are some limitations and challenges to the reimbursement landscape of digital health technologies, Livongo Health, a leading digital therapeutics company that simplifies diabetes management, has shown that it is possible to gain reimbursement for your product if you have compelling evidence.

Livongo Health achieved successful reimbursement with many insurers in the US for their $50 per month diabetes program with 220,000 members for its diabetes program at the end of 2019. Furthermore, Livongo expanded its strategic agreements with Express Scripts and CVS Health, two of the leading health insurers and pharmacy benefit management (PBM)companies in the US, to drive continued sales velocity. So how did Livongo Health Achieve this? Here are the key success factors:

- Successfully reached early adopters, who paid out-of-pokcet and helped the company to establish their product as valuable and user-friendly.
- Generated substantial evidence for a broader population's insurance coverage of its diabetes program.
- Generated meaningful evidence like cost savings data, reduced hospitalizations, and reduced hypoglycemia to allow payers to evaluate the value of their technology and make reimbursement decisions during the clinical trials stage.

As a result, Livongo has successfully contracted with the full continuum of the payer universe— National PBMs (Pharmacy Benefit Managers) Health Plans and enrolled with CMS (Centers for Medicare and Medicaid Services) as a provider.

Livongo merged with Teladoc Health, the global leader in whole-person virtual healthcare, on October 20, 2020, to improve the delivery, access, and experience of healthcare for consumers globally.

(Source: Livongo Annual Report 2019)

Digital Therapeutics (DTx) Enablers

There has been a perceptible shift from the curative aspect of the diseases to preventative one during the last 15 - 20 years. Digital therapeutics can help identify and treat diseases and be a first line to prevent chronic conditions from occurring or worsening. Torreya, a global investment banking boutique serving the life sciences industry, has identified factors enabling the evolution and growth of digital therapeutics. These are:

- The capability to demonstrate clinically meaningful outcomes.
- Providing easy access to patients for therapies on-demand.
- Shorter development timelines and lower costs than traditional pharmacological interventions.
- Favorable pharmaco-economics, aligning with healthcare's overall shift to value-based care.
- The ability to combine technology with evidence-based medicine to deliver personalized patient care.

These enablers indicate a promising future for digital therapeutics. However, early biopharma adopters will have a first mover advantage, like in any other industry.

Digital Therapeutics (DTx): Challenges

While digital therapeutics are very promising in many ways, a few challenges in the near term do exist. These are:

- The optimal pathways to scale and commercialize are still unchartered.
- Although digital therapeutics provide significant economic value to providers and two of the largest Pharmacy Benefit Managers (PBMs) in the US have created digital formularies, securing reimbursement from payers and healthcare systems can still be challenging.
- The intellectual property (IP) and product protection are not yet fully vetted and tested.

- Not many digital therapeutics product launches in the recent past.
- Several digital-biopharma partnerships have been dissolved in the recent past.

However, these are not insurmountable challenges. DTx companies must integrate their platforms within the electronic health record (EHR) or software that physicians already work on to ensure faster adoption. Therefore, the DTx companies must focus on these and resolve them to ensure growth for digital therapeutics in the future.

DTx: Future Positive!

Digital may appear to offer only minor incremental improvements today but has the potential to create a paradigm shift in the biopharmaceutical sector. Torreya, a leading global investment banking boutique serving life sciences companies, foresees a promising future for digital therapeutics. Here is how digital therapeutics will likely evolve (Table).

Table 2.24 Evolution of Digital Therapeutics

2020	2025	2030
Early days: incremental benefits to existing pharmacological treatments, such as: • Improvements in behavior-mediated indications • Improved adherence • Real-time access to therapy	Real-world data and analytics will drive R&D and patient treatment decisions: • Biomarkers used for clinical trials • Data generated recommendations for treatments	Continuous biomarker monitoring will be ubiquitous: • Remote monitoring and diagnosis • Digitally monitored drug delivery • Prediction of exacerbation risk

Source: Digital Therapeutics and the Future of Pharma, A Report by Torreya, February 2020

When you consider the patient-centric approach and the multiple benefits digital therapeutics offer to all healthcare stakeholders, DTx will most certainly play a vital role in transforming healthcare in the future. Consider, for example, these growth drivers:

- The way DTx delivers evidence-based therapeutic interventions and behavioral therapies via software to replace or complement the existing treatment of a disease.
- The increasing interest of biopharmaceutical companies in collaborating with DTx companies to create differentiation and value *around their pills*.
- A likely increase in merger and acquisition activities between big Pharma and digital therapeutics firms. The recent mega-merger between Teladoc and Livongo spotlighted the power of digital therapies and the virtual care market. Other Telehealth players are eyeing digital therapeutics platforms to enhance the value of their services.
- The regulatory agencies like the FDA in the US are paving the way for rapid digital therapeutics development, empowering DTx vendors to launch their products quicker than ever before.
- Insider Intelligence estimates digital therapeutics to be a $56 billion global opportunity by 2025.

In the next eight to ten years, digital therapeutics will likely impact every aspect of healthcare, driving value-based care and precision medicine in diagnosis, treatment, and ongoing patient monitoring.

Here is a case of the recent merger of two leading players in the digital health space that indicates digital therapeutics' important role in transforming patient-centric healthcare.

CASE

28

Teladoc and Livongo's $18.5 Billion Merger Creates A Digital Health Giant Valued at a Whopping $37 Billion!

The merger of Teladoc Health and Livongo Health not only creates a new healthcare giant with a value of $37 billion but also pushes Teladoc Health into the forefront of next-generation healthcare. The combined company is expected to have pro forma revenue of $1.3 billion, representing 85 percent year-on-year growth. It expects adjusted EBITDA (Earnings Before Interest, Taxes, Depreciation, and Amortization) of $120 million.

The merger achieves synergies by expanding the reach of Livongo's pioneering Applied Health Signals platform via Teladoc's end-to-end virtual care platform and helps transform the healthcare experience from preventive care to the most complex cases, bringing whole person health to consumers and greater value to all stakeholders, says Jason Gorevic, the chief executive officer of Teladoc Health.

Teladoc Health is changing how patients access healthcare by delivering a wide spectrum of patient care, from on-demand urgent care to supporting chronic and complex health challenges.

The Teladoc and Livongo merger indicates the important role that digital therapeutics will play in transforming healthcare in the future.

(Source: Company website and press releases)

CASE

29

The *Digital Pill*!

What is a digital pill? A digital pill is a capsule or tablet with embedded sensors. When the tablet or capsule is taken, these embedded sensors track the movement as it makes its way through the body and communicates data about it to a mobile app, which can be accessed by the patient, caregiver, or healthcare practitioner. For example, pairing medication with an ingestible sensor can help clinicians track how often patients take prescription drugs.

Every year, non-compliance with prescription drugs causes losses of billions of dollars worth in healthcare in the US and elsewhere in the world. Digital pills can help improve compliance by patients.

The US FDA approved the first-ever digital pill, *Abilify MyCite* (aripiprazole with a sensor), in November 2017. Abilify MyCite tablets have an ingestible sensor embedded in the pill. These tablets are useful in treating schizophrenia, episodes of bipolar disorders, and also treat depression. How does the drug work, and how can track it in the body once it is ingested? When a patient takes the *Abilify MyCite* pill, a message is sent from its sensors to a patch worn on the arm. The data is forwarded to an app on the patient's smartphone, and that is how one can track the ingestion of the medication. Besides, patients can also share the data with their carers and doctors, via a web-based portal.

Otsuka Pharma markets *Abilify MyCite* tablets. Proteus Digital Health provides sensor technology and the patch. The US FDA first approved Abilify in 2002 for the treatment of patients with schizophrenia. A decade later, it gave marketing approval for the digital sensor used in *Abilify MyCite*. Here's the timeline of Abilify marketing approvals by the US FDA:

- US FDA first approved Abilify in 2002 to treat schizophrenia.
- Abilify MyCite was first permitted for marketing by the US FDA in 2012.
- The US FDA approved Abilify MyCite for Otsuka Pharmaceuticals on November 13, 2017.

Tatsuo Higuchi, President and representative director of Otsuka Pharmaceuticals, described the approval of *Abilify MyCite* as *a potentially transformative junction in our more than 25 years of experience in the field of mental health therapies*.

While speaking on occasion, John Kane, Chair of Psychiatry at the Donald and Barbara Zucker School of Medicine at Hofstra, Northwell in New York, said: *For the first time in my years of experience as a psychiatrist, there is an innovative way to provide individuals with serious mental illness, and selected members of their families and care teams, with information on objective medication-taking patterns to help inform patients' illness management and personalized treatment plan*.

(Source: Adapted from an article by Debbie Andalo, FDA approves first digital pill, The Pharmaceutical Journal, November 16, 2017)

3D Printing

3D (Three-dimensional) printing technology is not new. It has been around for over thirty years. It was developed at the Massachusetts Institute of Technology in the 1980s as a rapid-prototyping technique. 3D printing, also known as additive manufacturing, makes three-dimensional solid objects from a digital file. It is called additive manufacturing because creating a 3D printed objective is achieved using an additive process. In an additive process, an object is created by laying down successive layers of material until the object is created. Each layer can be seen as a thinly sliced horizontal cross-section of the eventual objective.

3D Printing Basics

The creation of a 3D printed objective is achieved using additive processes. In an additive process, an object is created by laying down successive layers of materials until the object is created. For example, you can see each of these layers as a horizontal cross-section of the eventual objective.

The 3D printing process starts with making a virtual design of the object you want to create. This virtual design is, for example, a CAD (Computer-Aided Design) file. This CAD file is created using a 3D modeling or 3D scanner (to copy an existing object). A 3D scanner can make a 3D digital copy of an object. Next, a 3D model is prepared before it is ready for 3D printing. Therefore, preparing a 3D model creates a path for 3D printing called slicing. Slicing divides a 3D model into hundreds or even thousands of horizontal layers and needs to be done with software. When the 3D model is sliced, you are ready to feed it to your 3D printer. Although 3D printing technology was developed many years ago, it is only recently that the core technology for 3D printers has become available at prices many individuals and smaller companies can afford. Integrating 3D printing into your workflow can improve productivity and manufacturing efficiency and increase your competitive advantage. 3D printing achieves these with its three distinct features significantly different from almost any other manufacturing process.

1. Printed parts are grown in layers.
2. Material is added rather than subtracted.
3. Eliminates often the need for complicated or expensive production tooling.

3D Printing in Healthcare

While 3D printing has beneficial applications across many industries and businesses, it has enormous potential in the healthcare and pharmaceutical industries. 3D models mean that physicians and diagnosticians can bring patient scans to life by precisely identifying what is required before performing a procedure. As a result, it results in less time under anesthetic for the patient, reduced costs involved with the operation, and improved outcomes. Besides, 3D Printing offers more advantages. Consider these, for example:

- Improved surgical planning. It allows surgeons to prepare better before surgery, which impacts overall results.
- Better patient communication. A 3D model improves patients' understanding of the procedure by providing them with something they can see and touch.
- Medical and research devices can be prototyped quickly and easily, and tools can be printed when required.
- 3D Printing improves the quality of clinical training. 3D printed anatomical models help students better understand anatomy and surgical procedures.
- 3D Printing allows the production of devices such as hearing aids. Sonova, the hearing aid company, can mass-produce hundreds of thousands of custom-made products annually. Despite high quantities, each product is tailored for its wearer's individual needs.
- 3D Printing is used in producing dental implants for Invisalign® aligners. The Invisalign System comprises a series of doctor-prescribed, thin, clear plastic removable orthodontic appliances (aligners) and proprietary 3-D software. The Invisalign System is an alternative to conventional wire/bracket technology and fixed devices for treating patients with malocclusion. An

estimated 500,000 custom-fit Invisalign braces are printed daily.

- Also, 3D Printing enables the production of prosthetic limbs tailored to meet the patient's specific needs while adhering to a narrow regulatory framework.

3D Printing in the Pharmaceutical Industry

3D Printing technology can open doors in product development, manufacturing, research and development, and clinical trials in the pharmaceutical industry. It has excellent potential for controlled release and on-site printing at pharmacies. 3D Printing could add a whole new dimension of possibilities to personalized medicine, producing personalized 3D dosage form in its most simplistic form. Picture the following scenario, for example: *Imagine a pediatrician talking to a four-year-old child who has trouble adjusting to taking daily doses of steroids after being diagnosed with Duchene muscular dystrophy the previous month, "What is your favorite animal," she asks. "A zebra," quietly replies the child, whom we will call Sam. The pediatrician smiles as she makes a note on her office computer. "But not a black and white one, a blue and green one," Sam adds a little more confidence. Later, the toddler watches with wide eyes as the uniquely colored, zebra-like tablets appear from a three-dimensional (3D) printer in the hospital pharmacy.*

Science fiction? Today, it may seem like one. However, it is possible in the foreseeable future. It is just one example of how personalized one's medicine can be in its simplest form. 3D printing may allow even higher levels of personalization, such as printing pills in a complex construct of layers and using a combination of drugs to treat multiple ailments at once. Here is a brief list of what can be done in Pharma with 3D printing technology.

- Personalized drug dosing
- Unique dosage forms
- Complex drug release profiles
- Printing living tissue

World's First 3D Printed Drug, Spritam

3D Printing in pharmaceuticals has many possibilities, but are there any concrete examples of results? In 2015, Aprecia Pharmaceuticals produced the first tablet manufactured through 3D and approved by the US FDA. The company used 3D Printing to reformulate the anti-epileptic drug *levetiracetam*. The new 3D Printed product, *Spritam*, has a highly porous structure that traditional manufacturing could not achieve. This structure allows the pill to dissolve in seconds upon contact with saliva, helping elderly and young patients suffering from trouble swallowing pills, known as dysphagia.

Aprecia achieved this innovative development through a proprietary powder bed and inkjet 3D Printing technology known as ZipDose®. In manufacturing, a powdered layer containing the drug itself is laid down. That first layer passes under an inkjet printhead, and a binding liquid is printed along with the powdered sheet at specific locations. Successive layers are then printed up to 40 times or more, depending on the size of the tablet. Printing the layers allows the drug to be packed tightly. A single tablet typically holds 200 mg and can be layered to contain 1,000 mg. The result is a high-dose medicine that is easy to swallow for epileptic patients and breaks down inside the body to administer a steady dose over time.

Pioneering the Point-of-Care Drug Making

Here's the case of FabRx, a company determined to make point-of-care drug making a reality.

CASE

30

FabRx and the Promise of Point-of-Care Drug Making!

Abdul Basit and Professor Simon Gaisford, scientists at the University College of London, saw the huge potential in 3D printing for medicines. They believed they could commercialize printed tablets in the foreseeable future, say, within the next ten years, and started FabRx in 2014.

While the technology for 3D printing is not a major issue, the regulatory environment is the biggest challenge for 3D printing. First, you need to persuade the regulators to adapt and accept printing as a method of manufacturing pharmaceuticals. It was partly achieved when the US FDA approved Apprecia's Spritam, the world's first 3D printed drug. Second, to gain the Federal Regulatory Agencies' approval, 3D printing has to make the drug production process predictable, calculable, and safe from every regulatory point of view.

3D printing can make the drug absorption process more effective. Gizmodo, a design, technology, science, and science fiction website, reported in May 2015 that researchers of FabRx experimented with pills of different sizes and shapes and observed that a pyramid-shaped pill is absorbed by the body the fastest while a cylinder-shaped pill takes much longer. The basic principle here is when you increase the surface in contact with the dissolution media while keeping the volume of the printlet constant, you increase the drug release.

How do patients and physicians perceive 3D printing? Patients are not concerned about the technology behind the manufacture of the pills. Instead, they want easily swallowable pills, and doctors see 3D printing far from the market yet. On the other hand, many physicians consider 3D printing personalized medicines as the desired advancement. However, they are also skeptical about 3D printing as they are not used to this technology.

How long do we have to wait before 3D printing is widely available? The FabRx team is optimistic and expects to place the first printers in five years for the first *in situ* trials. However, the adoption of 3D printers will be slow and gradual as they need to address the regulatory compliance requirements. Initially, some large hospitals and community pharmacies will have printers, and patients will go there to collect their medications printed especially for them.

(*Source*: Adapted from Dr. Bertalan Mesko's article, *The Future of 3D Printing is Closer Than You Think*, published on May 4, 2017, in the medicalfuturist.com)

3D Printing in Pharma Marketing

While there are many possibilities for Pharma marketers to participate in and contribute to educational programs for HCPs and patients through innovative 3D Printing programs, pharmaceutical companies are rather slow in adopting this technology, unlike their counterparts in manufacturing and R&D. However, AstraZeneca has made a pioneering effort in grabbing and retaining the attention of many physicians at an international diabetes congress through its creative and innovative use of 3D Printing.

CASE

31

AstraZeneca's *Patient Profiler* Touch Table!

American Diabetes Association (ADA) and the European Association for the study of Diabetes (EASD), two of the world's leading organizations in diabetes, recommend individual treatment options for the disorder. Following this approach, AstraZeneca, which markets six products to treat type2 diabetes, wanted to communicate its commitment to personal care in diabetes treatment in an innovative way. Therefore, it has chosen the diabetes congresses to demonstrate how patient preferences and characteristics could influence the type2 of diabetes treatment they receive.

The company has chosen diabetes congresses because thousands of physicians attend them. To catch their attention, AstraZeneca needed an educational yet eye-catching experience. To create an engaging and memorable experience, the company developed an interactive application taking the physicians through the treatment pathways of 16 distinct patient cases using 3-D printed patient characters, each designed to showcase AstraZeneca's products.

Physicians could identify the most suitable AstraZeneca products based on the patient's clinical and personal profile. The 3-D printed figurines of 16 patients acted as triggers on a touch table surface, allowing for an engaging experience and a tangible representation of the patient-centric ethos. The touch table experience wowed all the physicians with its fantastic interactivity. It brought patient profiles to life and communicated AstraZeneca's commitment to individual patient care. AstraZeneca's touch table experience of individual patient care was innovative and interactive simultaneously, drawing physicians' admiration.

(Source; Adapted from the article: AstraZeneca patient profiler Touch Table, AstraZeneca with support from Ogilvy Communications, Finalist: Post Launch Experience, PMLiVE, Case: 3-D Printing)

3D Printing: The Way Forward

Dr. Alvaro Goyanes, director of development at FabRx, believes that the future is personalized medicine, thus personalized drug making. But, first, drug regulatory agencies must prepare for the change by familiarizing themselves with new technologies and trends such as 3D printing and introducing appropriate checks and balances.

3D Printing drugs could significantly impact how drugs are created and distributed and the efficiency of medical treatments. It is the way to go for Pharma!

Agile Marketing in Pharma

Pharma's customer landscape has increasingly become complex. As a result, pharma companies find it harder to meet the needs of all stakeholders. Consider, for example, the following changes that are evolving:

- Declining access to customers through traditional channels, reduced margins, increased research and development costs and decreased productivity.
- Empowered patients demand more holistic and customized solutions beyond drugs.
- Patient stratification leads to smaller launches.
- The increasing power of provider networks, prescription guidelines, and growing patient influence reduce the decision power of individual physicians. As a result, HCP (Healthcare Professional) influence on drug choice is declining.
- The continued focus of payers and regulators on affordability makes market access difficult for pharma companies. Furthermore, the payers' cost-saving approach creates hurdles to market access.
- The growing competition from biosimilar and generic pharmaceutical companies is gaining a share of the prescription drug market from the big pharma companies.

On top of these factors, non-traditional players like tech giants and startups are driving disruption by creating value beyond drugs in the healthcare market, forcing established players to develop new capabilities. Therefore, pharmaceutical companies need to identify, develop and acquire the differentiating capabilities to compete in the changing business environment. Agility is critical in this changing landscape, and organizations must design themselves to support continuous learning and development. Pharma companies can continue to be successful if they adapt to the changing needs of the stakeholders and apply innovative and Agile ways of working.

What is Agile?

Neil Osmond, Distinguished VP and Advisory at Gartner, one of the leading global research and advisory company described Agile as a *mindset of doing more for less. At its heart, it embraces you to deliver what the customer actually needs earlier while reducing wasted time, effort, and resources on the journey*.

Sarah Elk, a senior partner at Bain & Company, a global consultancy major and co-author of the book, *Doing Agile Righ*t, emphasized the customer-centric nature of Agile when she answered the question, Why is the customer so important in Agile: *The customer is really at the heart of an Agile enterprise. A mechanism for gathering customer feedback is always designed into any Agile Team's work, and customers are often consulted early. Sometimes it is internal customers being consulted, perhaps on changes to a business process, for example. Otherwise, it is external customers giving feedback may be on a new product. Agile is about testing and learning. It requires pivoting and adjusting based on what the customer says, not what the executive might have thought the right answer was.*

Origins of Agile

Solutions evolve from a collaboration between the self-organizing, cross-functional teams in an Agile approach. It evolved from a technology experts' conference in Utah in 2001, where seventeen software experts were seeking a solution to remedy the delays, low quality, and getting over the budgets in software technology projects and to get them back on time scope, budget and specifications. They developed four key values and twelve principles, which are known as Agile Principles.

Four Key Values

The four key values of Agile are:

1. Customer collaboration over Contract negotiation
2. Individuals and interactions over processes and tools

3. Responding to change over following a plan
4. Working software over full documentation

12 Principles

The twelve principles of Agile are:

1. Customer Satisfaction
2. Welcome Change
3. Deliver Frequently
4. Working Together
5. Motivated Team
6. Face-to-face
7. Working Software
8. Constant Pace
9. Good Design
10. Simplicity
11. Self-Organization
12. Reflect and Adjust

However, these values and principles are not new and have roots in the lean manufacturing principles developed in the 1940s and 50s in the Toyota Manufacturing Company.

Agile Methodologies

The Agile approach is based on the Agile Manifesto. Scrum is the most popular Agile methodology today. It involves a set of well-developed practices for innovation.

Scrum, Rugby, and Teamwork

Scrum is derived from an activity that occurs during a rugby match. What is common between a rugby match and Scrum? Creation of unique teamwork. The spirit of teamwork made people draw parallels between a successful rugby team and a Scrum team.

The origins of the rugby metaphor can be traced back to a 1986 Harvard Business Review article, *The New, New Product*

Development Game, by professors Takeuchi and Nonaka. They refer to the old, less effective way as the 'relay race' approach. Angela Anderies explained the parallels between Scrum and Rugby teams in *The Agile Mindset Blog* published on June 12, 2012. Here's the gist:

Rugby's simple yet game-defining role is *No forward passing*. In a Rugby match, players must pass the ball from player to player many times down the field as the team attempts to push through the opponent's defense and score. That is how and why a Rugby team moves down the field as a unit, much like a wave. No player how skilled can score without the support of the team. Similarly, a Scrum team understands that they must collaborate and pass work from one person to another. There is no place for the superstar who works alone.

Usually, there are fifteen players on a Rugby team, and each position requires a slightly different body type and skill set. There is room for short, tall, and all skill types such as slow but powerful, quick and fast, good hands, kicking ability on the field. Blending these different skills makes the team much more effective than a similar group with identical skillsets. All the players use their abilities regardless of their position in the field to further the team goal. Scrum teams are very similar to Rugby teams. They are cross-functional with self-managed roles. They adapt to complete the work and do not get stuck in rigid roles.

According to the Rugby Football Union, the governing body of the sport in England, Rugby's core values are teamwork, respect, enjoyment, discipline, and sportsmanship. Scrum also has values such as commitment, focus, openness, respect, and courage. And as in Rugby, these values shape the behaviors of Scrum team members.

In Rugby and Scrum, cross-functionality and flexibility become a competitive advantage.

Four Important Roles

Scrum's core principle is empowering the team and advocates working in small teams. Agile and Scrum have four important roles:

1. *Scrum Master* is responsible for setting up the team, Sprint meeting, and remove obstacles to progress. The scrum master does not assign tasks to team members. Task management is a team responsibility. The scrum master's role is to encourage and facilitate their decision-making and problem-solving capabilities. The Scrum Master will create a culture where everyone stays focused on the objective and collaborate radically.
2. *Product Owner* (Brand manager) creates product backlog, prioritizes the backlog, and is responsible for the deliverables in each Sprint or iteration. He is the interface between the business, the customers, and the product-related needs and the team on the other. He is responsible for:
   A. Action items to be completed daily
   B. Sprint planning
   C. Facilitating the Sprint planning meeting
   D. Reviewing the Sprint meeting
3. *Scrum Team:* Manages its work and organizes the work to complete in the sprint cycle.
4. *User Representative*: This often forgotten role is very important, as it takes on the user's voice. You need this person on the core team to ask difficult questions, such as *has anyone actually spoken about this to the customer*? However, depending on the project, this role may not be full-time on every project, but it is important.

How Scrum Works?

Scrums organize the work in time-boxed Sprints. Sprints should not be shorter than five days but might run up to thirty days. The idea of Scrum is that every morning at the same time, the whole team gathers for a Standup meeting for no more than fifteen minutes to answer three questions:

1. What did we do yesterday?
2. What will we do today?
3. What obstacles do we anticipate in what we are doing today?

There is a common goal for the Scrum Team to overachieve, and there needs to be a common excitement during each Sprint when the goal is achieved.

Sprints

Sprints are a set amount of time to achieve specific tasks in a project. They allow everyone to focus on the agreed amount of work in the agreed amount of time. Sprints should be long enough to see significant progress that you can tangibly measure but short enough to concentrate minds on achieving a goal. To achieve its objectives, each Sprint conducts three types of meetings:

1. *Sprint Planning*: The tasks at the top of the to-do list (product backlog in Agile terminology) are ratified, estimated, agreed and assigned with the whole team during this important meeting. It also sets a goal for the Sprint so that the team knows when it is done, what success will look like, and whether they can celebrate each Sprint's end.
2. *Sprint Review*: Each core team member gives an update in this meeting, showing their work wherever possible. The team reviews each of the Sprint tasks and whether they have been completed successfully. If they have not completed, the team moves them to the to-do list.
3. *Sprint Retrospective*: In line with the Agile principle of the team regularly reflecting on how to become more effective and adjust accordingly, Sprint holds a retrospective meeting at the end of each Sprint. The retrospective meeting of Sprint seeks to answer two important questions:

   A. What went well that we would repeat?

   B. What would we do differently in the future?

Kanban

Kanban, a framework that falls under Agile methodology, is a simple, visual means of managing projects that enables teams to see the process so far and what is coming up next. Kanban projects are primarily managed through a Kanban board which segments tasks into three columns—*To Do, Doing, and Done*. The visualizing process of Kanban helps increase transparency and collaboration between team members.

Agile Marketing

Agile marketing focuses on the customer, validated learning, short adaptive iterations, and cross-functional collaborations. Thus, it differs significantly from traditional marketing. Jim Ewel, one of the leading voices of Agile and a co-author of the book *Agile Marketing Manifesto,* highlights the important differences between traditional and Agile marketing. Here are the key differences:

1. Traditional marketing has an inward focus. It focuses on the producer and the product. The four Ps (Product, Price, Place, and Promotion) are inward-looking levers under the producer's control. In contrast, Agile marketing focuses on the customer and the customer value chain. For example, Robert F. Lauterborn's Four-C model, where customer experience replaces the product, cost replaces price, convenience replaces place, and communication replaces promotion, is a more appropriate model for Agile marketing.
2. Traditional marketing focuses on the producer's sales cycle and Agile marketing on the customer's buying process.
3. Traditional marketing focuses on the Spin, controlling the message owning the brand. Agile marketing focuses on transparency and engagement and recognizes that ultimately customers own both the message and the brand, and only through honest interaction can a company influence customers.
4. Traditional marketing relies on measurements like Total Addressable Market (TAM), market share, unaided recall of a

brand or ad, Gross Rating Points (GRP), and Target Rating Points (TRPs). In contrast, Agile marketing proceeds via a series of *experiments* forming a hypothesis of what might work and testing that hypothesis. Agile marketing chooses measurements appropriate to the hypotheses at hand, and measurement that aligns with the business and sales goals of the organization. Traditional marketing is measured in terms of success and failures, whereas Agile marketing is measured in terms of the pace of learning.

5. Traditional marketing believes that markets and customers are like a lump of clay you can mold into their idea of what the customer and the market should be with the marketing tools (four Ps, advertising, and public relations). In comparison, Agile marketing treats markets and customers as a complex system of individuals trying to learn what works for them and is not surprised when they don't react as expected.
6. The traditional marketing philosophy is to find a big idea, get it right and launch it with a big splash. It relies on a series of campaigns, yearly, quarterly, and big launches. In contrast, Agile marketing focuses on a series of short Sprints, emphasizing getting a good enough idea, testing it, and perfecting it over time.
7. Traditional marketing is often organized around internal functions such as Public Relations, Advertising, Product Management, Search Engine Optimization (SEO), and Search Engine Marketing (SEM). In comparison, Agile marketing tends to be organized around the customer value cycle (need recognition, information search, evaluation of alternatives, purchase decision, post-purchase behaviors). Often, in Agile marketing, different functions sit in the same space and collaborate to meet customer needs.

Agile Marketing: What it Means?

Agile marketing involves short-term planning and speedy execution cycles—typically a few weeks, allowing marketing teams more visibility and flexibility in prioritizing tasks and meeting objectives.

In addition, agile marketing uses the bite-sized decision-making approach, allowing a course correction to be on target due to its iterative process.

Agile marketing also means using data and analytics to guide opportunities and solutions to problems, continuously developing tests, quickly evaluating the results, and rapidly iterating.

Furthermore, Agile marketing enables quick decision-making and seamless collaboration by breaking down the organizational silos with its cross-functional team approach.

Agile for Pharma

Without a doubt, the Agile approach offers many advantages over traditional models and makes a compelling case for pharma to adapt. In today's rapidly changing and increasingly challenging marketing environment, pharma marketers need to respond rapidly to both market events and the needs of their stakeholders—patients, physicians, and payers. But can pharma adapt the agile way of working? However, it may not be easy for pharma to adapt as it faces many challenges. Consider these, for example:

1. *Overcoming the Traditional Mindset* is a significant hurdle as it requires a culture change to accept the Agile process as better than what they have been doing till now. Since the old way is still working in many ways for many years, there is a natural resistance to change.
2. *Working around the Organizational Structure* is another major challenge as it involves breaking away from structured practices and breaking down the silos that have made marketers successful.
3. *Coping with the slow pace of Regulatory Review* is a big issue stopping many conservative pharma companies from adopting Agile.

Despite these challenges, some pharma marketers aware of Agile's benefits are starting to think about moving to a more agile approach. For example, McCullum Keeler, managing partner and chief strategy officer at Calcium, a full-service independent healthcare marketing agency, has rightly observed that *executing in alignment with Agile principles in the pharma might be feasible, albeit with some caveats. The entire structure of internal marketing teams would have to be re-thought to amplify a cross-disciplinary style and assigns to a lead, the Scrum Master. He should have the authority to make autonomous decisions*.

Breaking Silos

Pratap Khedkar, chief executive officer of ZS Associates, a leading global management consulting and professional services firm, sums up the Agile approach in three steps: *Anticipate, Decide, and Act*. And to capitalize on those actions faster, some pioneering pharma companies are developing ways to break down the communication silos to foster an Agile approach.

According to Mr. Khedkar, the new paradigm of the future is to imagine a room where all three of these activities happen together. At ZS Associates, they call it the *launch room*. The following case presents a brief picture of the launch room and what happens there.

CASE

32

Launch Situation Room Breaks Communication Silos!

ZS Associates implemented Launch Situation Rooms for real-time post-launch analysis. The standard practice in the pharmaceutical industry is that every sector is doing its research in separate offices and then communicating the results every couple of weeks with a PowerPoint presentation in a meeting with other stakeholders. Instead of engaging in such an elaborate and time-consuming process, Mr. Khedkar came up with the idea of putting all the players in the same room—the brand team, the analysts, market researchers—and as they collect the data, instead of developing the reports they participate side-by-side in intense working sessions that occur every few days. They review the information, and everyone in the room speaks to how the group should respond to the data. Such a centralized process with all the people in the same room enables them to work with a group mindset and not an individual mindset, which changes how they function. As Mr. Khedkar says, *this lack of silos is really important; otherwise, it just means getting reports faster, but it still takes a long time to communicate the intel from one group to another*.

Source: Adapted from Robin Robinson's article, Trending 2018: Agile Marketing, published in PharmaVoice, November/December 2017

What is Driving Agility in Pharma?

Pharma companies are beginning to realize that they need to react quickly to the market and customer needs, adapt within three to six months, and course-correct as they go. Some of the important factors that are driving agility in pharma are:

- The number of market events has increased. Some brands can have up to eleven launches in their category in one year. In the past, there used to be a new competitor every three or four years, and marketers had time to prepare for this. As a result, there were no big shocks to the system as often as today.
- Today, product launches face many challenges and have to put out more fires during launch. As a result, marketers need to get to the root of a problem sooner, say, in two months instead of the traditional two years to course-correct.
- Forecasting future outcomes is much more complicated today, and spending the time to determine all possible scenarios and prepare for them is a lot of work that does not necessarily result in any solutions.
- Pharma companies increasingly realize that waiting for six to nine months to find out how a launch or campaign is going is pointless when you can make changes in a matter of weeks instead of months using the Agile approach.
- The shifting of focus to acting on data instead of having a long-range plan in place that does not have the flexibility to change. The Agile approach gives that flexibility.

Agile Opportunities across Pharma Value Chain

The Agile approach offers several opportunities across the entire pharmaceutical value chain. Consider the following opportunity areas, for example:

1. *Drug Discovery and Research*: Agile offers many opportunities in the drug discovery space. For instance, Agile enables the decentralization of innovation across organizational boundaries. For example, companies can create internal

independent research teams that compete against each other for funding and thus creates a research environment that fosters success. In addition, collaborations and partnerships with academic research organizations can accelerate drug discovery.

2. *New Product Launch*: Agile's culture of experimentation and customer-centric ways of working can help improve pharma's new drug launches. The Agile approach lets pharma companies collaborate with patients and physicians to co-create prototypes for comprehensive, beyond-the-pill solutions.
3. *Market Access*: Agile's fully integrated, cross-functional teams can improve market access by bringing strategic market access experts, pricing and reimbursement stakeholders, and field forces together to develop innovative pricing and reimbursement models.
4. *Marketing and Sales*: Agile principles can energize the marketing and sales teams of a pharma company. For instance, rapid prototyping allows the rollout of marketing plans and initiatives to be fast and adaptive. In addition, modular brand plans increase flexibility by allowing marketing departments across several small budgets instead of a single large budget.
5. *Medical Affairs*: The medical affairs teams need to become Agile because new advances in medicine and communication technologies build new expectations to effectively communicate science in newer ways, rapidly responding to changes in the scientific and competitive landscape.
6. *Production*: The growth of precision medicine requires a transition to agile production because batch sizes are shrinking and drugs are more tailored to patients' individual needs.
7. *Supply Chain*: Agile helps pharma companies to create supply chains that are more flexible and responsive. For instance, Merck US is installing an agile, end-to-end integrated supply chain by utilizing technologies such as IIoT (Industrial Internet of Things) and RFID (Radio Frequency Identification). What is more, the evolution of precision medicine calls for more responsive supply chains.

How Agile can Benefit Pharma?

Agile can benefit pharma in several ways. Neil Osmond explains five types of benefits that Agile can offer pharma in the PharmaField article, *Implementing Agile Working in Pharma*, published on August 5, 2019.

1. *Customer/Patient*: As you need to bring the voice of the customer or patient into the project from the very beginning and throughout the project, Agile helps create outcomes that are highly relevant to the customer and patient needs.
2. *Visible Delivery*: The Agile approach ensures a team's focus on shorter-term and enables tangible deliverables over grand plans that rarely realize benefits.
3. *Harmonizing Benefits*: Self-organizing Agile teams who take on shared responsibility help reduce the bottlenecks. Agile teams win together and lose together.
4. *Decisions and Transparency*: Agile encourages decisions to be made when the team is wiser, not before. It brings transparency to project risks, progress, and delays that can be caught and addressed earlier.
5. *Minimizes Waste*: As the Agile approach focuses on what needs doing next rather than being distracted by lower priority tasks, it minimizes waste.

Implementing Agile in Pharma

If you are convinced about what is possible with Agile, the next step is to start the journey with Agile. So how do you start the journey? Where will you begin? Here are some useful suggestions from Neil Osmond, a leading expert on agile ways of working:

- Get the buy-in from your team and train them.
- Start small. Start with a pilot in one project. You can even start with using a Kanban board and then build from there.
- Get your roles right. Role clarity is very important. Be clear about who makes the decisions, who has the expertise, and who is the voice of the customer and patient for running the project effectively.

- Develop Team Spirit. If you live by Agile's *success as a team, fail as a team* philosophy, it makes the blame game irrelevant.
- Develop a minimum viable solution faster. While this can be challenging, it can unlock significant value by not committing to work and expenses until you have learned in the real world rather than guessing at the planning stage.
- Get support functions on board. You must get all the functions that sign off your tasks, such as medical, legal, regulatory, and IT (Information Technology), and convince them. Once they get the hang of it, they will find Agile liberating.

Three Building Blocks of Agile Marketing

While the desire to catch the agile wave among pharmaceutical companies is increasing, many still struggle to take full advantage of the value agile can offer. However, some biopharmaceutical companies are experiencing success with riding the agile wave. Jake Beesley, managing director, and Lukasz Kowalczyk, senior manager, digital marketing, Interactive at Accenture, a leading global management consultancy firm, have identified three value principles and building blocks that enable successfully adopting agile and realize its benefits in their Accenture Blog article, *Can Life Sciences Companies Catch the Agile Marketing Wave*? The core of Agile marketing rests on these three value principles. These are:

1. *Relevance* is about delivering experiences that meet the customers' individual needs according to their preferences. So how do you build relevance into your strategy? Creating modular content is an important building block to make your communication relevant because traditional ways of creating content developed in the pre-digital era cannot meet the needs of today's HCPs (Healthcare Professionals) and patients. Today, the pharma companies have to address the needs of individual HCPs and patients, which increases the demand for unique sets of content. Therefore, companies need to create more versions of content at a faster pace while remaining compliant. It means developing modular content that is a pre-approved content fragment into the customer's channel in real-time.

2. *Speed* is about creating and delivering those experiences quickly. So how do you build speed into delivering experiences? Suppose you need to design, produce, deliver and measure customer interactions faster. In that case, you have to form cross-functional teams consisting of these functions with the singular purpose of spearheading the end-to-end process of creating and delivering a superior customer experience.
3. *Optimization* means improving the process of delivering experiences every day. One way to achieve this is to organize diverse yet focused teams is to set up *pods*, small teams working together towards a goal for a given amount of time. These small, highly focused teams combine the traditional roles such as content strategy, creative assembly, and marketing analytics conventionally provided by third parties. These multi-disciplinary teams enable accelerated knowledge sharing, transparency, and providing rapid solutions. Marketers can achieve a deeper level of analytics as they can track the performance of each content fragment with digital interaction, whether it is the web, email, advertisements, or any other channel. In addition, marketers can now test the performance of several content fragments in digital interaction, allowing the improvement of a campaign quickly, say, within minutes by optimizing messaging for the next interaction. Furthermore, measuring the interaction components allows marketers to understand customer preferences more deeply, leading to much richer customer segmentation and personalization of messaging. When you have a deeper understanding of individual customer preferences and influence interactions, you can create customer experiences that they value most.

From Principles to Practices

The authors, Jake Beesley and Lukasz Kowalczyk suggest simple steps for putting these three principles into practice:

- Start small. Start with a brand or product team. Assess the potential of modular content to reduce waste and deliver messages that are highly relevant to customers.

- Assemble a test pod (small, multi-disciplinary team) to walk through the end-to-end process of creating and delivering a customer interaction and experience. Use that to identify skill and capability gaps.
- To optimize, define the data you need, and simulate your workflow to capture performance data and deliver insights to decision-makers.

Agile Transformation

Most organizations mistakenly think that Agile adoption and Agile transformation are the same. However, they both differ significantly. Agile adoption is *Doing* Agile. Adoption is the act of taking up or putting something into effect. Whereas, Agile transformation is *Being* or *Becoming* Agile.

Agile transformation is more difficult to achieve because it involves changing the complete cultural and organizational mindset to embrace a culture of a self-organizing, collaborative way of working instead of the siloed. Therefore, pharma companies will have to switch from a traditional to an Agile model based on four organizational building blocks to achieve Agile transformation. The following table presents a snapshot of these.

Table 2.25 Traditional and Agile Models: Organizational Building Blocks

Organizational Building Blocks	Traditional Model	Agile Model
Culture	• Stable organization and risk-avoiding culture • Process-oriented work with strong pre-defined work • Working within tasks and silos and employees do their tasks • Best-in- class	• Learning organization and culture of experimentation • Result and product orientation of empowered employees • Strong collaboration across silos and employees enabled to find a way • Best and First-in-class

Contd...

Organizational Building Blocks	Traditional Model	Agile Model
Organization	• Homogenous, segregated teams with a strong hierarchy and slow decision-making • Pre-defined career paths • Execute within the structure	• Cross-functional, integrated, and empowered teams with a flat hierarchy for faster decision-making • Unpredictable, rapid careers with life-long learning • Innovative beyond the lines
Ways of Working	• Stability based on experience matters • Application of traditional methods • Good understanding of analogous customer	• Agile Methods (Process Mechanics): Scrum, OKR (objectives and Key Results), Product Ownership, Product Backlog, Technical practices, Continuous Delivery foster innovation and learning • Customer-centric development
Technical and Physical Work Infrastructure	• Traditional office applications • Focus on office work and sitting at desk	• Innovative collaboration tools and systems such as Google Apps for global, virtual teams • OpenOffice culture and work infrastructure together with flexible work models, mobile hardware

Source: Adapted from an article by Dr. Clemens Freytag, Director and Executive Board member at Strategy&, Building an Agile Pharma Organization 4.0 published on LinkedIn blog on April 30, 2019.

Culture Above All

Agile transformation is, first of all, involves a cultural transformation. Bart Schlatmann, chief executive officer at Allianz Direct, is very emphatic about this fact when he said in a McKinsey interview: *Culture is perhaps the most important element of this sort of change effort. We have spent an enormous amount of energy and leadership time trying to role model the sort of behaviors—ownership, empowerment, customer-centricity that is appropriate in an Agile culture.*

Implementing Agile Transformation

Successful implementation of Agile transformation requires the senior leadership team of your company to become actively involved in the planned transformation. In addition, they need to champion the cause of Agile transformation and become strong advocates of the three laws of agile.

The Three Laws of Agile

Stephen Denning, the author of the book, *The Age of Agile*, describes the three laws of Agile. Further, he says: *Agile means embracing fundamentally different assumptions. Thus Agile operates under three laws*. These are:

1. *The Law of the Small Team*: Here, the key principle is that small autonomous, cross-functional teams work in short cycles and on relatively small tasks, getting continuous feedback from the customer.
2. *The Law of the Customer*: In truly Agile organizations, everyone is passionately obsessed with a continuous and relentless focus on delivering value for the customer. Thus, they eliminate any activity that does not contribute to value for the customer.
3. *The Law of the Network*: Breaking down the silos, Agile teams take the initiative on their own and interact with other teams to solve common problems, becoming a network of high-performing teams.

Agile Fluency

Agile transformation means mastering the Agile approach. Mastery comes when Agile becomes the natural way of working for the whole organization. Martin Fowler, software developer and international speaker on software development, has applied the Japanese martial arts concept of Shu-Ha-Ri to Agile to explain the three phases of maturity a person goes through as they gain Agile knowledge in his blog article, *Shu-Ha-Ri published in martinfowler.com on August 22, 2014.*

Shu-Ha-Ri

In Shu-Ha-Ri, the early stages of learning focus on concrete steps to imitate. The focus then shifts to understanding the principles and finally into self-directed innovation. Here are the steps:

- *Shu*: In this beginning stage, the student follows the teachings of one master precisely.
- *Ha*: With the basic practices working, he now learns the underlying principles and theory behind the technique and explores alternatives.
- *Ri*: Now, the student learns from his practice and adapts to what he has learned to his particular circumstances.

Key Steps

Start small with a team or two, learn from their mistakes, and then iterate quickly, applying what you have learned. The success of your Agile teams will be your best advocates for moving forward. Thus, establishing a team to pioneer the transformation is the first step. When successful teams start talking to other teams, inspiring them, it creates a snowball effect, enabling them to create a new future and become champions to encourage others.

Unlearning what you have been doing before learning the new ways of Agile is another important step. Many senior leaders who transition the Agile, state that they had to unlearn what they thought it meant to be a leader, changing from the role of a commander to empowering others.

Once Agile teams establish the Agile way of working as their normal way of working, the organization needs to ensure all corporate functions are also transformed to become agile. Moving support functions to Agile breaks the silos and bureaucracy, which slows the organization.

Cases

Here are two cases showing how pharma companies have adopted Agile practices.

CASE

33

Agile Practices at MSD (Merck Sharp & Dohme), UK!

MSD introduced Agile practices of developing, adapting, and reinventing the content to support its digital ambitions. The result? By adopting Agile practices, MSD achieved far more than fast-moving, effective digital campaigns. Teams functioned better together, and work was prioritized more clearly, delivered earlier, and with greater confidence that outputs would translate into better outcomes for patients and healthcare professionals.

Nick Williams, the director of the business unit that implemented the Agile initiative, became an Agile advocate and started helping pharma teams develop their unique versions of Agile strategy after leaving MSD.

Source: Adapted from Neil Osmond's article, Implementing Agile in Pharma, published in PharmaField on August 5, 2019.

CASE 34

Agile Practices at Novartis, UK!

The leadership at Novartis, UK, decided to identify ways to support their teams' work through complexity, rationalize workloads, and achieve results. As a result, the company conducted a pilot with a single multichannel marketing project in one integrated franchise team. Initially, they trained the team and gave ongoing support. And The pilot project has tangible objectives, which the team achieved successfully. The team achieved:

- Delivery time—reduced by half compared to internal benchmarks.
- Production of materials—70 percent reduction in time spent in approvals, and costs were 50 percent lower than expected.
- Team Satisfaction—rated highly, with confidence to repeat the achievement in future work.

Calitriona Walsh, business franchise head at Novartis, UK, said on thoccasion: *Our pilot team delivered an outstanding result by adopting an agile approach. Their experience has directly influenced our decision to use Agile across more of our business*.

Source: Adapted from Neil Osmond's article, Implementing Agile in Pharma, published in PharmaField on August 5, 2019.

The Way Forward

According to a recent McKinsey study, 90 percent of executives identified agility and collaboration as critical to the organizations' success. What's more, organizations that adopt agile processes do financially better than those that do not. Consider, for example, that the world's largest and fastest-growing companies such as Amazon, Apple, Facebook, Google, and Microsoft are all agile organizations.

The Agile transformation results in intangible benefits to organizations and their customers in both quantitative and qualitative terms. Consider these benefits, for example:

- Agile thinking empowers employees by abolishing silos
- Enables broad shifts in culture and mindsets which attract the best employees
- Improves customer experience through customer-centric ways of working.

In sum, Agile is the way of the future, and pharma companies need to start planning for that future today.

Big Data and Analytics

In 2006, British mathematician Clive Humby coined the phrase, *Data is the new oil*. Like oil, data is valuable, but if unrefined, you cannot use it. Similarly, data also has to be refined and converted into actionable insights and knowledge.

Today, digital transformation is sweeping across industries, including pharmaceuticals. So what is the fuel that feeds the engine of the digital revolution? Data. Big data, and analytics.

Gartner, a leading global research and advisory consultancy firm, defines big data as *high-volume, high-velocity, and high-variety information assets that demand cost-effective, innovative forms of information processing that enable enhanced insight, decision-making, and process automation*.

Further, big data is a term applied to data sets whose size or type is beyond the ability of traditional relational databases to capture, manage, and process the data with low latency.

Four 'V's

You would observe that there are four **V**'s in Gartner's definition of big data. These are:

1. **Velocity:** This group comprises the forms of data constantly coming into the system, often in real-time. This data helps in knowing what is happening now in the real world and can help make effective decisions. Consider, for example, the data generated by medical devices and sensors constantly and in real-time, which, if not tracked on time, may become useless. Another example of this type of data is social media, which generates megabytes of data per second, giving a sense of velocity in the data flow.
2. **Volume**: As the number of sources increases by the day, the amount of data collected becomes huge, and it cannot be handled by traditional methods of data storage, processing, and analysis.

3. **Variety**: Variety refers to the different types of data collected, which may be structured, semi-structured, or unstructured. For example, data can be text, an image, or video, among others. It could also be from different sources, such as social media, blogs, web searches, wearables and any other as long as you can capture it.
4. **Veracity**: Veracity which means authenticity is the, fourth 'V' because authenticity or reliability of data is very important. However, social media, an important source of big data, may not be authentic as per present regulations and yet is meaningful and important, providing valuable insights.

Big data includes all types of data that a company can collect from all sources, such as internal company processes and various external sources that the company deals with. Therefore, big data can be divided into these broad categories:

- *Demographic Data*: information regarding age, gender, marital status, employment, and income status
- *Psychographic Data*: behaviors, beliefs, values, interests, lifestyles
- *Geographic Data*: geolocation, which is important for sales territory planning and managing in the pharmaceutical industry
- *Behavioral Data*: data based on users' web surfing behaviors, extracted from cookies
- *Contextual Data*: a wide field concerning the context and environment surrounding us. For example, from news to sentiment and market fluctuations. Essential for communicating timely and relevant messages to customers across all touchpoints in their journey.
- *First Party Data*: Data that a company collects directly from its users and customers through CRM (Customer Relationship Management) systems

As you can see, not only organizations but individuals and devices are also producing data in huge volumes, even up to terabytes per second. Further, artificial intelligence (AI), mobile, social media, and the Internet of Things (IoT) are driving data complexity through new forms and sources.

Although big data gathered from internal processes and external sources have different applications, it is important to integrate them to make meaning out of them and develop insights. That is when technological advancements like digitalization, Cloud computing, cheaper storage, and faster processing speeds come into the picture.

Data: Three Different Uses

We can divide data into three broad categories based on how we can use it. These are:

- *Descriptive Data* describes a situation, such as reporting, which describes what happened and why.
- *Predictive Data* uses past data to predict future outcomes. It answers the question— *what will probably happen in the future?*
- *Prescriptive Data* takes a look at *cause-and-effect* analysis and tells you what to do. It answers questions like— *what will happen, when, and why?*

Big Data Analytics

Big data analytics is the use of advanced analytic techniques against very large, diverse data sets that include structured, semi-structured, and unstructured data from different sources and in different sizes, from terabytes to zettabytes. Organizations can use advanced analytics techniques such as text analytics, machine learning, predictive analytics, data mining, statistics, and natural language processing (NLP) to gain new insights from previously untapped data sources.

Big Data Analytics in Pharma

Big data analytics is revolutionizing many processes such as research & development, drug discovery, clinical trials, sales, and marketing in the pharmaceutical industry, improving efficiency across the board. Here is a brief account of how big data analytics can help pharmaceutical companies in these areas:

Research and Development

Pharma companies can generate informative analytics with the insights gained from historical and real-time sources such as social media, IoT sensors, log files, and patient data. The large volumes of data gathered from these various sources at different stages, from drug discovery to real-world usage, can help Pharma gain useful insights to develop and discover new drugs that are highly relevant to the needs of the patients.

Drug Discovery and Development

Traditionally, drug discovery has been an iterative process of physically testing various compounds to discover new drugs, which requires more resources and is very time-consuming and cost-intensive. However, big data analytics help researchers through predictive modeling for drug discovery, enabling them to predict drug interactions, toxicity, and inhibition, speed up the whole process and cut down the developmental costs.

Clinical Trials

Clinical trials are essential in the pharma and life sciences industries as they help determine whether a specific treatment is safe and effective for patients. But, they involve huge costs, even up to $2.6 billion, for developing a single drug from bench to bedside. Also, they are time-consuming, taking about 8 to 10 years, almost half the patent life of the new drug. Further, recruiting the right patients for clinical trials is crucial for the success of these trials is very difficult, and this could be a major reason why many clinical trials fail. Big data can help pharmaceutical companies to recruit the right patients for clinical trials, using data such as genetic information, personality traits, and disease status, which will increase the success rate of the drug.

Precision Medicine

In addition, big data enables precision medicine as it uses relevant data on a patient's genetic make-up and behavioral patterns to diagnose and treat disorders. Thus it can help pharma companies develop personalized medicine specific to an individual patient's genes and lifestyle.

Sales and Marketing

Big data can significantly help Sales and Marketing in the pharmaceutical industry to maintain their competitive advantage in today's hyper-competitive marketplace. Today, thanks to big data analytics, Pharma can analyze the information from social media, demographics, EHR (Electronic Health Records), and other data sources, spot, and tap into the underserved and new markets. Furthermore, big data analytics can help pharma companies analyze the effectiveness of sales efforts and make key decisions to improve their marketing and sales strategies.

Future Outlook

Thus, big data analytics have revolutionized the pharmaceutical industry enabling them to develop more effective treatments and their sales and marketing teams to be smarter and more efficient. Therefore, to stay ahead of the competition and optimize their performance, Pharma companies should develop a strategic plan that integrates big data analytics with the infrastructure and enterprise systems.

The future outlook for Big Data Analytics? It could only be better and brighter as big data analytics has the potential to transform the way healthcare providers use sophisticated technologies to gain insights from their clinical and other data repositories and make informed decisions leading to better patient outcomes. Every way you look at the future of big data analytics, it is indispensable!

Real World Data and Evidence

Increasingly, pharmaceutical and life sciences companies are embracing real-world data (RWD) and real-world evidence (RWE) as it presents a significant opportunity to improve efficiency and innovation. It is because they are looking to sources beyond randomized clinical trials (RCTs) to measure and demonstrate the value they bring as the healthcare industry's focus on outcomes is increasing.

Real World-Data is the data relating to patient health status and the delivery of healthcare routinely collected and, therefore, reflects the experience of individuals through their routine interactions with the healthcare system (claims data, electronic health records) or data collected in surveys, registries, and, more recently, from sensors (wearables).

According to a 2018 Benchmarking Survey by Deloitte, a leading international consultancy firm, *approximately 90 percent of global pharmaceutical companies are using or have plans to use real-world data in the near future*.

Many Uses

Pharmaceutical and life sciences companies can use Real-World Data in many ways to maximize clinical study enrollment and even shorten clinical trial timelines. Consider these, for example:

- Real-World Data can help Pharma increase the quantity, quality, and timeliness of useful, trustworthy research results.
- It can help sponsors understand how treatments perform and assist in clinical trial planning.
- By using digital records to map specific patient populations, sponsors can determine where the largest patient population exists within a specific therapeutic area.
- Sponsors can also cross-reference patient data with relevant investigator sites to determine the correct physicians specializing in the treatment or study of the disease of interest.

Challenges in Using Real-World Data

Although Real-World Data has many significant uses for pharmaceutical companies, some challenges exist in using it. Erin Booth, Senior Manager, Regulatory and Medical Writing at MMS, a data-focused clinical research organization, explains four major challenges in her MMS Blog article, *How Real World Data is Changing the Pharmaceutical Industry*. These are:

1. **Availability of data**: Data focused on patient characteristics and outcomes is not always accessible. Also, baseline values may be absent in many cases, and follow-up after treatment may be missing.
2. **Concerns about quality/precision**: The designation of a particular indication in some cases may not be as precise as in a clinical trial, as there are no guidelines to follow for designations. For example, if a sponsor were collecting data on heart attacks or strokes, and if there is no adjudication committee to review and categorize the designation, it may lead to underreporting of the severity.
3. **Different EMR Systems**: Interoperability is an issue as different health systems have different EMR (Electronic Medical Records) platforms. Updating systems is not simple or cost-effective, making data pooling and statistical analyses required for regulatory reviews nearly impossible.
4. **Governance Issues**: If patients have not consented to use their data in an application for an indication, many concerns such as patient privacy, data security, transparency and confidentiality, access, conflict of interest, intellectual property, and integrity can come into play, leading to governance issues.

Pharma and biotech companies using Real-World Evidence (RWE) must address these issues to ensure their findings are strong and precise as these problems, if not addressed, it can reduce the amount of power of in a study intended to show a difference between treatments, giving a bias toward no difference in a comparison study.

Overcoming the Challenges

In the above-cited MMS blog article, *How Real-World Data is Changing the Pharmaceutical Industry*, Erin Booth also suggests ways to overcome the challenges the industry faces in using Real-World Data. To overcome the challenges, Pharma must:

- Engage healthcare providers and patients by promoting adherence to practice guidelines and adherence to prescription drugs
- Establish a framework for confidentiality and security
- Adopt a common approach to configuring digital healthcare data
- Eliminate barriers that promote complexity while ensuring appropriate safeguards
- Establish a regulatory framework that provides stakeholders

What is Real-World Evidence (RWE)?

Real-World Evidence (RWE) is the clinical evidence regarding the usage and potential benefits or risks of a medical product derived from analysis of Real-World Data (RWD). Real-World Evidence can be generated by different study designs or analyses, including randomized trials, large simple trials, pragmatic trials, and observational studies (prospective and retrospective).

Although Real-World Evidence (RWE) has been in use for many years, it is the recent advances in analytics allow it to be employed in new ways to understand how patient characteristics and behaviors affect health outcomes, helping to predict the progression of a disease, a patient's responses to therapy, or the risk of adverse events. Furthermore, it also helps increase the efficiency of R&D investments by accelerating time to market.

Why Real-World Evidence?

Like in everything else, there is a difference in what we expect and what happens, even in healthcare. What could be the reason for this difference? One way to explain this is because there is a gap between what we learn (research) and what we do (practice).

But it is what happens in practice that matters. Real-World Evidence fills those gaps by gathering data from the real world— from patients' interactions across the healthcare system.

Recently, several forces such as cost and competitive pressures, scientific advances, increasing digital adoption by stakeholders, regulators' positive attitude towards emerging technologies, and the increasing breadth and interoperability of data and technologies are driving participants in the healthcare ecosystem to intensify their focus on value and patient outcomes. Consider these changes, for example:

- Payers are gradually shifting to outcomes-based contracts, and providers are vying to gain privilege status with each other.
- Patients are taking more ownership of their outcomes.

The changing environment makes it almost mandatory to gather insights from real-world evidence and get the right treatment to the right patient at the right time by measuring outcomes and demonstrating the value of interventions.

Uses of Real-World Evidence (RWE) in Pharma

Real-World Evidence can provide pharmaceutical, and biotech companies value across the entire life cycle product. Consider these uses. For example, RWE can:

- Help researchers in pre-trial design by identifying potential patients and creating proper inclusion criteria for clinical trials
- Help researchers expand the scope of a clinical trial by providing information about a broader cross-section of a real-world patient population. It can help clinicians, researchers, and industry partners better understand their products and how they work in the real world.
- Supplement traditional outcome measurement with patient-generated data such as patient-reported outcomes (PROs) or biometric data that is easier to collect between doctor appointments.

- Help post-marketing surveillance activities such as— detecting adverse events or risks as they arise during real-world usage of a drug or device; comparing new products or treatments with existing options and the standards of care; updating clinical guidelines as certain populations or groups more benefit than others; complying with regulatory requirements.
- Help expand an indication profile for a product. For example, Pharma companies can study safety and outcomes data from RWD disease or product registries for their products which they can use to supplement a submission to regulatory authorities like the US FDA or EMA (European Medicines Agency) without going through a very lengthy and costly process of conducting clinical trials for every new indication.
- Facilitate shared decision-making between a patient and physician by providing individualized decision support tools through advanced analytics. For example, The Michigan Bariatric Surgery Collaborative uses a tool that predicts, based on individual characteristics, how a patient might respond to different types of bariatric surgery.

Advanced RWE Analytics

In the past few years, the introduction of advanced real-world evidence (RWE) analytics has made real-world data an even more powerful resource for pharmaceutical companies. Unlike traditional RWE analytics, advanced RWE Analytics uses state-of-the-art data engineering approaches to building large data sets with rich information on thousands of patient variables. Also, it uses predictive models, machine learning, and more to extract deeper insights from these data sets. RWE Analytics thus enable pharma companies to draw on thousands of patient characteristics to understand what drives outcomes better.

McKinsey, a leading global consultancy firm, estimates that *an average top-20 pharma company that adopted advanced RWE analytics across the whole value chain for in-market and pipeline products could unlock more than $300 million a year over the next three to five years*.

Growing Regulatory Acceptance

In March 2016, The US Food and Drug Administration released a statement outlining the goals and procedures for the Prescription Drug User Fee Act (PDUFA) VI for 2018-22 with notice that this would include the use of real-world evidence (RWE) in regulatory decision-making. Later, in December 2016, The 21st Century Cures Act became law in the US, to help accelerate medical product development, allowing innovations and advances to become available for patients who need them faster and more efficiently. Towards that aim, it included a provision for RWE to be used in place of evidence from randomized controlled trials (RCTs), if judged appropriate by the FDA.

Here is a case that shows how the US FDA approved a supplementary New Drug Application based on real-world data and evidence.

In 2015, Pfizer received US FDA accelerated approval of IBRANCE® (Palbociclib), combined with letrozole, for the treatment of postmenopausal women with estrogen-receptor positive, human epidermal growth factor receptor 2-negative (ER+/HER2-) advanced breast cancer as initial endocrine therapy for their metastatic disease. FDA reviewed and approved IBRANCE under Breakthrough Therapy designation and Priority Review Program.

Later, FDA Pfizer received regular FDA approval and expanded indication for first-line HR+, HER2-metastatic breast cancer in February 2016. Furthermore, in April 2019, Pfizer received a supplementary New Drug Application (sNDA) to expand the indications for IBRANCE®, combined with an aromatase inhibitor or Fulvestrant to include men with hormone-receptor-positive (HR+), human epidermal growth factor receptor 2-negative (HER2-) advanced or metastatic breast cancer. The approval is based on data from electronic health records (EHR) and post-marketing reports of the real-world use of IBRANCE in male patients sourced from three databases: IQVIA Insurance Database, Flatiron Health Breast Cancer database, and the Pfizer global safety database. Speaking on this occasion, Chris Boshoff, MD, Ph.D., said: *We appreciate that our partnership with the FDA has allowed us to take a significant step forward in using real-world data to bring medicines to patients most in need*.

(Source: US FDA Approves IBRANCE® (palbociclib) for the Treatment of Men with HR+, HER2-Metastatic Breast Cancer, pfizer.com, April 04, 2019)

Another notable example of real-world evidence is AstraZeneca's use of real-world data to demonstrate the real-world effectiveness of its diabetes therapy Farxiga (Dapagliflozin) compared to competitors.

Real World Evidence (RWE) and Pharma Marketing

Advanced real-world analytics could help pharmaceutical companies identify new targets for molecules, accelerate time to market, and improve formulary position and payer negotiations. Also, it can generate stronger evidence of differentiation and benefit/risk balance for products already on the market.

Furthermore, real-world evidence with its advanced analytical capability can help pharma companies to answer critical questions such as:

- Which patient subsegments respond best to the proposed therapy?
- What patient characteristics predict a switch from drug X to drug Y?
- On which indications in a biological pathway is a drug most likely to be effective?

Answers to these questions and more will equip pharma marketers to target their promotion and reap the benefits of data-driven marketing.

What the Future Holds for RWE?

Real-world evidence can help Pharma significantly to stay ahead of the competition. With insights derived into biology, unmet needs, real-world therapy usage, safety and effectiveness, drivers of healthcare professionals' choices, and other factors, RWE powered by traditional and advanced analytics can help decision-makers in Pharma in:

- head-to-head comparisons of effectiveness and safety
- cost-effectiveness analyses to support submissions to payers and regulators

- other forms of communication with external stakeholders, and
- improving patient outcomes

Companies that build real-world data generating capabilities will have a distinct competitive advantage over others that don't.

However, a word of caution, as a disruption in RWE space may be round the corner. Pharmaceutical and healthcare companies should address disruption from tech giants and payers. Already, the signs are emerging. Consider, for example, Google has engaged with one of the largest US healthcare systems to collect and analyze data from millions of patients. It signals growing interest among major tech players outside the healthcare sector.

Above all, real-world evidence can help accelerate pharma companies' shift from product-focused to patient-focused organizations.

Blockchain in Pharma

What is Blockchain?

Blockchain is a list of records—a ledger that's open and distributed. As new records (blocks) are added to the list (chain), they're verified cryptographically across the network, maintaining the blockchain. As a result, blockchain is inherently secure and allows for transparent consensus without putting any central party in charge. Furthermore, blockchain technology can fix many of the vulnerabilities of the conventional supply chain in any industry. The advantage of a blockchain-based system is that competitors can collaborate on a shared platform without sharing sensitive information. Companies can safely work together in a shared, permanent ledger without giving up control or revealing their data. A single company does not own the ledger in the blockchain system. Instead, it is governed by all members of a network. That is how the blockchain delegates the work of checks and balances to cryptography and code and helps reduce friction, expose fraud, and assure product authenticity with great speed.

The Pandemic Exposes Supply Chain Inefficiencies

The recent global pandemic, COVID-19, exposed the inefficiencies of the pharmaceutical and medical supply chains worldwide. For example, leading hospitals in almost all countries struggled with shortages of basic safety equipment such as masks, gowns, face shields, and sanitizers during the pandemic. The hospital authorities and government officials were not ready to meet the swift and sudden escalation in demand, bringing to light the long-festering problems in the medical supply chain. In the US, CDC and FDA officials were concerned that fraudulent respirators are circulating and fraudulent test kits for COVID-19 are being sold online. The Federal government in the US has placed more than $110 million in N95 mask orders at high prices with unproven mask vendors.

Blockchain has been a disruptive technology for a decade, and many industries have embraced it. However, when the Covid-19 pandemic struck, the pharmaceutical industry realized that its global supply chain lacked connectivity and data exchange and that only blockchain could help resolve it.

When China's manufacturing system almost came to a grinding halt, cracks in the global pharmaceutical supply chain started to appear. That's when the healthcare industry realized the urgency to improve the global supply chains worldwide that started crumbling, when borders worldwide were closed, followed by the reduced workforce, lockdowns, and an insatiable demand growing for goods and services internationally.

How Blockchain Can Help Pharma?

Arun Ghosh, a KPMG analyst, says that the primary use for blockchain in the pharmaceutical industry is to serve as a ledger of truth for sharing complex information with regulators, pharmacy benefit managers, contract manufacturers, physicians, patients, academic researchers, and R&D collaborators and others. Furthermore, blockchain can improve nearly every component of the pharmaceutical value chain, from increasing supply chain transparency to enhancing data collection in clinical trials and optimizing marketing and advertising expenditure.

Blockchain as a technology is crucial for pharma as it provides traceability throughout the product lifecycle by relating data, propagating it, and distributing it securely throughout the organization. In addition, the pharma industry requires transparency in its clinical trials, supply chain control as it scales up, product validation, and quality assurance in the approval process and commercialization. But, perhaps, the most important advantage that blockchain technology can offer the pharmaceutical industry is to help solve the long-festering problem of counterfeit drugs.

The pharmaceutical industry loses billions of dollars annually due to counterfeit drugs. Currently, it is the most pressing issue worldwide, especially in the developing world. Apart from this, interoperability, drug traceability, and data security are among the urgent issues that need to be resolved. Blockchain can change and improve the situation by making the processes more transparent and easier to trace. Akeo, a consultancy firm specializing in blockchain technology, globally summarized the advantages of blockchain in the pharmaceutical industry in their ebook, *Blockchain in Pharmaceuticals*. Here is the gist:

1. *Increase Trust*: Blockchain will make it easy for manufacturers, wholesalers, and retailers to track the complete supply chain. It will not only provide better visibility but will also maintain the high trust factor amongst the parties.
2. *Enhanced Security*: Blockchain, the immutable ledger, is considered one of the most secure systems in the world. Blockchain will ensure the drug information stored on the ledger remains safe and unmodified, for example, patients' records.
3. *Added Visibility*: Visibility and privacy are amongst the top concerns for the pharma supply chain. Blockchain, a distributed ledger, is the best technology to make the stored data visible to every party.
4. *Prevent Drug Counterfeits*: Registering drug information on the blockchain will allow manufacturers and regulatory authorities to track, trace, and authenticate drugs at any stage. It will make it impossible to make counterfeit goods.

What is more, blockchain can make clinical trial management more secure and streamlined. Clinical trial management has been facing numerous challenges related to the design model and security of the personal data of enrolled patients. Blockchain can help clinical research professionals in addressing these and other challenges.

The MediLedger Network

The MediLedger is a classic example of how competitors in the pharmaceutical industry can collaborate on a shared platform without sharing sensitive information. The MediLedger Network is a blockchain consortium focused on pharma supply chains, including Gilead, Pfizer, Amgen, Genentech, Americsource-Bergen, and McKesson. Chronicled, a tech start-up, provides the underlying technology to the network.

MediLedger's first solution is a product verification system that makes it easier to verify that a returned drug is authentic, a common but difficult process. The task of verifying that returned salable drugs are authentic falls to wholesalers, who must contact the manufacturers to track down serial numbers. This process can take up to forty-eight hours. However, the wholesalers can make the same verification in less than a second using blockchain. Hospitals and pharmacies can also use this rapid serial number verification with as little infrastructure as a web browser and barcode scanner.

The next solution that MedicalLedger is working on is applying blockchain technology to *track and trace*. *Track and Trace* is the process of identifying a specific box of drugs and where it has been at any time. This process can be done with blockchain without revealing confidential and sensitive information to anyone in the ecosystem. MediLedger recently completed a pilot using a blockchain for track and trace with 25 participants, including Walgreens and Walmart, transportation provider FedEx, Standards organization, GS1 (Global Standards), wholesale drug distributors in America, including Americsource-Bergen and Cardinal Health, etc.

Blockchain's Potential

Ultimately, blockchain participants will be able to enforce a set of rules in real-time as a box of drugs travels from one handoff point to another across the entire supply chain. Along the way, auditing is automated and embedded, flagging problems and who has custody as it happens. When drugs reach their final destination, it's as though they arrive with a BlackBox of data to assure authenticity and compliance with the business rules during their entire journey.

Blockchain and Digital Ads

Pharma companies in the US spend billions of dollars on prescription drug ads, especially on TV and print. For example, the pharma industry's advertising expenditure in 2016 increased to $5.2 billion from $3.2 billion in 2012, a sixty-percent increase over the last four years.

Many pharma companies still use spray and pray tactics in TV ads and billboards. However, these are expensive and not target-specific. By leveraging artificial intelligence and blockchain technologies, pharmaceutical companies could implement highly focused and segmented ads and generate superior results at a fraction of the cost.

Especially for digital ads, blockchain can bring transparency to the advertising supply chain, optimize advertising expenditure and help reduce ad tech tax. According to 2017 data from the Association of National Advertisers (ANA) in the US, about forty cents of every dollar goes to fees. That fee is the tech tax. It goes to a range of tech providers, data sellers, potentially inventory arbitrageurs, and several others, many of whom may not add value. However, cutting out the ones that don't add value is difficult when the brand behind the buy has little visibility into where its dollars go, who all the parties to the transaction are, and whether they are necessary to the campaign. Blockchain can allow brands to track exactly where all their advertising dollars go and help optimize the ad spend.

What it Takes?

Undoubtedly, blockchain technology offers many advantages like decentralized data structure, unprecedented data security and integrity standards, and maintaining tamper-proof data records. However, there is one catch. Blockchain is an ecosystem technology, and it can only benefit when the technology is broadly adopted and when physical systems work with it. More industry standards are needed to make it all truly interoperable. For example, the visibility of technology is limited by manufacturers' packaging. In some countries with the greatest fraud, serialized numbers are not yet required on a box of drugs. Full track and trace would need to connect the network to these systems.

However, things are changing for the better. New regulations are in place to pressurize the pharmaceutical industry to work better together in developing standards. For example, in the US, the Drug Supply Chain Security Act (DSCSA), signed into law in 2013, has a deadline of 2023 for manufacturers to track and trace all transactions involved in transporting medicines from factory to patient. Likewise, the EU's (European Union) Falsified Medicines Directive lays out rules to combat fake medicines in the region and includes anti-tampering security on packaging and tracking requirements.

Changes Everything

Marc Andreessen, inventor of the internet browser, summed up the true potential of blockchain technology and what it can change when he said: *The practical consequence is, for the first time, a way for one Internet user to transfer a unique piece of digital property to another Internet user, such that the transfer is guaranteed to be safe and secure, everyone knows that the transfer has taken place, and nobody can challenge the legitimacy of the transfer. The consequences of this breakthrough are hard to overstate.*

Design Thinking

Design Thinking

Think differently is what we would usually say when trying to find a solution to some difficult problems. But, how do you think differently? When you think of it, *Design Thinking* is thinking differently!

Design thinking is not a new concept. Its origins can be traced to Herbert A. Simon's 1969 book, *The Sciences of the Artificial*. Later, Stanford University taught a course on the design aspects in the 1980s. Design thinking is another method to identify all parameters of a problem to create a solution at its core.

Shawn Nason, one of the pioneers of design thinking and founder of The Nason Group, specializing in helping companies become more innovative, says design thinking is a limited term. He says *design thinking is only a part of a much bigger process in this co-creation and human-centered design aspect. It's about putting the customer in the middle of your process, product, or solution. Co-creating means bringing the consumer in and using an open innovation process. You may use other companies and competitors, aligning your organization outside your own, to bring this process about.*

Traditionally, design is a concept that has been linked to creative professionals. However, design is now strongly integrated into the business. Today, design is not limited to artists, graphic designers, or architects, but it is a tool for innovation that businesses, including pharma organizations, most necessarily integrate. Tim Brown, President, and CEO of IDEO, an innovation company that aims to make an impact through design, hit the nail on the head when he defined Design Thinking as *a human-centered approach to innovation that draws from the designer's toolkit to integrate the needs of people, the possibilities of technology, and the requirements for business success*.

Pharmaceutical companies can use design thinking to drive ideas to better connect with and serve the patient experience. As Pharma is becoming more patient-centric, design thinking can become a core competence and a competitive advantage.

Design Thinking: Basic Steps

Dr. Nicolas Davies briefly describes the basic steps of design thinking in her eyeforpharma article titled *Design Thinking: A Human-Centered Approach for Pharma*, published in EyeforPharma on September 15, 2015. Here is the gist of what she wrote: The basic steps are Empathizing, Defining, Ideating, Prototyping, and Testing.

1. **Empathizing**: Empathy is always used on the end-users, and understanding them is vital. Tools like contextual inquiry and having people with ethnographic backgrounds help. A general observation is pharma companies often fail to empathize with patients. To be empathetic, pharmaceutical companies will do better if they start treating patients, not just the disease.
2. **Defining**: The second step, defining, refers to identifying the problem, while **Ideating** is brainstorming alternative solutions to that problem. According to George Petroff, GE's Chief Patient Officer: *Design Thinking is mostly about problem-framing. It generates ideas, narrowing them down to a set of concepts to develop further. It can help Pharma stakeholders by defining the problem they are trying to solve before resources are allocated to solving it.* The key questions to ask during the defining step are: What pain points do patients with a particular illness have to deal with, like when visiting the doctor, picking up the prescription, or taking the medication? How is their relationship with their doctor? What causes them to miss a dose or not follow the doctor's instructions? Who do they trust for information? Marie Hartmann, Design Director and Partner at *Designit* says: *The two steps, Defining and ideating, are the stage for constant questioning. We should seek to answer questions related to the patients and their contexts. The questions will always reveal opportunity areas, often with big potential for improvement*.
3. **Ideating**: The key questions to ask during the Ideating stage are: What can we do to ensure that medication is taken correctly and works better? Can we, somehow, influence the patients to change their lifestyles to improve the effectiveness

of the drugs? What else can we do to help the patient to live a better life? In addition to asking several questions, we must also deploy visualization tools to help stakeholders comprehend the situation. We can use design artifacts such as mind maps, patient journeys, and diagrams to provide a physical representation to help stakeholders grasp the problem and its potential solutions. As a result, the stakeholders can visualize both the current situation and envision what it could look like in the future. Thus, visualization allows us to understand how the patient experience looks today and work collaboratively with healthcare providers and pharmaceutical companies to create the ideal experience.

4. The final two steps of design thinking, **Prototyping** and **Testing** go hand in hand by ensuring that an idea doesn't simply stay as an abstract and unused idea. Whereas design artifacts represent the problem, prototypes represent the chosen solution. Moreover, Prototyping allows getting rapid feedback on each of the prototypes, collecting the pros and cons, rejecting them, or accepting them for further improvement. The key here is to think like real users and decide on how real users would experience the prototype. We are moving from 'belief,' 'behave,' and 'feel' users have to the current solution to understanding the desired 'belief,' 'behave,' and 'feel' with the finished product.
5. **Testing** then involves transparent experimentation so that Pharma can immediately see and assess the solution's real-world feasibility. Testing involves 'real people,' which reveals valuable insights to improve the solution further.

Design Thinking: Opportunities for Pharma

Pharma has several touchpoints with patients that provide opportunities to apply design thinking, including clinical trials, diagnosis, treatment, and medication delivery. In addition, many companies are using innovative designs to improve the self-management experience for patients. Examples of design thinking in Pharma include:

- GE healthcare's Sensory Suite is a mammography exam machine that distracts patients from feelings of anxiety and discomfort. This innovation was driven by research showing that one out of four women avoids mammography due to the fear of the problem.
- Bayer's Diabetes Care, for example, partnered with IDEO to develop the design, interface, and on-the-shelf packaging for a self-management gadget called Contour USB Blood Glucose Monitor. On the one hand, it is a rod that touches and measures blood; on the other, it is a USB, which can provide a blood sugar levels summary using GE software.
- Through a long-term collaboration with Designit, Novo Nordisk has developed several solutions that enable diabetes patients to take their medication less scarily with a device looking more like a pen than a needle.
- In collaboration with Smart Design and OXO, UCB also created Cimzia (Certolizumab pegol), which rethinks the self-injection process for arthritis patients.
- Beyond machines and technological gadgets, design thinking can provide solutions in many other ways, such as packaging to support patient self-management. IDEO, for example, assisted a specialized pharmacy, PillPack, in developing a system to provide quick and simple home deliveries to patients who lose track of their medication for various reasons. IDEO designed every interaction with the patient as straightforward and reassuring, sorting out the medication into separate and personalized packets with time, date, and an image of the pill.
- Design thinking also detects and solves experiential problems throughout healthcare programs. Designit recently helped improve and design the experience of breast cancer patients by reducing their waiting time between learning of their lump and getting a specialist's formal diagnosis. They managed to reduce time by 90 percent, from up to 12 weeks to an average of 7 days, at the Oslo University Hospital in Norway.

Despite the many advantages that design thinking offers, It will take time before the pharmaceutical industry becomes truly design-driven. Shifting the culture is a major hurdle they need to cross. Pharmaceutical companies are wired to technology and business and are not known for their experiential approach.

Nonetheless, design thinking remains critical to potentially improving patients' experiences across Pharma, and it begins with empathizing. Firstly, companies should invest time and resources in understanding their users' needs. And they need to ask and answer two vital questions: How can the patient's quality of life be improved and not how the diseases are cured? How do we as an organization need to change to deliver this experience?

Here are some cases showing how some pharmaceutical and healthcare organizations have applied design thinking to improve patient experiences:

CASE

36

Monash Watch Reduces Hospitalization With Design Thinking!

Australia's Monash Health had a **Monash Watch** program to use telemedicine to keep vulnerable populations healthy at home and reduce hospitalization rates. It used detailed storyboards to help hospital administration and government policymakers envision this new approach in practice. They did not build a digital prototype but used visualization through a detailed storyboard and achieved the desired outcome.

(Source: Edouard Demeire's book, KICCASS Pharma, 2020)

CASE

37

The Case of a Twice Yearly Infusion, An Innovation that Was Slow on Its Diffusion Curve!

Here is one application of design thinking whose innovation was slow on its innovation diffusion curve. A company engaged in selling large volume parenterals developed a drug delivered as a twice-yearly infusion against competitors' daily orals. As a result, the product has a distinct competitive advantage against its competitors. The advantage of a twice-yearly infusional drug is that you are not reminded of your disease daily every time you have to take your oral medication. However, the flip side of it is most people dislike infusions.

The team identified two reasons for disliking infusion through the first phase of the design thinking process. One was some form of needle phobia, which could be hard to resolve. The other was that the infusion took three to four hours sitting in an infusion seat. Otherwise, active patients were annoyed with spending half a day in an infusion seat in a less hospitable environment such as a clinic. So the whole design process then centered on how to make this a positive experience. And the ideation phase came up with the idea to create a Starbucks-like friendly environment, which would involve music being played. However, one participating design team member argued that this was a lot of effort to develop an idea that some patients were already applying, coming to the hospital with an iPad to watch a movie they hadn't time to watch yet!

(Source: Edouard Demeire's book, KICCASS Pharma, 2020)

CASE

38

UCB, An Early Adopter of Design Thinking!

The Belgium drug major, UCB, adopted design thinking in a big way inside its teams. The company has a very rigorous process to unite the right brain thinking (feelings, intuition, visualization, imagination) and left brain thinking (logic, fact-based, linear, mathematical). They say the process is not just useful for product development but tasks as varied as distributing drugs directly in East European countries instead of going through local partners and for internal tasks such as the staff's compliance training which has previously been run as e-learning where staff members were clicking through the next button.

(Source: Edouard Demeire's book, KICCASS Pharma, 2020)

Scenario Planning

A scenario is a description of possible actions or events in the future. In business planning and strategy, a scenario is a potential event or a combination of events that could be relevant to the organization as it could provide a significant opportunity or create a risk. Apart from this definition of scenarios, it is important to understand what scenarios are not. For example, scenarios are not:

- Compelling descriptions of possible futures
- Intended to forecast the future
- Neither predictions nor contingency plans
- The same as strategic options

Scenarios are external and fall outside the organization's control, unlike the strategic plan.

The future is unpredictable and uncertain. However, a reasonable knowledge about what the future will look like will help businesses to prepare for it. Enter scenario planning. Scenario planning helps you define critical uncertainties and develop plausible scenarios for discussing the impacts and responses to give for each one of them. Scenario planning is a very useful tool because if you know what could happen, you are more likely to deal with what will happen.

Scenario Development Model

Although Herman Kahn is credited with using Scenarios for the first time in the 1950s, through his work for the US Military, the Royal Dutch Shell Company (Shell) adopted Scenario planning as a strategy in 1972. However, scenario development processes are generally undertaken in facilitated groups and rely heavily on the subjective judgments of the group members. So how do these groups develop scenarios, and on what basis? The following table presents a broad process framework for developing scenarios.

Table 2.26 Scenario Development Process Framework

Stage 1: Project Orientation	Stage 2: Environmental Exploration	Stage 3: Synthesis and Story development	Stage 4: Scenario to Strategy
• Establish the scenario purpose • Identify the focal/strategic issues • Surface potential scenario themes • Establish the scenario horizon year	• Identify the driving forces • Segregate *Uncertainties* from *Predetermined* • Establish Critical *Uncertainties* • Identify linkages and causal relationships	• Define the scenario *logics* • Create scenario end states • Construct scenario storylines • Elaborate/ embellish storylines to create narratives	• Identify *Early Warning Signs* for each scenario • Establish implications across and within the scenarios • Assess Strategic Fit and identify strategic options

Source: Ron Bradfield and Hany El-Sayed, Four Scenarios for the future of the pharmaceutical industry, Technology Analysis and Strategic Management, Vol 21, No. 2, February 2009, 195-212

Scenario Planning Objectives

Leaders of all functions must understand what scenario planning is and use it as a tool to drive immediate actions, decisions, and longer-term plans. So, the objectives of scenario planning for a given function are the same as at the corporate level. Jackie Wiles at Gartner describes key objectives of scenario planning in her July 8, 2022, article on the Gartner blog. The objectives are to:

- Maintain focus on critical growth and transformation initiatives during disruption
- Identify surefire strategic decisions to pursue, regardless of which future unfolds
- Perform due diligence on critical short-term decisions, and make strategic course corrections as needed
- Prepare the team to mitigate potential risks and provide timely risk-aligned guidance for different scenarios

Scenario Planning at Corporate and Functional Levels

While the purpose and objectives of scenario planning are similar at corporate and functional levels, their roles in implementation are different. The scenarios created and prioritized at the corporate level are cascaded down at relevant functional levels. The various functional levels then define implications, risks, and opportunities for each Scenario relevant to their respective functions, create action plans, and monitor them.

When leaders of the various organizational functions understand their roles and cascade the corporate scenarios as applicable to their respective functions, it can make the strategy execution more resilient. If the scenario changes, functional leaders can substitute the original actions with scenario-specific ones they already envisaged.

Scenario Planning Process

The six steps of scenario planning are:

1. **Brainstorm future scenarios**, but you must decide the time frame first. Once you decide on the time frame, say at least a decade, you need to consider factors that can impact your business and organization, like political and economical conditions, technological advancement, and competitors' landscape.
2. **Identify trends and driving forces**. While identifying trends and driving forces, the focus should be on understanding who will be affected by them. Who and what can influence those?
3. **Create a scenario planning template**. The scenario planning template should cover societal structure, demographic, economic, and political factors, public opinions, markets, consumer behavior, technology, innovation, competitive industry structure, and your organizational capacities and core competencies.
4. **Develop a scenario**. Developing an actual scenario is a crucial task in the whole process. First, you need to evaluate each

factor and create a situation of the plausible traits and trends of the market. It is akin to writing a movie scene where you build a plot and develop a story around it. Also, you have to define touch points around which your story will revolve.

5. **Evaluate a Scenario**: Following a systematic step-by-step procedure, the scenario planning team can balance wild imagination and sound judgment based on collective knowledge and experience. Identify the issues that are likely to impact your business in the future and come up with strategies to deal with those potential issues. For example:

- Today, patients, particularly millennials, are taking a proactive role in their healthcare. Some progressive pharmaceutical companies are accordingly becoming more patient-centric. Healthcare is becoming more patient-centric, and this will only accelerate. Therefore, Pharma must change its strategy from being product-centric to patient-centric. How should you plan for this big change or transformation?
- How will increased adoption of Telehealth impact pharmaceutical companies in the future?
- With physician access decreasing, how will Pharma improve their engagement with HCPs and other stakeholders?
- The cost-containment pressures by governments, payers, and providers are driving a shift from cost-plus to value-based pricing of pharmaceutical products. How will Pharma deal with such a situation?
- The digital revolution is already impacting the pharmaceutical industry, which will likely intensify in the future. How prepared is your company to undergo a digital transformation?
- Transactional marketing practices in branded-generic markets such as India rule the roost forming a Pharma-Physician nexus. There are strong indications that the governments in these countries are determined to end these unethical practices. What will be the impact of such governmental decision on your business and the industry? If you have been practicing transactional marketing with a *quid-pro-quo* approach, how will you change them to transformational marketing practices?

How must you prepare for that?

6. Update strategies and policies based on the evaluation. You must evaluate and update your strategic plans periodically as the market situations are changing according to the Macro-environmental factors defined.

   Thus scenario planning and analysis give us a more explicit picture and help us prepare for an uncertain future. In other words, it helps us in making our strategies future-proof!

Cloud Computing

What is Cloud Computing?

Cloud computing is a technology where the software is not installed on individual desktops. Instead, it is hosted on a web-based server, offering on-demand software availability.

Cloud Computing in Pharma

Early adopters of cloud computing among pharmaceutical companies, such as Pfizer, Johnson & Johnson, and Eli Lilly, used Amazon Web Services (AWS) and Amazon EC2 (Elastic Computer Cloud) in many areas like R&D, process proteomics, bioinformatics, statistics, and adaptive trial design to improve performance and reduce costs. While pharma has been relatively slow in adopting cloud technology due to some security concerns initially, the subsequent improvisation in security features and the COVID-19 pandemic are driving the companies to embrace cloud like never before.

According to Healthcare Information and Management Society analytics survey report, the adoption rate of cloud computing in the pharma industry has increased significantly, with over eighty percent of companies leveraging cloud services. Lower infrastructure costs, efficient management of workloads, and improved business agility are some of the main reasons for this increasing cloud adoption.

Cloud is more than just a storage solution. Leading biopharmaceutical companies increasingly recognize that the cloud can help them shrink innovation cycles, standardize processes across global operations, scale up rapidly, and enable analytics, among other benefits.

Over eighty percent of pharmaceutical companies say they apply cloud technology in many areas across the value chain, such as research and early development, market access, and commercial and medical applications.

Furthermore, we can see the transformative nature of cloud technology from the fact that Moderna delivered its first clinical batch of its COVID-19 vaccine candidate to the US National Institutes of Health for Phase I trial only 42 days after the initial sequencing of the virus using cloud technology. So how did Moderna do it? According to Stéphane Bancel, Moderna CEO, *because you don't have to reinvent anything. You just fly*!

What Pharma Leaders Say about Cloud?

Andrea Del Miglio, Tobias Hlavka, Jeffrey Lewis, Manuel Möller, and Pablo Prieto-Munoz highlight the biggest advantage cloud technology can offer to pharmaceutical companies in their article, *The Case for Cloud in Life Sciences*, published in McKinsey.com on October 28, 2021. Here's what they wrote: *Cloud technology can help life sciences companies deliver brand-new services in less than six months, increase release frequency from quarterly to weekly, and slash deployment-lead times from days to hour*s.

In addition, they quote what some of the big pharma leaders said on what Cloud technology has done and could do to the pharma industry. Consider these, for example:

- Jim Swanson, Chief Information Officer at Johnson & Johnson: *Ubiquitous data, together with elastic, scalable cloud and edge computing, is part of what's enabling us to innovate and scale in such unprecedented ways*.
- Christopher Weber, CEO of Takeda**:** *My vision is to deliver transformative therapies and better experiences to patients, physicians, and payers faster than previously possible*.

CHAPTER

3

Reimagine Stakeholder Engagement

Winning with New Rules of Engagement

We see our customers as invited guests to a party, and we are the hosts.

It's our job everyday to make every important aspect of the Customer Experience a little better.

— *Jeff Bezos*

Tablet Detailing

For a very long time, pharmaceutical companies have been using paper-based detail-aids to promote their products to physicians. Later, pharma companies have started using laptops for detailing their products to physicians to gain better attention. While the laptop detailing has some advantages over the paper detail-aids or visual aids regarding audio and video content and some graphic links, it was not very convenient to use. The time taken for the laptop to boot was longer, and the navigation too was challenging. Furthermore, internet speed also was grossly inadequate. The laptops were suitable for offline presentations of PowerPoint and videos. The detail-aids, as a result, were mere electronic versions of paper-based detail-aids or visual aids. Some multinational and large Indian pharma companies used laptops to detail their new products and significant products by their managers in the field.

However, the introduction of the iPad by Apple in 2010 changed all that. iPad, by its capabilities, has become the most convenient, versatile, and useful tool for detailing, and the pharmaceutical industry quickly embraced it. Within six years of its introduction, the iPad has achieved a phenomenal adoption rate. Over 80 percent of Pharma companies use it as their device of choice for detailing their products in North America and some European countries. While iPad has become the numero uno digital tactic for the pharma industry, some companies have started using other tablets too as detail aids. The share of other tablets, however, is meager.

Why is iPad Pharma's Device of Choice?

Pharma has embraced the iPad as their device of choice for detailing by their sales force as it offers many advantages. Consider these for example:

1. Excellent visual quality with a large screen for delivering video, graphics, and animation content
2. Sleek touchscreen and lightweight make it easy to carry
3. 3G or 4G wireless connectivity built into the device for speedy internet connectivity

4. Capability to combine Customer Relationship Management (CRM) system that includes content visualizing, call planning, signature capture, tracking, scheduling, showing videos, presenting detail-aids, GPS, integrated e-mail, and Closed-Loop-Marketing (CLM) system into the device making it an ideal tool for sales force automation.

Furthermore, it is also possible to do on iPad the sales management side of sales force effectiveness such as territory planning, sales operation, sales forecasting, promotion response planning analysis, and some return on investment (ROI) calculations and marketing planning. Besides, the Pharma industry can measure why sales campaigns are getting the most response rates or leads with the data input captured through the closed-loop-marketing system on iPad.

3 Ways to Get the Best Out of Your iPad Detailing

Here are three essential success factors that can significantly improve your sales reps' performance of iPad detailing.

1. Use the iPad detail-aid to support the verbal conversations of your sales reps. Spelling out everything leads to an overload of presentation slides or PDF pages. Experienced Pharma sales reps used the printed detail-aids to strengthen their detail talk and never read the text verbatim. Likewise, iPad detail-aid, too, should make the conversation impactful and not replace it. A good tablet detail-aid helps strengthen the delivery of the message with a logical structure, examples, and cases and support to the product story. The rep should always lead the conversation.
2. Stop broadcasting your message and start engaging. The tablet is an ideal device to capture data on treatment practices and brand perception of physicians. Continuous content refinement will get the attention and, more importantly, sustain the attention of HCPs (Healthcare Professionals) and reinforce Pharma sales representatives' motivation.
3. Maximize the graphical opportunities of the iPad to strengthen the marketing message. iPad and other tablets have enormous

potential to go beyond text and images. You can, for example, include treatment class, mode of action animations, video statements by key opinion leaders (KOLs), patient cases, and much more. You can make the content come alive and make the detail-talk interactive, and memorable experience with the help of the iPad.

Common Mistakes to Avoid

The three most common mistakes to avoid while implementing tablet detailing are:

1. Do not create a digital version of a paper visual-aid. The early adopters of iPad detailing made the mistake of creating exact copies of their visual aids without utilizing any additional functionalities such as video, animation, and data capturing that iPad has.
2. Do not overload the iPad with too much content. It is possible to add almost an infinite stream of content. Therefore, it is tempting to equip the sales force with almost encyclopedic information to handle any objection and any question. That will only make it difficult, if not impossible, for the sales reps to search for the relevant content during the 'detail call.' Furthermore, it is observed that most reps use only three to five pages or slides of tablet detail-aid to support their conversation. However, when you want to add more content, make sure that it is not a part of the main navigation stream and add it in a sub-menu. Always ensure that the main detail-talk flows are short and to the point. Let the rest of the content be a part of the sub-menu.
3. Do not overdo it. Never use animation for the sake of animation video content just because it can be done well on an iPad. Use them only when they are strengthening the key messages.

Implementing iPad Detailing Effectively

Many sales reps feel somewhat uncomfortable about the tablet detailing platform because one can monitor if and how much the detail-aid is being used in the field. Therefore, you need to explain the benefits of making their message more effective and their engagement with the physicians much better.

Remember to involve your sales reps right from the beginning when launching a tablet detailing program. As they have to use the device and the detail-aids every day, they are best positioned to provide valuable input on what is required to make tablet detailing a success.

Leverage the call expertise of your sales reps and show them how iPad detailing can support their conversations with the physicians and take it to the next level. The best way is to demonstrate how it will help them engage physicians, which is getting increasingly difficult.

Train your sales reps on how and when to use the iPad or any other tablet that you may be using. Use role-play as part of the training exercise, record the *role play* sessions and show it to reps to precisely know where and what they need to correct. It is observed that many representatives today look more at the visual aids rather than at the physician they are detailing to. The same is the case with the sales reps who were early adopters of tablet detailing. It is observed that they, too, were looking more at the iPad than at the doctor they are presenting to.

Winning with iPad Detailing

The iPad has become the number one digital tool for over eighty percent of pharmaceutical companies in North America and some European countries. However, many of them have yet to unleash the iPad's real potential to engage physicians and healthcare professionals. In addition, the iPad has the potential to be the single device for sales force automation and customer relationship management and closed-loop marketing for the pharmaceutical sales force.

Closed-loop marketing captures information on every interaction with the physicians regardless of the channel being used. It acts on the information gathered in designing subsequent messages, thus ensuring target-specific and highly personalized marketing messages. Tablet detailing can be an excellent tool to start the closed-loop marketing experience with additional channels integrated later.

Designing and Delivering Segment-Specific Content

Your iPad can deliver the content specific to the segments in each of your physician segments across the stages of their adoption of your product. Stages of adoption, also called the *ladder of adoption*, are the step-wise overview of a doctor's possible steps when considering a brand. Consider the following segments (based on stages in which the physicians currently are) for example:

1. Physicians who are unaware of the treatment or brand or using a different brand
2. Physicians who have just started prescribing and sent their first prescriptions
3. Physicians who have taken up your brand and prescribing more or less regularly
4. Physicians, who are high volume prescribers and brand advocates who influence peers proactively to prescribe the brand

Each of these segments require a different marketing message to meet their communication needs. For example, during their calls, the sales representatives will try to determine the stage at which their physicians are. Brand managers accordingly design specific communication messages targeted to meet all physicians' communication needs as per their relative positions on the stages of adoption. The sales representatives can thus access the right information and the required presentation slide-decks or videos on their tablets quickly and deliver an engaging detail. Without the segment-specific content, it would be much harder for the sales force to use their tablets effectively and engagingly.

How to Create an Engaging 'Tablet Detail'?

Brand managers usually create the tablet-detailing communication strategies which are used by their sales forces. Here are four major areas to consider when designing engaging tablet details:

1. *Target Audience Segmentation*: You need to cover all customer segments in your detail aid, including your customers' position on the adoption ladder. Also, pre-structure the detailing talk for each of the positions on the ladder of adoption. When the sales rep identifies the position of a physician on the ladder of adoption during a call, he can select the appropriate detail that best fits the customer's position on the adoption ladder. Without segmented content, sales reps will find it difficult to use the tablet effectively, thus limiting the impact of the call.
2. *Creating Segment-Specific Content*: Once you define the segments and relative positions your targeted physicians may occupy on the ladder of adoption, tailor all content according to the behavioral objectives (what you want the physicians to do after the call) and messages. It increases the interest of the physicians and motivates your sales reps to use the tablet detail. There may be many messages that apply to these segments. However, it is important to limit the messages between two and three. More may be confusing for the sales force and be complex in a call with the physician.
3. *Different Content Types to Suit Different Customer Profiles*: While it is possible to create many different types of content in terms of graphics, videos, animations, methods, all the content may not be liked by all physicians. Some may prefer medical, scientific content such as guidelines and publication downloads, while others may prefer more patient-oriented content such as patient cases and support programs. Differentiation of customers according to their interests holds the key so your sales force can quickly choose a content piece that matches the physician's interest and preferences.
4. *Enabling for a Successful Closure*: Closing the call is perhaps the most difficult part of the conversation. Therefore, a strong closure screen will be a useful tool. It could consist of presenting different patient profiles or suggesting to the physician to agree to prescribe a product to a new patient profile before the next call. Other possibilities are that a sales rep could summarize the conversation or invite the physician to a follow-up activity. A strong closure sets up a future

interaction, which could also be delivered by another channel than the sales representative.

Improving Tablet Presentation Skills

While the iPad is a versatile digital tool for effectively engaging the physicians during a detail, it requires considerable skills and practice. Training to enhance the presentation skills in using a tablet is essential. Consider training your sales force on these areas:

A. When to use an iPad and when not to use
B. How to segment physicians
C. How to use and handle the iPad properly?
D. How to properly use the iPad? A representative, for example, should not be looking at his tablet while presenting a detail talk but should be looking at the physician.
E. Which message to address first, preferably for each segment?
F. How to close the conversation?
G. What to do if no segmentation can be determined?
H. What to do if the physician gives only 30 seconds? What is his elevator pitch?

Elementary and straightforward as they may seem, these basics are essential as they make the representative resourceful regarding conducting themselves in any situation.

The critical question is, how are you using your iPad or tablet? The effectiveness of iPad or tablet detailing depends on whether you are trying to unleash its full potential or not. David Ormesher, CEO of Closerlook, one of the leading digital marketing consultancy firms in the US, puts it succinctly when he says: *If the tablet is not part of an authentic, closed-loop strategy, it simply replaces a glossy presentation with a shiny one. It is like replacing a traditional hammer with an auto-hammer: it's cool, it's electric, but in the end, it still does the same thing*.

Tablet Detailing: Future Outlook!

The Indian Pharma companies are rather slow to adopt tablet detailing. The continued heavy reliance on the transactional business model and quick success tactics based on massive rewards—monetary, expensive gifts, and substantial discounts for purchasing physicians may be one of the critical factors. The few companies which are investing in technology are the ones that are implementing tablet detailing. However, the tablet detailing in India is currently a digital version of the paper-based visual-aid with a few bells and whistles. It is not yet exploiting the full capabilities that tablets in general and iPad, in particular, can offer. It is like a glossy presentation being replaced by a shiny one.

As competition intensifies and when the current arms race of discount and gratification-based selling begin to recede because they no longer can deliver, Pharma companies that have ignored the telltale signs of the changing landscape of the marketplace would realize the need to invest in technology, development, and implement the best practices. The innovators and early adopters of technology are sure to reap the rich rewards in the changing marketplace.

Virtual Engagement

Doctors often rely on pharmaceutical companies for drug information. However, for the past few years, doctors cannot find time to meet with Pharma sales reps for various reasons. In addition, many large hospitals and Group Practices have been restricting their access to pharmaceutical companies.

COVID-19 Drives Virtual Engagement of Customers

The recent global pandemic, COVID-19, has caused many biopharmaceutical companies to rethink their customer engagement practices more critically. Although well underway before COVID-19, the pandemic accelerated the pace of change in how they operate and engage their customers. As a result, the pharmaceutical industry that relied on the traditional face-to-face sales force and physicians' interactions before the pandemic was forced to change significantly by reinforcing virtual communication approaches.

From the start of the pandemic traditional in-person sales reps' visits sharply declined due to social distancing and lockdown measures. As a result, pharma companies had to adapt rapidly to this new world and start or increase the process of engaging their customers virtually. In addition, they had to train their sales reps in using virtual tools to stay connected with physicians. As the restrictions around in-person interactions and hospital visits continued, the relationships between physicians and pharma sales reps were changing, creating a substantial increase in demand for virtual and online meeting software tools.

According to a GlobalData poll conducted with pharmaceutical industry professionals in April and May 2020, three-fourths of the 456 respondents opined virtual interactions remain either a stand-alone option or a mix of in-person and virtual interactions even after COVID-19 recedes.

When asked if he prefers remote visits or online visits at an Online Veeva Summit, Dr. Andrew J. Moore, hematologist, and oncologist at Southeast Cancer Center, said: *Without a doubt, digital is the way to go. The biggest impact COVID has had on our clinics is the efficiency and workflow of our day. I would like to see virtual visits continue absolutely*.

Video Calls Preferred

In another GlobalData poll completed with healthcare providers in the same period as physicians this time, about thirty percent of the 317 respondents believed that video calls are the best tools for virtual interactions between sales reps and HCPs, followed by messaging (20 percent) and phone calls (16 percent). Many respondents saw video calls as the best alternative to traditional in-person interactions with pharma sales reps. Although video calls cannot fully capture the body language, they can still provide information and facial expressions, giving some non-verbal cues to help establish rapport.

Virtual Engagement is the Way!

Every way you look, virtual engagement seems to create a sustainable engagement with stakeholders in the pharmaceutical industry.

Virtual or remote engagement is sometimes referred to as *tele-detailing*, a *web call*, *eDetailing*, *eRep*, or *eMedical Science Liaison*, depending on whether the presenter is a sales rep or a medical science liaison (MSL) interacting with the customer. In essence, virtual engagement is conducting an interactive, real-time meeting with a healthcare provider online.

Virtual Engagement Adoption Increasing

Changing customer behavior drives the increasing adoption rate of virtual engagement in the pharmaceutical industry. Here are the main reasons:

1. Access to physicians is becoming increasingly difficult and has come to a grinding halt with COVID-19, resulting in a drastic decline in sales rep productivity. These trends are increasing pressure on the pharma industry, and virtual

engagement could be a good alternative to extend reach and contact frequency to sustain the business.

2. Virtual engagement allows physicians to interact from the comfort of their homes, and as such, physicians are also more prepared to spend time with sales reps and MSLs (Medical Science Liaisons).
3. Since 2014, when the tipping point between digital immigrants and digital natives among physicians was reached, more than sixty percent of doctors today, are very familiar with digital communication channels such as Skype, FaceTime, and Zoom, in their personal lives.

When you consider all these factors, virtual sales reps and physicians' engagement is likely to remain a new standard even after COVID-19 recedes.

Factors Influencing Virtual Engagement

There seems to be a strong relationship between remote participation and specific parameters.

1. Age. Healthcare professionals participating in virtual engagement are slightly younger than physicians on average.
2. Physicians who own a tablet or smartphone are likelier to accept an invitation for remote engagement.
3. A relationship with a sales rep or MSL (Medical Science Liaison) makes a difference. Physicians are three times more likely to accept an invitation to interact remotely if they already have a good relationship with the sales rep or medical science liaison.
4. Physicians who visit pharma-owned websites, or are active on social networks for professional purposes are more likely to accept an invitation than those who don't.

Tele-Detailing

Tele-detailing allows drug companies to provide this interaction remotely on the doctors' terms. Tele-detailing (also known as 'e-Detailing), or 'remote or virtual detailing' or 'web calls,' is engaging remotely with doctors and Healthcare Professionals (HCPs). It is an interactive, online, real-time meeting with a physician. As physician access for Pharma companies is increasingly getting restricted, Tele-detailing or e-detailing help extend reach and contact frequency to create a more significant impact.

Two Basic Types

There are two basic types of eDetailing. One is Interactive (Virtual or Remote) detailing. A physician can access the interactive detailing at his convenience. A typical virtual eDetailing call contains multimedia content such as a slide deck, video, or animation that lasts between 5 and 15 minutes. It is mainly used by many pharmaceutical companies in North America and some European countries. However, its adoption is increasing in many emerging markets such as India, China, Brazil among others. The virtual detailing offers an advantage to the physician as he can control the detailing time and the contents he would like to access. He can also request a face-to-face detailing with a company sales representative and samples of the products he would want to try at the end of the detailing session.

Live or video detailing, on the contrary, is a face-to-face video conference with the physician speaking to a pharmaceutical sales representative on a smartphone, a tablet such as an iPad, or a computer webcam. The Pharma sales rep directs the detailing and leads him through the presentation containing similar multimedia elements as virtual or live detailing. It is more or less similar to the traditional detailing, except that it is a video and not real.

Three Models

Currently, the pharmaceutical industry follows three models for implementing e-Detailing.

1. The *Outsourced Model*, where an external agency manages all components and activities of e-Detailing of a company. External sales reps are contracted to make the remote detail calls.

2. The *Dual Model* is where an external agency conducts most activities such as scheduling and arranging appointments with physicians except the actual call delivery.
3. The *Hybrid Model* is where an external agency does the initial setup, training, and platform configuration. The call scheduling and call delivery are done internally by the company employees.

Implementing e-Detailing

The three necessary steps in implementing an e-detailing program are scheduling a meeting, running the meeting (e-Detail), and evaluating the meeting.

1. Scheduling a meeting involves taking a prior appointment from the physician when he would like to log in at the appointed website to participate in the company's e-Detail.
2. Running a meeting presents the e-Detail by the Pharma company's representative or MSL if the meeting is about only clinical or medical issues, not the product. The meeting takes place over Skype, FaceTime, or a similar web-based platform or at the designated website.
3. Evaluating e-Detail is the final step in the process. It is for collecting the essential feedback to improve the future e-Details and provide the physician with additional information such as clinical trial reports, web links, and samples.

Following the e-Detail, most physicians would like new product information, educational programs, links to other sources, and drug formulary updates (mainly for the reimbursement status of the prescribed products).

e-Detailing Strategies

e-Detailing offers many advantages to a pharmaceutical company. The most common strategies followed by Pharma companies are:

1. Coverage means extending the reach towards customer groups currently not seen by the field force.

2. Frequency, the number of calls a Pharma sales rep makes can be increased compared to face-to-face calls as there are no commuting and waiting times in web-based, remote calls.
3. Vacant Territories can be covered adequately.
4. Companies can offer Services On-Demand to physicians by addressing their online requests for product or clinical information and samples.
5. e-Detailing makes Differentiated Messaging possible. With e-Detailing, you can target your message specific to the individual physicians based on the feedback from the previous interactions, whether face-to-face or e-Details.

Objectives of e-Detailing

It is essential to set clear goals before implementing an e-detailing program. Consider these objectives, for example:

1. To increase the length or duration of an e-Detail. When the e-detail is more interactive and intuitive, it is more enjoyable with appropriate animation and video built into the communication.
2. To increase the effectiveness of e-Detail by delivering a personalized, target-specific communication that is relevant to each physician.
3. To decrease the cost of sales force without losing effectiveness.

Training is Important

Prior training of the Pharma sales representatives who deliver e-Detailing is vital as it involves new technology. The training focuses mainly on two broad areas. One is on How to Present the Content using the technology right and how to manipulate the webcam and the audio headset, give the physician access to the meeting, and share the relevant content securely. The second aspect of training focus is on Remote Communication. Pharma reps will often not be able to see the physician during an e-detail call and still have to ensure that physicians pay attention to them instead of doing something else during the call.

Three Key Factors for e-Detailing's Success

Three main factors influence the success of e-Detailing. One is the cost. On average, per physician, the e-Detailing cost is estimated to be between US $100 - 150 compared to the face-to-face detailing cost of US $200 - 250 per physician. Secondly, e-Detailing is more effective. The duration of an e-Detail is about 10 minutes on average compared to 2 minutes of a face-to-face detail. Increasing physician acceptance is the third success factor. A quintiles study observed that a whopping 97 percent of physicians are likely to repeat an e-Detail. Almost three-quarters of them agree that e-Detailing is the future of pharmaceutical contact.

Why Do Physicians Like e-Detailing?

Here are some reasons why physicians like e-detailing.

1. Ease of scheduling.
2. Fits into the physicians' schedule better
3. Convenient, as they have the option to take the detail at the office or home.
4. Saves time.

e-Detailing in Branded-Generics Markets

So far, we have discussed e-Detailing in research-based Pharma markets such as the US and Europe. e-Detailing, as we have discussed here, is not yet practiced by the Indian pharmaceutical industry. One primary reason could be that e-Detailing is not a one-size-fits-all strategy. e-Detailing is more beneficial in the pre-launch and post-launch phases of a product lifecycle. In the pre-launch phase, to create and increase awareness, and in the post-launch to accelerate the adoption rate. During these stages, there is a great need for product and clinical information. Perhaps, marketers in branded generic markets may not yet feel a pressing need for e-Detailing. The current transactional model of pharmaceutical selling, which is based more on gratification and the consequent complacent attitude by some Pharma marketers, maybe another reason.

That said, e-Detailing is undoubtedly important as it offers the same advantages in branded generics markets as in research-based Pharma markets. The new product launches are crucial for companies in branded-generics markets too. Moreover, physician access is increasingly getting restricted, even in branded-generics markets such as India. e-Detailing offers a cost-effective solution to reach the difficult-to-see or even no-see physicians.

Pharma Marketers, who are progressive and forward-looking, would be better off understanding the best practices of e-Detailing to stay ahead of the curve and reap the rewards of e-Detailing.

Virtual Engagement: Future Outlook

Mark McLaughlin and Brian Mahoney outline the future outlook for virtual engagement in the Pharmaceutical Executive article, *Opening Digital Doors: Remote Selling During COVID-19*. Here is the summation of what they say:

1. Relationship selling will continue to be important. However, reps must also operate in a digital, virtual environment, given the dramatic shifts in face-to-face access and HCP preferences to digital.
2. Digital opens the door for reps to become more flexible and engage more effectively to deliver what the healthcare professionals need at any given moment.
3. As the industry moves ahead, digital channels will complement in-person visits in a significant way. From remote meetings to email, virtual engagement strategies will become more useful in improving and sustaining customer relations.
4. Biopharma companies have finally found the flexibility to engage customers on their terms and get doctors the information they need, when they need it, and how they need it. The industry is entering its greatest era of effectiveness and efficiency in serving its many stakeholders.

Webinars

What is Webinar? A webinar is an interactive presentation given to a large, geographically dispersed audience who can engage with the presenter and each other in some way. A webinar is more like an interactive seminar conducted on the internet. For example, a webinar may contain audience polls, Q&A (Question&Answer) chat functions, and whiteboards.

A webcast is a one-to-many presentation conducted on the internet. It is much like a traditional TV broadcast but shown live via an internet stream. The recording is then stored on a web page for future viewing.

Webinars are one of the most effective channels in the pharmaceutical industry today because they can extend reach and frequency. Besides, they can save customer time and money and offer a convenient means of receiving relevant communications. As a result, healthcare professionals (HCPs) can consume more educational material over time in bite-size chunks that are accessible with the ability to replay the content right from their office, house, or even on their smartphones.

Use of Webinars in Pharma

Pharmaceutical companies predominantly use medical education webinars and engage HCPs in research or treatment discussions. They are also great for connecting HCPs with key opinion leaders (KOLs) more frequently. Pharmaceutical companies may also use webinars for brand promotion, as they are not the main drivers of the channel's success. Hosting a webinar requires using specialized software that connects the presenter and audience PCs (personal computers), tablets, or smartphones. Above all, a webinar requires the most suitable content. Therefore, good, relevant content remains the core of a webinar's success.

Webinar channels can provide a significant opportunity to showcase your organization's expertise in a disease area or a portfolio of products and create or renew interest among your targeted HCPs.

The formula for winning through webinars? Start with understanding your target customers' journey and ensure that you have the relevant content they value and deliver an engaging experience.

How to Conduct Engaging Webinars?

How to get the most out of your webinars? How to conduct highly engaging webinars? The key to providing more engaging and interactive webinars is to allow attendees to personalize their experiences. When busy physicians agree to exchange their precious time for informative content, they expect to find the value they could not readily receive otherwise. Targeting the right audience and posting excellent pre and post-marketing of the event, know-how, and using the best technology, determine the success rate of your webinar.

Content is the king, even in webinars. Your content should provide the value that they are seeking. Gurpinder Singh, Head of Digital Marketing at GlaxoSmithKline, India, offers valuable tips to improve engagement and involvement in his insightful article titled, *Webinars in pharmaceutical marketing*, published in the LinkedIn blog on June 18, 2018.

1. *Planning your webinar*: Planning is crucial. Before you plan your webinar, it is essential to create a detailed plan and define key performance indicators (KPIs) that you will measure in the webinar. Proper planning improves the chances of success significantly.
2. *Run surveys*: Ask your customers and find out their pain points and wants. Your webinar topics should address these pains and wants. Remember to ask your customers the right time and day for the webinar.
3. *Choose the right platform*: Choosing the right platform to run your webinar is very important. Your audience will stay long from various locations and multiple devices, where they might experience fluctuations in internet connectivity. Therefore, ensure the platform supports low-bandwidth streaming and is viewable on devices without additional plug-ins.

4. *Bring the expert speaker*: Once you decide on the topic, engage the expert who can deliver value to your audience. Ensure the speaker is aware of the surveys you ran so they know the pains and wants of the target audience to deliver a highly relevant and engaging presentation.
5. *Promote your webinar*: Your webinar is not an isolated event. It is a vital part of your marketing campaign. It is the core of your content strategy, and you must promote it appropriately across all your marketing channels. Start promoting your webinar at least one month before the event. Create a landing page for registration and spread the word about the event using all possible channels. Make a detailed communication plan for your webinars. Here are some crucial points to ponder and act upon while promoting your webinar:
    1. Record a one-minute video of the expert speaker to describe what to expect from the webinar.
    2. Send the initial invite 3 to 4 weeks before the webinar. This communication should have similar content to the landing page, letting your target audience know about the webinar — when it is, and giving them an effortless way to register. Let every webinar communication include the following text: *Can't attend the webinar? Register, and we'll send you the recording*.
    3. Send a targeted reminder just two weeks before the event. This communication is for the audiences who opened your invite email but did not register. It should remind them about the upcoming webinar and ask for feedback on why they haven't registered yet. Embed a survey in the email asking for their reasons. For example— maybe the day or time doesn't work for them, or perhaps they're not interested in that topic. Whatever the reason is, you can take this feedback and use it to plan your next webinar. Use SMS (Short Messaging Service) as one of the channels in your webinar marketing campaign. Mobile has become the most convenient channel for communicating transnational information and marketing messages.

4. Now, you need to send the reminder just one day before or on the day of the webinar. Once you have the desired number of HCPs registered doesn't mean they will show up. If you promote your webinar 2 to 4 weeks in advance, most of the registered HCPs will likely forget the exact date on which the webinar goes live. Remember to send out reminder emails or SMS one day before and on the day of the live event to ensure a high attendance rate.

Here are five important points to consider while conducting an engaging webinar:

1. *What is the right duration of the webinar*: Webinar audiences prefer attending webinars that run between 30 to 45 minutes and not longer. Plan your webinar, therefore, no longer than 30 to 45 minutes. If you are dealing with a complex topic, break it down, run a series of webinars and ensure that the related information is available on your website.
2. *Keep it interactive*: Use Q & A (Question & Answer) and polls throughout the presentation to get a feel of your audience's engagement level and to keep them involved. See if you can offer to download, or read more material during the event. Think of any VAS (Value Added Service) you can provide during the live event. Let your customers feel the value of attending live versus on-demand.
3. *Start and end on time*: Be respectful of your audience's time by starting and ending at the designated times.
4. *Ensure your webinar is viewable on-demand*: Please make the on-demand available as soon as possible for customers unable to attend the live version.
5. *Marketing after the webinar*: Do not let the webinars you have created end on the event date. Since you have created valuable content, plan a post-webinar communication proactively for HCPs who attended or missed the webinar. Plan, for example, a summary of the webinar and some FAQs (Frequently Asked Questions) based on the Q & A session along with the on-demand link, which your customers will perceive as an excellent

value. Also, share a calendar of all past and future webinars with your engaged customers.

Pharma's Webinar Strategy

How can pharmaceutical companies benefit from webinars? Many pharma marketers recognized that they must go beyond banner and search ads and reinvent their strategy. Pharmaceutical companies must broaden their vision to gain insights from the HCP community. Here are some important reasons why webinar channel is best suited to provide these insights and reach their target audience with highly relevant and valuable content.

1. Webinars offer the best real-time exchange of queries from physicians. Doctors tend to ask questions during webinars, which Pharma can analyze and effectively communicate to their target audience with the best solutions.
2. Webinars help pharmaceutical companies identify clinical dilemmas and address them immediately. Through webinars, Pharma can understand major clinical dilemmas from the specialties they want to promote their products and deliver the solutions they have already identified to a large audience through key opinion leaders (KOLs) convening webinars.
3. Webinars help pharmaceutical companies earn recognition as knowledge partners and bring a significant shift in the perception of the physician community from the current banner and flyer marketers. The relationship with HCPs as a knowledge partner is an excellent opportunity for Pharma to project its values and communicate its outstanding contribution to healthcare.

Effective Engagement

How should Pharma engage HCPs in Webinars? Phanish Chandra, CEO of Docplexus, a leading doctors' network from India, offers three valuable suggestions for engaging with HCPs through webinars in his Docplexus blog article titled, *How to be successful with KOL webinar*, published on July 5, 2016. As he rightly says,

Pharma already has a lot of clinical insights and resources to conduct webinars on a vast range of topics. However, it needs a comprehensive strategy to unleash the power of the webinar channel. He suggests that Pharma's webinar strategy should incorporate the following points.

1. *Identify key therapeutic areas and novel treatments*: Pharma should identify key therapeutic areas where most practitioners face practical problems. It will help them unearth the unmet needs of doctors. Also, Pharma should identify any discovery or solution they can offer to address the problems of practicing physicians.
2. *Address the questions of the physician fraternity by recognized KOL (Key Opinion Leader)*: Identify key opinion leaders (KOLs) in target specialties to present pertinent topics in that specialty. Doctors are inclined to learn from recognized peers in their community. Furthermore, eminent KOLs can help resolve the dilemmas that practitioners face and address their questions immediately, thus enabling other doctors to better patient care.
3. *Provide additional resources to doctors*: In addition to live streaming of their webinars, Pharma should provide other resources like presentations or videos to help the audience better equip themselves with clinical knowledge. Pharmaceutical companies can also promote their proprietary insights, which can, in turn, change physicians' prescription behavior.

Website Engagement

A website is the foundation of digital marketing. For many companies, the website (mobile optimized) is the heart of their digital strategy. It is the hub to which all other marketing activities are directed. According to Inbound Marketing Best Practices, 60 percent of all leads generated should come from inbound traffic, and that traffic needs a home. The website is that home.

In the early days of the internet, a website was more like a simple online business presentation. However, it has evolved from a one-way promotional channel to an integrated two-way service and educational platform over the years. Today, a website can fulfill many functions in pharmaceutical companies. Consider these, for example:

1. Corporate Websites give general company information, information for investors, and information about employees. Often, It has limited information for Healthcare Professionals (HCPS) and patients. Some pharmaceutical companies have a comprehensive website with multiple sections containing information about their products, research pipeline, and other activities.
2. Product Websites inform HCPs on specific products giving all the relevant product information.
3. Disease Websites inform patients about a disease condition, the possible treatment options, and the implications of not starting treatment.
4. As the name suggests, Campaign Websites are separate websites for specific campaigns, although temporary. However, the campaign websites of late are becoming less popular. Pharmaceutical companies seem to be making their main websites flexible enough to cover the campaigns.
5. The HCP Self-service Portals are more comprehensive sites providing full service across products with features that help develop a 360-degree personalization. For HCP websites, validation is required in most countries. Two options are commonly used for validation. One is to embed a third-party

validation tool in your website. The other is a validation system run by the pharmaceutical company itself. The advantage of the company's system is that the validation takes place against the CRM database, based on a few fields such as HCP's name and license number. Whatever option you choose, make sure you make the validation process hassle-free.

6. Corporate Websites contain mostly general company information and investor and employee information.

How to Build an Engaging Website?

To build an engaging website, one needs to define the strategy and goals of the proposed website and its target audience. The key questions to ask when building an engaging website are:

1. Who is the desired target audience for the website? For whom is this website being built?
2. How do we know that the website is engaging enough? Successful? What will success look like?
3. Which KPIs (Key Performance Indicators) should we monitor and use?
4. What are the conversion points? What is the desired behavior that we want from our visitors? What do we want the visitor to do when she visits our site?

Only after answering these questions should the site structure and content be defined. These processes are highly interrelated. For instance, a series of videos will require a different site structure than a library of text documents. In addition, we must keep our websites updated and fresh; therefore, we need a plan to update the website with new content continuously.

Creating the design of the website and building it are the next steps. These should happen in tandem with continuous user testing and testing for bugs. Now, the site is ready for launch. However, a website launch is not the endpoint of a website journey. Four follow-up actions are crucial:

- Firstly, you must ensure that the site is well promoted.

- Secondly, measure all traffic coming into the website and monitor the usage pattern of visitors.
- Thirdly, build up further content based on usage results. Also, continuously optimize and maintain the site.
- Ensure feedback on all these points into a continuous learning process, which you can use to refine the strategy, KPIs (Key Performance Indicators), content, and editorial plans.

Continuous Updating of the website can be a challenging task. Therefore, create both pre and post-launch content plans before launching the site.

Also, to optimize your website engagement ensure that you:

- Create multiple types of content and include personalization and segmentation options to keep your website robust after launch.
- Integrate your website into your overall content marketing plan rather than leaving it as a separate entity.

Measure What Matters

Websites can be great trackers. They have a significant advantage in that you can track almost everything you want to. There are three types of metrics that are important. They are Exposure metrics, Interaction metrics, and Engagement metrics. You can develop KPIs for each of these metrics.

1. *Exposure Metrics* looks at the reach of your websites by measuring the number of visitors you can draw to your website or the number of pages they visit on average.
2. *Interaction Metrics* access specific content items you have identified as key for your visitors to interact with.
3. *Engagement Metrics* look at how optimal the user experience is for your website visitors. These include the number of visitors returning to your site or the duration they spend watching your videos. You could also launch a mini-survey on your site that measures the willingness of your visitors to recommend your site to peers. It is also known as the Net Promoter Score (NPS).

How to Optimize Your Website?

While a detailed discussion on optimizing your website is beyond the scope of this book, here are twelve critical points to make your website more effective. Consider these, for example:

1. Before designing a website or any web project, ask yourself two questions:

   A. Why should people come to your website?

   B. Why should people return to your website?

2. What is the most important page of your website? Every page. Visitors can enter any page of your website through search engines and social media referrals. Create engaging content on every page.
3. Research suggests that less than 20 percent of visitors go to the home page. It is, therefore, essential to include a Call to Action (CTA) on every page. Remember, a webpage without a Call to Action (CTA) is a lost opportunity.
4. Physicians prefer independent, third-party websites to those pharmaceutical companies provide as they perceive them to be more trustworthy. It is, therefore, better for pharmaceutical companies to partner with independent websites to engage with physicians more effectively.
5. Good design matters. Remember that your visual design will determine visitors' first impressions in many cases, no matter how valuable your content is. First impressions are crucial. A visitor decides whether to stay on your website or go to a competitor in a split second.
6. The entire site should scale to different devices. If the visitors find the site fiddly or annoying, they will leave regardless of its quality. It is also called *Responsive* design.
7. Monitoring your website results and adjusting when needed is crucial for success.
8. A/B Testing is essential. Try out different designs, wording, and flows. Changing the wording in a button can significantly impact conversion rates. Therefore, never stop testing.

9. Testing the usability of a website is vital. No matter how visually pleasant or content-rich a site is, users will get frustrated and abandon it if it does not work or is challenging to navigate.
10. Customize your web pages. Adjust content to match visitors' needs. Develop multiple landing pages, depending on the nature of the visit.
11. Optimization of your website is vitally important. Your website should scale according to the device and screen being used. Ensuring every visitor browsing your website irrespective of the device he uses be it a smartphone, tablet, or laptop, has a great user experience. As Steve Jobs famously said: *Design is not just what it looks like and feels like. Design is how it works*.
12. Combine content with services. You can build enduring customer relationships by combining your compelling content on your website with services such as continuing medical education (CME).
13. Continuous management of your website is not something nice to do but mandatory. Management of website, not just from a technical point of view but also concerning its content. Update your content regularly.
14. Finally, ensure that every page has credibility, trustworthiness, and professionalism. The tone of voice of your website should resonate consistently on every webpage.

A website is a vital tool for many companies, which has many purposes, including brand building, fostering customer loyalty, and 360-degree customer engagement. The following cases show the discerning pharmaceutical marketer, how some global Pharma majors have effectively created and managed their websites and offer valuable insights.

CASE

39

Dr. Reddy's Laboratories' Unbranded Russian Website on Pain Management!

Dr. Reddy's achieved a leadership position in the pain management area in the Russian market. The company garnered every second prescription written for alleviating pain in the market. The company's six brands enjoy the leadership position. Not content with this, Dr. Reddy's wanted to achieve the status of one of the most respected companies. To defend its therapeutic leadership in the pain management segment and stay on the top, the company conducted market research to identify the unmet needs of physicians in the Russian Federation. The company found that all the physicians wanted to acquire knowledge and update themselves about the latest medical developments related to their specialties in the Russian language because doctors in Russia study medicine in the local language, Russian, in the medical colleges in the country.

Dr. Reddy's created an unbranded portal on pain management to meet this unmet need. They chose an unbranded website because an unbranded website is seen as more credible by physicians. The company created compelling content about the latest pain management advances and thousands of articles and key opinion leader (KOL) videos in Russian. The company updated the content at regular intervals, almost daily, and more than once a week without any break. The company sourced its content from the most respected scientific publishers worldwide. More than 18,000 physicians, six thousand of whom were neurologists, registered themselves on the website enabling the company to have a phenomenal reach of physicians that it could not cover.

The website was an unprecedented success and set a new benchmark. It achieved a Click-through-Rate (CTR) of 20 percent against the industry standard of about 3 percent. Even the email open rate was a phenomenal 6 percent, six times more than the industry's 1 percent.

Dr. Reddy's had also started closed-loop marketing with analytics at the back end and engaged physicians meaningfully with relevant messages that resonated with physicians. As a result, medical representatives of Dr. Reddy's can engage their physicians far more meaningfully.

The unbranded portal has significantly impacted the company's presence in the Russian market, reinforcing its strong leadership position.

CASE

40

Galderma's *Mom Genes* Campaign!

That the mother and daughter bond is profound is universally acknowledged. Mothers pass down wisdom, advice, and inspiration to their daughters. Also, mothers even pass down a predisposition to age like them. Still, it is observed that many women do not talk about it. Galderma, one of the world's leading companies, focused on skin health and dermatology, conducted a study on mother and daughter facial aging in the US recently and found that:

- 82 percent of moms hope facial aging is easier for their daughters, but more than half never talked about it together
- 73 percent of daughters think they are more likely to age like their moms
- Ninety percent of moms and 88 percent of daughters said: "There is more pressure to look younger longer nowadays."
- More than two-thirds (67 percent) of moms and daughters said, "I frequently worry about my face showing signs of aging."
- Seventy-seven percent of daughters said, "they worry even more if I am aging just like mom."
- Sixty-six percent of moms and 77 percent of daughters said, "I'd be more interested in treatments with natural-looking results."

Mom Genes Campaign

Based on the research study findings, Galderma launched a *Mom Genes* Campaign in February 2016, to educate women on the genetics of facial aging and inspire mothers and daughters everywhere to face the future with more optimism and open dialogue. The survey helped contextualize the need to start a conversation about mom genes among women. In addition, the branded campaign website featured a *Mom Genes* Gallery of photo recreations and encouraged visitors to join the ASPIRE Galderma Rewards loyalty program for rewards and savings.

Why *Mom Genes* Campaign? Miles Harrison, president and general manager of Galderma North America, explained convincingly. In this context, he said that *Galderma had been committed to women's skin health and dermatologic needs at all stages of life for more than fifty years. We know that the skin ages, and the phrase like the mother, like daughter, holds. We celebrate those genetic bonds — and Galderma is a global leader studying them to design and provide innovative medical solutions for long-term skin health. This campaign aims to ignite a new and dynamic dialogue about facial aging*.

Dr. Doris Day, a board-certified dermatologist, said about the *Mom Genes* campaign: *Genetics and nurturing good skin health practices are big factors influencing how the face ages. Women can learn a lot about how the process may affect them by observing and discussing their moms' changes. The great news is that both moms and daughters have more options than ever before to address facial aging, thanks to recent innovations in skincare and treatments that can help maintain skin health and natural beauty. Talking to a specialist can help at all stages, from providing advice to those in their 20s that will set the stage for skin health to supporting people in their 30s, 40s, and 50s to age well and truly gracefully. Significant advances have been made to help women maintain their natural beauty and look as good as they feel. Galderma, a leading skin health company globally, makes many of the trusted aesthetic treatments I recommend to my patients, such as Restylane®'s family of products and Sculptra® Aesthetic.*

Galderma kicked off their *Mom Genes* campaign on an encouraging note to all women asking them to celebrate Moms and the role of *Mom Genes* in their lives by posting a recreation of a favorite photo of their mom to www.momgenes.com. For every photo posted, Galderma will donate $5 (up to $50,000) to National Charity League Inc., a non-profit organization dedicated to fostering the mother and daughter relationship through hands-on volunteerism that promotes leadership development and a legacy of social awareness and compassion.

Also, Galderma arranged a professional photoshoot media event in New York City and engaged nearly 30 editors in recreating family photos of their moms to make the story personal and relevant. Robust website traffic, media coverage, outstanding feedback from HCPs (Healthcare Practitioners), and social media postings from reporters, consumers, and HCPs have significantly helped the campaign resonate with its target audiences.

The spirit of the *Mom Genes* campaign and the way its impact can be best understood in the words of Kelli Bender, who participated in the recreation of a family photo of her mom, Judi Bender, in her article in People Today in February 2016: *I learned a very important lesson. I want to age like my mom. She is beautiful inside out, in a way that always makes me feel lucky to be her daughter. I will be ecstatic to look anything like her 30 years from now! But more important, I want to grow up to resemble the woman my mom is today — confident, dedicated, loving, and altruistic. And if that happens, it won't just be from Judi's mom's genes but all the work she has put in.*

(Source: Adapted from articles: 1. New Galderma campaign encourages women to love their 'mom genes,' News provided by Galderma and published in CISION PR Newswire on February 4, 2016; 2. Article by Kelli Bender, We tried it: Getting a makeover to become my mother, in People on February 17, 2016.)

CASE
41

Your Cancer Game Plan by Merck!

Even the toughest person in the world goes through some low times. But you have got to create a game plan and stick to it.

— Jim Kelly, Head and Neck Cancer Survivor.

Merck launched *Your Cancer Game Plan*— a new awareness campaign focused on helping people with cancer. Their loved ones tackle the emotional, nutritional, and communication needs and encourage people with head and neck cancer. The campaign collaborates between Pro Football Hall of Famer and head and neck cancer survivor Jim Kelly, Head & Neck Cancer Alliance (HNCA), and Support for People with Oral and Head and Neck Cancer (SPOHNC). These are the leading patient organizations, which have been supporting the head and neck cancer community for nearly six decades combined, and Savor Health, a service dedicated to supporting the nutritional needs of people surviving cancer.

The head and neck cancer organizations partnered with Merck on Your Cancer Game Plan work tirelessly to raise awareness and meet the needs of people living with head and neck cancer through their resources, support, and programming. The tools and resources included a guide to help people living with cancer talk to family and friends to get the support they need, strategies to help them cope emotionally with issues such as anxiety and depression, recipes to help enhance nutritional health, informational videos to help people stay positive through their cancer journey and much more.

Head and neck cancer describes the many tumors in or around the throat, larynx, nose, sinuses, and mouth. Each year, more than 60,000 head and neck cancer cases are diagnosed in the US. Many people with head and neck cancer face unique challenges resulting from surgeries and treatments that impact a person's appearance, speech, smell, taste, ability to swallow, and sight.

People with head and neck cancer may experience different physical and emotional challenges than other forms of cancer. Your Cancer Game Plan provides support and resources to help address these challenges. It also provides Kelly's tips on remaining positive and healthy recipes for those facing head and neck cancer.

Know Your Game Plan

Jim Kelly's personal experience as a head and neck cancer survivor is a source of great inspiration for many people living with the disease. Jim Kelly explains his experience in his own words: *I know first hand the special challenges people with head and neck cancer and their families face. My experience taught me the importance of emotional support and taking care of myself, and I hope that by sharing my experience — I can inspire others to take action and know their game plan.*

Many people may know and recognize Jim Kelly's struggles on the football field as a former quarterback for the Buffalo Bills, but not many people would know about his battle with head and neck cancer and what he learned along the way. So here is his message on the website: *I am proud to share my personal experience as a head and neck cancer survivor. I encourage those facing head and neck cancer and their loved ones to visit the website www.yourcancer-gameplan.com to find my Kelly Tough Tips — which helped me through my journey with cancer — and the other resources available through this campaign helpful.*

What is Your Cancer Game Plan?

Your cancer game plan is about three things:

1. Always let your doctors and the people around you know how you feel.
2. Number two, eat right. Make the right choice with food and exercise.
3. Number three, and probably most important, it's about having the right attitude. Stay positive.

Expanding Cancer Awareness

As Merck expands indications for its cancer fighter, Keytruda, it also adds the treatment areas for its cancer awareness umbrella campaign. The recent additions to Your Cancer Game Plan focus on melanoma with a former major league baseball star and melanoma survivor Mike Schmidt in September 2017; and lung cancer fronted by a former college recruit and lung cancer survivor, Taylor Bill Duck. Taylor Bell Duck best summed up the state of awareness about lung cancer when he said: *The way people think about lung cancer is that you don't think it will happen to you — and I was the picture of health*. Later, Merck also added bladder cancer to its umbrella campaign – Your cancer game plan.

Each focus area on the home website, www.yourcancer-gameplan.com, includes the story of a starring spokesperson. It also includes everyday patients and survivors in videos talking about their support systems, healthy eating and exercise, adjusting to a new normal with a cancer diagnosis, and more. Along with the expanded focus on new forms of cancer, Merck also expanded its collaboration with CancerCare and five lung cancer patient associations — Bonnie J. Addario Lung Cancer Foundation, LUNGevity, Lung Cancer Alliance, Lung Cancer Foundation of America, and Lung Cancer Research Foundation. Speaking about the expanded collaboration and Your Cancer Game Plan Campaign,

Jill De Simone, Senior Vice President of Merck Oncology in the US, said: *At the center of Your Cancer Game Plan is the person with cancer, which is why we are thrilled to work with this group of lung cancer survivors on expanding the program. Each of these advocates bring a shared commitment and passion that Merck and our partners hold for educating and supporting the community of people impacted by this devastating disease.*

(Source: Adapted from articles: 1. Beth Snyder Bulik, Merck drafts game plan for lung cancer with awareness campaign expansion, Fierce Pharma, November 29, 2017; 2. Merck's website www.yourcancergameplan.com)

CASE

42

Sanofi Launches *Highs & Lows* Diabetes Awareness Campaign!

Sanofi, one of the global Pharma majors, has launched *Highs & Lows*, a diabetes awareness campaign to help people with diabetes better control their condition. The campaign highlights the emotional and psychological factors that negatively impact patients' diabetes self-management, such as fear of a drop in blood sugar levels and public perception of the disease. The campaign aims to help people achieve what they need – a better balance for a better future. Sanofi launched the *Highs & Lows* campaign based on the results of a survey it conducted among type 2 diabetes patients in the UK, What is more, the U.K, has the highest number of people with type 2 diabetes in Europe, with almost 3.5 million people currently diagnosed with type1 or type 2 diabetes — a figure that is forecast to rise to five million by 2025.

Sanofi found that a quarter of participants in their survey feel anxious or fearful of having low blood sugar levels— or hypos — with 42 percent actively preferring to have high blood glucose than risk a hypo, despite potential life-threatening disease prognosis. Furthermore, 15 percent of those surveyed said they believe others are to blame for having the condition, while 14 percent said they think people with diabetes are perceived as greedy!

Speaking on occasion, Dr. Mike Baxter, medical therapy expert at Sanofi UK, said: *Our research shows that there is a need in the UK for better support for people with type2 diabetes — not just in terms of the medical management of the disease but also the emotional and psychological aspects of the condition. Consequently, the level of diabetic control in a large number of people with diabetes in the UK remains unacceptably high, exposing them to high risks of developing preventable diabetic complications*.

That is the reason why Sanofi has launched the Highs & Lows campaign. To support its campaign, Sanofi has created a patient support website (www.diabeteshighsandlow.co.uk) with symptom checklists, guides for discussions with healthcare professionals, videos, and further resources to improve people's knowledge about diabetes.

Sanofi staged a tightrope walking stunt at London's Southbank to draw the public attention to its *Highs & Lows* campaign. This show symbolically helped raise awareness of the difficulty of successfully balancing diabetes self-care.

Sanofi believes *Highs & Lows* can help prevent almost a million serious medical complications associated with diabetes, such as eye disease, kidney disease, foot ulcer, and amputations, that occur each year due to poor diabetes management.

(Source: Adapted from an article by Rebecca Clifford, Sanofi launches Highs & Lows diabetes awareness campaign, PMLiVe, November 24, 2016)

CASE

43

Merck's *Everybody Versed* Campaign for Gardasil!

Merck launched a new campaign — VERSED, to raise awareness of human papillomavirus (HPV) recently in 2018, ten years after its first awareness campaign for the same disease. In the new campaign, VERSED, Merck debunked two common misconceptions that its earlier campaign had stoked:

1. That Gardasil (Merck's vaccine for HPV first approved in 2007) is a female-specific vaccine for cervical cancer, and
2. That sexual transmission is not important, or at least is not worth talking about

However, the fact is that there are more than 100 different strains of the human papillomavirus (HPV) identified. They infect 80 percent of women and 66 percent of men at least once throughout their lives. While most HPV infections disappear without treatment, prolonged infection with high-risk strains can develop into various cancers: cancers of the mouth, throat, cervix, and genitals, including penile and vaginal cancers.

A Short History of HPV Vaccine

The US FDA approved Merck's vaccine, Gardasil, for female use in 2007 and approved GlaxoSmithKline's vaccine Cervarix two years later. The FDA approved the vaccine only for female use because Merck included only females in its efficacy trials for Gardasil — even though researchers knew that males could transmit the virus and be harmed by it. The initial approval and promotion of Gardasil turned HPV vaccination into a health issue for young women. As a result, pharmaceutical companies marketed it to this population. The consequent physician and public dialogue socially constructed Gardasil (and later versions by other firms) as the girl's vaccine.

This completely jeopardized herd immunity. It occurs when the vaccination of a significant portion of a population (the herd) protects individuals who have not developed immunity. It ignored that nearly 50 percent of those carrying the virus in heterosexual interactions are male. As a result, females who could not access the vaccine were not protected from male HPV transmissions. Merck did not change its aggressive female-specific promotion even after the FDA approved Gardasil for males in 2009.

Gardasil Gets It Right with VERSED

With the VERSED campaign, Merck did it right this time around. The VERSED campaign mentioned that HPV is a sexually transmitted virus and that Gardasil is equally effective in men and women. The original Gardasil campaigns did not talk about sex, using gender stereotypes in a way that disempowered women. In addition, Merck's ads of earlier campaigns depicted mothers and daughters expressing shock at the connection between HPV and cervical cancer. Thus, Merck finally addressed to correct earlier misperceptions as they have undermined the HPV vaccine's ability to promote health for all.

The New VERSED Campaign

Merck created a very informative, educative, and interactive website for the campaign and promoted it across social media channels such as Facebook, Instagram, Tumblr, and website. You can access all the valuable information by logging on to www.versedhpv.com or clicking on a Snapchat ad, for example. Here are some examples of what you can get from the website:

VERSED.

Everybody is VERSED.

Get Smart about HPV.

It starts with knowledge: Human papillomavirus (HPV) can cause certain cancers and other diseases. Let's be the ones that know what HPV can do. Get VERSED on HPV.

Get Vocal.

Knowledge looks good on everyone.

Put your knowledge to the test. Then get your friends in on it too, because you're VERSED like that.

VERSED Vs. Not

How much do you know about HPV?

Click to Begin

@versedHPV — Instagram

VERSED on HPV?

Now Get Vocal.

HPV is widespread. For most people, HPV clears on its own. For others who don't clear the virus HPV can cause certain cancers and diseases.

HPV facts are not always pretty. So, if there was something you could do to help prevent certain HPV-related cancers and diseases, wouldn't you?

Ask your doctor to learn more. Then get others to do the same. Get smart on HPV.

Learn what you can do now.

Lessons from Gardasil Campaigns

The most important lesson from Gardasil's approach to promotional campaigns is that pharmaceutical companies should not wait for things to become socially acceptable before they embrace them.

Instead, the priority needs of people's health should be the primary focus, and they should find ways of persuading the public.

HPV can affect anyone, regardless of sex, gender, or sexuality. Marketing to a certain demographic or not including all the facts can exclude individuals from reaping the health benefits of a product. The pharmaceutical industry has an important stake in and responsibility for public health. Therefore, it has to consider avoiding societal biases and deciding on the strategy that promotes health for as many as possible when marketing a drug.

(Source: Adapted from articles: 1. Ashley Anderson, After a decade, new Gardasil ad campaign gets it (mostly) right, STAT: First Opinion, June 18, 2018: 2. www.versedhpv.com)

CASE 44

Novartis Launches *24 Life Hacks in 24 Hours*!

Novartis launched a #MSLifeHacks campaign on May 27, 2015, World Multiple Sclerosis Day, and joined the global multiple sclerosis (MS) community. In addition, the company launched a new initiative, 24 Hacks in 24 Hours, on this world MS day. The Multiple Sclerosis International Foundation (MSIF) created World Multiple Sclerosis Day in 2009 to raise global awareness of multiple sclerosis. You can follow #MSLifeHacks on Twitter, Facebook, and Pinterest.

The theme of world MS Day in 2015 was access — in other words, Living Like You — the equality of access to diagnosis, treatment, and support; access to travel and leisure facilities; and access to education and employment. Living Like You aims to empower and support those with and impacted by multiple sclerosis.

The new initiative, 24 Hacks in 24 Hours by Novartis, offers many helpful tips for all people with multiple sclerosis. For example, Novartis shared one helpful tip on World Multiple Sclerosis Day in 2015 and created a shortcut or a smart idea to live well with multiple sclerosis online every hour for 24 hours. That's why the initiative is named 24 Hacks in 24 Hours. Novartis is committed to releasing 365 bright ideas — one a day for an entire year — for the MS community.

Novartis hosted an ongoing #MSLifeHacks campaign on the living like you global online platform. Launched in February 2014, the campaign has garnered 130,000 site visits in three months to May and provided access to a wide range of supportive information for many people living with multiple sclerosis and all who the condition has touched.

Speaking about the #MSLifeHacks campaign and their global online platform, Living Like You, David Epstein, Division Head, Novartis Pharmaceuticals, said: *Giving people with MS access to more than treatments and bringing the MS community together to share stories is vital to helping people with MS live a better life irrespective of their circumstances with this debilitating disease. #MSLifeHacks and our online platform, Living Like You, are examples of how we use digital and social media to give people access to information written by people with MS, for people with MS, to help them understand the complex nature of the disease.*

The Novartis-supported Living Like You (www.livinglikeyou.com) is an online resource community that features magazine-style content detailing the journey through the realities of life with multiple sclerosis by offering insights from people who live with the disease. Providing online information about MS, is very important because people with MS, are up to three times more likely to be online than people with other diseases. In addition, MS is mentioned online every 13 seconds. Since its launch in February 2014, Living Like You has garnered more than half a million site visits and over 60,000 social engagements in fifteen months.

Novartis is doing more than driving access to information online about multiple sclerosis. The company supports a Europe-wide initiative to provide employment opportunities for young people with MS and is a part of the Believe and Achieve program of the European Multiple Sclerosis Platform (EMSP). Believe and Achieve provides young people with MS, opportunities in paid, supported, and mentored work placements across the European Union.

www.livingwithyou.com

Here are some sample hacks from the Novartis-sponsored website livingwithyou.com:

365 days of #MSLifeHacks

A real look at life with multiple sclerosis.

Ever heard of a hack? Quite simply, life hacks are creative ways to make everyday tasks simpler. And when MS, can lead to some pretty unique challenges, simplicity is golden. So for the next 365 days, we share a new trick, shortcut, or clever way to live well like you. Stay tuned for a new life hack released every day for the next year, and be sure to follow us on Facebook, Twitter, and Pinterest with the hashtag #MSLifeHacks.

Here are some Sample hacks:

- Clear your makeup brushes using baby shampoo.
- Try on shoes in the afternoon or evening for a more accurate fit.
- Make remembering passwords easy — Give yourself a hand with remembering passwords. A trusted app will keep them all in one place — with one master password to access them.
- Remember your talking points by preparing notes before important conversations. Keep the essential details straight with notes you take before important conversations— whether with your families, friends, or doctor.
- Pedal your feet under your desk to keep blood circulation. If you spend most of your day sitting or lying, move your feet regularly as if you are pushing pedals to help your blood circulation.

(Source: Adapted from articles: 1. Novartis, Novartis launches '24 Hacks in 24 Hours' showing commitment to people with MS, access guidance and advice, News Medical Life Sciences, May 28, 2015; 2. www.livinglikeyou.com)

CASE

45

Salix Launches *Let's Talk 2* IBS Awareness Campaign!

A wholly owned subsidiary of Valeant Pharmaceuticals International, Salix Pharmaceuticals is a leading specialty pharmaceutical company committed to preventing and treating gastrointestinal disorders. To reinforce its position in the segment, Salix launched a national educational campaign called 'Let's talk2 on April 3, 2018. April is the month of IBS (Irritable Bowel Syndrome). 'Let's talk2, the campaign endorsed by the International Foundation for Functional Gastrointestinal Disorders (IFFGD), encourages patients and their healthcare providers to have 2-way conversations about their irritable bowel syndrome with diarrhea (IBS-D).

The International Foundation for Functional Gastrointestinal Disorders (IFFGD), founders of the IBS-D awareness month, is dedicated to encouraging and empowering 'patients' 2" to talk openly with their healthcare providers about their irritable bowel syndrome with diarrhea (IBS-D) and its associated symptoms.

Over Sixteen million Americans suffer from IBS-D and often live with debilitating symptoms, including abdominal pain and diarrhea, for years before being correctly diagnosed. A microbial imbalance has been linked to symptoms of IBS-D. It is also the seventh most common diagnosis by primary care physicians. To make matters worse, over 75 percent of IBS patients are under-diagnosed. In addition, women are more likely to be affected by IBS-D in a ratio of 2: 1. 'Let's talk 2' is designed to help patients communicate better with their healthcare providers. Better two-way conversations can help lead to better patient outcomes.

To kick off the campaign, Salix created a let' stalk2.com. On this new website, patients can go for more information on IBS-D, including common triggers, possible causes, different treatments, and tips on preparing for a discussion with healthcare providers. With its resources, the *Let us talk 2* campaign will support the shared goal of helping people go from symptom onset to diagnosis much faster by educating them about IBS-D's potential causes and symptoms and encouraging more direct conversations with physicians. In addition, research conducted in 2017, by the Journal of Neurogastroenterology and Motility suggests that many IBS-D patients feel stigmatized; healthcare providers should be aware of the stigma in IBS patients.

Besides, Mark Pimentel, MD, Program Director, Medically Associated Technology (MAST) Program, Cedars-Sinai, observed: *Patients may feel embarrassed to discuss their bowel habits, especially when there is a diarrheal component. However, doctors must know all the details of their 'patients' symptoms to provide them with the best treatment option. Patients should pay close attention to any change in their bowel habits, such as an urgent need to go to the bathroom and abdominal pain, as these can be signs of IBS-D.*

www.letstalk2.com

The following copy on the landing page explains everything you want to know about IBS-D.

'Let's Talk2

Because the talk 'shouldn't be as uncomfortable as the symptoms.

It may not be easy for you to discuss diarrhea. But your healthcare provider needs to know all of the details of your symptoms to give you the best treatment options. So 'Let's make the conversation comfortable.

Click here to learn about an IBS-D treatment option.

(Source: Adapted from articles: 1. Salix launches Let'sTalk2" IBS awareness campaign, CISION PR Newswire, April 3, 2018, 2. Kate Scarlata, 'Let's Talk 2, For A Digestive Peace of Mind Blog, June 4, 2008; 3. www.letstalk2.com)

CASE

46

UCB Creates a New Destination for the Parkinson's Community with its *More Than Motion* Website!

UCB, a multinational biopharmaceutical company headquartered in Brussels, Belgium, has a strong focus and presence in the neurology therapeutic area. In 2012, UCB introduced a new online community at the American Academy of Neurology (AAN) annual meeting for the millions of people living with Parkinson's disease worldwide. The Parkinson's *More Than Motion* community launched at the American Academy of Neurology Brain Fair included a Facebook page, where people affected by Parkinson's could come together to share experiences, consult experts, register for *More Than Motion* magazine, and watch videos featuring real people living with Parkinson's disease. In addition, it included a reality-TV-style video series showing how patients and their families are affected by this severe disease.

The name of the project — *More Than Motion*, gained the appreciation of the Parkinson's community right from the start. People often think of the disease as a movement disorder. Doubtless, Parkinson's disease is characterized by motor difficulties, and many patients experience tremors — but there is more to Parkinson's than Motion. In addition to difficulties in walking or talking, many people experience memory, digestion, and sleeping problems. Therefore, the project's name — *More Than Motion*, is appropriate. It reflects a holistic view of how this severe disease affects people rather than focusing on a single aspect of complex conditions.

In 2017, UCB launched a new desktop and mobile responsive website that brings great content from the *More Than Motion*™ magazine to an even wider audience. Visitors can sign up for the publication and download a digital version to their desktop.

Above all, *More Than Motion* remains a community as it encourages families affected by Parkinson's to share their stories with others. It can be particularly valuable to those newly diagnosed with the disease. In addition, it helps patients find comfort in knowing that so many other families are living with the same experience as they are.

The *More Than Motion* website allows patients to upload their photos, bringing them into an active support group from the comfort of their homes or wherever they may take their mobile devices.

More Than Motion **™ Website Contents**

Here is the gist of the website's contents: www.parkinsonsmore thanmotion.com, to give you an overview of how it is useful in serving people with Parkinson's disease.

Welcome to *More Than Motion*

Welcome to More Than Motion™, *a community dedicated to portraying the full realities of living with Parkinson's disease (PD). You probably already know if you or someone you love lives with PD. It's the most recognizable symptoms — tremors, stiffness, or slowness, which can affect movement. However, you may not realize that PD affects more than Motion. Other symptoms of PD, can include sleep disturbances, fatigue, or trouble with memory. Join the More Than Motion conversation and get a glimpse of people's real lives with PD to find out how they cope day-to-day and aim to keep active and involved with life despite the challenges that Parkinson's disease can present.*

We hope these stories inspire you to share your story, learn from others, and get involved in the PD community.

Other Sections on the Website are:

- Get the Magazine
- Get helpful resources
- Join our community
- Patient Journeys
- Link to the blog, Facebook page, and YouTube channel. Blogs for More Than Motion have useful articles published frequently.
- Train Your Brain: Give your brain a workout! Try these puzzles and challenges from nationally syndicated puzzle columnist and author of 47 Puzzle books, Terry Stickels. Find many more at his website, terrystickels.com.

(Source: Adapted from articles: 1. Eric Puntel, U.S. Corporate Communications, UCB, Parkinson's disease website: More Than Motion, UCB.com, May 8, 2017; 2. www.parkinsonsmorethanmotion.com)

CASE

47

This Bike has MS!

How do you raise awareness of a lesser-known chronic disease with very vague, common symptoms and, therefore, difficult to recognize and easy to ignore? Unlike many diseases that attract public attention, Multiple Sclerosis (MS) is not fatal. It is not a life-threatening disease. Instead, it is a disease that threatens everyday living with often invisible symptoms and is difficult to understand. The major problem with MS is that people don't understand why you're sick because you don't look like you're sick. If people do not understand the illness, how will they care for it and seek treatment? To make them realize the seriousness and consequences of multiple sclerosis, they first have to understand it. Then, they need to be aware of it. The key question is, how will you raise their awareness of multiple sclerosis?

MS, a not-for-profit organization in Australian Capital Territory (ACT), New South Wales, Australia, has launched This Bike has MS, an integrated advertising campaign to precisely do that. To raise the awareness of multiple sclerosis and funds for improving the well-being of patients with the disease. Hosted online at thisbikehasms.com, the campaign features a specially designed bike, which helps educate people and improve their awareness of multiple sclerosis.

Why a bicycle ride to raise funds for improving treatment options and providing resources to support people with multiple sclerosis?

Rides seem to be very common and popular in Australia for fundraising activities. There seems to be a ride for almost everything. In 2015, for example, there were roughly 67 rides in Victoria alone, 33 of which were fundraising events. At the same time, most of these rides are inconsequential and are often unrelated to the cause it is raising funds for. The activity is merely a means to an end, raising money for a cause. Most of these fundraising activities were missing a significant opportunity. The opportunity of making the ride relevant to the cause it is raising funds for. To make people understand and be aware of the disease, its symptoms, consequences, and outcomes for donating money. How do you make people understand multiple sclerosis, an invisible disease whose symptoms are so vague and common that they are difficult to link to the disease specifically? You need to create a campaign wherein people can feel, experience, understand the symptoms and visualize the invisible disease.

MS Australia has teamed up with Grey Australia, a well-known advertising and marketing communications agency, to exploit this opportunity. Grey Australia was not content collecting funds for new research and patient services. It wanted to make people understand multiple sclerosis and what it was like to live with it. That is how the campaign idea — *This Bike has MS,* was born.

This approach would resonate with the donors and create more advocates and involvement in participants, news outlets, and supporting businesses. There is an opportunity to create something ownable and sharable.

This Bike has MS

The idea of creating a bike that has MS is born out of a creative brainstorming process and a thorough analysis of the situation surrounding the disease. Here is a snapshot of the birth of This Bike has MS:

Strategy

1. Language seems to be a major problem as it is difficult to describe the symptoms that link them to the disease as they are vague and common. What could be the solution when language is a problem? Stop talking. If words don't do justice to multiple sclerosis, show people what you mean. Bring the symptoms to life in an unmissable way.
2. There is little motivation for people to understand multiple sclerosis as a disease unless they are personally affected. It creates an interesting education idea people want to spend time with. The idea should spark curiosity and talkability and maintain the interest level for a longer period.
3. Turn a generic charity ride into educating people about MS and its symptoms and understand how everyday living challenges people with multiple sclerosis.

Execution of Strategy

Grey Australia has executed the strategy brilliantly by building a bike with symptoms of M.S. hidden inside its parts. The team that created this unique, first-of-its-kind Bike representing the symptoms of multiple sclerosis needed a multi-disciplinary team. The team led by Carol Cook, a Paralympian Gold medalist diagnosed with MS in 1998, included neurologists, a physiotherapist, a sports scientist from the Victorian Institute of Sport, bike mechanics, and several people living with multiple sclerosis. They worked hard to build the symptoms of MS into a bike. The team has put together the MS Bike Manual, a written resource accompanying *This Bike with MS*, as a 74-page book and an online resource. It presents a detailed breakdown of the Bike's components and explains how each element has been calibrated to replicate multiple sclerosis's physical effects and symptoms. Here is a brief account of how they did this:

- The wheels are weighed down by fatigue. Heavy materials used in the Bike's wheels add to the resistance to the rider making it more challenging to move the Bike forward.

- The gears of the Bike are made to battle spasticity. The Bike has gears with broken teeth that make them slip unpredictably, reducing the rider's ability to control speed, direction, and momentum.
- The Bike's frame has no balance. A bend in its steel frame structure disrupts the Bike's equilibrium, causing it to sway randomly from side to side when ridden at speed.
- The seat, with its ultra-thin cushion, is riddled with pain. Incorrectly designed for distance riding and adjusted to a level that causes discomfort, the seat will become increasingly painful over time.
- The fork with a straight bend in its length, combined with its Un-trued wheels, will cause the Bike to move erratically. As a result, the rider will be unable to maintain a steady line.
- The handlebars are full of pins and needles. Ball bearings hidden beneath the tape of these handlebars accentuate vibrations throughout the rider's upper body. It will lead to pins and needles that will progress to complete numbness.
- Carol Cook, the leader of the MS Bike Project, speaking on the project, said: *Cycling is a precision sport. We've taken everything you'd look at in a good bicycle and did the opposite. We wanted to know how close we could get to recreating the symptoms of multiple sclerosis. I certainly would not want to ride this Bike.*
- Marion Simpson, the neurologist and M.S. specialist closely involved in the project — this Bike has MS. while speaking about the project said: *I am very interested in what this Bike can do for treatment and education. I was encouraged to focus on the potential unpredictability of the Bike. MS's symptoms vary for various reasons, and we wanted to ensure the Bike was erratic and uncomfortable. I want to get closer to understanding MS and MS patients.*

Finally, Michael Knox, chief creative officer and managing partner of Grey Group Australia, had to say about the MS. Bike: *This Bike is a nasty piece of work. It sucks. We're looking forward to seeing how much money it can raise, how much pain it can inflict, and how much closer it can get us closer, and to a better understand and treat multiple sclerosis.*

Strategy in Action

Grey has created an online film entitled This Bike has MS to communicate its strategy loudly and widely. The film introduced the experts who created the Bike that was terrible to ride and walked the audience through the symptoms and design. The online video was viewed 171,529 times on YouTube as of February 16, 2019. The agency also created a beautiful parallax website with sharing features, a memorable name, and *thisbikehasms.com* that allowed visitors to delve further into the human and mechanical stories behind the campaign. However, that was not enough to make the members understand the impact of MS. They had to demonstrate the Bike in action and needed riders for this terrible-to-ride Bike. The agency has demonstrated the impact in a way that words could never do. They created a Pester Campaign targeting past and current elite cyclists to take the challenge and ride the Bike in MS Melbourne Cycle.

The call for a rider took a massive effort. It took a series of online films, including a testing sequence at the Victorian Institute of Sport, social media, public relations, and an outdoor poster campaign — all relying on donated space. Finally, after five weeks of searching, the agency found their rider in Shane Kelly, a five-time Australian Olympian.

Campaign Results

This Bike has MS, debuted on the tenth anniversary of the Melbourne Cycle Race, held on March 6, 2016. The results of the campaign were remarkable. The campaign has surpassed every objective set.

1. *Objective #1*: Increase public awareness and engagement of MS. The campaign reached 24.9 million people against a set objective of 4 million in just three months and relied on donated media.

2. *Objective #2*: Help the MS Melbourne Cycle reach its target of $3 million. The Bike with multiple sclerosis raised $3.8 million, which is twenty-seven percent above the target.
3. *Objective #3*: Generate $500,000 in earned media (PR, Buzz, and sharing) around the symptoms of MS Result? The Bike has MS achieved $ 7 million in earned media. This Bike has MS garnered international coverage, including 5 to 7-minute segment coverage on SBS (Special Broadcasting Services) International News, The ABC Breakfast Show, Fox News, and the front page of the Huffington Post. It was not just covered. It was revered. Fox News said it was Brilliant. Huffington Post wrote: *Powerful education tool that has enabled people to get a glimpse into what sufferers of MS deal with*.

Other Results

Also, *This Bike has MS* achieved great success, which significantly improved the involvement and engagement of the audiences. Here are some of the important ones:

- Five of the largest pharmaceutical companies globally, such as Roche, Biogen, Merck, Genentech, and Mylan, have used the Bike and the manual to help improve engagement and understanding of MS.
- The Bike has been used by twelve other MS organizations worldwide to promote, raising nearly $1 million.
- New bikes are now being built in Mexico, Hungary, Turkey, Germany, and the US to spread the understanding of MS and its symptoms.

Four Lessons

What can we learn from *This Bike has MS* Campaign? The campaign teaches us four valuable lessons. Danish Chan of Grey Group explains these four lessons in their general entry form for the Australian Effie Awards for 2016. These lessons, as described by Danish Chan, are:

1. *Stop trying to write headlines and start making them*. When you cannot afford to pay for people's attention, turn your focus to pop culture. Shift your focus from storytelling to story-making. MS Australia and Grey Group Australia did not have big budgets for massive multichannel advertising campaigns to make people understand the invisible symptoms of multiple sclerosis. They thought about creating and raising awareness, educating people, and making them understand MS, and how it impacts people's daily living with the disease. They came up with a brilliant idea to create a unique experiential vehicle — This Bike has MS.
2. *Bake in the marketing*. Too often in big businesses, the product tells one story, and the marketing and advertising tell another. However, if you bake an idea into the product, then the product is transformed into something more than something you buy. It becomes something that you buy into. The creative team baked the strategy of This Bike has MS, and transformed a generic charity ride into a successful marketing tool that people bought into.
3. *Play to human nature*. As humans, we need to be excited by something to wake up. We need something important to engage with and give the attention it deserves. Putting a disease into a bike and putting a five-time Olympian on that Bike to a ride did precisely that. It got our undivided attention because it was worth it.
4. *Embrace the power of the experts*. Advertising may be very attractive and appealing but flippant. Experts can be enlightening but boring to cut through the media noise. This Bike has MS, a communications agency, neurologist, physiotherapist, bike mechanics, sports scientists, Olympic cyclists, and people living with MS, with all different skill-sets working together for the common good. To produce something educational, entertaining, and above all, unexpected. Real, committed collaboration made the campaign unique.

(Source: Adapted from articles: 1. Danish Chan, This Bike Has MS, The Australian Effie Awards: General Entry Form, 2016, PDF; 2. Duncan Macleod, This Bike Has MS, Inspiration Room, December 9, 2015; 3. Angela Natividad, Ad of the day: Grey just designed a bicycle that has the symptoms of MS: Brilliant Australian campaign makes the disease feel real, AdWeek, December 29, 2015)

CASE

48

Tylenol's *Smile it Forward* Campaign!

McNeil Consumer Healthcare, makers of Tylenol (acetaminophen), teamed up with the pediatrician, Tanya Altman, and MomCentral to help mothers by giving them tips for managing childhood milestones to reveal those feel better smiles in 2013. Every new experience is a critical step along a child's journey, from the first fever to the first tooth and bike ride. Some milestones are more challenging for the mom and the child than others. momcentral.com is a one-stop online source that provides influential moms with knowledge, compelling content, and connectivity with their mom community.

Tylenol launched its *Smiling It Forward* Campaign to help moms get through the most difficult moments and enjoy the relief that comes. The campaign encourages moms to visit the website *www.smilingitforward.com* to experience this from pediatrician Tanya Altman, M.D., and share photos of their children's smiles. Each smile shared will benefit the Children's Health Fund, which provides healthcare services to underserved children throughout the US.

Founded by singer and songwriter Paul Simon and Irwin Redlener, MD, a pediatrician and child health advocate, Children's Health Fund is a national leader in healthcare for vulnerable children. The Children's Health Fund has a fleet of 50 mobile medical clinics serving hundreds of locations across the country, including schools, community shelters, and homeless shelters, so every child in need can be healthy and learn.

The Tylenol *Smiling It Forward* Campaign, dedicated to families across the country, was launched to help bring children in need the healthcare they deserve through the support of the Children's Health Fund. Parents can upload photos of their growing children at www.smilingitforward.com, and a $1donation for every photo uploaded will be made to the organization up to $100,000 by the company. In addition to sharing their child's healthy smile, parents can also visit the website for tips from Dr. Tanya Altman on preparing for those major childhood milestones. In 2013, over 10,000 infant smiles were shared.

Moms looked forward and loved to share their children's progress as they grew. However, a MomCentral survey after the campaign revealed that:

- Eighty-seven percent of moms take photos of their children's accomplishments from the first steps to the first day of school, and
- Seventy-four percent post photos on social media

However, every milestone brings a host of aches and pains — a child's first tooth can bring on teething pain, the first day of school can mean exposure to cold and flu virus, and minor scrapes and bruises often accompany the first bike ride. Although these are natural, many moms feel ill-equipped to manage the discomfort of many children's 'firsts.' Yet, for all moms, the top two most challenging moments when caring for their newborn are the baby's first fever and teething issues. So whose advice would they seek about these early milestones?

- Sixty-four percent turn to their family and
- Eighty-two percent are most likely to turn to their pediatrician

McNeil Consumer Healthcare teamed up with pediatrician Tanya Altman for its Smiling It Forward Campaign. Dr. Tanya Altman said in the campaign context: *Aches and pains are an inevitable part of childhood. As a mom and pediatrician, I know it's important to ease the potential discomfort that might come their way. There are many smiles throughout childhood worth celebrating — but something special about the smile comes after a fever breaks or pain has been relieved. I am excited to partner with the Tylenol Smiling It Forward team to help moms across the country achieve and celebrate their child's 'Feel Better' smile through various milestones.*

(Source: Adapted from the article: Tylenol® Smiling It Forward™ celebrates "Feel Better" smiles to benefit Children's Health Fund, CISION PR Newswire, August 12, 2014)

CASE

49

Allergan's Female Empowerment Campaign: # *She Can*!

The Allergan Pharmaceutical Company, as we know it today, is a result of a whirlwind of acquisitions that began in 2013. Actavis, a leading international specialty pharmaceutical company, is more known for its acquisitions than its research and development investments. So the company chose the acquisition route to grow. And grow it did. Allergan Pharmaceuticals is a specialty Pharma company with a clear customer focus on ophthalmology, women's health, and dermatology.

Actavis acquired Allergan in November 2014 for a whopping US $70.5 billion, creating one of the world's largest pharmaceutical companies by sales. The combined company adopted the Allergan moniker in June 2015. The following table presents a snapshot of how Actavis became Allergan.

Table 3.1 How Actavis became Allergan?

Year	Details of Acquisition
2012	Watson buys Actavis for US $5.9 billionWatson officially adopts Actavis monicker.
2013	Actavis buys Warner Chilcott For US $5 billion
2014	Actavis buys Forest Laboratories for US $28 billion.Actavis buys Allergan for US $70.5 billion.
2015	Actavis officially adopts Allergan monicker

Women, millennial women in particular — are a crucial segment for Allergan's business. According to the company estimates, sixty-two percent of patients on Allergan's products are women. Its US sales force covers more than 30,000 gynecologists each year. What is so special about this segment? Firstly, this generation of women is more educated and successful than earlier generations. The generation of women is determined to break the glass ceiling. They are looking for ways and means to overcome the negativity and the obstacles in their life and are determined from *I can't even* to *you can*. Allergan wanted to ride on this mindset and aptly launched the #ActuallySheCan campaign in 2015.

Allergan, a leader in women's healthcare in North America, has a strong presence in the oral contraceptives market with its Loestrin Fe (norethindrone acetate and Ethinyl estradiol tablets). The company also received 2015 another contraceptive, Liletta, a long-term hormonal intrauterine device. To reinforce its already strong position and build a formidable franchise among millennial women, Allergan launched the #ActuallySheCan campaign to answer the emotive, inundated declaration adopted by young women across the country: I can't even, #ActuallySheCan is a playoff of a common phrase used by millennial women — *I can't even* — and aims to instill confidence in women.

So, what is so different about #ActuallySheCan? It is not the first healthcare campaign focused on empowering women. Other campaigns such as Proctor & Gamble's #LikeGirl campaign and FCB Inferno London's #ThisGirlCan won at the Cannes and Lion Health Creativity Festivals in Cannes, France. However, for Allergan, #ActuallySheCan is more than a campaign. It is about fostering a discussion among women, not at them. Herm Cuckier, vice president of Women's Healthcare at Allergan, explained the campaign's purpose and said: *This is a platform and medium for women to get more educated. It is not just a traditional social media platform with standard banner ads and tweeting content about a product. Instead, the campaign's main aim is to help young women learn and share information about healthcare and wellness, including contraceptive options*.

Also, the #ActuallySheCan campaign is not a one-way dialogue between a company and its customers, as Bill Meury, president of Branded Pharmaceuticals at Allergan, says. But, he adds, "*Millennials don't want to receive information that way. They want to seek and source information in their way, style, and approach from sources they believe in and find credible. We know that, and it is certainly multifactorial and fully integrated with a surrounding sort of feel. Typically, the communication channel in healthcare used to be between a physician's office and a hospital — now, it is everywhere and 24/7. Moreover, millennials represent a quarter of the population, and in the not-so-distant future, they will consume more healthcare than baby boomers*."

#ActuallySheCan is an unbranded campaign that engaged its customers across multiple social media platforms such as Facebook, Twitter, and Instagram, incorporating interactive elements to the campaign's online platform. The interactive elements of the campaign include facial recognition software that assigns users emojis based on their facial expressions, which they can share with their friends. In addition, women were encouraged to visit *#ActuallySheCan.com*, upload a selfie, and read more about their healthcare options. It also featured live events and panel discussions through *HerCampus.com*, a website for college-age women. The website has three components — a place to upload selfies where users can convert them to Shemojies, information about contraceptive options (including details about Loestrin Fe), and information about upcoming events about the campaign.

Besides, the #ActuallySheCan campaign featured an essay contest in Cosmopolitan magazine and a partnership with online magazine HerCampus to host live events and panel discussions. Allergan tapped Faith Popcorn agency's BrainReserve to develop the campaign. Herm Cuckier says: *this is just the starting point. This isn't just a three-month campaign. I hope we'll look back in five years and see that this is a starting point to a more transformational approach*.

Allergan partnered with celebrities such as Lea Michelle (of Glee fame) and social media stars Le Bosworth and iJustine to raise awareness of the campaign. In addition, these celebrities share what she can actually mean to them.

To make the #ActuallySheCan campaign even more successful and memorable, Allergan released a limited edition of #ActuallySheCan tank tops created in partnership with lifestyle brand, LeMotto. By selling the #ActuallySheCan tanks on *LeMotto.com*, the campaign aimed to spread awareness and support an organization that shares the same mission of female empowerment. Most of the tank tops sale proceeds will be donated to AcademyWomen, a non-profit organization created by and for military women to provide mentoring services and extensive networking and development opportunities.

Jourdan Dunn, a well-known international model, was the face of the #ActuallySheCan collection, and she embodied the #ActuallySheCan spirit through her many achievements. In addition to an illustrious modeling career, Jourdan is an influential advocate for diversity in the fashion industry, a cooking show host, a mother, and a philanthropist. Regarding the collection, Jourdan said that the #ActuallySheCan tanks are the perfect way to inject positivity into your life, with motivational slogans that encourage the best in all of us.

The fashionable collection of LeMotto tanks came with trendy slogans with an inspirational #ActuallySheCan message — one of the campaign's Less / More mottos. These mottos encourage women to enable the positive in their lives and eliminate the negative. Consider some of these inspiring mottos, for example:

Less Drama, More Karma

Less Regret, More Sweat

Less Hesitation, More Meditation

#ActuallySheCan has amassed a national following with a female empowerment message that resonates with contemporary young women. The campaign created a meaningful, confidence-fueled experience and context for millennial women. Through their official hashtag, #ActuallySheCan, the campaign has built a national platform for women to express their own goals and facilitate a larger conversation around female achievement and well-being. #ActuallySheCan started a movement around modern female empowerment, celebrating young women and their ambitions.

(Source: Adapted from articles: 1. Kevin McCaffrey, Allergan debuts #ActuallySheCan campaign, MM&M, July 21, 2015, 2. Nathalie Tadena, Allergan launches 'Actually She Can' Ad campaign, The Wall Street Journal, July 21, 2015; 3. News provided by Allergan, ActuallySheCan (Social Media) by Allergan launches limited edition #ActuallySheCan (S.M.) Tank Top shirts, A charitable initiative supporting military women, CISION PR Newswire, June 9, 2016)

CASE

50

Allergan Teams with Star Paratriathlete to Boost its IBS-D Med *Viberzi*!

Viberzi is Allergan's horse in the IBS-D (Irritable Bowel Syndrome with Diarrhea) race. Its major competitor is Xifaxan of Salix pharmaceuticals, a product that won US FDA approval on the same day as Viberzi in May 2016.

Allergan teamed up with Amy Dixon, the world champion paratriathlete, motivational speaker, and IBS-D sufferer, to raise awareness around the disease and its treatment, Viberzi. The partnership aims to spark and improve conversations about IBS-D between patients and doctors. According to the latest survey, about 65 percent of those afflicted with IBS-D experience GI symptoms for at least a year before speaking with a physician, and 46 percent wait at least three years. Amy Dixon counts herself among those who waited longer than they needed to. She said in a statement that her partnership with Allergan was driven by the desire to let people know that they don't have to go through life this way. I experienced abdominal pain and diarrhea for years before I decided to go to the doctor.

To help steer patients toward medical help, Allergan has set up IBSDandAmy.com, a website featuring Amy Dixon's story, a discussion guide for broaching the subject with a doctor, and resources detailing how to manage the disease's symptoms. Allergan, of course, hopes some of the patients leave their doctors' offices with prescriptions of Viberzi, its therapeutic solution for IBS-D.

Allergan has planned to do more to improve its share of the IBS-D prescriptions. For example, the company has inked a pact with population health management specialist, SonarMD to develop tools to help doctors monitor and manage patients using the drug. Allergan also brought together a group of experts — IBS CounSel — to provide doctors support, education, and leadership.

Also, Allergan rolled out IBSDontract.com, an online resource for patients complete with information on identifying symptoms, managing the conditions, and speaking with a doctor about IBS-D.

(Source: Adapted from the article: Carly Helfand, Allergan teams with star paratriathlete in yet another effort to boost IBS-D med Viberzi, Fierce Pharma, November 23, 2016)

CASE

51

Synergy Pharmaceuticals' *Poop Troop* Take Poop Emojis to a Whole New Level!

Certain things are frowned upon discussing in polite company. Sex, politics, and poop are surely at the top of the list. Still, Chronic Idiopathic Constipation (CIC) affects approximately 33 million Americans and an estimated 14 percent of the global population, estimate the Edelman Specialist Agency Salutem. In addition to causing infrequent, hard stools and other physical symptoms such as straining, abdominal bloating, and discomfort, CIC can adversely affect an individual's quality of life, including increasing stress and anxiety. Unfortunately, as Julie Holcombe, senior director of marketing at Synergy, says, many people with CIC feel embarrassed or uncomfortable talking about their symptoms with those closest to them, so they often suffer in silence. That is why Synergy Pharmaceuticals launched a *Poop Troop* campaign. To make difficult conversations easier for people with CIC (chronic idiopathic constipation) while raising awareness around the impact of CIC beyond those living with this complex disorder.

Synergy has reimagined poop emojis as a series of distinct emojis for people with the gastrointestinal disorder— CIC (chronic idiopathic constipation). The primary reason is that Synergy has a drug called Trulance (plecanatide) approved by the US FDA for treating chronic idiopathic constipation.

The *Poop Troop* Campaign featured fourteen animated poop emojis to encourage people to talk to their family, friends, and healthcare providers about CIC's physical and emotional impact. According to a press release, each character (emoji) represents a type of bowel movement — from constipation to normal to diarrhea — and an emotion that people with CIC often associate with each, including strained, depressed, angry, relieved, cool, euphoric, surprised, concerned and embarrassed. Moreover, members of the *Poop Troop* have memorable names like — Left out, Lumpy, Miss La Poop, Mr. Smooth, Ploptimistic Peter, Runny Ron, and Sausage Sally.

The Poop Troop has been a part of a broader disease education campaign, ConfrontConstipation, launched by Synergy. The company created a website, confrontconstipation.com, which recommends using the Poop Troop to determine treatment goals and have a more productive dialogue about constipation with healthcare professionals or sharing them with friends to take your texts to a whole new level! The ConfrontConstipation site also includes a discussion guide.

The emoji keyboard containing the fourteen emoji characters of the Poop Troop is available on both iOS and Android platforms for a free download. Once installed, the Poop Troop can be accessed directly from the standard keyboard page on a user's smartphone.

Research has shown that more than 90 percent of people use emojis in their day-to-day digital conversations. Surely, emojis are most likely to make difficult and embarrassing, and stigmatized conversations such as poop talk make it easier and effective.

(Source: Adapted from the article: Lisa Lacy, Synergy pharmaceuticals' Poop Troop' take Poop Emojis to a new level! The Drum, April 11, 2017)

CASE

52

1 Mission, 1 Million! Getting to the Heart of Stroke!

Boehringer Ingelheim, one of the world's leading research-driven pharmaceutical companies with an experience of over 130 years, sponsored a 2010 global disease awareness initiative, *One Mission, One Million*. The *1 Mission, 1 Million* campaign is a unique and innovative disease awareness campaign that will allow people, patients, clinicians, and others around the world to put forward their projects for disease awareness about atrial fibrillation so that we can educate and inform the general public, patients and clinicians about atrial fibrillation and what can be done to prevent stroke.

Atrial fibrillation (AF) is the most common sustained heart rhythm abnormality worldwide, with one in four adults over 40 developing A F in their lifetime. Patients with atrial fibrillation have a five-fold higher risk of stroke than those without atrial fibrillation. The AF-related strokes are estimated to be around 3 million annually worldwide.

This massive global disease awareness campaign, One Mission, One Million: Getting to the Heart of Stroke, is unique in many ways. When the campaign was announced in 2010, asking for project submissions — individuals, patient and professional groups, and healthcare centers across as many as 36 countries submitted many projects on the campaign website www.heartofstroke.com. After reviewing these, The expert panel put 184 projects to vote by public members for projects that they believed would make a difference in preventing Atrial Fibrillation (AF)-related strokes. The public engagement was massive, with over two million people voting for the projects. Another significant feature of the One Mission, One Million campaign was that as many as forty-five third-party organizations worldwide supported it.

Jane Seymour, the well-known English actress, supported the campaign and invited votes from the general public for the projects that made a difference in preventing AF-related strokes. She said: *I'm thrilled that so many countries are set to benefit from* One Mission, One Million. *I have very personal reasons for being involved with this as my mother had AF and unfortunately had a stroke due to the condition. AF-related strokes can be incredibly debilitating, and I am proud to be a part of this initiative, which has given the public the power to allocate € 1 million to projects that will make a difference in the lives of people with AF and their families*.

Winners of the *One Mission, One Million* campaign were from worldwide and included individuals, patients, professional groups, and healthcare professionals from 18 countries. The winning projects include, for example:

- An iPhone app to detect an irregular heart rhythm
- The production of a disease awareness video
- The local provision of electrocardiogram monitoring
- An online social media platform

Spain led the way with five winners, followed by France and Germany with four winners. There were 32 awards, ranging from € 10,000 to €100,000, totaling €1 million.

(Source; Adapted from articles: 1. Press Release, €1 million awarded to winning projects which aim to prevent atrial fibrillation-related stroke, Business Wire, August 29, 2011, 2. Press release for non-UK, non-US, non-Canada media, Actress Jane Seymour takes up the fight against common heart rhythm disorder, atrial fibrillation and its link to stroke, Business Wire, March 22, 2011)

CASE

53

I'm Me in EndoMEtriosis!

AbbVie, a global pharmaceutical company, launched a national campaign in the United States with the help of Julianne Hough, a well-known actress and Emmy-award-winning choreographer, to raise awareness about endometriosis. The campaign is called Get in the Know about ME in Endometriosis. The campaign, supported by AbbVie, is dedicated to inspiring women to learn about and understand endometriosis, a disease affecting an estimated 1 in 10 women, and address their symptoms with a healthcare professional. Although endometriosis is one of the most common gynecological disorders in America, there is a lack of awareness and prioritization of endometriosis as an important women's health issue. In addition, surprising as it may seem, it can take up to six to ten years to diagnose endometriosis.

Julianne Hough, best known as a two-time professional champion and judge on Dancing with the Stars, is the right person to be the face of the campaign as she had endometriosis earlier. Here's what she said about the campaign: *After I was diagnosed with endometriosis in 2008, I talked about my symptoms with family and close friends, leading some of them to talk to a doctor about the symptoms.* I am ME in endoMEtriosis, *and I'm here to show women what the face of this chronic and painful disease looks like. Endometriosis is a part of me, and it could be affecting you and many other women in your life*.

The campaign encourages women to learn more about endometriosis at *MEinEnd.com* and join the conversation online by sharing the hashtag #Me in Endo. Endometriosis is associated with pain symptoms, which can be very debilitating and may interfere with day-to-day activities. Without proper communication about endometriosis, it may take longer for women to receive a diagnosis. The Get in the Know campaign website (www.MeInEndo.com) aims to increase awareness about endometriosis, elevate understanding, and facilitate conversations between women and healthcare professionals.

The website features a wide range of information, such as an endometriosis checklist, which provides a simple overview of symptoms so women can identify those that apply to them. In addition, a symptom-tracker is meant to help women understand the impact endometriosis symptoms have on their daily lives.

How does the sponsor, AbbVie, feel about the campaign — Get in the Know about ME in Endometriosis? Here's what Michael Norton, vice president, and head of US medical affairs at AbbVie, said about the campaign: *AbbVie is proud to work with Julianne Hough and make this education campaign possible. Although endometriosis cannot be cured, the pain associated with endometriosis can be managed upon proper diagnosis. With the Get in the Know about ME in Endometriosis campaign, we hope to educate about endometriosis and empower women to engage in dialogue with physicians, family, and friends to help bring awareness to symptoms and change the way the disease is understood.*

(Source: Adapted from the article; AbbVie News Center, Julianne Hough empowers women to Get in the Know about endometriosis, March 23, 2017)

CASE

54

Astellas' *Transplant 360*!

The *Transplant 360* program by Astellas demonstrates how the pharmaceutical industry can make a valuable contribution to patient health, aside from its product offerings. It is a classic example of a beyond-the-pill solution that pharmaceutical companies can offer.

The *Transplant 360* strategy was straightforward. To become the number one resource for patients preparing for or receiving an organ transplant. Astellas has a very ambitious reason for launching this program. The company wanted to directly improve clinical outcomes for organ transplant patients by encouraging them to lead healthier lives, face better tracking of their key measures, and connect them seamlessly with their healthcare team improving communications.

What can a transplant patient do to keep their new organ longer and save a life? Adherence to immunosuppressant medication is the most important thing on the list. Unfortunately, non-adherence is complex and was unacknowledged mainly by healthcare professionals (HCPs), despite its catastrophic implications for organ transplant failure. Also, where non-adherence was recognized, HCPs felt powerless to address it. In 2011, the Astellas program targeted adherence to immunosuppressant medication. What is significant about Transplant 360 is that patient focus directed every stage of the program's development and implementation so that the solution delivered supports transplant patients directly and via their HCPs in a 360° approach. In addition, the campaign had a dedicated website, www.transplant360.com, as an important resource for patients and HCPs.

The uptake of *the Transplant 360* program across Europe was impressive, with about 80 percent of UK transplant units adopting the program leading to a ten-fold increase in visitors to the transplant 360 website, www.transplant360.com. The program has also raised the profile of non-adherence, as demonstrated by the leading international meeting agenda going from zero mentions of adherence to widespread coverage between 2010 and 2012. The Transplant 360 program also helped patients get full support in maintaining their health and the health of their new organ.

The *Transplant 360* campaign won the PM Society Awards Gold for Digital Patients Initiatives.

This highly targeted patient support program should become the template that others follow in terms of Its :

1. Lack of commercial objectives
2. Patients' focus, and
3. Robust engagement of the whole clinical community

(Source: Adapted from the article: Excellence in Patient Focus; Finalist: Transplant 360, Astellas Pharma Europe in association with Choice Healthcare Solutions, PM Live)

CASE

55

AbbVie's *Uncover Your Confidence* Campaign Empowers People Living With Psoriasis!

AbbVie, a global, research-based biopharmaceutical company, teamed up with Stacy London, style expert and co-host of TLC's (The Learning Channel) What Not to Wear, on July 8, 2013, to launch a new Psoriasis social media campaign called Uncover Your Confidence. The campaign featured psoriasis-friendly style advice and educational resources designed to encourage people living with psoriasis to confront their condition proactively. Psoriasis is commonly mistaken as just a skin condition. However, psoriasis is a chronic disease of the immune system that appears on the skin. Psoriasis affects an estimated 125 million people worldwide. It is a non-contagious disorder that speeds the growth cycle of skin cells and results in thick, scaly areas of the skin. Currently, there is no cure for psoriasis, but treatment can help control the condition.

Stacy London is the most appropriate face of the campaign as she has lived with psoriasis since the age of four and deeply understands the disease and its impact on one's life. While speaking about the campaign, Stacy London said: *Through* Uncover Your Confidence *campaign, I hope to inspire others living with psoriasis to be self-assured through their style, stay positive and find the right dermatologist to help them manage their disease. I always strive to empower people to feel more confident in their skin, and psoriasis is a cause that is particularly near and dear to me.*

Dr. Maria Rivas, vice president of global medical affairs at AbbVie, clearly explained the campaign's purpose when she said: *It is incredibly powerful to hear Stacy speak about her personal experience. Through this partnership, we aim to educate, provide resources and tools, and bring Stacy's style of expertise to people living with this chronic condition so they can confidently confront their disease every day*.

The campaign's central website, www.UncoverYourConfidence.com, provides psoriasis-friendly advice and educational resources to both men and women. The website provides:

- Stacy's Guide to Style, complete with seasonal style tips for home and wardrobe for people living with psoriasis
- Videos with Stacy answering common questions of interest for people with psoriasis
- Video series featuring Stacy's psoriasis journey and stories from other individuals living with psoriasis
- An online search tool to find a local dermatologist who manages psoriasis
- Access to the Psoriasis Patient Advocate program pairs those with psoriasis with trained professionals in their local area who can provide one-to-one support, education, and other resources. The Psoriasis Patient Advocate program is not replacing a medical professional or a dermatologist trained in treating psoriasis. The patient advocates will not provide medical advice.

(Source: Adapted from the article: News Provided by AbbVie, Stacy London launches Uncover Your Confidence campaign to empower people living with psoriasis, CISION PR Newswire, July 8, 2013)

CASE

56

a:care: Abbott's Digital Initiative to Improve Patients' Health in India!

Abbott, a global pharmaceutical company, has a significant presence in India. It is the second-largest pharmaceutical company India, generating about one-third of Abbott's $4.4 billion global established products business. The global major gained its foothold in India by acquiring Piramal Healthcare's formulation business in a $3.7 billion deal in 2010. In addition, Abbott launched a new digital platform to improve patient awareness and doctor engagement and aid adherence with a treatment plan to drive better health outcomes.

The digital platform called *a: care* enables consumers to grant their doctor access to the health information they input. Also, it provides reliable healthcare information, reminds patients to take pills, tracks medication consumption, and uses gamification tools and reward points to incentivize patients for the right behavior by offering discounts on the purchase of medicines.

Abbott has partnered with *1mg.com*, an online pharmacy, and plans to include such partners, possibly even health insurance companies going forward. Speaking about their new digital initiative, Jawed Zia, Head of Abbott's pharmaceutical business in India, said: *It is a neutral platform designed to bridge the communication gap between doctors and consumers. He also said Abbott wants at least one million consumers to use their platform in five years. In addition, the company plans to add enhancements such as regionalizing content and personalized health coaching to equip patients to better manage their health conditions.*

The *a: care*, a global platform, currently includes three specialty chronic illnesses — diabetes, thyroid, and osteoarthritis with plans to include more therapies in a phased manner later this year. The platform can be accessed by web or mobile for free. To activate full service of *a: care*, a consumer would need the activation code that usually comes with a doctor's prescription.

www.acare.co.in

Abbott's*: a: care* initiative has a dedicated website to provide all the needed resources to improve patient outcomes. The following copy of the web pages from their website meant for patients and doctors clearly explains the scope of its capabilities and services in improving health outcomes.

For Patients

Better Health, Our Mission

Meet a: care. Nothing is more important than health. The *a: care* is dedicated to guiding you toward better health outcomes with personalized resources, tools, and tips designed to make a real difference.

1. *Why You Are Here*: The path to better healthcare isn't simple. a: care's innovative and engaging solutions are designed to personalize the process and make it more enjoyable.
2. *What You Will Get*: Knowledge. Support. Resources. All designed to equip you better to make the right decisions about health.
3. *How You'll Engage*: Sign up to start your personalized journey, including fun ways to learn, quizzes, surveys, and health calculators.
4. *Explore*: See the many ways a: care provides support. When it comes to solutions, one size doesn't fit everybody. That's why

we've developed personalized ways to engage with *a: care*. With a resource center that will make managing your healthcare more efficient and more enjoyable.

5. *Learn a: care* would like to help you learn more. The more you know, the easier it is to have good conversations with your doctor and make better decisions. *a: care* helps with key information that is easy to access, reliable, and relevant.
6. *Play*: You've probably never enjoyed learning this much. Learning about topics related to health doesn't have to be boring. It can be fun and engaging. *a: care* has developed tools that allow you to learn where and when it is easiest for you. The tools are straightforward and, therefore, easy to understand.

For Doctors

1. *Valuable Resources in a Single Spot*: the more you visit *a: care*, the more valuable you'll find us. Our resources run the gamut, assisting you throughout your busy health journey.
2. *Your Day is About to Get Less Complicated*: Now, there's a place to find the latest information on therapies and conditions, connect with patients, and watch videos on important health topics.
3. *You can gather your patients in one place*. *a: care* can help by bringing your patients together in a single spot and helping you help them.
4. *Explore the latest therapy topics*. Read articles and newsletters and watch conference videos relevant to your practice.

(Source: Adapted from articles: 1. Viswanath Pilla, Abbott takes digital route in India to improve patient health outcomes, MoneyControl, March 19, 2019; 2. www.acare.co.in)

Search Engine Marketing

With a 78 percent share of the global search engine market, Google processes about a whopping 3.5 billion searches on the net every day. Also, there are over one billion websites on the world wide web today. This milestone was first reached in September 2014. It is quite a challenge to make your website stand out in this huge clutter. So how do you make a presence in this densely crowded cyberspace? Enter Search Engine Marketing (SEM).

Search Engine Marketing (SEM) is a form of internet marketing activity that promotes websites by increasing their visibility in search engine result pages (SERP). Search Engine Marketing covers two key tactics: Search Engine Optimization (SEO) and Search Engine Advertising (SEA).

Search Engine Optimization

Search Engine Optimization (SEO), also known as 'organic results,' is mainly achieved by optimizing the content of websites so that they are ranked among the top of the search engine result pages. This is very important for your website because over 90 percent of all search engine traffic visits or clicks the links on the first page of search engine results. The second page receives a mere 5 percent of the traffic. What is more, no one types an URL (Uniform Resource Locator) or web address anymore. While URL remains vital to the web's structure, web users, healthcare professionals, and patients alike use search engines virtually. With effective search engine marketing, you make sure you are found on the internet. Because if you are not found, you may just as well not exist.

Search Engine Advertising (SEA)

Search Engine Advertising (SEA), also known as *Sponsored Results*, shows specific search-related ads and works on a Pay-Per-Click (PPC) basis. You can get your ads placed by a search engine in certain search results. These advertisements, however, do not appear in natural search results. Instead, they usually appear on the right-hand side of the results page in response to a corresponding search term. The fee for these ads is calculated by the number of clicks the advertisement attracts. Hence the name pay-per-click ads.

Search engine advertising is particularly useful if a website does not appear at the top of the search results because it is still new and not yet well known, or there is a lot of competition for the search terms or keywords being used.

If Pharma marketers can't compete in the natural search results of SEO (Search Engine Optimization), they can still consider SEA (Search Engine Advertising). Here are some important advantages that SEA offers marketers:

A. Firstly, search engine advertising is based on value. You pay for clicks and not for views. Therefore, you can consider it as results-driven advertising.
B. You can also consider it relevant advertising because ads are only shown when people search for the keywords you have defined. This is different from mass media advertising such as television or radio that targets everyone.
C. In addition, search engine advertising is very cost-effective. Many keywords in healthcare are very specific, and therefore competition is generally low on those keywords. Some of the keywords, for example, are sold for less than ten euro cents.
D. Furthermore, you can control your costs on SEA (Search Engine Advertising). You can decide at the beginning of a campaign how much budget you want to spend. Once you reach your budget limit, your ads will simply stop showing.
E. Search Engine Advertising (SEA) is transparent as it is based on the auction. Therefore, the *Cost per Click* (CPC) is determined by the level of competition, and this is transparent to advertisers.
F. Search Engine Advertising (SEA) can provide valuable insights into which keywords your target audience is using, thus helping the advertisers' campaign relevancy.

G. With search engine advertising, you can also extend the reach of your campaigns. Apart from being the most visited site, Google can also extend the reach of your campaign beyond its own website in placing your ads on relevant third-party websites. This is called Google AdSense.

H. One major advantage of search engine advertising is that people perceive text advertising as less intrusive than traditional banner advertising.

I. Above all, you can monitor your campaigns with SEA (Search Engine Advertising) in real-time and improve them continuously.

Which CPC to Measure?

Which is the ideal metric to measure when you are using SEA (Search Engine Advertising)? Cost-per-Click (CPC), or Cost-per-Conversion (CPC)?

Many marketers use cost-per-click as one of the metrics to measure the success of a campaign. However, the number of clicks does not tell about the quality of the visitors and visits. Instead, consider the goals of your campaign. Always. What do you want your visitors to do once they are on your web page? How visitors convert? Do they download a factsheet, a pdf of an article, register for an event, or subscribe to your newsletter and so forth. You can track these activities and calculate the cost per conversion and compare those across different channels.

Search Engine Marketing (SEM) versus Display Advertising

Search engine marketing (SEM) and Display advertising (banner advertising) are distinctly different. SEM is a pull tactic. It pulls people in. Display advertising is a push tactic. It pushes ads towards people. Display advertising is used more frequently in the early stages of the customer journey when they are not actively looking for a solution to a problem. On the other hand, search is more frequently used in the latter stages of the customer journey, such as closer to the treatment and product decision and drug adherence. Google Analytics can help you monitor how well your brand is performing across channels in real-time.

SEM and the Customer Journey

It is essential to understand how patients and healthcare professionals search throughout the customer journey. Studying your customers' search behavior will give you actionable insights and enable you to align the content of your website and your search engine marketing strategy. In addition, it will help you make your content more relevant for healthcare professionals and patients alike and place it more prominently on the result page of search engines.

Search Engine Optimization (SEO)

You need to optimize your website and content if you want to be found on the world wide web. And it is very difficult to be found on the web with over a billion websites. It is not enough if you are found on the web. You have to be listed on the first page of the search engine results page (SERP). Because if you are not on the first page of search engine results, you will likely get a mere 5 percent of the traffic. Optimization of your website and content, therefore, is no longer a matter of choice. It is rather mandatory. Search engine optimization (SEO) can optimize your website and other digital channels for search engines. Search engines are the starting point for everything for most web users.

How Search Engines Work?

A search engine works basically through a web crawler, which is also called a web spider. A web crawler is an automated software application that systematically browses (or crawls) the world wide web. Web crawlers copy all the pages they visit and store them in a web index. It is because of this web index, a search engine can generate result pages in a split second. When we perform a search, the search engine flips through this index, which is like a massive book, and locates all the relevant pages and selects the pages it thinks are the best to show first. The algorithm defines the selection logic.

Search engines create their result pages based on a series of algorithms. These algorithms determine whether your page gets a high ranking or not. Therefore, you need to monitor the positioning of your web pages and your competitors' continuously as search engines regularly update their algorithms, which can impact the ranking of your web pages. With most traffic (over sixty-one percent) coming via search engines, a position drop can significantly impact your traffic and, hence, your business.

Choosing Keywords

Choosing the right keywords is crucial for success in search engine marketing. The keywords you use in your content determine your rankings on search engine result pages (SERPs). To help you select the right keywords, Google has developed a Keyword Planner tool. It generates a list of relevant keywords and their monthly search volumes for a therapeutic area or product. The tool helps you select the right keywords for search engine optimization(SEO) and search engine advertising (SEA).

SEO Success Factors

Surprisingly, only 42 percent of pharmaceutical companies actively optimize their websites to improve their search engine visibility. However, search engines are the starting point for most web users to search everything. Here are some critical success factors for optimizing your search engine and improving your position on its result pages:

1. *Value of Keywords*. SEO is free. You don't have to pay to be shown on search engine result pages (SERPs). The keywords you choose and use in your content determine the position of your website and other channels in search engine result pages. Selection of the right and most relevant keywords that match your customers search for does take time and effort. Your keywords are very valuable.
2. *Content is king*. Search engine optimization (SEO) is content-driven. You optimize your content for search engines by

incorporating the most relevant keywords. Besides, you also need to update your content at regular intervals continuously. The more relevant and recent your content is, the greater the chances of attaining higher rankings in search engine result pages. The higher your content appears in the result lists, the greater the probability of visiting your content.

3. *Technology is Important*. In addition to relevant keywords, technology too is crucial for optimizing your search engines. You need to make sure that your website is easily accessible to search engines. It is essential to optimize your site structure to facilitate both surfing and crawling. Search engines only interpret the text, and content tagging (text descriptions) enables them to interpret and index those visual elements. It is, therefore, important to tag all the visual elements on your sites, such as images, videos, PDFs, and others. Also, optimize your website for mobile. Mobile optimized websites get better positioning in search engines.
4. *Credibility is crucial*. Credibility ensures better rankings on search engine result pages. One simple way to improve the reliability of your website is to have other websites link to your site. When other important websites link to your site, that enhances your site's credibility leading to an improved ranking in search engine results. Remember to enable social sharing because these additional links help you improve your page rankings and traffic to your site.
5. *Optimize your website*. To optimize your website, first of all, you need to create quality content. Sites with interesting and engaging content will have better search engine traffic. Easy to read text that is frequently updated and appropriately tagged content is highly engaging.
6. *Optimize linking*. Link all your other websites and also optimize them. The More the links are the more the clicks.
7. *Combine channels*. Combining channels facilitates multichannel engagement and can create a seamless experience.

8. *Make your content shareable*. People share content they find useful, trendy, engaging, credible, and trustworthy. Also, make it easy to share by creating social sharing links.
9. *Promote your website*. The more traffic the websites get, the better position they will get in the search results.
10. *Monitor*. Monitor your search engine rankings continuously. When search engine algorithms change, or competitors become more active, your position on the search engine results may fall.

SEO in Pharma Industry

Pharmaceutical companies, being highly regulated, face some challenges in implementing their search engine optimization strategies. While these are not insurmountable, pharmaceutical marketers should keep them in mind when planning their SEO strategies.

- *Copy approvals* for all types of content in the pharmaceutical industry take time as they involve multiple functions such as legal, medical, and regulatory. Keeping content fresh and up-to-date can, therefore, be challenging. It is essential to start the search engine optimization simultaneously as soon as content development starts.
- *Right Keywords*. You may not include the most appropriate and relevant keywords such as your product names as organic search on your website as they will not be allowed.
- *Password challenges*. Most websites for healthcare professionals are password-protected. However, search engines cannot index password-protected content. Search engines, therefore, index only the landing pages of HCP sites, and due to this limited access to your content, these sites are unlikely to show up high in search results. What is the alternative? How can you improve your page ranking? Include as much descriptive content as possible on the landing page of every password-protected site. You can also add a section for patients that can be publicly accessed from your landing page.

To achieve success in SEO (Search Engine Optimization) and Search Engine Advertising (SEA), analyzing the traffic to a website and other channels is crucial. Google Analytics can help you analyze conversions, optimize keyword bid prices, look at bounce rates and the cost-effectiveness of your campaign.

Finally, continuous optimization of your campaign as it is running holds the key to success. You can do this by adding more relevant content to your website, identify new keywords, and optimize budgets accordingly.

■

E-Mail Engagement

An email address or Digital ID is the most widely used form of digital verification. It can tell marketers about online people, where they have been, what they have done, and even what they like. This information enables marketers to improve personalization, deliverability and target their marketing messages to the right customers.

Customers today are more likely to respond to personalized interactions with brands and companies when and where they are most engaged. Technology today uses customers' digital ID as the core of who they are, where they have been, what they like, and where they might go possibly. When you consider the usage of emails today, you would understand how important they are as digital IDs. Research by Radicati Group indicates that there are four billion email users at the start of 2020 worldwide, who collectively send 306 billion emails every day. Statista, the German company specializing in market and consumer data, estimates the number of email users to go up to 4.6 billion by 2025.

An email has an ability that many other channels do not have. It can create valuable, personal touches at scale. Different types of emails are sent to different target groups through email marketing to build and maintain customer relationships. The three main types of emails are:

1. *Marketing Emails* such as newsletters, sales, and promotional announcements are commercial.
2. *Notification Emails* are more informative. These include registration confirmation emails, status update changes such as updates from free to premium services, notification on recently browsed products, feedback request emails, and subscription abandonment.
3. *Transactional Emails* are sent confirming the customer relationship. These include welcome messages, account opening, shipment tracking and order status updates, and more. The recipients expect these.

Research indicates that about 60 percent of Pharma marketers consider email marketing a standard practice in their marketing activity. Best Practices research suggests that Pharma companies would do well with their email strategies if they do three basic things:

A. The subject line of your email determines whether your email will be opened or not. It is because your recipient's first impression of your email communication is through the subject line. Considering the number of emails we all receive every day, the subject line must be persuasive to generate an action. Research suggests that subject lines of under 49 characters make the best open rates. You must start your subject lines with information-carrying and descriptive words. Also, avoid generic, meaningless words in the subject line.

B. Make it easy to subscribe and make it easy to unsubscribe your emails. When you make it difficult to unsubscribe, people get annoyed and may even mark you as spam, which can be more harmful.

C. In the Pharma industry, open rates for rep-triggered (sent from sales representatives) emails can be twice as high as those for mass campaigns.

4-*U* Approach to Subject Lines

Subject lines are crucial for the success of email marketing campaigns as they determine the open rates and click-through rates (CTRs) of your emails. Therefore, you have to prepare your subject lines carefully. A 4-U approach is a useful tool in this regard. Rudd Kooi, Fonny Schenck, and Beverly Smet proposed this 4-U Approach in their insightful book, *Evidence-Based Multichannel: Delighting Pharma Customers in the Omnichannel Age*. Consider these 4-'U's, for example:

A. *Useful*: In what way is the message of value to the recipient? Follow the WIFR-Rule: What's-in-it-for-the recipient?

B. *Ultra-Specific*: Make it immediately clear to the recipient what he can expect from the email?

C. *Unique*: In what way is the message compelling and inviting?

D. *Urgent*: Can you create a need to read it now?

Effective Email Engagement

The life span of an email is very short. Twenty-four percent of all email opens happen during the first one hour after delivery. The chances of your email being opened after twenty-four hours are less than one percent. So how do you ensure that your audiences open your emails? How can you engage them effectively? Here are two factors that can help you significantly in engaging your audiences effectively.

A. *Personalize your messages*. Knowing how, where, and when to personalize messages is the vital first step. As more and more people are worrying about cyber-security, personalization has to be used with caution. Trust is essential in personalization. Like in real life, you build a relationship of trust over time. Any insincere familiarity can put the readers off. Personalization should go beyond addressing the reader with classic Dear followed first and last names. Personalizing content is more important. Use customer journey information to suggest the content, products, or services. Giving people what they want helps forge closer ties. What parts of the email can be personalized? Virtually every part! Consider these, for example, Subject line, Content blocks, Offers, discounts and offers, specific information relevant to that consumer, CTA (Call-to-Action) links, or buttons.

B. *Communicate Segment-specific messages*. Research suggests differences in email behaviors between general practitioners (GPs) and Specialists. GPs usually generate a higher open rate of 27 percent compared to specialists with 22 percent. While this may not be a big difference, it is significantly different for the click-through rates (CTRs). Specialists showed a 21 percent CTR on average, GPs displayed a considerably lower 13 percent CTR. Therefore, you should design your mails using subject lines and segment-specific content to GPs and specialists. Additionally, it would be best if you keep the following factors in mind while designing segment-specific emails:

- You need to customize content for different personas of customer segments.
- Towards loyal customers, for example, content should be focused on expanding prescription use in a new group of patients.
- In Non-prescribers, the focus of content may be on overcoming the hurdles to prescribe for the first time.
- Also, you can send different content depending upon the orientations of the customers. You can design science-focused content for a more science-oriented specialist physician and a different type of content for a more relationship-oriented GP.

Measure What Matters

The basic metrics that you should measure and monitor in your email strategy are:

1. **Exposure Metrics** looks at exposure, or how many people you can potentially reach with your message. Good exposure metrics are the number of opt-ins you collected, the number of emails sent, and the number of email permissions obtained over time.
2. **Interaction Metrics** looks at interaction levels. Good interaction metrics are the number of emails opened, and the number of emails bounced.
3. **Engagement Metrics** looks at engagement levels. These are the most important as they measure the true impact of an email. Good engagement metrics are the number of click-throughs or call-to-actions responded to, the number of opt-outs, referrals, and shares.

A to Z of Email Marketing: Winner's Checklist

How to win with email marketing? What are the critical success factors? Here's a checklist of essential steps to pay attention to and act upon. Finally, here's a list that can help you win with your email marketing.

A. Who will receive your emails? Define your target audiences clearly.
B. Define relevant customer segments so that you can customize messages.
C. Define your email content. Prepare a detailed content strategy. Which type of email to be sent to whom? Consider all kinds of emails, such as marketing, notifications, and transactional.
D. What are your frequency goals? How often do you plan to send your emails? What are your key performance indicators for each type of email?
E. Prepare a schedule covering all your email messages.
F. Use an actual person's name as the sender of an email. Having a generic 'info@' sender address can hurt open rates.
G. Have a clear, attention-grabbing subject line that tells the recipient exactly what they should expect in the email.
H. It is vital to have a personal salutation for each email.
I. Anchor your email with the value proposition mentioned in the subject line. It could be a downloadable report or an article.
J. Personalize your email offering to the extent possible.
K. Make your CTA (Call-to-Action) easy to recognize and understand, so the recipient knows what she needs to do.
L. Ensure that all images for the mailing are relevant to the content and the subject because images will not be shown automatically in the majority of email clients. People need to download them. So avoid putting your CTA (Call-to-Action) buttons in the image of an email.
M. Include social sharing buttons that allow the recipients to share your message with their network in your email.
N. Prepare your designs and content for your emails. Test them and ensure that they work equally well on all devices. Optimize your emails for mobile devices. Over fifty percent of people open their emails on their mobiles today.
O. Now about your header and footer of the email. Ensure every email contains a link to your privacy policy, an unsubscribe option, and a link to your website. In addition, always provide an option to view the email on a webpage in the header of your email, in case of recipients, who cannot open it in their email client.

P. Make sure your email message contains a sufficient amount of actionable links. More links mean more clicks.

Q. Make sure that you receive all the emails, which are sent, so you can get a better idea of how your target audience receives them.

R. Try to standardize your email templates as much as possible. It will save development time while at the same time will ensure a consistent look and feel.

S. New subscribers are often more engaged. Do keep track of the date when people subscribe to your program. It will help you adjust your content, as subscribers' interest may start to wane after a while.

T. Facilitate subscription. Make it easy for recipients to subscribe and unsubscribe.

U. Make it easy to share and forward your email content.

V. Email is an essential part of every brand team's communication mix. Therefore, this channel should be owned by the marketing, not by the IT department.

W. Measure results. Track open rate, click-through rate (CTR), unsubscribe rate, bounce rate, website traffic, and signups since the previous campaign.

X. Continuously test different features of your email campaigns such as design, different call-to-actions, or different wordings, as these things can significantly impact campaign outcomes.

Y. Continue to optimize audiences' content, design, and frequency.

Z. Finally, email is an essential part of every company's communication mix. Investing time, effort, and resources in email marketing is a 'must-do despite the advent of newer social media sharing channels.

Display Advertising

What is Display Advertising?

Display advertising is an online advertising model where marketers use banner ads with other visual ad formats to advertise their products and services on websites, apps, or social media channels. Sonia Veres presents a simple definition of display ads in Creatopy's blog article titled, What is a Banner Ad and how does it work? *A display ad or banner ad is an advertisement displayed on a webpage. The advertisement consists of text or an image (jpg, png,or gif) or a multimedia object usually created in flash. Thus banner ads can be static or animated depending on the technology used to make them.*

Wired magazine (hotwired.com in the 1990s) launched the first-ever banner ad when it launched the AT&T ad on October 17, 1994. It was a simple banner that said, "*Have you ever clicked your mouse right here? You will,*" and the banner sent the user to an AT&T campaign.

All banner ads share the same basic function. When you click on the web page or multimedia object you see on a web page, your internet browser takes you to the advertiser's website or landing page.

Display advertising or bannering is a popular and effective format of digital advertising. Display ads are a cost-effective method of advertising for marketers looking for ways to reach and acquire customers. From what used to be a blanket coverage tactic, display advertising has evolved into a more accurately targeted due to its integration with wider advertising networks and its increasing sophistication.

Display ads are usually placed in designated corners of web pages and social media platforms. In addition, they are usually showcased in the form of a banner ad (graphic or text). While display ads or banner ads and search engine ads may appear simultaneously, they serve very different purposes. In contrast, search engine ads are best suited when a customer or patient searches for information.

Display ads are designed to create awareness or develop a specific need. They are often used early in the customer or patient journey as a form of *push* advertising. Therefore, search engine ads should be considered *as pull* advertising and will more likely occur later in the customer's journey.

Why Display Advertising?

There are three main reasons why companies choose display advertising:

1. *Brand Awareness:* You can grow your brand awareness using banner ads so people can easily recognize your product or service.
2. *Generate Leads:* Helps you generate leads, and it's a great way to build a customer base.
3. *Retarget Your Audience:* If somebody came on your website and did not respond to your CTA (Call-to-action), you can retarget them with your banner ads.

Types of Display Advertising

The main aim of display ads is to automatically draw users' attention to the ad when visiting a website or a social media platform. Therefore, marketers have been experimenting with different formats of display ads to win the users' attention. The different types of display ad formats are:

1. *Banner Ads*, named after their shape, which is banner-like, are the most commonly used display advertising format, and they stand out on any web page. They are hyperlinked, image-based ads in the shape of a strip usually placed on the top of a web page to immediately draw the users' attention.
2. *Rich Media* is an innovative display advertising tactic involving interactive elements such as video and audio features to make the advertising more engaging.
3. *Interstitial Ads* are those ads that appear as a separate web page before you are directed to the original page that you

wanted to visit on the internet. Since they take up the entire screen, they are effective in capturing the user's attention.

4. *Video Ads* (video ads in a banner) are more engaging and attract a lot of attention. Platforms like YouTube and Instagram have made it convenient for marketers to run video ads.

As M. Laurence Light, former chief marketing officer of MacDonald, said: *It no longer makes sense to send an advertising message to the many in hopes of persuading the few*.

These days, display ads use sophisticated targeting methods to ensure maximum reach and that the right advertisements land in front of the eyeballs of the right audience. But then, How do you target your display ads?

Targeting Display Ads

Target feature in display advertising ensures that your ad reaches the right target audience resulting in avoiding your ad spend on a demographic not interested in your product or service. ChiradeepBasuMallick suggests six vital steps in the targeting process for maximizing returns on display advertising in a blog article titled, *What is Display Advertising? Definitions, Targeting Process, Management, Network Types, and Examples* in toolbox.com on May 20, 2020. Here is the gist:

1. *Define Your Demographic*: You can segment the audience based on their basic demographic details like age, gender, interests, etc.
2. *Identify Target Keywords*: Target keywords allow you to reach your target audience. The Display Ad Network, such as Google, will match your keywords with words and phrases present in the publisher's site where your ad will be displayed.
3. *Zero-in On the Topic*: This feature lets you choose a group of websites that fit a specific topic or category within which your business operates.
4. *Formulate the Ideal Placement*: You can choose the website you want to display your ads on.

5. *Show Ads Based on the Interest*: Google collects data on its users' behavior. Depending on what users are searching for, you can run your display ads that resonate with specific interest areas.
6. *Retarget Based on Past Interest*: Also known as retargeting, this display ad retargeting feature lets you target users who have already visited your website, thereby reinforcing the brand's impact and recall.

Performance-based Pricing

As Peter Drucker, the management guru, famously said: *What's measured, improves*.

During the early days of internet advertising, you could only buy ads on a cost per 1000 basis, also known as CPM (Cost per 1000 Impressions). However, with the arrival of search engine marketing (SEM), pricing models have moved to performance-based pricing. These include:

Cost-per-Click (CPC)

Cost-per-Lead (CPL)

Cost-per-Acquisition (CPA)

The significant thing about performance-based pricing is that the risk shifts from the advertiser to the publisher. Today, about two-thirds of all online advertising campaigns are performance-based.

Counting What Counts

How do you know your display advertisement strategy is working? How do you measure its impact? Are you counting what counts? Here are four key performance indicators (KPIs) to measure the outcomes of display advertising:

1. *Reach* is the number of views your display ads attract. It helps you assess the effectiveness of your display ad management and targeting effort. If ads are not reaching the desired audience, you need to readjust your targeting parameters.

2. *Impressions* indicate the number of times your display ad has been served to a user on a website or social media platform. Every time an ad is displayed, it counts as an impression. Once you quantify the impressions, you can measure and map ad performance against the conversion rates. If you observe that your impressions are growing and not the conversion rates of your display ad, you need to rethink about display ad strategy and plan.
3. *Click-Through-Rate (CTR)* is a crucial indicator of engagement. It indicates the number of people who have clicked on your ad. It is the ratio of impressions to clicks. For example, if your ad receives 1,000 impressions and generated 100 clicks, that is a click-through ratio of 10 percent. Low CTR calls for a relook at the strategy and targeting parameters.
4. *Conversion Rate* is the most important metric to consider. Conversion rate quantifies the number of people who click through to your landing page and perform the action as per your call to action (CTA), such as downloading your app, opting into a newsletter.

How Display Ads Work?

The inner workings of display advertising may be complex. However, the process itself is simple. So let's take a sneak peek into how display ads work.

When you visit a web page with space for an online advertisement, an impression is announced. And from every impression, the exchange system sends a bid request. In addition, the information about the impression, such as which website or web page it is and information on the surfer, is provided to the exchange platform so the system can decide whether to bid or not. The system decides whether to bid or not within milliseconds. Finally, the exchange system that runs the auction evaluates all of the bids and assigns a winner. The winning ad is then shown on the website. The whole process takes an instant almost since it takes less than 100 milliseconds.

Major Tactics to Maximize Impact

There are several major tactics to maximize the impact of display advertising. Here are some important ones:

1. *Geo-targeting* is the first tactic. Based on the geographic location of the surfer, you promote the most relevant offering. For example, suggest the nearest hospital or doctor or list the feedback of nearby patients with a similar condition that uses your service.
2. *Contextual Targeting* is another tactic where you place your ad near relevant context. For example, if you want to raise awareness of a program for hypertension patients, make sure you display your ads on the blogs and other health websites that discuss this topic.
3. *Behavior Targeting* uses a person's behavior to push the most relevant ads. For example, undiagnosed patients display a different online behavior compared to diagnosed patients. Therefore, you need to display different ads meeting their specific needs.
4. *Social Targeting* is about engaging patients and physicians on social media. It can be challenging. However, social networks such as Facebook and LinkedIn offer some great advertising opportunities. You can target your customers at specific demographic profiles and interest categories on social media.
5. *Variety in Ad Design* is another important tactic. People ignore your ad if you display the same ad repeatedly. Even if the suggested offering does not change, change the ad design to grab the surfer's attention.
6. *Use Different Formats*. To move beyond simple text and images, you may consider using different formats like the in-banner video, making interesting offers with a CTA (Call-to-Action), and interactive ads.

   A. The in-banner video ad can help generate more views and clicks. You can add, for instance, the video footage of one of your webinars to a display ad.

B. You can make an interesting offer to encourage the viewers to click. For example, you can promote through your display ads relevant content that's downloadable for free.

C. Polls or simple games embedded in your display ads can create an interaction with the surfer, which in turn, can help build engagement.

How to Get Most from your Display Advertising?

While all the good marketing and advertising communication principles are applicable to display advertising, here are some points to consider when designing display advertising.

1. Define your target audience and decide what you want from them.
2. What is your value proposition? A clearly defined value proposition will help you write the copy of your banner ad and choose a good CTA (Call-to-action) button text.
3. Ensure your copy is simple and easy to comprehend. Most audiences viewing your web page have limited time and attention. They are already consuming a lot of content. Therefore, your copy needs to be crisp and direct to stand out on the overcrowded internet. In addition, since display ads let you identify and target specific demographic and psychographic profiles, make sure to formulate your copy relevant to the audience to resonate.
4. Decide on your budget. How much money do you want to invest in display advertising?
5. Make sure that the color scheme and design are in sync with the corporate and brand image. In addition, it is important to keep your ads clutter-free, and the textual content should be visible.
6. Do not use too many formats for your display ads. Remember, less is more when it comes to display advertising. A successful campaign is minimal, direct, and crisp.
7. Avoid display overload by producing multiple variations of your ads because over three-fourths (77 percent) of all display ads are completely ignored.

8. Lastly, ensure that display advertising is appropriately integrated with the rest of the campaign. Most often, marketers consider display advertising as an extending and supplementary tactic to others in the marketing mix. It is a supportive tactic and not supplementary.

Mobile Engagement

Mobile is one of the most recent disruptions in the digital space today. Every digital activity that you can think of, such as social sharing, searching the internet, buying things, making payments, has gone mobile. As a result, mobile, one of the recent innovations in digital technologies, has enormous potential in almost every industry, including the pharmaceutical industry. However, mobile is not without challenges. Companies get only one chance to make a first impression, which is mostly via a mobile device. If your website is not mobile optimized and does not scale up properly to your customers' mobile devices, you are on a sure path to losing your customers. Therefore, it is important to follow a mobile-first approach.

Mobile-First Approach

As the name suggests, the Mobile-First approach is about designing a desktop website starting with mobile and then scale it up to larger screens. Thus, the mobile-first approach is contrary to the traditional approach of starting with a desktop website and then adapting it to the mobile. Instead, a mobile-first approach means building your website with mobile in mind with the main objective of improving the mobile users' experience on your site.

The rapid adoption of mobiles makes it mandatory for companies to adopt a mobile strategy. Consider these facts, for example:

1. According to GSMA (Global System for Mobile communication Associations), over two-thirds (66.85 percent) of the world's population has a mobile device as of August 2021. In 2017, for example, a little over half (53 percent) of the world population had mobile devices.
2. Statista, the world's leading business data platform, predicts the number of mobile device users will increase to 7.33 billion by 2023 from 5.27 billion in 2021.
3. The rise of mobile devices has led to an *always-on* mentality, blurring the lines between private and professional lives.

4. Research indicates 9 out of 10 smartphone users have their mobile within arm's length round the clock.
5. Also, eighty-seven percent of smartphone users read personal and work-related emails on the same mobile device.

How to Develop a Mobile-First Mindset?

Here are five key questions you need to answer to develop a mobile-first mindset.

1. What is your level of mobile maturity? Are you a beginner or already have taken some mobile initiatives? If you are not a novice, how many mobile initiatives do you currently have, and how well are they integrated into your overall marketing strategy?
2. How do you compare with your closest competitors on mobile maturity?
3. Is your website mobile responsive? If it is not, make it now. Then, after building a mobile-optimized website, you can start creating apps when there is a specific need.
4. Are you considering mobile as an *add-on* to your strategy or fully integrating it into your overall marketing strategy?
5. Are you capturing learnings from your mobile initiatives and building them into your future strategies?

Mobile in Pharma

Pharma companies need to have a clear mobile strategy and mindset to survive and grow in the rapidly changing marketplace. Therefore, mobile is a must for Pharma. Consider, for example, the following reasons:

1. There are 5.27 billion mobile users globally.
2. More than one-half of all online searches take place on mobile. Fifty percent of all web activities are mobile.
3. Fifty-two percent of smartphone users gather health-related information on their phones.

4. Even HCPs (Healthcare Professionals) are turning to mobile. About 80 percent of physicians use smartphones and medical apps.
5. The mobile health app market was valued at $47.7 billion in 2021 and projected to grow to $149 billion by 2028.

In addition, most healthcare professionals actively search and consume professional content outside normal business hours. Therefore, pharmaceutical marketers should design their mobile services with different user contexts and times in mind.

When your target audience is on mobile more often, you cannot afford to ignore mobile. Going mobile is a way to engage them when they want it where they want it. It's no longer an option.

State of Mobile Marketing

While most pharma marketers acknowledge the importance of mobile, only seventeen percent of them have their mobile strategy fully integrated into their overall marketing strategy. And only half of them have a mobile-first mindset.

The variety of devices and operating systems make it difficult for marketers to embrace a mobile-first mindset. That is probably why many of them are stuck in a mobile-campaign mode, and very few reach a mature mobile digerati state. For example, Research2Guidance, which studied the pharma app field in 2017, found that Johnson & Johnson was the only pharmaceutical company with a good mix of breadth (number of apps) and depth (usage).

COVID-19 Accelerates Mobile Health Growth

The global pandemic COVID-19 has led to a significantly increased utilization of mobile health platforms across the globe. In addition, the pandemic made remote patient monitoring, patient data analysis, and diagnosis and remote engagement of pharma sales reps and physicians an absolute necessity.

Mobile health or medical application downloads during the peak month of the pandemic recorded an unprecedented increase. According to Statista, the leading business data platform, there was a 135 percent increase in medical application downloads in South Korea and around 65 percent at a global level during the peak month of COVID-19. Thus, the pandemic has certainly boosted mobile medical app adoption fueling its market growth.

Mobile Marketing: Key Tactics

Out of the many tactics mobile marketers use to reach and engage their customers, three have a *must-have* status. Consider for example these tactics:

1. A responsive website or a mobile-optimized website has become the norm today. Websites that do not scale properly to whatever mobile device their customers are using are bound to lose customers.
2. The second most important mobile tactic is a mobile-optimized landing page.
3. Outbound SMS (Short Messaging Service) is another popular tactic for using text for multimedia messages and notifications. Short-code SMS replying is a tactic that allows customers to reply to an SMS sent during a marketing campaign with a short-code.
4. Mobile bar codes such as QR codes are convenient for redirecting customers from offline channels, such as brochures, to the online space. QR codes are graphics that can be scanned by a mobile device and then redirect customers directly to an URL.
5. Geo-targeting allows marketers to deliver specific and relevant content on a mobile device based on the website visitor's geographic location. For example, a website visitor can receive a targeting message about a flu outbreak when entering a geographic location with a flu outbreak.
6. Wearables are another very important mobile tactic. Wearables are mobile devices with sensors that track motion, heart rate, sleep, or other physiological metrics. You can find them on smartphones or dedicated devices such as wristbands, watches, and even shirts.

Wearables and Disappearables

Wearables and devices that are worn on the body continually collect data such as biofeedback and physiological data. They then upload the data automatically to the cloud to make it available for review by HCPs or patients. This automatic upload allows for greater accuracy and consistency of health data collection. However, there is a long way to connect and integrate this data directly into a more holistic healthcare record system.

There is an increasing trend towards becoming the quantified self or life-logging group. There is a growing interest among people to keep track of their health records to adjust their behavior and stay healthy without the input of a physician.

There is another trend that is increasing. *Wearables* are giving away to *disppearables*. Disppearables are biodegradable sensors inside the body. Some biopharma companies are taking to the internet of things in a big way and introducing disppearables as a solution around the pill.

mHealth

mHealth is a term used for the practice of medical and public health, supported by mobile devices. It refers to mobile communication devices such as mobile phones, PDAs, and tablets for health services and information. Mobile devices are changing the way patients and healthcare professionals access the internet and find health information.

mHealth is helping track some of the healthcare challenges such as the aging population, non-compliance (patients not taking medicines), management of chronic diseases, and even helping with strategies for prevention of chronic diseases. Here is a partial list of areas where mobile device applications are used:

1. Reference
2. Decision Support
3. Monitoring

4. Compliance
5. Disease Management
6. Chronic Disease Prevention

Increasingly patients depend less on HCPs and more on online for healthcare information. It is, therefore, important that pharmaceutical companies and other healthcare organizations provide accurate information. In addition, pharmaceutical firms and healthcare marketers can use new technologies such as geofence locations, video assets, and text messaging to reach their audiences, even while they are in the doctors' offices or near a pharmacy.

Furthermore, mobile phone and tablet applications have provided a new and easy way for patients suffering from chronic diseases to manage their conditions and guide them toward healthier lifestyles.

More Apps

Pharmaceutical companies realize the importance of gamification as yet another tool to engage their key stakeholders, such as patients and HCPs, and started developing more and more apps. Here are some examples of successful apps:

A. *Respimat inhalation demonstrator by Boehringer Ingelheim*. Designed for HCPs, the app provides medical information on the next-generation device and facilitates physicians training patients on using Respimat. The app enables inhaler interaction, a vital issue, offers hands-on experience with an intuitive interface, and is available at no additional cost.

B. *Back-in-Play by Pfizer*. Designed as a game, this app aims to boost knowledge of a little-known disease, ankylosing spondylitis. Through this, patients in Europe learned about this condition that causes inflammation in their spine and pelvic joints.

C. *Boehringer Ingelheim's HealthSeeker* is a game that helps those with diabetes make better lifestyle choices about their condition and overall wellness.

D. *Bayer created the diabetes Didget* game using Nintendo's DS handheld game system to regularly encourage children with diabetes to test their blood glucose levels. Players receive rewards for testing consistently. Bayer's Didget blood glucose meter fits in with the Nintendo's handheld game system. It allows children with diabetes to play Knock-'em-down, the World's Fair Board Game, inspiring pediatric patients to keep up with their testing schedule.

E. *Johnson & Johnson's Care4Toda*y is designed to improve adherence to treatment regimens through reminders to take medication, refill prescriptions, and visit healthcare providers. The mobile adherence program can be used for any prescription or OTC medication or nutritional supplement, including but not limited to the Johnson & Johnson group of companies.

F. *Janssen's 'Sorted App'* is designed for patients with attention deficit hyperactivity disorder (ADHD) in the UK. The app acts as a daily organizer to help patients create, categorize, and prioritize daily tasks with a point-scoring element to motivate the users. Janssen's key product for ADHD is Concerta XL. Developed with the concurrence of Physicians in the U.K., the app is designed to utilize the functionalities of the iPhone, such as its calendar, reminders, and voice memos. The app's targeted at people above 12 years.

G. *Sun Pharma's RespiTrack App* is a mobile application that connects doctors with their asthma patients. The app's focus is to improve treatment compliance and minimize non-adherence and dropouts in the asthma treatment regime. RespiTrack allows complete monitoring of asthma attacks, symptoms, medications prescribed by the physicians. It enables patients to record time, place, duration, and triggers of attacks along with medication details on the mobile app. The patient can easily send this data to his physician through over-the-air mode weekly or monthly. In addition, a review dashboard in the app provides a snapshot of all parameters for monitoring over periodically. Also, through RespiTrack, a doctor can access his patient's details through a personalized tracker module, which is directly synced with the patients' app. This module allows doctors to access patients' ailment history, attack patterns, symptoms, medication patterns, and reports. In addition, a doctor can remotely view patient reports, and connect with him through an integrated messaging app.

A research study by Research2Guidance (R2G) observed that between 2008 and 2016, the top Pharma companies had 65 apps in the Apple and GooglePlay app stores on average compared to 1 or 2 apps from other health app publishers. However, even the Pharma companies with the most downloaded apps have accrued 6.6 million downloads since 2008, had less than a million active users. So why is the rate of adoption slower in the case of Pharma as compared to other healthcare and fitness apps?

Mobile App Cases

The following cases show how some global pharma majors have developed mobile apps with a patient-centric approach to improve their health monitoring and adherence.

CASE

57

Alkem's initiative into Digital Marketing with *DonApp* is Successful!

Alkem is the latest example of what digital marketing can do for your brand's success. Moreover, digital marketing can do a lot for your brand. For example, digital marketing has helped Alkem to grow its DonApp brand's market share from 37 percent to 43 percent in one year.

DonApp is the Alkem brand of Donepezil, a drug that effectively treats dementia and Alzheimer's disease. Donepezil is originally discovered by Eisai Pharmaceuticals, a Tokyo-based international drug company. So naturally, Eisai was enjoying the brand leadership in the Donepezil market with its brand Aricept.

Alkem started its digital marketing foray in 2016 and never looked back. The company launched a patient-focused digital campaign to its marketing, a departure from the doctor-focused industry norm. In addition to its conventional transactional mode of marketing, the company did four things in the digital space.

First, it formed a 'Dementia and Alzheimer's Community of India' Facebook group with 75,838 members as of September 18, 2018.

A. It started sharing emotional videos on WhatsApp.

B. In early 2016, Alkem launched an *I Remember* campaign that helped in achieving its dual objectives. One is the company spread awareness about dementia, a mental condition that people are hesitant to talk about, and allowed it to lead a growing prescription drug segment.

C. Alkem launched a mobile app with its brand name - DonApp, specially made for Alzheimer's' patients and their caregivers. It can provide your loved elders with helpful reminders about medicines, food, doctors' appointments, and a location tracker.

Alkem's digital marketing initiatives are noteworthy when you consider that only 7 percent of Indian drug manufacturers delve into digital marketing. Whereas for multinational companies operating in India, it is becoming a way of life as their respective parent companies have been practicing digital marketing for some time now. Indian drug laws, however, do not allow a pharmaceutical manufacturer to promote a prescription drug to the public. However, it does not stop the company from helping dementia and Alzheimer's patients with GPS - tracker-enabled free apps if patients go missing. That's why Alkem chose to launch a mobile app with its brand name - DONApp for both IOS and Android mobile users.

More than 4.1 million Indians suffer from dementia, the most common being Alzheimer's disease, which causes a gradual decrease in remembering and thinking clearly, eventually affecting a person's daily functioning. However, the awareness of the disease and its consequences are low due to social stigma, lack of awareness, and that people often confuse forgetfulness associated with normal aging. Alkem is also partnering with the Alzheimer's and Related Disorders Society of India (ARDSI), Mumbai Chapter, to spread awareness. The society conducted a three-kilometer Awarathon on December 3, 2017, at Mumbai's Worli sea face.

The potential shift of power from doctor to patient is evident from the Government's determination to stop the physician - Pharma nexus by legalizing the Uniform Code of Pharmaceutical Marketing Practices (UCPMP) and the internet explosion bringing all information, which was privy only to the healthcare professionals till now, easily accessible to the public. Thus, the pharmaceutical industry in India and the world over have an excellent opportunity to share medical information with patients through social media channels and educate the patients.

Pharmaceutical companies in India, even today, rely heavily on transactional marketing and are following the conventional methods of engaging physicians with high-value gifts, sponsorships and vacation packages, cruises, and even cash payments. For all such pharmaceutical companies, digital marketing necessarily could be a rite of passage into a patient-centric, information-driven, and corporate-brand-building-focused approach from the conventional quid pro quo relationship with the doctors.

While this path is not easy, Alkem has shown that it is possible. Alkem grew its DonApp brand's sales from Rs. 23 crores in 2016 to Rs. 26 crores in 2017. It may not be much in value, but the unit-wise sales increase has been impressive because the drug's price was capped in March 2016 by the regulator. Much of this growth can be attributed to its social media campaign.

Alkem's digital marketing initiative certainly paid rich dividends in every which way you look. It indeed shows what can be done with digital marketing.

(Source: Adapted from Ruhi Kandhari's article, Indian Pharma doesn't have a choice but to market digitally, The Ken, November 1, 2017)

CASE

58

Mobile App Success Story: How *One Drop* Did It!

How did *One Drop* become so successful an app for monitoring and managing diabetes? Because it offered solutions that match users' needs by paying close attention. It is built to help people who struggle with diabetes every day. It is created by Jeff Dachis, who was a diabetic himself.

Jeff Dachis discovered in September 2013 that he had diabetes. He started to search for solutions for managing his condition but found many gaps in the medical system. Finally, he understood how scary it could be for a person to be diagnosed with diabetes and clueless about it, and that is when he decided to build his app to help all patients with type 1 and type 2 diabetes log the required data to improve their health. That's how the mobile app, One Drop, for managing and monitoring diabetes effectively was born.

Jeff Dachis launched the mobile app, *One Drop* for iPhone in April 2015 on Apple App Stores, and after a year and a half for Android users. Today, it continues to be a trustful partner for those who need a great amount of information about type 1 and type 2 diabetes.

What Makes *One Drop* Unique?

What makes *One Drop* unique? There are at least four things that come to mind. *One Drop's* success rests on these four pillars: Simplicity, Community, Technology, and Business Model. These factors have not only made *One Drop* very successful, but they have also been responsible for its winning the best design award at its launch festival in 2015, one month before it hit the market. After that, every important publication such as TechCrunch, Mashable, CNN, Diabetes Daily, Fortune, the Washington Post, Gizmodo, and many others revealed the impact of this app on its customers. So what made One Drop the big success it is today? Here are the four pillars that made One Drop the big success that it is today.

1. *Simplicity*: When you are dealing with a massive amount of data, providing the right information at the right time becomes crucial for making your life easier. Management of diabetes involves the processing of a lot of data. Data such as your dosing schedules, monitoring of blood sugar levels, and nutritional and caloric values of the various foods you take, your walking and exercise moments, among others. With One Drop, you can schedule specific reminders for medication, and you will receive insulin pump data. The same app will calculate the carbs for each recipe, and it will allow you to have a better overview of your progress.
2. *Community*: As Jeff Dachis, the CEO of One Drop, says: *Diabetes is hard; it doesn't have to be. It is especially true when a great group of people who share the same concern allows you to check their evolution of progress, their recipes, and other information that becomes useful to you on you are determined to live a healthy life. Their social support can be of immense help, even when you are not confident about your progress. Interacting with other members of the same community makes you feel a little better. Also, what others accomplished makes you see that you can also reach the same level. What is more, the news feed of the One Drop app keeps you abreast of all the developments and events that are happening in the area of diabetes. The app helps you build a lifelong relationship with the community.*
3. *Technology*: One Drop is more than just an app for diabetes management. It helps all categories of people who are

interested in managing their overall health. For example, if you usually forget to take your meds no matter what reason, this is an app to use. At the same time, if you want to keep your weight in check, One Drop is a suitable solution. Also, the app's smart tools help you with accurate data to help you eat right and exercise appropriately. One Drop is an app that allows users to maintain a positive lifestyle and attitude.

4. *Furthermore, One Drop has recently added an Augmented Reality (A R) toolkit* that presents advanced data visualization technology to help users to analyze their graphs better. An engaging interface offers a pleasant experience while customers understand the stats displayed. One more recent additional feature of One Drop to take its technology to a higher level is its integration of the blood sugar monitoring system with Apple Watch and an Automated Decision Support System. One Drop became the first and only wireless blood sugar glucose monitoring system to connect directly to Apple Watch. The app allows users to transfer blood glucose data from One Drop Chrome directly to the Apple Watch companion app. With its new Automated Decision Support system, One Drop forecasts blood glucose prediction values over time and offers behavioral recommendations. One Drop's proprietary Artificial Intelligence (AI) generates accurate predictions for a single user based on over 1.3 billion aggregate longitudinal Diabetes health data of all people utilizing the One Drop platform. Uniquely, this allows One Drop to provide a user with accurate predictions after entering a single data point and improves over time.
5. *Subscription Model*: While the basic app of One Drop is available free to its users on Apple App Stores and Google Play, there is a subscription model which offers many value-added services. The basic app provides everything that people with diabetes need to manage their data required for healthy living. For those who need more and require 24/7 assistance, for a monthly subscription, they receive:

A. Personalized help and they will be coached by a certified diabetes educator(CDE). It is essential to count on specialized support whenever you need it. With One Drop —Experts, users have two options: on-track and on-call. Whatever their choice, experts will be there to encourage and help them continue the program.

B. Additionally to this in-app chat feature, users who pay for extra services will receive test strips and those who will take a One Drop - Chrome, a blood glucose meter that uses Bluetooth to sync data with the One Drop mobile app.

It is tough to control chronic conditions such as diabetes, but with the new technology that appears daily, everything gets easier for patients and their families. One Drop has become one of the most robust solutions for diabetes, weight loss, hypertension, and diabetes prevention. As one of its customers described: *One Drop* can be a lifesaver!

Speaking about the empowering nature of their latest application of proprietary technology of Artificial Intelligence and Augmented Reality to their already famous diabetes management system, One Drop, Jeff Dachis, CEO of One Drop, said: *For too long a time, the diabetes industry has operated on point solutions and closed systems focused on the needs of healthcare providers in the clinic; rather than on the needs of the people using the systems to manage their disease every day. We are excited to further empower One Drop users with their addition to the* One Drop *experience*.

(Source: Adapted from articles: 1. Felicia, Mobile App Success: How One Drop did It, App Samurai, October 2, 2017; 2. News Provided by One Drop, One Drop became the first diabetes glucose monitoring platform to integrate directly with Apple Watch, CISION PR Newswire, September 12, 2016)

CASE

59

Tylenol's Mobile Campaign Drives 3,000 App Downloads!

Johnson & Johnson's McNeil Consumer Healthcare Division launched a mobile campaign using Google's AdMob platform to drive the discovery of its free, branded mobile app for iPhone, *Tylenol PM Sleep Tracker*. Deutsch Creative Agency created the app, which is available as a free download in the App Store and is promoted with the tagline: *See how beneficial a goodnight's sleep can be!* The company ran a 'click-to-download' banner ad campaign across iPhone sites driving about 3,000 downloads. In addition, the campaign pushed the Tylenol Sleep Tracker app's ranking in the App Store from 120 to 14, which drove the additional organic viral spread of the application.

As Tony Nethercutt, vice president of sales at AdMob, says: *With tens of thousands of apps in the App Store, promotion is crucial to getting your app highly ranked, which is critical for discovery. Consumer discovery is difficult with 50,000 apps, so being ranked in the top 25 most popular apps in your category is crucial to getting more downloads. That's why the company used the AdMob platform. To enable* the Tylenol Sleep Tracker *app's discovery on the App Store, pushing its rank up*.

AdMob is Goggle's advertising platform for promoting and monetizing mobile applications. AdMob Mediation, the platform's unique feature, allows developers to promote their apps through in-app ads, monetizing their applications by ensuring in-app advertising and provides intelligent insights through Google Analytics. Also, your AdMob account connects with your Adwords account to distribute your ads for your iPhone applications. By combining AdMob with Adwords, you can create mobile app install campaigns. These campaigns are specific to getting more people to download your app, with Adwords on your app and other information.

Evaluating your campaign performance by tracking installs as conversations are very easy with AdMob. AdMob fully integrates with Google Analytics, allowing you to access all the metrics and dimensions that matter to your application, such as user acquisition, engagement, revenue, screen views, sessions, app version, screen size, and more. You can also segment your audience to gain perspective on how people use your application.

Now about the application itself: The *Tylenol Sleep Tracke*r iPhone application lets users track their sleep hours and moods, see their sleep history over time, add notes and customize their icons and get tips to help them sleep better. Tylenol is promoting the application as part of its *Get Ready for Bed* campaign.

Before launching the mobile campaign, AdMob asked two critical questions in a survey: *How do you usually download apps from App Store? And How do you discover the apps you decide to wish to download?* AdMob found 93 percent of consumers download applications using their iPhone, with only 7 percent using their computer. The response to the second question was:

- 62 percent were searching for a specific type of application
- 60 percent were browsing through the top App Store rankings
- 46 percent heard about the application via word of mouth
- 20 percent see ads while using other applications, and
- 19 percent discover the application from press stories or blog reviews

Tylenol PM Campaign

In 2009, Tylenol focused on the insight that getting ready for bed is an all-day activity. So the campaign ads encouraged people to *Get Ready* for Bed throughout the day by making more sleep-friendly choices. In addition, they prioritized digital and outdoor media to speak to people in the context of their daily activities. A bus shelter ad, for example, says:

Get Ready for Bed. Block out bright lights and distractions with heavy shades.

Feel Better. Tylenol PM

During their month-long Sleep Campaign, McNeil Consumer Healthcare, the makers of Tylenol PM, wanted to help people develop better sleep habits. So they created an integrated campaign to get people thinking about how their daily choices affect their sleep and the importance of getting a good night's rest. For example, they used 3-D bus shelters to remind passers-by that their afternoon coffee may be keeping them up at night. These ads were featured in The New York Times and Curbed.

Bus shelter wraps in Chicago City gave the illusion that commuters were sitting inside their bedroom and let them explore the different ways they could make their bedroom a more sleep-friendly environment. In addition, a magazine ad allows people to track a week of sleep to see how getting better sleep could affect their mood. Here is what the ad says:

How are you feeling today?

Draw the face that lifts your mood and record the number of hours you slept.

(Faces: Grumpy Sad Happy)

Does sleep have an impact on how you feel during the day? Take our 7-day challenge to find out. Chances are you'll see that getting enough sleep can help you manage stress, improve your concentration and memory, and may even help lift your mood. Tylenol PM Rapid Release Gels relieves aches and pains and helps you fall asleep with a non-habit-forming sleep-aid when used as directed. And more sleep could mean more happy days ahead.

F*eel Better Tylenol PM*

Tylenol PM Sleep Tracker App

The Tylenol PM Sleep Tracker iPhone app lets people see for themselves how beneficial a good night's sleep could be. It allows users to track their previous night's sleep and corresponding mood, keep a sleep journal, and access dozens of tips for getting a better night's sleep.

Time-targeted online banners deliver tips on what you could do during the day to improve your chances of a good night's sleep and things you can do at night if you still have trouble falling asleep.

The campaign's companion website, getreadyforbed.com, consolidated all the sleep tips and tools into one place, with sections focusing on things you can do throughout your day to help you sleep at night, how to get your bedroom ready for bed, and the benefits of sleep in improving your mood. The copy of the ad on the website says it all:

Not getting enough sleep?

Making simple changes to your daily routine and sleep environment can help make it easier to

get a good night's sleep.

Get yourself ready for bed

Get your bedroom ready for bed

Why sleep is important

When you have nighttime aches and trouble sleeping, Tylenol PM Rapid Gels can help.

(Source: Adapted from articles: 1. Tylenol mobile campaign drives 3,000 app downloads, Mobile Marketer; 2. Tylenol PM, Creative Director, and Art Director, Steven Emry, stevenemry.com)

CASE

60

GlaxoSmithKline Rides Piggyback on the *FluTracker App* of the Weather Channel!

GlaxoSmithKline's (GSK) consumer healthcare unit makes over-the-counter (OTC) treatment, Theraflu. Theraflu, as the name indicates, is a cold and flu remedy. In addition, GSK has sponsored the new cold and FluTracker, the weather channel app on the weather company, weather.com site. IBM, the weather company owner, told eWeek that with this tool, users can find out in real-time when virus activity is rising in their areas — and take whatever action they see fit to protect themselves. With this app, GlaxoSmithKline shows people how many in their geographic area suffer from colds or flu — and what to do if they are among the afflicted.

GSK's OTC division launched in 2016 Theraflu ExpressMax Caplets, a product with a specially formulated coating that provides a warming sensation you can instantly feel, letting you know that powerful relief is on the way, according to the Theraflu website. The weather company is also helping out with the launch of Theraflu ExpressMax caplets. It is working with GSK's over-the-counter division to market the new formulation using local sentiment data. Speaking about the marketing strategy of its new product, Theresa Agnew, chief marketing officer of GSK Consumer Healthcare, said: *The combination of social sentiment and cognitive learning will not only inform and advise consumers, but it will also provide valuable insights for the marketing team in terms of knowing when to merchandise and market Theraflu brand in different areas throughout the country.*

GlaxoSmithKline has been looking for ways to stay ahead in the consumer healthcare market that is growing ever more competitive. So it teamed up with Novartis in 2015 to launch an OTC joint venture to effectively compete with Johnson & Johnson, Bayer, and Sanofi. The new technological initiative, FluTracker, is a step to stay ahead and competitive in the market.

The FluTracker app has its share of critics as well. For example, Mauricio Santillana, Assistant Professor of computational health informatics at Harvard Medical School, expressed his concern over the app: *If the information is displayed on this platform is not presented in context, I am concerned that this tool could be used to promote their products more than inform the population*.

Whatever may be your viewpoint on the app and its value to people who are likely to catch a cold or flu, there can be no two opinions on the fact that GSK's piggyback ride on FluTracker for its TheraFlu is a brilliant strategy.

(Source: Adapted from the article: Carly Helfand, GSK backs controversial FluTracker in TheraFlu launch deal with weather channel, Fierce Pharma, October 17, 2016)

CASE

61

Pfizer Israel: *Public Restroom iPhone App* Rated Top 25!

The absence of public restrooms can be a major challenge for patients with overactive bladder. So how do you find a public restroom where there is none?

Tali Rosin, public affairs & policy manager with Pfizer Israel, says that there are no public toilets in Israel. Identifying this unmet felt need, Pfizer launched a GPS (Global Positioning System) app — *Public Restrooms iPhone app* that locates the nearest toilet — restaurants included. The app has some interesting features. Consider these for example:

- The app was available in the Hebrew language for markets in Israel.If public toilets are difficult to locate in Israel, it might also be difficult for Pfizer to develop and maintain data quality on individual facilities. Here's where the social power of smartphones has been put to good effect. Users can add toilets not already in the app's database.They can also grade toilets they visit for criteria such as cleanliness, availability of toilet tissue, or whether they needed to ask for the key.
- The app even provides a daily news bulletin, automatically fed using RSS (Really Simple Syndication) to complete functionality.
- Facilitates integrated telephone dialing to Pfizer's helpline, which received over 1,000 calls.

Pfizer's *Public Restrooms app* was part of a campaign with mostly TV commercials that dealt with the situation (overactive bladder) and not the solution. Also, the app addresses Pfizer's goal to promote health information while encouraging people to take action and seek help from a medical professional.

The main problem for people with overactive bladder (OAB) is that they often avoid leaving their homes for a long time with the fear of not finding a restroom when they need it. Pfizer, therefore, thought that they would help, so they will know where the nearest toilet is because they do suffer from urinary incontinence (UI). And while doing that, maybe they'll conclude that they might suffer from an overactive bladder, and then they will perhaps go to the doctor and ask for help.

The *Public Restrooms app* is designed to raise awareness about the overactive bladder (OAB). People with OAB, therefore, will find it very beneficial. The app will also benefit mothers with little children and tourists in Israel.

The app has become very successful with over 15,000 downloads from Apple App Stores and reached the top 25 position on the app stores within three months of its launch in September 2011.

With the combination of innovative features such as location-based services, social engagement, and ratings, and integrated telephone dialing, Pfizer's *Public Restrooms app* broke new ground for pharmaceutical engagement with patients even in a highly regulated environment.

(Source: Adapted from articles: 1. Daniel Ghinn, CEO, Creation Healthcare, Pharma gets social: Social, mobile app helps Pfizer engage consumers in Israel, Pharmaphorum, December 23, 2011; 2. PharmaGuy, Pfizer mobile public toilet app rated top 25 by George Costanza, Pharma Marketing Blog, February 21, 2012)

mHealth: Future Outlook

Many factors drive the greater uptake of mobile technologies among patients and healthcare professionals. Consider the following factors, for example:

1. Growing adoption of smartphones
2. Increasing penetration of 3G and 4G networks, and 5G networks
3. Increasing usage of the connected devices and mHealth apps for the management of chronic diseases
4. Increasing Focus on patient-centric healthcare delivery, and
5. Increasing demand for home healthcare services.

At the same time, certain factors are restraining the growth of mobile adoption in healthcare. These are lack of standards and regulation, limited guidance from physicians in selecting healthcare apps for patients, and resistance from healthcare providers. However, these are not very difficult to overcome. Considering the significant advantages that mHealth can offer, the future outlook seems brighter for mobile health technologies. Consider, for example, the following indicators that will drive the growth of mobile health in the coming years.

1. Rapid growth in the usage of smartphones
2. Development in coverage of networks
3. Increasing prevalence of chronic diseases requiring remote monitoring
4. Rising geriatric population
5. Increasing demand for health and analytical solutions leading to increased adoption of such applications by healthcare providers and others

According to Markets and Markets Research, the global mobile health market is expected to reach USD 213.6 billion by 2025 from USD 50.6 billion in 2020, with a CAGR of 33.3 percent over the forecast period of 2020 2025. The forecast reflects the optimism and confidence of a robust outlook for the future of mobile.

Gamification

You can find Gamification everywhere today — from boardrooms to classrooms and social media. Over the last few years, Gamification has gained wide acceptance and recognition in many areas such as marketing, healthcare, business, politics, and technology design. The pharmaceutical industry has embraced this trend in healthcare gamification to meet the ever-increasing challenges of creating value and brand building. Initial research and case studies prove that Gamification improves patient compliance and health outcomes.

Five Key Elements

Gamification uses the mechanics of gaming to engage users and solve problems in a non-game context. There are five critical elements in a gamification strategy:

1. Reward or recognition for the players' achievements.
2. A goal and a sense of purpose.
3. Rules and a framework for participation motivate participants to tackle challenges strategically.
4. Continuous challenge. Achieving each next step should be harder but not too hard. The best option is that level one prepares the user for level two. There should be a flow that will keep the users fully engaged.
5. The feedback that tracks the players' status informs them how close they are to the end goal.

How Gamification is Beneficial?

1. Gamification can promote therapies. By creating interactive, educational health content, Gamification can promote new and existing therapies.
2. Gamification can increase engagement between Pharma, HCPs, and patients. HCPs' use of interactive technology to communicate with their patients is gradually growing. With

Gamification, Pharma can provide responsible, educational health content and improve health awareness among patients. Consider the case of Sanofi-Aventis, which has successfully used Gamification as a strategy to improve patient adherence.

3. Gamification allows showing patients firsthand how their daily habits and choices affect their condition.
4. Gamification helps create and regulate virtual patients by inserting medical record information.
5. Gamification can facilitate physician education. Physicians are interested in improving the health outcomes of their patients in less time. Pharma companies can help achieve this by implementing Gamification.

The next three cases show how some pharma companies have used Gamification to increase patient awareness and improve adherence.

CASE

62

Sanofi has Got Game!

Sanofi's *GoMeals* mobile app is an excellent example of Gamification in pharmaceutical marketing. *GoMeals* is a set of applications developed by Intouch Solutions, a specialized digital Pharma marketing agency for Sanofi-Aventis, in the US.

GoMeals is designed for people living with diabetes to promote Sanofi's diabetes drug, Acomplia. The app, available on the web and for smartphones, encourages users to make healthy choices concerning nutrition, as *GoMeals* suggests. The app features eating healthy, staying active, and tracking blood glucose levels. *In addition, GoMeals* allows patients to see how their daily habits regarding nutrition and exercise impact their diabetes.

GoMeals uses the game design elements to provide users clear reports on calorie intake from their meals, calories burnt from their exercise and physician activity, and glucose readings.

Sanofi-Aventis has developed a game, *Monster Manor,* with Vancouver-based Ayogo that rewards children with Type 2 diabetes for checking their blood glucose regularly. The app uses short mini-games that add up to unlock features and characters. It automatically sends the results to the parents' smartphones. The parents can give kids rewards to the children directly through the app.

Sanofi Diabetes, a Sanofi-Aventis division, has launched another mobile game in the UK called *Mission T1D* to educate and teach children and their parents, caregivers, and friends about Type 1 diabetes.

The game is set in a school. Players who complete levels and get points to unlock short practical messages about living with Type 1 diabetes and longer shareable educational videos. The videos cover important topics such as:

1. What is Type 1 diabetes?
2. Everyday life with diabetes
3. What is hypoglycemia and how to help
4. What is hyperglycemia and how to help
5. How to have a healthy diet with or without Type 1 diabetes

The entire program can run on a PC and a smartphone designed to be used by individuals or in a classroom setting.

Sanofi has certainly made a pioneering effort in developing these apps for diabetes and in engaging patients and HCPs.

(Source: Mobile Health News)

CASE

63

Packy and Marlon!

Packy and Marlon is an educational platform video game that is designed to improve self-care behavior in children with type 1 diabetes. It was developed by WaveQuest and published by Raya Systems for the Super Nintendo Entertainment System. The game achieved some success with treatment groups.

Packy and Marlon were designed to help remove the stigma of being different. Young people with diabetes who played the game with their friends and saw that their friends did not consider diabetes a big issue were more willing to do important self-care throughout the day, even when their friends were around.

Game Play

A gang of rats has invaded Camp Wa-Kee, and stolen the food and medical supplies, hiding them in different areas of the camp. Two diabetic elephants — Packy and Marlon, are entrusted with the task of retrieving the stolen goods and clearing out the malicious rodents, remembering at the same time to take their insulin and check their blood glucose levels. At the end of the game, they face the evil Bosses Beets and Yebur of the lunchroom crew.

The plot provided the kind of compelling struggle based on current events that every child craves. Evil, sadistic rats have left food all over the place and set up a puppet government with rigged elections.

Totalitarian anti-diabetic laws have been enacted that require all creatures to stuff food down their throats greedily. Unfortunately, the sinful and greedy animals of Camp Wa-Kee are all too willing to comply. Packy and Marlon are rebels in the eye of the law and are hunted down like dogs.

The game *Packy and Marlon* has eighteen grueling levels to be played. After about six stages, you will notice the levels repeat themselves. Each level contains many friends you must run into and answers questions regarding diabetes. Packy and Marlon appear quite popular with friends such as Lions with a hat-on, Zebras with a hat-on, dolphins with a hat-on, and an Eskimo. Each level includes questions such as — what insulin does to your blood sugar levels, when you should take insulin, and a rotation of injection sites. If you get your answers right, you will get a star.

Your weapons in the game are limited to peanuts and blasts of water. You can get the upgraded version of either of these powers if you pledge loyalty to the dark lord, Inlusin . However, despite the number of weaponry upgrades, no item will eliminate your diabetes.

In the game villains, you will encounter giant rats with boxing gloves, spirited rodents, flaming blowfish, and ghosts who shoot out little ghosts from their hands, whom you must overcome with your knowledge of diabetes and peanut physics.

The game *Packy and Marlon* is important in the history of therapeutic gaming, a concept that originated in the mid-1990s. For example, a six-month study undertaken in 1997 on behalf of Click Health by researchers at Stanford University's Medical Center on 59 diabetic children aged between 8 to 16 found that, after playing the game, the children were four times less likely to require urgent care visits than children who had played other games. Furthermore, a three-month study found that for kids with diabetes, the game decreased their diabetes-related emergency room and urgent care visits by 77 percent. Packy and Marlon were also tested in Kaiser hospitals, where it was shown to have given important information to people with diabetes and encouraged patients to offer to support each other.

(Source: Adapted from articles: 1. Packy and Marlon, Wikipedia, 2. Kevin, "The Goblin" Wilson, Packy and Marlon, Something Awful, February 4, 2006)

CASE
64

Bronkie, The Bronchiasaurus Raises Asthma Awareness!

Bronkie, the Bronchiasaurus, is an educational platform game developed by Wave Systems and published by Raya Systems for Super Nintendo Entertainment System. It is part of the educational video game series from Raya Systems, including Captain Novolin, Rex Roman: Experimental Surgeon, and Packy and Marlon!

Gameplay and Plot

The game attempts to teach children about asthma. Years ago, the meteors struck the prehistoric city of San Saurian, and the explosions covered the earth with clouds of dust, thus causing asthma in the dinosaur world. The dinosaurs built a mighty wind machine to clear the air, but their plans were thwarted by Mr. Rexo, who stole the machine, hid its pieces over San Saurian, and forced other dinosaurs to protect them. The two friends, Bronkie, and Trackie, with the help of their sidekicks — Sam and Kyler, must find the missing machine parts before the dust returns and save the planet.

Bronkie and Trackie can develop shortness of breath from tar, cigarette smoke, flurry animals, and other obstacles. Bonus games include learning the proper use of the inhaler and other daily facts of life for people with asthma.

Back to the plot. When Bronkie and Trakie are looking for parts to build a giant wind machine that had previously kept the asthma-inducing dust away, however, Bronkie has only a limited number of strong breaths at his disposal, which can be replenished with lung items found around each level. There are a few dinosaurs who are helpful but on one condition. That is, you must answer their asthma trivia questions correctly. Once you do that, these helpful dinosaurs give you transportation, items, or windmill parts.

What Makes Bronkie, The Bronchiasaurus Different?

Eric Bigras points out the typical educational efforts of asthma and its management in his insightful article, *Bronkie, The Bronchiasaurus: An epistemological Review in High-Level Gamer*. He states that many educational efforts surrounding asthma revolve around the proper use of medication and inhalers to control asthma. The typical model of asthma education has three characteristic features:

1. It is medicalized. Asthma is understood as a pathology possessing its epidemiology and etiology.
2. It is technologized, involving most solutions for acquiring and utilizing some form of technology.
3. It's aimed almost exclusively at asthmatic people and focuses on personal responsibility or self-care.

What makes Bronkie, The Bronchiasaurus, different from the rest of asthma educational efforts is that it introduces environmental concerns into asthma education in addition to self-care. Throughout the game, the player must guide Bronkie through a series of levels filled with enemies and asthma triggers such as chemical drips and dust clouds while simultaneously collecting peak flow meters and inhalers. Also, they must repair the windmill because the entire city of San Saurian is covered by one all-encompassing dust cloud. The wind machine must be repaired to bring the environment back to a state where the city's inhabitants can live healthy lives. Thus, Bronkie ultimately attributes the causation of asthma to the environment.

This premise focuses the player's attention on the environment. Playing Bronkie, The Bronchiasaurus teaches the players that while medication can control asthma attacks, only environmental intervention can prevent them entirely.

(Source: Adapted from articles: 1. Bronkie, The Bronchiasaurus, Wikipedia, 2. J. C. Fletcher, Virtually overlooked: Bronkie, The Bronchiasaurus, Engadget, April 26, 2007, 3. Eric Bigras, Bronkie, The Bronchiasaurus: An epistemological review, High-Level Gamer, January 7, 2014)

Slow Rate of Adoption

If Gamification offers so many benefits, why are there relatively fewer downloads for Pharma apps compared to other healthcare apps? Here are the possible reasons:

- Many of the Pharma apps have highly targeted audiences like HCPs.
- People with specific disease states.
- Pharma apps tend to target local markets, say in three or fewer countries, making them unlikely to compete on download numbers with fitness, health, or diet tracking apps that appeal to a larger market segment.

Engagification, not Gamification!

While Gamification positively impacts participant engagement, message recall, and patient outcomes, there is one problem. It is the name itself - Gamification. When you say that you will gamify the participants' interaction with your content, the term - Gamification lends itself to trivializing the most serious experience related to improving health and wellbeing. Patients, physicians, and other pharmaceutical industry stakeholders still cling to the idea that games should not be part of the conversation in such a serious realm as healthcare. In Pharma marketing, it is crucial to steer the discussion away from the word Game - and towards terms like engagement, retention, and adherence. Therefore, please do not call it a game. Call it an app. More importantly, your strategy is not Gamification. It is engagification!

Closed Loop Marketing

Digital and multichannel marketing are often tied to closed-loop marketing (CLM) because CLM can integrate different digital channels, such as websites and social media, as part of the detailing efforts of a firm.

Pharmaceutical companies identify and refine the marketing promotional materials their physicians find exciting and resonating. Then, they seek to adapt their promotion efforts and direct them back to the physician - closing the loop. For example, consider the following steps a Pharma company may take in implementing closed-loop marketing.

A pharmaceutical sales representative (PSR) is provided with an iPad or tablet containing the detailing software. This software enables the PSR to present an engaging, detail-talk about his product through a multimedia presentation that may include PDFs of clinical article reprints, a slide deck, and a video featuring a key opinion leader or mode of action, the drug or interactive graphs, among others. While the physician is engaged in the detail-talk and viewing these materials, a record is made of which ones are used and what length of time was spent on each page, slide, graph and video.

The recorded information is sent immediately to a central system at the firm's head office via the internet. The feedback data from the tablet is analyzed with the customer relationship management (CRM) data that the company has (companies that implement CLM strategy will most certainly have CRM in place). The insights derived from this integrated analysis are used to prepare content that meets that particular physician's needs, which is then communicated to the PSR and brand manager. PSR delivers the message via the preferred channel of the physician and at the time and place the physician wants. This process ensures the delivery of the right message that the physician can resonate with at the right time, on the right channel, and at the right place.

Thus, CLM (Closed Loop Marketing) can be a powerful way to improve customer-centricity by incorporating real-life customer insights into marketing strategy and messaging in real time. In the same way that consumer retail websites update customer recommendations based on past activity, pharma can customize Healthcare Professional (HCP)-marketing strategies and messages based on individual preferences learned from past customer interactions. For example, pharmaceutical companies implement CLM in the sales representative channel via tablet detailing, capturing insights from the representative's interactions with HCPs, such as the content that the HCP found most engaging electronically. Pharma marketers then customize future messaging for HCPs based on those insights.

At the same time, pharma has been exploring the use of channels beyond the traditional field force, such as tele-detailing, video-detailing, physician communities, websites, email, and others. Pharmaceutical companies hope to increase and improve physician engagement by offering multiple interaction options through smaller, single-channel pilots and some coordinated MCM (Multichannel Marketing) programs.

With these insights derived from gathering and analyzing data from customer interactions that come from real life, not from marketing research, the brand manager may develop branding strategies nationally or for specific geographical regions based on physician preferences. Combined with meaningful segmentation, these insights allow accurate customization of content quickly achieved in digital channels and allow pharma marketers to send the right message and the most relevant content to customers via their preferred channels.

When you practice closed-loop marketing, you are engaging the physicians optimally because there is continuity in conversations. Every interaction becomes meaningful as it takes the physicians' needs, concerns, and wants into account and addresses them promptly.

Closed loop marketing thus can help pharmaceutical firms prepare communication strategies that their customers find compelling. With CLM, we can give customers what they want, how they want it, and when they want it.

Social Media Engagement

The times are changing for the healthcare scenario in general and pharmaceutical marketing in particular.

Like all other media, pharmaceutical marketing media was unidirectional and relied only on broadcasting carefully crafted marketing messages to its target audience, mostly physicians and doctors with good prescribing potential. However, since the mid-1990s, the growing popularity of the internet has offered a vast choice and freedom of access to content dynamically from millions of websites. Content generation during these early years of the internet revolution was no doubt massive, but there was not much difference in the type of content. Most of them resembled their traditional websites, which were more like online brochures, and e-commerce sites were merely looking like online versions of their earlier catalogs. This period was later termed web 1.0.

Later, Web 2.0 or Social Media emerged as a buzzword with the advent of user-generated content such as blogs and wikis. People started participating actively by using the internet discussion boards, rating the content, and posting comments, making it a hub for social communities. What is most interesting about web 2.0 is that some of the most consumed and engaging information was not coming from a small number of media channels but a large number of regular internet users. As a result, early social networks emerged, enabling people to connect more easily. These networks matured and gave rise to services like Twitter and Facebook. Facebook today dominates the social media scene with a whopping two billion users.

What is Social Media?

Social media generally refers to Internet-based tools that allow individuals and communities to gather and share information, ideas, personal messages, images, and other content. It also facilitates real-time collaboration with other users. Social media is referred to as Web 2.0 and Social networking. Social media includes blogs, social networks, video and photo-sharing sites, wikis, and many other media. Here's an example that shows some of the media grouped by purpose and functions. The list is only indicative and not exhaustive

1. Social networking (Facebook, MySpace, Google Plus, Twitter, and others)
2. Professional Networking (LinkedIn)
3. Physician Social Networks (Sermo, Quantia, MD, Doximity, Docplexus)
4. Media sharing (YouTube, Flickr)
5. Content production (blogs, Blogger, WordPress, Tumblr, and Microblogs such as Twitter)
6. Knowledge / Information aggregation (Wikipedia)
7. Virtual reality and gaming environments (Second Life)

Social Media Marketing and Pharma

Social media marketing in the pharmaceutical industry combines various social media tools and platforms to establish conversations with physicians, patients, and other stakeholders. These online conversations help pharmaceutical companies build relationships with customers as you can spread brand messages through electronic word-of-mouth.

While traditional marketing media was more of a monologue, social media has created an opportunity for engaging in a dialogue and conversation with consumers. Consumers can express their questions and concerns, enabling the brand to build a relationship. Social media users, in the process, generate a lot of content. They post over 30 billion comments on Facebook and more than two billion tweets on Twitter monthly. Moreover, about twenty percent of this vast generated content mentions a specific drug or disease. When one in every five conversation pieces is in the pharmaceutical and healthcare space, can Pharma afford to remain a silent spectator?

Physicians on Social Media

While the exact numbers vary, most studies indicate that about 80 percent of physicians use social media for personal interactions, professional communication, and research. Physicians' social media usage seems to follow a typical 1-9-90 pattern.

- Approximately 1 percent of physicians using social media are content producers creating and publishing original content to other healthcare professionals and ePatients. They provide this information on blogs, forums, and information-sharing websites.
- A further 9 percent of physicians engage with others on social media by commenting on posts, participating in online discussions and chats, sharing useful information, and linking to other members online.
- The remaining 90 percent of physicians consume information. They use the internet and social media to find and read relevant information about their patients and practice.

Patients are in Control

More and more patients are turning to sites such as *Patients Like Me* and other patient and disease communities online to research their symptoms and arrive at a self-diagnosis before visiting their physicians. The availability of extensive healthcare information on the social web impacts the relationship between patients, physicians, and brands. Increasingly, doctors face self-diagnosing patients who have already researched their symptoms and are seeking prescriptions for conditions they think they have. The patients may even post reviews of their experiences in case of pushback by their doctors. Patients today are taking greater responsibility than ever for their health.

Insights from Social Media Conversations

Patients seem more forthright and descriptive in their online conversations about their disease conditions and treatment feedback as they afford greater privacy than in-person consults. These conversations benefit Pharma Marketers as they better understand how patients perceive the current product or service offerings and their unmet needs. With insights from this deep understanding, marketers can develop better, more relevant marketing materials, including packaging, educational, and promotional tools aimed at physicians and patients.

Challenging Regulatory Environment

Pharmaceutical companies, as they operate in a highly regulated industry, face many challenges, such as handling incomplete and misinformation about their products offline and online. According to the US Federal Drug Administration (FDA) Guidance on how Pharma should use social media, pharmaceutical companies should provide fair and balanced information about their products in their social media posts. In addition, they need to include the side effects, adverse reactions, and contraindications in their product information.

Furthermore, the FDA clearly stated that it wouldn't be taking a lenient approach towards either tweets or sponsored links. Social media posts must incorporate full and balanced information about their products, even on sites with limited character spaces like Twitter. It is not enough to provide links in the post to your web pages for detailed product information. Pharmaceutical companies face severe penalties by the FDA if they don't make the proper disclosure. Drug firms must be careful not to mislead consumers on Twitter, Facebook, or any other social media channel. Otherwise, they will open themselves to liability. Kim Kardashian's Instagram post is a classic example of what happens when you don't follow social media regulations. Here are three cases highlighting the importance of regulatory compliance.

CASE

65

How Kim Kardashian's Instagram Post Got Drug Firm that Makes *Diclegis* into Trouble with the FDA?!

In July 2015, Kim Kardashian, a leading supermodel with a massive following on social media, posted to her 45 million followers on Instagram and 35 million followers on Twitter about Diclegis, a prescription drug brand of a morning sickness tablet manufactured by Rosemont-based Pharma company, Duchesnay in the U.S. Here's a transcript of that post:

OMG. Have you heard about this? As you guys know, my #morning sickness has been pretty bad…I tried changing things about my lifestyle, like my diet, but nothing helped, so I talked to my doctor. He prescribed me #Diclegis, and I felt a lot better; most importantly, it's been studied, and there was no increased risk to the baby. I'm so excited and happy with my results that I'm partnering with Duchesnay USA to raise awareness about morning sickness. If you have morning sickness, be safe and sure to ask your doctor about the pill with the pregnant woman on it and find out more:

www.diclegis.com; www.diclegisImportantSafetyInformation.com

It is not a typical post by an average morning sickness sufferer who recommends a product online. Kim Kardashian is a celebrity with a massive online following and is paid to endorse the brand. The FDA took objection to this post as it failed to mention important information like the drug's side effects, adverse reactions, and contraindications. The social media post is false and misleading in presenting efficacy claims for 'Diclegis' but fails to communicate any risk information. The FDA demanded that Duchesnay immediately cease its 'misbranding' of the drug and has given time until August 21 to respond to the Agency. The company withdrew the social media posts. Here's what Dean Hopkins, general manager of Duchesnay, said in this regard: *In the original post, which we developed with Kim, we provided her with a link to risk information and limitation of use for Diclegis. But the post did not meet the FDA requirements for communicating important product information*.

Kim Kardashian posted a long corrective ad on August 30, 2015.

(Source: Sharon Lurye, How Kim Kardashian's Instagram Post Got Rosemont Drug Company in Trouble with the FDA, PhillyVoice, September 1, 2015)

CASE

66

Facebook-Share Function Gets a Warning from the FDA!

Novartis, one of the global Pharma majors, got approval from the US FDA on October 29, 2017, and launched Tasigna (Nilotinib) to treat chronic myeloid leukemia with resistance or intolerance to existing therapies.

In 2010, Novartis used a Facebook share function as one of the marketing tactics for promoting its leukemia drug, Tasigna, on individual consumers' profile pages and news feeds. The company shared through this functionality a short description of the drug, relevant visuals, and website links on an individual's Facebook profile page, and upon their approval of the posting, some specific networking newsfeeds. The FDA found this objectionable as it did not present the risk information about the drug in these postings. The Agency's primary concern was that these postings could imply that the drug was effective in treating all types of leukemia patients. Instead, the medication was effective only in a narrow subset of leukemia patients, for which it got approval. The company duly withdrew the Facebook share function.

(Source: Grant Gross, US FDA Warns Pharma Firm About Facebook Promotion, Reuters, August 7, 2010)

CASE

67

Suprenza's False Claims Ring an Alarm!

Suprenza's case shows how false and misleading pharmaceutical advertising in digital media can land the company in Trouble.

The Citius pharmaceutical company obtained approval from the US FDA in June 2011 for its Suprenza (phentermine chloride), a prescription drug for use as an adjunct for the short-term in the weight reduction regimen based on exercise and behavioral modification in the management of exogenous obesity.

The landing page of Suprenza's website, www.leanonsuprenza.com, contained an image of an attractive woman, holding the lettered blocks of the word, 'LEAN' and eye-catching efficacy claims such as: Stay on course for success with Suprenza Lean Program. However, the web page conspicuously omitted all the relevant information regarding side effects, contraindications, and risk factors. There was no information substantiating the product claims. The site only revealed one warning about the risk of simultaneously using Suprenza with other drugs for weight loss. It ignored all other warnings and precautions. There was no information regarding the approved indications and required body mass index (BMI) for starting the treatment.

On June 9, 2014, the FDA sent a warning letter urging the company to stop violating the FDA rules and respond promptly with a plan for discontinuing such promotional materials. The letter stated that the information presented on the website was false and misleading as it did not contain any risk and safety information. The letter also noted violating the Federal Food, Drug, and Cosmetic Act.

Citius promptly removed the website from the internet search. The company moved it to a new website, www.suprenza.com, and eliminated its Lean program. Later, Citius Pharma withdraws Suprenza to focus on the company's core assets.

(Source: Pharma and Life Sciences: FDA Tells Citius that Suprenza Web Page is False, Misleading in Untitled Letter, Bloomberg Law, June 17, 2014)

FDA Guidance on Social Media: Implications for Pharma

Pharmaceutical companies won't be able to send a series of tweets containing a product's full benefit and risk information. Instead, they will need to provide the complete information in a single tweet.

How can Pharma Comply with the FDA Guidance on Social Media?

Pharmaceutical companies must connect with patients and physicians on social media to offer reliable information about their products and improve health and wellbeing. However, how can they comply with the FDA regulations while providing this information and controlling the conversations on various social media platforms, and ensuring the delivery of fair and balanced information? Henniger Bullock and Collen Tracy Jones suggest a five-way approach to achieve this in their Law 360 article of April 21, 2017, *5 Social Media Pitfalls in the Pharmaceutical Industry*.

1. *Set A Clear Internal Policy*: Develop a clear policy that includes a centralized social media hub such as a company-sponsored website, Twitter handle, and Facebook page for posting messages on behalf of the company. Create a concrete social media advertising policy and clearly define who may engage on social media on the company's behalf. Ensure that all employees understand their role on social media, whether in their personal or official capacity, and how they must conduct themselves on social media sites. The legal department must clear the content for regulatory compliance.
2. *Create A Controlled Environment*: When its consumers (patients) and customers (HCPs) are frequently on social media, can Pharma afford to shy away? Not. Pharma should embrace social media but maintain control of it. A pharmaceutical company can create a controlled environment, foster relationships with patients, and communicate useful, fair, and balanced information about its products and services by creating a company website or a company-initiated chat area.

3. *Create A Compliance Strategy*: It is not enough if you define the roles of engagement and rules of conduct on social media for your patients in your social media policy. You need to ensure compliance. A compliance strategy and a monitoring system are put in place to ensure total compliance.
4. *Comply With All HIPAA Act Privacy Laws*: Pharmaceutical companies need to do more than comply with the FDA Guidance on social media. They must comply with HIPAA (Health Insurance Privacy, Portability, and Accountability Act). Complying with patient privacy laws is equally important. Therefore, educate all employees on patient privacy laws and how they relate to business. Remember, even an individual posting a patient's picture violates privacy. Create a social media working group to discuss any concerns and issues.
5. *Keep Future Litigation in Mind*: Ensure that you prepare a carefully coordinated message and have it approved. Ensure compliance with social media standards and policies before embarking on a social media campaign.

Pharma Must Embrace Social Media

Although many regulations over how pharmaceutical companies should conduct themselves on social media are challenging, Pharma must find a way to comply with them and participate actively in social media as it offers many opportunities. Therefore, Pharma must embrace social media. Consider these reasons, for example:

1. More and more patients are using social media as a significant source of information and an integral part of their healthcare research journey. Typically, their journey begins when they notice their symptoms. It leads to their searching social channels often before they visit a physician or simultaneously with their visit to the doctor. The second phase of online search follows the diagnosis to seek more information about their condition from credible sources and people like themselves. Patients who share their stories on social channels become a significant source of information to those actively seeking their perspectives. This information, at times, could be unbalanced and even irrelevant.

2. The information on social media may not always be from reputable and accredited sources. It may be marginally accurate at best and significantly harmful at worst.

Therefore, Pharma companies must provide balanced and credible information on social media where their patients are seeking meaningful information and help them get balanced, accurate information that is essential for their wellbeing.

6 Ways Pharma may use Social Media

Dr. Kevin Campbell, an internationally recognized cardiologist, suggested six ways pharmaceutical companies can use social media in an interview with Joanna Belbey, a columnist with Forbes magazine. He said that Social Media is an ideal channel for pharmaceutical and device companies to educate, market, listen to, and connect with customers. Moreover, pharma firms can do all this while complying with the guidelines of industry regulators. Here's a summary of what he suggested:

1. *Education*: Pharmaceutical firms may offer consumers disease-specific, unbiased educational information on broad topics. The purpose of such educative information is to help patients better understand their disease state and engage with their healthcare professionals for improved outcomes.
2. *Marketing*: Pharma can use social media to share press releases on new products, clinical trial results, community service, significant charity contributions, and their major commitment to developing new and better treatments.
3. *Connecting with Physicians*: Social media is an efficient and effective means of connecting with physician customers. It is also less expensive than sales force costs. Through social media, Pharma can engage with many physicians at once with its best and brightest scientists and researchers. It is also an excellent opportunity to ask questions and have a dialogue with each other rather than being 'detailed-to' by a sales representative, simply a regurgitation of a memorized script

of a new study. The physician would have already read it in all probabilities.

4. *Connecting with Patients*: Pharma can use social media to create patient support groups and communities. These groups allow patients with common interests and need to connect and discuss their conditions, treatments, and experiences.
5. *Clinical Trials*: Social media can become a powerful tool to enroll patients in clinical trials. Clinical trial enrollment is one of the biggest barriers to completing a clinical trial.
6. *Listening*: Social media can be a big help for Pharma in gaining insights into the unmet needs of the patients through social listening. These insights can be of immense use to Pharma in developing its communication strategies with physicians and even directing the future course of its product development.

Important Social Networks

Physicians-only Networks

Social networks are dedicated websites or other applications which enable users to communicate with each other by posting information, comments, messages, and images. Initially, social media outlets were designed to attract individuals who use the platform for personal reasons. However, there seems to be an influx of social networks that cater to specific professions.

For doctors, physician-only social networks are becoming a valuable resource. These online communities are becoming a useful resource to turn to for many professional purposes. They help physicians to communicate and collaborate in a secure environment. There is more to these physicians-only social networks than sending and receiving messages. They also provide opportunities for CME (Continuing medical education) credits and to compete against peers for various rewards. The features differ from site to site. Here are the top four social networks for physicians at a glance (Table 3.2).

Table 3.2 Top Four Social Networks for Physicians

Physicians' Social Networks	Important Features
1. Doximity	One of the best physician social networks. Over 50 per cent of U.S. physicians are verified Doximity members. Mobile friendly physician platform giving the ability to instantly connect with their peers in a secure, HIPPA-compliant environment. Offers the opportunity to receive CME credits for reading medical journals provided by the site.
2. Sermo	The most trusted and preferred social network for doctors with over 800,000 doctors in the U.S, and select countries in the West. Exclusively for licensed physicians. High level of anonymity available for physicians who post on the site. Sermo allows the media to conduct polls among its physicians and interview them.

Table 3.2 *Contd...*

Physicians' Social Networks	Important Features
3. Quantia MD	Launched in 2006. One of the best online resources doctors can utilize for collaboration and career development. 1 in 3 physicians visit Quantia MD to keep with new medical information and to learn from their colleagues. Has several features that reward users with CME credits or 'Q' points that can be redeemed for Amazon gift certificates. Another interesting feature is that members can compete against their peers in the monthly general medicine puzzle, the monthly cartoon caption contest and by solving weekly clinical cases and image contests.
4. Docplexus	Largest online community of doctors in India with over 3,80,000 members. Docplexus aims to provide value to the Indian medical community through innovative, technology-driven offerings. Provides audio-visual coverage for major medical events. Also offers CME courses to fulfill the educational needs of the physician community.

Abbott is the first pharmaceutical company to launch a digital-only campaign through physicians' network, doctors.net.uk. Consider this case.

CASE

68

Abbott's Established Products Division Launches the First Digital-Only Campaign in Pharma!

Abbott Established Products Division (EPD) launched its low-dose hormonal replacement therapy (HRT) brand, Femoston - Conti. What is unique about this launch is that it is probably the first-ever, digital-only launch in the pharmaceutical industry.

The launch campaign reached 9,000 doctors, or 45 percent of the NHS population of obstetricians and gynecologists. Abbott EPD's low-dose HRT brand, Femoston-Conti (estradiol and didrogesterone tablets), engaged these doctors via the British online professional network, doctors.net.uk. The campaign included interactive case studies, clinical paper summaries, and can ask the 'experts section.'

How did Abbott decide on a digital-only launch via doctors.net.uk? The decision was based on the findings of Abbott's research on the likely impact of professional networks on pharmaceutical brand promotion. Research indicated that online professional networks could provide a more effective method of engaging doctors than traditional sales and marketing channels. It is because they enable them to take a more targeted and measurable approach and deliver a mix of promotional and educational messages that readily benefit doctors' clinical practice.

Physician professional networks are increasingly becoming popular, and an estimated three million physicians use them worldwide. Statistics from doctors.net.uk show that 59 percent of them visit these channels specifically to update their medical knowledge, while 38 percent do so to get information on new products.

Abbott, which is already very active in the digital space, partnered with doctors.net.uk for its Femoston-Conti launch in 2013 and has won the PM Society 2013 award for the best HCP website for their Femoston - Conti low-dose created by doctors.net.uk. The judges of the award praised the winning entry for its excellent educational content. They said it was nice to see the industry take this step — and clearly, it was a good decision, judging by the impressive results.

The campaign was a success. Enjoy Mann, commercial marketing manager for Abbott EPD (Established Products Division), said while speaking about the campaign results to PMLiVE: *The results speak for themselves. The coverage and frequency of the campaign exceed current national call rates by sales reps. What pleases us the most is our increase in market share and continued sales growth. Doctors return to the website, indicating that they find it a valuable resource*.

(Source: Adapted from the article: Piotr Wrzosiñski, Abbott EPD: The first digital marketing-only launch in Pharma, Pharma Marketing, K - Message, November 25, 2013)

Patient Communities

Social networks focused on patients suffering from a specific disease condition have come up over the past few years. They can be vital for people who feel alone in their health struggles. They are particularly helpful to those who cannot leave home because of their disabilities. These social networks are their social life. At the same time, despite all the benefits and support they offer, patient social networks are not without challenges. Firstly, many physicians are concerned about these networks as most of the medical advice comes from them from other users or unverified articles on the internet. Secondly, many patient networks do not generally moderate comments to verify the accuracy. They, however, try to make it clear where the content comes from and whether it is from medical professionals or fellow patients. Table 3.3 presents some of the more influential and important social networks that focus on and serve the needs of patients.

Table 3.3 Some Important Social Networks for Patients

Patient Networks	Their Focus
1. Patients Like Me	Used to be primarily for some neurological conditions, but their fabulous software is available for many conditions now.
2. CureTogether	Has patient communities for a number of conditions
3. SmartPatients.com	An online community where patients and their families learn from each other.
4. CancerConnect.com	Offers comprehensive cancer information organized by disease and stage. A free social network for patients, survivors, and caregivers.
5. TuDiabetes.org	A space on the web where people with diabetes or their loved ones can find support, help each other and share their experiences and what they do everyday to stay healthy with this condition.

Here is a ground-breaking case showing how a global pharmaceutical company engaged its patients through a social media campaign.

CASE

69

Pfizer's *can You Feel My Pain* Social Media Campaign!

Pfizer, a global Pharma major, launched on January 29, 2013, Pain Exchange, an online forum designed to promote conversation about pain between patients to help them find appropriate language when describing their pain symptoms accurately and with confidence when talking to their general practitioner (GP) so they can arrive at a correct diagnosis of their condition. The Pain Exchange was developed as the UK, and Ireland pilot under the wider Pfizer-funded European awareness campaign *Can You Feel My Pain*?

Why a campaign about pain awareness? The subjective nature of pain and patient challenges in accurately describing their symptoms to general practitioners (GPs) find it hard to define, measure, and accurately diagnose chronic pain, explains Roger Anderson, a G P, and Pain Exchange supporter. Because research has shown that more than a quarter of people affected by chronic pain suffers in silence as they find it difficult to effectively communicate their experience of pain to general practitioners, and so are not diagnosed. Therefore, if patients are better able to express their symptoms during a consultation, GPs will be more likely to diagnose the condition and thus offer appropriate treatment and support. Also, the pressure on GPs to treat chronic pain is more in the UK as the number of pain specialists is very low. There is only one pain specialist per 32,000 sufferers to support the work of primary care. Therefore, the need to understand chronic pain and how to effectively manage and treat it at the point of consultation at the general practitioner level is stretched.

Unmet Need

Research data from a survey called *The Painful Truth* conducted among more than 1,000 chronic pain sufferers in January 2013 indicated that:

- Millions of patients were still suffering daily despite trying several treatment options.
- More than a third of sufferers struggle with routine daily tasks affecting their work and personal lives, relationships, and the ability to care for their children.
- For many patients, conventional medication or surgery is not the answer, and there is a greater need to explore how best to use innovative and cost-effective technologies as they emerge to manage chronic pain.

When you listen to or read the comments made by internet users who have engaged in the campaign using social media channels, including Flickr and Care2, an online petition tool, it is clear that many people living with chronic pain feel neglected and misunderstood.

Louise Clark, Associate Director, Communications UK, and Europe, said: *We know that patients are not getting to the right diagnosis and management of pain, and there is a lot of frustration about not being able to voice their thoughts and opinions*.

Can You Feel My Pain? Social Media Campaign

Pfizer has set up *Can You Feel My Pain* as an engagement tool across Europe to galvanize support and mobilize the voice of patients across the region online in a way accessible to everybody in six European languages. Pfizer partnered with nine Patient Advocacy Groups (PAGs) across Europe to create a social media campaign — Can You Feel My Pain? These Patient Advocacy Groups are:

1. Action Pain
2. Arthritis Care
3. Back Care
4. Cystitis and Overactive Bladder Foundation
5. Pain Association Scotland
6. PainConcern
7. Pain U.K.
8. Action on Pain, and
9. Trigeminal Neuralgia Association

The initiative was designed to give a collective voice to people living with chronic pain that they can use to support a broader initiative to communicate the plight of pain patients to European-policy makers and drive change in attitude. *Can You Feel My Pain* initiative includes social media interfaces in six European languages overcoming the language barriers, which has often been a challenge in international healthcare engagement strategies. The campaign had a significant level of engagement, with 75 percent of outcomes such as online petition signatures coming from engagement in languages other than English.

First of its kind!

Can You Feel My Pain? It is one of the most groundbreaking examples of a pharmaceutical company engaging in a healthcare issue through social media. The campaign has many firsts to its credit. Consider these, for example:

- The first campaign to use the photo-sharing platform Flickr as a powerful cross-language visual communication tool
- Facebook Campaign in six European languages with content in three sections — Raising awareness; signing the Bill of Rights (of patients with chronic pain) online petition, and; sharing your personal story about chronic pain.

- The First campaign encourages patients to share their experiences in multiple language environments openly.
- Connecting to an international network of patient organizations around a common cause
- Empowering them to engage effectively using social media
- Running an online petition in support of a Bill of Rights proposed for people suffering from chronic pain in six languages hosted on a social cause site — Care2

Pfizer's digital engagement strategy for *Can You Feel My Pain*, as we can see, was a break from convention. It was not designed to attract users to a campaign website but to engage them right where they were. Internet users on a patient advocacy group website, for example, can directly participate in the social media components from there, or those using social media channels including Facebook, Twitter, or Flickr can engage using these platforms. Pfizer's strategy was to create a groundswell of public voice about living with chronic pain, allowing patients and carers to express themselves via whatever channel and language they felt most comfortable — from email to social media using text or images.

Research-Led Strategy

Before formulating the strategy for *Can You Feel My Pain*, Pfizer researched the behavior of internet users around chronic pain in Europe. Here's what a Pfizer spokesman said about the preparation before the campaign: *We carried out some research to look at who was talking about what, in which places, and those greatest places of engagement opportunity were our initial target to ensure that the uptake of the campaign was good… so we're reaching out to people in the right way and the right language and the right environment*.

Bill of Rights

One in five adults in Europe is living with chronic pain; where Pfizer defines chronic pain as pain that lasts for more than three months and can be unbearable, making everyday activities difficult and, in some cases, impossible. Chronic pain is often misunderstood, misdiagnosed, and inappropriately managed, leading many people to suffer in silence. Therefore, Pfizer took the help of Care2, a cause site, to file its Bill of Rights as an online petition. Pfizer's Bill of Rights for people affected by chronic pain focused on five areas:

1. Right to be understood as a condition by the public and employers.
2. Right of access to accurate and improved information about their chronic pain.
3. Right to access healthcare professionals who have been adequately trained and fully understand chronic pain, specifically how to diagnose and appropriately manage the condition to limit worsening.
4. Right to have early intervention and optimal pain management from access to healthcare professionals who can identify the best possible pain management and support for each patient at the earliest possible stage.
5. The right to pain relief is a fundamental human right.

Successful Campaign

The results of the campaign have been significant. Over 11,000 people have shared their experiences of living with or caring for a patient with chronic pain; over 1,700 patients have initially signed a petition in support of the Bill of Rights to help improve the lives of people affected by chronic pain. The number of petitions grew by 400 during the next month. Moreover, over 65 percent of people who have signed *Can You Feel My Pain's* online petition have also commented about their experiences of chronic pain.

Key Lessons

One can learn three vital lessons from Pfizer's groundbreaking campaign — *Can You Feel My Pain*?

1. *Preparation is the key to success*. The idea for *Can You Feel My Pain* first emerged in 2009 when Pfizer brought together European Patient Groups working in the area of chronic pain to create an advisory board working in partnership with each other sharing a common ground, says Ruth Wilson, Pfizer's team leader, patient relationship management.
2. *Effective partnerships are vital to success*. The partnerships with the nine patient advocacy groups played an essential role in shaping the campaign strategy. Pfizer learned a lot from talking with the partners and understanding in taking the campaign forward. Pfizer provided practical support by equipping patient groups to play a more active role in social media and teaching them new skills that enabled them to go beyond supporting the *Can You Feel My Pain* initiative. You have to engage with partners early and ensure that they share the same belief in the direction that you want to go. You must ensure they are engaged and active throughout the planning process. Above all, find out what their expectations are and exceed them.
3. *How to effectively engage with your audience on social media*? Pfizer did not follow the conventional route to using social media, such as campaign website, Twitter handle, etc. Instead, it followed a different strategy to engage the target audience effectively and creatively. The company had Facebook pages in three languages — English, German, and Dutch. Pfizer's use of Flickr is novel for a pharmaceutical firm, and the company looked for photos that illustrate what your pain is like on a good day and what your pain is like on a bad day. Another important lesson from Pfizer's social media use is that you must work effectively with medical and legal colleagues in a highly regulated environment like the pharmaceutical industry. Don't assume that everybody — whether a partner or people within your organization — understands or knows what these platforms for engagement are, how they work, or how they will work within a campaign. It would be best if you spent some time educating people early on. You must empower your team

and your partners who need to engage your audience on social media so they can participate effectively and passionately. Remember that social media is a moving target, and continuously upgrading your skills and capabilities is crucial for effective engagement.

Pfizer identified pain medications as one of the six key invest-to-win areas in its 2010 R&D streamlining process. The company already makes Lyrica (pregabalin) for neuropathic pain, which tallied US $2.8 billion in 2009 sales.

Can You Feel My Pain has been a groundbreaking initiative that united patients across Europe and gave them a voice. As a result, the campaign received Healthcare Engagement Strategy for Empowering Patients in 2011 by Creation Healthcare.

(Source: Adapted from articles: 1. Daniel Ghinn, Can you feel my pain: Pfizer with European Patient Groups, Creation Knowledge; 2. Pfizer Launches Chronic Pain Forum: Twitter-style comments are used to help patients describe their conditions, PMLiVe, January 29, 2013; 3. Dominic Tyer, Digital Pharma: Pfizer socializes pain campaign, Pharmafile, Eye for Pharma, October 5, 2010; 4. Selina McKee, Pfizer launches chronic pain campaign, Pharma Times, January 29, 2013)

Online Forums

An online forum is an internet forum or a message board, an online discussion site where people can hold conversations in the form of posted messages. Since the dawn of the internet, Online Forums have been a significant social outlet that has had a tremendous effect on online society. As a result, they have become commonplace today.

Increasing infiltration and use of the internet and changes in the health care system have resulted in a heavier reliance on the internet for disease and health education. Every day, millions of users log on to their favorite online health communities and interact with others to get advice and discuss everything related to their symptoms, disease condition, and treatment options. This trend has increased the expectation and reliance on peer education and support in many areas, including medical, to precede, supplement, or even replace professionals.

Online health forums have become so popular and influential that most often, even before they call a doctor, patients go online when they are facing a health crisis or ongoing illness. As a result, more people today than ever before are turning to social media before, during, and after diagnosis. Sixty-nine percent of doctors in a survey conducted by Cello Health Insights said that many of their patients look up their conditions online before a consultation.

Online health communities, also referred to as – treatment, disease state, or patient communities – represent a tremendous opportunity for pharmaceutical companies to educate patients and create goodwill among them.

By creating or partnering with online health communities, Pharma firms have an opportunity to connect with their patients and consumers. They also provide the Pharma brands an avenue to give the much-needed factual information and patient-centered care and generate goodwill in the process.

Through their partnerships with online health communities, pharmaceutical companies can help improve patients' awareness of certain diseases, which take a long time to diagnose. As a result, they can reduce the diagnostic timeline earlier in their disease journey, and this early diagnosis would ensure a better quality of life for the patients.

Understandably, a business cannot and should not be on every social network. At the same time, you cannot afford to ignore influential social networks. So, what are the right social networks for your company? To know that, you must consider what each network is good at and how you should participate in the conversation meaningfully. It is important to remember that the social media landscape changes very quickly; therefore, keeping abreast of new channels is part of a good long-term social media strategy.

Multi and Omni Channel Engagement

As the name indicates, multichannel marketing (MCM) uses multiple channels to reach a target audience. In the case of pharmaceutical marketing, the target audience is physicians, followed by healthcare professionals, patients, and other stakeholders. The communication channels include both traditional and digital ones. Pharmaceutical marketers, however, have always operated in a multichannel environment that included personal selling, direct mail, journal advertising, meetings, and conferences, even before the internet era. However, these channels tended to be marginal and not necessarily integrated with the dominant channel, the field force.

Multichannel marketing involves multiple channels — offline, online, and personal and non-personal. As the internet has grown exponentially, the number of channels too increased dramatically. The following table presents personal and non-personal pathways in the pharmaceutical industry.

Table 3.4 Customer Engagement Model in the Pharmaceutical Industry

Personal Interactions	Non-personal Interactions
Tablet Detailing	Website
Face-to-Face Meetings	Email
Local Physician Meetings	Direct Mail
Call Center Service to Customers	Short Messaging Service (SMS)
Medical Science Liaison (MSL)	Mobile Apps
Medical Conferences	Webinars
	Virtual Detailing
	Display Advertising
	Social Media Platforms

One of the main challenges for Pharma is to select the right set of channels and, more importantly, the right content for these channels per segment or even at the individual level. Some of these channels, such as remote detailing and tablet detailing, are more personal, but most can be considered non-personal.

There is more to multichannel marketing than multiple channels. It is essential to understand the difference between multiple channels and multichannel. Multichannel means getting synergies from connected channels. Simply adding channels without integrating them doesn't bring additional benefits. Your digital channels should be a connected network rather than a series of isolated silos of information. One channel should lead to the next.

According to Healthcare Dimensions, a firm specializing in Health Management Solutions, about seventy-five percent of Healthcare Professionals (HCPs) want to receive information about continuing medical education opportunities from pharmaceutical companies in an easily accessible manner and on demand. Integrated multiple channel communication is the way to do that. Multichannel marketing offers three significant advantages over traditional ones.

1. *Relevant Communication*: Different people want to consume content in different ways. Advanced multichannel and omnichannel communication enables this by providing flexibility to deliver your content in the channel that best suits your audience's needs. The data gathered from the interactions with the tablet detailing or e-detailing presentation will inform the microsite content for each doctor. In effect, each doctor can now have their tailor-made channel and immediately connect to it. Pharma marketers, thus, can provide a better experience for HCPs.
2. *Better Clinician Education*: Multichannel communication offers another significant advantage. It enables you to demonstrate value with digital clinician education. The flexibility of multichannel allows HCPs to benefit from on-demand educational content and guided e-learning tools. The pharmaceutical industry can better understand its products and services by providing relevant and high-value information. It will help them raise their reputation and earn much-needed trust.
3. *Improves Treatment Outcomes*: Besides clinical education, you can use multichannel communication to help physicians to support patients throughout their healthcare journey by assisting them in improving adherence to medications.

Benefits for Pharma

Pharmaceutical companies, too, can benefit significantly from multichannel marketing. Consider these advantages, for example.

1. *Increasing Marketing Return on Investment (ROI)*: Data drives multichannel marketing. It allows you to measure the return on investment (ROI) of your marketing materials and efforts. Because the channels are connected, you can also connect the data with a complete overview of what, when, and how content is being accessed. You can see what is working and act quickly to make improvements.
2. *Empowers Field Force*: Multichannel empowers the customer-service teams in the field. Your medical representatives can supplement their face-to-face meetings with physicians with online remote contacts such as virtual detailing, eMSL (electronic-Medical Science Liaison) meetings, and other forms of virtual engagement. Besides, medical representatives can help physicians access different channels with on-demand content and offer personalized content to suit their individual needs.
3. *Refining Segmentation*: Many pharmaceutical companies are realizing and recognizing the need to refine their segmentation strategies by targeting high-priority customers with smaller field forces. Multichannel enables a key account strategy by delivering customer experiences that match your refined market segmentation. You can, for example, use high-value, one-to-one channels with priority targets by supplementing them with on-demand information relevant to their needs and wants.

Common Pitfalls

There are many misconceptions about multichannel marketing which can prevent you from achieving your objectives. One should be aware of them and develop a more precise understanding of what multichannel marketing is and what it is not. Here are some common pitfalls you need to be aware of.

1. Multichannel, as such, is not about adding digital channels to your marketing mix. Some offline channels continue to do well, and they should be given their due importance.
2. Digital is a strategy, first and foremost. A failure to see digital as a strategic investment will lead to overall failure.
3. Digital is often associated with innovation. When we do something digital, we do something innovative. No, it is not necessarily so. Digital is rapidly becoming the way we do business.
4. Many marketers seem to see digital as a channel in isolation. You need to activate and integrate all the channels — online and offline, along the customer journey, in a well-orchestrated way to achieve success.
5. Pharmaceutical marketers often see digital as a way for their field force to enhance engagement with physicians. However, such a stance is very limited. Digital offers a transformational opportunity to engage healthcare practitioners (HCPs) and all the new stakeholders. They are becoming increasingly important in healthcare decision-making, such as patients, caregivers, nurses, and pharmacists. Digital helps you to reach audiences that previously were not reached effectively through traditional and costly Pharma channels. It helps you to reach all the stakeholders cost-effectively.

Winner's Checklist

How to succeed with multichannel marketing? What are the critical success factors? Here's a checklist that can help you win with multichannel marketing.

1. *Determine your target audience*: Who are your target audience? Do you want to target patients, physicians, or payers? You can target as many audience segments as you want as long you have the necessary logistics to cover their entire customer journey.

2. *Measure your multichannel marketing success*: You cannot improve what you cannot measure. Set two or three key performance indicators (KPIs) and a measurable objective for each channel. Track the progress against the set objectives. You need to set goals to measure your reach, acquisition, and conversion. Monitoring the progress and making the necessary course corrections along the way is the key to achieving success.
2. *Integrate all your channels*: Integration of all your channels is vital for success. Channels need to connect naturally and not compete. Consider, for example, your blog post leads to a subscription box, a newsletter, and a landing page. Remember that your message is uniform across all channels. It is crucial.
3. *Engage with your stakeholders*: In today's Attention Economy, customers are used to instant engagement and personalized messaging and content. Your Pharma brand, therefore, needs to have a conversation online and not just a static presence. You can use live chat, mobile apps, email, chatbots, and more to engage with your customers with messaging that is as personalized as possible.
4. *Involve your representatives*: Pharmaceutical sales representatives continue to be a significant driving force in multichannel pharma marketing even though their numbers in the marketplace are dwindling. As such, you need to involve them in all aspects of the marketing process. Remember that emails sent by your representatives (Rep-triggered emails) have much higher open rates than those sent by pharmaceutical companies.
5. *Focus on the patient*: Patient-centricity is no longer a buzzword. Patients are increasingly playing an influential role in healthcare, and pharmaceutical marketers need to acknowledge this.
6. *Stay up-to-date*: There were few surprises with traditional marketing channels. It is not the case with multichannel marketing. Digital marketing changes rapidly, and you can sometimes be out of the loop in just a few months. Pharmaceutical marketers need to stay updated with global

marketing trends and not just stick to their industry. Moreover, you can adapt to change if you stay up-to-date with market and marketing trends. Today, in the digital era, you can get data and learn from it almost instantaneously. The key questions to ask and answer are:

- Are physicians not engaging with your website enough?
- Don't patients find the information on your website useful?
- You can learn from the data you have at your fingertips and tweak your marketing strategy.

Omni-Channel Marketing

The dictionary defines Omni as universal or of all things, whereas Multi means many. The literal translation of Omni-channel, therefore, means to communicate across all channels rather than just many channels, as in the case of Multichannel.

What is the difference between omnichannel and multichannel marketing? The difference between omnichannel and multichannel comes down to a company's approach to digital channels. Stacy Schwartz, a digital marketing expert, succinctly puts the difference between omnichannel and multichannel marketing, when she says: *Companies that focus on maximizing the performance of each channel - physical, phone, web, mobile - have a multichannel strategy. They are likely to structure their organizations into swim lanes focused on a channel, each with its reporting structure and revenue goals*.

The result is competition that sometimes creates friction between the teams and misalignment. But, on the other hand, sometimes it may work for the good. In multichannel marketing, channels are

Table 3.5 Multichannel Marketing and Omni-channel Marketing: Key Differences

Multichannel Marketing	Omni-channel Marketing
1. Brand is at the center of the strategy. Starts with the brand's view of the world and is then projected on the customer. 2. Basically a tactical approach. Marketers manage each channel independently and implement tactics that work best for that channel. 3. Multichannel marketing is a brand's effort to interact with customers across multiple channels and platforms.	1. Customer is at the center of the strategy. Considers how the customer sees the world and then determines internal marketing. 2. Internal departments work together and are in-tune with the overall messaging and strategy. The focus is on creating a consistent, cohesive overall strategy. 3. Omni channel marketing offers a seamless, integrated customer experience, no matter where or how the individual customer engages with the brand. That's why it is called *Omni-channel.*

managed and optimized independently. It may result in competition within the marketing department or lead to a disconnected marketing experience. In contrast, an omnichannel marketing strategy puts the customer, not the corporate silos, at its center. It is thus more about customer centricity than anything else. The critical differences between multichannel and omnichannel marketing are presented in Table 3.5.

Omnichannel marketing uses data across all touchpoints to build a customer profile to enable the purpose of contextual marketing. Contextual marketing is an online marketing model in which people are served with targeted advertising based on terms they search for or their recent browsing behavior. In the context of omnichannel marketing in the pharmaceutical industry, this means that if a physician seeks clarification or some additional evidence in a face-to-face detailing session with a Pharma rep and when he next visits an e-detailing site of that company, he should continue the journey, and not start from the beginning. That is a seamless customer experience.

It is important to remember that whether it is multichannel or omnichannel marketing, you should consider using traditional and digital channels in a mutually reinforcing way. Today there are many channels to reach the customer. The multiple channels that have cropped up in the digital era are the website, email, SMS (Short Message Service), Search Engine Marketing, Pay-per-click advertising, eDetailing, online forum, blogs, and microblogging, social networks, big data and analytics, and mobile applications.

Winning with Omnichannel: A Checklist

How do you improve your chances of success and enhance omnichannel customer engagement? Here's a list of questions that can show how to formulate a winning omnichannel strategy for engaging your stakeholders effectively.

1. What is your current understanding of the channels your customers are using?
2. What are the channels' reach, impact, and cost?

3. Do you have clear, measurable objectives for each channel?
4. What is the competitive landscape? How are your major competitors engaging their customers on these channels?
5. Have you looked beyond your traditional customer groups in your current strategy? Have you considered the increasing influence of other stakeholders?
6. How deep is your current customer segmentation? Have you considered the power of finer segmentation capabilities of digital marketing? Have you developed strategies based on personalization technology, or are you still focusing on mass outreach?
7. Have you put strategy first and channels second? Also, have you put content before channels? Do you have uniform communication that is consistent across all channels?
8. Have you considered cost per engagement across all channels — digital and traditional ones?
9. What is the level of integration of your customer-facing organization (sales, marketing, medical affairs, digital)? Can it provide a seamless experience for your customers?
10. Do you have an effective monitoring mechanism to track progress against objectives for each channel?

Some of the leading Pharma majors increasingly have been using multichannel strategies for their marketing campaigns for some time now. Therefore, studying them will be of immense use for pharmaceutical marketers who want to practice multichannel and omnichannel marketing strategies for their brands and companies. The following cases show how they have been leveraging multi and Omni channels.

CASE

70

Got Ladyballs? Ovarian Cancer Campaign is a Bit too ballsy for some!

Ovarian Cancer Canada (OCC) launched a rather ballsy campaign in 2016 to raise awareness of ovarian cancer. It's a campaign with cojones or Ladyballs. One of the videos produced by the group states that: *women have balls too, and they're at risk. So have the lady balls to do something about it. Because equating courage and strength to the male anatomy is what every woman wants. Many women say the tagline left them stunned and offended.* One woman even wrote on Facebook about the ad, saying it is sexist and insulting. She wrote: *Yes, I am aware that ovarian cancer needs to be discussed. Got it: You're trying to be clever. I am a woman with ovaries, not a woman with Ladyballs.*

Speaking about the campaign, Karen Cinq Mars, VP of Marketing at Ovarian Cancer Canada, said: *Some love it, some hate it, but either way, people are talking about it, which is always the goal of cause-related campaigns*.

Speaking on the campaign's effectiveness, Angela Y-lee, Chair of Northwestern University's Kellogg School of Management, said: *In the past, campaigns could win awards based on artistic characteristics, whether or not they were effective in delivering the desired objectives*. Marketing experts agree that based on the increased awareness alone, the campaign seems to be a success. That has changed. Campaigns should be and are evaluated on effectiveness. And the Got Ladyballs campaign appears to be getting on peoples' radar even though the reactions are not all positive.

Behind the Campaign

Ovarian Cancer Canada tested for a year before the campaign five different themes with a sample group of 1,000 Canadians. The Ladyballs campaign performed the best. Those surveyed described it with words like empowered, strong, curious, proud, and important. Seventy-seven percent of the respondents said the campaign was compelling. Seventy percent said it made them think of ovarian cancer in a new way. Based on the survey results, the team at Ovarian Cancer Canada decided that rather than focusing on sad facts to elicit sympathy to focus on the strength of survivors and power, we all have to do something about women's most fatal cancer.

Why name the campaign Ladyballs? Because to say that someone has the balls to do something automatically elicits thoughts of an individual who is daring, brave, or courageous. While some assign this term to men, these traits, when you think of it, apply to people regardless of gender. Women have balls too, and literally, female gonads are, in fact, ovaries. Whether you call them ovaries or lady balls — the more important thing is to talk about them.

Ovarian Cancer

Ovarian cancer has been called a silent killer as it claims the lives of five Canadian women daily. There is no reliable test for it yet. Women over 50 are generally more at risk for ovarian cancer, but those in their 30s have also been affected by it. Because there's no awareness about it, and because symptoms are so vague, it gets caught too late. That is why a campaign to raise awareness of this deadly disease.

What makes the Ladyballs Campaign Unique?

1. While other cancer foundations boast high awareness, high spending levels, and significant corporate sponsorships,

Ovarian Cancer Canada relies almost exclusively on private donors. Unaided awareness of ovarian cancer in Canada was very low at 4 percent compared to other forms of cancer, with over 60 percent of Canadians utterly unfamiliar with the disease. Therefore, the campaign's purpose was to get people to talk about ovarian cancer so that more women would ask their doctors about it.

2. Cause-related campaigns are successful when they permeate the culture with something memorable. However, people were uncomfortable talking about their ovaries beyond acknowledging their existence and anatomical location. In contrast, with the male equivalent (testes), the literal meaning takes a back seat to what they colloquially represent: courage and boldness. Ovaries, however, had no such alternate usage, name, or meaning. So Ovarian Cancer Canada (OCC) decided to position ovaries as female balls (Ladyballs).
3. The Ovarian Cancer Canada (OCC) launched the Ladyballs Campaign in December 2015 nationally and ran almost for six months until May 2016. The videos and ads depicted situations that a modern woman might find herself in — such as a business meeting or a social gathering — where she has to make brave decisions, reminding women that they have balls too, and leading to the line: *Do you have the Ladyballs to do something about ovarian cancer?* The many formats of the campaign were:

   - A 30-second Public Service Announcement (PSA) video
   - A 60-second Cinema version video and an on-premise film in restaurants, bars, and salons
   - Print and digital ads featured strong women of varying ages and ethnicities to show that the disease does not discriminate. Show us your Ladyballs — a user-generated activation — was deployed in social, digital, and search, allowing the public to display their support for the cause. PR and community outreach amplified the message. National Television and Radio news featured OCC representatives and Ovarian cancer survivors.

4. The campaign results were impressive. There was a year-over-year increase of 118 percent in inquiries about ovarian cancer from women, along with an average increase of 22 donor calls per week. Seventy-five percent of donations received during the campaign were from new donors. There were also significant improvements in the number of calls to OCC regional offices (35 percent), and social engagement increased by 22 percent.
5. The Ladyballs Campaign registered a significant increase in earned media for Ovarian Cancer Canada. The campaign generated a whopping $12 million in donated media compared to a few thousand dollars in the past.
6. There was more to the Ladyballs Campaign than effectiveness in raising awareness of ovarian cancer and earned media. There were awards galore. Here's a list of awards won by the campaign:

   - Cannes 2016 winner: Silver Lion, Fundraising and advocacy, Health and Wellness
   - Cannes 2016 winner: Bronze Line, PR
   - Cannes 2016 Shortlist: Glass Lion
   - Canadian Marketing Association 2016 winner: Gold, Advertising, Fundraising, Public Service
   - Cassies 2017 winner: Gold, Underdog
   - Cassies 2017 winner: Silver, Cause, Creative Effectiveness

(Source: Adapted from articles: 1. Patricia Kozicka, Got Ladyballs? Ovarian Cancer Campaign a bit too "too ballsy" for some, Global News, January 6, 2016, 2. Strategy Staff, Cassie's Gold: Taking cancer by the Ladyballs: Ovarian Cancer Canada raised awareness and increased donations with a ballsy campaign, Strategy, February 22, 2017)

CASE 71

Dr. Reddy's Launches a Spate of New Campaigns to Revive the OTC Brands it Acquired from Novartis!

Dr. Reddy's, one of the leading international generic companies, started breathing new life into the over-the-counter brands it acquired from Novartis. These brands, which were a force to reckon with in their heydays, are — Doan's (magnesium salicylate), Bufferin (Aspirin buffered with magnesium oxide, calcium carbonate, and magnesium hydroxide), and Nupercainal (Dibucaine) ointment. The New Jersey-based Ducere Pharma acquired these brands from Novartis. Later in 2016, Dr. Reddy's acquired these brands and three more brands from Ducere.

As these brands were very popular a few years ago when they were being promoted and became even household names, Dr. Reddy's wanted to capitalize on their brand equity. As the brand image was fading out as they did not actively promote these brands in the past, Dr. Reddy's decided to breathe new life into them. The challenge before Dr. Reddy's was — how do we bring it back to the current market but also bring it to a new generation of potential sufferers? So, the company decided to launch a digital campaign to revive these heritage brands. The campaign included a website revamp, digital and search ad placements, and TV spots. It started its first national TV campaign in August 2017.

Doan's had been a very popular brand in the past and a trusted name for pain relief in the US. So Dr. Reddy's had decided to revive this once-well-known back-pain brand with a digital campaign. The

15-second TV spot for Doan's begins with Doan's — *We have had your back's back since way back*.

The initial results were promising, according to Lauren Schulz, director of OTC (over-the-counter) brand marketing at Dr. Reddy's in the US. Doan's awareness, for example, went up from 35 percent to 43 percent in eight test markets surveyed.

Dr. Reddy's had also updated the product adding a New Doan's Cream targeting the younger users, while the traditional analgesic tends to track the older. In addition, the company also started a digital-only campaign for the other two popular OTC brands — Bufferin and Nupercainal. The reason why the company is investing in these brands is that it is keen to grow them. Because these brands were very popular in the past, and as people knew these brand names, there was room to grow, but somehow they have been ignored.

The challenge Dr. Reddy's faces is formidable with many established competitors in OTC pain relief such as Advil, Tylenol, Aleve, and Excedrin. The US market for internal analgesics in 2016 was $4.12 billion, while sales of external pain relievers were $734 million, according to the consumer healthcare product association.

(Source: Adapted from an article by Beth Snyder Bulik, Dr. Reddy's Revives ex-Novartis OTC brands with a late of new ad campaigns, Fierce Pharma, August 21, 2017)

CASE

72

Gaming Tackles Back Pain: Pfizer's *Back-in-Play*!

How do you reach the difficult-to-reach audience among men aged between 18 to 40 that too at the right frequency if you have to deliver a very important message? Take, for example, the patients suffering from ankylosing spondylitis in Europe. It is barely pronounceable, and the condition affects 1 in 200 people, the most common in men aged 18 to 40. It is also frequently confused with common back pain leading to substantial delays in diagnosis. In addition, there is a considerable lack of awareness among the general public about the symptoms of ankylosing spondylitis. Early diagnosis can help minimize the long-term impact of this excruciatingly painful and even debilitating condition.

Pfizer Europe found an answer to this reaching-the-difficult-to-reach question, and the company understood what makes its target audience (men aged between 18 to 40 in Europe) tick. The answer was that you could reach them via the gaming and video channels. The company has used these channels effectively to raise awareness of ankylosing spondylitis among men, its target audience. Complimented by a targeted media strategy and capitalizing on world cup fever, the campaign used football, online, gaming, and video to cast a wide net and motivate those most likely to have ankylosing spondylitis yet unaware of it to seek information and reduce confusion with common back pain.

Pfizer launched its most appropriately named campaign, *Back in Play*, with the most appropriate timing — around the FIFA world cup 2010 to capitalize on the football fever among its target audience of men aged between 18 to 40 and delivered a simple, subtle message about the symptoms of ankylosing spondylitis. *Back in Play* was a perfect strategy because the company's message reached its target audience 38 million times across multiple channels.

Seeding a game online, where levels of concentration are very high, ensured excellent message retention. *Back in Play* proved to be the perfect channel to reach vast numbers of the relevant audience quickly with the symptoms. Research indicated that multiple channels were critical for success as men wanted entertainment, not education online. They need insights, not information. And more importantly, the information had to find them — they were not going to seek it.

Pfizer complemented its integrated multichannel campaign, Back in Play, with professional footballer endorsement, online promotion, a dedicated YouTube channel, and a targeted online and offline media campaign driving large numbers of potential patients to the campaign website and successfully exposing them to simple messaging about ankylosing spondylitis.

The results of the campaign speak for themselves of *Back in Play's* great success. Consider these facts, for example:

- Sixteen million plays of Back in Play game on over 450 websites
- 450,000 + website visits with an average of 1 in 5 website visitors viewing specific ankylosing spondylitis information
- Triple the target number of potential patients seeking ankylosing spondylitis information
- Over 47,000 views of 11 videos on YouTube featuring international footballers and opinion leaders

- 12 Active European affiliates
- 20 + million reached with print and broadcast coverage
- Six national patient groups engaged across the European Union

Speaking about the phenomenal success that Back in Play had achieved, Rupert Watts, Senior Manager, eMarketing Pfizer Specialty Care said: *We are delighted with the results of Back in Play, which has exceeded our expectations, as well as the objectives set. It has made a significant impact, both internally and externally, using an innovative and integrated multichannel approach. In addition, it has proven longevity and secured a real active engagement with an audience that is traditionally not easy for a disease awareness campaign to reach.*

(Source: A PMLiVE article, Gaming tackles back pain — Case Study: Raising awareness of ankylosing spondylitis among men aged 18–40 via online, gaming, and video channels, published on November 30, 2011)

CASE

73

Novartis Launches *See Me to Know* Campaign for Cosentyx!

Novartis worked with Hill Holiday, a Boston-based marketing and communications agency, to launch its *See Me To Know* campaign for its brand Cosentyx (secukinumab), a drug used in treating psoriasis. The campaign focuses on making the brand real, using real patients, speaking from real experiences, relating to sufferers on a human level, and evoking feelings of empathy, understanding, and inspiration.

Psoriasis, a chronic inflammatory condition, which is considered the most common autoimmune disease in the US, affects an estimated 7.5 million people. Cyndi Lauper, a celebrity in the music world, hid and struggled with her psoriasis for many years to find a treatment that worked for her. She started taking Cosentyx.

When Cyndi Lauper, the celebrated pop icon and winner of Grammy, Emmy, and Tony awards, started taking Cosentyx, Novartis spotted an opportunity to partner with her in a campaign to raise awareness of psoriasis. In addition, they could use Cyndi Lauper's voice and story to help patients with psoriasis. This partnership allows Cyndi to connect with patients and create buzz for the brand in a highly competitive market. Novartis carefully considered and executed the celebrity partnership keeping patients in mind and ensuring that the brand kept its promise to be real. Cyndi Lauper is sharing her story to demonstrate the impact plaque psoriasis has had on her life and why she saw a dermatologist and decided to start treatment with Cosentyx (Secukinumab) first 1L-17A antagonist approved by the US FDA to treat moderate to severe plaque psoriasis.

What is noteworthy about this *See Me To Know* campaign is that Cyndi is not the only spokesperson in the campaign, as is typical of celebrity sponsorships. Instead, she was one of the many advocates who spoke about their struggle with psoriasis and how they overcame it. Cyndi's story is genuine, which makes her authentically connect with the community. Her reassurance to patients with psoriasis was spontaneous when she said: *It took me a long time to get to where I am today, but I made it — so can others who are struggling with psoriasis.*

The campaign featured Cyndi in a 60-second TV spot with two other patient advocates. Besides, the *See Me To Know* campaign created a six-episode web series of Cyndi's story and surrounding content culminating in an original song and music video — Hope, which can be viewed on www.seemetoknow.com. Novartis supported the campaign with a surround sound paid media plan, including broadcast, print, digital, and social, via Twitter, Facebook, and YouTube, and online video, Tumblr.

Novartis released the Hope song by Cyndi Lauper in honor of world psoriasis day in October 2017. Inspired by psoriasis patients and Cyndi Lauper's experience of living with the disease, Hope is part of the *See Me To Know* campaign. The campaign is a celebration of patients' success stories and encourages others living with plaque psoriasis to seek ways to get back to doing things they want to do. Speaking about the song, Cyndi Lauper said: *I have met many people with psoriasis and drew inspiration for the song from their stories of struggle, courage, perseverance, and Hope. I know first-hand the impact psoriasis can have, and my goal is to give it a voice to the millions of Americans who may struggle with their psoriasis. We don't need to hide, and we don't need to be embarrassed.*

(Source: Adapted from articles: 1. IPG (Inter Public Group), Hill Holiday Novartis collaborate with Cyndi Lauper for World Psoriasis Day, November 7, 2017, 2. Novartis Pharmaceutical Company News, Novartis collaborates with pop icon Cyndi Lauper to release a new song in honor of World Psoriasis Day, CISION PR Newswire, October 24, 2017)

CASE

74

Lundbeck's Multichannel Depression Awareness Campaign —*Lean on Me*!

Lundbeck, the Danish international pharmaceutical company making Cipralex (escitalopram), launched the first multichannel depression awareness campaign, *Lean on Me*, specifically targeting friends and family to identify those with depression to seek help. In addition, it has utilized facial recognition technology for the first time, allowing users to share personalized *Lean on Me* videos via email, Facebook, and Twitter. A post-launch survey revealed that 63 percent of consumers found the campaign helpful in recognizing depression in a friend. Eleven percent of those identified with depression sought help from a healthcare provider. Besides, Lundbeck partnered with over ten patient and professional groups, including the World Federation for Mental Health, European Depression Association, and Aware, among others, for its *Lean on Me* campaign.

Depression, a Major Challenge

Depression affects 33 million people in Europe, yet approximately half of people with depression are not diagnosed, partly due to the high stigma surrounding the disease. That is the major challenge. To help overcome this, Lundbeck teamed with Ogilvy Health PR to develop a disease awareness campaign to break down the stigma around depression and encourage those affected to seek treatment. In addition, some of the major symptoms of depression — a feeling of hopelessness, lack of energy, and volition, mean that people are difficult to reach and mobilize. Research also indicates that 68 percent of people with depression withdraw from friends and family, who can offer significant help in recouping.

The Solution: *Lean on Me*!

Ogilvy Health PR found the answer to the problem from the inspiring and motivational lyrics of Bill Withers' much-loved song, Lean on Me. *Lean on Me! When you're not strong, and I'll be your friend, I'll help you carry on.* These lines reverberate throughout the campaign. Here are the lyrics of the complete song that can lift you from your blues:

Lean on Me Lyrics by Bill Withers

Sometimes in our lives, we all have pain

We all have sorrow

But if we are wise

We know that there's always tomorrow

Lean on me when you're not strong

And I'll be your friend

I'll help you carry on

For it won't be long

'Til I'm gonna need

Somebody to lean on

Please swallow your pride

If I have things you need to borrow

For no one can fill those of your needs

That you won't let show

You just call on me, brother, when you need a hand

We all need somebody to lean on

I just might have a problem that you'll understand

We all need somebody to lean on

Lean on me when you're not strong

And I'll be your friend

I'll help you carry on

For it won't be long

'Til I'm gonna need

Somebody to lean on

You just call on me, brother, when you need a hand

We all need somebody to lean on

Lean on Me!

The campaign contained an engaging and colorful online platform, including educational content, personal stories, offline and online advertising, live events, and media campaigns. In addition, for the first time in a healthcare campaign, *Lean on Me* has used facial recognition technology, the friend clip allowing users to share personalized *Lean on Me* videos via email, Facebook, and Twitter.

Results of the Campaign

In a survey conducted four months after the launch, over half of the HCPs reported seeing more patients presenting with depression. Sixty-six percent reported more patients being diagnosed, and fifty-six percent reported more patients being treated with depression. Eleven percent of consumers who remembered the campaign said they sought help for themselves or a friend as a result of the campaign. Two-thirds of consumers surveyed said that *Lean on Me* made them recognize by a friend or family.

The online results of the campaign, too, were impressive. The website has had more than 95,000 visits, with more than 180,000 pages being viewed. More than 7,400 people also engaged with the Friend-clip videos.

Lundbeck seems to be satisfied with the campaign outcome. Fredric Jerre, Head of Global Marketing Lundbeck, said about the success of their *Lean on Me* campaign: *The* Lean on Me *campaign destigmatizes depression and delivers for those affected by it and the ones closest to them. We are proud of the campaign and the innovative elements that make it unique. In particular, the Friend-Clip technology, which has never been used in a hea*lthcare campaign before, has proven to be a valuable tool for engaging with our target audience.

(Source: Adapted from the article: Case Study: Multichannel depression awareness campaign — Lean on Me, PMLiVE, March 9, 2012)

CASE

75

Allergan's *EyePowerment* Campaign!

Before we had our voice, we had our eyes. So there you have it — a simple yet powerful way of noting that a person's eyes can say as much about them as anything they speak. A person's eyes speak volumes and are often one of the fastest ways to read between the words and discover a person's real intent, belief, or true motive. This insightful message is at the core of Allergan's new campaign — EyePowerment.

The eyes are the first facial features we, humans, notice about another person. Sounds obvious? To validate this, Allergan, the international specialty Pharma company conducted, *A Look at our Eye Language*, a new online eye language survey of 1,019 adult Americans in 2017. More than half of the respondents (53 percent) agreed with the statement. In addition, research shows that the eyes provide a powerful form of nonverbal communication about who we are and what we feel. To help interpret our eye language, Allergan has partnered with Patti Wood, a body language expert with more than 25 years of experience.

Kelton Global, an Insights and Strategy consultancy, conducted *A Look at our Eye Language* on behalf of Allergan to support its new EyePowerment campaign to raise awareness for chronic eye disease.

Patti Wood says: *Eye language is a powerful form of communication that can reveal a lot about us, but chronic dry eye symptoms like red or itchy eyes may unintentionally interfere with the message you want to send. My passion for interpreting our language of eyes aligns with Allergan's EyePowerment campaign, which aims to empower people who might be experiencing symptoms of chronic dry eye and talk to their doctor about treatment options.*

A Look at our Eye Language revealed several insights. Here are some of the more important findings:

1. Approximately ninety-seven percent of Americans surveyed say they are comfortable making eye contact with those they know.
2. Those who see the value in maintaining eye contact say holding a direct gaze makes them feel respected (53 percent), understood (45 percent), and appreciated (44 percent).
3. Many feel eye behavior creates a shared connection (36 percent), leaves a positive impression (35 percent), and increases one's likeability (29 percent).
4. Women are more likely than men to feel eye behavior shows sincerity (53 percent vs. 41 percent) and creates a shared connection (42 percent vs. 30 percent).
5. More than half of Americans (57 percent) can tell if someone is listening by looking into their eyes.
6. Over a quarter (28 percent) of respondents believe that others know how truthful they are by looking into their eyes.

Recognizing the importance of eye language and the messages our eyes can send, Allergan launched the EyePowerment campaign to raise awareness of chronic dry eye disease and its consequences. It is estimated that 33 million Americans suffer from chronic dry eye disease. The EyePowerment campaign aims to empower them by raising their awareness and persuading them to talk to their doctor. In addition, the campaign encourages people suffering from chronic dry eye disease to join the conversation by following @eyepowerment on Twitter and using the hashtag #eyepowerment. Allergan also has created a campaign website, eyepowerment.com, where visitors can learn more about symptoms and treatment options for chronic dry eye disease.

Chronic dry eye is usually caused by reduced tear production due to inflammation. Dry eye is often a chronic disease that can occur because of advanced age, contact lens wear, certain medications, eye diseases, and other medical conditions or environmental factors. Without enough tears, the film protecting the eye can break down, creating dry spots on the cornea. Allergan believes that it is important to have an informed conversation with your doctor regarding your chronic dry eye disease (CDE). Certain external conditions that can worsen CDE include sitting too long at the computer, pollen and allergies, dry air or wind, dust or smoke. Also, chronic eye disease tends to occur more frequently in women than in men. CDE can be associated with hormonal changes, common among women who are experiencing menopause or post-menopausal.

FCB (Foot Cone & Belding), one of the largest global advertising agency networks, created an eye-catching television commercial to grab people's attention for Allergan's EyePowerment Campaign. The commercial featured a striking montage of images of famous personages whose eyes — as we viewers can readily see — speak volumes about their personages. It included close-up images of celebrities such as Lucille Ball, Bette Davis, Amelia Earhart, Maya Angelou, Rosa Parks, Frida Kahlo, and Tig Notaro, among others. They are all in their own right, game-changers, trailblazers, and statement makers. The faces of the campaign embody the spirit behind Eyepowerment, whose presence — and eyes helped tell their personal story, reveal their character, and leave their mark on the world. Their images were on television and social media platforms like Twitter, Facebook, and Instagram. The TV spot ended with a few simple lines of copy about chronic eye disease and the suggestion that viewers see their doctor for their eye exam.

Allergan's EyePowerment movement was timed perfectly. The campaign kicked off on February 24 during the 2017 Academy Awards events. The celebrity influencers at the awards show were encouraged to take selfies of themselves and post them on Twitter to demonstrate that a person's eyes are way more powerful than any designer dress on the red carpet. The EyePowerment Campaign played out on digital, social, and print platforms for several weeks and was backed by a strong public relations push.

Allergan encouraged its target audience through their campaign EyePowerment to tweet a selfie of their eyes with #eyepowerment and #donate. For every #eyepowerment shared with an 'eye selfie,' Allergan will contribute $10 for Dress for Success up to $25,000. Why Dress for Success? Because in addition to Eyecare, women's healthcare too, is a significant focus area for Allergan, and Dress for Success is an organization dedicated to empowering women to achieve economic independence by providing a network of support, professional attire, and development tools to help women thrive in work and life. The mission of the Dress for Success organization matched the essence of the EyePowerment Campaign. Dress for Success's mission of empowering women is accomplished by its many services beyond the outfit. The Dress for Success organization, too, like Allergan, does work to empower women to reach their full potential. Remember, our eyes play such a powerful role in representing us, so making sure our eyes are healthy can also help us feel confident and capable of achieving our goals.

Allergan's US eye care unit generates more than the US $2.5 billion in annual sales. It has one of the deepest eye care pipelines in the industry, with more than 20 programs in various stages of clinical development. Allergan's EyePowerment Campaign is built on a 60-year heritage in ophthalmology of fulfilling its mission to make healthcare a public health imperative.

(Source: Adapted from articles: 1. Lewis Lazare, The eyes have it in Allergan's new ad campaign from FCB Chicago, Chicago Business Journal, February 27, 2017; 2. Sheila Shayon, EyePowerment: 5 questions with Allergan's SVP Herm Cuckier, Brand Channel, April 11, 2017; 3. Allergan Plc: Allergan's EyePowerment Campaign releases survey revealing the importance of eye language and the crucial role it plays in our communications, CISION PR Newswire, May 16, 2017)

CASE

76

Takeda, Lundbeck Plan US Test for Depression App in their Latest Beyond-the-pill Foray!

Can keep track of medication doses and mood swings help improve depression treatment? Takeda Pharma, the Japanese International drug major, has set out to find out that in a beyond-the-pill tech project. Takeda Pharma teamed with Lundbeck, a Danish international pharmaceutical company, and Advocate Healthcare on a study that uses an app with a conversational text interface to track and measure patients' experience with antidepressant therapies. During the study, users will record medications, moods, side effects, and other general well-being measures every day for 12 weeks. All study participants will have been prescribed some antidepressants by their physician.

The recorded information in the app serves two purposes. One is it serves as a feedback mechanism for patients — to inform them of their progress or problems. Secondly, patients can also use the app to communicate with physicians. For instance, if a patient who is not doing well records thoughts about suicide, the app will trigger a message to their healthcare provider.

What is Takeda's interest in testing a depression app? Takeda holds the US marketing rights to Trintellix (vortioxetine) under a marketing deal with Lundbeck and launched a multichannel marketing campaign titled Tangles to promote the drug after a name change from Brintellix to Trintellix. The multiple channels for engaging healthcare professionals (HCPs) include TV, digital, in-office TV, and print campaign. The multicolored tangles pictured in the advertisements across the channels represent the multiple symptoms of major depressive disorders beyond merely being sad. In addition, Takeda created two distinct versions of their TV creatives — one with a female lead and the other with a male lead. While two-thirds of depression patients are female, a sizable proportion of patients are male, and one cannot ignore or overlook them. That is why Takeda included both populations to represent and best communicate with the entire patient community.

Takeda is also running an unbranded disease awareness campaign about depression at www.lighterblue.com and on Facebook. The campaign highlights the variety of symptoms depression can cause and includes patient and family stories.

Having developed great real-world experience with Trintellix among HCPs with campaigns like Tangles, Takeda has now decided to raise patient awareness and engagement to support their dialogue with healthcare professionals about Trintellix as a possible solution to help untangle their multiple symptoms of depression.

Advocate Healthcare, a faith-based non-profit, is the largest health system in Illinois and a leader in the medical field dedicated to changing patient expectations by giving them easy access to all that they need to stay well, live well and achieve outstanding treatment outcomes.

Takeda Pharma's Study on the Advocate Pathway app builds on another pilot study that the company launched with a cognition kit in the UK in early 2017. Participants in that test wore Apple watches with an app that collected both passive and active data from people with major depressive disorder. In 2016, Takeda sponsored a Shark-tank like innovation contest to draw submissions for digital solutions for depression. Dr. Darryl Sleep, vice president and head of Takeda's US medical office and US medical affairs, said in an interview: *Our interest here is to improve the wellness of patients, and our medicine is only part of that. We recognize that we can't do this alone and need to be a partner in the broader healthcare system. For example, a prescription for an antidepressant for a patient with depression is not addressing the fundamental problem of depression.*

Advocate Healthcare is handling patient recruitment and marketing to attract patients now. If the app works, Takeda will take a more active approach in getting it out to patients who need it.

Speaking about the commitment to improve outcomes and the patient-centric approach of Takeda, Dr. Darryl Sleep added: I*f this does improve outcomes based on well-defined, standard-of-care measurements for patients with treatment for depression, we would want to partner with other stakeholders in the healthcare community to make sure it's utilized widely — although again, not linking it to any particular medicine.*

(Source: Adapted from articles: 1. Beth Snyder Bulik, Takeda, Lundbeck plan the US to test for depression app in the latest beyond-the-pill foray, Fierce Pharma, November 13, 2017; 2. Beth Snyder Bulik, Takeda launches new DTC campaign for renamed depression med, Trintellix, Fierce Pharma, July 24, 2016)

CASE

77

GSK's Prevacid OTC Gets a New Spokes Character — A Fireball!

Guess who the new spokes-character for GlaxoSmithKline's (GSK) over-the-counter heartburn drug, Prevacid (lansoprazole), is? An animated ball of fire with a mischievous glint in its eye. It is *Lurker,* the fireball, and it is popping up in TV, digital and trade ads, and promotions for the heartburn-relieving drug from GSK, Prevacid. GSK has the US marketing rights for Prevacid from Takeda.

In the TV ad that launched *Lurker,* the fireball earlier in January 2017, it (the fireball character) hides in the bushes as two women drink coffee and chat as they eat lunch on a nearby bench. The flame with legs never talks. Instead, it just giggles as it chases off one of the women who didn't take her heartburn medicine.

GlaxoSmithKline's consumer healthcare division developed the *Lurker* character to communicate the risk of recurrence of frequent heartburn interestingly. They explored several options and decided on Lurker due to its ability to convey the idea in a truly engaging way. The agency that created the campaign is Havas Adrenaline. The target audience is people with frequent heartburn, defined as two or more days per week.

The heartburn market in the US has been hot for the past few years. That's because top proton pump inhibitor drugs such as Prevacid went over the counter (OTC) yet continued with their aggressive marketing strategies. In addition, Pfizer, with its rights for OTC

Nexium and Proctor & Gamble with its OTC Prilosec, make the market fiercely competitive and aggressive marketing mandatory to win in the marketplace.

(Source: Adapted from the article: Beth Snyder Bulik, GSK debuts new Fireball character for Prevacid OTC heartburn drug, Fierce Pharma, January 20, 2017)

CASE

78

Bristol-Myers Squibb Sponsors *Thriver Thursdays*, a New Docuseries by TV Host, Robin Roberts!

Bristol-Myers Squibb (BMS), a global Pharma major, teamed up with ABC's Good Morning America co-anchor Robin Roberts to spotlight ordinary yet extraordinary people who have risen above and beyond major challenges. Robin Roberts, a two-time cancer patient, prefers the word Thriver to the survivor. Roberts celebrating her six-year bone marrow transplant birthday in September 2018, encouraged people to use the hashtag #thriverThursday to share stories about how they not only survived life-altering circumstances but continued to persevere, achieve goals and surpass them. Roberts' production company, Rock'n Robin Productions, turned some of those into digital series that ran for six weeks.

Bristol-Myers Squibb, as a part of the public relations effort, sponsored these digital docuseries by Roberts titled *Thriver Thursdays*. The company's brand name as a sponsor appears on screen once during the video stories superimposed in simple sponsored by tag. The company said that it sponsored the series because the spirit of the series is in line with its mission, which is to help patients prevail over serious diseases. BMS said in a statement to Fierce Pharma: *We are incredibly inspired by Robin Roberts' mission to support and celebrate thrivers in our community — people who achieved despite life-altering circumstances*.

Roberts thanked the Pharma in a Twitter post on the launch day, writing: I *want to thank the entire @bmsnews family... I have enjoyed going to your headquarters and meeting such wonderful, caring people! Thank you for helping us profile these individuals who are making their message of hope and perseverance. #thriverThursdays.com*

Here are three brief profiles of these ordinary yet extraordinary people featured in the *Thriver Thursdays* series:

1. The first episode featuring Winnie Harlow, the trail-blazing fashion model, was aired on November 15, 2018. Winnie Harlow was the first model with the autoimmune skin condition vitiligo who will walk the runway in the annual Victoria's Secret fashion show in December 2018.
2. The second episode of #thriverThursday featured Duronne Walker, a New Orleans native, sharing his story of tragedy and triumph. He credits faith, family, and friends as his saving grace.
3. The third episode featured Clarie Griffith, who, at age 13, was diagnosed with bipolar disorder. During her darkest times, she developed an eating disorder, hallucinated, and at her worst, attempted suicide. Through treatment, Clarie has gotten better and is now sharing her story, working to change the stigma of a mental disorder.

(Source: Adapted from the article: Beth Snyder Bulik, Bristol-Myers Squibb signs on as the sponsor of TV host Robin Roberts' new digital docuseries, Fierce Pharma, November 28, 2018)

CASE

79

Canesten's *Code Word*!

Three in four women will experience a yeast infection at least once in their lifetime. Bayer's over-the-counter medication, an easy and effective solution for this common condition, is available in any local pharmacy in Hong Kong. And yet, Bayer faced a significant barrier in this market. Chinese women are embarrassed to discuss the topic with anyone, let alone to mention it to a pharmacist in a public area. To be successful with Canesten, Bayer had to remove the taboo on the subject and empower women to speak up to get help.

How do you clear a big cultural hurdle like asking for medication for a stigmatized condition such as yeast infection by women in a pharmacy, particularly when it is stigmatized? By leveraging an even bigger cultural trend. What is the most significant cultural trend in Hong Kong? Korean Pop and Korean drama are, in fact, an obsession in Hong Kong. While women in Hong Kong refuse to open up about their health conditions even to their closest girlfriends, they do not hesitate to talk about their Korean Pop and Korean drama obsession in public. Based on this insight, Bayer developed a code word by twisting the word for yeast infection, *yum to-yin*, into a hunky Korean-sounding name *KumTou-Yin* to pique interest, make people smile, and eliminate the discomfort about saying the word out loud. The company then created an online Korean-style drama series revolving around a woman with a secret she was hiding from her friends to help lift the taboo and get people talking.

What is so unique about this Code Word strategy? Code Word is a distinctly different and very creative strategy. Here are the major factors that were responsible for its success:

1. Instead of a leaflet or message, Bayer delivered a Code Word to customers. Apart from being unique, this offers a direct solution to their embarrassment of telling the pharmacist about their yeast infection. The Code Word campaign removed the discomfort of having and talking about a yeast infection.
2. The company reached its target audience — women aged between 25 to 44 through teaser posters and web banners to make them engage in the online video. After learning the Code Word from the video, they can feel free to speak up with friends and pharmacists about yeast infection.

The results were beyond expectations. The web series received over 200,000 views in the first few days, with the online search for the clever Code Word skyrocketing. The campaign even made it to the front cover of one of Hong Kong's most popular magazines. What is more, with additional print and out-of-home support, KumTou-Yin became a hot topic of conversation for women across all of Hong Kong. The sales too increased significantly during the campaign period by 25 percent, and traffic to pharmacies increased by 41 percent.

(Source: Cannes Contenders: J Walter Thompson, Hong Kong, Bayer Canesten: The Code Word, Campaign Brief Asia, May 9, 2016)

CASE

80

Who Pneu? Pfizer Joins the American Lung Association in a Disease Awareness Campaign!

Pfizer, the global drug major and maker of Prevnar 13 (pneumococcal 13-valent conjugate vaccine), joined the American Lung Association (ALA) in a disease awareness program for pneumococcal pneumonia. The duo put a patient at the center of the campaign by replacing their celebrity spokesman with a patient in their new awareness campaign, *Who Pneu*?

Actor Tim Daly was the face of the initial campaign when it was launched in September 2015. In the ad, which was on television and also ran in movie theaters, he spoke about his mother's bout and hospitalization with pneumococcal pneumonia. The ad prompted some unusual responses on Twitter, including a call from doctors without borders for Pfizer and GSK to cut the cost of their pneumococcal vaccines.

In the new, *Who Pneu* disease awareness campaign on TV, Tim Daly makes way for a 51-year older woman named Pam who contracted the disease. In the new ad, Pam and her two daughters talk about her experience with the infection — how surprised they were when she was diagnosed.

Research indicated that people aged 50 years and older are at increased risk of contracting pneumococcal pneumonia, which results in hospitalizations for 250,000 adults of 50 years plus every year. As a result, Pfizer and the American Lung Association set out in 2015 with a mission of the *Who Pneu* effort to make people aged 50 years and older aware of this increased risk.

There seems to be a popular misconception among adults aged 50 and older that you have to be older and sicker to contract pneumococcal pneumonia. However, the reality is that even if they feel healthy, people over 50 years of age and older are at increased risk for this potentially serious lung disease due to their age alone. With their *Who Pneu* campaign, Pfizer hoped to raise this awareness and remove the misconception about this severe infection.

Through television, radio, and print public service announcements (PSA), Pfizer and the American Lung Association shared information about the severity of pneumococcal pneumonia. In addition, they encouraged adults of 50 years and older to take an online risk assessment and learn more about their risk for pneumococcal pneumonia at *WhoPneu.com*.

Prevnar 13, a blockbuster for Pfizer, reached a whopping US $6.3 billion in 2015 sales. However, its sales are expected to decline in the next five years as more people get the vaccine and the audience size shrinks.

(Source: Adapted from articles: 1. Beth Snyder Bulik, Who Pneu? Pneumonia awareness campaign by Pfizer and American Lung Association, Fierce Pharma, November 9, 2016; 2. Who Pneu? A pneumococcal pneumonia awareness campaign, American Lung Association, September 30, 2015)

CASE

81

Drive4COPD: Take Action Today, Breathe Better Tomorrow!

DRIVE4COPD is America's single most massive awareness campaign for chronic obstructive pulmonary disease (COPD), the nation's fourth leading cause of death. The principal purpose of this landmark campaign, launched in February 2010, has been to raise awareness of COPD among people by helping them recognize the signs and symptoms of COPD and take action to see if they may be at risk and talk to their healthcare professionals.

What is remarkable about the DRIVE4COPD campaign is the wide spectrum of its participants. Leading health, business, entertainment, and sports organizations embraced this campaign with a common goal of driving fundamental change in COPD awareness in the United States. A robust network of organizations, including the American Association of Respiratory Care, COPD Alliance, COPD Foundation, Country Music Association, US COPD Coalition, and funding sponsor Boehringer Ingelheim Pharmaceuticals drove this massive campaign. What is more, DRIVE4COPD is the official initiative of NASCAR® (National Association for Stock Car Auto Racing).

Pinwheel is the campaign's icon, which symbolizes the movement and momentum of DRIVE4COPD. Because the effort of DRIVE4COPD is racing to find people who may be at risk and driving to change the way people think about COPD. Besides, the pinwheel icon also has relevance to the disease as an emblem of a person's ability to breathe, as people with COPD may struggle to get enough air to make a pinwheel spin.

Race for the Missing Millions with COPD

While Danica Patrick is readying the members of the DRIVE4COPD race team — who have close family members touched by COPD — to drive 6,000 miles across the country in four days in the Race for the Missing Millions, the primary purpose of the race is to call on the people, millions of them to complete a five-question screener to see if they are at risk for COPD. It is to find the missing millions with COPD.

The race started on February 13, 2010, after Patty Loveless debuted the song she composed in memory of her sister, who died at a young age from emphysema, to inspire others with COPD to take action to continue to live their life. After the song, Patty Loveless joined her fellow DRIVE4COPD race team members for a ceremonial drive on the track. The celebrity drivers took off after that on four routes across the country, making pitstops in 14 cities to screen as many Americans as possible to see if they were at risk for COPD.

COPD Population Screener®

Most people believe their symptoms, such as shortness of breath, are just typical signs of aging, so they are not diagnosed until they have already lost half of their lung function, according to Dr. Charles D. Connor, president and CEO of the American Lung Association. Dr. Connor further said: *It is important to recognize symptoms and see a doctor early before the lungs become severely damaged. We believe DRIVE4COPD will encourage people to take action regarding this progressive disease*.

COPD includes chronic bronchitis, emphysema, or both. It is a progressive disease that causes irreversible lung damage, so early diagnosis and management are critical to helping patients breathe better. DRIVE4COPD campaign offers a brief five-question screener, as it is a mostly unrecognized disease. The five-question validated COPD population screener®, culled from an extensive 52-question initial survey, was found to be most likely to predict COPD. Here are the five questions:

1. During the past four weeks, how often did you feel short of breath?
2. Did you cough up any stuff, such as mucus or phlegm?
3. Please select the answer that best describes you in the past 12 months. I do less than I used to because of my breathing problems.
4. Have you smoked at least 100 cigarettes in your entire life?
5. How old are you?

The survey questionnaire has instructions for participants and healthcare professionals, along with a scoring guide.

Celebrity Ambassadors Drive Engagement

The campaign has engaged a strong network of celebrity ambassadors to help drive national attention to the disease. The celebrity ambassadors list of the 2010 DRIVE4COPD campaign looks like a list of who's who in the United States. Consider these names, for example — Billy Ray Cyrus, multi-platform recording artist, and television star; Patty Loveless, Grammy-Award winning country music star; Olympic gold medalist Bruce Jenner; former pro-football great Michael Strahan; Danica Patrick, GoDaddy, and NASCAR® National Series™ driver. In addition, each of these ambassadors had a personal story of a loved one who struggled with COPD. Throughout the year, the ambassadors reach audiences across the country through appearances, media interviews, and public service announcements, informing, educating, and encouraging the public to learn about their risk of the disease.

Speaking about the campaign, Danica Patrick, whose grandmother suffered from emphysema, one of the two-forms of COPD, said: *I remember my grandma struggled to breathe and how it limited her life. So that is why our goal is to get at least one million people to take the five-question screener to find out if they are at risk for COPD and talk to their doctor. Because the sooner you act, you can get on the road to breathing better.*

Key Initiatives

How does DRIVE4COPD work to put brakes on COPD to stop in its tracks? What are the key initiatives of the campaign? The campaign has been working through diverse channels, including art, music, sports, live events, and online activities, to expand its reach and increase its engagement with its target audience. Here are some of the key initiatives

1. The campaign has partnered with internationally renowned artist and sculptor Michale Kalish to create *24M: the DRIVE4COPD Monument*. Inspired by the iconic pinwheel, 24M is a visual representation of the impact of COPD in the United States to encourage the public to take action to see if they may be at risk. Kalish used 2,400 license plates to construct the 24 large-scale pinwheels, each standing between eight to fourteen feet tall with a six-foot span. The number of license plates from each of the 50 states reflects the percentage of that state's population affected by COPD. Visitors can walk through the monument following a self-guided tour to learn about its creation, the impact of COPD, and the DRIVE4COPD campaign. The general public can access tour dates and locations, an exclusive video of Kalish's creating 24M, a downloadable walking tour script, and an audio tour by visiting DRIVE4COPD.com or using the QR or Quick Response codes found at the 24M display.
2. DRIVE4COPD designated November 4 as a one-day wakeup call to inform the American public about the importance of early COPD screening and detection called The Great American Screen-off. On this day, people 35 years of age and older are

encouraged to take the COPD Population Screener™ in their healthcare professional's office or online at DRIVE4COPD.com to know their risk for COPD. Also, the general public can lend their support for COPD awareness and DRIVE4COPD by wearing the color orange on this day.

3. Online, DRIVE4COPD.com provides information about COPD and highlights campaign news and happenings. Besides, people can find through this website upcoming events, 24M tour dates, and pitstop locations where DRIVE4COPD will be taking its message on the road to bring education and screening opportunities directly to communities from coast to coast. DRIVE4COPD is also on Facebook, Twitter, Flickr, and YouTube, where people can track COPD news and COPD updates.
4. People 35 years of age and older can take the COPD Population Screener and discuss the results with their healthcare professionals if they are at risk. Those younger than 35 can engage by making the Pinwheel Promise, a pledge to learn about COPD, and recognize the importance of early screening by encouraging friends and loved ones to take a screener to determine their risk.
5. For healthcare professionals, DRIVE4COPD offers an HCP-focused website available at DRIVE4COPD.com/HCP. On the site, doctors and healthcare professionals may access unique resources, including a customizable toolkit with campaign assets and tailored screening materials.
6. The campaign partners, who embrace the campaign's mission as their own, drive the success of the DRIVE4COPD effort. DRIVE4COPD has made it convenient to host its screening events and raise COPD awareness for its partners from diverse fields such as sports, art, entertainment, music, healthcare, and business. The campaign provides customized assets to all its partner organizations.

Committed Partners

The most important reason for the great, continued success of the DRIVE4COPD campaign is the commitment of its partners. All partners owned the same mission: to find Americans at risk for COPD and encourage them to take action today so that they can breathe better tomorrow. Here is what Steve Phelps, senior vice president, and chief marketing officer of NASCAR, said about the campaign: T*his is an important cause for NASCAR, and we are committed to helping our fans and millions of Americans who have COPD by increasing public understanding of the disease. We are thrilled that this campaign has become the official health initiative of NASCAR, making its first pitstop during the popular Dayton Weekend and coming to many other races during the season*.

J. Martin Carroll, president, and CEO, of Boehringer Ingelheim USA, had the final word on the campaign when he said: *As a leader in respiratory health and a company committed to improving the lives of patients and their families, we are proud to be the founding sponsor for this important awareness initiative and to be collaborating with ambassadors and organizations who share our goal of shining a much-needed spotlight on COPD. Someone dies from COPD every four minutes, yet most Americans still don't know what COPD is. We are committed to helping people learn about their risks, recognize early symptoms, and encourage them to take action today so that they can breathe better tomorrow*.

(Source: 1. DRIVE4COPD: Take action today. Breath better tomorrow. DRIVE4COPD.com, PDF, 2. News provided by Boehringer Ingelheim Inc., DRIVE4COPD sheds light on the nation's 4th leading killer through unprecedented public health initiative, CISION PR Newswire, February 5, 2010)

CASE

82

Breast Cancer Campaign Using Lemons goes Viral!

A campaign using lemons to teach women to recognize breast cancer symptoms and to break the taboos of discussing the condition has gone viral and has been used to educate people around the world. The charity, Worldwide Breast Cancer has created a remarkable campaign, Know Your Lemons, that uses easily understandable visuals — altered pictures of lemons to illustrate 12 key changes in the breasts that could indicate the presence of breast cancer.

#KnowYourLemons campaign was the brainchild of a young designer, Corrine Ellsworth Beaumont, who lost both her grandmothers to the disease. She used lemons to depict breast changes that could be cancer. The campaign has gone so viral that over 200 million women in 2017 viewed the illustrations of the changes in lemons depicting symptoms of breast cancer. The social media statistics, too, are very impressive. The image that illustrates breast changes has been viewed more than three million times on Facebook and has been shared more than 40,000 times. Also, the campaign has been featured by media outlets worldwide. Dr. Beaumont did not expect the campaign to go viral in such a huge way. She was simply hoping that it would reach as many women as possible.

The Secret of Success

But, what is the secret of the campaign's phenomenal success in reaching so many people? Dr. Beaumont, who founded the charity

— Worldwide Breast Cancer and created the visual campaign #KnowYourLemons, believes visuals rather than reams of text can harness the power of modern design principles. Also, the visuals in the campaign cut through taboo and discomfort in talking about breasts and discussing the subject of cancer with friends, family, and even doctors. The visuals in the campaign are friendly and easily approachable, and patients can look at them. When they see lemons, they interpret them as breasts. The campaign has become so popular and widespread because it is not overt, and people understand in seconds without having to combat all those hurdles of taboos and fear and large amounts of text.

Significant Effort behind the Campaign

Dr. Beaumont began working on the #KnowYourLemons campaign more than fifteen years ago, after the death of both of her grandmothers from breast cancer. Those deaths prompted a need to know more about the disease. So Dr. Beaumont was in her twenties when she went to a cancer library and asked them these basic questions:

- What do I need to know about breast cancer?
- Am I at risk?
- When do I start getting scanned?
- And what does a lump feel like?
- What should I be looking for when it comes to breast cancer?

The person working at the library could not answer any of these questions. Further, she said: *I don't know what to tell you because no one your age comes here.* Dr. Beaumont later read all leaflets and browsed through all the websites she could find and was left with more questions than answers. Finally, she said: *There wasn't one resource that said, Corrine, this is everything you need to know right now as a woman in her early 20s. So I thought the design could make a difference here. And the seeds for #KnowYourLemons were sown then.*

Dr. Beaumont initially began working on the visuals as part of her master's degree project and then for her Ph.D. Since then, the visuals have gone through many iterations. They have been tested on hundreds of patients and are being refined continuously. She always puts herself into the patient's shoes to see the problems from their perspective. She also talks to healthcare practitioners and those involved, like caregivers, who understand the issues and then develop visual solutions based on their needs.

The visuals of the campaign and the leaflets have been translated into 16 languages. However, Dr. Beaumont is looking forward to more donations to expand the campaign into more languages and develop more materials to extend the campaign's reach.

Breast Cancer Prevalence

Breast cancer is top cancer in women worldwide and is increasing, particularly in developing countries where the majority of cases are diagnosed in late stages. Also, one in 8 women, or 12 percent, will develop invasive breast cancer throughout their lifetime. In 2015 alone, over 570,000 women died of breast cancer globally. As of January 2019, there are more than 3.1 million women with a history of breast cancer in the US, according to a research estimate.

Dr. Beaumont explained when she spoke to MedScape Medical News that a lot of research has shown that people recall as little as 14 percent of what they are told during consultations, even for non-life threatening conditions. Furthermore, she said that a substantial proportion of patients have low health literacy, and many feel uncomfortable talking about breast cancer even with their friends and family.

Although breast cancer is more common in older people, it is a good idea to get to know your breasts and what is normal for you because early diagnosis increases the chances of survival significantly.

Later, Worldwide Breast Cancer developed a Know Your Lemons mobile app for breast health. The following press release explains the purpose and how the app offers significant help to the millions of women who are likely to face the challenges of breast cancer.

Know Your Lemons Mobile App

Worldwide Breast Cancer enlisted the help of DogTown Media, a mobile app development company, to develop a mobile app for their 2017 award-winning *Know Your Lemons* campaign to optimize its impact and reach as many women as possible worldwide. The result is *Know Your Lemons*, a versatile tool that expands on the original campaign with humorous video and audio guides to do self-exams. The app was released on March 8, world women's day in 2019.

The *Know Your Lemons* app is backed by a decade of research and has been designed to address major gaps in breast health communication. Despite many awareness campaigns in the past, a 2017 survey by the Avon Foundation for Women among 19,000 women globally found, among other things, that:

- only 2 percent of women can recognize all the signs of breast cancer
- 42 percent of women don't feel confident in their ability to spot a change indicative of breast cancer

The new Key the *Know Your Lemons* mobile app addresses many gaps in the knowledge about breast health. Its key features are:

1. Education about the symptoms of breast cancer and the difference between healthy and unhealthy lumps found in the breast
2. Exam coaches such as Mona Lisa explains step-by-step how to self-exam in an entertaining and informative way.
3. Booking mammograms or screening appointments with local FDA-certified screening centers

4. Questions for users to ask clinicians or doctors at screening appointments, as well as advice on what (or not) to wear and how to prepare for different breast tests.

The *Know Your Lemons* app was made possible with support from Celgene, Avon Foundation for Women, and Genentech. The app is available for download on iTunes and Google Play under *Know Your Lemons.*

Dr. Beaumont's commitment to the cause of breast health resonates as she walks her talk. She explained the app's purpose clearly when she said: *Even though over 200 million people saw our 12 lemons image in 2017, we dream of empowering 2.2 billion women regardless of race, language or location, so they can know what to do to detect breast cancer better*.

(Source: Adapted from articles: 1. Liam Davenport, Breast cancer campaign based on Lemons goes viral, Medscape, January 19, 2017, 2. Social media campaigns: The good, the bad, and the sprinkled, PaloCreative, May 23, 2017, 3. Digital media client Worldwide Breast Cancer releases innovative breast health app, March 8, 2019, CISION PR Web: 4. Press Release, Know Your Lemons: Worldwide Breast Cancer releases new Know Your Lemons app because breast cancer awareness doesn't end October 31, KnowYourLemons.com)

CASE

83

Novo Nordisk Partners with Charles Kimball for its *Race with Insulin*!

Novo Nordisk, the Danish multinational pharmaceutical company and a leader in the diabetes therapeutic area, has built an enduring partnership of more than one hundred races and counting with IndyCar race driver, Charlie Kimball to promote education and raise awareness about diabetes. While every race car driver has sponsors, not every driver depends on his sponsor the way Charlie Kimball does: He has type1 diabetes and uses Novo Nordisk's meds daily. Another unique feature of this partnership is that not every sponsor gets the articulate marketing backup that Kimball provides.

Enduring Partnership

The enduring partnership that is going great even after 100 races of Novo Nordisk with Charlie Kimball began in 2009, two years after he was diagnosed with diabetes. Kimball was diagnosed with type1 diabetes in 2007 and started using Novo Nordisk's treatment — Tresiba (insulin degludec injection). A year later, in 2008, Kimball's endocrinologist thought the Pharma company might be interested in the young race car driver and introduced him to Novo Nordisk. Sarah Spielvogel, senior manager for diabetes brand communication at Novo Nordisk, said about their first meeting: *We hit it off from the get-go. After five minutes, we got the sense that he is very passionate about what he does.* So the company and Kimball struck a partnership in 2009, starting with the brand on his racing suit and a few speaking engagements.

Why sponsor sports car racing? Why the partnership with a race car driver? Entering into such a partnership is great, according to Sarah Spielvogel. While Novo Nordisk is a well-recognized leader in diabetes care, its insulin portfolio faces fierce competition. Besides, few US doctors at the time were prescribing a pre-filled insulin delivery device like Novo's Flexi-pen to patients with diabetes as an alternative to a vial and syringe, even though insulin delivery devices were globally used in as many as 85 percent of diabetes patients. Further research revealed that IndyCar fans are 23 percent more likely to have diabetes. While the reasons for such a statistic are unknown, Novo Nordisk knew that they were the right target audience, and the company needed to be smart as to how to send those messages and engage the audience.

Novo Nordisk first signed on as Kimball's primary car sponsor in 2011 under the Chip Ganassi Racing team. While the details of the deal are not public, Bloomberg estimated that the cost of a primary IndyCar sponsorship starts at $5 million to $ 9 million for the side pod, another $ 1 million to $2 million for the front wind, and $300,000 to $900,000 for the cockpit and tail.

What makes Kimball standout among many race car drivers who depend on sponsorships is he is as knowledgeable about marketing as he is about car mechanics and driving techniques. He worked to make sure Novo Nordisk became comfortable with him as a brand ambassador — and with the idea that motor car racing could be an effective marketing tool.

Kimball's commitment and dedication to car racing and diabetes awareness can be seen in what he told during an interview with Fierce Pharma: *I love racing. There is nowhere I feel more active than in a race car. Diabetes is along for the ride with me every time I climb into the cockpit. So diabetes, and talking about diabetes means I get to talk about racing too.*

Race with Insulin Campaign

Impressed with Kimball's combination of driving grit and genuine dedication to fans and diabetes awareness, Novo Nordisk expanded the partnership and rolled out the Race with Insulin campaign in 2013. That same year Kimball became the first driver with type1 diabetes to win a major IndyCar race. Later in 2016, Charlie Kimball became the first driver to have the same sponsor for 100 starts with the same team in the history of car racing.

Before launching the Race with Insulin, the communications team at Novo Nordisk set three main objectives for the campaign:

1. Increase visibility and share of voice for the Novo Nordisk portfolio of Insulin products
2. Motivate patients with diabetes to speak with their doctor about treatment with Novo Nordisk products
3. Position Novo Nordisk as a leader in diabetes care

The Race with Insulin campaign of Novo Nordisk has evolved from the earlier races. After racing in the IndyCar Light Series in 2009-10, Kimball ascended to the majors — the Izod IndyCar series in 2011. By then, Novo Nordisk's communication program was track tested. However, it required meticulous planning because messaging is everything in the communications business. Therefore, the focus has been on — what is it that Charlie will be communicating and why? It has been the basic purpose of its entire communication strategy from which the company has arrived at a three-step tactical plan:

1. *Media Relations*: This included coordinating trackside video and photo shoots for use with media, developing press materials, and conducting local, regional, and national media outreach.
2. *Social Media Engagement*: Novo Nordisk launched the first-ever pharmaceutical branded Twitter page in 2009 with its partnership with Charlie Kimball. @racewithinsulin would regularly share information about Kimball's partnership with Novo Nordisk and his use of products to help manage his

diabetes. Unlike some sporting celebrities, Kimball does all Twitter posts himself. He says: *It's important for fans to know that it is my voice, and there is no wizard behind the curtain*. As he tells, the mobility of Twitter gives him a way to interact with fans while he is at the track, posting about the weather conditions and when he is about to climb into the car. It's like pulling the curtain back on my life as a racing driver.

3. *Local Market Events*: Novo Nordisk secured direct-to-patient speaking opportunities at venues where patients actively seek information about diabetes management, including national conferences through its partnerships with the American Diabetes Association (ADA) and Taking Control of Your Diabetes. Also, Kimball would sign autographs and participate in meet-and-greets encouraging patients to work closely with their physician and not let diabetes stop them from pursuing their dreams, as a face-to-face platform is the most effective. These appearances also drive social media engagements. When the patients get home, they can send Kimball a tweet. Thus begins a long cycle of engagement between patients, Kimball, and the company, Novo Nordisk.

Campaign Results

The campaign results clearly show the tactical plan's success on all parameters — media relations, social media, and awareness and engagement.

1. *Media Relations*: Race with Insulin generated more than 393 million media impressions; 306 original placements, including two with service stories (Associated Press); 47 print, including Los Angeles Times, USA Today, Diabetic Living, and Today's Dietician; 106 TV and Radio and 306 online placements.
2. *Social Media*: The Twitter page @racewithinsulin has increased its number of followers by 75 percent from January to December 2011. There were 2,418 followers in January 2012.
3. *Awareness and Engagement*: Kimball directly engaged more than 42,000 patients with his story at 15 diabetes conferences. Preliminary research indicated a correlation between engagement (branded PR) and an uptick in sales in two key markets.

4. *Position Novo Nordisk as a Leader In Diabetes Area*: Kimball's appearances at 33 local market events further increased brand and company visibility to patients and key opinion leaders (KOLs). Based on feedback from the sales force, these visits created partnership opportunities among key stakeholders.

Lessons Learned

The race with Insulin campaign offers a couple of valuable lessons for marketers. The first lesson is about the importance of collaboration with so many groups and partners playing a role in the campaign. Good communications from each one of them are critical. Messaging, therefore, is everything. The second lesson (not in terms of its importance, both the lessons are equally important) is that, just like driving a race car, nimbleness in PR is essential. You need to adapt your strategies to whatever happens next continually. Above all, your brand ambassador, in addition to his celebrity status, should walk the talk and be responsible and responsive. Like in the case of Kimball, he feels a connection between success on the track and his effectiveness as a diabetes awareness and product spokesman. He says: *I'm a competitor, and I want to win. But having this relationship with fans who have diabetes gives me a perspective that helps me. When I get out of the car, someone asks me to sign their insulin pen. It's a feeling that is very rewarding*.

Whether Charlie Kimball wins on the track in future races or not, as a role model for diabetes awareness, he is a winner and will always remain one!

(Source: Adapted from articles: 1. Scott Van Camp, Case Study: Passionate spokesman, nimble communications, and trackside tweets power winning IndyCar sponsorship, PR News, February 20, 2012, 2. Beth Snyder Bulik, Novo Nordisk, and Indy driver Charlie Kimball drive partnership to the 100-race mark and counting, Fierce Pharma, September 28, 2016)

CASE

84

A Feisty Social Media Campaign by Novartis: *Hey, MS, Take This*!

Novartis, the Swiss drug major, took a bold, spirited new tack to win in the multiple sclerosis (MS) therapeutic area with conversions to its oral MS drug, Gilenya (fingolimod). It's *Hey, MS, Take This!* The campaign showed patients sticking their tongues with Gilenya capsules on them to show their willingness to fight back against multiple sclerosis.

The campaign is aimed at younger people with multiple sclerosis, a chronic autoimmune disease with symptoms like fatigue, difficulty walking, and blurred or double vision. What is more, two-thirds of those with multiple sclerosis are women, and many are diagnosed when they are young, say between 25 to 44 years of age; a majority of these women patients use blogs, Facebook, Twitter, and YouTube to find information and to connect with fellow sufferers. That is why Novartis is targeting its campaign mainly to young women on channels where they are present and when they are present. *Hey, MS, Take This* was a multi-channel campaign with the channels being:

- National print outlets, including a half-dozen national news magazines like *People, Shape, and Self*, and the websites of Women's magazines
- An online video featuring on social media outlets

Novartis is using real patient stories, gleaned from about a dozen patients, on its website, gilenya.com, and in brochures and other marketing materials.

Multiple sclerosis strikes in the prime of life, and many patients use the web and social media to connect. Many are now being diagnosed in their 20's and 30's. Early treatment makes the most impact. That is why Novartis is targeting those people who are young and digitally savvy.

How did Novartis choose such a feisty theme as Hey, *MS, Take This*? The company's upbeat theme came from social listening and sentiment analysis. Novartis observed that the patients expressed on blogs and other social media where people said that this disease (MS) would not stop *me*. Those spirited words and the attitude to fight the disease gave the campaign a bolder tone. Hence *Hey, MS, Take This*!

Novartis tried to make this bold campaign significantly different from other pharmaceutical campaigns. As Mike Delvin, Creative Director of the campaign's ad agency, DraftFCB, part of the Interpublic Group, which interviewed multiple sclerosis patients, says: *The campaign,* Hey, MS, Take this *is all about attitude. There were many nuggets reflected in their voice and attitude and an outpouring about the impact Gilenya had on their lives. In addition, the agency has designed 60-second commercials and print ads for Novartis to get people thinking about their treatment choices*.

Novartis licensed Gilenya from Mitsubishi Tanabe Pharma in 1997, conducted clinical trials, and found that the drug was more effective than interferon treatments. Still, severe side effects included elevated liver enzymes, headache, diarrhea, and back pain. Novartis marketed this drug immediately on approval for oral treatment of multiple sclerosis from the US FDA on September 22, 2010. Initially, Novartis conducted a smaller marketing effort, with ads in magazines aimed at those with multiple sclerosis and a limited placement in national magazines. *Hey, MS, Take This* is the first significant and broad marketing campaign for Gilenya, which became a finalist in the 2014 Effie Prescription Healthcare DTC (Direct-to-consumer) category.

Featuring real patients has become a contemporary way to get patients to recognize their symptoms and to be more in control. However, pharmaceutical companies need to tread a fine line so that they are not seen as promoting their prescription drugs directly to the patients. They can only encourage patients to ask their doctor for a prescription for the drug.

Since its approval in September 2010, Gilenya achieved US $1.2 billion in 2012 sales. In 2012, the total market for multiple sclerosis was around the US $9 billion, with firms such as Bayer, Biogen, and Teva actively competing for a slice of the market.

Gilenya's *Hey, MS, Take This* campaign empowered young patients suffering from multiple sclerosis, who used phrases like — *No needles for me* and *Take this, you bully*, to show their defiant attitude towards the disease as they cope with it.

What can we Learn?

When you are the first oral medication for multiple sclerosis, it just sells itself, right? Wrong. The world will not beat a path to your door even if you have the best mousetrap to paraphrase Emerson. Market place, behavioral and business hurdles stood between Gilenya, the groundbreaking therapy, and the people hungry for it. What is the solution, then? How do you ensure that the drug reaches its potential in the marketplace? The solution was to tap the passion, frustration, and optimistic patients themselves. That's what Gilenya had done with its campaign. The *Hey, MS, Take This*! The campaign gave them an unprecedented platform for support. It allowed them to open up, shape, reflect, support, and shout. This approach significantly helped Gilenya to change their behaviors.

Hey, MS, Take This broke the barriers. The results speak for themselves. Gilenya requests jumped 21 percent, and being a peer-recommended brand jumped 82 percent.

Gilenya's 2016 sales grew by 14 percent to US $3.1 billion.

(Source: Adapted from articles: 1. Elizabeth Olson, An MS-drug takes a feisty approach aimed at younger patients, The New York Times, April 3, 2013, 2. Gilenya: Hey, MS, Take This! Campaign, 2014 finalist Healthcare— Rx-Consumer/DTC, effie.org)

CASE

85

Flonase's *#FallOfFame* Among the AdWeek's Top Ten Healthcare Brand Geniuses!

There is more to allergies than meets the eye. Allergies are more than runny noses, watering eyes, and skin rashes and are also a severe blow to a country's economy. In the US, for example, costs associated with allergies, including doctor visits, medication, and other expenses, exceed $18 billion each year, according to the CDC (Centers for Disease Control and Prevention). In addition, according to the Asthma and Allergy Foundation of America, 1 in 5 suffer from allergies in the US, and they miss roughly 6 million work or school days each year.

Flonase Sensimist 24 HR Allergy Relief OTC Launch

GlaxoSmithKline (GSK) has been marketing Flonase (fluticasone propionate) Allergy Relief nasal spray over-the-counter (OTC) since February 2015. The company got FDA approval for Flonase Sensimist 24-Hour Allergy Relief in August 2016 and launched it in February 2017. GSK built a coordinated multichannel marketing campaign for its Flonase Sensimist 24 Allergy Relief, spanning print, TV, and social media channels such as Instagram, Twitter, Facebook, Twitter, and Vine. Here are the critical elements of GSK's Flonase campaign — #Fall of Fame.

1. The company used TV to introduce people to the brand as it provided a wide reach to the most general audience.

2. GSK used the digital route to explain more about how the product worked and build a platform for conversations with the customers.
3. The company listened to its customers as they wanted to drive more organic searches. Their research gave them critical insights into what allergy sufferers were looking for. It revealed that the allergy sufferers were not getting relief with their current allergy meds and did not like missing out from activities when allergies were triggered. This simple yet powerful insight helped GSK to arrive at the perfect tagline that encourages allergy sufferers — Be Greater Than Allergies!
4. One of the most significant features of GlaxoSmithKline's Flonase Sensimist OTC launch was that the company used Instagram for its campaign. Using Instagram for a campaign was not only the first for GSK but also the first time that any pharmaceutical company had used the Instagram channel to engage their audience.
5. Besides, GSK roped in Derek Hough, the Emmy-award winner and New York Times best-selling author, and six-time champion in franchise history of the hit ABC show, *Dancing with the Stars,* to help raise the awareness of the distressing effects of allergies.
6. In spring 2016, Flonase worked with a YouTube-famous family, the *Eh Bees*, to go on an allergy road trip to 10 of the worst cities for allergy sufferers. The *Eh Bee* family is the funniest family on social media. With papa bee and mama bee at the helm, they create family-friendly content across all platforms. The *Eh Bee* family has amassed a loyal following of over 18 million followers and over 300 million views per month worldwide. A Follow-the-journey button takes you to the road trip details and trip itinerary.

Flonase Campaign on Instagram — Fall of Fame

GlaxoSmithKline launched its first online content for Flonase Sensimist with Instagram used six, and it was right the first time! It was an immense success. The company used six Instagram photographers with allergies who snapped photos along 24-hour journeys outdoors — hay fields, dandelion patches, and hanging out with pets. These photographs served as visual confirmation that Flonase worked with them round-the-clock, fueling the 24 Hours of Being Greater campaign. GSK, to create and sustain interest, came with a celebrity dog, Doug the Pug, and asked people to share their photos on Instagram with the hashtag #Fall of fame. Here is one such invite:

When you're greater than your fall allergies with Flonase Allergy Relief, you can make it to the Fall of Fame. Show us photos and videos of you and your pet at your best — outside or inside thoroughly enjoying what Fall has to offer — and you may have one of many $250 gift cards or the $5,000 grand prize.

Think your pet is Fall of Fame worthy?

Check out the competition. Upload your photo and tweet — I just entered my best buddy into the @FlonasePet #Fall of Fame #Contest

The response has been very good, with about 6,000 people sharing their photos on social media channels. So what made GSK's social media campaign so successful? In a highly regulated industry such as pharmaceuticals, humanizing Flonase and leveraging customers' experiences made GSK's social campaign a great success. GSK, through its well-coordinated multi-channel social media marketing strategy, was able to achieve two objectives —build awareness, and start a convincing conversation with potential users.

Finally, in a very personal business, like healthcare, which touches many powerful core human emotions, it is essential to understand your current customer base and tap into the emotions they already have instead of guessing for every media campaign. That is what GlaxoSmithKline did and reaped rich rewards. Flonase has generated sales of $100 million in the first sixteen weeks after its launch and captured a 10 percent market share in the first year of launch in a highly competitive and saturated market space such as allergy relief.

(Source: Adapted from articles: 1. Kim Radefeld, Healthcare: Doug the Pug does digital right. Does your consumer healthcare brand? Paragon, August 30, 2017; 2. Matthew Libassi, Dancing with the Stars Derek Hough reveals the one thing that affects his performance, Fox Business, March 24, 2017)

CASE

86

Show Stopper Exposes Taboo in Astellas' *A Matter of Urgency* Campaign!

Nearly one in five people in the UK over 40 have an overactive bladder (OAB) and live with the urgent need to go to the toilet. However, many feel too embarrassed to talk about it, believe nothing can be done, and consider it an inevitable part of aging.

Astellas Pharmaceuticals, a Japanese multinational Pharma company that manufactures medicines for the treatment of overactive bladder (OAB), wanted to destigmatize and raise awareness among people about the condition and educate them about the treatment options available. Therefore, the company asked Red Door Communications (RDC), a specialist consultancy dedicated to developing and managing healthcare communication programs to devise an educational program to encourage people with OAB to ask their GP (General Practitioner) for advice. The stigma attached to bladder problems has made it a taboo topic; therefore, the campaign needed to encourage them to set aside their embarrassment, speak up about OAB and seek help.

A Matter of Urgency Campaign

Red Door Communications developed a campaign theme — *A Matter of Urgency*, to reflect the main symptom of overactive bladder (OAB) — the urgent need to go to the toilet. It was decided to engage with people by generating intrigue at Hampton Court Palace Flower Show, the largest flower show in the world, to overcome the media taboo and embarrassment associated with OAB, supported by printed materials and the privacy of online information.

Award-winning designer Jill Foxley designed a bright pink tap magically suspended three meters high in the air — incorporated the waterworks theme and secured significant media attention and interest from national television to online gardener's blogs. The giant pink tap became one of the iconic images of the 2010 Hampton Court Flower Show. It got people talking about their waterworks and removed the taboo associated with bladder problems.

The agency secured TV doctors — Dr. Christian Jessen and Dr. Dawn Harper, the presenters of Channel Four's program Embarrassing Bodies, to spearhead the A Matter of Urgency campaign. They developed a multichannel campaign with many elements to support. Here are some of the more important aspects of the campaign:

- Patient information leaflets
- The microsite is a home to the campaign, amatterofurgency.co.uk, offering further information
- A key message carousel
- A downloadable patient leaflet, and
- Video clips of Dr. Christian Jessen and Dr. Dawn Harper explaining OAB treatment options

Campaign Results

The results of the campaign were quite impressive. The following results illustrate how successful the campaign has been.

- 41,000 leaflets distributed
- 28 pieces of UK media coverage with a total circulation of over 32.8 million
- Twitter and Facebook posts exceeded 30,000
- The microsite had more than 1,180 unique visitors
- Google Analytics showed that traffic to the site peaked as a result of the traditional media coverage and Twitter posts

Client's Perspective

Astellas Pharma was quite happy with the success of the campaign. Here is what Claire Holman, marketing manager at Astellas Pharma, said about the campaign: It was a fantastic experience to witness *A Matter of Urgency* garden generate such a high level of public interest – both from the media exposure that Red Door Communications secured and from the crowds that gathered ten people deep at the garden itself. Our ultimate goal was to encourage people to take action, and we have already seen an increase in patients asking for help and finding out more from the *A Matter of Urgency* website. The team did a great job of tying our campaign message with creativity, ensuring patients could articulate their symptoms of urgency in a meaningful way when they did present, as OAB can be challenging to describe.

(Source: Adapted from the article: Claire Holman, Marketing Manager, Astellas Pharma, Case Study: Show stopper exposes taboo: Overcoming the media embarrassment associated with OAB, PMLiVE, June 1, 2011)

CASE

87

GSK Launches *What's Your Why?* Campaign to Encourage Quit Smoking!

GlaxoSmithKline (GSK) Consumer Healthcare is a leading player in the smoking cessation therapy area with brands such as Nicorette® range and Nicoderm® (nicotine transdermal). The company wanted to raise awareness about the importance of quitting smoking and how they can do it.

The company understands smokers don't need to be told why they should quit — they already know Why. So, in December 2014, GSK launched a branded campaign, *What is Your Why?* To hear every single one the whys from the smokers who want to quit. The campaign kicked off in New York City with Mark Ballas, a professional ballroom dancer on the ABC program, *Dancing with the Stars*, and a former smoker. Having quit smoking successfully with Nicoderm CQ a year before, Ballas shared his *Why* with top-tier reporters and on social media.

Building on this momentum, in May 2015, just before one of the most significant smoking awareness days, GlaxoSmithKline created the first-ever, mid-year branded campaign of its smoking cessation-aiding brands' activation to reach the heights of quitting smoking. The *What's Your Why* smoke swap was held in Time Square, New York, and encouraged smokers to share their *Whys* in exchange for free quit-smoking resources. In addition, Ballas and his mother, Shirley, a former 40-year smoker who quit smoking with Nicorette, spoke to national media about their Whys, Quit-Support and performed a Quit-Step dance.

Later in September 2015, the campaign sparked conversations and encouraged smokers to turn September into SELFtember, a time for smokers to begin their smoke-free journey. In addition, mark Ballas interviewed with top entertainment press about quitting and encouraged Los Angeles residents to attend What's Your Why Smoke-Swap in Santa Monica.

Besides, the campaign's traditional in-store and direct outreach efforts invited quitters to visit the brands on Facebook and Twitter to share their Why stories. nicorette.com, nicoderm.com, and the unique GSK smoking cessation destination quit.com provided a home for a selection of Why stories while directing quitters to helpful resources.

MyQuit.com Resources

GlaxoSmithKline created a dedicated website, www.quit.com for the campaign. The website offers many useful resources for those who want to quit smoking. Here are some of those important resources.

- What is Your Why?
  - Plan Your Quit
  - Quit Advice
  - Support Hub
  - FAQs
  - Celebrating over 20 years of helping smokers quit with a badge that says Fighting Smoking Over 20 Years — Nicorette® and Nicoderm® CQ
  - How smoking affects you
  - Inspiring stories from quitters
  - Personalize your Quit with the My Quit Board
  - Get Your Coupon
  - Cravings can be tough — You are tougher! Get tips on how to control cravings.

- Join My Quit. Stay motivated with a support program that delivers advice, tips, coupons, and more — straight into the box.
- What's Your Why takes you to a page that details the effects of smoking on your body
  - Smoking and your immune system
  - Smoking and your bones
  - Smoking and your heart
  - Smoking and your lungs
  - Smoking and your eyesight
  - Cigarettes and cancer
- Why Are You quitting smoking? The key to a successful quit is to have a reason. A personal, compelling reason to want to quit smoking can help fuel your determination to realize a smoke-free life.

My Quit App

The road to quitting smoking is different for everyone, but research shows you are more likely to succeed with a support program. GlaxoSmithKline launched a mobile app. My Quit for iOS and Android platforms is a support program for all who want to quit smoking. The app has exciting and useful features such as:

- Track your cravings
- Support, advice, and tips from successful quitters
- Get rewards and savings
- Find your inspiration
- See how much your quitting is saving you
- Customize your quit
- Celebrate every cigarette you don't smoke
- Get the right support when you need it
- Personalize your dashboard

- Sophisticated data charts
- Works with your nicotine replacement therapy
- Log slip-ups
- See your progress

Effective Engagement

The What is Your Why? The campaign is a classic example of how to engage your audience effectively. The effectiveness can be seen when you look at what the campaign has achieved. Here are some indicators (January 2016) of the campaign's successful engagement:

- A 54 percent increase in fans for Nicorette's Facebook page
- A 107 percent increase for Nicorette and Nicoderm CQ combined with the Twitter following
- 71,000 Why stories shared

Key Lessons

1. *Every quitter's journey is unique*. Treat it as such. GlaxoSmithKline clearly understood that every quitter faces his challenge and has a unique way of celebrating his victories. Although there are some shared experiences, quitting can often feel tougher when the quitter feels no one understands or appreciates his struggle.
2. *Those who want to quit (your target audience) need not be educated on the health risks associated with smoking*. They all are aware of health warnings. They have been pressed by their doctors, friends, and families. Still, many smoking cessation products focus on telling smokers why they should quit. GSK has got this insight and decided it was time to ask them — instead of telling their Whys — their motivation for quitting. This fresh and differentiated approach drove a shift in thinking for Nicorette and Nicoderm CQ, putting the quitter at the center of the strategy and allowing the brand to make a more personal and emotional connection with all smokers.

3. *We need a shift in conversations from rational to emotional to make a difference*. GSK knew its job was to inspire and support smokers who want to quit while providing an effective method of quitting. They had an opportunity to create a point of difference for their brands by shifting the beginning of the conversations from the rational to the emotional side of their journey.
4. *User-generated content, when authentic, enhances credibility, engagement, and conversion*. Realizing this, GlaxoSmithKline drove quitters' engagement with the campaign by creating authentic, user-submitted content and highlighting some of it in official branded communication. The company included the user-generated content in a series of interviews that showcased the Why of specially selected quitters. The stories and voices of fellow quitters' What is Your Why created a supportive online community and earned greater credibility for the brands. The brands became trusted friends and advisors.

GlaxoSmithKline (GSK) has creatively elevated quitting smoking conversation using its game-changing step of emotion in differentiating its smoking cessation brands — Nicorette and Nicoderm CQ and made them trusted friends and advisors of the quitters.

(Source: Adapted from articles: 1. Alyssa Leys, What's Your Why? Campaign: GSK Consumer Healthcare, Innovators 2015: Strategies, PM 360, December15 2015; 2. Content from the website, www.quit.com; 3. What's your why? Nicorette & Nicoderm CQ Create emotional connections to drive brand engagement, Epsilon Marketing, January 15, 2016, 4. My Quit App features from Apple App Stores)

CASE

88

What a Dragon can Teach us about ADHD!

Attention-deficit hyperactivity disorder (ADHD) affects around 2 to 5 percent of school children in the UK, according to research estimates. ADHD is typically associated with inattentiveness, hyperactivity, and impulsiveness and can be coupled with sleep and anxiety disorders. Despite being a common condition, ADHD remains somewhat misunderstood as to its nature and effects on children.

Patients and healthcare providers find it challenging to discuss ADHD. How do you describe a child with ADHD? The current information used by doctors in explaining the condition continues to be a difficult task. Although there are many patient information brochures and leaflets to explain symptoms and treatment to some degree, there is a problem. Children with ADHD know they are different. For a child of six or seven, this is a huge mountain to climb. Parents and teachers, too, find it a difficult path to tread on. For both, there was no relevant support on resources readily available. They are all shrouded in medical terminology and not in a format and language familiar to a child of 6 or 7.

Shire Pharmaceuticals AG, a global leader in ADHD treatment, wanted to live up to its company mission of being a truly patient-centric organization. So the company approached the problem differently. Shire Pharmaceuticals stripped away the medicalized, rational world perspective of ADHD in a way that is identifiable to a child. The company teamed up with McCann Manchester, the largest and the most successful integrated marketing communications company in the UK, to develop a communication strategy that resonates with children with ADHD in a humanized way.

McCann Manchester created something that humanized ADHD. A campaign called — The Trouble with Dragons. Speaking about their campaign, Sarah Fleming, senior account director and part of the health and wellbeing team at McCann Manchester, said: *We created something that allowed a child to explore the condition and how it affected them in a way that was relevant to their world and way of thinking.* The team at the agency did not want to stick to a traditional campaign. They wanted to do something different. They wanted to put a face to ADHD because a face on ADHD makes it recognizable and easier to understand, something that you can humanly relate to.

Initially, the team devised a printed storybook featuring characters Olly and Red — two protagonists in a tale entitled *The Trouble with Dragons*, which described a young boy's struggle with ADHD. Olly is the child affected, and Red, a dragon, personifies Olly's condition, acting out the behaviors and challenges faced by a child with ADHD. The book takes the reader through specific scenarios that children with ADHD find particularly difficult, such as getting dressed in the morning or sitting still in a class. Development of *The Trouble with Dragons* storybook included input from professionals in the education sector and children.

Multichannel Campaign

Shire Pharmaceuticals and McCann Manchester decided to take *The Trouble with Dragons* campaign further from the print medium. They had gone multichannel complete with an app and awareness efforts like a healthcare professional-targeted email campaign. They had developed promotional materials such as posters for doctors' clinics and coloring sheets and stickers around the campaign theme to educate and engage children with ADHD in the clinics.

The Trouble with Dragons App

The Trouble with Dragons storybook is made into an interactive mobile app enhanced with short games and additional functionality to further its use in children with ADHD. The agency has carefully considered short and focused tasks as they help to occupy the user while they learn about their condition. It also gives the child a rewarding sense of completing the game, meaning they are more likely to remember what they achieved.

The Trouble with Dragons interactive app is mainly created to help young children diagnosed with ADHD understand a little more about their condition.

Delivering Value

The Trouble with Dragons mobile app has been appreciated by parents, teachers, and doctors. Many healthcare professionals (HCPs) felt that the app delivered a truly valuable experience — not only to their patients but to doctors themselves when discussing ADHD with a parent or family. Digital technology has once again proved its ability to deliver value in therapeutic management and as a better patient educational resource.

The Trouble with Dragons program achieved great success. It has been translated into ten languages and distributed to physicians, teachers, parents, and children with ADHD. In addition, it has gone on to win several healthcare industry awards.

The Trouble with Dragons campaign won a *gold* at the PM Society Digital Award in the multichannel campaign category in 2016 and a bronze in the digital patient initiatives category. It was also a finalist in the innovation category.

(Source: Adapted from articles: Marco Ricci, What can a dragon teach us about ADHD, Pharmaphorum, May 31, 2017)

CASE

89

Pfizer takes Counterfeit Medications Head-on with its *Get Real, Get Prescription* Campaign!

Counterfeit prescription drugs have been a big menace for the pharmaceutical industry for many years. Counterfeit drugs pose a significant threat to public health. The World Health Organization (WHO) estimates that 10 percent of all medicines available worldwide are counterfeit. For the counterfeiters manufacturing and selling fake medicines, the rewards are high, and the risks are low. In Europe, customs and border police had discovered unprecedented quantities of counterfeit medicines — over 4 million items in 2007. However, many people remain unaware of the dangers of fake medicines, and large numbers of people, particularly men, continue to fuel the multi-million-pound counterfeit medicines business.

Counterfeiters have heavily targeted Pfizer's medicines over the years. Fake versions of popular drugs like Viagra have become big business for organized crime as they are probably more than 2,000 times more profitable than dealing in hard drugs.

Speaking on counterfeit medicines, Jim Thompson, founder of the European Alliance for Access to Safe Medicines, said that the prospects of high profits are attracting criminals to the fake Viagra market. He also said: *You can buy a kilo of sildenafil, the active ingredient of Viagra, on a website for about £33 and make a lot of tablets from it. According to a Pfizer report, one in ten men has admitted to buying drugs over the Internet without a prescription, and one of the most popular drugs purchased online is Viagra of Pfizer.*

Pfizer, as a company bearing the brunt of counterfeit versions of its drugs to a large extent, has worked extensively with regulators, law enforcement authorities, and healthcare professionals to stem the tide. Besides, Pfizer decided to launch an unprecedented direct-to-consumer (DTC) type of campaign to alert the public to the risks and raise their awareness of the consequences of buying medicines without a prescription and from illegal websites. The company knew it needed the highest level of support from all key stakeholders and the creative execution of a strategy that would allow a public health message to cut through the consumer space.

Pfizer planned very meticulously a multichannel campaign detailing every step of the process to take the counterfeit drug menace head-on.

1. As a first step, the company measured the extent of the problem and tried to understand why people were reluctant to engage with their healthcare professionals and buy their medicines online without a prescription. The firm's research showed that a tenth of the men had purchased a prescription-only medicine without a prescription. Fifty percent of these were men buying online, of which nearly one-third saw this behavior as having a low or neutral risk.
2. Armed with this insight into why people buy prescription medicines from illicit sources, Pfizer developed their research study into a detailed report entitled, Cracking Counterfeit with a foreword by respected media medic Dr. Mark Porter. The company briefed all key stakeholders such as the Medicines and Healthcare Products Regulatory Agency (MHRA), The Patients Association, Men's Health Forum, and HEART UK on the report and got their approval and support on the media statement.
3. Dr. Mark Porter and Pfizer's medical director had led the Media Outreach program, which helped create public awareness messages.

4. Having laid the foundation and obtained the support for its ongoing public awareness activities to fight counterfeit medicines, Pfizer took the next step of launching a major campaign against counterfeit prescription drugs in the form of a creative consumer-facing roadshow — Cracking Counterfeit messages across the UK. Western-style snake oil salesmen, led by Professor Chancetaker, entertained crowds with sales pitches for miracle elixirs before delivering the patient safety message. It was supported by extensive regional media outreach, photo calls, and radio interviews in hosting cities.
5. The logical next step after delivering the patient safety messages was to influence people to change their behavior of buying medicines without prescriptions from illegal websites. Pfizer discussed various options with their agency, Red Health marketing communications consultancy, and decided on a hard-hitting cinema advertising that shocks the viewers into changing their online behavior of buying prescription drugs without prescriptions. Determined to take its behavior-changing advertisement to a new level, Pfizer conducted several workshops to evaluate previous shock campaigns, particularly those from the Department of Health. The company selected the advertising agency, Langland, to execute the campaign. Langland's uncompromising approach to executing the video led to the birth of the Ratty video. Pfizer discussed the advertising strategy with all their campaign partners and ensured that it upheld the ethical and regulatory principles. All the governmental, regulatory, and patient organizations supporting the Cracking Counterfeit program also signed up as campaign partners.
6. The *Get Real, Get A Prescription* video upped the volume and impact of the core messages shockingly. Langland used some of the latest cinematic techniques to create a graphic advert featuring a man pulling out a dead rat from his mouth to reflect that the fake medicines have been found to contain rat poison.

7. Pfizer arranged a premiere show of the *Get Real, Get A Prescription* at the Odeon cinema in London's Shaftesbury Avenue to bring existing and new stakeholders together for this groundbreaking launch. Over seventy attended from the government, law enforcement, regulatory, and health sectors. Key consumer and trade media, including advertising journalists, also participated. The launch became an excellent opportunity for all the stakeholders who briefed journalists on their perspectives.
9. Dr. Mark Peter chaired the launch presentation, and speakers from MHRA and The Patients Association discussed the campaign's significance. Pfizer presented an attention-grabbing media kit containing the news release, DVD, and other resources to maximize media coverage.
9. Besides, the company also developed an exclusive Independent Television Network (ITN) feature in the run-up to launch. In its science edition, Lawrence McGinty used the stakeholder event to put his final interviews in place.
10. What is more, a regional radio day, led by Men's Health Forum's Dr. Ian Banks, increased the penetration of messages at a local level. Also, The Metro carried a four-page advertorial with rat campaign images.

Digital Messages

Pfizer utilized a series of digital tools for its *Get Real, Get A Prescription* campaign. The first one was a campaign website, www.realdanger.co.uk, which provided an online destination for audiences beyond the cinema-goers. The company created online buzz and excitement with its advertising imagery, designed to create a shock. The company developed excellent material for its viral outreach and launched a YouTube channel. Also, the company engaged men's interest bloggers and social networks to drive interest online. Proactive linking with partner organizations viral outreach through social media included Facebook, Delicious, and Stumble upon. The *Get Real, Get A Prescription* campaign became a topic of online conversation, and the social media community widely distributed links to the advert.

Campaign Effectiveness

The *Get Real, Get A Prescription* campaign shocked a lot of people. Some people were so shocked that they complained to the Advertising Standards Association (ASA). However, in its ruling, the ASA said the advert did show images that some people might find offensive and distressing. Despite that, the agency thought the image of a rat being regurgitated was justified because it was designed to highlight an important issue, the dangers of which could result in damage to health or fatality. The campaign was very effective. Consider the following pointers that indicate the effectiveness of the campaign.

- The audience clearly understood the message and saw the elements of the campaign. Ninety-seven percent of men questioned leaving the cinemas confirmed that the campaign would impact their online behavior.
- Medicines regulators also felt the impact. The MHRA experienced a significant increase in calls to its counterfeit helpline immediately following the campaign's launch.
- *Get Real, Get A Prescription* became the number one education video, and over 49,000 people visited www.realdanger.co.uk 25 days after the launch. Traditional media coverage was equally extensive, with 93 articles creating 296 million opportunities to view.

One of the most important outcomes of the campaign was that it brought all the leading health stakeholders in the UK to take a unified position against counterfeit medicines. The resolve to root out the counterfeit trade of prescription drugs is reflected in what Mick Deats, Group Manager of Enforcement at MHRA, said: *The MHRA will not hesitate to take action against those who undermine public health. There is a considerable risk to the public from obtaining medicines through unregulated websites. If you feel your medicine may be counterfeit, contact the dedicated 24 Hour anti-counterfeiting hotline or counterfeit email enforcement at MHRA.*

Pfizer has every reason to be happy about the success of the *Get Real, Get A Prescription* campaign. The company's feelings about the campaign are best summed up by their medical director, Dr. David Gillen, when he said: *We are thrilled to be collaborating with the MHRA and leading UK patient organizations to tackle the industry-wide problem of counterfeit medicines. The time has come to issue a clear, unified message to people about the dangers of purchasing medicines from illicit and unregulated sources.*

(Source: Adapted from articles: 1. Pat Pearson, Hard to swallow: How to create an award-winning campaign that shocks audiences into a behavior change, PMLiVE, October 5, 2009; 2. Rebecca Smith, Medical Editor, Man coughs up the rat in advert warning over fake drugs, The Telegraph, January 15, 2009; 3. Nikki Sandison, Pfizer's dead rat ad campaign against fake Viagra to be investigated, Campaign, March 4, 2009, 4. Mike Huckman, Pfizer smells a rat in drug counterfeiting, CNBC, June 22, 2009)

CASE

90

Pfizer's *Get Old* Campaign Gets Youthful!

Since 2012, Pfizer has brought together community experts and leading partner organizations to share new insights on a diverse range of aging topics, from new research on chronic conditions to lifestyle changes that help people age well. Thus, *Get Old*, a multi-year campaign, was born.

Get Old is not just a campaign. It is a movement. Pfizer created *Get Old* to challenge people of all ages to rethink what it means to *Get Old* and take a more active role in their health. *Get Old* seeks to challenge the misperceptions of aging and drive new conversations that inspire people of all ages to take action on their health, explore new opportunities, and look forward to what's to come as they get older. The main aim of the *Get Old* campaign is to inspire individuals to take a new attitude towards aging and realize that getting old is not about an end but a beginning — a time to fulfill old dreams and make new ones a reality.

Pfizer partnered with Huge, a full-service digital agency headquartered in Brooklyn, New York, with offices worldwide, to disrupt perceptions about growing older as part of an effort to strengthen the company's brand image. The resultant multi-year campaign, *Get Old*, featured innovative ways to celebrate aging and wellness, engaging the general population and fostering cultural change within the organization.

The Inspiration for *Get Old*!

What inspired Pfizer to launch a campaign such as *Get Old*? There are at least three factors that inspired Pfizer to launch the campaign. Consider these, for example:

1. By 2030, one in five Americans will be 65 or older, and chronic conditions accompanying aging are rising. While chronic diseases are the leading cause of disability in the US, many could be prevented or delayed through simple lifestyle changes.
2. The 65+ population is projected to more than double in size to 98 million by 2060, with the 85+ population projected to almost triple from 6 million to 14.6 million in 2040.
3. For 165 years, Pfizer has been working to help people live longer, healthier lives. As one of the oldest pharmaceutical companies, it knows and respects the challenges and opportunities that experience can bring. Pfizer works with healthcare professionals, healthcare systems, insurers, and the government to help people age well.

Support from Many Groups

Several partnership organizations supported Pfizer's *Get Old* program. Here are some of the leading organizations that support the program:

1. Alliance for Aging Research
2. American Sexual Health Association
3. Caregiver Action Network
4. Generations United
5. Men's Health Network
6. National Alliance for Caregiving
7. Services and Advocacy for GLBT Elders
8. Society for Women's Health Research, and
9. Women Heart

Get Ready. Get Set. Get Old!

In June 2015, Pfizer updated its *Get Old* campaign with a creative video and a new tagline — *Get Ready. Get Set. Get Old*. *Get Old* wants to help individuals understand that every day is an opportunity to begin again, start new adventures, and experience firsts! The new updated campaign has been a continuation of its earlier themes, building on the momentum it generated earlier. In 2014, the campaign addressed people's #FOGO or *fear of getting old* and challenged their cultural stereotypes and perceptions around experiences as they age. In addition, the yearlong campaign provided inspirational stories of individuals that have defied what is expected as well as tools and a series of challenges aimed at spurring people to change their attitude toward aging.

In addition, the campaign provided many resources supporting their *Get Old* movement. For example, the campaign website, www.getold.com, is updated continuously with a range of updated content to engage users.

The program's mission has also been revised to reflect this direction: It's time to tell the truth about aging: the more you embrace it, the more you'll enjoy it. So join us today with a new attitude so those later years can be the best time of your life.

Engaging Multichannel Campaign!

Get Old has been the most engaging multichannel campaign ever for Pfizer. Speaking about the campaign, Brenna Robinson, Director, Global Reputation, Digital Content and Media Strategy with Pfizer, said: *We want people to think of Pfizer differently. If people view and interact with us differently, that will maintain and hopefully improve the reputation of Pfizer as a company*.

Here's a partial list of some of the important resources, including the updated content:

The programs mission

1. *Video*: The video played a significant part in engaging the audience. None of us can escape the fact that the longer we live, the older we get, and yet in popular culture, the idea of getting older has many negative implications, as shared by the children in Pfizer's videos. A child in one of the videos describing his grandmother says: *My grandma can pick up a piano and fish and police officers and dogs.* The video was viewed more than 11,000 times in the first few months of 2015.
2. *Website*: www.getold.com has been designed as the home of the campaign, which contains highly engaging content with links from all the social channels driving the visitors. The website continuously updates a wide range of content to engage users, such as:
    - Personal stories and images from the branded campaign, *Get Old*.
    - New articles from notable bloggers
    - Guest blog entries by experts in key subject areas such as caregiving and a variety of health conditions
    - Tools and resources from various partner organizations, including National Alliance for Caregiving, Society for Women's Health Research, Generations United, and American Sexual Health Association
3. *Content Marketing*: Pfizer, in its *Get Old* campaign, has made liberal use of shareable content in a refreshing way. Content shared carries a subtle and optimistic message about hope, health, and long life. Pfizer's decision to prioritize engagement over direct commercial messages made the campaign content very popular. Even more significant is that Pfizer's *Get Old* campaign engaged very effectively with its heartwarming original and third-party content. Pfizer's *Get Old* campaign was significantly different from other corporate campaigns. In fact, *Get Old* was more ambitious than any other corporate campaign because it was more like an open platform where

content shared ranges from Pfizer's materials to a diverse range of third-party loosely aligned with the campaign's values.

4. *Facebook*: We are challenging people of all ages to rethink what it means to get old, reads the campaign's Facebook page. The content of the campaign on Facebook was designed to make the idea of healthy aging aspirational. Pfizer's *Get Old* Facebook page was one of the most followed pages in the pharmaceutical industry, with 348,059 followers and 357,846 likes.
5. *Twitter*: The campaign's dedicated Twitter profile has 37,800 followers as of December 5, 2018.
6. *Paid Media*: Also, Pfizer used paid media to promote outreach.

Improved Reputation Too

The campaign marked the beginning of new leadership at Pfizer. Ian Read took over as the chief executive of Pfizer from Jeff Kindler in 2011. It was at a time Pfizer's reputation had dipped low due to a list of reputation-related legal issues such as a $2.3 billion settlement over the marketing of anti-inflammatory drug Bextra (valdecoxib) and a $14 million settlement for illegally marketing the overactive bladder (OAB) medication Detrol among others.

Ian Read, the new chief executive, set himself a goal of taking charge of the company, which was to shore up the firm's reputation. Pfizer, a global major with a 165-year legacy, had great relationships with policymakers and advocacy groups. However, they never really had been communicating about the significant contributions they made towards improving the health and wellness of humanity and never really tried to build relationships with consumers. They conducted a perception study among people living in the US to understand their views about aging and created the now-famous campaign, *Get Old*.

Launched in 2012, *Get Old* engaged and inspired millions of people to develop a positive attitude about aging. Corporate campaigns such as Pfizer's *Get Old* do more than create a feeling of goodwill.

Research shows that cultivating a positive corporate reputation has been shown to improve balance sheets as well. A poll conducted on behalf of Pfizer found the campaign was associated with a 45 to 55 percent uptick in how consumers felt about Pfizer's reputation as a trustworthy company.

In the process of conceiving and executing an ambitious campaign such as *Get Old*, Pfizer tested a lot of stuff, took big risks sometimes, do things that no other Pharma company had ever done before. But then, that's what pioneering is all about. The most important lesson is that organizations can apply the learnings from campaigns like *Get Old*.

(Source: Adapted from articles: 1. Pfizer News, Get Ready. Get Set. Get Old. Prizer challenges conventional views of aging through a new campaign, June 4, 2015, 2. Deborah Weinstein, Pfizer's 'Get Old' Campaign gets youthful! Medical Marketing & Media, June 10, 2015, 3. Daniel Ghinn, Pfizer breaks new ground with its Get Old campaign, Pharmaphorum, January 19, 2015)

CASE 91

Janssen's *Psoriasis 360!*

The Internet has indeed changed the landscape of healthcare engagement, creating an environment of participatory medicine, where patients are taking responsibility for their health. Access to better information and awareness about diseases and treatment options are making this increasingly possible. Some pharmaceutical companies are proactively taking initiatives to stay at the forefront of this changing landscape and social media to share important and relevant information on the channels that patients use to engage them in enabling and empowering conversations. Janssen's Psoriasis 360 campaign is one such groundbreaking initiative.

Janssen Pharmaceuticals, one of the leading research-based pharmaceutical companies that is a part of the global drug major Johnson & Johnson, has a leadership position in the psoriasis therapy area. The company makes Stelara ((ustekinumab) as a treatment option for adults with moderate to severe plaque psoriasis. An estimated 7.5 million American men and women have psoriasis. Psoriasis is commonly mistaken as just a skin condition, while it is a chronic disease of the immune system that appears on the skin.

Website and Twitter Account

Janssen Pharmaceuticals launched *Psoriasis 360* campaign across multiple channels such as a central website, Facebook, Twitter, YouTube channel, and a mobile app for iPhone to help patients understand the severity of their disease and help them discuss their condition with their physicians. The website www.psoriasis360.com provides access to simple tools designed to help patients understand their condition better and support them in communicating with their physician. In addition, its Twitter account posted regular updates about psoriasis to connect with interested patients using this channel.

Facebook

Janssen, in a first for the pharmaceutical industry, has taken the bold move of configuring the Facebook wall to allow open comments, which are only moderated after they are published. Psoriasis patients seemed comfortable talking about their condition in this environment. *Psoriasis 360* wanted to use all aspects of social media to help with its disease awareness campaign about psoriasis, and it established its Facebook page to allow online discussions about the disease. The wall posts included dialogues between patients giving advice and sympathizing with each other. The *Psoriasis 360* Facebook Page was well received by patients and has reached over 30,000 post views.

The *Psoriasis 360* Facebook page hosted patient-to-patient engagement. However, according to Alex Butler, digital strategy and social media manager at Janssen, out of the first one hundred comments posted on the Psoriasis Facebook page, four had to be removed due to content that was either inappropriate or would not allow Janssen to remain compliant with regulators. While removing these comments, the company contacted the individual users in these cases and explained why they deleted the comments.

Psoriasis 360 wanted to use all aspects of social media to help with its disease awareness campaign about psoriasis, and its Facebook page allowed an online discussion about the disease. In addition, the company consulted with The Psoriasis Association, a charity it helps fund, and agreed that their Facebook page would be a good place to visit for patients with psoriasis.

In 2012, Janssen decided to take down its award-winning *Psoriasis 360* Facebook page due to the ever-increasing number of troublesome comments. The company said: *Whenever a post on this page mentions a specific drug by name or talks about the efficacy of a particular treatment or its side effects, we have to ask for it to be changed or pull it.* The firm said this has been stifling worthwhile discussions, and having to keep removing these posts had become too cumbersome for the firm. However, Janssen said it remained committed to providing balanced information and resources on its Psoriasis 360 website, Psoriasis YouTube channel, and Twitter account, as these have not been affected by its Facebook discussion.

Psoriasis 360 iPhone App

The *Psoriasis 360* iPhone app, designed for use by healthcare professionals and patients, provides tools for assessing and tracking the severity and impact of psoriasis. In addition, the app encourages Patients to seek appropriate levels of medical care. In contrast, the app's functionality for healthcare professionals (HCPs) includes a PASI (Psoriasis Area and Sensitivity Index) calculator tool that can assess the severity of a patient's condition.

A New Standard of Engagement

Psoriasis 360 is not a me-too social media campaign but addresses a real need. People are responding and engaging. What the company wanted out of the campaign was that patients should get the right treatment, whatever the severity of psoriasis. That's why the company provided the correct information. The campaign has set a new standard of engagement for Janssen and demonstrated that a pharmaceutical company could host an open Facebook wall dedicated to a therapy area outside of the United States.

Although others are providing an engaging environment for psoriasis patients to talk about treatment, Janssen wanted to give a place to talk about the disease itself. As Alex Butler said: *If you have credibility and useful content, this content must reach the people who need it. But you cannot do that now unless you use social media, the communication that people take part in, or else it will not be possible to achieve anything like the reach you need.*

The *Psoriasis 360* program has been very successful, and Janssen picked up two awards for it from the PM Society's Digital Media Awards in 2011. The campaign also won the Healthcare Engagement Strategy 2011 Award for Engaging Patients for meeting patients' needs for information and pioneering in a regulated environment.

Key Lessons

Janssen's Psoriasis 360 campaign offers four valuable lessons to make a social media campaign successful.

1. *Credibility is vital for success*. You should only launch a campaign where you have credibility, where you have something different from what is out there which are relevant to the patient and physician communities.
2. *Passion fuels the campaign*. What are the significant resources you need to make your social media campaign successful? According to Alex Butler, it is not merely about money, but people skills, passion, and commitment to the cause. It also takes tremendous desire and passion among your cross-functional colleagues, including medical, legal, and regulatory, to make things happen.
3. *Clear focus*. It is essential to focus on the things that are working to make the best use of available resources. If something is not working, it needs to be stopped so that you can put more resources behind those that are working well.
4. *Content is crucial*. Meticulous planning to produce content is essential for the success of a social media campaign. Community and engagement don't mean anything without content. You need to have a model that can ensure relevant content is continuously in place to make your social media campaign successful.

(Source: Adapted from articles: 1. Ben Adams, Janssen to remove its Psoriasis 360 Facebook page, Pharmafile, March 28, 2012, 2. Daniel Ghinn, Psoriasis 360, Janssen, Creation Knowledge)

CASE

92

Salix Pharmaceuticals Hooks up with Lifetime Channel to Talk IBS-D!

Irritable Bowel Syndrome (IBS) can be embarrassing to talk about. However, Salix Pharmaceuticals, a division of Valeant Pharmaceuticals, one of the leading Specialty Pharma companies in the US, found even a bigger problem. That is, the number of people who potentially have IBS is undiagnosed. A research study commissioned by the company revealed that up to 75 percent of patients with IBS lack a formal diagnosis.

That research finding got Salix thinking about how it could better educate people about the condition. And right around that time, Access Health, an American Healthcare consultancy company, approached Salix. Access Health was to produce a 30-minute show for the Lifetime TV health segment on IBS-D (Irritable Bowel Syndrome that causes Diarrhea). Salix recommended Dr. Mark Pimentel, a key opinion leader (KOL) in gastroenterology, to Access Health for the show. It was the right fit at the right time. The show featured two of Dr. Pimentel's female patients, along with the doctor telling their stories about years of difficulties and over-the-counter remedies on their way to diagnosis. The show aired on October 11, 2017.

While most of the show focused on education and awareness, Dr. Pimentel and the patients also talked about Salix'sXifaxan (Rifaximin) as the specific medication that worked for them. For those brand mentions, the show's last-minute presented a standard list of possible risks and side effects used in brand advertising. Although Access Health owned the content, Salix didget to show the segment at the recent American College of Gastroenterology (ACG) conference. It helped Salix in twoways; one is that it showed the physicians what Salix was doing about patient education. Secondly, it also pointed out the issue of many undiagnosed patients.

The primary issue was that patients might not know more options available than they could get over the counter. One of the patients in the video says it took her five years to get a diagnosis. IBS is a condition that is not only embarrassing to talk about, but patients don't think there is anything that can help them.

Another major fit for the Lifetime TV show on IBS-D was the target audience. The target audience for Salix products — females in the 25 to 44 age range — matched well with Lifetime's predominantly female audience. Salix's research found that 78 percent of diagnosed patients in its study were women, while 64 percent of undiagnosed patients were women.

To reinforce its strategy, Salix scaled up its sales force earlier this year (2017) by nearly 40 percent to boost the lagging Xifaxan sales by hiring 250 experienced sales team — representatives and managers.

(Source: Adapted from the article: Beth Snyder Bulik, Valeant's Salix hooks up with Lifetime Channel to talk IBS-D, Fierce Pharma, October 22, 2017)

Content Marketing

The internet is the starting point for most people researching health information. Digital Pharma reported that over 12 months, 72 percent of internet users mentioned in a survey that they looked online for health information. Pharmaceutical companies can use this opportunity to create informative and engaging content on health information related to their therapeutic areas and brands.

Who and what rules the internet? Content, of course! Content is the king when it comes to marketing online. Content is the fuel that drives your digital marketing activities, such as Search Engine Optimization (SEO). Content is what gets you noticed on social media. Content gives you something of value to offer your customers in emails and paid search ads.

Creating content that is not promotional but educates and inspires gets you noticed. Content that offers valuable and relevant information ensures that your customers stay tuned in. The key to good content is that it avoids being overtly promotional and is useful or valuable to the customer. Because if the content is not relevant to the consumer, whether it is the patient or HCP, they go elsewhere. They want to understand the condition and the treatment options available to them. Therefore, you need to give the information they need to decide on a language they fully understand, through the medium they want, and when they want it. Quality of content is crucial to engaging them on their terms. The excellent quality content aims to create a two-way engagement rather than delivering a one-way sales pitch. Once you generate good quality content, you need to market it effectively. How do you market your content? Content marketing, as defined by the *What is* website, is: *Content marketing is the publication of material designed to promote a brand (or service), usually through a more oblique and subtle approach than that of traditional push advertising. The essence of good content marketing is that it offers something the viewer wants, such as information or entertainment*. Content marketing can take many forms, including Youtube videos, blog posts, and articles. Sometimes, it shouldn't seem like marketing; it should only be identified because the advertiser is identified as the content provider.

Modular Content

In the pharmaceutical industry, marketing and sales teams can build on the existing content and adapt it to suit the new markets while retaining the essential elements consistently. With a modular content approach, pharma marketers can repurpose their content across markets and channels, ensuring the same quality.

What is modular content? Modular content is creating pre-designed blocks of content modules to create marketing assets. These modules cover all the elements required to provide a detailed picture of the content, including product benefits, claims, references, graphics, and logos. In addition, each module has specific business rules on how to use it, resulting in the content you can deliver as a standalone or in combination with other content modules.

Creating modular content helps pharma marketers in developing content quickly and reduces inefficiency. In addition, modular content allows scientific content management facilitating content reuse to create effective omnichannel content quickly. The important benefits of modular content are:

- The sales and marketing teams can engage with customers more effectively by having marketing assets ready at their fingertips.
- Pharma marketers can develop MLR (Medical, Legal, and Regulatory)-approved content modules without MLR constantly reviewing marketing assets. As a result, they can focus more on new features and experiences, repurposing the content more effectively.
- Creating content structure in advance allows users to reinforce customer perception about the brands with consistent content across multiple channels, creating an omnichannel experience. Furthermore, modular content allows you to create effective omnichannel strategies since you can assemble the content modules quickly and in different configurations to build personalized customer journeys, allowing you to tell your product story across channels.

Creating Modular Content: Important Steps

How do you develop modular content that is consistent across channels? Consider the following steps.

1. Create a generic content template with core brand assets, so your teams can generate customized content faster per promotional strategies.
2. Make the content creation process consistent across all teams through documentation.
3. Involve your MLR (Medical, Legal, and Regulatory) team early in the modular content creation process so everyone is onboard and understands the nuances of promotional strategies and possibilities.
4. It is important to assess the technology requirements for integrating modular content. For example, you need a digital asset management solution where content is stored, shared, and managed. Also, a content authoring tool for modular content can help create and manage content faster.

Optimize Your Content

It is not enough to create great content. You must optimize it because a strong online content marketing strategy is also the key to SEO (Search Engine Optimization). Google's algorithm keeps evolving to promote web pages with high-quality content better. As Karim Binon, digital marketing manager of Oceasoft, a leading provider of high-quality temperature monitoring solutions based in Montpellier, France, rightly observed: *Posting great content on a website that is technically not optimized is like riding a Harley Davidson equipped with a scooter's engine. It won't go very long and not very fast*.

Pharmaceutical marketers must provide engaging content that meets the needs, wants, aspirations, and goals of all their key stakeholders, namely, patients, HCPs, providers, and payers. Meeting the needs and interests of the target audience is crucial for success. Pharma should create different content for each customer segment in a way that speaks directly to their particular issues. A one-size-fits-all approach is outdated now. The key questions to ask and answer are:

1. Who is your target audience? Are they patients or general practitioners? Specialist physicians?
2. What information do they want?
3. What issues do they have, and how can you solve them?

Remember to be engaging; content should be interactive, interesting, informative, and shareable. Your content should not seem like a marketing strategy or be promotional. However engaging, content cannot promote itself unless at least you share it on social media.

A successful and sustainable content strategy for a pharmaceutical company hinges on developing a trusted relationship using the content. Remember, trust is an emotion based on credibility. It can be built only on aligned values. Therefore, pharmaceutical marketers must be very objective in developing their content and focus more on building credibility than grabbing attention. Of course, you need to grab attention and sustain it, but credibility is more important in building a trusting relationship. In healthcare, it is even more critical. You can draw attention and build trust only when you have a strong point of view based on facts in your content. Otherwise, it would be a series of mere facts that anyone can find with a google search. Your content must resonate with all your key customers – patients, physicians, and payers. All of them should feel that the pharmaceutical company understands their values and beliefs, and that it is not just educating them on a prescriptive solution.

Ramya Sriram outlined the seven essential steps in the content marketing strategy titled *Content Marketing for Biotech & Pharma: The Ultimate Guide*, written by Christopher Oseh, an experienced science content writer. Here is a gist of the seven-step process of content marketing in the life sciences industry:

1. *Content Goals*: Set specific goals you want to achieve with your content, set milestones for your goals and track the progress.

2. *Define Your Audience*: Outline specific characteristics such as pain points, challenges, problems, and need that match your audience to determine the type of content to create so that your audience engages optimally with your content.
3. *Content Research and Plan*: Use appropriate research tools to discover the topics of your audiences' interest, and schedule a calendar for publishing the selected topics.
4. *Intentional Content Creation*: Create search engine optimized content that communicates with your audience at every stage in the customer's journey.
5. *Content Distribution*: Decide on the appropriate channels where your ideal audience can easily see and engage with it.
6. *Content Performance Analysis*: Analyze all published content periodically to identify top-performing content and focus only on them. Measure common indices like the number of unique visitors, likes, shares, comments, and leads.
7. *Types of Content*: As there are many types of content you can create to engage your audience effectively, matching the content type with the audience's needs and preferences are important. Here are some types of content that your audience would be interested in:
   - *Case Studies* are a type of content that involves interviewing customers who have used your products and services. It involves asking the right questions, using multimedia content, and creating a resource page to engage the audience effectively.
   - *White Papers* are compelling special reports written to solve problems faced by a target audience, usually written by subject matter experts.
   - *Press Releases and Blog Posts* are a great way to communicate any event, product launch, company news, or industry-related discovery to the public.
   - Social Media Posts are more suited for short, catchy content with well-designed images and short videos to improve interaction with your audience.

A Sage Advice

Robert Rose, the chief strategist at Content Marketing Institute and co-author with Joe Pulizzi of the book, *Managing Content Marketing,* advised that:

Content marketers should start thinking of themselves as media companies— with a distinct point of view. Their goal is to develop an audience for their content. However, they must balance that with how, when, and where they will show their distinct and unique point of view.

MSL (Medical Science Liaison)

The Upjohn company in the USA first introduced the concept of Medical Science Liaison in 1967. They created the position of Medical Science Liaison to provide educational awareness and to build rapport with the leading doctors (Key Opinion Leaders or Thought Leaders) for their new drug Tolbutamide (Orinase). Because their peers perceive the Key Opinion Leaders as experts in a given therapeutic area, they wield considerable influence among their peers. Therefore, the critical task of Medical Science Liaisons is to influence the influencers!

Medical Science Liaisons have significantly grown in importance and size during the last fifteen to twenty years. What are the reasons for this growth? Samuel Dyer, CEO of Medical Science Liaisons, says, "The Key Opinion Leaders are demanding it!"

The Eureka Moment

The Cutting Edge Information conducted a benchmark study a few years ago and found that the average time the Pharma sales rep spent with a doctor was less than two minutes, while the MSL spent a little over an hour on average with a doctor. That made companies sit back and realize that doctors valued that exchange.

Growing Importance of MSLs

Today's thought leaders seek detailed information as they engage in clinical conversations with Pharma, Biotech, and Medical Device companies. Increasing scientific sophistication is another reason for this increasing role of medical science liaisons, as it requires scientifically trained medical experts.

The traditional sales force is suffering from restricted access to physicians. MSLs, despite their non-promotional role, provide a valuable link between doctors and the company.

Moreover, a field-based MSL may provide a strong strategic asset for any company. They can collect crucial insights from the field on current and new therapeutic approaches and generate significant new data.

What's in a Name?

Although initially called Medical Science Liaisons (MSL) by Upjohn, pharmaceutical, biotechnology, and medical device companies have used different titles to describe the MSL job over the years. The job titles vary, though they typically have the same roles and responsibilities. Some of the more commonly used job titles for the MSL function are:

1. Clinical Liaison
2. Clinical Science Consultant
3. Medical Liaison
4. Medical Manager
5. Medical Science Consultant
6. Medical Science Manager
7. Scientific Affairs Manager

Tasks and Responsibilities of MSLs

Whatever the job title may be, the primary responsibility of an MSL remains to establish and maintain a peer-to-peer relationship with leading doctors who influence other doctors. Therefore, most of MSLs' activities revolve around engaging Key Opinion Leaders, building and strengthening ties with them, and educating them about the company's product development and research activities. Here are some of the essential activities that the MSLs perform:

1. KOL relationship management
2. Educating KOLs and other leading HCPs
3. Identifying and training speakers
4. Attending medical conferences
5. Coordinating company-sponsored clinical research

6. Delivering scientific presentations
7. Organizing and participating in Continuing Medical Education (CME) activities
8. Medical publications
9. Gathering competitive intelligence
10. Training or supporting the sales force

MSL: Prerequisites and Key Competencies

To perform such a wide range of scientific and academic activities, what qualifications and competencies should MSL-aspirants have? Consider these, for example:

1. Advanced degrees such as MD, Pharm D, or Ph.D. in life sciences
2. Understanding of Clinical Trial and Drug Development guidelines
3. Demonstrated Scientific Aptitude
4. Strong Communication Skills - both oral and written
5. Strong Interpersonal Skills
6. Ability to Collaborate, Persuade and Motivate
7. Ability to Teach and Learn
8. Working knowledge of the internet, computers, and technology
9. Strong Scientific and Business Acumen
10. Creativity

Different Roles

Both the Sales and Marketing function and Medical Science Liaison are field-based. Both functions interact with Healthcare Practitioners. Some of the customers may even be common. However, that is where the similarity ends, and the difference begins. The following table presents the critical differences between Pharmaceutical Sales epresentatives and Medical Science Liaison Managers at a glance.

Table 3.6 Roles of Pharma Sales Reps and MSLs at a Glance

Pharmaceutical Sales Rep	Medical Science Liaison
1. Part of Sales and Marketing Department	Part of Medical Affairs or Regulatory Department
2. Trained to sell and persuade prescribers to prescribe the company's products	Non-selling function. Establishing and reinforcing relationships with KOLs through a number of scientific activities
3. Prescriber focus	KOL Focus
4. Works with 'doctors in the trenches' or clinically based physicians	Works primarily with the physicians researching and teaching
5. Redirects unsolicited complex inquiries to Medical Affairs	May respond to unsolicited complex questions from KOLs and HCPs
6. May have technical background	Most often have technical background
7. Sells products based upon integration of key brand messages and appropriate use of product	Works on scientific education and clinical research studies to disseminate product related and non-product related scientific information in therapeutic areas of KOLs' interest
8. Performance and goals are based on sales of a product	Performance and goals are based upon outcomes with academic thought leaders and Continuing Medical Education Objectives as per organizational goals set

MSLs must be perceived as neutral scientific experts on the company's products. They should respond when KOLs and other HCPs have technical questions about a company's products or studies. They should not act as a surrogate sales force.

What MSLs Don't Do?

Since pharmaceutical sales representative and MSL positions are field based and visit some of the same customers, it is essential to clearly define what sales representatives do and don't do and what MSLs do and don't do. It is even more important to draw a clear boundary regarding what MSLs don't do. If you remember that' S' in MSL stands for 'Science and not Sales,' what MSLs should not do becomes very clear. Consider these 'Don'ts' for example:

- MSLs do not generate noise; the buzz about products before approval

- MSLs do not drive sales or otherwise promote products
- MSLs Do not proactively discuss off-label information
- MSLs do not make patient-specific therapy or treatment recommendations
- MSLs do not render general practice-related medical, or business services

It's All about Providing Value

MSLs, too, are facing physician access issues today. The only key to opening the physicians' doors is delivering information that the physician values. MSLs consistently create value and differentiate themselves from the rest of the pack, and get FaceTime with thought leaders.

How does an MSL deliver value? They can deliver value in many ways. Consider these, for example. Understanding the doctor's needs and targeting the right KOL with the correct information can improve credibility and build trust. If MSLs are approaching KOLs with clinical information only, they may be missing the value proposition, which lies in the insights.

As Mr. Paul Meade, President, Thought Leader Select, says, "*If doctors are closing to sales reps at healthcare systems, then closing the door to MSLs is probably not far behind unless they can create value in that conversation. The value is not in the data. It is in the insights the MSL can bring to the discussion. It is a necessary skill for today's MSL.*"

e-MSL (Medical Science Liaison)

Although the digital revolution has been impacting every aspect of the pharmaceutical business, medical affairs or medical science liaisons are relatively slow in adopting the digital ways of working.

While pharma marketers have quickly adopted digital, their medical colleagues continued to rely more on traditional customer engagement methods such as publications, scientific congresses, and in-field MSLs. However, the recent pandemic, COVID-19, accelerated MSLs' (Medical Science Liaisons) digital adoption as in-person visits, meetings, and medical congresses had come to a standstill.

Moreover, the increasing demand from HCPs to receive medical information anytime, anywhere, reduced access rates to physicians, and increasing limitations on in-person congresses, even after COVID-19, escalate the need for digital alternatives in medical education.

In addition, the arrival of 'disruptive' trends such as real-world data, wearables, and physician communities will further accelerate the strategic importance of eMedical programs across the product lifecycle.

Gone are the days when specialists and general physicians accessed the latest clinical information only during their lunch breaks or working days, with the tipping point of digital native versus digital immigrant HCP reaching in 2014. Today, the HCPs (Healthcare Professionals) can access information anywhere, anytime with their triple screen—PC, Tablet, and Smartphone. Therefore, pharma needs to understand the information-seeking behavior of always-on physicians to reach them effectively.

It is important to remember that not all physicians are the same—not only in terms of age and technical savviness but also in how and when they access information. For example, you can see that different specialists and general physicians have distinct patterns for their preferred timings. Here are some research findings on the information-seeking behavior of physicians:

1. These days, HCPs are over three times more likely to access medical information outside than during office hours.

2. The evening hours are the most preferred time for HCPs to access medical information, such as watching educational webinars.
3. HCPs access most of their medical information outside office hours, but Pharma tends to focus its efforts on HCPs during their office hours, creating multichannel opportunities.

e-MSLs and Product Launch

MSL plays a crucial role as medical education touches all phases of the product lifecycle, and e-MSLs (also known as e-Medical in some markets) is no different in disseminating knowledge and information about products and diseases they treat. They provide a very important service to HCPs, being the face of Pharma at national scientific and medical education conferences. Therefore, HCPs see e-MSLs (and MSLs) as a valuable resource for delivering global medical education fitting to their needs.

However, there is a small difference in the way they do that. First, they provide the information virtually to physicians where and when they are present. That is why they are called e-MSLs. e-MSLs deliver the information through digital channels and in-person whenever it is necessary.

The information needs of HCPs vary at each stage of the product lifecycle. Consider these needs at each stage, for example:

A. Medical education has the most important role during the pre-launch phase. You can start it during phases two and three of drug trials to establish unmet needs, demonstrate thought leader advocacy, and position the main scientific proposition of a product and use all these strands to maximize impact at launch.
B. You need to build awareness of new product at the launch phase by disseminating information with complete research data, supporting what it can do to patients. The launch phase requires support from all channels, supporting education for internal and external audiences.

C. During the post-launch phase, educational initiatives could target a broader range of audiences, including nurses, general physicians, specialists, pharmacists and other stakeholders, who have an increasing influence on the prescribing and decision-making process.

D. Finally, as a product comes to maturity, the need is two fold: you must hold onto early adopters while moving other stakeholders along the adoption ladder. In addition, e-MSLs can also support new clinical trials to pave the way for future indications.

Changing Landscape

The e-MSL trend is increasing mainly because of two reasons. One is that digital-savvy physicians are increasing and prefer virtual engagement to in-person ones. The other reason is that physical attendance at medical congresses at national and international levels is steadily decreasing. There are several reasons responsible for this drop in physical attendance at medical congresses. Consider these, for example:

- Rising costs of hosting satellite symposia, exhibit booths, and other traditional costs
- Increasing compliance pressures on HCPs making them reduce their conference and speaking engagements
- Digitally native HCPs increasingly accessing medical events on line as they are very convenient—anytime, anywhere
- Dwindling satisfaction levels with traditional medical congresses
- Virtual conferences are becoming more convenient, with software, broadband speed, robustness, and cost-effectiveness improving with each year significantly

Therefore, the medical associations must change their operational model to preserve and protect their prestige and revenue by engaging their members continuously throughout the year with deeper personalized immersion and providing more social and professional networking opportunities.

Virtual Meetings, or Webcasts

Virtual meetings or webcasts have become an impactful medical tactic for e-MSLs (Medical Science Liaisons) as they provide an excellent opportunity to deliver medical content and build customer engagement. Here are some major benefits they offer:

- Extend Pharma's reach beyond the limited groups of in-person participants
- Allow Pharma to increase contact frequency while reducing the cost per contact
- Allow HCPs access content when and where they want to

Webcasts can be quite an impactful tactic, when you follow these important steps:

1. Define your target audience and set behavioral objectives. For example, what do you want them to do after the event?
2. Create compelling content aligned with the objectives. Consider CME (Continuing Medical Education)-accrediting.
3. Ensure speakers allow sharing of their presentations online.
4. Define and execute a cross-channel promotional plan for maximizing the reach.
5. Decide who will host the sessions? Internal, or third-party? If you decide on third-party, select a robust platform vendor and an experienced content agency.
6. Follow a multichannel, automated webcast reminder process.
7. Decide and execute a follow-up plan with delegates, and close the loop with MSLs and Reps.
8. The most important step before you begin is getting the buy-in from your legal and regulatory to ensure compliance.

Usually, Medical Affairs, or MSL programs tend to focus on third-party channels, as physicians tend to perceive them to be more credible. Indeed, third-party channels, such as scientific websites, newsletters, online journals, and virtual congresses have a stronger impact than the Pharma-owned medical channels. The disadvantage with third-party channels is that you may miss the opportunity of engaging with your customers in a 360-degree manner. However, you can use third-party channels to maximize reach and trigger customer to further engage with Pharma-owned content or events. It is critically important that you close the loop, follow-up where appropriate, by defining individual customer journeys and act upon.

Getting Participants for your Webinar

How to get more participants for your webinar? First, you must actively promote your webinar and recruit participants to attend it, even if it's science-based and not sales-oriented because if you just broadcast, nobody will come to you. You cannot just fill up your webinars from your email lists.

- Pickup a highly relevant topic
- Choose the headline with care. The headline should be inspiring and tell people what they can gain from the webinar
- Choose a good time and day that is most convenient for most participants as there are good and less optimal times to send out an invite or host a webcast. Research suggests that a different time of the day can mean doubling response and participation. So, A/B-testing the timing of all your activities is very useful.
- Make use of your email list
- Don't forget to remind people
- Provide a replay of the webcast
- Request and encourage participants to share the webinar information
- When sending a reminder to people, ensure that the event URL is embedded in the reminder as an 'add to my calendar' functionality.
- Also, send the reminder to people that have not opened it after three days.
- Also, consider SMS notifications just before the start of a live webinar.
- During the live webcast, it is always advised to allow interaction from the participants to live Q and A, or Poll.

- Also, ensure that a chaptered recorded version of your webcast is provided after the live event, as this typically doubles the webcast viewer rates. It's also crucial to do it within the week after the live event; otherwise, the momentum will be gone.
- Ensure that viewers can also evaluate your event afterward and try to close the loop by, for example, allowing an MSL to deliver a viewer certificate after your event

Once the participant recruitment process of the webinar is completed, it is important to deploy an automated process to remind participants about the forthcoming event. The following table outlines a reminder process flow that has been found successful.

Table 3.7 Process Flow for Webinar Reminders

Time Line - Before the Event	Reminder Type
Before one Week	eMail reminder
Before one Day	eMail reminder
Before one Hour	SMS Text
Webcast Goes Live	Web Cast Goes Live
Time Line - After the Event	Activity Type
Immediately After the Event	A Quick Evaluation Survey Questionnaire (Keep it simple) or A Poll about the event
Two Days Later	On-demand Webcast (Replay)
One Week Later	Access to High Lights or Executive Summary of the Webinar (downloadable Link via eMail and SMS)
Ten Days Later	Evaluation Survey Report via eMail
	Webinar Participation Certificate— To be delivered by MSL / Rep

It's worthwhile to consider a combination of third-party and Pharma-owned recruitment channels, both on and offline, as they will generate the highest impact. Although many pharmaceutical companies only use reps or MSLs for recruitment, often there is not enough time for reps and MSLs to invite customers face-to-face, or even online. Complementing these invitations with other channels will increase reach and improve recall and participation levels.

e-MSL Roll Out: Two Models

How do you roll out your MSL strategy? Two popular models exist—*In-office Activation* and the other is *e-MSL On-Demand*.

A. In-office Activation is where sales reps can connect remotely through their tablet with an MSL as soon as a medical question is asked that the sales are not supposed to answer. If an MSL is available, then the interaction can occur right away. If not, an appointment is set up and carried out at a time convenient to the HCP.

B. MSL On-Demands where sales reps can connect remotely through their tablet with an MSL as soon as a medical question is asked that the sales are not supposed to answer. If an MSL is available, then the interaction can occur right away. If not, HCP can book an appointment at his convenient time, using online calendar functionality.

Content Rules

Content, credible, authentic content holds the key to success for Pharma's medical education and scientific communication programs. Therefore, the success of e-MSLs hinges on the quality of content they can create and deliver. So, what sort of content should they create? Content that HCPs can use to improve their practice because, according to research HCPs seek and prefer information that can impact their medical practice.

In today's information overloaded world, time and attention have become the drivers of engagement. Here are some key success factors that can help Pharma develop compelling, attention-grabbing content.

- First and foremost, content should be relevant to the needs of your target audience while at the same time being in alignment with your medical strategy.
- Content should be highly searchable. Make it easy for physicians to find information quickly when they need it. No complicated links or access details.

- Make it interactive and engaging, allowing viewers to dive deep— but only if they want it. Engaging content will keep HCPs coming back.
- Make the content current and authentic with the latest information in their area of interest. Also, provide options for HCPs to access content from experts and peers.
- Provide bite-sized, easily digestible, and actionable information online at the point-of-care. HCPs will find it extremely useful.
- Make the information available on-demand whenever needed.
- Create your content in different digital formats to suit different learning styles and preferences of HCPs. For, example, General physicians prefer broader, less specialized content and are generally more favorable toward practical case studies than in-depth video formats. On the other hand, specialists prefer deep dives on one topic with multiple opinions and generally prefer video formats.
- Consider presenting your content in the story format by weaving individual content items into an overall medical 'story' to increase its stickiness and memorability.
- Ensure that there are as few technical barriers to access as possible. Also, make your content accessible through different channels and devices to suit the needs and preferences of digitally savvy physicians.

The RIBS Test

A message becomes successful when people remember it. So how can you craft messages that stick and are memorable? Caryn Marooney, Head of Technology Communications for Facebook, suggests people test their content's stickiness with the RIBS Test. The RIBS test is a framework designed to help create a message with a better chance of resonating (in short, *stick to your ribs*). RIBS is an acronym for Relevant, Inevitable, Believable, Simple. When your content meets these four criteria, it becomes stickier and memorable and improves recall value. The key questions to ask are:

- Are we solving a problem the physicians care about? (Relevant)

- Is our content part of a trend? Does it make intrinsic sense to the audience? Does it resonate with them? (Inevitable)
- Is our content credible? (Believable)
- What is the one line we want our audience to remember? (Simple)

Short Messages for Short Attention Spans

The attention spans of people in general, and physicians in particular, are getting shorter by the day. We might even beat the goldfish's attention span of nine-seconds at the present rate of our shortening attention span. Therefore, It would help if you grabbed customers' attention instantly with short teasers instead of presenting the full story straight away. But, unfortunately, these teasers are getting shorter and shorter— from an executive summary to an email, to a 140-character Tweet, to just one infographic or image. However, once you have the customer's attention, their capacity to access digitized information is limitless.

e-MSLs : Future Outlook

Although research suggests that most physicians find pharma-owned eMedical initiatives more impactful than a face-to-face visit with a sales rep, Pharma-owned eMedical channels are still on a low maturity level, especially when compared to offline medical activities.

However, due to changing customer needs and regulations, increasing physician-access restrictions, cost controls, technological advancements, and increasingly digitally native physicians, one can expect that eMSLs in Pharma will rapidly mature in the coming years.

DOL (Digital Opinion Leader) Engagement

Daniel Ghinn, CEO & Founder of Creation.Co, who coined the phrase— Digital Opinion Leaders (DOLs) in 2012, explains the origin of the phrase and its similarities and differences with Key Opinion Leaders (KOLs) in their ebook, *Digital Opinion Leaders (DOLs) are More Important than Ever: The rise of online influencers and what it means for healthcare.* Here are the highlights:

Key Opinion Leaders (KOLs) are considered KOLs based on their experience, seniority, and role, whereas Digital Opinion Leaders (DOLs) are a term coined by creation.Co in 2012 is considered in the context of their online *Influence*, which does not necessarily reflect the level of professional seniority. Here, *Influence* is determined by the *crowd* of other experts. It is like a mass peer review where physicians trusted by their peers develop a strong network of influence among themselves. That is how the Digital Opinion Leaders (DOLs) emerged first, and being trusted by their peers online, they can significantly impact learning, health systems, and health outcomes, often all over the world.

Digital Opinion Leaders (DOLs) are becoming an increasingly important stakeholder group for Pharma companies to engage and consult with our growing dependence on social media over the past decade. It is also a trend of a new breed of influencers that has mastered the art of scientific communication in a digital world predating the COVID-19 Pandemic and is now accelerated.

Who are DOLs?

We all know that traditional Key Opinion Leaders (KOLs) are established physicians who are well-known and admired in their fields, publish regularly, and are active in clinical research. They attend and speak at major conferences and sit on multiple Pharma Advisory Boards. Here is one of the common definitions of DOLs. They are *influential members of an online community to whom others turn for advice, opinions, and information*. In other words, DOLs are those individuals whose ideas and behavior serve as models for others via social media.

Sebastian Sorsaburu, vice-president of global medical affairs at Amgen, defines DOLs as having established their presence in a platform with their unique signature style and cadence of posting regular updates. However, they do not just post data. Instead, they've understood how to get the point across well with the medium and make themselves an important part of a growing digital ecosystem. He adds that three emerging channels of importance for DOLs are— podcasting, video casts (YouTube mainly), and Twitter.

While there is some overlap with KOLs, DOLs can be anyone, from physicians, nurse practitioners, pharmacists, researchers, patients, caregivers, journalists, and science writers. One thing that sets DOLs apart from typical social media influencers is that they are not interested to self-promote. Instead, they want to educate, engage, and challenge their followers. They are experts with professional credentials and credibility, and virtually provide clear and concise scientific communication.

You can find DOLs on many digital platforms, with Twitter being the platform of choice for many, especially for conference coverage and discussions with the public and peers. Further, Podcasts and YouTube, and Vimeo videos are also gaining popularity. Of late, we are also seeing many DOLs using newer platforms like TikTok to reach a younger audience.

You can identify DOLs through three metrics:

- **influence**: indicates the number of followers
- **Resonance**: tells us about the frequency with which their content is shared
- **Relevance**: how appropriate their content is to a particular objective

However, some Digital Opinion Leaders (DOLs) are also Key Opinion Leaders (KOLs), but the majority are not. Instead, they are passionate individuals from various roles, who use the online space to connect with their peers globally and make a difference. For example, Sarah Flanagan, or Nurse Sarah, as she calls herself online, is a nurse practicing in the US who uses TikTok—where she has more than

72,000 followers and 2.6 million likes— to talk frankly about life on the healthcare frontlines. For example, she tells the world how much she loves 'FIGS Scrubs.' Another example is Katy, a pediatric nurse practitioner in California, US, with more than 45,100 followers. She frequently posts about the life of a nurse and supports product promotion for brands, including a plant-based meals company.

So, the question is— Are nurse influencers like Sarah and Katy Digital Opinion Leaders? creation.co has developed a series of metrics for considering how to qualify a Digital Opinion Leader based on a set of measurable indicators like social media presence, peer or public following, and relevance of content, these nurse influencers would qualify for the brands that they sponsor.

Traditional KOLs build their reputation over time, becoming role models and someone their peers admire. At the same time, online forums such as social media create more of a level playing field for other physicians and HCPs (Healthcare Professionals) irrespective of their roles and seniority. COVID-19 Pandemic accelerated this trend and encouraged more HCPs to move into the digital space. Some KOLs have taken to social media and digital networks and became DOLs. It is unfortunate not to see other traditional KOLs embrace the growth of digital networks and create an online presence because they have much to offer, considering their experience and expertise. Their online presence will enable them to reach peers globally.

According to Christopher Nugent, Associate Director, Digital Marketing & Strategy at Alkermes: *Some KOLs (Key Opinion Leaders) have not fully embraced digital yet— but given current events, the writing is on the wall. As a result, they see the need to adapt and become more of DOL or fade away*.

Pharma has a great opportunity to create mutually beneficial partnerships between traditional KOLs and DOLs where they can learn from one another. For example, DOLs can share information on how social media can best support KOLs, and KOLs can share their knowledge and experience if the DOL has less experience. Pharma can also help and support traditional KOLs by providing necessary training in relevant social media skills they may be lacking.

While Digital Opinion Leaders have been playing an increasingly influential role in advancing care in their specialty areas, it is intriguing to observe that many are playing the role of sponsored influencers. These HCPs are developing their online networks, and commercial brands are using the HCP's Influence to target product advertising to their professional peers and consumers, and patients.

Classifying DOLs

creation.co has classified Digital Opinion Leaders into two broad categories—Scientific DOLs and Brand Ambassadors. However, it is not easy to classify all HCPs into these two broad categories. Because some doctors with strong scientific credentials are also on TikTok, playing an important role in health advocacy and education among the TikTok demographic. Most TikTok users are under 30, whereas most Twitter users are much older. For example, Austin Chang, MD, is a professor and gastroenterologist with more than 400,000 followers and 19.8 million likes on TikTok.

The following table presents the two broad categories of DOL classification and its criteria:

Table 3.8 Digital Opinion Leader Classification

DOL Category	Scientific DOL	Brand Ambassador
Scientific credentials	Usually high (senior role, publications, trials)	Not usually high
Most active channels	Likely to include Twitter, Sermo, Blogs	Likely to include instagram, TikTok
Who they influence	Peers; people with similar special interests	Younger people; public; peers on these channels (to some extent)
Use Social Media for	Peer learning and collaboration; developing their profile	influence; fun; engagement; developing their profile

(Source: Daniel Ghinn, CEO& Founder, **creation.co**, The rise of influencer marketing in healthcare: why context is key when considering Digital Opinion Leaders)

Identifying the New HCP Thought Leaders

Over the past twenty years, there has been a steady increase in HCPs' social media use for professional purposes, which increased about 50 percent in the year of the COVID-19 Pandemic resulting in the rise of the HCP Digital Opinion Leader (DOL).

Also, more and more medical teams are recognizing the significance of social media in capturing insights directly from customers and communicating the treatment value. Many Digital Opinion Leaders (DOLs) have become the New Key Opinion Leaders (KOLs). These are driving health policy decisions, defining the views of their online peers, and may be shaping your brand well before the launch. Pharma companies are trying to understand how to engage these new thought leaders and leverage their influence online.

Laura McIntyre, senior health strategy analyst at **creation.co** suggests a three-step process for identifying these new influencers in her article, *Medical Affairs: Best Practice for Identifying online HCP Thought Leaders:*

1. **Start With The End in Mind**: What challenge or opportunity are you looking to address by identifying DOLs? Your objective for identifying the thought leader is vital and must align with your organization's overall strategy. What do you want to achieve with your collaboration with the DOL? Is it educational collaboration to reach primary care physicians by co-creating content? Building early advocacy? Or using a DOL's voice to reach patients? Or to ensure that the most influential HCPs online have up-to-date information on the product and raise the awareness of new treatment data? Answering questions like these will help you determine the kind of DOLs that is right for you.
2. **What Do You Need To Know About These Individuals To Meet The Challenge You Are Facing**: Who are the DOLs nice to have, and who are the ones you must have? For example, a Digital Opinion Leader with a large public following and passionate for general awareness but with little or no interest in the scientific conversation is a nice-to-have but might not

be right to consider strategic partnerships for communicating the science behind the treatment. Also, DOLs suitable for marketing or commercial teams may not be the appropriate ones for the medical affairs teams. Digital Scientific Leaders (DSLs) are the HCPs who possess all the qualities of a DOL and have a scientific focus and expertise to influence the scientific conversation within the therapy area. DSLs (Digital Scientific Leaders) usually have higher scientific credentials and use their media for peer learning, education, and collaboration. So, they drive the discussion around the latest study and trial data, testing, diagnosis, and MOA (Mechanism of Action) of treatments to lead and shape the scientific dialogue amongst their peers online.

Finally, here are some useful questions you will find helpful when considering your DOLs.

1. Does the Digital Opinion Leader have the same interest in the topics that matter to you? Is he on the same page with you on topics such as a particular disease, treatment approach, issue, or cause?
2. What is the follower network of the Digital Opinion Leader and their specialties? Where are they located?
3. What level of influence does the Digital Opinion Leader have among his peers?
4. Know who or what influences your Digital Opinion Leader.
5. What key topics, other than the topics you both are interested does the Digital Opinion Leader discuss?
6. Which social media channels are the Digital Opinion Leader influential on? If he is not active on channels you are already using, do you need to rethink your channels or your Digital Opinion Leader?
7. What are the media preferences of the Digital Opinion Leader? Understanding the media preferences of the Digital Opinion Leader is important as it helps you to decide and determine the tools for potential engagement and collaboration.

8. Is your DOL also a Key KOL? Knowing this will help you plan for online and offline channels to engage more effectively as he can be influential on both.
9. Is the DOL open to collaboration?
10. Do you already know the DOL? If so, It can greatly impact your understanding and relationship.

DOLs: Pharma's Perspective

What is the view of Pharma about the emergence of Digital Opinion Leaders? Here are the views expressed by two industry leaders, which are indicative of the industry's perspective on Digital Opinion Leaders and how the industry can engage them effectively.

1. **Sebastian Sorsaburu's (Vice-president, Global Medical Affairs at Amgen) take on DOLs**:

   We are seeing a new type of DOL emerge. In the past, only certain people could become KOLs and have a voice in the scientific community. They would need the podium presentations, the research pedigree, and the network to become influential. A DOL today may not be a Key Opinion Leader (KOL) by classic standards in the pre-digital era, but has become so due to their mastery of digital communication. Perhaps these DOLs do not do a lot of research on their own, yet can stay up-to-date with all the research being done and package it so the general audiences can understand. They can edit it compellingly, being true to the facts and credible. How do you engage DOLs? Well, the first challenge is to discover them. But then, discovering DOLs is not very difficult. Once you begin to engage and signal your interests within a certain area, the algorithm does the hard work of discovery. Today, social networks have become so smart that once you take some initial steps to build the fields organically, the right DOL influencers will start showing up. The fundamental capabilities that come with digital— the speed, the ability to crowdsource, and easily run analytics— all have radical potential to upend how we collaborate with KOLs to do research.

   However, we need to address some issues in the new digital way of working. First, how do we ensure that healthy network effects occur instead of harmful ones? A case in point is the recent controversial promotion of hydroxy-quinolone for treating COVID-19 by individuals outside the scientific mainstream, which was picked up by non-scientist twitter aficionados and then snowballed. Another related and less obvious problem is someone becoming an expert on a particular topic and starting to comment and editorialize in other areas. In this case, it would be much harder to tell the difference, even for those within the medical community. The key issue is— while KOLs are regulated by many forms of checks and balances, how to create similar protections for the emerging world of DOLs. The challenge is how legislation and governance evolve in the online world that all industries and society face.

(Source: Andrew Stone, The Age of the Digital Opinion Leader, Reuter's Events-Pharma, July 28, 2020)

2. **Christopher Nugent, Associate Director, Digital Marketing & Strategy, Alkermes**

Dr. Vincent Rajkumar is a notable example of a DOL which has mastered the medium. He is very active in Blood Cancer research, with over 74,100 followers on Twitter who pay close attention to his postings, whether he is sharing pre-or-post-congress thoughts, or initial response to a recent research publication. DOLs such as Dr. Rajkumar are in the mold of a traditional KOL but have become savvy to digital media. We can expect to see more of them make this transition.

Investing internally and building digital capabilities in-house is important to engage with DOLs and influence the conversations. We have invested in technology and added headcount to have that subject matter expertise in-house. In addition to significant cost savings versus outsourcing, building capabilities in-house has enabled us to have a conversation. Rather than waiting on an agency, we can engage and pivot the conversation on a dime.

(Source: Andrew Stone, The Age of the Digital Opinion Leader, Reuter's Events-Pharma, July 28, 2020)

Why Should Pharma Engage DOLs?

Digital Opinion Leaders can help pharmaceutical and biotech companies to:

- Spread the word about clinical trials recruitment and new data,
- Provide feedback on marketing materials and messaging,
- Co-Create marketing, medical, educational, or patient support resources
- Share disease awareness initiatives, and
- Share their unique insights and educate their peers

You can reach a large number—tens of thousands— of potential customers by engaging DOLs to co-create programs, share their unique insights, and help educate their peers. And if you engage them longitudinally and build authentic relationships, you will have someone on your side who has the power to reach all your potential customers at the click of a button. In addition, DOLs can help you increase the medical community's awareness of new data, or treatment algorithm changes, with Twitter mentioning driving citations now.

To build an enduring relationship, you need to provide value. And you can provide value only when you listen to and understand your DOLs. The answers to these questions mentioned above will help you better understand them. One more thing, it is important always to consider the HCP's (Healthcare Practitioner) perspective. Melissa Fellner, Global Marketing Director at AstraZeneca, emphasized this need at the 2020 eyeforpharma conference in Philadelphia when she said: *It is less about the story that you want to tell and more about understanding your customer and their needs and how you can provide value to them, in the right way.*

How to Engage DOLs?

Being digital pioneers, Digital Opinion Leaders are already tech-savvy and familiar with virtual meetings and events. However, you need to meet with them on their terms. It is not about merely virtually engaging with them but doing so in the most effective manner. Think, for example, instead of involving them in multi-hour web meetings with long presentations, you may consider asynchronous (over-time, anytime) touchpoints where you can present data or materials in short video form as interactive slide decks. Natalie Yeadon, CEO & Co-Founder of Impetus Digital, a leading company focused on delivering virtual collaboration experiences for life sciences companies, suggests four main areas where partnering with DOLs can help life sciences companies significantly in her blog article, *Digital Opinion Leaders (DOLs): Who are they and how Pharma engages them*, in Journal of Mobile Health Published on April 4, 2022.

1. **Online Advisory Boards and Insight-gathering**: Creating separate advisory boards with DOLs in addition to your traditional KOL advisory boards or inviting a mix of KOLs and DOLs and community providers on your advisory board can help you get more diverse and representative feedback. Moreover, DOLs bring a unique perspective from their practices as they understand what other providers and patients are saying and sharing online. Further, DOLs being tech-savvy, will be able to push Pharma teams to leave their comfort zones and explore new avenues.
2. **Medical Education and Knowledge Dissemination**: DOLs can help pharmaceutical and biotech companies design, develop, and execute medical education and other learning activities because of their ability to bring attention to new studies or resources. They can help you design a series of educational web meetings, videos, podcasts, or learning modules. DOL advisors are more likely to share the studies discussed at advisory board meetings, which resonate with them in their networks. Monitoring these social media interactions can help you identify unanswered questions, unmet needs, or areas where additional research is needed.
3. **Conference - and Post-Congress Debrief Sessions**: DOLs often live-tweet about the different sessions, abstracts, and posters. You can use their clear and concise reporting skills by inviting them to e-huddles exclusively on a secure portal

so they can share their learnings from the event with your Medical Affairs teams. Also, you can invite them to participate in post-congress debrief sessions to discuss the key takeaways from different presentations and the next steps.

4. **Peer-to-peer Collaboration, Best Practice Sharing, and Document Co-creation**: You must engage DOLs also longitudinally as you do with your KOLs to build authentic and long-lasting relationships. Also, consider creating a sense of virtual community, where they can share best practices and collaborate on projects by giving them access to a safe, secure, and compliant online portal outside of their social media followings.

Effectively Engaging

Katie Kennedy, Head of Client Marketing at **creation.co** suggested fourteen ways for Pharma to engage with HCP Digital Opinion Leaders effectively:

1. Train and educate your HCP DOLs in areas where they may be expressing a lack of certainty, and empower them to share the learnings with their followers.
2. Provide educational resources published in their preferred format, which they could easily digest and re-purpose.
3. Be where your HCP DOL customers, such as the congresses they are attending, sites they are using, and social media platforms, to focus your outreach to them in the right place.
4. Send your field representatives to engage with your HCP DOLs. You can provide personalized insights for each DOL to ensure your sales representatives discuss the topics and areas that matter most to them.
5. Correct any misinformation you see in your HCP DOLs sharing. If they are saying something incorrectly, this could spread very quickly.
6. If some of your HCP Digital Opinion Leaders leading and driving the online conversation in your therapy area turn out to be in roles that you do not traditionally engage with, it could be an

opportunity to rethink.

7. Help your HCP Digital Opinion Leaders develop a new social media channel /community for their therapy area.
8. Reinforce your relationship with those HCP DOLs, who you now know are your advocates.
9. Understand which HCP DOLs are your competitors' advocates and why, and revise your messaging strategy accordingly.
10. Run your digital conference, encouraging your HCP DOLs to spread the word.
11. Collaborate with your HCP DOLs in live streaming.
12. Consider hosting a Twitter chat with your DOL chairing the Q&A.
13. Pre-record an interview with the DOL, and share it on social media, encouraging the DOL to also share with their community to expand reach.
14. Collaborate with your DOL to engage HCP peers through a Twitter poll or chat.

The Future of DOL Engagement

Digital Opinion Leaders are here to stay; if anything, their influence only increases. If you have not already started engaging them, it is time to engage them. Engaging a combination of Key Opinion Leaders (KOLs) and Digital Opinion Leaders will help you gather more representative insights and will help you with a much broader and deeper reach than what would be possible with only one.

Engaging DOLs is not much different from engaging with other stakeholders. You need to be open and authentic and take their feedback and constructive criticism. Show them how you are acting on the insights collected. Engage them frequently, not only during conferences or when a new study crops up. If you think there is nothing significant to talk about, ask them what matters to them and how the industry can help.

Phygital: The Future of Engagement

What is Phygital?

Chris Weil, Chairman-CEO at Momentum Worldwide, an international practice in consulting, strategy, analytics, and experience design, first coined Phygital in 2007 to describe the inseparable connection between the physical and digital worlds. Phygital is derived from the contraction of two words (Physical and Digital) into a single word (Phygital). Phygital is the concept of using technology to bridge the digital world with the physical world to provide a unique interactive user experience.

The physical and digital boundaries have been blurred for some time, creating a seamless omnichannel experience in the retail, transportation, hospitality, and entertainment industries. Successful companies today do not follow a physical or digital strategy but a united phygital strategy that unites both sides to create an immersive digital experience for the customer.

The phygital trend accelerated during the COVID-19 pandemic, as life moved online and brands, companies, and work itself had to pivot to digital channels quickly.

Blake Morgan, a globally recognized keynote speaker and the author of the bestselling book, The Customer of the Future, wrote in an article, *The Rise of the Phygital Experience*, published on forbes.com on May 16, 2022, that *Marketers must make every interaction of their brands with customers count and unite what customers want most in a digital channel and what they want most in a physical experience to create a united phygital experience*.

How do you create a strong phygital experience? Like all aspects of customer experience, creating a great customer experience starts by understanding your customers, what matters to them most, and how they like to acquire and interact with that. A quality phygital experience understands customers' needs and provides excellent digital tools and in-person experiences to move between channels seamlessly.

Pharma and Physical Marketing

Traditionally, pharma marketing relied heavily on physical marketing and on— in-person channels— mainly sales reps, physical meetings, and congresses- pushing messages about their products and services. However, the pharma marketing landscape has been changing over the past few years, and the pandemic has increased the speed of change, causing many challenges. Here are the main reasons and challenges.

- Digital natives among HCPs (Healthcare Professionals) are increasing, with the tipping point (51 percent) being reached in 2014. Digital native physicians are estimated to be about 75 percent of total physicians by 2030. These physicians are digitally savvy, prefer digital channels, and want to receive relevant communication conveniently on the channels they want.
- Pharma marketers in the off-patent space find it difficult to differentiate their products and continue to stick to sales pitches and push messages. As a result, initiatives beyond the pill are missing.
- Pharma companies cannot gain adequate attention from doctors as they are unwilling to spend more than a few minutes with sales representatives as they are not meeting their information requirements.
- Unable to provide compelling reasons for physicians to prescribe their products, many pharma companies in the branded-generics markets are resorting to the soft option of transactional marketing. However, with some rules and guidelines in place, it is also becoming difficult to provide upfront benefits to HCPs on a *quid pro quo* basis. Instead, it forces the industry to move to a relationship-based approach to engage physicians with persuasive, evidence-based communication.
- Even offline, physical marketing events such as seminars and conferences through key opinion leaders are becoming difficult for pharma companies to engage physicians.

- Empowered patients are demanding seamless customer experiences that they are used to from other sectors of health care too.

Digital is the Way Forward

A steady decline in the quantity (reducing access to physicians) and quality of engagement and an increasing adoption rate of physicians to digital channels have been pushing pharmaceutical companies to use digital channels for improving physician engagement.

When the digital revolution is changing doctors' behavior in seeking information, can pharma continue with its communication strategies and not go forward with digital ways?

Furthermore, a Docplexus study on understanding what information HCPs want from pharma and how they want it revealed that:

- 79 percent of physicians are unable to get full information during visits of medical representatives
- 75 percent of physicians go online for more information
- The preferred schedule of physicians for online communication is once a week between 1 to 4 PM or 7 and 10 PM.
- As regards the types of information, 42 percent of HCPs want medical types, with 35 percent looking for new treatment regulations and 23 percent wanting to know the services by pharma.

Common Multichannel Pitfalls

There are some common misconceptions about digital, and marketers will do better by avoiding these:

- Most people believe that multichannel is digital only. It is not.
- Some marketers think and use digital only as a playground and use it for some pilots and small projects. However, Digital is not a playground but a mainstream.
- Do not equate digital with innovation.

- Do not place digital in isolation. Make it an integral part of your strategy.
- Do not see digital only as a way to enhance sales rep engagement with the target group. Instead, think of a much larger role for Digital in your total strategy.
- Remember, Digital is not a substitute for face-to-face communication. Use it right, and it can augment your overall strategy significantly.

Is Phygital the New Omnichannel?

Phygital blurs the line between physical and digital channels to create a consistent omnichannel experience. There is no longer a separate physical and digital strategy but an integrated phygital strategy that unites physical and digital sides to create an immersive customer experience no matter which channel they access information, product, or service.

Every multichannel or omnichannel strategy should contain a balanced mix of the three media types—Owned, Paid, and Earned. Here is a brief account of each media type, what it is, its role, and its benefits:

- **Owned Media** comprises those channels that the company fully controls. For example, a website, mobile site, blog, newsletter, and press release form part of the owned media. Owned Media helps build longer-term relationships and establish a continuous presence. The advantages of owned media are— full control, cost efficiency, longevity, versatility, and addressing different target audiences. The downside of owned Media is that it often lacks trust among HCPs, the source being the company or the brand and their perceived vested interests.
- **Paid Media** is the presence of your company acquired through buying space on these channels. Display advertising, SEA (Search Engine Advertising), and sponsorships are some examples of paid media. Paid Media is used essentially to drive traffic to your owned media. The advantages of Paid Media

are that it gives you control over costs and immediate impact and is easily scalable. However, the response rates with Paid Media are declining, and banner blindness is increasing.

- **Earned Media** is when your customers become the channel. Notable examples of Earned Media are Word-of-Mouth (WoM), Buzz and Viral marketing, and Retweets and Likes on social media platforms. Earned Media is very important in establishing stronger credibility and improving engagement. However, the company does not have any control over Earned Media. Also, it is hard to measure and scale up.

Here is a table giving you an illustrative list of the various channels available for you to engage your customers.

Table 3.9 The Phygital Channel Mix (Offline and Online)

Offline or Physical Channels	Online or Digital Channels
• Promotional call • Direct Mail • Newsletter • Sales rep visit • Sales rep tablet detailing • Samples • Promotional SMS • Local scientific meeting • International scientific meeting • Medical Journal • CME • Congress Booth for displaying company's products • MSL (Medical Science Liaison) • KOL meeting • Medical Education • Phase IV Clinical Trail	• eDetailing • eNewsletter • Remote Engagement • Website • eMSL • Webcast • eCME • Smartphone App • KOL webinar

In sum, Owned Media enables you to engage with customers, Paid Media with strangers, and Earned Media with advocates. Therefore, you must use a balanced mix to reach and engage your target audience effectively.

Implementing Phygital

Now that we know the importance of phygital marketing, how do we implement or practice it? Firstly develop a phygital strategy by understanding the target audience thoroughly regarding their needs, wants, and channel preferences and a convenient time for interacting. Consider the following steps:

1. Develop a brand strategy covering all key aspects, such as brand objectives, positioning, business opportunities, and key stakeholders.
2. Translate the strategy into something actionable by identifying leverage points, behavioral objectives, and differentiated messages.
3. Decide on the conversion points— what content or services will drive the action and change we want?
4. What are the ideal channels to achieve this—physical and digital?
5. Prioritize your action plan by deciding on what is feasible. Also, study the impact of these tactics.
6. Measure what matters. How can we measure the interactions and engagement?
7. Invest adequately in creating the necessary digital and physical infrastructure.
8. You must blend insights from offline and online behaviors into physician perception about the therapy area, your molecule, and your competition. It would help you develop compelling communication strategies for your brand.
9. Develop and create various types of relevant, modular content that is channel-specific yet integrated to ensure uniformity and consistency of messaging across the channels to create a seamless experience.
10. Train your sales representatives thoroughly on scientific and technical aspects to build their capabilities for orchestrating multiple channels— physical and digital in effective physician engagement.

11. Implement closed-loop marketing to provide your sales representatives with the relevant next-best action tactics based on continuous measurement and monitoring of the impact of their interactions with HCPs.
12. Finally, creating holistic engagement with your audience through various channels is crucial to succeeding with phygital. An integrated approach will help you seamlessly improve the experience of your customers (HCPs) and consumers (patients). Studies show that good omnichannel engagement results in up to 90 percent retention of customers.

CHAPTER

4

The Future of Pharma
A Look into the Crystal Ball

The only thing we know about the future is that It will be different, and the best way to predict is to create it.

— *Peter Drucker*

Digital Transformation

What is Digital Transformation?

Digital transformation in healthcare is not about technology but people. Digital health solutions can help us remove the friction from healthcare experiences, allowing healthcare professionals to focus on patient care and patients to take an active role in their health and well-being with easy and intuitive tools.

Lindsay Herbert, the author of the book Digital Transformation: Build Your Organization's Future in the Innovation Age, identified and dispelled three misconceptions about digital transformation:

- **Misconception 1**: Digital Transformation needs a big budget before it can even start. **Reality**: You don't need a big budget to start a digital transformation. You can start a digital transformation regardless of your current size and sector. You can start with a simple question— How do we drive value, and what does the organization design need to look like to enable that?
- **Misconception 2**: Everyone knows what I'm talking about when I say *Digital Transformation*. **Reality**: No, they don't. Everyone you have spoken to about digital transformation has a slightly different definition of its focus, extent, and purpose. It is one of the major reasons why many digital transformation programs fail.
- **Misconception 3**: When digital transformation is over, we can return to business as usual. **Reality**: *Transform*, by definition, means something is no longer the thing it was before. In that case, how can one think that digital transformation will allow us to continue doing what we have always done? Digital transformation is to understand the rules of the game have essentially changed. Digital transformation is not just putting your existing practices on the internet. Also, it is not about adapting to new technology at all. It is about directing an organization to be more adaptive to change itself.

What is Real Digital Transformation?

Real digital transformation is not about getting your company to use a specific set of new and emerging technologies. Instead, it is about transforming your company's capabilities to react and successfully utilize new technologies and procedures now and in the future. It's about making your company future-proof!

Most organizations are stuck in their ways, siloed, isolated, slow to react, and bogged down by old processes. Moreover, its complex approval processes slow down decision-making and make it difficult to reach a consensus, let alone pursue a collective goal. Real digital transformation helps break down these barriers, removing the constraints imposed by outdated logic, leveraging technology to improve revenue streams, drive down costs and enhance the customer experience. But, like any professional sportsperson undergoing rigorous training, successful digital transformation begins with small changes, including using new devices, platforms, systems, and networks. It helps the organization create:

- More profitable business models
- More efficient operating processes
- Greater access to markets
- Better customer experiences
- increased revenues

Three Major Areas

Digital transformation addresses all key elements intrinsically linked to your business as a whole by tackling three major areas:

1. **Business Model**: How revenue is generated, how customers are acquired and retained
2. **Customer Experience**: How you deliver customer experiences by engaging with them with your products and services
3. **Internal Processes:** Ways of working, operations, analysis, and Decision-making

These three critical areas of your digital transformation program will help you increase revenues and competitive advantage and get done more, faster, and with less.

Why Digital Transformation?

Pharmaceutical companies, known for their innovative capabilities, whether developing from scratch or incremental innovation of existing products, now face a different challenge of dealing with a disruptive innovation driven by inventions outside the healthcare sector. In addition, new players from the technology and digital arena are redefining how healthcare is delivered. Their innovations are forcing the pharmaceutical industry to change its business models or even create completely new ones in their industry. Consider, for example, pharma companies such as Merck and AbbVie taking initial steps towards offering a range of basic services to improve patient compliance and adherence through interdisciplinary collaboration. Merck, for example, created a patient engagement platform, MerckEngage, and AbbVie developed a video solution for managing Parkinson's Disease with Karolinska University Hospital.

The innovative solutions developed by non-traditional entrants into the healthcare ecosystem rapidly change individual patients' engagement. For example, many new biosensor technologies, smart devices, portals, and physician guidance tools allow enhanced self-monitoring capabilities and patient adherence. All these digital health solutions help solve the major long-term issues of patients, providers, and payers who are pharma's key stakeholders. Also, healthcare providers and payers demand better health outcomes and greater cost-effectiveness from payers and providers, forcing pharmaceutical companies to engage more actively in the opportunities arising from the digital revolution and patient-centered care. Therefore, pharma companies must think of ways to engage their stakeholders directly to stay relevant in the future healthcare system, or they may be left behind.

The Real Challenge of Transformation

Paradoxical as it may seem, as humans, we all love convenience, but at the same time, we naturally avoid new processes and resist change. Therefore, resistance to change, a major challenge of digital transformation, is rooted in our DNA. These hardwired genetic attributes that make us avoid changing make new technology slow to take off initially. However, once adopted, the same evolutionary trait makes the system hard to leave because we have become comfortable with it, and the process is convenient. That is why transforming to keep up with technology is not the real problem. The real challenge is changing attitudes towards *change* itself. The real challenge of digital transformation is putting new ways of working in place to ensure continuous change and improvement at your company's core.

What Pharma should do?

The competitive pressure from healthcare systems and non-traditional players in the evolving healthcare ecosystem dictates that pharma companies must ensure that they:

- Respond faster than ever before with more comprehensive approaches to change
- Embrace new technologies and strategies with increased flexibility
- Accelerate development programs that foster new skill sets, new mindsets, and new behaviors
- Open up to greater collaboration with new partners, including connecting and sharing information with others in the competitive space, as individual patients will increasingly require a combined approach to treatment.
- Take advantage of cost-effective and efficient devices that collect health data, such as the Apple Watch, Fitbit Fitness Tracker, continuous glucose monitors, and portable electroencephalogram (EEG) monitors, as they become available.
- Increase transparency to earn the trust of regulatory bodies and patients

How Digital Transformation Impacts the Pharma Industry?

Digital transformation can impact the pharmaceutical industry positively in many ways. Vijay K Veera shows many ways in which digital transformation impacts pharma in a blog article, Perspective: *How Digital Transformation is Impacting the Pharma Industry,* published in CXO Bytes a few months ago:

- *Faster drug discovery with new age digital technologies*: Pharma scientists can create digital versions of potential molecules to accelerate drug discoveries by simulating models in the R&D labs using artificial intelligence and machine learning, and predictive analytics.
- *Clinical Trials— Data is the new drug*: Digital transformation can help pharma companies solve the perennial problem of recruiting candidates for clinical trials, with digital initiatives such as electronic consenting and passing of information electronically.
- *Re-imagining data—Advent of the external arm*: Today, scientists can leverage data and plumb databases by combining with emerging technologies such as artificial intelligence and machine learning and find patients who were controls in past treatment trials for similar conditions to create an *External Control Arm*.
- *Clinical trials— Anytime, Anywhere, Anyone*: The proliferation of self-monitoring devices, wellness gadgets, and wearables augmented decentralized clinical trials. Pharma companies are yet to harness this huge data in real time and realize its potential value. Pharmaceutical companies can store the data in cloud-based metadata repositories. They can readily access and analyze clinical trial data that helps them develop more potent and safe drugs and treatments.
- *Real-time data visibility is indispensable for pharma supply chain efficiency*: Digital transformation helps pharma companies break down their silos, enabling data across the organization in a harmonized manner and enriching it with

external data such as weather, regulatory, and customer data. In addition, companies can capture robust real-time data insights, plot measures, and countermeasures in planning and scheduling their deliveries. In addition, with technologies such as IoT and RFID (Radio Frequency Identification), decision-makers can have a single view of the entire supply chain from manufacturing to delivery.

- *Blockchain— Unblocking pharma bottlenecks*: Blockchain helps partnering companies with competing interests collaborate and safely work together in a shared, permanent ledger without giving up control or revealing proprietary or sensitive data.
- *Bolstering drug supply chain security with blockchain*: The influx of spurious drugs claims the lives of thousands of patients globally, affects sales, and harms the reputation of pharma companies. Blockchain technology can bring about radical security measures, reinforcing the supply chains of pharmaceutical companies with its barcode tracking system that tracks a drug from the conveyor belt to a customer.
- *Reinventing HCP engagement with Artificial Intelligence (AI) and Machine Learning (ML) and omnichannel experience*: Pharma companies can optimize their brand performances by mining healthcare datasets and deploying machine learning algorithms to plot and fine-tune promotional strategies to capture and captivate the HCP minds.

How Pharma can Transform?

The game-changing digital technologies that are increasingly available today will help pharmaceutical companies to improve their efficiencies significantly throughout the value chain. Companies that are proactive today will stay ahead, leaving behind those that are not.

The best way to be proactive on this journey is to start the transformation in a targeted way by focusing on key long-term technologies and, simultaneously, on specific pilot projects to build practical experience and expertise before fully operationalizing them.

The Human Factor in Transformation

Companies must be agile enough to reinvent and transform themselves in today's hyper-competitive business environment. At the same time, it is important to understand the importance and significance of human factors in change management, for they can determine whether transformation takes place or not. In 1996, John P. Kotter suggested eight steps to successfully steer a corporation through times of change in his insightful book, Leading Change. He says Transformation programs require:

- a compelling story— a Sense of Urgency
- a strong cross-hierarchical team—a Guiding Coalition
- a clear vision of where to go
- good communication
- empowered employees rather than top-down procedures
- quick-wins and consolidated gains to keep the momentum, and
- a refined organizational culture that recognizes the right new behaviors

Do's and Don'ts

Arthur D. Little, a leading global management consulting firm, suggests three important do's and don'ts for effective organizational transformation.

1. **Do** focus on precise management of the *hard facts* of the change: organizational charts, role descriptions, and processes, but **Don't** underestimate the importance of the *soft factors* and hidden cultural barriers– the unwritten rules in your organization.
2. **Do** apply state-of-the-art change management methods, but **Don't** skimp on the initial assessment to tailor the change approach to your context.
3. **Do** use formal approaches where these are effective, but **Don't** underestimate the need for informal and unconventional approaches in many situations.

Digital Transformation: Closing the Gaps

While most pharmaceutical companies recognize that digital is disrupting healthcare, very few companies have a quantified, granular understanding of how digital affects their competitive environment and business model. As a result, Pharma certainly lags in adopting digital transformation. Why so? McKinsey, a global management consulting major that developed a Digital Quotient (DQ) assessment tool, observed that while many pharma industry leaders believe that the gap in data analytics is what has been holding them back in their digital strategy, the fact is that there are additional elements related to their strategy, culture, and organization responsible for not embarking on a company-wide digital transformation. Brain Fox, Nisha Subramanian, Amit Paley, and Michelle Prevost of Mckinsey and Company identified three practices that represent pharma's biggest barriers to improving their digital performance in their article, *Closing the digital gap in pharma, published in Mckinsey.com on November 23, 2016.* These are:

1. Ensuring a customer mindset
2. Linking digital to the broader mindset
3. Maintaining an efficient operating model

Five Stages of Successful Digital Transformation

Lindsay Herbert, the author of the book Digital Transformation: Build Your Organization's Future in the Innovation Age, introduced a five-stage model for a successful digital transformation, BUILD, an acronym for **B**ridge, **U**ncover, **I**terate, **L**everage, and **D**isseminate. Why BUILD? Two reasons. First, BUILD symbolizes digital transformation's scale, permanence, and impact. Secondly, these five steps spell something meaningful and are easy to remember, and they come from the distinctive phases present in most large-scale and small-scale digital transformations.

1. **Bridge**: Bridging the gaps between your company, the people it is meant to serve, and the changes happening around it. The first step of digital transformation is figuring out how much you need to change and how quickly.

2. **Uncover**: Uncovering your company's hidden barriers, useful assets, and needed resources to plan and prioritize its routes transformation forms the second stage. It involves investigating your company, challenging outdated logic, and prioritizing needed fixes.
3. **Iterate**: Iteration is about building in short cycles, testing with real users, and improving as you go to know which innovations you can scale. It involves switching from insight gathering and consensus building to producing actual results, working through cross-functional teams collaboratively.
4. **Leverage**: During this stage, you leverage successes to access greater resources, influence, and space to scale new solutions, ways of working, and the innovation mindset.
5. **Disseminate**: In this final stage, you disseminate innovations and new ways of working systematically to make thriving in changing environments the new *business as usual*, incrementally scaling digital transformation across every area of the organization.

Pharma's Digital Transformation: Key Success Factors

Over eighty-one percent of healthcare executives say that the COVID-19 pandemic has accelerated digital transformation with a surge of innovations in their organizations. However, technology is only part of the equation in digital transformation. It is important to address people, processes, data, and other factors to achieve digital transformation throughout the organization from the current stage of innovation in isolated pockets. The article, *Seven Key Success Factors for Digital Transformation in Healthcare*, published in Philips Global blog on April 13, 2022, highlights what it takes to implement a successful digital transformation. Here's the gist:

1. Designing digital health solutions for better human experiences
2. Bringing everyone on board through effective change management
3. Training staff to help them get the most out of digital technology

4. Taking an inclusive approach that leaves no patient behind
5. Adopting cloud-based platforms for data access anytime, anywhere
6. Building digital trust by safeguarding privacy and security
7. Joining forces through strategic partnerships and ecosystem collaboration

Digital Transformation in Pharma: Some Examples

Digital transformation can fundamentally change the way pharmaceutical companies do business. It can help organizations significantly improve patient care, customer experience, cost-effectiveness and manufacturing counterfeit-proof medications, productivity, and profitability. The following cases show how some pharma companies have successfully implemented digital transformation.

CASE

93

Four Tips from Pfizer on Going with Digital Pharma Marketing!

Pharmaceutical companies are embracing the digital way of working to empower their most valued resource—customer-facing teams to enhance their relationships and create a more effective engagement by delivering content the way customers want it.

Pfizer's successful experience in digital marketing teaches us four lessons on how to implement digital pharma marketing strategies

1. **Pick the right mix of markets**: The choice of pilot markets is very important to assess how well your digital solution works and impacts your business. It is useful to select your most challenging market with a complex health system and hard-to-reach physicians to gauge your solution's real-world effectiveness.
2. **Train on business scenarios**: Do not just focus your field teams' training on the virtual interaction programs built into your CRM system. They work on it every day, anyhow. Instead, focus on use cases and building soft skills to take advantage of the new channel. In addition, it would be better to encourage them to embrace digital capability and use it to maximize customer-facing time by modeling different business scenarios.
3. **Ensure global-local collaboration**: It is important to establish the role, and goal clarity across marketing organizations, analytics, business, and IT teams to create a best practice

template for digital engagement and ensure organizational alignment.

4. **Set the right measures of success**: It is important to set the right measures. For example, Pfizer created three metrics to assess virtual communication's real-world impact and success in establishing and nurturing new relationships to improve flexibility for HCPs and operating costs when you enable field force capabilities.

   1. Customer Engagement:

   - What is the impact of our virtual meetings? Are they contributing to the total number of customer-facing hours?
   - What is the average duration of a virtual call?

   2. Customer and User Experience:

   - Is our customer solution positively impacting our customer perceptions?
   - Do our customer-facing teams find the solution usable?

   3. Business Efficiencies:

   - Are there any operational improvements with our integrated solution?

(Source: Nicole Salis and Manuel Lima, 4 Tips from Pfizer on Going on Digital with Pharma Marketing, veeva.com, April 16, 2018) — Reduce the font size by one point for the entire text in 'Source')

CASE

94

UCB's Erik Janssen shows the Way to Take Your Company to the next level With Digital Transformation!

Do you want to take your company to the next level? If you want to, follow this advice from Erik Janssen, vice president and head of digital care transformation for immunology at UCB. He is making a difference by creating successful healthcare partnerships.

Here is his take on digital transformation and how they have been doing it at UCB.

The guiding principle at UCB is delivering value to the patients who are at the core of everything they do. The company understands that it must amplify the power of scientific innovation through digital transformation to create sustainable value, ensuring that patients can live the lives they choose.

UCB's digital portfolio includes ten transformational projects within neurology and immunology. The company uses digital technologies in all these projects to create new or modify existing business processes, cultures, and customer experiences to meet changing business and market requirements.

For example, UCB, the global leader in epilepsy management, launched a new independent digital health company, Nile AI Inc., created to improve care for people with epilepsy. The mission of this company is to make the journey of every epilepsy patient predictable. Nile, the first company of its kind in this space, aims to improve the interaction between physicians and patients to optimize care delivery

In addition, UCB focuses on people with rheumatological, dermatological conditions, and osteoporosis, where early diagnosis is a hurdle. For example, axial spondyloarthritis, a chronic inflammatory rheumatic disease, could take up to nine years until people are diagnosed and treated for the condition. UCB believes that developing digital solutions alone or with partners in this area can greatly impact patients.

Furthermore, on January 5, 2021, UCB filed a trademark application for MY JASMINE with the United States Patent and Trademark Office (USPTO). MY JASMINE is a care coach app with a screening algorithm where patients log in to the program and see a questionnaire about their disease, social context, and personality. This screening process helps the company identify unmet needs that a patient with rheumatological conditions faces and tie them to another solution.

UCB is also developing an AI (Artificial Intelligence) radiology algorithm that runs on scans of vertebrae to detect fractures and identify potential patients who may develop osteoporosis, helping physicians augment their ability to diagnose patients much earlier.

UCB focuses relentlessly on high unmet needs, be they from the patient, physician, or healthcare system, to create highly relevant and meaningful solutions either as a company or with their trusted partners.

UCB is going through a full-scale digital business transformation that includes digitalizing its core business to establish simpler and more efficient new ways of working.

UCB's definition of digital transformation is embracing digital to augment how it delivers value to patients. By applying technologies to transform care. Accordingly, the company has embarked on transformative initiatives to seamlessly integrate technologies by connecting to peers, partners, and the patients they serve.

What takeaways from UCB's digital transformation journey can we use to transform our companies to take them to the next level? Here are five takeaways suggested by Erik Janssen in his interview with Jason Hartman for Authority Magazine:

1. Empower a digital mindset
2. Use data and technology with a purpose
3. Partner for a greater impact
4. Accelerate better outcomes through a deeper understanding
5. Transform the way care is delivered by transforming your work

(Source: Adapted from Jason Hartman's article, Erik Janssen of UCB On How To Use Digital Transformation To Take Your Company To The Next Level, published on February 14, 2021, in Authority Magazine)

CASE

95

Takeda Accelerates Digital Transformation!

In October 2020, Takeda Pharmaceutical, a global Japanese pharma company, entered into a five-year strategic agreement with Amazon Web Services (AWS) and Accenture, a global consulting major, to accelerate Takeda's digital transformation. The collaboration will leverage cloud and data-driven insights to accelerate drug development, increase operational agility, reduce technology costs and develop the workforce of the future.

Furthermore, the collaboration is a win-win for all as it increases Takeda's ability to respond with greater speed, agility, and insights across the value chain, benefiting customers, employees, partners, and patients.

Takeda can increase connectivity and collaboration with the life sciences ecosystem and external partners by accelerating the delivery of data services and capabilities. For example, the collaboration has already helped Takeda harness the cloud to launch a secure data sharing and clinical trial acceleration for the COVID R&D Alliance in less than five days which would have taken up to three months otherwise.

In addition, Takeda's Plasma-Derived Therapies Business Unit, which develops critical life-saving and life-sustaining therapies for patients with rare and complex diseases, is creating state-of-the-art, digitally connected donation centers and modernizing the donor experience, optimizing the plasma collection process.

According to Andy Jassy, chief executive officer of AWS (Amazon Web Services), by leveraging the most comprehensive set of cloud services in the industry, innovators like Takeda can cut costs, time to insight and discovery, and improve patient experiences. Also, the cloud services enable Takeda to quickly and efficiently discover, develop and manufacture therapeutics securely and compliantly.

Julie Sweet, chief executive officer of Accenture, has this to say on this: *Takeda's bold move to become a cloud-first company, 80 percent in the cloud, is a powerful example of how transformation benefits all— from accelerating therapies for patients to empowering employees with new ways of working, creating new jobs, and up-skilling people for the digital world, to the sustainability benefits of moving to the public cloud.*

Finally, Christopher Weber, president, and chief executive officer of Takeda, said about the collaboration and his vision: *By combining the power of three organizations, Takeda is making a bold move to be at the intersection of human health, technology, and business growth. My vision is that, in less than ten years, every Takeda employee will be empowered by an artificial intelligence assistant to help him make better decisions, enabling us to deliver transformative therapies and better experiences to patients, physicians, and payers faster than previously possible. Together, Accenture and AWS will propel Takeda further than we could alone make this vision a reality.*

(Source: Company press release: Takeda Accelerates Digital Transformation with Accenture and AWS, December 13, Osaka, Japan, New York, and Seattle)

CASE 96

Astellas Utilizes the Digital Transformation to Maximize Value for Patients!

Astellas, a leading Japanese pharmaceutical company with a global presence (operations in 70 countries worldwide), embarked on a digital transformation program to create and maximize value to patients.

Astellas wants to be at the forefront of healthcare change to turn innovative science into value for patients. Therefore, the company's approach to digital transformation is not just streamlining operations through digital technology but considering digital transformation as a key enabler.

Astellas is committed to providing value to patients through their journey by integrating innovative medical technologies with cutting-edge technologies in different fields to develop solutions across the whole spectrum of medical care, including diagnosis, prevention, therapeutic and prognostic care.

The company is proactively developing solutions that maximize patient outcomes and reduce costs by implementing digital transformation across all areas of the pharmaceutical value chain, including R&D, manufacturing, sales, and marketing.

Astellas' vision for digital transformation is to become a world-class intelligent enterprise that accelerates digital transformation to turn innovative science to value for patients. The company has identified four sources of value centered around digital and data to realize its vision:

- **Sense**: Use sensory devices to collect various types of events as data
- **Analyze**: Utilize and analyze all data to forecast the future and support bold and accurate decision-making early on
- **Automate**: Use digital for high-quality, fast operations
- **Engage**: Use a combination of digital and analog to connect people across time and space

Shinya Suda, senior vice president of information systems at Takeda, gives his perspective on Takeda's digital transformation when he says: *For me, DX (Digital Transformation) is about evolving the way we conduct business; it's about utilizing digital technology to increase value for patients dramatically. Even if we introduce a small system, it is an excellent example of DX if it leads to increased patient value. Conversely, if we decide to work with cutting-edge technology or use an extensive system, we can't call it DX if it does not evolve the way our business is done and lead to increased value*.

(Source: Astellas DX Strategy Series: Utilizing DX to create and maximize value for patients, the company website, astellas.com)

CASE

97

Digital Transformation at Pfizer!

Over the past few years, Pfizer has been undertaking an organization-wide digital transformation aligned with its mission. Pfizer's Mission? Albert Bourla, CEO of Pfizer, defined Pfizer's mission as *driving breakthroughs that change patients' lives.* Digital plays a part in every aspect of how they will achieve that transformation.

3 Bold Moves

Pfizer created three bold moves supporting its purpose-driven blueprint to win the digital race in pharma. Its focus is on:

1. Applying digital technologies to help speed up the discovery and development of medicines and vaccines
2. To enhance the patient and customer experience for improving outcomes
3. To make work faster and easier through automation

Digital Companion Strategy

As a part of Pfizer's digital transformation strategy, Digital Companions provide solutions and tools over digital channels to help providers and patients in various ways, such as educating, improving compliance, and adherence leading to improved patient outcomes. Pfizer aims to create a supportive digital companion with every breakthrough they deliver to the market to drive engagement and help patients and healthcare providers. Here are some examples of Pfizer's Digital Companions and how they help drive the engagement of customers (Providers) and consumers (Patients):

- Mabu, the wellness coach, is artificial intelligence (AI)-powered patient engagement robot from Catalia Health. Mabu talks with patients about how they are feeling and helps answer their questions about their treatment. The Mabu Care Insights Platform, then delivers data and insights to clinicians at a specialty pharmacy provider to help a patient's caregivers initiate timely and appropriate outreach to the patient. Thus, Mabu helps to manage symptoms better and address patients' questions in real-time.
- LivingWith™ is another digital companion of Pfizer. It aims to connect cancer patients with an oncology support system, enabling them to share information with caregivers, friends, and family and remember important information from doctor's visits.
- In addition, Pfizer completed a drone pilot program in the Dominican Republic to deliver medications to patients in remote, hard-to-reach areas by partnering with WeRobotics and the Dominican Republic's Ministry of Health. The company is considering other locations that could benefit from this program.

Change Management

Driving change in any organization is very difficult as we humans are naturally hardwired to change. The older and more established the organization, the greater the resistance. Pfizer has been around for over a hundred years. So, the key to a successful transformation effort is change management. It is not easy to get people to adapt to a new way of doing things. The best way to get people to come to the transformation journey is to share the vision of the future: What does the future look like? Why do we need to change? How will it benefit the company, our customers, and each of us? And once people start to see tangible outcomes during the transition, they often become advocates of the transformation process.

Pfizer has successfully engaged its employees and brought them on the transformation journey. So how did the company achieve it? The first thing is to bring all colleagues, whether they are change-averse or eager to jump in into the transformation journey.

For those that are change-averse, the company introduced mini roadshows, focusing on presenting the vision of the future.

And for those eager to change, the company ensured that there were lunch-and-learns, Agile sprint retrospectives, and ideation sessions with team members on projects and work streams where they could bring input and become a part of the change programs. Pfizer addressed the concerns of the change-averse and change-eager, sharing success stories and celebrating incremental wins to make the transformation successful.

3 Strategic Themes

Pfizer followed a three-pronged strategy to achieve digital transformation across the company.

The first key theme is scaling new ways of working — working smarter and faster with agile processes, simplifying how the teams learn and develop.

Secondly, the company focused on powering the core, driving the organization of drug discovery and development, deepening patient and healthcare provider engagement through things like its digital companions, driving manufacturing and supply chain excellence, and leveraging real-world data and evidence in its R&D pipeline.

Finally, the company is transforming its business with initiatives such as virtual clinical trials, virtual core go-to-market mode, and engaging patients longitudinally to drive improved outcomes.

Lidia Fonseca, Pfizer's Chief Digital and Technology Officer, says about their digital transformation: *Pfizer is starting to support patients, physicians, and payers in a very different way than in the past. We are learning about blind spots in patients' journeys and working on using insights from data and digital solutions to deliver a more integrated experience. We want patients, caregivers, and healthcare providers to sync in real-time to improve experiences and outcomes meaningfully*.

(Source: Adapted from Stan Gloss's interview with Bill Leister, Senior Vice President Pfizer, Pfizer's Digital Strategy and Transformation published on Bio-IT World, on July 20, 21; and the company website pfizer.com)

CASE

98

Johnson & Johnson's Digital Transformation!

Johnson & Johnson is an American multinational medical device, pharmaceutical, and consumer packaged goods manufacturing company founded in 1886. The company operates over 250 companies. In recent years, the company has reimagined itself as a health-technology innovator in many ways.

With over 132,000 employees and $93.3 billion in worldwide sales in 2021, Johnson & Johnson is the largest drug firm in the world.

While technology has always been central to J&J's mission, it was still considered a cost center until about ten years ago. However, in 2012, when the company brought on a new CIO (Chief Information Officer), Stuart McGuigan, things changed, and the company embarked on a digital transformation program.

In 2017, McGuigan explained the company's vision of digital transformation in an interview. He said that *true digital transformation touches every part of the organization— from core IT back to the supply chain. So in our view, it has to be an integrated effort rather than a separate one. You're going to run into trouble at some point, for instance, if you're implementing user-centered development and design thinking on the front end. But, still, you haven't digitized your business processes on the back end. So we brought everyone together and said we would take an end-to-end view of digitization— from how we consume electricity in the data center to how we interact with customers. And we invited everyone in the company to look at what we were doing— at any point— to see what sort of progress we were making.*

J&J has been an early adopter of intelligent automation, artificial intelligence (AI), robotic process automation (RPA), and data science, completing 60 global processes. Joaquin Duato, Vice Chairman of the Executive Committee, Johnson & Johnson, wrote an essay, *Johnson & Johnson: Bettering Health Through Tech in a New COVID-19 World*, for Deloitte's Wall Street Journal Page. He wrote: *Intelligent automation reduces repetitive and routine work while generating insights that employees can use to improve decisions, compliance and quality, and speed. For example, our finance collections team automates routine tasks, giving members more time to engage with customers to address their concerns. It has led to improved cash flow, increased productivity, greater efficiency, higher customer satisfaction, and enhanced job satisfaction. In addition, intelligent automation has helped us support the well-being of our employees and their ability to work remotely during the COVID-19 crisis and to execute critical business processes like payroll, sourcing virtually, and financial close.*

Digitalizing Products

J&J created several digital tools to guide people on their healthcare journeys by leveraging their clinical knowledge and technology. Here are some examples showing how J&J has been digitalizing its products to improve healthcare outcomes for patients:

- RA-RA (Remote Assessment in Rheumatoid Arthritis) mobile app can work with wearable trackers like Fitbit to collect behavioral and health information such as heart rate, sleep duration, and daily levels of joint pains and help indicate how well the medication is working and whether the patient's condition is improving or worsening.
- One-touch Reveal is another mobile app that helps diabetic patients monitor and manage their blood glucose levels.

- Another mobile app helps accelerate surgical consults for people with knee pain. The app starts by asking several questions about knee pain levels and will then use the results and predictive analytics to provide personalized treatment advice. Surgical candidates can download another app to help prepare them for surgery and recovery with targeted tips.

Robotizing Surgery

J&J formed a joint venture, Verb, with Google's Verily in 2015. When Google exited the joint venture in 2019, J&J acquired its stake and took over Verb entirely. Nevertheless, J&J is very optimistic about the future of robotic surgery, which can be seen from what Verb Surgical's CEO said some time ago. He said: There are 10—20 million surgeries a year, and only 5 percent are done robotically. We believe the number should be 75—90 percent. Currently, most robotic surgeries are performed by Da Vinci, a machine with large precise arms controlled by surgeons. But Verb's goal extends beyond hardware— it aims to be a platform for digital surgery, leveraging five technology pillars— robotics, visualization, advanced instrumentation, data analytics, and connectivity— and using a large amount of data to help the surgeon make highly informed fast, and accurate decisions. Verb calls this Surgery 4.0 the next evolution of surgery.

In addition, Johnson & Johnson plans to weave digital innovations into the organization's DNA, including its culture and processes. As Stuart McGuigan said, T*rue digital transformation touches every part of the organization—from core IT back to the supply chain. So, in our view, it has to be an integrated effort rather than a separate one.*"

(Source: Adapted from articles— 1. Elizabeth Mixson, Johnson & Johnson: A Crash Course in Tech-Enabled Business Resiliency, Intelligent Automation Network, March 23, 2021, 2. Ting, Alumni, Johnson & Johnson: Embracing Digital Transformation, Digital Innovation, and Transformation, MBA Student Perspectives, Harvard Business School)

CASE

99

Dr. Reddy Gears Up for a Digital Transformation!

Mukesh Rathi, Senior Vice President and Chief Information Officer at Dr. Reddy's Laboratories, foresees a huge opportunity for digital transformation in the primary value chain and the customer / patient journey. The opportunities exist across the value chain, from selecting a portfolio with analytics-based insights, drug development with *in-silico* experiences, and automated lights-out manufacturing using industry 4.0 technologies to dynamic supply chain management.

The aim of digital transformation in the customer and the patient journey is primarily to create a differentiated value proposition. The company aims to bring together four key touchpoints through various collaborations. These touchpoints are:

- in the journey of outpatient healthcare and wellness
- doctor consultations
- pathology laboratories and diagnostic services
- pharmacies and insurance

Dr. Reddy's plans leverage key opportunities to provide personalized services using digital technologies under customer and patient journeys. The company understands that digital transformation in pharma is much about people transformation and mindset shift as it is about the use of technology. Therefore, the company focuses on building digital capabilities, inspiration from success stories, and effective orchestration of change management.

Collaborative Models

The boundaries between technology and pharmaceuticals are blurring, enabling digital native companies to venture into pharma digital space. In addition, it is making pharma companies look at digital native solutions to address end-to-end solutions to consumers' pain points and enhance customer experience. Therefore, it is important to be open to collaborative models to leverage expertise from other players.

Extracting Insights is Vital

In pharma and life sciences companies, the term customer denotes a large audience ranging from healthcare professionals, doctors, and institutional buyers to patients or end consumers. Interactions with all these stakeholders take place in various forms, such as physical (in-clinic), virtual (tele-calls and remote calls), unsupervised visits of customers to websites, or digital platforms.

It is important to identify customer journeys with all their key touchpoints and understand the nuances and friction points, ensuring compliance with laws and regulations, including data privacy.

Empowering Customer Experience

Dr. Reddy's major focus is empowering customer experience with digital infrastructure, analytics, and personalization models. The company is building an underlying infrastructure through many initiatives, such as iPads for their field colleagues, collaboration platforms for remote engagement, and digital/web platforms for pull-based engagement.

Speaking about their strategy to improve customer engagement and experience, Mukesh Rathi, CIO at Dr. Reddy's, says: *We are creating data and analytics engines for insights with strategic aspects of Collect, Connect, and Analyze. In addition, we enable experience personalization with initiatives such as in-clinic message, remote, omnichannel message, and on-platform for all three physical, virtual, and unsupervised interaction formats. The human-centric design has also started to play an increasingly important role in our digital offerings regarding customer and patient journeys as we move from physical to unsupervised interactions with increasing digital innovation. Deeper customer relationships happen when we know the customer and personalize the engagement. For example, an omnichannel message or a remote conversation with a stakeholder may throw up multiple data points on the content, channel, and context. The outcome of deep insight is to personalize the message for the stakeholders that hits the right note and addresses the uncommunicated and unmet needs.*

In addition, technology can help identify evolutions to recommend personalized diet plans, share behavioral nudges, etc., to improve the treatment outcome when every patient goes through a journey throughout the process of disease therapy, from consultations to therapy adherence.

Cloud-native Platform

The company is deploying emerging technologies like Cloud and aims to achieve more than 70 percent workload transformation to Cloud by FY 2025. In addition, the company would like to transform its landscape into Cloud-native in the next few years.

Digital Approach

Furthermore, Dr. Reddy's has taken several initiatives as part of its digital transformation. Consider these, for example:

- *Digital Science Initiative* to help the company significantly reduce drug development cycle time, improve bio study success rate, and improve cost savings to enable first-to-market products, using data and analytics across the product development cycle.
- *Smart Rep Platform Initiative* for sales and marketing effectiveness has multiple platforms to improve the productivity of field force through smart scheduling calls, improving detailing quality with personalized nudges, reviewing call performance, virtual calls with doctors, etc.,

- *Digitalize the Core* to simplify and digitalize the processes that would enable the company to scale up without adding complexity. Their journey on paperless plants, Enterprise Resource Planning (ERP) upgrade, tablet-based detailing in the field, etc., would fall under their digital initiatives.
- Transform with Digital through conducting programs across the value chain that leverage digital and analytical use cases.

Three Core Areas for a Digital Future

Mukesh Rathi, CIO at Reddy's, believes that the future of Digital at Reddy's will continue to evolve around three broad areas.

1. *Enable business* with Digital through a relentless focus on digitalizing all core processes of their value chain to create a digital operating system that enables scale and efficiency.
2. *Building business with Digital* by being a partner of choice with all stakeholders, including patients, providers, and customers, in the entire journey from illness to wellness. It involves working on patient services, digital therapeutics, and new digital business model platforms such as SVAAS to cater to the unmet needs of patients.
3. *Leading business* with Digital keeps a dual focus on productivity platforms that help deliver differentiated service to customers and healthcare professionals for a seamless user experience. It provides a competitive advantage for the organization.

(Source: Adapted from articles—1. Salvi Mittal, Dr. Reddy's Gears Up For A Massive Digital Push, ET CIO, June 2, 2022, 2. Sneha Jha, Mukesh Rathi Uses Digital to Give Dr. Reddy's A Competitive Edge, ET CIO, September 21, 2018)

CASE

100

UCB's Digital Transformation of R&D!

UCB's central mission is to deliver value for people with severe immunological and neurological diseases now and into the future. The company recognized that leveraging digital technology is necessary and not a nice to have to realize its mission because digital allows you to create transformative projects that meet patients where they are.

Today's empowered patients are active participants in their care journey and increasingly demand more personalized and convenient healthcare solutions. Therefore, UCB is creating digital initiatives to unlock holistic, personal, and efficient value solutions generating value for patients from more than just drugs.

UCB's Digital Care Transformation Approach aims to use data and technology with purpose throughout the whole value chain for both drug and non-drug solutions because patient value extends beyond the molecule.

Here's an indicative list of UCB's transformational initiatives:

- The UCB Moonshot effort is being developed in partnership with PostEra— a start-up biotech company that maps routes for drug synthesis using Artificial Intelligence (AI) algorithms. Apart from providing better research data-driven insights to fast-track the discovery of therapeutic molecules and improve patient journeys, it is also helpful to find *pockets* that may not have been seen before and re-envision *undruggable targets*.

- The Statistical Science & Innovation group at UCB recently filed a patent application centered on an improved machine learning method. The application has been designed to search through a large hypothesis space to identify the most valuable pieces of information that allow AI to predict an outcome or provide decision guidance.
- UCB uses data analytics to optimize clinical trial design, including patient selection, automated analysis of trial data, and enhanced logistics operations.
- UCB believes collaborations are essential to innovation and achieving scientific breakthroughs. For example, UCB partnered with Microsoft to combine its deep knowledge in bioscience with Microsoft's expertise in computer science and artificial intelligence for discovering new correlations and patterns critical to finding innovative and highly individualized medicines.

(Source: Lévina Claufriez, Research and Development Communications, UCB, published on ucb.com, on May 30, 2022)

CASE

101

Cipla's Learning Transformation Journey!

Cipla, a pharmaceutical company, operating in more than eighty countries worldwide, embarked on a massive project a few years ago to transform itself from disconnected and decentralized to an engaging, accessible, and scalable organization.

In 2016, Cipla created MiCipla— the standardized global induction program to provide a uniform onboarding experience across all levels, functions, and geographies. Later, COVID-19 pushed Cipla to move to a virtual induction across the company, whose success accelerated the company's vision to create excellence in onboarding experience with a fully digital, automated, and self-directed MiCipla.

In 2017, the company constituted Cipla University with a centralized approach to unify enterprise-level learning and development initiatives and incorporate partnerships with business stakeholders across the organization. In addition, under the aegis of Cipla University, the company created transformational learning academies to deliver customized yet standardized learning solutions across verticals, aligning them with the organization's long-term business goals.

Cipla used digitalization as the main tool to make its vision a reality. The company focused its digital transformation strategy on creating a complete learning experience, integrating cutting-edge learning technology with tools such as inter-connected learning apps, and portals with deep integration with LMS (Learning Management Systems). As a result, it has simplified, standardized, and automated learning.

A 3-Phase Process

Cipla's digital transformation journey of learning involved three phases. In Phase 1, the company introduced enterprise-level digital learning platforms under the umbrella of Cipla University to address the needs across functions like India Sales Business, Supply Chain, Integrated Product Development, and Corporate functions, deploying device and platform agnostic learning apps. In addition, the company partnered with—

- CEB (Gartner), an online global best practice and insights tool,
- Percipio (Skillsoft), a Learning Experience Platform, and
- Kwench, the Phygital Library

These partnerships drive self-directed learning addressing the micro and deep learning needs of the Cipla Team.

Later in Phases 2 and 3, the company strengthened its digital learning vision, focusing on the organization's specific challenges and demands aligned with Stakeholder Experience, Operational Agility, Culture, and Leadership.

Cipla's LMS (Learning Management System) platform, *MiLearning*, has over 23,000 users, benefitting from its high-impact blended learning, with custom content, simulations driven through apps, knowledge and application check using gamification, AI-enabled tools, and live behavior tracking checklists.

6D's (Disciplines) of Learning

The established six disciplines of breakthrough guide the learning intervention at Cipla University. These are:

1. D1: Define the business outcomes
2. D2: Design the Complete Learning Experience

3. D3: Deliver for Application
4. D4: Drive learning for transfer
5. D5: Deploy performance support
6. D6: Document results

Tangible Outcomes of the Transformation

Here are a few tangible examples of the impact that the digital transformation of learning at Cipla University created, indicating the program's success:

- Eighty-eight percent of Cipla employees say I have an opportunity to learn and enhance my skills continually. Also, The 2020 scores place Cipla 21 percent above the Global Industry Average and 12 percent above the India Industry average.
- Cipla's learning programs focus on applying the learnings to business problems into Breakthrough Projects (BTPs). Each BTP has clearly defined success criteria and leads to cost optimization. The estimated cost saving from BTPs implementation was INR 25 Crores.
- Sharing success stories of successful application of the learnings is an important part of the program. For example, participants shared 500 plus customer conversion stories within 90 days of application from a sample representing 25 percent of the business.

(Source: Adapted from Blog articles— 1. Suryakant Pandey, Senior director, head - learning and development, Cipla's Learning Transformation Journey— from disconnected & decentralized to engaging, accessible, and scalable, peoplematters.in , February 27, 2021, and 2. What are the 6D's? published on the6d.com)

CASE

102

Cipla's Digital Transformation!

For the past four years, Cipla, the Indian pharma major with a global presence in over eighty countries, has been dabbling in machine learning (ML), data analytics, robotic process automation(RPA), and other new-age technologies as a part of its organization-wide digital transformation.

Cipla's digital transformation journey started with IT moving to the front end of the business. Realizing that building a digital culture is crucial for the transformation, the company decided to reskill and up-skill the organization, digitizing several processes in HR, manufacturing, supply chain, product development, and sales & marketing.

The company set goals and milestones for its digital transformation effort. Consider these, for example:

- Move the entire field force to a digital detailing platform in 12—15 months.
- Reduce downtime at Cipla's global manufacturing units by 20—30 percent.

At the same time, Cipla has introduced several innovations to keep up with the changing digital landscape:

- *Laboratory Information Management System (LIMS)* helps to control better, manage and organize and document lab data, improve efficiencies by providing more analytical results at lower cost, improve accuracy, enhance customer service and reduce cycle times.

- *Electronic Lab Notebooks (ELN)* capture data during research and track product development phases by automating the documentation process, enabling the company to transit towards paperless R&D.
- *The Closed Loop Marketing System* enables the 8,000-strong Cipla field force to have a meaningful discussion within the short face-time with the doctor, automatically analyzing a physician's preferences and arms the salesperson to deliver personalized content that closely matches the physician's interests. More importantly, the accompanying e-detailing software displays and manages visual aids such as presentations, reprints, and animations. Simultaneously, it captures the interactions between reps and physicians by recording which items are viewed and for how long. It uses this for information to create the next best action steps.
- *Manufacturing Execution Systems (MES)* help the company achieve replicated manufacturing processes and provide real-time feedback on any changes in requirements. It also ensures paperless workflow by automating material flow and capturing cost information.

Progress To-date

Cipla has integrated over 400 instruments through the Internet of Things (IoT)with Electronic Notebooks (ELN) and Laboratory Management Systems (LIMS), which help in generating valuable, actionable data.

In 2019, the Company digitized its B2B network system, using the reverse auctioning tool to procure direct and indirect materials worth Rs. 2.6 billion.

In February 2019, Cipla became the first company in the Asia Pacific to upgrade to a cloud-based pharmacovigilance solution.

An 8000-strong ground field force uses Closed Loop Marketing to improve its interaction with around 1.2 million HCPs across India.

More Innovation

Cipla recently entered into a partnership with Wellthy Therapeutics to offer a combination of pharmacotherapy and digital therapeutics for improved patient outcomes in chronic therapies of diabetology and cardiology.

Cipla is one of the few pharmaceutical companies in the Asia Pacific to embrace organization-wide digital transformation.

(Source: Adapted from an article by Nikhar Aggarwal, A Look at Cipla's Tech Innovations as it Embarks on Digital Transformation: ETCIO Interview with KedarUpadhye, Jt President & Global CFO, Cipla, published in ETCIO.com, on September 10, 2019)

The Future of Health

The ubiquitous digital technology has already linked many aspects of individual lives to digital platforms for service, communication, and social sharing, affecting us in many ways, such as economic, productive, psychological, behavioral, and much more. In addition, the new technologies have already disrupted many industries like music, entertainment, transportation, hospitality, and retail. Similarly, healthcare is in for a radical transformation with an even greater scope than music or travel. What drives this transformation?

Consider the following drivers, for example:

1. Growing global population: Demographers estimate that the world's population will be 8.6 billion by 2030, compared to 7.86 billion in 2021, impacting the world economically, industrially, nutritionally, and politically. In addition, an increase in life expectancy and the consequent health problems of an aging population impact caregiving mechanisms significantly. As a result, the unsustainable costs of providing healthcare to 8.6 billion people accelerate transformation.
2. It's a connected world today. The ever-growing connectivity with five billion people having internet access— an increase of one billion over 2021. Furthermore, the new mobile broadband, 5G, will connect even territories that lack infrastructure, providing access to schooling for children in remote regions of Africa and Asia. Such omnipresent connectivity will enable access to telemedicine and even robotic telesurgery. For example, in 2019, a Chinese neurosurgeon could operate on a patient with Parkinson's disease 3,000 kilometers away.
3. The technological and digital revolution empowers the patient by making the patient central to healthcare. Today, individuals can monitor their health and access dedicated digital services anytime, anywhere. The increasing availability and affordability of genetic screening combined with our digital health profile— all the data actively or passively collected about our health via several wearable devices— enables physicians to make

accurate predictions about the probability of developing a disease before it happens and implement countermeasures, leading us to preventative healthcare.

4. There are already several digital solutions to support patients, caregivers, and healthcare professionals in adherence to therapies or the diagnosis and treatment of certain chronic conditions, shifting the focus from cure (therapy) to care of people.
5. The rapid growth of wearables and network-connected devices indicates a radical healthcare transformation. Several connected and cognitive devices are portable, wearable, ingestible, and implantable devices that can monitor health and fitness information, engage patients and their community of caregivers and deliver self-regulated therapies autonomously. According to *Forbes*, the wearables market was worth $27.9 billion in 2019 and is estimated to reach $74.03 billion in 2025.
6. Digital therapeutics are preventive and therapeutic evidence-based interventions driven by software for a broad spectrum of physical, mental, and behavioral conditions. These are powered by artificial intelligence, patient data, and behavioral science, which can help patients adopt and sustain healthy behaviors through gamification and other forms of engagement.
7. Artificial intelligence (AI) significantly impacts healthcare by providing *reasoned* information to healthcare professionals, assisting them in their work, and allowing them to prescribe the best possible care.
8. The future of healthcare will include products that generate and deliver medical interventions directly to patients using software to treat, manage, and prevent diseases and disorders. But, policymakers, payers, and clinicians must first develop frameworks and pathways for scale-up and integration into healthcare systems, along with clinical guidelines and technical training for optimizing Patients' product use.

9. What would a future pharmaceutical company look like? Brendan Frey, a co-founder of Deep Genomics, believes that the future of medicine will be based on artificial intelligence (AI) because biology is too complex to be understood by humans. Further, he says that *in the vision of Deep Genomics, the future pharmaceutical company will resemble a computer company, with an incredible team of biologists, chemists, and experts in clinical and non-clinical trials, unlike a traditional pharmaceutical company with biologists and chemists using IT tools. It's a matter of culture, a culture of computer science*.
10. Today, with precision medicine integrating whole genome sequencing, comprehensive metabolomics, and advanced imaging, it is possible to identify the potential risk of chronic diseases in adult patients. Furthermore, C. Thomas Caskey, Chief Medical Officer of Human Longevity and member of the National Academy of Sciences says that the goal of precision medicine is to provide a path to assist physicians in achieving disease prevention and implementing accurate treatment strategies.
11. The pharmaceutical industry is shifting from its earlier closed innovation approach, where it was doing all research and development inside the company, to an open innovation approach, collaborating with other research firms, including contract research organizations. Many big pharma companies are practicing open innovation. Roche Healthbuilders, Pfizer Healthcare Hub, Novartis BIOME, and Bayer GSA are examples of big pharma's open innovation approach, demonstrating that large traditional organizations can respond to the needs of patients and all the stakeholders innovatively.
12. Digital Health seems to be on a rapid growth path, with over 20,000 companies pursuing innovation from many angles trying to innovate all aspects of the care processes, such as remote patient monitoring services, mobile healthcare applications, and advanced healthcare information systems. As a result, the global digital health market is expected to reach $884 billion by 2030, with a compound annual growth rate (CAGR) of 21.8 percent between 2020 and 2030, according to a Research and Markets report.

13. Artificial intelligence, blockchain, data, virtual reality, mobile connectivity, advanced predictive analytics solutions, and new business models are changing healthcare, creating an unprecedented wave of innovation.
14. The growing number of digital-native consumers who do not accept the level of information and services that past generations have accepted are demanding seamless care experiences, forcing pharma companies to develop innovative solutions.
15. The Digital revolution will likely change the current *problem-symptom-diagnosis-solution* paradigm to one based on a large amount of patient data from devices, apps, and software received by the doctor with the patient's consent. With this data aided by additional software and algorithms, the doctor can make diagnostic and therapeutic interventions instead of making hypotheses and inferences like in the past.
16. The digital tools will also help HCPs save time on the administrative tasks he is currently spending on and allow them to deal with patients holistically, humanely, and more empathetically than now.

The digital health revolution allows pharmaceutical companies to differentiate their offerings with digital therapies while offering customized therapeutic solutions that improve adherence to therapy and patient outcomes. First, however, they must transform the way they work to realize this opportunity.

The Future of Pharma

Charles Dickens opens his great novel, *A Tale of Two Cities*, with:

It was the best of times, and it was the worst of times; it was the age of wisdom, it was the age of foolishness, it was the epoch of belief, t was the epoch of incredulity, It was the season of light, it was the season of darkness, it was the spring of hope, it was the winter of despair.

The opening words of Charles Dickens's novel, *A Tale of Two Cities*, perfectly encapsulate pharma's current situation. The outlook has never seemed more promising, more ominous.

The Best of Times

First, let us consider the best of times. It is the best of times because:

- Rapidly strengthening and technological base
- Growing demand for medicines, and
- The removal of former impediments to free trade

The Worst of Times

Now, let us look at the worst times. It is the worst of times because:

- The decline of innovation and poor scientific productivity
- Regulations are becoming more onerous
- Market conditions are getting harsher
- Rising healthcare costs
- A shift from unit-based pricing to value-based pricing in mature markets. New products will be priced based on the value buyers accord to them. It's what the customer thinks— not what the manufacturer thinks that matters most

Two Major Challenges

1. Tomorrow's challenge is to develop new medicines that can prevent or cure conditions that are currently incurable
2. Today's challenge is to get to tomorrow

Six Fundamental Shifts

Brian D. Smith, Managing Director, Pragmedic, UK, identified six great shifts transforming the pharmaceutical industry. Each one is a shift from the world used to be to how it is transforming.

Life sciences leaders should develop the ability to *see the forest for the trees* (discerning the big picture from little details). We are bombarded daily with the news of innovative technology, tighter regulation, and new approaches to controlling healthcare. The challenge is to see how these myriad factors combine the sector's shape. Only then do the industry leaders stand any hope of preparing for the future.

In his scholarly book, *Darwin's Medicine*, Brian Smith describes how understanding evolutionary science can provide this necessary foresight. Here is the gist:

Darwin's profound insight— evolution by natural selection, which is used to explain the profusion of species on our planet, is also useful in understanding the behavior of industries. Because biological and economic systems have a lot in common. For understanding organisms or organizations, the basic science is the same.

Six Great Shifts

1. **The Great Value Shift**

   In the Value Shift, the definition of value shifts from the outcomes of treatments, products, services, and interventions to a much more complex, context-specific definition that includes clinical, economic, and other factors by multiple healthcare stakeholders such as HCPs, payers, and patients and caregivers.

2. **The Global Shift**

   The Global Shift is a shift in the demand patterns for treatments, products, services, and interventions which is currently focused on western economies where demand is relatively more homogenous and less heterogeneous to a much broader world that covers the rest of the world where demand is very heterogenous along multiple dimensions, including clinical requirements, payer preferences, and patient needs that are clinical and non-clinical.

3. **The Network Shift**

   The Network Shift is a profound change. It is about how firms and other organizations structure themselves. The shift from big organizations to networked business entities is more complex and fluid, applying pressure simultaneously in favor of business models that can build and manage dynamic, agile networks, using their structures to create better returns and manage risk across the entire value chain. The networked organizations create selection pressures against business models that are hierarchical, siloed, and unicentric.

4. **Systeomic Shift**

   Systeomics, in biomedicine, is the integration of proteomics (a study of a complete set of proteins expressed by an organism) and transcriptomics (a study of the full range of messenger RNA or mRNA, molecules expressed by an organism). The drug discovery business is witnessing a Systeomic Shift wherein the new therapies are taking the Systeomic route, using the genomic data at the pathway level for discovering novel gene targets and biomarkers for many diseases hitherto thought of as untreatable.

5. **The Information Shift**

   The biopharmaceutical industry is witnessing a turning point in the type of information we collect, how we apply it to discover and develop drugs, devices, and other medical technologies, and how we understand our customers' needs, produce products and deliver services to meet those.

6. **The Trimorphic Shift**

   Trimorphic means occurring in or having three distinct forms. The pharmaceutical industry is currently witnessing a three-way polarization in how companies focus their resources. Consider these, for example:

   - Research-based firms are becoming even more innovative.
   - Low-cost firms are becoming incredibly lean, highly cost-efficient, and
   - Efficient and customer-centric firms are excelling at personalization, tailoring their value propositions to *a segment of one.*

These six great shifts are fundamental and real. Firms will only survive if they adapt to the selection pressures created by the shifts.

AsLeon C. Megginson of Louisiana State University rightly observed, *it is not the strongest or the most intelligent who will survive but those who can best manage change*.

How to Respond?

How do you respond to these fundamental shifts?

1. Recognize these great shifts and don't become too focused on individual factors in the market
2. Understand that these shifts are inevitable and that you can only adapt to them, not stop them
3. Use the selection pressures as guides, allowing them to shape your choice of markets, strategies, and structures

Remember, it's easy to lead a market in times of change— look where it's going and get in front!

How Pharma is Responding?

Here are three examples showing how pharma is responding to these great shifts:

1. Recent acquisitions show Roche, for example, is evolving into an outcome-oriented, research-intensive firm.
2. Medtronic is pushing toward a customer-intimate firm in which product development complements rather than leads its strategy.
3. Mylan ((now, Viatris due to its merger with Pfizer Established Products) has been specializing in becoming a hyper-efficient cost leader.

Many other firms are evolving into networked entities, keeping only their differentiating activities in-house. How they respond to the six shifts varies according to their chosen habitat.

How Technology is Shaping Pharma? Ten Trends

Dr. Bertelan Mesko, the medical futurist and Director of the Medical Futurist Institute wrote an ebook, Technology Shaping Pharma, describing the future trends and how they impact the industry and healthcare. Here are the key points discussed in the book:

1. **Empowered Patients**

   As digital health enables patients to take their health and future into their hands, pharmaceutical companies and healthcare providers should treat them as equal partners and not as passive healthcare recipients in the past. Pharma companies should include patients in their advisory boards so that they can develop products in the future, taking into their exact needs and experiences they want, making product development highly relevant.

2. Digital Health Strategy: '*Around the Pill*'

In the future, pharmaceutical companies will emphasize using technology to appeal more to providers and payers, building services around the pill to differentiate their offerings. Around the pill is essentially building patient service programs that are usually non-clinical around the medication to improve patient outcomes and patient adherence.

3. Digital Pills

Digital pills are ingestible medications with embedded electronic circuits rather than smartphone logging apps. *Abilify Mycite* was the first digital pill approved by the US FDA. It contains Aripiprazole, a drug indicated in the treatment of psychiatric conditions like bipolar disorders and schizophrenia. As a patient swallows the pill, the acidic environment in the stomach activates the pill's sensor, which sends Bluetooth signals to an external patch. It will then notify the smartphone app that the patient took the pill.

4. *In Silico* Trials

In Silico trials are clinical trials conducted by computer simulation. They are cost-effective, safe, and free from side effects, as there are no human and animal participants in these trials. However, it was only since COVID-19 these trials became more widely used.

5. Virtual Reality (VR)

Virtual Reality (VR) is increasingly being used in hospitals in the US and other advanced countries today. Virtual reality can help doctors and patients in many ways. Consider these, for example. VR could:

- assist doctors in the OR (Operating Room)
- help medical students study the human body more closely and prepare better for real-life surgeries
- help patients with mental problems fight their phobias, schizophrenia or paranoia more successfully
- help patients with stress and chronic pain release stress and relieve pain

Brennan M. Spiegel, Director of Health Services Research at Cedar-Sinai Medical Center, a non-profit hospital in Los Angeles in the US, believes the future will be VR pharmacies with specialists prescribing appropriate VR treatments to patients.

6. Augmented Reality (AR)

Augmented Reality (AR) has many useful applications in healthcare, including the following:

- Nurses can find veins easier with an AR vein scanner, Accuvein.
- Patients can describe their eye condition better to their doctor through EyeDecide.
- AR helps patients see how their drug works in 3D in front of their eyes instead of reading long descriptions on the product packs.

7. 3-D Printing of Drugs

Many researchers globally are working on possible 3-D printing solutions. Consider these, for example:

- Researchers at Organovo, a biotech company in the US, and Murdoch Children's Research Institute (MCR) in Australia produced several artificial kidneys with stable quality, making bio-printed kidneys for human organ transplantation a possibility soon.
- In 2015, Aprecia Pharmaceuticals received FDA approval for its 3-D printed Spritam tablets for treating seizures in people with epilepsy.
- The UK-based specialist biotech company, FabRx, believes they can commercialize 3-D printed tablets within 5–10 years. They also foresee that 3-D Printing will be available in every major hospital in the next decade.

3-D Printers as home-based pharmacies may not be considered science fiction twenty years from now.

8. **Artificial Intelligence**

   Artificial Intelligence (AI) has capabilities that can revolutionize healthcare. For example, artificial intelligence can:

   - mine medical records, design treatment plans
   - speed up medical imaging
   - make finding new drugs faster and cost-effective

9. **Precision Medicine and Pharmacogenomics**

   Precision medicine is about tailoring medical treatment to each patient's characteristics. However, it does not mean creating unique drugs or medical devices for a patient but subpopulations that differ in their susceptibility to a particular disease or response to a specific treatment. For example, the GeneSight test evaluates multiple genetic variations influencing people's response to antidepressant and antipsychotic medications. Currently, many precision drugs in oncology with target-specific pathways are at various stages of development.

10. **Need for New FDA Regulations**

    The new waves of digital innovation will drive the currently unprepared regulators to accelerate their technology adoption. Customers are unwilling to wait for regulators' approval to adopt innovations. Here are two recent cases where customers embraced innovations before the regulators did.

    - Diabetes patients started using artificial pancreas (a system made of thee parts that work together to mimic how healthy pancreas control blood glucose in the body, mainly in type I diabetes) even before the FDA approval, as is evident from their *#wearenotwaiting* twitter movement.
    - Another case in point is regulations going after innovation involve direct-to-consumer testing companies, particularly 23andMe Services, which appeared more than fifteen years ago in the market. However, The FDA finally approved it in 2017.

How Digital Technologies are Transforming Pharma?

New technologies such as artificial intelligence (AI), machine learning (ML), big data analytics, predictive analytics, augmented reality (AR), virtual reality (VR), 3D Printing, cloud computing, natural language processing (NLP), and others are disrupting the pharmaceutical industry.

It's a top-toe disruption affecting everything from patient interaction within the health system to how they are treated.

As Scot Brinker, blogger and marketing technologist, rightly observed, *marketing has become a technology-powered discipline. Marketing organizations, therefore, must infuse technical capabilities into their DNA.*

The Digital Imperative

With digital technology reaching a tipping point in 2014 when 51 percent of healthcare practitioners became digital natives and expected to grow to 75 percent by 2030, digital is no longer an option for pharma marketers. It has become imperative. Digital is imperative today.

If this is not convincing enough, consider these additional factors:

- Manhattan Research conducted a few years ago suggested that doctors who participate in online patient communities write an average of 24 prescriptions per week than those with no interest in online communities.
- Research also suggested that a third of the doctors have changed a patient's treatment due to an internet search.
- An Accenture estimate suggests that effective digitization fuels growth by about 33 percent and profitability by about 40 percent.
- Research conducted in North America has found that the average American goes to the doctor three times a year but spends 52 hours searching for health-related information. With

internet speeds and penetration growing rapidly worldwide, it won't be long before consumer-searching for health-related information gains speed even in the rest of the world.

The question, therefore, is not whether to go digital but how.

The Future of Pharma Marketing

The pharma marketing landscape continues to evolve with the emergence of a technological and digital revolution. Traditionally, pharmaceutical companies have focused mainly on physicians, but now the access restrictions from hospitals and physicians increasingly challenge face-time opportunities to sell directly.

Meanwhile, the internet has become an extended source of health information for all pharma stakeholders, such as patients, caregivers, and providers. They have immersed online, surfing from health portals to pharma companies' websites, health advocacy sites, blogs, and chat rooms, fundamentally changing how pharma marketers must interact with their customers.

Pharma must understand that digital communications are not just a channel but an entirely different way of doing business, influencing everything from gaining strategic insights to tactical execution.

Pharma marketers must understand by listening to the changing environment with their ears close to the ground by embracing and responding to it with relevant and meaningful strategies and tactics.

Stephen Towers, Ph.D., presented the future of pharma marketing in his article, *Pharma Marketing's DATA-Driven Omnichannel Future: Four Interconnected Themes from Reuters Pharma Marketing USA 2021*, published in Pharma-Marketing Network blog—pharma-mkting.com on December 17, 2021.

Here is an indicative list of some of the major changes that are already happening and those on the horizon:

- The future of pharma marketing will be data-driven by the huge data from multiple sources, including patient-generated through wearables and sensors powered by advanced analytics and technologies like artificial intelligence and machine learning.
- The future of pharma marketing is engagement, interactivity, and user control. Pharma marketers will continue to improve their profiling of healthcare professionals and patients by

creating user personas and mapping customer and consumer journeys. Their messaging will be target-specific, personalized, and highly relevant.

- Creating a better customer experience than competitors will be the new strategy, shifting marketing focus from the traditional product-centric approach to customer-centric.
- Content is still king. However, pharmaceutical companies must deliver dynamic, relevant content to HCPs at different stages in their journey.
- While omnichannel engagement is the key to creating personalized customer experiences, some challenges remain, and pharma should address them. First, you need a deep understanding of customer needs and channel preferences and use those insights to tailor all content to individual HCPs, with orchestrated delivery and engagement across channels. The challenge here is that the current siloed organizational structures do not allow a seamless customer experience. What is needed is organization-wide governance that works to break down silos and usher in a data-driven culture.
- Omnichannel engagement requires a deep understanding of the type of content that HCPs need and how that changes over time so that you can deliver a steady stream of relevant and value-added content incrementally throughout their customer journey. Such a hyper-personalized approach requires a much higher volume of content than traditional approaches. It also requires greater agility to ensure the delivery of content that is relevant to physicians *now* rather than content that was relevant six months ago. Accordingly, companies must step up their internal content creation and review processes.
- Pharmaceutical companies must up-skill their commercial teams as they significantly contribute to the insight-generation process. It is as important as growing the analytics function in a company.
- While the novel tactics and channels, such as rep-generated text messages and expanded video content, are most exciting, it is important to refrain from using them to ensure that these

new tactics or channels are not disconnected from the rest of the customer experience.

- As Chatrick Paul, Senior Vice President and head of the US Oncology Business Unit at AstraZeneca pointed out that the opportunity here is not to think of it at the level of tactics, but to really shift to think about an end-to-end approach, identify the relevant main points along the journey, and start creating the right content through the right channels that really have an impact.
- Pharma's data-driven decision-making approach will not displace the field force but reaffirms that the critical position of sales reps and MSLs (Medical Science Liaisons) is central to the organization. It is because most sales-and-marketing-led capabilities will only reap the benefit of advanced analytics if there is also significant human input. While data collection and processing will remain highly automated, the more sophisticated capabilities, such as AI-enhanced customer journey design and next-best-action strategies for marketing, require the expertise and insights of the field force and other stakeholders.
- The future of pharma marketing will be phygital (physical + digital) or hybrid to deliver superior customer experiences throughout the customers' and consumers' journey. The new data capabilities will enable reps to become superheroes in the field by empowering them with greater insights, increasing their relevancy, and helping to elevate their relationship with HCPs. Finally, as Samer Ansari, Head of Digital & IT, Global Oncology Business Unit at Takeda Pharmaceuticals, says: *At the end of the day, it's still about connections and relationships, and our field reps are critical in all of that. They are the ones that own the relationship and create that trust when it comes to engaging with our customers. We can always have other experiences (send more emails, have slick websites), but it's how we channel all of our data and digital thinking and capabilities to elevate that relationship experience with the rep.*

Winner's Checklist

Under conditions of complexity, not only are checklists a help, they are required for success.

— *Atul Gawande*

You can never overemphasize the importance of a checklist as a vital tool for improving productivity. In the book, The Checklist Manifesto: How to Get Things Right, the author, Dr. Atul Gawande writes that: *Good checklists are precise, to the point, and easy to use even in the most difficult situations. They do not spell out everything—a checklist cannot fly a plane. Instead, they provide reminders of only the most critical and necessary steps—those that even the highly skilled professional using them could miss. Good checklists are, above all, practical.*

The Winners' Checklist, in our context, is about asking some of the essential questions that should signal to a company how the change is taking place and how much 'it' needs to change.

You can't do today's job with yesterday's tools and still be in Business tomorrow is an accessible business saying of unknown authorship. Some companies have realized this and have been able to sharpen their tools and use new tools that are relevant today. May others did not and perished. One reason for the ineffectual response is that business leaders have not appreciated the rate and pace of change—how the 'has become' is becoming.

The key to success is anticipating change before it arrives, evolving, and planning strategies to ride it and master it.

When you carefully examine, you find that the *Major Drivers* of change are in areas like:

- Information technology
- Global perspective for global markets
- Ethical corporate behavior
- Responsibility to society at large, not just shareholders
- Total customer solutions and customer-centricity

The rate of change in the global pharmaceutical industry is so high that incremental improvements will not work, let alone maximize your potential. Gone are the days when you could gain a competitive advantage by developing a slightly better way of doing things. The pace of change is so rapid that it is almost like a gale-force wind. You will probably go backward if you aim to take a small step. You need to take a big step into the teeth of the gale merely to hold your position. To move forward, you have to take more than one big step at a time. The change has to be revolutionary, not evolutionary.

Consider what Gary Hamel said while discussing strategy as a revolution: *Let us admit it. Corporations around the world are reaching the limits of incrementalism. Squeezing another penny out of costs, getting a product to market a few weeks earlier, responding to customers' inquiries a little bit faster, ratcheting quality up by one or more notch, and capturing another point of market share—these are the obsessions of managers of today. But pursuing incremental improvements while rivals reinvent the industry is like fiddling when Rome burns*.

While the usual is no longer usual, a business-as-usual approach will fail. Moreover, the rate of change offers opportunities for competition to exploit if you fail to do so. John O'Keefe, Group Vice President, Proctor & Gamble, in his highly stimulating and thought-provoking book *Business Beyond the Box: Applying Your Mind for Breakthrough Results*, says that: t*oo many organizations use the past as the sofa. The past should be used as a springboard and not as a sofa*. The critical question is how your organization sees the past—as a sofa or a springboard.

Lindsay Herbert asks many essential questions for executing digital transformation in her insightful book, *Digital Transformation: Build Your Organization's Future for the Innovative age,* which makes a useful checklist.

Here are thirty such questions, which act as a checklist for arriving at the significant steps needed to move forward in this era of tumultuous change. All the successful companies have found answers to these and planned their strategies accordingly.

The Winners' Checklist

1. Do we have a well-defined *Mission* (not just a statement) that all team members understand? How do our senior management team members see themselves as – revolutionaries or evolutionaries in our industry? Do they contend with the status quo? Or do they want to rewrite the rules for the industry? What is our leadership quotient? What is their foresight about our industry?
2. Do we have a clear *Vision* and a detailed blueprint for action on how we will achieve what we want? How detailed are our action plans? Do they indicate responsibility centers and timelines for each key objective?
3. Do all our employees share organizational optimism and aspirations? Do they have a clear sense of urgency and a sense of ownership of our organizational goals and objectives?
4. Is our top management allocating as much time for pre-market competition as market competition? How much of their time goes into running and managing the current Business compared to that spent to visualize, anticipate changes, and plan for future business opportunities? How much time do they spend on maintenance instead of building our Business?
5. Does our current customer experience match with the desired customer experience? What is the gap, and do we have a time-bound specific action plan to bridge it?
6. Can our existing digital estate deliver to customers their actual needs?
7. Could technology innovations improve customer experience and decrease competitive threats? If so, what innovations?
8. What business innovations could improve customer experience and decrease competitive threats?
9. How have our competitors and peers adapted to new conditions shaped by customers' digital expectations?
10. How are competitors or alternatives in the marketplace meeting customers' needs better than ours?

11. Could technology innovations add business value or enhance customer experiences? If so, what innovations?
12. What new business models and ways of working resonate with the target consumers we could leverage through digital technology?
13. What relationships should exist between staff and departments to meet customers' needs?
14. What processes should be in place to respond to changing external needs and conditions?
15. How are we measuring success in each business area? Which of these are at odds with our customers' needs?
16. What are the natural crossover points in our company's internal operations where digital technology and new ways of working could lead to greater success externally?
17. What are the current attitudes towards digital and innovation?
18. What attempts did we make to innovate in the past? What succeeded and why?
19. Why did certain attempts at innovation fail?
20. What areas of our business present the greatest barriers to digital transformation?
21. What areas of our business require the most transformation?
22. What digital opportunities exist that can transform our current customer experiences?
23. What are the critical barriers to achieving our digital transformation vision?
24. What are the immediate opportunities to start transforming our current customer experiences?
25. What skills, capabilities, and resources are we missing to undertake transformation efforts?
26. What assets can we use to start transformation efforts, even on the short-term and small scale?
27. Do our business goals align with our shared transformation vision? Are they linked to drivers of the organization's success?

28. How do we stack up against the competition? Are our competitors' product and service offerings similar to ours? What is our competitive advantage?
29. Can the goals be measured against the five-point evaluation criteria— customer value, competitive advantage, business impact, technical feasibility, and scalability?
30. What is the cost and impact of transformation on the existing systems?

Winning Leadership for an Era of Change

Lawrence A. Bossidy, an American author and former CEO of Allied Signal (later Honeywell), suggested four action steps for making a company a winner in an era of change through effective leadership many years ago, which are relevant even today as they are axiomatic.

1. Firstly, determine the task by honestly assessing where you stand with customers, employees, and competitors.
2. Two, articulate a vision of where you want to be and the values for how you want to behave. Set aggressive goals and keep everyone focused on achieving them.
3. Three, fill your company with people bursting with energy and creativity— people with diverse talents who can work together in a team setting. Give people constant, candid feedback, and let them know that the organization can fulfill their highest career aspirations.
4. And finally, create a culture obsessed with customers, and build your organization and incentive systems around the customer's interests.

Epilogue
You're Gonna Need a Bigger Boat!

He who studies medicine without books sails an unchartered sea, but he who studies medicine without patients does not go to the sea at all.

— William Osler, The Father of Modern Medicine

You're Gonna Need a Bigger Boat!

What has a line from a Hollywood blockbuster of the 1970s, Jaws, and the present healthcare scenario have in common?

Chief Brody in the movie Jaws speaks the iconic line—*You're gonna need a bigger boat,* minutes after the eponymous twenty-five feet white shark appears behind their vessel *Orca,* which is too small to catch the giant shark. He realizes that he needs a bigger boat.

Ned Russel, the managing partner of healthcare at Alliance Stagwell, draws an interesting parallel between this scene and the predicament pharma marketers face today in his article, *'Jaws' as an allegory for today's healthcare marketing? Yes, 'You're gonna need a bigger boat'* in mmm-online.com on October 30, 2018.

Think of Chief Brody as the marketer and Captain Quint as management. And Chum, as the traditional marketing plans and tactics pharma marketers used to engage customers, and the great white shark is the digital, technological revolution, and rising consumerism sweeping the pharmaceutical marketplace and changing its landscape.

The all-pervading technology is making every business a technology business, transforming all industries. Consider, for example, Amazon transforming retail, Airbnb transforming lodging, and Uber transforming transportation. It's now the Pharma's turn. Big tech companies are already foraying into healthcare with technology, changing healthcare delivery, making it a seamless experience across the consumer's journey. Pharma leaders and marketers cannot keep their heads in the sand for long.

The first bite (of the metaphorical great white shark) will be to a healthcare system geared toward population health and grounded in electronic health records, making data as important to our industry as it is to a trader on Wall Street. And the sheer size of the shark is symbolic of a broader meaning of health that puts every disease in the context of how a life is really affected—all in the name of creating a better outcome.

While most healthcare marketers realize that change is happening, their response is tepid, like Chief Brody kept throwing *chum* (traditional engagement tools) upon seeing the shark. At the moment, the evolution in healthcare marketing is slow and incremental, and we all must prepare for the wave of disruption. It's rather ironic that the industry which needs to change most for the well-being of the population it serves is perhaps the most ill-prepared for the type of transformation that is likely to turn the industry upside down.

Pharma needs a bigger boat— a *bigger boat* thinking to navigate the change successfully. Ned Russel, managing partner of healthcare at Alliance Stagwell, identified five critical areas where you can apply this bigger boat thinking:

1. *Look beyond the traditional talent pool*. Now that you need to transform digitally and technologically to stay competitive in the changing environment, you must acquire relevant talent from non-pharma, technology, and even other industries to inject new thinking and challenge legacy ways of working.
2. *Embrace technology*. There is more to embracing technology than creating a patient app or a nice-looking, fully functional website, although they may be necessary. It is about treating technology as an extension of your product and adding value. For example, Takeda and Johnson & Johnson took initiatives and entered into partnerships to add value *beyond the molecule* to their products. Pharma marketers must rethink technology. Suppose you are marketing a fertility drug or other woman's healthcare products. In that case, you may consider partnering with the company that makes *Ava Fertility Tracker*, which is wearable and tracks five physiological signals using machine learning algorithms and extracts data from the five most fertile days of the menstrual cycle.
3. *Get smart about data*. Data is the new sales force for healthcare. To leverage the huge data from various sources such as electronic health records, wearables, and devices the patients wear in real-time. Building capabilities with data scientists and analysts who can turn numbers into actionable insights and marketing strategies is important.

4. *Embrace consumerism*. The empowered patients of today are taking more control of their health. They are increasingly aware of the benefits and costs associated with them and demand convenience and seamless experiences from healthcare that they are used get from other sectors.
5. *Broaden your organization's definition of health*. Pharma companies must broaden their definition of health and their role in healthcare, for many lifestyle diseases cannot be cured by drugs alone. A broader definition of health and its purpose will help pharmaceutical companies broaden their role in health management. They should remember what Theodore Levitt, professor emeritus of marketing at Harvard Business School, said in his classic article, *The Marketing Myopia* published in Harvard Business Review in 1960, about sixty years ago, because it is still very relevant. When you think of it, it is not an article but a manifesto. He said it is important to ask a fundamental question and understand a deceptively simple question: What business are we in? If you define your business narrowly as the railroads did way back in time, you are sure to lose your business to the disruptors like the railroads lost to road and aerial transportation. Likewise, the pharmaceutical industry is disrupting, with big tech firms such as Amazon, Apple, Alphabet, Microsoft, and some agile startups trying to creep into the healthcare space by delivering services that improve customer experience. Therefore, it's time for the pharma leadership to redefine health and its purpose and ask themselves—What business are we in? Are we in the business of producing medicines and therapies or improving the health outcomes of patients? Their answers would determine the role that they will play in the rapidly changing healthcare ecosystem.

Suppose the pharma leaders' definition is broader, taking a holistic view of all the elements that factor into managing a disease—emotional, nutritional, and economic. In that case, they can create more valuable and enduring brands.

Pharmaceutical companies who turn a blind eye to the impending disruption will be caught in the jaws of disruption.

References

1. Eric Topol, The Patient Will See You Now: The Future of Medicine is in Your Hands, Basic Books, New York, 2016
2. Harley Manning, Josh Bernoff, Forrester Research, Outside In: The Power of Putting Customers At the Center of Your Business, New Harvest, 2012
3. Sean McDade, Listen or Die: 40 Lessons That Turn Customer Feedback into Gold, LionCrest Publishing, 2018
4. Charlene LI Josh Bernoff, Groundswell: Winning in A World Transformed by Social Technologies, Harvard Business School Press, Boston, MA, USA
5. Letizia Affinito, Empowering the Connected Physician in the E-Patient Era: How Physician's Empowerment on Digital Health Tools Can Improve Patient Empowerment and Boost Health (Care) Outcomes, Routledge, Taylor & Francis Group, New York, 2019
6. Edouard Demeire, KICCASS Pharma: Keep it Customer Centric, Agile & Strategically Simple in Pharma & Diagnostics Management, 2020
7. Jordi Bernal-Figo and Joaquin Bernal-Fuertes, Pharma 2027: Evolve or Disappear, Published by Jordi Bernal-Figo, 2013
8. Paul Hellman, You've Got 00:00:08 Seconds: Communication Secrets for a Distracted World, AMACOM, American Management Association, 2017
9. Philip Kotler, Hermawan Kartajaya, Iwan Setiawan, Marketing 5.0: Technology for Humanity, Wiley, 1st Edition, April 2021
10. Philip Kotler, Waldemar Pfoertsch, Owe Sponholz, H2H Marketing: The Genesis of Human-To-Human Marketing, Springer, 1st Edition, 2021
11. Sean McDade, Pharma Customer Experience: 20 Secrets to 10X Your CX and Boost Patient Outcomes, Lion Crest Publishing, 2021
12. Ernest Hemingway, The Sun Also Rises, Simon & Schuster Classic Edition, 1996
13. Paul Hudson, Pharma needs to stop chasing shiny objects and start embracing practical technology, Fortune, January

7, 2020, https://fortune.com/2020/01/07/pharma-health-tech-digitization-sanofi/

14. Mike DeLone, Vice Chairman, US Life Sciences Leader, Deloitte LLP, The COVID-19 Pandemic Could Forever Change Biopharma, Deloitte Blog: Health Forward, April 7, 2020, https://www2.deloitte.com/us/en/blog/health-care-blog/2020/covid-19-pandemic-could-forever-change-biopharma.html
15. Greg Reh, Jonathan Fox, Christine Chang, Tacking Digital Transformation: How Biopharma Companies Can Realize, the Power of Digital and Prepare for a New Reality, deloitte.com, July 17, 2019, https://www2.deloitte.com/us/en/insights/industry/life-sciences/biopharma-company-of-the-future.html
16. Gaurav Agarwal, Hemant Ahlawat, and Martin Dewhurst, Winning Against COVID-19: The Implications for Biopharma, McKinsey & Company, April 15, 2020, https://www.mckinsey.com/industries/pharmaceuticals-and-medical-products/our-insights/winning-against-covid-19-the-implications-for-biopharma
17. David Bell,The Wharton Business School, Brian Fox, McKinsey&Co, Ryan Olohan, Google, Pharma 3D: Rewriting the Script for Marketing in a Digital Age, http://www.pharma3d.com/#chapter-856435
18. Blue Latitude Strategic Marketing Consultancy, Customer Experience: The Essential Guide for Pharma, http://cdn2.hubspot.net/hub/230479/file-645840154-pdf/Blue_Latitude_Customer_Handbook__March_2014_.pdf?t=1397045610220
19. Mohanbir Sawhney, Northwestern University, Re-imagining Pharma Marketing, December 2016, http://www.mohansawhney.com/wp-content/uploads/2016/12/ReimaginingMarketing_v4.pdf
20. Sarah Armstrong, Dianne Esber, Jason Heller, Björn Timelin, Modern Marketing: What it is, What it isn't and How to Do it, mckinsey.com, March 2, 2020, https://www.mckinsey.com/business-functions/marketing-and-sales/our-insights/modern-marketing-what-it-is-what-it-isnt-and-how-to-do-it

21. Erin Fitzgerald, SERMO, Today's Healthcare Professionals are Leveraging Social Media Conversations for Collaboration, Global Reach, and Real-Time Learning, Health IT Outcomes, November 15, 2018, https://www.healthitoutcomes.com/doc/today-s-healthcare-professionals-are-leveraging-social-media-conversations-for-collaboration-global-reach-and-real-time-learning-0001
22. Suzanne Gamwell, Breaking from Tradition—Social Media at Medical Congresses, PMLive, July 8, 2019, http://www.pmlive.com/pharma_intelligence/Breaking_from_tradition_-_social_media_at_medical _congresses_1292138
23. Life Sciences, How to Reach HCPs on Social Media: Are You Missing Out? March 6, 2020, https://lifesciences.stickyeyes.com/how-to-reach-hcps-on-social-media-are-you-missing-out/
24. Life Sciences, How Pharma Can Harness the Influence of Digital Opinion Leaders, February 17, 2020, https://lifesciences.stickyeyes.com/how-pharma-can-harness-the-influence-of-digital-opinion-leaders/
25. Sarah Morgan, HCPs—They are Just Like Us! InTouch Solutions, August 1, 2017, https://www.intouchsol.com/blog/hcps%E2%80%8B-theyre-just-like-us/
26. Jonathan Catley, Study Shows Patient Influencers Turn to Social Media Over HCPs, MDConnect, May 16, 2019, https://www.mdconnectinc.com/medical-marketing-insights/patient-influencers-turn-to-social-media-over-hcps
27. Alessandro Di Fiore, Kendra West and Andrea Segnalini, Why Science-Driven Companies Should Use Agile, Harvard Business Review, November 4, 2019, https://hbr.org/2019/11/why-science-driven-companies-should-use-agile
28. Paul Tunnah, Eye-on-Innovation: Can 'Design Thinking' Revolutionize Pharma's Culture? Pharmaphorum, May 3, 2018, https://pharmaphorum.com/views-and-analysis/can-design-thinking-revolutionise-pharmas-culture/
29. Sascha Lehmann, Nils Liedtke, Phyllis Rothschild, Eloy Trevino, The Future of Brand Strategy: It's Time to 'Go Electric,'

McKinsey & Company, May 27, 2020, https://www.mckinsey.com/business-functions/marketing-and-sales/our-insights/the-future-of-brand-strategy-its-time-to-go-electric

30. Linda Watts, 10 Reasons to Build Healthcare Journey Maps, Perficient Healthcare, August 15, 2020, https://blogs.perficient.com/2020/08/15/10-reasons-to-build-healthcare-journey-maps/
31. PM 360 Staff, The Keys to Delivering Superior Digital Customer Experience, PM360, June 21, 2018, https://www.pm360online.com/the-keys-to-delivering-superior-digital-customer-experience/
32. J. Clement, Percentage of Mobile Device Web Traffic Worldwide from 1st Quarter 2015 to 2nd Quarter 2020, Statista, July 21, 2020, https://www.statista.com/statistics/277125/share-of-website-traffic-coming-from-mobile-devices/
33. Madeline Good, How Customer Centricity is Changing Pharmaceutical Customer Experience, PeopleMetrics, January 19, 2018, https://www.peoplemetrics.com/blog/the-patient-experience-how-customer-centricity-is-changing-the-pharmaceutical-industry
34. Pete Gale and Will Myddleton, Customer Experience for Pharma Companies, PMLiVE, March 21, 2013, http://www.pmlive.com/pharma_thought_leadershipcustomer_experience_for_pharma_companies_468166
35. Victoria Summers and Vijay Unnikrishnan, While Telehealth Continues to Evolve, Pharma Needs to Keep an Eye on the Future, zs.com, August 3, 2020, https://www.zs.com/insights/telehealth-continues-to-evolve-pharma-keeps-an-eye-on-the-future
36. Kevin Dolgin, Digital— Teaching An Old Dog New Tricks: Car Maker Tesla Has Few Lessons for Pharma On Truly Putting Digital First, Reuters Events, March 20, 2017, https://www.reutersevents.com/pharma/column/digital-teaching-old-dog-new-tricks

37. George Underwood, Beyond 'beyond the pill,' PharmaTimes Magazine, January, 2018, http://www.pharmatimes.com/magazine/2018/janfeb/beyond_beyond_the_pill
38. Robin Robinson, Moving Beyond The "Beyond The Pill" Conversation, PharmaVoice, March 2018, https://www.pharmavoice.com/article/2018-03-beyond-the-pill/
39. Chris Round, How Merck Is Stepping Up For Patients, Pharmaphorum, May 8, 2018, https://pharmaphorum.com/views-analysis-patients/how-merck-is-stepping-up-for-patients/
40. DMI Blog, Ethics, Regulation & Customer Experience in the Pharma Industry: Why It Matters, digitalmarketing institute.com, https://digitalmarketing institute.com/blog/ethics-regulations-customer-experience-in-the-pharma-industry
41. Dr. Nicola Davies, Design Thinking: A Human-Centered Approach for Pharma, Reuters Events: Pharma, September 15, 2015, Design Thinking: A Human-Centered Approach for Pharma
42. Lucy Fulford, Design: Pharma's Next Frontier, Reuters Events Pharma, September 16, 2019, https://www.reutersevents.com/pharma/patients-and-medical/design-pharmas-next-frontier
43. Erin Henkel and Jarrod Ryhal, 5 Principles for Making Digital Healthcare More Human-Centered, IDEO, November 08, 2019, https://www.ideo.com/blog/5-principles-for-making-digital-healthcare-more-human-centered
44. Ash Rishi, Applying Design Thinking to the Pharma Digital Environment, Pharmaphorum, March 4, 2014, https://pharmaphorum.com/views-and-analysis/applying-design-thinking-to-the-pharma-digital-environment/
45. Debprotim Roy, How Healthcare, Pharma Cos Evolve in Current Digital Age, PHARMABIZ.com, November 13, 2019, How healthcare, pharma cos evolve in current digital age, http://pharmabiz.com/ArticleDetails.aspx?aid=119310&sid=9

46. A J. Ploszay, IQVIA's Vice President of Digital Strategy, Communicating With Healthcare Professionals in the Time of COVID-19, European Pharmaceutical Review, October 7, 2020, https://www.europeanpharmaceuticalreview.com/article/129827/communicating-with-healthcare-providers-in-the-time-of-covid-19/

47. Dane Mitrev, "Ping An Good Doctor" Showcases First AI-Powered Booth Clinic, Neurohive, December 11, 2018, https://neurohive.io/en/news/ping-an-good-doctor-showcases-first-ai-powered-booth-clinic/

48. Alexander Aboshiha, Sam Marwaha, Julius Neiser, and Christopher Weyrer, Biopharma's Remote-Health Imperative, BCG.com, August 27, 2020, https://www.bcg.com/publications/2020/biopharma-remote-health-imperative

49. Brady Walcott, Executive Vice President, Intouch Group, Mark Bard, Co-Founder, DHC Group, DHC Group, The Aftermath: COVID-19 Insights & Recommendations—How the Pandemic Will Forever Change Pharma Sales & Marketing, https://digitalhealthcoalition.org/whitepaper-aftermath-covid-19-intouch-group-june-2020/

50. Will Reese, A Practical Guide to Personalization, Pharma Marketing Network, December 8, 2020, https://www.pharma-mkting.com/articles/a-practical-guide-to-personalization/

51. Robin Robinson, Segmentation and Personalization Brings Targets into Focus, Pharma Voice, October 2012, https://www.pharmavoice.com/article/segmentation-personalization/

52. Marcin Kozlowski, 6 ways Pharma Companies Can Standout with Personalized Video, VINTOM, April 29, 2019, The Medium, https://medium.com/vintom/6-ways-pharma-companies-can-stand-out-with-personalized-video-670bc31c1f71

53. Simple, Not Easy: 3 Fundamentals of Data-Driven Pharma Marketing, Acxiom, https://www.acxiom.com/resources/pharma-marketing-fundamentals-ebook/

54. Rebecca, D'Ippolito, Global Compliance Manager, Sermo, Here's How to Balance Both HCP Privacy and Personalized Experiences, Sermo, October 28, 2020, https://

www.sermo.com/blog-balance-hcp-privacy-and-personalized-experiences/

55. Anton Morrison, The Evolving World of Pharma Marketing, Pharmacy Times, May 28, 2020, https://www.pharmacytimes.com/news/the-evolving-world-of-pharma-marketing
56. Rasmus Bech Hansen, What Pharma Can Do to Win in Virtual, Pharmaphorum, May 4, 2020, https://pharmaphorum.com/views-analysis-sales-marketing/what-pharma-can-do-to-win-in-virtual/
57. Tyler Clifford, Veeva Systems Sees Product Usage Increase Tenfold As Biotech Companies Race to Find COVID-19 Cure, CNBC: Mad Money, March 26, 2020, https://www.cnbc.com/2020/03/26/veeva-systems-crm-usage-increased-tenfold-amid-race-to-find-covid-cure.html
58. Andrew Matthius, The Opportunity to Reimagine the Patient Experience, PM 360 Online, September 8, 2020, https://www.pm360online.com/the-opportunity-to-reimagine-the-patient-experience-during-covid/
59. M. Szmigiera, Impact of the Coronavirus Pandemic on the Global Economy—Statistics and Facts, statista.com, May 7,2021, https://www.statista.com/topics/6139/covid-19-impact-on-the-global-economy/
60. Paula Bellostas, Johanna Tybus, Carsten Pasolick, A COVID-19-Led Healthcare Digital Transformation, kearney.com, https://www.kearney.com/health/article?/a/a-covid-19-led-healthcare-digital-transformation
61. Julian Upton, The Road to Digital Transformation: Roles and Requirements for Organizational Success, PharmExec.com, May 11, 2021, https://www.pharmexec.com/view/the-road-to-digital-transformation-roles-and-requirements-for-organizational-success
62. Angie Tran, Paid Social vs. Organic Social: Creating A Hybrid Strategy, The AdRoll Blog, Last Updated: December 14, 2020, https://www.adroll.com/blog/growth-marketing/paid-social-vs-organic-social-creating-a-hybrid-strategy

63. Nadia Khatri, Brand Insights Contributor, Director of Omnichannel Strategy, Biopharm Communications, Engaging and Educating HCPs with KOL-Based Paid Social, PharmExec.com, May 1, 2021, https://www.pharmexec.com/view/engaging-and-educating-hcps-with-kol-based-paid-social?utm_source=sfmc&utm_medium=enews&utm_campaign=mktg_brandinsights
64. Amanda Barrell, How Modular Content Provides 'Light Speed' Review and Boosts Engagement, Pharmaphorum, July 23, 2020, https://pharmaphorum.com/views-analysis-sales-marketing/how-modular-content-provides-light-speed-review-and-boosts-engagement/
65. Robb DeFilippis, What is Modular Content and Why Do Pharma Marketers Need it NOW? Pharmaphorum, May 24, 2021, https://pharmaphorum.com/views-analysis-sales-marketing/what-is-modular-content-and-why-do-pharma-marketers-need-it-now/
66. Pharma Guy, 3 Insights from Re:Imagine Pharma Marketing 2020, Pharma Marketing Network, November 11, 2020, https://www.pharma-mkting.com/blog/3-insights-from-reimagine-pharma-marketing-2020/
67. Mircea FUCIU, Luigi DUMITRESCU, Lucian Blaga, From Marketing 1.0 to Marketing 4.0—The Evolution of the Marketing Concept in the Context of the 21st Century, DE GRUTER Open, Vol. xxiv, No. 2, 2018, https://sciendo.com/article/10.1515/kbo-2018-0064
68. A Forrester Consulting Thought Leadership Paper Commissioned by Adobe, April 2018, The Business Impact of Investing in Experience: Experience-Driven Business Drive Superior Business Performance by Investing Broadly in CX Across the Customer Lifecycle, The Research is conducted by Karin Fently, Senior Marketing Consultant and Forrester's Customer Experience Research Group, https://www.adobe.com/content/dam/acom/en/experience-cloud/research/roi/pdfs/business-impact-of-cx.pdf
69. Kartagya Pandey, Why is Customer Experience the New Marketing Strategy, DATAFLOQ, May 25, 2020, https://

datafloq.com/read/why-customer-experience-new-marketing-strategy/8431

70. Qualtrics, The Digital Experience Playbook: a 3-Phase Approach to Delivering Digital Experiences that Drive Business Impact, https://www.qualtrics.com/au/lp/ebook/digital-experience-playbook/?utm_lp=hub-design-cx-program
71. Simon Grime, Director of Fendix, Collaborative Working is the Key for the NHS and Pharma, Pharmaphorum, August 20, 2018, https://pharmaphorum.com/views-and-analysis/collaborative-working-key-nhs-pharma/
72. Anne-Sophie Royer, How Pharma Can Amplify Design Thinking to Connect More with Consumers? Pharma-IQ, June 11, 2020, https://pharmaphorum.com/views-and-analysis/collaborative-working-key-nhs-pharma/
73. Experience Point, Why Pharma Needs Design Thinking? October 11, 2019, https://blog.experiencepoint.com/why-pharma-needs-design-thinking
74. Megan Golden, Customer Experience: What It Is, Why Companies Fall Short, And How To Satisfy Expectations? LInkedIn Marketing Solutions Blog, July 25, 2018, https://business.linkedin.com/marketing-solutions/blog/sales-and-marketing/2018/how-b2b-companies-can-deliver-indispensable-customer-experiences
75. Mike Weir, What is A Customer Journey Map And Why Are They Important? LinkedIn Marketing Solutions Blog, December 7, 2021, https://business.linkedin.com/marketing-solutions/blog/sales-and-marketing/2018/customer-journey-map-definition-benefits-examples
76. Nicolas Machier, Kevin Neher, and Robert Park, From Touchpoints to Journeys: Seeing The World As Customers Do, McKinsey & Company, March 2016, https://www.mckinsey.com/business-functions/marketing-and-sales/our-insights/from-touchpoints-to-journeys-seeing-the-world-as-customers-do
77. McKinsey Pharmaceuticals & Medical Products (PMP) Launch Service Line, From Products to Customer Experience: The New

Way to Launch in Pharma, McKinsey & Company, August 2018, https://www.mckinsey.com/industries/pharmaceuticals-and-medical-products/our-insights/from-product-to-customer-experience-the-new-way-to-launch-in-pharma

78. Ashutosh Gupta, Healthcare Product Launch: Designing CX for High ROI, docplexus, December 3, 2020, http://docplexus-insights.com/blog/customer-experience-pharmaceutical-product-launch/

79. Matt Salvetti, Pharma CX: The Most Important Part of Product Launch That You Aren't Planning For, PeopleMetrics, https://www.peoplemetrics.com/px-blog/pharma-cx-the-most-important-part-of-product-launch-that-you-arent-planning-for

80. Scan McDade, PhD, What Pharma Can Learn From CX Leaders, PeopleMetrics, 5 Tips For Improving Customer Experience In Pharmaceutical Industry, Customer Think, December 7, 2020, https://customerthink.com/5-tips-for-improving-customer-experience-in-pharmaceutical-industry/

81. Gareth Pickering, Micro-Moments And the Pharma Customer Journey, Orientation Marketing, August 15, 2019, https://www.orientation.agency/insights/micro-moments-and-the-pharma-customer-journey

82. Rafael Natanek, Christoph Schlegel, Michael Retterath and George Schlegel, How To Make Your Drug Launch A Success, Bain & Company, September 6, 2017, https://www.bain.com/insights/how-to-make-your-drug-launch-a-success/

83. Oliver Ehrlich, Herald Fanderi, and Christian Habrich, Mastering The Digital Advantage In Transforming Customer Experience, McKinsey & Company, May 2017, https://www.mckinsey.com/business-functions/operations/our-insights/mastering-the-digital-advantage-in-transforming-customer-experience

84. Alfonso Pulido, Ron Ritter, Ewan Duncan, The CEO Guide To Customer Experience, McKinsey Quarterly, August 2018, https://www.mckinsey.com/business-functions/operations/our-insights/the-ceo-guide-to-cu

85. Dr. Eric Schadt, The Role of Big Data in Medicine, McKinsey & Company, November 2015, https://www.mckinsey.com/

industries/pharmaceuticals-and-medical-products/our-insights/the-role-of-big-data-in-medicine

86. Jan Ascher, Daniel Höglund, Arafat Milka, Ivan Ostojic, and Maxence Vancauwenberghe, From Product to Customer Experience: The New Way To Launch In Pharma, McKinsey & Company, August 15, 2018, https://www.mckinsey.com/industries/pharmaceuticals-and-medical-products/our-insights/from-product-to-customer-experience-the-new-way-to-launch-in-pharma
87. Brooke Boyarsky, Will Enger, and Ron Ritter, Developing A Customer Experience Vision, McKinsey & Company, March 4, 2016, https://www.mckinsey.com/business-functions/marketing-and-sales/our-insights/developing-a-customer-experience-vision
88. Cynthia A. Challener, Ph.D, Astellas Takes Patient Care To Next Level, Pharma's Almanac, September 20, 2019, https://www.pharmasalmanac.com/articles/astellas-takes-patient-centricity-to-the-next-level
89. Kirstie Pickering, UCB: Patient Centricity Should Move Business Forward, PMLive, March 23, 2015, http://www.pmlive.com/pharma_news/ucb_patient_centricity_should_move_a_business_forward_688527
90. Optimizing Patient Centricity: An Actionable Guide, Cordence Worldwide, https://static1.squarespace.com/static/5d9b8b970aa01f728168dbdf/t/5e0d5531bb6d5e7d706ec428/1577932099618/Optimizing+Patient+Centricity+-+An+Actionable+Guide
91. Andrea Levin, Public Relations & Communications, UCB, Parkinson's Disease: A Patient Centric Approach, UCB.com, July 18, 2012, https://www.ucb.com/our-company/magazine/article/Parkinsons-disease-a-patient-centric-approach
92. Marco Ricci, What's The Value of Patient Centricity? Pharmaphorum, November 14, 2017, https://pharmaphorum.com/views-and-analysis/whats-value-patient-centricity/

93. Paul Simms, Turning Patient Centricity From Theory Into Practice: UCB Case Study, Reuters Events Pharma, March 6, 2015, https://www.reutersevents.com/pharma/patients/turning-patient-centricity-theory-practice-ucb-case-study
94. Robin Robinson, Patient-Based Culture, PharmaVoice, April 2019, https://www.pharmavoice.com/article/2019-04-patient-centricity/
95. Nicola Davies, A Structural And Cultural Transformation For A Patient-Focused UCB, Reuters Events Pharma, January 14, 2016, https://www.reutersevents.com/pharma/commercial/structural-and-cultural-transformation-patient-focused-ucb
96. Corinna Cornejo, Patient-Centered Business Growth: The Value Delivered to Pharma, WEGOHEALTH, March 9, 2018, https://www.wegohealth.com/2018/03/12/patient-centered-business-growth/
97. Hensley Evans, Sharon Suchotliff, and Jennifer Ntiri , What's The Secret To Becoming Patient-Centric? Look Outside Pharma, ZS, August 12, 2020, https://www.zs.com/insights/whats-the-secret-to-becoming-patient-centric
98. Hensley Evans, Sharon Suchotliff, and Jennifer Ntiri, Pharma's Roadmap To Patient Centricity, ZS, https://www.zs.com/content/dam/pdfs/Pharma_Map_Patient_Centricity.pdf
99. Patient-Centered Culture By Design: Embedding Patient-Centered Focus With The Culture Of Pharmaceutical Companies, eyeforpharma, https://www.ashfieldhealthcare.com/wp-content/uploads/2016/01/Patient-Centred-Culture-WhitePaper.pdf
100. Rachel Diebner, David Malfara, Kevin Neher, Mike Thompson, and Maxence Vancauwenberghe, Prediction: The Future of CX, McKinsey Quarterly, February 2021, https://www.mckinsey.com/~/media/mckinsey/business%20functions/marketing%20and%20sales/our%20insights/prediction%20the%20future%20of%20cx/prediction-the-future-of-cx-v2.pdf?shouldIndex=false
101. Jacob Ader, Julien Boudet, Marc Brodherson, and Kelsey Robinson, Marketing & Sales Practice: Why Every Business

Needs A Full-Funnel Marketing Strategy, McKinsey & Company, February 2021, https://www.mckinsey.com/~/media/mckinsey/business%20functionsmarketing%20and%20salesour%20insightswhy%20every%20business%20needs%20a%20full%20funnel%20marketing%20strategy/why-every-business-needs-a-full-funnel-marketing-strategy.pdf?shouldIndex=false

102. Liz Harrison, Dennis Spillecke, Jennifer Stanley, Jenny Tsai, Marketing & Sales Practice: Omnichannel in B2B Sales: The New Normal In A Year That Has Been Anything But, McKinsey & Company, March 2021, https://www.mckinsey.com/~/media/mckinsey/business%20functionsmarketing%20and%20sales/our%20insightsomnichannel%20in%20b2b%20sales%20the%20new%20normal%20in%20a%20year%20that%20has%20been%20 anything%20but/omnichannel-in-b2b-sales-the-new-normal-in-a-year-that-has-been-anything-but.pdf?shouldIndex=false

103. Chase Bibby, Jonathan Gordon, Gustavo Schüler, and Eli Stein, Marketing & Sales Practice: The Big Reset: Data-Driven Marketing In The Next Normal, McKinsey & Company, March 2021, https://www.mckinsey.com/~/media/mckinsey/business%20functions/marketing%20and%20sales/our%20insights/the%20big%20reset%20data%20driven% 20marketing%20in%20the%20next%20normal/the-big-reset-data-driven-marketing-in-the-next-normal.pdf?should Index=false

104. Dr. Olivia Kessel, UK Director of AbbVie Care, How AbbVie Care Is Putting Patients At The Centre, PMLive, March 15, 2016, http://www.pmlive.com/pharma_thought_leadership/how_abbvie_care_is_putting_patients_at_the_centre_951351

105. Amanda Barell, How People Power Is Building Patient-Centric Pharma, Pharmaphorum, September 19, 2018, https://pharmaphorum.com/views-analysis-patients/how-people-power-is-building-patient-centric-pharma/

106. Amanda Barell, Embracing Next Generation Patient Centricity, Pharmaphorum, May 16, 2019, https://pharmaphorum.com/patients/embracing-next-generation-patient-centricity/

107. Ed Miseta, Chief Editor, Clinical Leader, Janssen Uses A Dashboard To Monitor Patient Engagement Process, Clinical Leader, November 12, 2019, https://www.clinicalleader.com/doc/janssen-uses-a-dashboard-to-monitor-patient-engagement-progress-0001

108. Nicolas Davies, Janssen Leads On Patient-Centric Innovation, Reuters Events Pharma, January 11, 2016, https://www.reutersevents.com/pharma/commercial/janssen-leads-patient-centric-innovation

109. Taren Groom, Editor, Patient-Based Business Strategies, PharmaVoice, April 2018, https://www.pharmavoice.com/article/2018-04-patient-based-business-strategies/

110. Amanda Barrell, 2018 in Review: How Patient-Centricity Led To New Drugs That Tackle Unmet Need, Pharmaphorum, December 17, 2018, https://pharmaphorum.com/views-analysis-patients/2018-in-review-how-patient-centricity-led-to-new-drugs-that-tackle-unmet-need/

111. Andrew McConaghie, No Safety Concerns So Far In Sangamo's Groundbreaking Gene-Editing Trial, Pharmaphorum, February 7, 2018, https://pharmaphorum.com /news/no-safety-concerns-far-sangamos-groundbreaking-gene-editing-trial/

112. Deborah Borfitz, Takeda Using Chatbot To Improve Patient-Centricity And Trial Design, Clinical Research News, March 29, 2021, https://www.clinicalresearchnewsonline.com/news/2021/03/29/takeda-using-chatbot-to-improve-patient-centricity-and-trial-design

113. David Champagne, Amy Hung, and Oliver Leclerc, How Pharma Can Win In A Digital World, McKinsey & Company, December 2015, https://www.mckinsey.com/industries/pharmaceuticals-and-medical-products/our-insights/how-pharma-can-win-in-a-digital-world

114. Alexander Bedenkov, Andrey Ipatov, Ryan James Bale, From Pill To Platform: The Future of Pharma Lies Beyond Illness, LSE Business Review, October 22, 2020, https://blogs.lse.ac.uk/businessreview/2020/10/22/from-pill-to-platform-the-future-1-of-pharma-lies-beyond-illness/

115. Sarah Neville, Digital Disrupters Take Big Pharma 'Beyond the Pill', Financial Times, April 24, 2017, https://www.ft.com/content/d7a60642-0361-11e7-ace0-1ce02ef0def9
116. Jason Bloomberg, Digital Transformation Moves Pharma 'Beyond the Pill', forbes.com, April 15, 2014, https://www.forbes.com/sites/jasonbloomberg/2014/08/15/digital-transformation-moves-pharma-beyond-the-pill/?sh=20e5eb241c58
117. Using Actions, Not Words, To Reimagine Medicine, Phesi, https://www.phesi.com/using-actions-not-words-to-reimagine-medicine/Using Actions, Not Words, to Reimagine Medicine
118. Dr. Joseph Sgroi, 4 Key Ways To Reimagine The Future of Healthcare, Clinic Cloud, December 10, 2020, https://www.clinictocloud.com/blog/four-key-ways-to-reimagine-future-healthcare
119. Roshan Karunaratane, 3 Quick Tips For Better Patient Engagement, Clinic Cloud, October 20, 2020, https://www.clinictocloud.com/blog/three-quick-tips-for-better-patient-engagement
120. Why Dr. Joseph Sgroi Engaged Clinic To Cloud, Clinic Cloud, https://www.clinictocloud.com/case-studies/dr-joseph-sgroi
121. Enabling Market Access Through Outcome-Based Pricing, PMLive, February 17, 2020, http://www.pmlive.com/pmhub/market_access/valid_insight/white_papers_and_resources/enabling_market_access_through_outcomes-based_pricing
122. Jef Williams, The Changing Role Of The Patient, ICE Magazine, January 31, 2020, https://theicecommunity.com/the-changing-role-of-the-patient/
123. Sandra Sánchez, Health: Reimagining The Pharma Sales Rep Model, Mexico Business News, April 28, 2021, https://mexicobusiness.news/health/news/reimagining-pharma-sales-rep-model
124. Andrew Stone, Blended And Augmented: Reimagining The Role Of The Rep, Reuters Events Pharma, December 18, 2020, https://www.reutersevents.com/pharma/commercial/blended-and-augmented-reimagining-role-rep

125. Mary Assimakopoulos, The Power of Observation in Gathering Patient Insights, Reuters Events Pharma, April 10, 2014, https://www.reutersevents.com/pharma/column/power-observation-gathering-patient-insights

126. StartUp Health, Power To The Patients: 3 Companies Driving Patient Empowerment, STARTUP+Health, October 19, 2018, cC

127. Marrie Ennis-O'Connor, What Does It Mean To Be An Empowered Patient? Patient Empowerment Net Work, May 22, 2018, https://powerfulpatients.org/2018/05/22/what-does-it-mean-to-be-an-empowered-patient/

128. Hayden LIndskog, Maria Strom, and Christian Zebri, Using Ethnography To Translate Behavior To Value In Medical Devices, Pharmaceuticals & Medical Practice, McKinsey & Company, January 2021, https://www.mckinsey.com/industries/pharmaceuticals-and-medical-products/our-insights/using-ethnography-to-translate-behavior-to-value-in-medical-devices

129. Debbie Fletcher, The Impact of Market Research on Digital Marketing, Market research.com, April 8, 2015, https://blog.marketresearch.com/the-impact-of-market-research-on-digital-marketing

130. Tony Tran, What Is Social Listening, Why It Matters, And 10 Tools To Make It Easier, Hootsuite, March 3, 2020, https://blog.hootsuite.com/social-listening-business/

131. Kavi Bhandari, Digital Adoption Is No More An Option But A Necessity For Pharma Companies, BW Healthcare World, June 04, 2021, http://bwhealthcareworld.businessworld.in/article/Digital-Adoption-Is-No-More-An-Option-But-A-Necessity-For-Pharma-Companies-/04-06-2021-391985/

132. Mayank Agarwal, Karel Eloot, Matteo Mancini, and Alpesh Patel, Industry 4.0: Reimagining Manufacturing Operations After COVID-19, McKinsey & Company, July 29, 2020, https://www.mckinsey.com/business-functions/operations/our-insights/industry-40-reimagining-manufacturing-operations-after-covid-19

133. Sponsored Content By IQVIA, Moving Pharma Marketing From Multichannel To Omnichannel, BiopharmaDive, June 7, 2021, https://www.biopharmadive.com/spons/moving-pharma-marketing-from-multichannel-to-omnichannel/601275/
134. Shailendra Sinhasane, Digital Healthcare Ecosystem: The New Era Of Medical Care, MOBISOFT, October 12, 2020, https://mobisoftinfotech.com/resources/blog/digital-healthcare-ecosystem-the-new-era-of-medical-care/
135. Sebastian Hermes, Tobias Riasnow, Eric K. Clemons, Markus Böhm, Helmut Krcmar, The Digital Transformation Of The Healthcare Industry: Exploring The Rise Of Emerging Platform Ecosystems And Their Influence On The Role Of Patients, Business Research, 1033-1069 (2020), September 11, 2020, https://link.springer.com/article/10.1007/s40685-020-00125-x
136. Umesh Mohanty, Vinod Sankarnarayanan, Building A Digital-First Healthcare Ecosystem, Thought Works, March 11, 2021, https://www.thoughtworks.com/insights/blog/building-digital-first-healthcare-ecosystem
137. Terence Ryan, Making Sense Of the Healthcare Ecosystem And How Technology Is Enabling People-Driven Health, HealthChampion, October 11, 2019, https://myhealthchampion.com/making-sense-of-the-healthcare-ecosystem-and-how-technology-is-enabling-people-driven-health/
138. Mathis Friesdorf, Ulrike Deetjen, Ajit Sawant, Greg Gilbert, and Florian Niedermann, Digital Health Ecosystems: A Payer Perspective, McKinsey & Company Healthcare Systems & Services, August 2, 2019, https://www.mckinsey.com/industries/healthcare-systems-and-services/our-insights/digital-health-ecosystems-a-payer-perspective
139. Enabling Market Access Through Outcomes-Based Pricing, PMLiVe, February 17, 2020, http://www.pmlive.com/pmhub/market_access/valid_insight/white_papers_and_resources/enabling_market_access_through_outcomes-based_pricing
140. John LaMattina, Outcomes-Based Pricing Not A Panacea for High Priced Drugs, Forbes, March 27,2019, https://

www.forbes.com/sites/johnlamattina/2019/03/27/outcomes-based-pricing-not-a-panacea-for-high-priced-drugs/?sh=68d384c25c23

141. Elodie Adida, Outcome-Based Pricing For New Pharmaceuticals Via Rebates, Management Science, August 6, 2020, https://pubsonline.informs.org/doi/abs/10.1287/mnsc.2019.3574
142. Nimer S. Alkhatib & Ivo Abraham (2020) The Six Delta platform for outcome-based contracting for pharmaceuticals, Journal of Medical Economics, 23:11, 1209-1214, DOI: 10.1080/13696998.2020.1824161
143. Paul Grant, 'Agile' Content Approvals In The Pharmaceutical Industry, Creation Knowledge, May 28, 2015, https://creation.co/knowledge/agile-approvals-pharmaceutical-industry/
144. Maria Aquirre, During WCLC 2020, HCPs Divisions On Twitter Need For Novel EGFR & NSCLC Treatments, Creation Knowledge, May 7, 2021, https://creation.co/knowledge/during-wclc-2020-hcps-discuss-on-twitter-need-for-novel-egfr-nsclc-treatments/
145. Laura Meyer, Understand, Identify and Partner With HCPs To Improve Patient Support, Creation Knowledge, March 19, 2021, https://creation.co/knowledge/understand-identify-and-partner-with-hcps-to-improve-patient-support/
146. Daniel Ghinn, Ten Questions To Ask About Your HCP Digital Opinion Leaders, Creation Knowledge, November 27, 2020, https://creation.co/knowledge/ten-questions-to-ask-about-your-hcp-digital-opinion-leaders/
147. Erica Bartlet, Meeting The Three Biggest Challenges of Pharma Value-Based Agreements, Model N, October 25, 2019, https://www.modeln.com/blog/pharmaceuticals/meeting-the-three-biggest-challenges-of-pharma-value-based-agreements/
148. Javier González, PharmD, Chief Operating Officer, Abraca Health Duluth, GA, Accountability Is Everything: Outcomes-Based Pharmaceutical Agreements, AHDB: American Health & Drug Benefits, October 2012, Vol. 12. No 6, https://

www.ahdbonline.com/issues/2019/october-2019-vol-12-no-6/2849-accountability-is-everything-outcomes-based-pharmaceutical-agreements

149. Alaric Dearment, Outcome-Based Contracts Likely To Keep Growing, Evolving Despite Challenges, MedCity News, January 24, 2020, https://medcitynews.com/2020/01/outcome-based-contracts-likely-to-keep-growing-evolving-despite-challenges/
150. Steven G. Morgan, Hannah S. Bathula, Suerie Moon, Pricing of Pharmaceuticals IS becoming A Major Challenge For Health Systems, The BMJ, January 13, 2020, https://www.bmj.com/content/368/bmj.l4627
151. Justin McCarthy, Big Pharma Sinks To The Bottom Of the US Industry Rankings, GALLUP, September 3, 2019, https://news.gallup.com/poll/266060/big-pharma-sinks-bottom-industry-rankings.aspx
152. Bertalan Meskó, Zsófa Drobni, Èva Bényei, Bence Gergely, Zsuzsanna Györffy, Digital Health Is A Cultural Transformation of Traditional Healthcare, Mhealth, 2017:3:38, Published online September 14, 2017, https://www.ncbi.nlm.nih.gov/pmc/articles/PMC5682364/
153. PHILIPS, Rise of Digital Health During Pandemic Energizes Commitment And Expectations of Younger Doctors, Healthcare IT News, October 28, 2020, https://www.healthcareitnews.com/news/emea/rise-digital-health-during-pandemic-energises-commitment-and-expectations-younger-doctors
154. Wendy Sue Swanson, MD, Healthcare's Digital Revolution: How Pop Culture's Tech Tools Are Impacting Patients And Providers, Physician's Insurance, https://www.phyins.com/magazine/healthcares-digital-revolution-how-pop-cultures-tech-tools-are-impacting-patients-and, Accessed on June 9, 2021.
155. Global Data Healthcare, Virtual Sales Reps' And Physicians' Engagement To Remain A New Standard Post-COVID-19, Pharmaceutical Technology, May 21, 2021, https://www.pharmaceutical-technology.com/comment/virtual-engagement-covid-pharmaceutical-companies/

156. Chris Neuner, Pharma: 3 Ways Data-Driven Technology Is Powering The Pharma Sales Evolution, PULSEPOINT, September 21, 2020, https://pulsepoint.com/blog/3-ways-data-driven-technology-is-powering-the-pharma-sales-evolution
157. Richard Staines Interviews Rebeca Silver, General Manager, Veeva, Pharma's Digital Transformation Journey And The Role of Customer Reference Data, Pharmaphorum, December 4, 2020, https://pharmaphorum.com/views-analysis-digital/pharmas-digital-transformation-journey-and-the-role-of-customer-reference-data/
158. Vikram Kotnis, The New Rules Of Doctor Engagement In The New Normal, AmuraTech, July 12, 2020, https://www.amuratech.com/blog/the-new-rules-of-doctor-engagement-in-the-new-normal
159. Featured Article, Price Waterhouse Coopers (PWC), Reorganizing Pharmaceutical Supply Chains Post-COVID-19, HealthcareGlobal, https://healthcareglobal.com/procurement-and-supply-chain/reorganising-pharmaceutical-supply-chains-post-covid-19
160. Rakesh Sharma, Reimagining Bio Pharma R&D And Clinical Trials In The Age of AI, Express Pharma, May 15, 2019, https://www.expresspharma.in/reimagining-biopharma-rd-and-clinical-trials-in-the-age-of-ai/
161. Dr. Nandita Bhargava, Reimagining Healthcare Supply Chain Through Automation, LinkedIn.com, September 16, 2020, https://www.linkedin.com/pulse/reimagining-healthcare-supply-chain-through-dr-nandita-bhargava/
162. Rajagopalan Subramanyam, How Pharmaceutical Serialization Can Help Reimagine Business Models, SAP Community, March 22, 2017, https://blogs.sap.com/2017/03/22/how-pharmaceutical-serialization-can-help-reimagine-business-models-part-1/
163. Rajagopalan Subramanyam, How Pharmaceutical Serialization Can Help Reimagine Business Models, SAP Community, March 22, 2017, https://blogs.sap.com/2017/03/22/how-pharma-

ceutical-serialization-can-help-reimagine-business-models-part-2/

164. Arthur D. Little Global, Barnik Chitran Maitra, Thomas Kuruvilla, Bernd Schreiber, Lokesh Dadhich, Harinarayanan S, Radhika Shah, Arunabh Podder, India's Supply Chain: A Bold Vision For 2030, September 11, 2020, https://www.adlittle.com/en/insights/report/reimagining-india's-supply-chain

165. Luca A. Fineli and Vas Narasimhan, Mini Review: Leading A Digital Transformation In The Pharmaceutical Industry: Reimagining The Way We Work In Global Drug Development, Clinical Pharmacology and Therapeutics (A Wiley Journal), 2020 Oct: 108 (4): 756-761, PMC, US National Library Of Medicine, National Institutes of Health, NCBI Resources, https://www.ncbi.nlm.nih.gov/pmc/articles/PMC7540662/

166. Pharma And Life Sciences, Impact of Amazon's Entry in Pharmaceutical Distribution Industry, GEP.com, December 7, 2017, https://www.gep.com/blog/mind/impact-amazons-entry-pharmaceutical-distribution-industry

167. Nirmala Iyengar, Angela Radcliffe, CapGemini Invent: Five Predictions For COVID-19 Driven Agility Across The Life Science Value Chain, CapGemini, June 1, 2020, https://www.capgemini.com/2020/06/covid-19-predictions-for-life-sciences/

168. Katie Kennedy, 14 Ways Pharma Can Engage HCP Digital Opinion Leaders, Creation Knowledge, October 14, 2020, https://www.capgemini.com/2020/06/covid-19-predictions-for-life-sciences/

169. Katie Kennedy, Add Value To Engage Effectively With Your Digital Opinion Leaders, Creation Knowledge, April 14, 2021, https://creation.co/knowledge/add-value-to-engage-effectively-with-your-digital-opinion-leaders/

170. Katie Kennedy, The Difference Between DOLs and KOLs And Why It Matters To Pharma, Creation Knowledge, March 29, 2021, https://creation.co/knowledge/the-difference-between-dols-and-kols/

171. Laura McIntyre, Medical Affairs: Best Practice For Identifying Online HCP Thought Leaders, Creation Knowledge, May 10, 2021, https://creation.co/knowledge/the-difference-between-dols-and-kols/

172. Daniel Ghinn, Digital Opinion Leaders In Diabetes: The Worldwide HCP Social Media Study, Creation Knowledge, June 23, 2014, https://creation.co/knowledge/digital-opinion-leaders-in-diabetes-the-worldwide-hcp-social-media-study/

173. Dr. Nicola Davies, The Sales Rep Of The Future, Reuters Events Pharma, December, 16, 2016, https://www.reutersevents.com/pharma/commercial/sales-rep-future

174. Chris Ross, Combining Hard Technology With Human Skills, PMLiVE, November 6, 2019, http://www.pmlive.com/pharma_intelligenceCombining_hard_technology_with_human_skills_1315749

175. Jaideep Bajaj and Saby Mitra, Conducting The Sales Symphony: How the "Orchestrator Rep" Addresses A Restricted-Access, Multichannel World, ZS Sales+ Marketing, https://www.veeva.com/wp-content/uploads/2011/12/ZS-WP-The-Orchestrator-Rep-in-Pharma.pdf

176. ZS interview With Jaideep Bajaj, Pharma Sales: Why You Need Orchestrator Reps Now, ZS Sales+Marketing, https://www.zs.com/content/dam/pdfsPharma_Sales_Orchestrator_Reps.pdf

177. Saby Mitra and Jaideep Bajaj, Sales Reps Take On 'Orchestrator' Role To Deliver Superior Customer Experience, PharmaLiVE.com, https://www.pharmalive.com/sales-reps-take-on-orchestrator-role-to-deliver-superior-customer-experience/

178. Abheek Singh, Namit Puri and Amit Mittal, Reimagining Go-To-Market Strategies After the Pandemic, BCG, May 28, 2020, https://www.bcg.com/publications/2020/reimagining-go-to-market-strategies-after-covid-19-pandemic

179. Neil Osmond, Implementing Agile Working In Pharma, PharmaField, August 5, 2019, https://pharmafield.co.uk/opinion/implementing-agile-working-in-pharma/

180. Neil Osmond, A Guide To Implementing Agile In Pharma, PharmaField, August 5, 2019, https://pharmafield.co.uk/in_depth/a-guide-to-implementing-agile-in-pharma/

181. David Edelman, Jason Heller, Steven Spittaels, Agile Marketing: A Step-By-Step Guide, McKinsey & Company, November 9, 2016, https://www.mckinsey.com/business-functions/marketing-and-sales/our-insights/agile-marketing-a-step-by-step-guide

182. Sarah Elk, Customer's Role In Agile, Bain & Company, October 09, 2020, https://www.bain.com/insights/why-is-the-customer-so-important-in-agile/

183. Karan Shah, Why Does Pharma Sector Need Digital Transformation, IID Blog, https://iide.co/blog/digital-transformation-in-pharma-industry/ Accessed on June 09, 2021

184. News, COVID-19 Accelerated Digital Transformation Of The Pharma Industry By Five Years: Poll, Pharmaceutical Technology, March 09, 2021, https://www.pharmaceutical-technology.com/news/covid-19-accelerated-digital-transformation-of-the-pharma-industry-by-five-years-poll/

185. Paul Tunnah, Interview with George Miller, Vice President and Global Health Innovation Accelerator COE At UCB, Can 'Design Thinking' Revolutionize Pharma's Culture, Eye On Innovation: Pharmaphorum, May 3, 2018, https://pharmaphorum.com/views-and-analysis/can-design-thinking-revolutionise-pharmas-culture/

186. Andrew Mathius, How Design Thinking Helped One Life Sciences Company Attract More Customers, PM360, January 25, 2016, https://www.pm360online.com/how-design-thinking-helped-one-life-science-company-attract-more-customers/

187. Abhishek Shankar, Enhancing The Patient Experience: How Life Sciences Companies Use Design Thinking To Deliver Better Outcomes, HCLTech, March 29, 2018, https://www.hcltech.com/blogs/enhancing-patient-experience-how-can-life-sciences-companies-use-design-thinking-deliver

188. Andrew Stone, On the Journey From Pill To Platform, Reuters Events Pharma, June 3, 2021, https://www.reutersevents.com/pharma/medical/journey-pill-platform

189. Pushparajah, D.S, Making Patient Engagement a Reality. *Patient* **11,** 1–8 (2018), https://www.researchgate.net/publication/318660420_Making_Patient_Engagement_a_Reality

190. Dr. Nicolas Davies, A Structural And Cultural Transformation For A Patient-Focused UCB, Reuters Events Pharma, January 14, 2018, https://www.reutersevents.com/pharma/commercial/structural-and-cultural-transformation-patient-focused-ucb

191. Amy Turnquist, The Customer Experience Roadmap Is Paved in Empathy & Emotion, DHC—Digital Health Coalition, June 2021, https://digitalhealthcoalition.org/insights/article-customer-experience-roadmap-paved-in-empathy-amy-turnquist-june-2021/

192. Kaitlyn Clark, Associate Digital Strategist, Anika Patel, Digital Strategist, EHR, Ogilvy Health, How Pharma Can Benefit From The EHR, PharmaVoice, November/December 2018, https://www.pharmavoice.com/article/2018-11-ehr/

193. Beth Snyder Bulik, Ogilvy CommonHealth Takes A Deep Dive On EHR AS A Marketing Strategy For Pharma Clients, Fierce Pharma, May 9, 2016, https://www.fiercepharma.com/marketing/ogilvycommonhealth-takes-deep-dive-ehr-as-a-marketing-strategy-for-pharma-clients

194. Jonathan Ziegel, VP, Engagement Strategy, and Stephanie, Neuwirt, Associate Director, Customer Experience (EHR) Ogilvy CommonHealth Worldwide, PharmaLiVE.com, https://www.pharmalive.com/interactive-digital-marketing-a-multi-channel-marketers-look-at-integrating-ehrs-into-the-digital-ecosystem/ Accessed on June 17, 2021

195. Liz Sporrer, Senior Media Planner, CMI, Samantha Bogus, Media Planner, CMI, Electronic Health Records And Pharmaceutical Advertising, CMI Media Group, February 23, 2021, https://cmimediagroup.com/resources/electronic-health-records-and-pharmaceutical-advertising/

196. Marketing, EHR Systems And The Power Of Data In Marketing, HealthLink Dimensions, January 9, 2019, https://healthlinkdimensions.com/uncategorized/ehr-systems-and-the-power-of-data-in-marketing/

197. Harshit Jain, MD, 5 Ways Pharma Marketers Can Enhance Physician Communications Without Call-to-Action Messages, PharmExec.com, March 22, 2021, https://www.pharmexec.com/view/5-ways-pharma-marketers-can-enhance-physician-communications-without-call-to-action-messages

198. Harshit Jain, Ways Pharma Marketers Can Boost Physician Engagement Via Telehealth, MedCity News, March 5, 2021, https://medcitynews.com/2021/03/ways-pharma-marketers-can-boost-physician-engagement-via-telehealth/

199. Scott Greenstone, How Pharma Marketing Is Overcoming EHR Industry Fragmentation, OgilvyHealth, January 9, 2019, https://ogilvyhealth.com/blog/how-pharma-marketing-is-overcoming-ehr-industry-fragmentation/

200. eConsultancy, Six Trends In Pharma Marketing: Embracing Digital Transformation In The Pharma And Healthcare Sectors—A Marketer's Guide, Created For The Attendees And Friends of ePharma 2017: The Art And Science Of Innovative Digital Strategy, worldpharmatoday.com, https://www.worldpharmatoday.com/wp-content/uploads/2017/01/whitepapers_Six-Trends-in-Pharma-Marketing.pdf

201. Ira Haimowitz, PhD, Vice President, Product Strategy, Crossix, and Whitney Kemper, Sr. Director, Analytics Products, Crossix, Applying Real-World Evidence Data For Measuring Pharmaceutical Digital Media Programs, PMSA, Pharmaceutical Management Science Association, https://pmsa.org/jpmsa-vol06-article06, Accessed on June 17, 2021

202. Andrew Mathius, How Pharma Can Help Ease The Growing Burden On Healthcare Professionals, PM360, May 16, 2019, https://www.pm360online.com/how-pharma-can-help-ease-the-growing-burden-on-healthcare-professionals/

203. John Kenny, InTouch Group, The Now And The Next: Advice For Pharma Marketers In the Now And The New Normal. WARC, May 2, 2021, https://www.warc.com/newsandopinion/opinion/the-now-and-the-next-advice-for-pharma-marketers-in-the-new-normal/4049

204. Christopher Manz, MD, Joseph S. Ross, MD, M. H. S. , and David Grande, MD, M.P.A., Perspective: Marketing To Physicians In A Digital World, The New England Journal of Medicine, November 13, 2014, https://www.nejm.org/doi/full/10.1056/NEJMp1408974

205. Steve Love, Principal, ZS Associates, Sudhanshu Bhatnagar, Business Consulting Manager, ZS Associates, Greg Rickman, Business Consultant, ZS Associates, Jody Wang, Business Associate Consultant, ZS Associates, The Value Of EMR Data: Unlocking Insights That Drive Pharma Sales, Spring 2016, MyOwnMed.com, https://myownmed.com/wp-content/uploads/2020/04/RGB-JPMSA-The-value-of-EMR-data-unlocking-insights-that-drive-pharma-sales.pdf#new_tab

206. Ashutosh Gupta, Healthcare Marketing: 3 Tips For Creating Tactically Sound Email Campaigns, docplexus, January 21, 2021, http://docplexus-insights.com/blog/3-email-marketing-tips-for-pharma/

207. Kevin George, A Guide To Email Marketing For The Pharma Industry, Uplers Email, January 13, 2021, https://email.uplers.com/blog/email-marketing-for-the-pharma-industry/

208. Ferdi Steinmann, Pharma and AI: 2021 And Beyond, PharmExec.com, December 4, 2020, https://www.pharmexec.com/view/pharma-and-ai-2021-and-beyond

209. Harshit Jain, CEO and Founder, Doceree, Hyper-Personalization To Drive Pharma Marketing Efforts By 2021, eHealth: The Enterprise of Healthcare, February 3, 2021, https://ehealth.eletsonline.com/2021/02/ai-and-hyper-personalization-to-drive-pharma-marketing-efforts-by-2021/

210. Using Artificial Intelligence (AI) For Better Doctor Segmentation For Pharma Marketing, Multiplier, AI Powered Healthcare

Marketing, https://multipliersolutions.com/using-artificial-intelligence-ai-better-doctor-segmentation-pharma-marketing/

211. Alex Dale, AI And Pharma Sales, PharmaTimes, March 28, 2019, http://www.pharmatimes.com/web_exclusives/ai_and_pharma_sales_1282806
212. Edit Lepine, Pharmaceutical ales Beyond 2020: Using AI To Fine-Tune Your Strategy, P360, Powered Possibilities, November 19, 2019
213. Dr. Andrea Bates, How AI Is Changing The Pharma Sales Force Model, EULARIS, https://eularis.com/how-ai-is-changing-the-pharma-sales-force-model/ Accessed on June 21, 2021
214. Kathleen Walch, The Increasing Use Of AI in The Pharmaceutical Industry, forbes.com, December 26, 2020, https://www.forbes.com/sites/cognitiveworld/2020/12/26/the-increasing-use-of-ai-in-the-pharmaceutical-industry/?sh=45aaeb1d4c01
215. Rasim Shah, Embracing AI in Pharma Sales. PharmaField, March 2, 2020, https://www.forbes.com/sites/cognitiveworld/2020/12/26/the-increasing-use-of-ai-in-the-pharmaceutical-industry/?sh=45aaeb1d4c01
216. Chloe Kent, Changing The Face of Pharma Sales With AI, Pharmaceutical Technology, May 7, 2021, https://www.pharmaceutical-technology.com/features/odaia-changing-the-face-of-pharma-sales-with-ai/
217. Codrin Arsene, AI For Pharma Marketing: It Really Works Right Now, PM360, June 5, 2020, https://www.pm360online.com/ai-for-pharma-marketing-it-really-works-right-now/
218. Dr. Andrea Bates, 16 Examples of Successful Applications of Artificial Intelligence in Pharma Marketing, EULARIS, https://eularis.com/16-examples-of-successful-applications-of-artificial-intelligence-in-pharma-marketing-part-2/ Accessed on June 21, 2021
219. Harshit Jain, AI is Vital for Pharma Marketers to Raise Engagement with Physician, forbes.com, April 7, 2021, https://www.forbes.com/sites/forbestechcouncil/2021/04/07/ai-is-

vital-for-pharma-marketers-to-raise-engagement-with-physicians/?sh=24361b2483d4

220. Antonio Gulli, AI is Vital for Pharma Marketers to Raise Engagement with Physician, forbes.com, June 18, 2021

221. Pratap Khedkar and Saby Mitra, White Paper: Boosting Pharmaceutical Sales and Marketing with Artificial Intelligence, ZS.com, https://www.zs.com/insights/boosting-pharmaceutical-sales-and-marketing-with-artificial-intelligence, Accessed on June 21, 2021

222. Beth Snyder Bulik, How Did Novo Nordisk's Sophia Chatbot Become A Pharma Industry Standard? Empathy, Timing and Relevance: Experts, Fierce Pharma, August 18, 2020, https://www.fiercepharma.com/marketing/ai-week-life-sciences-track-ai-and-pharma-marketing-reveals-keen-interest-chatbots

223. Dr. Andrea Bates, Utilizing the Power of Chatbots in Pharma Marketing, EULARIS, https://eularis.com/utilizing-the-power-of-chatbots-in-pharma-marketing/ Accessed on June 21, 2021

224. AI White Paper, Why Chatbots Will Become Commonplace in Pharma By 2025, Earthware, https://earthware.co.uk/ai-white-paper.pdf?v=1, Accessed on June 21, 2021

225. Adam Chapman, The Chatbots Are Coming! Reuters Events Pharma, May 15, 2019, https://www.reutersevents.com/pharma/commercial/chatbots-are-coming

226. Rise of the Chatbots: Bringing AI Into Pharma Marketing, Big Eye Agency, August 16, 2019, https://www.bigeyeagency.com/insights/rise-of-chatbots-bringing-ai-into-pharma-marketing/

227. Healthcare Advertising Blog, 5 Hypothetical Healthcare & Pharma Chatbot Examples, bfw life sciences, https://healthcareadvertising.gobfw.com/healthcare-pharma-chatbot-examples/#es_form_f1-n1 , Accessed on June 21, 2021

228. Chris Finch, AI is Transforming R&D—Now It Can Transform Pharma Marketing, PMLiVE, August 12, 2019, http://www.pmlive.com/pharma_thought_leadership/ai_is_transforming_pharma_r_and_d_now_it_can_transform_pharma_marketing_1297189

229. Andrew Grojean, Social Media Manager; Abid Rahman, Senior Director, Innovation and Technology Development at InTouchSolutions, White Paper, Compliant Chatbots on Social: Best Practices for Pharma, InTouchSolutions, 2018, https://www.intouchsol.com/wp-content/uploads/Blog/PDFs/Compliant_Chatbots_on_Social_POV.pdf
230. The Top 12 Health Chatbots, The Medical Futurist, January 16, 2020, https://medicalfuturist.com/top-12-health-chatbots/
231. Robin Robinson, The Uptick of AI Use Will Bring Pharma Into the Future Faster, PharmaVoice, November/December 2019, https://www.pharmavoice.com/article/2019-11-ai/
232. Samantha McGrail, AI in the Pharma Industry: Current Uses, Best Cases, Digital Future, PharmaNews Intelligence, April 30, 2021, https://pharmanewsintel.com/news/ai-in-the-pharma-industry-current-uses-best-cases-digital-future
233. Kechit Goyal, Artificial Intelligence in Pharma Industry: 8 Exciting Applications in 2021, upGRAD Blog, January 7, 2021, https://www.upgrad.com/blog/artificial-intelligence-in-pharmaceutical-industry/
234. Samatha McGrail, Impact of Medical Affairs on the Pharmaceutical Industry, PharmaNews Intelligence, February 22, 2021, https://pharmanewsintel.com/news/impact-of-medical-affairs-on-the-pharmaceutical-industry
235. Dr. Rajasekharan Karjagi, Head, Analytics Solutions, Wipro, and Manish Jindal, Manager, Analytics Solutions, Wipro, What Can IOT Do For Healthcare, wipro.com, https://www.wipro.com/business-process/what-can-iot-do-for-healthcare-/
236. Paul Hickey, Solving Problems in Healthcare With Alexa Skills: With Nate Treloar of Orbita, The Voice Series, November 25, 2020, https://voiceseries.com/solving-problems-in-healthcare-with-alexa-skills-with-nate-treloar-of-orbita/
237. Archana Oberoi, 7 Interesting Use Cases of Voice Assistants in Healthcare, daffodil.com, April 22, 2019, https://insights.daffodilsw.com/blog/7-interesting-use-cases-of-voice-assistants-in-healthcare

238. Johannes Beekman, IoT Technology is Making A Big Impact on Marketing, IoT Marketing, August 1, 2020, https://iotmktg.com/iot-technology-making-big-impact-marketing/

239. The Internet of Things in Marketing: The Integrated Marketing Opportunity, I-SCOOP, https://www.i-scoop.eu/internet-of-things-guide/internet-things-marketing/, Accessed on June 25, 2021,

240. Jo Best, Smart Pills And The Future of Medicine: Insights From Your Insides, ZDNet, February 23, 2021, https://www.zdnet.com/article/smart-pills-and-the-future-of-medicine-insights-from-your-insides/

241. Smart Pills Enable Convenient Diagnostics And Accurate Therapy, Alliance of Advanced BioMedical Engineering, 2017, https://aabme.asme.org/posts/smart-pills-enable-convenient-diagnostics-and-accurate-therapeutics

242. Elise Reuter, New 'Smart Pill' Maker Gains FDA Approval, MedCityNews, December 9, 2019, https://medcitynews.com/2019/12/new-smart-pill-maker-gains-fda-approval/?rf=1

243. Mike Thomas, IoT in Healthcare Applications: Leading To An Improved Industry, builtin.com, July 4, 2019, https://builtin.com/internet-things/iot-in-healthcare

244. Eme Sezgin, Yungui Huang, Ujjwal Ramtekkar, and Simon Lin, Readiness for Voice Assistants to Support Healthcare Delivery During a Healthcare Crisis and Pandemic, NPJ Digital Medicine, September 16, 2020, https://www.nature.com/articles/s41746-020-00332-0

245. HT Media Team, Extended Reality in Healthcare: Why Medical Marketers Should Be Excited, June 4, 2021, https://www.htmedia.in/archives/blog/extended-reality-in-healthcare-why-medical-marketers-should-be-excited

246. MM&M ebook Sponsored by PIXACORE, Virtual Reality Breaks Through the Healthcare Marketing, pixacore.com, April 2017, https://pixacore.com/wp-content/uploads/2017/04/Pixacore-March-2017-Virtual-Reality-Breaks-Through-in-Healthcare-Marketing.pdf

247. Craig Moore, Customer Centricity—The Key to Digital Engagement, AvantHC, August 27, 2020, https://avanthc.com/customer-centricity-the-key-to-digital-engagement/?utm_medium=email&utm_source=avanthc&utm_campaign=newsletter-0621&sslid=Mzc0t7A0NDOwNDMwAgA&sseid=MzIyNTYxt7A0NAEA&jobid=35a1ae43-121f-43d5-8d26-71dba4b66026

248. Craig Moore, Sign of the Times: The State of Digital Pharma Marketing Today, AvantHC, October 19, 2020, https://avanthc.com/sign-o-the-times/

249. Rob Spalding, Avant Healthcare White Paper, Come Together: How HCP-Focused Social Media Platforms Are Integral to the Future of Medical Education, Avant Healthcare, https://ss-usa.s3.amazonaws.com/c/308478374/media/34415f97 14b5272602688828679 4363/AvantHealthcare_ HCPSocial Networks_Whitepaper_091720.pdf, Accessed on July 1, 2021

250. Greta Rybicki, Crowd Sourcing Innovation in the Digital Workplace, AvantHC, June 17, 2021, https://avanthc.com/crowdsourcing-innovation-in-the-digital-workplace?utm_medium=email&utm_source=avanthc&utm_campaign=newsletter0621&sslid=Mzc0t7A0NDOwNDMwAg A&sseid=MzIyNTYxt7A0NAEA&jobid=35a1ae43-121f-43d5-8d26-71dba4b66026

251. Sponsored Content by IQVIA, Top Customer Engagement Trends in Pharma, BiopharmaDive, May 17, 2021, https://www.biopharmadive.com/spons/top-customer-engagement-trends-in-pharma 600047?utm_medium=email&utm_source=sharpspring&sslid=Mzc0t7A0NDOwNDMwAgA&sseid=MzIyNTYxt7A0NAEA&jobid=35a1ae43-121f-43d5-8d26-71dba4b66026

252. Laura Dix, Managing Director, Life Sciences, United Kingdom, Pharma's Role in Creating Quality in HCP Experiences, Accenture Life Sciences Blog, May 3, 2021, https://www.accenture.com/us-en/blogs/life-sciences/pharmas-role-in-creating-qualityhcpexperiences?utm_medium=email&utm_source=sharpspring&sslid=Mzc0t7A0NDOwND

MwAgA&sseid=MzlyNTYxt7A0NAEA&jobid=35a1ae43-121f-43d5-8d26-71dba4b66026

253. Bertalan Meskó and Dr. Pranavsingh Dhunnoo, Amazon's Dive Into Healthcare: A 2021 Update, The Medical Futurist, June 22, 2021, https://medicalfuturist.com/amazons-march-into-healthcare-a-2021-update?utm_source=The%20Medical%20Futurist%20Newsle tter&utm_campaign=c02d90fbd1EMAIL_CAMPAIGN_2021_6_29&utm_medium=email&utm_term=0_efd6a3cd08-c02d90fbd1-420567429&mc_cid=c02d90fbd1&mc_eid=fd3f67d550
254. Bernard Marr, What is Extended Reality Technology? A Simple Explanation for Everyone, forbes.com, August 18, 2019, https://www.forbes.com/sites/bernardmarr/2019/08/12/what-is-extended-reality-technology-a-simple-explanation-for-anyone/?sh=489552972498
255. Gunjan Bhardwaj, Five Use Cases for Blockchain in Pharma, Pharmaphorum, April 25, 2018, https://pharmaphorum.com/views-and-analysis/five-use-cases-for-blockchain-in-pharma/
256. Gunjan Bhardwaj, Why Pharma's Manufacturing Supply Chain Needs Blockchain Innovation, Pharmaphorum, April 17, 2018, https://pharmaphorum.com/views-and-analysis/pharmas-manufacturing-supply-chain-needs-blockchain-innovation/
257. Gunjan Bhardwaj, How Blockchain and AI Can Help Pharma Focus on Innovation Rather Than Advertising, forbes.com, June 8, 2018, https://www.forbes.com/sites/forbestechcouncil/2018/06/08/how-blockchain-and-ai-can-help-pharma-focus-on-innovation-rather-than-advertising/?sh=51212e322bdf
258. Toshendra Kumar Sharma, TOP Use Cases of Blockchain in Pharma, Blockchain Council, https://www.blockchain-council.org/blockchain/top-use-cases-of-blockchain-in-pharma/ , Accessed on July 2, 2021
259. Dashveenjit Kaur, How Blockchain Adds Value to the Pharmaceutical Industry, TechHQ Technology, February 17, 2021, https://techhq.com/2021/02/how-blockchain-adds-value-to-the-pharmaceutical-industry/

260. Yogesh Rawal, Blockchain-Based Solutions to Prevent Counterfeit Drugs, Akeo, April 14, 2020, https://medium.com/akeo-tech/blockchain-based-solutions-to-prevent-counterfeit-drugs-6e

261. Allison McCauley, Why Big Pharma is Betting on Blockchain, Harvard Business Review, May 29, 2020, https://hbr.org/2020/05/why-big-pharma-is-betting-on-blockchain

262. Nicole Perrin, What Blockchain Might Mean for the Digital Ad Supply Chain, Insider Intelligence, eMarketer, March 26, 2018, https://www.emarketer.com/content/what-blockchain-might-mean-for-the-digital-ad-supply-chain

263. Project Provenance Ltd, White Paper - Blockchain: The Solution for Transparency in Product Supply Chain, November 15, 2015, https://www.provenance.org/whitepaper

264. Sarah Cavill, Healthcare & Pharma See Big Uptick in Digital Advertising Spend, Insights: Digital Media Solutions, October 29, 2020, https://insights.digitalmediasolutions.com/articles/pharma-healthcare-digital-advertising

265. Marc Benjamin, Retargeting: A Roadmap for Pharma Marketers, Convergence Point Media, https:/www.convergencepointmedia.com/retargeting-a-roadmap-for-pharma-marketers/

266. Justin Freid, Director, SEM, Alya Sherman, VP, Partner Innovation at CMI Media Group, Advanced Display Targeting Options for Pharma, CMI Media Group, February 23, 2021, https://cmimediagroup.com/resources/advanced-display-targeting-options-for-pharma-brands/

267. Chiradeep BasuMallick, What is Display Advertising? Definition, Targeting Process, Management, Network, Types, and Examples, Toolbox, May 20, 2020, https://www.toolbox.com/marketing/programmatic-advertising/articles/what-is-display-advertising/

268. Sonia Veres, What is A Banner Ad and How Does It Work? Creatopy Blog, April 18, 2016, https://blog.creatopy.com/beginner-guide-banner-ad/

269. Robert Kotai, How Does Banner Advertising Work? Creatopy Blog, February 1, 2017, https://blog.creatopy.com/banner-advertising-basics/

270. Pharmaceutical Advertising for Brand Managers, ethoseo.com, https://ethoseo.com/pharmaceutical-advertising-strategy#.YP1Bti0RpZ0, Accessed on July 25, 2021

271. Mark McLaughlin, Brian Mahoney, Opening Digital Doors: Remote Selling During COVID-19, PharmExec.com, December 11, 2020, https://www.pharmexec.com/view/opening-digital-doors-remote-selling-during-covid-19

272. Shalini Shah, MD, Virtual Engagement During COVID Pushes Paradigm Shift in Physician Training and Patient Care, HIT consultant.com, December 2, 2020, https://hitconsultant.net/2020/12/02/virtual-engagement-during-covid-pushes-paradigm-shift-for-physician-training-and-patient-care/#.YQDtzi0RpZ0

273. Sermo, The Future of Physician Engagement, April 28, 2021, https://www.sermo.com/blog/insights/the-future-of-physician-engagement/

274. Ankit Singh, Big-data in mHealth Apps is the Future of Healthcare, TechUgo.com, September 8, 2020, https://www.techugo.com/blog/big-data-in-mhealth-apps-is-the-future-of-healthcare/

275. Alicia Phaneuf, How mHealth Apps are Providing Solutions to the Healthcare Market's Problems, Insider Intelligence, December 4, 2019, https://www.businessinsider.com/mhealth-apps-definition-examples?IR=T

276. Dr. Bertalan Mesko, The Future of Printing Drugs in Pharmacies is Closer Than You Think, The Medical Futurist, May 4, 2017, https://medicalfuturist.com/future-3d-printing-drugs-pharmacies-closer-think/

277. Robin Robinson, Trending 2018: Agile Marketing, PharmaVoice, November-December 2017, https://www.pharmavoice.com/article/2017-11-agile-marketing/

278. Jake Beesley, Lukasz Kowalczyk, Can Life Sciences Catch the Agile Marketing Wave, Accenture Life Sciences Blog, March 9, 2021, https://www.accenture.com/us-en/blogs/interactive-insights-blog/can-pharma-catch-the-agile-marketing-wave

279. Mike Stout, 5 Fundamentals of Agile Sales, PM360, May 16, 2021, https://www.pm360online.com/5-fundamentals-of-agile-sales/

280. Docplexus Editorial Team, Agile Marketing: Is Pharma Ready? Docplexus, January 22, 2018, http://www.docplexus-insights.com/blog/agile-marketing-pharma-ready/

281. Vaidyanathan Srikant, Grant Freeland, Maria Lopez, and David Greber, Agile Can Work Wonders in Pharma, BCG.com, September 09, 2019, https://www.bcg.com/en-in/publications/2019/agile-work-wonders-pharma

282. Neil Osmond, Implementing Agile Working in Pharma, PharmaField, August 5, 2019, https://pharmafield.co.uk/opinion/implementing-agile-working-in-pharma/

283. Justin Grossman, CEO & Partner at MeltMedia, Is Agile the Key to Mastering Journey Orchestration in Pharma Marketing? PharmaLive.com, https://www.pharmalive.com/is-agile-the-key-to-mastering-journey-orchestration-in-pharma-marketing/

284. Sarah Elk, Ask the Authors-Customers' Role in Agile: Why is the Customer So Important in Agile? Bain & Company, October 09, 2020, https://www.bain.com/insights/why-is-the-customer-so-important-in-agile/

285. Shantanu Ballal, How An Agile Model Can Help Marketing Teams to be More Customer-centric, ZS.com, https://www.zs.com/insights/how-an-agile-model-can-help-marketing-teams-be-more-customer-centric

286. Thomas Nacher and Abhishek Trigunait, Moving Pharma Forward: The Agile Imperative for Commercial Ops, ZS.com, August 20, 2020, https://www.zs.com/insights/moving-pharma-forward-the-agile-imperative-for-commercial-ops

287. Nikola Jurisic, Michael Lurie, Philippine Risch, and Olli Salo, Doing vs. Being: Practical Lessons on Building an Agile Culture, McKinsey & Company, August 4, 2020, https://www.mckinsey.com/business-functions/organization/our-insights/doing-vs-being-practical-lessons-on-building-an-agile-culture

288. Neil Osmond, A Guide to Implementing Agile in Pharma, PharmaField, August 5, 2019, https://pharmafield.co.uk/in_depth/a-guide-to-implementing-agile-in-pharma/

289. Barbara Stewart, Implementing Agile in Pharma, Hiya Marketing, November 3, 2020, https://www.hiya.marketing/post/implementing-agile-in-pharma

290. Agility in Pharma-Agility in Conditions of Heavy Regulations, kanbanize.com, https://kanbanize.com/agile/industries/agile-pharma

291. Nida Khan, Agile Product Launch in Life Sciences: The New Mindset and Approach for Launch Success-Part I, Cap gemini, November 30, 2018, https://www.capgemini.com/2018/11/agile-product-launch-in-life-science/

292. Nida Khan, Agile Product Launch in Life Sciences: The New Mindset and Approach for Launch Success-Part II, CapGemini, December 4, 2018, https://www.capgemini.com/2018/12/agile-product-launch-in-life-science-part-2/#

293. Nida Khan, Agile Product Launch in Life Sciences: The New Mindset and Approach for Launch Success-Part III, CapGemini, January 22, 2020, https://www.capgemini.com/pt-en/2020/01/agile-product-launch-in-life-sciences-the-new-mindset-and-approach-for-launch-success-part-3/

294. Agile: The New Active Ingredient in Pharma Development-An interview with Roche's Frank Duff, and Malte Schulz, McKinsey & Company, June 7, 2019, https://www.mckinsey.com/business-functions/organization/our-insights/agile-the-new-active-ingredient-in-pharma-development

295. Christian Zuberer, Agile Transformation in Pharma: How to Launch More Successfully in a Fast-Changing Environment, Homburg & Partner (Part of Accenture), https://www.homburg-partner.com/en/agile-transformation-in-pharma/

296. Shah, P. K. (2017). Adapting Agile in Regulated (Pharmaceutical) Environment. Retrieved from http://digitalcommons.harrisburgu.edu/pmgt_dandt/16

297. Gavin Llewellyn, An Introduction to the Agile Mindset, Smart Insights, October 4, 2019, https://www.smartinsights.com/

digital-marketing-strategy/an-introduction-to-the-agile-mindset/

298. Cosmina Pirlea, and Inês Batuca, Agile—The Art of Adapting to Change and Innovation, a-Connect, https://www.a-connect.com/knowledge/agile-the-art-of-adapting-to-change-and-innovation/

299. Jennifer Mariani, Is Agile the Answer to Big Pharma's Digital Revolution? ELIASSEN Group, https://blog.eliassen.com/is-agile-the-answer-to-big-pharmas-digital-revolution

300. Leanne Howard, What Does It Mean to Have an Agile Mindset? Agile Connection, April 1, 2015, https://www.agileconnection.com/article/what-does-it-mean-have-agile-mindset

301. Dr. Clemens Freytag, Director and Executive Board Member at Strategy&, Competing in a Tough Market—The Agile Pharma Organization 4.0, LinkedIn Blog, February 12, 2019, https://www.linkedin.com/pulse/competing-tough-market-agile-pharma-organization-40-clemens-freytag/

302. Dr. Clemens Freytag, Director and Executive Board Member at Strategy&, Building an Agile Pharma Organization 4.0, LinkedIn Blog, April 30, 2019, https://www.linkedin.com/pulse/building-agile-pharma-organization-40-clemens-freytag/

303. Steve Denning, Agile: The World's Most Popular Innovation Engine, forbes.com, July 23, 2015, https://www.forbes.com/sites/stevedenning/2015/07/23/the-worlds-most-popular-innovation-engine/?sh=7b87074e7c76

304. Agile Methodology: What is Agile Software Development Model and Process Testing? guru99.com, https://www.guru99.com/agile-scrum-extreme-testing.html#5

305. Paddy Corry, Scrum's Connection to Rugby, Serious Scrum: medium.com, July 30, 2019, https://medium.com/serious-scrum/scrum-s-connection-to-rugby-597405fed5ec

306. Angela, Scrum, Rugby and Teamwork, The Agile Mindset Blog, The druckmancompany.com, June 12, 2012, https://medium.com/serious-scrum/scrum-s-connection-to-rugby-597405fed5ec

307. Agile Transformation: Understanding what It Means to be Agile, castsoftware.com, Accessed on August 29, 2021.

308. Chris Daily, Is Agile Eating the World? belithe.com, September 21, 2018, https://www.belithe.com/is-agile-eating-the-world/

309. The 12 Stages of Agile Transformation—Synopsis of an article from Forbes, The 12 Stages of Digital Transformation Journey by Stephen Denning published on November4, 2018, Leadership Digest, innovation-thinking.com, September 30, 2020, https://innovation-thinking.com/2020/09/30/the-12-stages-of-agile-transformation/

310. Martin Fowler, Software Developer, Author, and International Public Speaker on Software development, ShuHaRi, martinfowler.com, August 22, 2014, https://martinfowler.com/bliki/ShuHaRi.html

311. Leslie Read, Principal, Deloitte Consulting LLP, and Leslie Korenda, Research Manager, Deloitte Center for Health Solutions, Segment By Behavior to Reach Healthcare Consumers, The Wall Street Journal, February 6, 2019, https://deloitte.wsj.com/articles/segment-by-behavior-to-reach-todays-health-care-consumer-01549504937

312. Kris Pettersen, Writer, Deloitte Insights for CMOs, In Life Sciences Marketing, COVID is a Call to Action, The Wall Street Journal, August 21, 2021, https://deloitte.wsj.com/articles/in-life-sciences-marketing-covid-is-a-call-to-action-01630084721?mod=cmo_relatedcontent_2&tesla=y

313. Matt Salvetti, Sales Manager at PeopleMetrics, Pharma CX: The Most Important Part of Product Launch That You Aren't Planning, PeopleMetrics.com August 21, 2019, https://www.peoplemetrics.com/px-blog/pharma-cx-the-most-important-part-of-product-launch-that-you-arent-planning-for

314. Behsad Zomorodi, The Patient Journey: A Tool for Market Access, Reuters Events, August 17, 2017, https://www.reutersevents.com/pharma/column/patient-journey-tool-market-access

315. Dr. Wided Batat, Professor and Doctor of Experiential Marketing, How Phygital is Humanizing the Customer

Experience, Inc. June 2, 2021, https://www.inc.com/brit-morse/biden-vaccine-mandate-large-employers-workplace-policy-covid.html

316. Ford Blakely, What Really Makes For A Great Customer Experience? Thoughts From Top CX Experts, customerthink.com, November 30, 2018
317. Racheal Diebner, David Malfara, Kevin Neher, Mike Thompson, and Maxence Vancauwengerghe, Prediction: The Future of CX, McKinsey Quarterly, February 24, 2021, https://www.mckinsey.com/business-functions/marketing-and-sales/our-insights/prediction-the-future-of-cx
318. Annette Franz, Bridging the Gap Between Product and CX, GetFeedback, July 20, 2020, https://www.getfeedback.com/resources/ux/bridging-the-gap-between-product-and-cx/
319. Nikoletta Bika, How to Create A Customer Experience Strategy: 14 Ways, Acquire, December 3, 2021, https://acquire.io/blog/customer-experience-strategy/
320. Colette Pomerleau, What is Brand Voice and How do You Establish a Successful One? 99designs.com, https://99designs.com/blog/marketing-advertising/brand-voice/
321. Matt Ellis, How to Create a Strong Brand Personality (and Why It is Important), 99designs.com, https://99designs.com/blog/business/understanding-brand-personality/
322. Irina Nica, Digital Marketer and International Speaker, How to Measure Customer Experience: Key Metrics and Tools, Acquire, Published on October 1, 2020 and Updated on December 7, 2021, https://acquire.io/blog/measure-customer-experience-metrics-tools/
323. Benedict Clark, How to Cultivate Customer Loyalty that Lasts, Acquire, December 16, 2021, https://acquire.io/blog/customer-loyalty/
324. Richard Buettner, The Top 10 Digital Customer Experience Tools for the E-Commerce Tech Stack, STYLA, https://blog.styla.com/en/top-10-digital-customer-experience-tools-for-the-e-commerce-tech-stack

325. Nigel Holloway, Five Lessons on Customer Experience From Pharma Giant Eli Lilly And Co, Forbes, December 8, 2020, https://www.forbes.com/sites/salesforce/2020/12/08/five-lessons-on-customer-experience-from-pharma-giant-eli-lilly-and-co/?sh=69095bbf5385

326. Heather Landi, Amazon and Crossover Health Expand Health Clinics to 2 More States, Fierce Healthcare, March 12, 2021, https://www.fiercehealthcare.com/tech/amazon-crossover-health-expand-employee-health-clinics-to-two-more-states

327. Sai Balasubramanian, MD, JD, Walmart May Soon Become the Largest Primary Care Provider in the Country, Forbes, February 16, 2022, https://www.forbes.com/sites/saibala/2022/02/16/walmart-may-soon-become-the-largest-primary-care-provider-in-the-country/?sh=3a77353873be

328. Tina Reed, Consumers Are Embracing Pharmacy Expansion into Primary Care, Says J. D. Power, Fierce Healthcare, August 11. 2020, https://www.fiercehealthcare.com/payer/consumers-are-embracing-pharmacy-expansion-into-primary-care-says-j-d-power

329. Brian Davies, Managing Partner, Movéo, Using Physician Specialty Personas as a Tool for Reputation, Movéo, https://www.moveo.com/white-paper/using-physician-specialty-personas-as-a-tool-for-reputation-management/

330. Health Commons Solutions Lab, Tool, Personas: Primary Care Physicians, https://www.mcmasterforum.org/docs/default-source/rise-docs/partner-resourceshcsl_primarycare physicianpersonastool.pdf?sfvrsn=aef557d5_3

331. Linda Watts, Healthcare: Your Guide to Healthcare Personas, Perficient, February 8, 2022, https://blogs.perficient.com/2022/02/08/your-guide-to-healthcare-personas/

332. Linda Watts, Healthcare: How to Build A Healthcare Journey Map, Perficient, February, 10, 2022, https://blogs.perficient.com/2022/02/10/how-to-build-a-healthcare-journey-map/

333. Perficient, Personas & Journey Maps: The Definitive How to Guide for Healthcare Providers, https://www.perficient.com/

insights/guides/2021/personas-and-journey-maps-the-definitive-how-to-guide-for-healthcare-providers

334. Hugh gosling, Through Thick and Thin, PharmaTimes Online, January 2017, https://www.pharmatimes.com/magazine/2017/januaryfebruary/through_thick_and_thin
335. Linda Watts, Understanding Healthcare Journey Maps, Perficient, February 9, 2022, https://blogs.perficient.com/2022/02/09/understanding-healthcare-journey-maps/
336. Pharma Digi Coach, Healthcare Personas for Pharma: Defining Target Market of Pharmaceutical Companies, pharmadigicoach.com, March 21, 2020, https://www.pharmadigicoach.com/customer-avatar-defining-your-ideal-customer/
337. Matt Breese, Perspectives on Prescriber Personas, MMIT, May 23, 2017, https://blog.mmitnetwork.com/perspectives-prescriber-personas
338. Matt Hummel, Chief Experience Officer, Using Personas to Develop Relevant Marketing Messages, PARAGON, August 3, 2020, https://paragon-inc.com/ideas/using-personas-for-messages/
339. Netigate, All You Need to Know About Customer Experience (CX), netigate.com, February 1, 2021, https://www.netigate.net/articles/customer-satisfaction/customer-experience-ultimate-guide/
340. Everise, The Evolution of Customer Experience, everise.com, December 9, 2021, https://insights.weareeverise.com/the-evolution-of-the-customer-experience
341. Andrew Stone, Reuter's Events-Pharma: The Age of the Digital Opinion Leader (DOL), July 28, 2020, https://www.reutersevents.com/pharma/medical/age-digital-opinion-leader
342. PharmaDigiCoach, Little Known Secrets to Great Customer Experience in Pharma, pharmadigicoach.com, July 15, 2020, https://www.pharmadigicoach.com/secrets-to-great-customer-experience-in-pharma/

343. Tracy Knight, Principal at Knight Strategic Communications, Using Patient Personas for More Effective Healthcare Marketing, linkedin.com, September 13, 2016, https://www.linkedin.com/pulse/using-patient-personas-more-effective-healthcare-marketing-knight/

344. David Tran, Customer Experience Manager, Boehringer Ingelheim ANZ, Five Steps to Embarking on a Customer Experience Transformation in Australian Pharma, Swipe Health, October 8, 2020, https://swipehealth.com/five-steps-to-embarking-on-a-customer-experience-transformation-in-australian-pharma/

345. Paula Fullman, Derek Evans, A More Holistic Approach to the Patient Journey, PM360, September 18, 2013, https://www.pm360online.com/a-more-holistic-approach-to-the-patient-journey/

346. Diane Eastabrook, New CVS, Uber Collaboration Could Be A Boon to Aetna MA Members, McKnight Home Care, January 21,2022, https://www.mcknightshomecare.com/new-cvs-uber-collaboration-could-be-a-boon-to-aetna-ma-members/

347. Heather Landi, Uber Commences Integration with Cerner EHR System for US Providers, Fierce Healthcare, October 28, 2019, https://www.fiercehealthcare.com/tech/uber-announces-integration-cerner-ehr-system-for-u-s-providers

348. Scot Adams, How to Map Your Content to the Customer Journey in Healthcare, ShareMovingMedia Inc, February 11, 2021, http://sharemovingmedia.com/how-to-map-your-content-to-the-customer-journey-in-healthcare/?utm_source=rss&utm_medium=rss&utm_campaign=how-to-map-your-content-to-the-customer-journey-in-healthcare

349. Lawrence Ganti, Why Data Analytics Should Be Pharma's New Core Competency, DATAFLOQ, June 18, 2018, https://datafloq.com/read/data-analytics-should-pharmas-new-core-competency/

350. Neil Grayson, Real-World Data Can Help Make Better Drugs and Do It Faster, STAT, May 2, 2018, https://www.statnews.com/2018/05/02/real-world-data-drug-development/

351. US Food & Drug Administration Blog, Real-World Evidence, https://www.fda.gov/science-research/science-and-research-special-topics/real-world-evidence

352. Jeffrey Pagnini, Senior Vice-President, 9 Ways Real-World Evidence is Changing Healthcare, ArborMetrix, August 9, 2021, https://www.arbormetrix.com/blog/9-ways-real-world-evidence-is-changing-healthcare

353. Yan Fang Liu, Senior Director, Hong Qin, Senior Director, Paul Stang, Senior Vice President, Jesse A. Berlin, Senior Vice President, Epidemiology, Johnson & Johnson Pte. Ltd, DIA Global Forum, November 2018,

354. PharmaVoice Team, Show Case: Real-World Evidence: Realizing the Benefits of RWE, PharmaVoice, March 1, 2021, https://www.pharmavoice.com/news/2021-03-realizing-the-benefits/612104/

355. Erin Booth, How Real World Data is Changing Pharmaceutical Industry, MMS Blog, https://www.mmsholdings.com/how-real-world-data-is-changing-the-pharmaceutical-industry/

356. Qin Ye, Todd Somsel, and Divya Babbar, Real-World Data and Evidence Industry Outlook Report, ZS Associates, April 24, 2021, https://www.zs.com/insights/real-world-data-and-evidence-industry-outlook-report

357. Beth Snyder Bulik, ASCO's Hot Marketing Topics: Real-World Data, Competition and Differentiation, Analyst Says, Fierce Pharma, June 4, 2019, https://www.fiercepharma.com/marketing/asco-non-clinical-topics-real-world-data-competition-and-differentiation-analyst

358. Hideki Maeda and Daniel Bin Ng, Regulatory Approval With Real-World Data From Regulatory Science Perspective in Japan, Frontiers in Medicine, April 15, 2022, https://www.frontiersin.org/articles/10.3389/fmed.2022.864960/full

359. Gil Press, Senior Contributor, The Landscape of AI and Real-World Evidence, Forbes, December 1, 2021, https://www.forbes.com/sites/gilpress/2021/12/01/the-landscape-of-ai-and-real-world-evidence-supporting-drug-approvals/?sh=23ac18b361a1

360. Jenni Spinner, Real-World Evidence 'Central' to Drug Development, Parexel, Outsourcing, February 7, 2022, https://www.outsourcing-pharma.com/Article/2022/02/07/real-world-evidence-central-to-drug-development-parexel

361. Stephen Towers, PhD, Pharma Marketing's Data-Driven Future: Four Inter-Connected Themes From Reuters Pharma Marketing USA 2021, December 17, 2021, https://www.pharma-mkting.com/articles/pharma-marketings-data-driven-omnichannel-future-four-interconnected-themes-from-reuters-pharma-marketing-usa-2021/

362. David Champagne, Alex Deverson, David Saunders and Lucy Pérez, Creating Value From Next-Generation Real-World Evidence, McKinsey.com, July 23, 2020, https://www.mckinsey.com/industries/life-sciences/our-insights/creating-value-from-next-generation-real-world-evidence

363. US FDA Approves IBRANCE® (palbociclib) for the Treatment of Men with HR+, HER2-Metastatic Breast Cancer, pfizer.com, April 04, 2019, https://www.pfizer.com/news/press-release/press-release-detailu_s_fda_approves_ibrance_palbociclib_for_the_treatment_of_men_with_hr_her2_metastatic_breast_cancer

364. Khosla S et al. Real-World Evidence (RWE) A Disruptive Innovation of Medical Evidence Generation? NIH, National Library of Medicine, Pub Med Central, August 29, 2018, https://www.ncbi.nlm.nih.gov/pmc/articles/PMC6039945/

365. Chris Stevenson, Osprey Health Consultancy, The Evolution of Scenario Planning and Simulation to Address Modern Market and Landscape Challenges, Pharmaphorum, April 9, 2019, https://pharmaphorum.com/views-analysis-sales-marketing/the-evolution-of-scenario-planning-and-simulation-to-address-modern-market-and-landscape-challenges/

366. Oleg Bestsennyy, Greg Gilbert, Alex Harris and Jennifer Rost, Telehealth: A Quarter-trillion Dollar Post-Covid-19 Reality? mckinsey.com, July 9, 2021, https://www.mckinsey.com/industries/healthcare-systems-and-services/our-insights/telehealth-a-quarter-trillion-dollar-post-covid-19-reality

367. Shiv Rao, Co-Founder and CEO of Abridge, Industry Voices - 3, Challenges Exposed in the New World of Telehealth (And How to Overcome Them), Fierce Healthcare, August 10, 2020, https://www.fiercehealthcare.com/tech/industry-voices-3-challenges-exposed-new-world-telehealth-and-how-to-overcome-them

368. Rami Ali and David Luther, Scenario Planning: Strategy, Steps and Practical Examples, Oracle NetSuite, May 14, 2020, https://www.netsuite.com/portal/business-benchmark-brainyard/industries/articles/cfo-central/scenario-planning.shtml

369. Hubert G. Leafkens, Zuaana Kusynova, Murray Aitkens, Jarno Hoekman, Pieter Stolk, Kevin Klein, Aukje K. Mantel-Teeuwisse, Four Scenarios for the Future of Medicines and Social Policy in 2030, Elsevier-Drug Discovery Today, Volume 27, Number 8, August 2022, https://www.sciencedirect.com/science/article/pii/S1359644622001283

370. Bozidar Jovicevic, Md, MBA, Vice President, Global Head of Digital Therapeutics at Sanofi, Ivan Ostojic, Partner, McKinsey, Zurich Office, Digital Therapeutics and Pharma: A Blue Print for Success From Sanofi's Bozidar Jovicevic— Interview, McKinsey & Company, February 14, 2020, https://www.mckinsey.com/industries/life-sciences/our-insights/digital-therapeutics-and-pharma-a-blueprint-for-success-from-sanofis-bozidar-jovicevic

371. Prof Scott H Kollins, PhD, Denton J DeLoss, PhD, Elena Cañadas, PhD, Jacqueline Lutz, PhD, Prof Robert L Finding, MD, Prof Richard SE Keefe, PhD et al. A Novel Digital Intervention for Actively Reducing Severity of Pediatric ADHD (STARS-ADHD): A Randomized Controlled Trial, The Lancet Digital Health, February 24, 2020, https://www.thelancet.com/journals/landig/article/PIIS2589-7500(20)30017-0/fulltext

372. Anuja Vaidya, What Are Digital Therapeutics and Their Use Cases, mHealth Intelligence, May 20, 2022, https://mhealthintelligence.com/features/what-are-digital-therapeutics-and-their-use-cases

373. Leslie Gautam, Executive Director, Tim Opler, Partner, Torreya, Digital Therapeutics and the Future of Pharma: Full Presentation, torreya.com, February 13, 2020, https://torreya.com/publications/digital-therapeutics-and-future-of-pharma_executive-summary.php

374. Francesca Boggio (Executive Insight), Stephen Focsa and Michele Casanova (Former Executive Insight Employees), Access & Reimbursement to Reward Innovation in Digital “BTP” Solutions, Executive Insight-Healthcare Consultants, April 11, 2018,https://www.executiveinsight.ch/en/insights/what-can-be-done-access-and-reimbursement-processes-reward-innovation-digital-btp-solutions

375. Anuja Vaidya, Senior Editor, Newly Approved VR Therapeutic for Back Pain Expands Scope for Home Health, mHealth Intelligence, November 23, 2021, https://mhealthintelligence.com/features/newly-approved-vr-therapeutic-for-back-pain-expands-scope-of-home-health

376. Susanna Gebauer, 14 Ways to Get More Participants for Your Webinars, The SocialMs, March 21, 2017, https://blog.thesocialms.com/14-ways-get-participants-webinars/

377. Introduction: Business Ecosystems Come of Age, deloitte.com, https://www2.deloitte.com/za/en/pages/strategy-operations/articles/introduction—business-ecosystems-come-of-age.html

378. Gianni Cardone, Design Director, Data and Ecosystems are the Future of Healthcare, Futurice, September 4, 2020, https://futurice.com/blog/data-and-ecosystems-are-the-future-of-healthcare

379. Daniel Kline, Mark Cuban Pharmacy Solves a Problem Politicians Can’t, The Street, May 22, 2022, https://www.thestreet.com/investing/mark-cuban-wages-war-on-drug-prices-cost-plus

380. Zachary Brennan, Senior Editor, Mark Cuban’s New Cost-Plus 15% Generic Drug Company is Really A Compounding Pharmacy, End Points News, January 31, 2022, https://endpts.com/mark-cubans-new-cost-plus-15-generic-drug-company-is-really-a-compounding-pharmacy/

381. Tina Reed, Mark Cuban is (Bleeping) Mad About Healthcare. Here's What He Wants To Do About It, Fierce Healthcare, October 19, 2019, https://www.fiercehealthcare.com/hospitals-health-systems/mark-cuban-bleeping-mad-about-healthcare-here-s-what-he-wants-to-do-about

382. Ned Russel, Managing Partner of Healthcare at MDC Partners, 'Jaws' as Allegory for Today's Healthcare Marketing? Yes, 'You're Gonna Need A Bigger Boat', MM+M, October 30, 2018, https://www.mmm-online.com/home/opinion/jaws-as-allegory-for-todays-healthcare-marketing-yes-youre-gonna-need-a-bigger-boat/

383. Elizabeth Mixson, Johnson & Johnson: A Crash Course in Tech-Enabled Business Resiliency, Intelligent Automation Network, March 23, 2021, https://www.intelligentautomation.network/resiliency/articles/johnson-johnson-a-crash-course-in-tech-enabled-business-resiliency

384. Ting, Alumni, Johnson & Johnson: Embracing Digital Transformation, Digital Innovation and Transformation, MBA Student Perspectives, Harvard Business School, https://digital.hbs.edu/platform-digit/submission/johnson-johnson-embracing-digital-transformation/

385. Salvi Mittal, Dr. Reddy's Gears Up For A Massive Digital Push, ET CIO, June 2, 2022, https://cio.economictimes.indiatimes.com/news/strategy-and-management/dr-reddys-gears-up-for-a-massive-digital-push/91953568

386. Sneha Jha, Mukesh Rathi Uses Digital to Give Dr. Reddy's A Competitive Edge, ET CIO, September 21, 2018, https://cio.economictimes.indiatimes.com/news/corporate-news/mukesh-rathi-uses-digital-to-give-dr-reddys-a-new-lease-of-life/65880621

387. Elizabeth Mixson, Abbott Labs: A Pioneer in Digital Behavioral Health—From Medical Device Company to Digital Health Innovation, Intelligent Automation Network, January 25, 2022, https://www.intelligentautomation.network/transformation/articles/abbott-labs-a-pioneer-in-digital-behavioral-health

388. Pharma and Life Sciences: FDA Tells Citius that Suprenza Web Page is False, Misleading in Untitled Letter, Bloomberg Law, June 17, 2014, https://news.bloomberglaw.com/pharma-and-life-sciences/fda-tells-citius-that-suprenza-web-page-is-false-misleading-in-untitled-letter
389. Grant Gross, US FDA Warms Pharma Firm About Facebook Promotion, Reuters, August 7, 2010, https://www.reuters.com/article/urnidgns002570f3005978d8852577700603e7e-idUS199529137420100807
390. Jessica Wong, How Digital Transformation Could Change Research and Development for Pharmaceutical and Beauty Companies, Forbes, November 12, 2021, https://www.forbes.com/sites/forbescommunicationscouncil/2021/11/12/how-digital-transformation-could-change-research-and-development-for-pharmaceutical-and-beauty-companies/?sh=3a3e17f41d6d
391. Sastry Chilukuri, Edd Fleming, and Ann Westra, Digital in R&D: The $100 Billion Opportunity, McKinsey, December 1, 2017, https://www.mckinsey.com/industries/life-sciences/our-insights/digital-in-r-and-d-the-100-billion-opportunity
392. George Underwood, How Digital is Reversing Fortunes in R&D, Pharmaphorum, February 20, 2020, https://pharmaphorum.com/views-analysis-digital/digital-reversing-fortunes-rd/
393. Nicolò Paraggio, Managing Director, Life Sciences, R&D Strategy Lead, Billions to Millions: Improving R&D Productivity, accenture.com, October 25, 2021, https://www.accenture.com/us-en/insights/life-sciences/from-billions-to-millions-transformation
394. The Docplexus Team, Phygital: The Holy Grail of Next-gen Pharma Marketing, Docplexus, October 8, 2019, https://docplexussolutions.com/physical-digital-phygital-way-pharma-marketers/
395. Life Sciences & Healthcare White Paper, Phygital: The Future of Pharma, hexaware.com, https://hexaware.com/resource/phygital-the-future-of-pharma/
396. Blake Morgan, The Rise of the Phygital Experience, forbes.com, May 16, 2022, https://www.forbes.com/sites/

blakemorgan/2022/05/16/the-rise-of-the-phygital-experience/?sh=31e127bf5b97

397. Phygital Transformation: Components, Challenges and Prospects, R&D Management, https://onlinelibrary.wiley.com/pb-assets/assets/14679310/R&DM%20-%20CFP %20 Phygital%20Transformation.pdf
398. Robb De Filippis, What is Modular Content and Why Do Pharma Marketers Need it NOW? Pharmaphorum, May 24, 2021, https://pharmaphorum.com/views-analysis-sales-marketing/what-is-modular-content-and-why-do-pharma-marketers-need-it-now/
399. Ramya Sriram, Content Marketing for Biotech & Pharma: The Ultimate Guide, Kolabtree Blog, November 20, 2020, https://www.kolabtree.com/blog/content-marketing-for-biotech-pharma-the-ultimate-guide/
400. Andrea Del Miglio, Tobias Hlavka, Jeffrey Lewis, Manuel Möller, and Pablo Prieto-Munoz, The Case for Cloud in Life Sciences, McKinsey & Company, October 28, 2021, https://www.mckinsey.com/industries/life-sciences/our-insights/the-case-for-cloud-in-life-sciences
401. Lévina Claufriez, Research and Development Communications, UCB, Let's Get Digital! A Look at UCB's Digital Transformation in R&D, ucb.com, May 30, 2022, https://www.ucb.com/Our-company/magazine/detail/article/Let-s-Get-Digital-A-look-at-UCB-s-digital-transformation-in-RD
402. Suryakant Pandey, Senior Director, Head, Learning and Development, Cipla's Learning Transformation Journey— From Disconnected & Decentralized to Engaging, Accessible, and Scalable, People Matters, February 25, 2021, https://www.peoplematters.in/article/training-development/ciplas-learning-transformation-journey-from-disconnected-decentralized-to-engaging-accessible-and-scalable-28590
403. What are 6Ds? The 6D Company, https://the6ds.com/what-are-the-6ds/
404. Nikhar Aggarwal, A Look at Cipla's Tech Innovations as it Embarks on Digital Transformation: ETCIO Interview with Kedar Upadhye, Jt President & Global CFO,Cipla, ETCIO, September

10, 2019, https://cio.economictimes.indiatimes.com/news/business-analytics/a-look-at-ciplas-tech-innovations-as-it-embarks-on-digital-transformation/71051298

405. Natalie Schibell, VP, Research Director, Kara Wilson, Researcher, Amazon Pulls The Plug on Amazon Care, Signaling A New Dawn of Healthcare Disruption, Forrester, August 28, 2002, https://www.forrester.com/blogs/amazon-pulls-the-plug-on-amazon-care-signaling-a-new-dawn-of-healthcare-disruption/
406. Grant Gross, US FDA Warns Pharma Firm About Facebook Promotion, Reuters, August 7, 2010, https://www.reuters.com/article/urnidgns002570f3005978d8852577700603e7e-idUS199529137420100807
407. Novartis Removes 'Share' Button for Tasigna, PMLive, August 9, 2010, https://www.pmlive.com/pharma_news/novartis_removes_share_button_for_tasigna_230395
408. FDA Tells Citius That Suprenza Web Page is False, Misleading in Untitled Letter, Pharma and Life Sciences, Bloomberg Law, June 17, 2014
409. Sharon Lurye, How Kim Kardashian's Instagram Got Rosemont Drug Company in Trouble With the FDA, Philly Voice, September1, 2015, https://www.phillyvoice.com/kim-kardashians-instagram-got-drug-co-trouble-fda/
410. Stephen Towers, PhD, Pharma Marketing's Data-Driven Omnichannel Future: Four Interconnected Themes from Reuters Pharma Marketing USA 2021, Pharma Marketing Network, December 17, 2021, https://www.pharma-mkting.com/articles/pharma-marketings-data-driven-omnichannel-future-four-interconnected-themes-from-reuters-pharma-marketing-usa-2021/

Index

A

B

C

D

E

F

G

H

I

J

K

L

M

N

O

P

Q

R

S

T

U

V

W

X

Y

Z

ABOUT THE AUTHOR

Subba Rao Chaganti has a masters in business administration and over fifty-two years of pharmaceutical marketing experience covering the whole gamut and all facets of the industry, from sales management to product management to heading the total marketing activity. His experience covers domestic and international marketing, and also Indian and multinational sectors.

For a few years, he also taught a course on Advertising and Brand Management at the GITAM Institute of Foreign Trade (now part of GITAM University) at Visakhapatnam as an adjunct professor. He also taught a course on Marketing at Jawaharlal Nehru Technological University (JNTU), Hyderabad, as a visiting faculty.

He lives in Hyderabad and can be reached at subbarao.chaganti@gmail.com.

Here is a list of his books published:

1. Pharmaceutical marketing in India: Concepts, Cases, Strategy
2. Game Plans for Post-Gatt Era: Action Agenda of Indian Pharmaceutical Industry
3. Compete or Forfeit: Strategies for Sustainable Competitive Advantage in Pharma Product Patents Era
4. Pharmaceutical Marketing in India for Today and Tomorrow - 25th Anniversary Edition
5. Bullseyes and Blunders: Lessons from 100 Cases in Pharmaceutical Marketing
6. Digital Pharma Marketing Playbook: Winning with the New Rules of Engagement
7. Cracking the Generics Code: Your 'Single-Source' Guide for Winning in 'Multi-Source' Product Markets

www.ingramcontent.com/pod-product-compliance
Ingram Content Group UK Ltd.
Pitfield, Milton Keynes, MK11 3LW, UK
UKHW020223290926
15470UKWH00001B/354

9 789395 039468